Two Steps Forward, One Step Back: The Deterrent Effect of International Criminal Tribunals

Jennifer Schense and Linda Carter (editors)

2017
Torkel Opsahl Academic EPublisher
Brussels

PREFACE BY SERIES EDITOR

The idea of the deterrence project originated in one of the Academy's Advisory Council meetings. Justice SONG Sang-Hyun, former President of the International Criminal Court ('ICC'), proposed that the Academy could conduct a study into whether the ICC has had a deterrent effect. A preliminary literature survey disclosed that no major study had been conducted on this area at this time, and thus the Academy decided to make a contribution to the ongoing academic and policy debates on various aspects related to the impact of the ICC.

Already at the initial stage of the project, it was decided to expand the focus to include prior international criminal tribunals – the International Criminal Tribunal for the former Yugoslavia, the International Criminal Tribunal for Rwanda and the Special Court for Sierra Leone – to provide a richer analytical frame and broader context for the study, and more useful inferences, conclusions and recommendations for enhancing the ICC's deterrent effect. Each case study aims to track the deterrent effect of the relevant tribunal or court from its point of entry into a situation through the convictions/acquittals and appeals stages, where these procedural steps have been achieved. The Academy engaged researchers with in-depth knowledge of the situation country and of the relevant tribunal or court operating there; most of them originated from the countries involved. During an initial workshop held in Nuremberg in February 2016 the authors and editors adopted a working definition of the term of deterrence and reached a common understanding of ideas and methodology.

The project on deterrence fits in the Academy's three-year research plan, and intersects with the Academy's inaugural research project on acceptance of international criminal justice. As the chapters of this volume show, numerous theoretical and practical linkages between deterrence and acceptance exist. One such linkage is explored through the study's focus on perceptions held by different sectors of society, which impact on the deterrent effect or the ICC.

The Academy's study is seminal because of its in-depth nature; other impact studies treat deterrence as one of several aspects of impact, and, consequently, pay it scant attention, although it is a core objective of the ICC. The deterrence project is important to the Academy for various reasons. First, the study involves fieldwork to gather first-hand information on those who have actually experienced (or not) the deterrence effect of international tribunals. These studies aim to showcase the new information collected rather than only survey what is already known. Second, the study brings together researchers from both legal and other disciplinary backgrounds, who seek to situate their studies within an interdisciplinary context to better understand how deterrence functions in the real world. Third, the study involves researchers who bridge the academic, the practitioners' and policy-making world to achieve a holistic approach.

Klaus Rackwitz
Director, International Nuremberg Principles Academy

Editors' Preface

We would like to thank, first of all, the International Nuremberg Principles Academy for conceiving and implementing this project. As the editors, we appreciated the opportunity to work closely with both Ambassador Bernd Borchardt and Klaus Rackwitz, the first and second Directors of the Nuremberg Academy respectively. Their commitment to the subject of deterrence, and their practical and intellectual support, helped to bring together an ambitious project in a short period of time.

We are grateful to Dr. Godfrey Musila who, as the Research Director of the Academy, conceived and organised the project based on an idea generated by the Academy Board member Judge SONG Sang-Hyun, former President of the International Criminal Court. We all relied as well on the steady guidance and good grace of Darleen Seda of the Academy who saw the project to its successful completion. Additional thanks must go to the external reviewer, Professor Mark A. Drumbl of Washington and Lee University School of Law. Professor Drumbl joined the project last, but with a wealth of professional experience on the subject of deterrence and international law, leavened with good humour throughout.

Finally, we must express our appreciation for the chapter authors, who undertook extensive and often difficult fieldwork to collect perceptions of deterrence from as many respondents as possible, and who found time for thoughtful analysis among the many other demands of their professional lives. These authors – all of whom are young professionals working in the countries about which they write – represent the future of international criminal law, insofar as the greatest deterrent effect must arise from the scene of the crime, so to speak, and from the communities that must grapple with these crimes most directly, and for the longest time. We must understand better both the failures and accomplishments of deterrence efforts because just as international crimes affect us all, so will the solutions we each find bind us more closely as a true international community. We look forward to continued contact with all participants in this volume, and to further discussion and implementation of its recommendations.

Jennifer Schense and Linda Carter

TABLE OF CONTENTS

1

Introduction

Jennifer Schense[*] and Linda Carter[**]

1.1. Origins of the Project

This introduction explains how this project came about and why it is timely. Conducted in 2016, it coincides with the seventieth anniversary of the conclusion of the Nuremberg trials on 1 October 1946, and the adoption of the seven Nuremberg Principles by the United Nations General Assembly by resolution 95(I) on 11 December 1946. The Nuremberg Academy's Second Annual Forum on 4–5 November 2016 commemorated the adoption of the principles and examined specific aspects in respect of each. The seven principles lay the foundation for addressing impunity for international crimes, underscoring a retributive approach to their investigation and prosecution. It is the search for a just punishment to fit the commission of international crimes.

The Nuremberg Academy recognises that retribution and deterrence are linked, in that the knowledge that commission of crimes carries the

---

[*] **Jennifer Schense** is the founding director of the House of Nuremberg and of Cat Kung Fu Productions, both dedicated to creating films and other popular, cultural works reflecting on justice. She has also worked with the International Criminal Court ('ICC') Office of the Prosecutor in the Jurisdiction, Complementarity and Cooperation Division since 2004, and is currently contributing to the ICC Registry's external relations and networking strategy. Prior to her work at the ICC, she served as the Legal Adviser for the NGO Coalition for the International Criminal Court from September 1998 until September 2004, and served for one year as a fellow at Human Rights Watch. She is currently completing her Ph.D. in international criminal law at Leiden University. She received her Juris Doctorate from Columbia Law School in 1997, and her B.Sc. in Russian language and Russian area studies from Georgetown University in 1993.

[**] **Linda Carter** is a Distinguished Professor of Law Emerita at the University of the Pacific, McGeorge School of Law, California, USA, where she teaches and researches on issues of domestic and international criminal law. Her most recent publications include, as co-editor, *International Criminal Procedure: The Interface of Civil Law and Common Law Legal Systems* (Edward Elgar, 2013) and, as co-author, *The International Criminal Court in an Effective Global System* (Edward Elgar, 2016). She has also participated in programmes in various international venues in teaching, research and programme development roles. She taught in the Nuremberg Summer Academy in 2016. She is a member of numerous professional organisations, including election to the American Law Institute.

risk of prosecution may deter current and potential perpetrators from committing crimes in the future. International justice may further help instil a new societal ethos, and thereby contribute more broadly to deterrence through legal, institutional and cultural influences at the national level. To this end, it may cultivate respect for human rights and the rule of law, and thereby influence behaviour of actors through the pressures exerted by public opinion about what is criminal or not, what is good or bad, or what is right or wrong.

This study is timely because more than 20 years have passed since the establishment in 1993 of the International Criminal Tribunal for the former Yugoslavia ('ICTY') and in 1994 of the International Criminal Tribunal for Rwanda ('ICTR'). The ICTR has already concluded its work and the ICTY is in the process of completing its mandate; a residual mechanism will handle any future issues. Nearly 15 years have passed since the 2002 establishment of the International Criminal Court ('ICC') and the Special Court for Sierra Leone ('SCSL'). Given that the Nuremberg trials arguably had their greatest impact several generations after their conclusion, the impact of international tribunals has yet to be fully felt. But the time is coming when the international community can take a step back and begin to assess the longer-term impact of these international institutions. Establishing a clear framework for making such an assessment will be essential. It is here that the Nuremberg Academy hopes to make a contribution.

1.2. Purpose of the Study

This study begins by acknowledging both the centrality and the elusiveness of deterrence as a goal. There is no clear agreement on what comprises deterrence, how it can be achieved and how it can be documented. The next chapter in this volume delves in greater depth into the definition of deterrence, how it differs from prevention, and how it relates to other goals of international or national justice mechanisms. It may be some comfort for supporters of deterrence to note that none of the goals of international or national justice are easy or even necessarily possible to achieve. All are intended to contribute to a process that at its best should be self-aware and continually self-appraising. There is a value in this respect even to goals that cannot be fully achieved. As the international lawyer Martti Koskenniemi argues in citing the importance of the aspirational as well as the practical functions of international law, "The justice that animates political community is not one that may be fully attained".[1]

With these limitations in mind, this project undertakes to conduct a study of the deterrent effect of international criminal tribunals through a selective study of ten conflict or post-conflict countries. The impact of the ICC is explored through studies of the Democratic Republic of Congo ('DRC'), Darfur (Sudan), Kenya, Uganda, Côte d'Ivoire and Mali. An examination of several non-ICC situations where other tribunals have been active provides a comparative perspective. In this regard, the project also analyses the role and effect on deterrence of the ICTY in Serbia and Kosovo, the ICTR in Rwanda and the SCSL in Sierra Leone.

1.3. Definition of Deterrence for Purposes of This Study

Deterrence is defined in this study to mean the capacity of prosecutions (or the work of the tribunals more broadly, including their mere existence) to elicit forbearance from committing further crimes on the part of those prosecuted, the 'similarly minded' and the general public. This approach presents a concentric circle effect, beginning with the perpetrator at the centre, and rippling out to his or her immediate peers, his or her political group, and beyond. The deterrent effect can be inferred from the ability of prosecutions to influence the interlinked views and behaviour of various groups, including those criminally inclined, and thus to prevent the commission of crimes. Deterrence may also be achieved through norm setting, in the strict sense, through adoption of national legislation that incorporates core international crimes into national law, and, in a wider sense, through the interventions of non-prosecutorial actors, including national governments and international or regional institutions such as the United Nations or the European Union, civil society organisations, journalists and others. Deterrence in its broadest sense overlaps significantly with prevention, and the boundaries between these concepts are explored further in the chapter on deterrence theory. The authors of these case studies examine only deterrence, but their findings will be relevant to any assessment of prevention in these situations over the long-term, but for now, that assessment is best left to the side.

---

[1] Martti Koskenniemi, "What is International Law For?", in Malcolm D. Evans (ed.), *International Law*, 2nd ed., Oxford University Press, Oxford, 2006, p. 111.

Deterrence may be divided into general deterrence, specific deterrence, targeted deterrence, and restrictive or partial deterrence. General deterrence refers to the discouragement of criminal activity through fear of punishment among the general public. Specific deterrence refers to the discouragement of subsequent criminal activity by those who have been punished. Targeted deterrence attempts to deter specific individuals or groups within a society, and restrictive deterrence refers to the minimisation rather than the abandonment of criminal activity which occurs when, to diminish the risk or severity of a legal punishment, a potential offender engages in some action that has the effect of reducing his or her commissions of a crime.

1.4. The Challenges of Measuring Deterrence

Deterrence, like many goals of criminal law, is elusive. Some have suggested that measuring deterrence is akin to proving a negative; to proving that something did not happen. To that challenge, a practical reply may suffice: the ICC for its part, as with many other tribunals, becomes involved in a situation after many crimes have been committed. In that case, there is rarely if ever only a true negative at play. Previous and ongoing crimes are strong indicators that additional crimes are likely to occur, helping to illuminate what would have occurred without the intervention of the relevant tribunal. As the former US ambassador-at-large for war crimes, David Scheffer, put it: "For people to say there will be no deterrence at all is as factually unprovable as to say there will be deterrence. You can't prove that. How do you prove that? How do you prove the state of mind of a perpetrator of these crimes?"[2]

Complex social phenomena like deterrence are difficult, and perhaps even impossible, to verify accurately, and causation of deterrence, where it occurs, is almost always going to be due to multiple factors. For the ICC's part at least, its founders never intended it to be a sole cause of deterrence, but rather for it "to put an end to impunity for the perpetrators of these crimes and thus to *contribute* to the prevention of such crimes".[3]

---

[2] David Scheffer, "Should the United States Join the International Criminal Court?", in *UC Davis Journal of International Law & Political Science*, 2003, vol. 9, no. 45, p. 51.

[3] ICC, Rome Statute of the International Criminal Court, 17 July 1998, in force 1 July 2002, Preamble ('ICC Statute') (emphasis added) (http://www.legal-tools.org/doc/7b9af9/).

With these challenges in mind, the parameters and methodology of the study were designed to explore available data, information and perceptions about deterrence in each case study, taking into account the multiple factors that influence the effect of the relevant international criminal court.

1.5. Parameters of This Study

1.5.1. The Courts

The courts covered in this study are the ICC, the ICTY, the ICTR and the SCSL. Some cases by national courts are also considered, where the authors deem them relevant or exemplary.

1.5.2. Stages of Proceedings

Each country study tracks deterrence along the procedural steps adopted for the relevant tribunal. For the ICC, the following stages are relevant: the preliminary examination, opening of investigations, arrest warrants (naming of suspects), confirmation of charges, trial, conviction and sentencing. The *ad hoc* tribunals have similar processes.

1.5.3. The Crimes

The study restricts its analysis to the core international crimes of genocide, crimes against humanity and war crimes. Although these three international crimes are also often codified in national penal codes, and there are other transnational crimes that could be included in an umbrella term of international offences, this project focused only on the crimes under the jurisdiction of the international criminal tribunals. As such, the study does not extend to what are often called 'ordinary' national penal code crimes, such as murder, corruption or organised crime, except for cases where national authorities have mounted prosecutions touching on the same factual basis as the international tribunal concerned.

1.5.4. The Respondents

The respondents include those prosecuted (suspects, accused and the convicted); those similarly placed (for example, politicians, rebels, businessmen, and 'foot soldiers' in situation countries); victims and victim groups;

and non-governmental organisation ('NGO') representatives and other experts.

1.6. Methodology of This Study

This study takes a mixed qualitative and quantitative approach, with a predominant emphasis on qualitative factors. On the quantitative side, the authors analysed first- and second-hand data about: 1) the increased or decreased number of casualties or dead during the period of the relevant tribunal's work; and 2) the increased or decreased incidences of violence and accompanying crimes or gross human rights violations. Quantitative data in this case provides important background information about whether human rights violations and criminality are in general on the rise or in decline. One cannot begin to discuss a potential deterrent effect of any investigation or prosecution without first knowing whether crimes are increasing or decreasing. Beyond this basic fact, it is generally acknowledged that drawing a direct correlation between prosecutions and a decline in criminality will always be troublesome. While the editors and authors appreciate the research of Kathryn Sikkink, Hyeran Jo, Beth Simmons and others, who search out the correlation between numbers and types of human rights trials and decreases in incidences of violence and criminality, this study takes a different approach.

On the qualitative side, the authors collected and evaluated information on three key factors: 1) discernible change in behaviour on the part of suspects, accused and like-minded individuals, including political and business elites and rebels; 2) changes in views and perceptions of victims about how or whether the relevant tribunal's effect has contributed to their safety; and 3) views of NGO members and experts on whether the tribunal has had a deterrent effect. In addition to discernible changes in behaviour, the qualitative factor of perceptions of the respondents is given particular emphasis. It is common sense that perpetrators, victims, bystanders and others act on their perceptions, for good or bad. Rational actor theory supports the argument that if perpetrators perceive that potential prosecutions threaten them, this perception will affect their choices. It matters less in the short term if those perceptions are correct, but more in the long term, as mainstream criminology supports the idea that primarily certainty of punishment, not swiftness or severity, has a deterrent effect. Other criminology and sociology studies complement rational actor theory in documenting how environments and the group dynamics that function therein affect an individual's perceptions of his or her choices, whether he or she views these choices as good or bad, and which ones he or she ultimately makes.[4]

Qualitative factors are paramount because trials do not take place in a vacuum, but in a social environment that results from the interaction of numerous political, social, economic, cultural and legal factors. A qualitative approach allows the researcher to explore the totality of a situation, using a case study approach to generate small but focused samples of data that illuminate how subjects interact with and affect the world around them.[5] It is a difficult task, as each interaction is akin to a stone thrown in a pond; multiple and ongoing interactions create multiple, overlapping ripples, until it becomes impossible to see the point of first impact or to attribute specific reactions to a single point of entry. But the better these interactions can be understood, the more the legal aspect – investigations and prosecutions in particular – can be tailored to have their greatest impact. This study aims to better understand these interactions and the complex environment in which prosecutions take place.

1.7. Sources for This Study

Sources for each country study differ, depending largely on availability. Authors draw quantitative data primarily from written and secondary sources, such as national statistics, reliable reports on specific incidents and general trends in criminality from national or international sources, and corroborated or reliable media reports on the same.

Authors draw qualitative data from first- and second-hand sources. In the case of first-hand sources, they rely on interviews with the categories of respondents noted above. Where authors were unable to obtain personal, one-on-one interviews, they used media or other public statements, typically those that could be corroborated or otherwise demonstrated to be reliable. Such sources can demonstrate both respondents' acknowledged changes in behaviour and changes in perceptions. Second-

---

[4] Malcolm Gladwell, *The Tipping Point: How Little Things Can Make a Big Difference*, Little Brown, Boston, 2000; Philip Zimbardo, *The Lucifer Effect: Understanding How Good People Turn Evil*, Random House, New York, 2007, p. 195.

[5] Kristin Reed and Ausra Padskocimaite, *The Right Toolkit: Applying Research Methods in the Service of Human Rights*, Human Rights Center, University of California Berkeley, 2012, pp. 9–11.

hand sources documenting reported changes in behaviour or perceptions may corroborate first-hand sources.

In some cases, authors have collected data from perpetrator or victim groups through focus group discussions and limited surveys, as well as through literature review and media analysis. Some authors were also able to use existing impact or deterrence studies and surveys.

1.8. The Role of Factors

While the goal of this introduction, and of this study's conclusion, is to draw out similarities between the country studies and the concomitant lessons and recommendations, such similarities cannot be forced. The Nuremberg Academy and this study's editors recognise that each country situation represents a unique combination of constantly evolving and interacting factors that influence whether international crimes are more or less likely to be committed. Recognising the uniqueness of each situation underscores the importance of developing unique solutions to achieve deterrence. This approach is consistent, for example, with what conflict resolution experts have written about the use of factors or indicators, that the "static labelling of conflict [...] is unsatisfactory, and in most cases creates a distorted picture of what is really at play".[6]

In the country studies in this volume, authors considered the relative presence of a number of factors, divided between court and trial-based, and external or contextual. Both sets of factors are further assessed in each situation between those that promote deterrence and those that undermine it. This list of factors or indicators is not intended to be comprehensive.

How can such a list of factors be derived and how should it further evolve? It is important to remember the purpose of factors or indicators, which is to "simplify raw data about a complex social phenomenon".[7] As

---

[6]   Luc van de Goor and Suzanne Verstegen, "Shooting at Moving Targets: From Reaction to Prevention", in Alfred van Staden, Jan Rood and Hans Labohm (eds.), *Cannons and Canons: Clingendael Views of Global and Regional Politics*, Royal Van Gorcum, Assen, 2003, pp. 272–73.

[7]   Kevin E. Davis, Benedict Kingsbury and Sally Engle Merry, "Introduction: Global Governance by Indicators", in Kevin E. Davis, Angelina Fisher, Benedict Kingsbury and Sally Engle Merry (eds.), *Governance by Indicators: Global Power through Quantification and Rankings*, Oxford University Press, Oxford, 2012, pp. 6–7.

such, they merely represent an entry point for understanding how we interact with the world around us.

Court/Trial-Based Factors	External/Contextual Factors
• Certainty/probability of prosecution • Speed of action of tribunal • Severity of punishment • Enforcement – police powers (ICC vs. ICTR) to compel co-operation or presence of supporting enforcer that is willing (e.g. UNSC) • Legitimacy of tribunal • Outreach (information awareness/transparency) • Prosecutorial strategies and exercise of discretion • Resources (financial/human/technical capacity) • Location of tribunal: one removed from theatre of violence could have diminished power of dissuasion	• Group dynamics: some perpetrators may not deterrable (system) "mob psychology" • The perpetrators (role of elites) • Cross-situation influence (e.g. impact of Taylor, al-Bashir, African Union on calculations by perpetrators in other situations) • Political economy (social norm) • Culture of impunity (social practices) responsible for witness/evidence tampering • Awareness of court and proceedings • Legitimacy/perception of court • Propaganda/ideology • National justice institutions (weak/strong) • Role of international community (action or inaction)

Figure 1: Factors Influencing International Crimes.

If justice as a complex phenomenon, as with deterrence itself, is viewed as "an ever-receding and ever-shrouded social ideal", one that must be constantly strived for, re-envisioned and reinvented, then these factors assessing progress towards deterrence must likewise be part of an ongoing, repetitive process for their construction. In short, just as efforts to achieve justice and deterrence must evolve, so must the indicators for measuring the successes and failures to achieve them. In the end, such indicators can in turn shape efforts to achieve justice and deterrence, acting as a rationale for action.[8] The process of producing such factors or indica-

---

[8]   Mark Goodale and Kamari Maxine Clarke, "Introduction: Understanding the Multiplicity of Justice", in Kamari Maxine Clarke and Mark Goodale (eds.), *Mirrors of Justice: Law*

tors is a collective one that is indivisible from standard-setting and decision-making, and even one that places those actors who generate them among the governors or wielders of power in global governance.[9]

Who are factors or indicators for? Indicators relating to international crimes are most specifically relevant for local actors, to empower them to take their destiny into their own hands. Indicators are also relevant to all those engaged with local actors, by dint of the interconnected nature of justice systems and the international dialogue on justice more broadly, as well as the cross-border nature of international crimes. The emphasis on dialogue between actors in the process of devising indicators is consonant with the need for the ICC and other actors to take account of the interconnectedness of court and trial-based factors, and external or contextual factors. One platform for that dialogue or communication, in the case of the ICC at least in large part, is the trial as didactic monument.[10] The effectiveness of these platforms relies on their ability to reach and retain various audiences: the societies most directly concerned, the international public, and components of each, including victims, police forces, armies, militias, states, NGOs and the UN. The long-term process is what matters the most, in particular to the societies most directly concerned.[11]

Indicators can provide crucial guidance to states and other actors, international tribunals included, seeking to understand the exact nature of their obligations, how far they extend, and how they might best attempt to fulfil them. This study will endeavour to provide useful and practical recommendations to states, the ICC and others, drawing from lessons learned in the country situations, on how to improve the chances for a deterrent effect from investigations and prosecutions, whether at the national or the international level.

---

and Power in the Post-Cold War Era, Cambridge University Press, Cambridge, 2010, pp. 10–11.

[9] Davis *et al.*, 2012, p. 15, see *supra* note 7.

[10] Carsten Stahn, "Between 'Faith' and 'Facts: By What Standards Should We Assess International Criminal Justice?", in *Leiden Journal of International Law*, 2012, vol. 25, no. 2, pp. 251–82; Mark Osiel, *Mass Atrocity, Collective Memory, and the Law*, Transaction Publishers, New Brunswick, NJ, 1999, p. 4; Pierre Hazan, "Measuring the Impact of Punishment and Forgiveness: A Framework for Evaluating Transitional Justice", in *International Review of the Red Cross*, 2008, vol. 88, no. 861, pp. 27–29.

[11] Hazan, 2008, see *supra* note 10.

1.9. Organisation and Recommendations

This book comprises 13 chapters. Following the introduction, Chapter 2 explores deterrence theory and positions deterrence analysis within the broader context of prevention theory and practices. Beginning with Chapter 3, each chapter through Chapter 12 presents a different case study. The case studies are in chronological order based on when an international criminal tribunal intervened. They examine Serbia, Rwanda, Kosovo, Sierra Leone, the Democratic Republic of Congo, Uganda, Sudan, Kenya, Côte d'Ivoire and Mali. Each case study analyses the effect of the relevant international criminal court, the factors that affect deterrence efforts, and the perceptions of those within the country. Recommendations for the ICC, states, and other international and national bodies are also explored in the case studies based on the experience of each situation. Finally, Chapter 13 synthesises the findings and recommendations in a conclusion.

2

Assessing Deterrence and the Implications for the International Criminal Court

Jennifer Schense[*]

2.1. Introduction

This chapter undertakes four tasks. First, it examines the goal of prevention or deterrence within the broader range of goals of the International Criminal Court ('ICC'), including whether this goal represents a general obligation to prevent crimes. Second, it examines how the ICC's efforts should fit in the broader context of the obligations and efforts of other members of the international community, in particular, nation-states. Third, it considers the role of indicators in assessing the potential deterrent or preventative effect of the actions of the ICC or others. Finally, it offers targeted policy recommendations that will make the approach to preventing crime more scientific, and create more objective benchmarks for assessing efforts to prevent crimes in the future. This chapter represents a distillation of a longer dissertation.

2.2. Deterrence and the Goals of the ICC

The chapter begins with an examination of the goal of prevention or deterrence within the broader range of goals of the ICC, including whether this goal represents a general obligation to prevent crimes.

---

[*] **Jennifer Schense** is the founding director of the House of Nuremberg and of Cat Kung Fu Productions, both dedicated to creating films and other popular, cultural works reflecting on justice. She has also worked with the International Criminal Court ('ICC') Office of the Prosecutor in the Jurisdiction, Complementarity and Cooperation Division since 2004, and is currently contributing to the ICC Registry's external relations and networking strategy. Prior to her work at the ICC, she served as the Legal Adviser for the NGO Coalition for the International Criminal Court from September 1998 until September 2004, and served for one year as a fellow at Human Rights Watch. She is currently completing her Ph.D. in international criminal law at Leiden University. She received her Juris Doctorate from Columbia Law School in 1997, and her B.Sc. in Russian language and Russian area studies from Georgetown University in 1993.

2.2.1. Goals of Criminal Law

Criminology, which in one form or another is almost as old as the commission of crime, has dabbled in deterrence, among the various purposes of punishment. Imprisonment arose originally in ancient Athens as an alternative penalty for those who could not afford fines, but eventually limits were set for those whose inability to pay led to indefinite imprisonment. The Romans were first to use imprisonment as a punishment, rather than simply for detention, but for the most part, punishment took physical forms, such as whipping, mutilation or slave labour, and prisons detained those either awaiting trial or awaiting punishment. In the 1700s, public resistance to torture and executions led to the development of mass incarceration, often coupled with hard labour, for two relatively contradictory purposes: first, to deter perpetrators, as prisons were meant to be so harsh and terrifying that they would deter people from committing crimes out of fear of going there; and second, to rehabilitate perpetrators, who were viewed through the prism of religious morality at the time as having sinned, and who therefore could be subjected in prison to instruction in Christian morality, obedience and proper behaviour.[1] These two purposes, deterrence and rehabilitation, demonstrate the broad spectrum of philosophical ideas underpinning criminology, which comprises at least three main schools and various additional social structure theories. International criminal law will have to begin to grapple with the same questions that have long faced national criminal law, in particular its goals and its priorities, and underpinning those goals, serious philosophical questions about what can best motivate and secure both individual growth and redemption, and societal change.

2.2.2. The Goals of the ICC

There is no definitive list of goals of the ICC, although the ICC Statute's Preamble describes the Statute's main purposes and results of the negotia-

---

[1] Mitchel P. Roth, *Prisons and Prison Systems: A Global Encyclopedia*, Greenwood Publishing, Santa Barbara, CA, 2006, p. xxvi; Peter Spierenburg, "The Body and The state: Early Modern Europe", in Norval Morris and David J. Rothman (eds.), *The Oxford History of the Prison: The Practice of Punishment in Western Society*, Oxford University Press, Oxford, 1998, p. 44; Michel Foucault, *Discipline & Punish: The Birth of the Prison*, Vintage Books, New York, 1995.

tion process, which form the basis for the Statute's acceptance.[2] Scholars have commented on the importance of further strategic thinking on the subject of why international criminal law punishes, or otherwise risk the ICC experiencing a perpetual stage of adolescence.[3] Goals can be categorised in myriad ways: teleological versus deontological; official versus operative; essential versus peripheral; process versus outcome; internally versus externally generated; proximate versus distant; short term versus long term; organisation-wide versus subsidiary; interim versus ultimate; implicit versus explicit.[4]

The most generally accepted goals drawn from the Preamble are: retribution; promotion of due process; encouragement of national proceedings under the rubric of positive complementarity; recognition of the interests of the victims; truth-telling and establishment of the historical record; reconciliation; promotion of the ICC and international law generally; promotion of the rule of law generally; maintenance of international peace and security; and individual and general deterrence or prevention. These goals must be viewed within the context of the most fundamental priority: for the Court to be and to be seen to be successful. None of these goals is easy or even potentially feasible to achieve, at least in full. There is a value though even to goals that cannot be achieved, as the international lawyer Martti Koskenniemi argues in citing the importance of the aspirational as well as the practical functions of international law: "The justice that animates political community is not one that may be fully attained".[5] Prevention deserves recognition as among the most important because if the Court and its partners can achieve it, many other goals would prove unnecessary.

---

[2] Morten Bergsmo and Otto Triffterer, "Preamble", in Otto Triffterer (eds.), *Commentary on the Rome Statute of the International Criminal Court: Observer's Notes, Article by Article*, Nomos, Munich, 1999.

[3] Kai Ambos, *Treatise on International Criminal Law*, vol. 1: *Foundations and General Part*, Oxford University Press, Oxford, 2013, p. 71; Mark A. Drumbl, "Collective Violence and Individual Punishment: The Criminality of Mass Atrocity", in *Northwestern University Law Review*, 2005, vol. 99, no. 2, pp. 539–610.

[4] Robert Cryer, Håkan Friman, Darryl Robinson and Elizabeth Wilmshurst, "The Aims, Objectives and Justifications of International Criminal Law", in Robert Cryer, Håkan Friman, Darryl Robinson and Elizabeth Wilmshurst (eds.), *An Introduction to International Criminal Law and Procedure*, 3rd ed., Cambridge University Press, Cambridge, 2014, pp. 28–45.

[5] Martti Koskenniemi, "What is International Law For?", in Malcolm D. Evans (ed.), *International Law*, 2nd ed., Oxford University Press, Oxford, 2006, p. 111.

2.2.2.1. Retribution

Retribution is the conduct of successful investigations and prosecutions, identifying perpetrators of ICC Statute crimes and submitting them for judgment and punishment, a goal supported explicitly in paragraph 4 of the Statute's Preamble. It is one of the most common rationales for criminal justice, extending back to biblical injunctions and the Code of Hammurabi. It finds more recent support from practitioners and scholars Rolf Fife, Diane Orentlicher, Robert Cryer, Håkan Friman, Darryl Robinson and Elizabeth Wilmshurst, citing among other sources an International Criminal Tribunal for the former Yugoslavia ('ICTY') impact study and the ICTY's *Alekšovski, Nikolić* and *Todorović* cases.[6] *Nikolić* emphasises that crimes will be punished and impunity will not prevail; *Todorović* stresses the need for a "fair and balanced approach" to ensure that penalties are proportionate to wrongdoing; and *Alekšovski* clarifies that retribution should not be confused with revenge.[7]

Of the ICC's four sentences thus far against Thomas Lubanga Dyilo, Germaine Katanga and Jean-Pierre Bemba, and the most recent plea agreement from and sentencing of Ahmad Al Faqi Al Mahdi, most of them address retribution among other goals. The *Lubanga* sentencing decision is fairly light in its reasoning, only briefly mentioning that the sentence must be in proportion to the crime,[8] but the other decisions are more detailed and borrow language from the previous decisions in succession, reinforcing the original reasoning of the Chambers. The Chamber in the *Bemba* decision draws from the ICC Statute's Preamble in arguing that

---

6. Rolf Einar Fife, "Penalties", in Roy S. Lee (ed.), *The International Criminal Court: The Making of the Rome Statute: Issues, Negotiations, Results*, Kluwer Law International, The Hague, 1999, pp. 319–20; Diane F. Orentlicher, *That Someone Guilty Be Punished: The Impact of the ICTY in Bosnia*, Open Society Institute, New York, 2010, pp. 34–46; Cryer *et al.*, 2014, see *supra* note 4.

7. International Criminal Tribunal for the former Yugoslavia ('ICTY'), *Prosecutor v. Momir Nikolić*, Trial Chamber, Sentencing Judgment, IT-02-60/1, 2 December 2003, paras. 86–87 (http://www.legal-tools.org/doc/f90842/); ICTY, *Prosecutor v. Stevan Todorović*, Trial Chamber, Sentencing Judgment, IT-95-9/1, 31 July 2001, para. 29 (http://www.legal-tools.org/doc/0cd4b3/); ICTY, *Prosecutor v. Zlatko Alekšovski*, Appeals Chamber, Judgment, IT-95-14/1, 24 March 2000, para. 185 (http://www.legal-tools.org/doc/176f05/).

8. International Criminal Court ('ICC'), Situation in the Democratic Republic of the Congo, *Prosecutor v. Thomas Lubanga Dyilo*, Trial Chamber, Decision on Sentence pursuant to Article 76 of the Statute, ICC-01/04-01/06, 10 July 2012 (http://www.legal-tools.org/doc/c79996/).

retribution and deterrence are the primary objectives of punishment at the ICC. It elaborates: "Retribution is not to be understood as fulfilling a desire for revenge, but as an expression of the international community's condemnation of the crimes", drawing as well from paragraphs 37 and 38 of the *Katanga* decision. It finds that the sentence must be proportionate to the crime and the culpability of the convicted person, then goes on to apply a comprehensive scheme to balance the relevant aggravating and mitigating circumstances pursuant to Rule 145(1)(b) and to pronounce a sentence for each crime, as well as a joint sentence specifying the total period of imprisonment, comprising a proportionate sentence and properly reflecting the culpability of the convicted person.[9] The *Al Mahdi* plea agreement likewise goes some way towards demonstrating that the sentence sought by the prosecution, to which the defence has agreed, is proportionate to the damage caused.[10] The same language in the *Bemba* and *Katanga* sentencings is used in the *Al Mahdi* sentencing.[11]

Some scholars have questioned whether retribution is an achievable goal for the ICC, given that the ICC under Article 77 of the Statute can generally issue only a maximum 30-year sentence, with a life imprisonment term "justified [only] by the extreme gravity of the crime and the individual circumstances of the convicted person". Given charges as extreme as genocide, can the punishment ever match the crime? This is a challenge at the national level as well.[12] Retribution, therefore, may be the most common official goal of national and international court systems, but its fulfilment remains a challenge everywhere.

---

[9] ICC, Situation in the Central African Republic, *Prosecutor v. Jean-Pierre Bemba Gombo*, Trial Chamber, Decision on Sentence pursuant to Article 76 of the Statute, ICC-01/05-01/08, 21 June 2016, paras. 10–12 ('Bemba Decision on Sentence') (http://www.legal-tools.org/doc/f4c14e/).

[10] ICC, "Al Mahdi Case: Accused Makes an Admission of Guilt at Trial Opening", Press Release, 22 August 2016; Ruth Maclean, "'I Am Sorry: Islamist Apologises for Destroying Timbuktu Mausoleums", in *The Guardian*, 22 August 2016.

[11] ICC, Situation in the Republic of Mali, *Prosecutor v. Ahmad Al Faqi Al Mahdi*, Trial Chamber, Judgment and Sentence, ICC-01/12-01/15, 27 September 2016, paras. 66–67 ('Al Mahdi Judgment') (http://www.legal-tools.org/doc/042397/).

[12] Drumbl, 2005, see *supra* note 3; Cryer et al., 2014, see *supra* note 4; Mark Osiel, *Mass Atrocity, Collective Memory, and the Law*, Transaction Publishers, New Brunswick, NJ, 1999.

2.2.2.2. Due Process

Due process does not appear in the Preamble, although it could be sub-sumed under "effective prosecution" in paragraph 4, but it is referenced explicitly in Articles 17(2) and 20(3)(b) of the Statute on admissibility. Due process emphasises in particular the rights of the defence. It is central in defining what will be successful investigations and prosecutions. The judges have a particular responsibility for ensuring its achievement, and this is reflected in all of the Chambers' judgments and sentences. For example, in the *Al Mahdi* sentencing, the Chamber endeavours to balance mitigating and aggravating factors, ensuring that aggravating circumstances are not double-counted towards the earlier assessment of gravity and towards sentencing, and that aggravating circumstances must be proved beyond a reasonable doubt, whereas mitigating circumstances must be proved only on a balance of probabilities.[13] This reflects an effort to ensure due process for the defence.

2.2.2.3. Positive Complementarity

Positive complementarity is unique to the ICC among international courts, although the ICTY's contribution to the creation of domestic war crimes chambers bears similarities.[14] Complementarity is reflected in preambular paragraphs 4, 6 and 10. Positive complementarity implies an active role for the Court in encouraging national proceedings, as reflected in Article 93(10)(a) of the ICC Statute, as well as Articles 15, 18, 53, 59, 83, 88 and 89; in short, articles that support communications and consultations between the Court and states. Positive complementarity also has strong roots in Office of the Prosecutor policy and practice.

2.2.2.4. Recognition of the Interests of Victims

The interests of victims are recognised in preambular paragraph 2, as well as Articles 15, 19, 53, 54, 68, 75, 79, 82, 93 and 110 on reparations, the Trust Fund for Victims, and the participation of victims in all stages of the proceedings. The ICC borrows victims' participation from the *partie civile* procedures in civil law systems; it does not have a history in common

---

[13] Al Mahdi Judgment, paras. 73–74, see *supra* note 11.

[14] Orentlicher, 2010, see *supra* note 6.

law systems unless it is considered aligned with the goal of protecting society.[15]

The *Bemba* sentencing decision argues that a proportionate sentence will acknowledge the harm to the victims, but the *Al Mahdi* plea agreement is particularly relevant. In his oral statement in court on 22 August 2016, Al Mahdi admitted guilt for the war crime of the destruction of historical and religious monuments. He apologised to Mali and to mankind more broadly, expressed his deep regret to the people of Timbuktu in particular, sought their forgiveness, and promised that it would be the last wrongful act he would ever commit.[16] The Chamber in sentencing Al Mahdi to nine years' imprisonment took into account a number of mitigating factors: among them in particular, that he showed "honest repentance [...] deep regret and great pain".[17]

The *Lubanga* and *Katanga* sentencing decisions by comparison shed further light on the impact of Al Mahdi's statement. Katanga made a similar apology to his victims, and the sentencing decision noted the victims' legitimate need for truth and justice, and for recognition of damage and suffering caused to them. It took into consideration the value of Katanga's apology, as well as the interests of victims more generally, in determining Katanga's sentence. By comparison, Trial Chamber I in the *Lubanga* case considered his involvement in attempts to negotiate peace as "of limited relevance" as a mitigating factor.[18] Although the *Lubanga* sentence does not address the goal of recognition of the interests of victims directly, it includes extensive language about the effects of crimes against children as a subset group of victims. Such apologies may be less than genuine, but

> [e]ven hypocrisy may sometimes deserve one cheer, for it confirms the value of the idea, and limits the scope and blatancy of violations...It responds to and generates forces that induce compliance, and it cannot long be maintained in the face of blatant noncompliance.[19]

---

[15] Fife, 1999, see *supra* note 6.

[16] Jason Burke, "ICC Ruling for Timbuktu Destruction Should Be Deterrent for Others", in *The Guardian*, 27 September 2016.

[17] Al Mahdi Judgment, paras. 86–105, see *supra* note 11.

[18] In 2015, Thomas Lubanga also expressed his desire following completion of his sentence to pursue a Ph.D. at Kisengani University on tribal conflict management.

[19] Louis Henkin, *The Age of Rights*, Columbia University Press, New York, 1990.

2.2.2.5. Truth-Telling and Establishment of the Historical Record

Truth-telling and establishment of the historical record is a goal that makes abuses harder to deny, tied to "the inalienable right to know the truth about violations",[20] but it is not one on which all judges agree. In the ICTY's *Krštić* judgment, the Tribunal expresses its intention to "counter denial and create a record of the Srebrenica massacre", but in the *Karadžić* case, the judges argue that "[t]he Chamber's purpose is not to serve the academic study of history". They also cite Judge B.V.A. Röling of the Tokyo Tribunal as enunciating a difference between the "real truth" and "trial truth".[21]. Most critics seem to believe that this goal is for the most part out of the reach of international courts. The *Lubanga* sentencing and *Katanga* judgment effectively have nothing on truth-telling. Al Mahdi's and Katanga's apologies to their victims may come the closest to truth-telling and establishment of the historical record at the ICC: as the Al Mahdi apology put it: "We need to speak justice even to ourselves. We have to be truthful, even if it burns our own hands".[22]

2.2.2.6. Reconciliation

The ICC Statute does not mention reconciliation, although some link it with the maintenance of international peace and security, and recognise it as a general goal of national criminal law.[23] The *Al Mahdi* plea agreement is to date the most relevant ICC finding, in that Al Mahdi seemed in his oral statement to the Court to recognise the importance of reconciling himself to the people of Timbuktu in particular, and of Mali in general. In the same vein, Katanga's apology to his victims is also potentially relevant to reconciliation, dependent also in part on how many of his victims will be aware of the apology. The *Katanga* sentencing itself very briefly references the restoration of peace and reconciliation of the people concerned, while the *Lubanga* judgment and sentencing say nothing about

---

[20] Orentlicher, 2010, see *supra* note 6; Cryer *et al.*, 2014, see *supra* note 4.

[21] Antonio Cassese and B.V.A. Röling, *The Tokyo Trial and Beyond: Reflections of a Peacemonger*, Polity Press, Cambridge, 1992; Robert Cryer, Håkan Friman, Darryl Robinson and Elizabeth Wilmshurst (eds.), *An Introduction to International Criminal Law and Procedure,* 2nd ed., Cambridge University Press, Cambridge, 2010, p. 26.

[22] ICC Press Release, 2016, see *supra* note 10; Maclean, 2016, see *supra* note 10.

[23] Fife, 1999, see *supra* note 6; Cryer *et al.*, 2014, see *supra* note 4; Orentlicher, 2010, see *supra* note 6.

reconciliation. The *Bemba* sentencing argues that a proportionate sentence will not only acknowledge the harm to the victims, but will also promote the restoration of peace and reconciliation.

2.2.2.7. Maintenance of International Peace and Security

Preambular paragraphs 3 and 7 reference the maintenance of international peace and security. The *Lubanga* and *Katanga* decisions have only vague references to the restoration of peace. The *Bemba* decision states that acknowledging the harm to the victims promotes the restoration of peace and reconciliation, and in paragraphs 71 and 72, lays out some concrete guidelines, in delving into the defence argument that Bemba contributed to the negotiation of ceasefire and peace agreements and that this should be considered in his favour. The Chamber responded that "promotion of peace and reconciliation may only constitute a mitigating circumstance if it is genuine and concrete".[24] In Bemba's case, the Chamber first expressed its doubt that Bemba's alleged peacebuilding and humanitarian efforts in the Democratic Republic of the Congo ('DRC') were sincere, genuine or ever implemented. Where one witness noted that the Movement for the Liberation of Congo's political goals and motivations translated into at least some humanitarian assistance, the Chamber argued that "assistance to persons other than the victims and selective assistance to the victims may be of limited, if any, relevance to the sentence". The Chamber also noted that any capacity Bemba may have for peacebuilding may not be a mitigating but rather an aggravating circumstance, where he refused to exercise that capacity. The Chamber found that:

> Mr Bemba's alleged contributions to peace in the DRC and the well-being of the population of Équateur demonstrate his experience and capacity to engage in peacebuilding efforts and assist civilians. However, despite invitations and repeated opportunities to make the same efforts in the CAR, he failed to do so.[25]

In this case, his choice to commit crimes rather than to exercise his peacebuilding capacity worked against him when it came time for the Chamber to render a sentencing decision.

---

[24] Bemba Decision on Sentence, paras. 71–72, see *supra* note 9.
[25] *Ibid.*, para.76.

2.2.2.8. Promotion of the ICC and of International Law Generally

Preambular paragraph 11 and Article 21 reflect promotion of the ICC and of international law, and of the rule of law more generally, similar to the affirmation of core values of international law.[26] The *Lubanga* sentencing decision has nothing to say on this, and the *Katanga* and the *Bemba* sentencing decisions are only slightly more forthcoming. Katanga cites one of the two functions of punishment as "the expression of society's condemnation of the criminal act and of the person who committed it"[27] and *Bemba* defines retribution as "an expression of the international community's condemnation of the crimes".[28]

This concept of expression (alternately described as demonstration, denunciation, explanation, education or didactive function) is key, more than their quantitative records, to international criminal courts maintaining faith in law and institutions.[29] The ICTY's *Kordić* and *Ćerkez* cases underscore "the educational function [... which] aims at conveying the message that rules of international humanitarian law have to be obeyed under all circumstances".[30] "Selectivity and indeterminacy are especially corrosive to the expressive value of the law".[31]

2.2.2.9. Ending Impunity

Preambular paragraph 5 reflects the goal of ending impunity. It is often cited in ICC statements and related commentary, but it is not specifically mentioned in the *Lubanga, Katanga* or *Bemba* sentencing decisions, or in the *Al Mahdi* plea agreement.

---

[26] Orentlicher, 2010, see *supra* note 6.

[27] ICC, Situation in the Democratic Republic of the Congo, *Prosecutor v. Germain Katanga*, Trial Chamber, Decision on Sentence pursuant to article 76 of the Statute, ICC-01/04-01/07, 23 May 2014, para. 38 (http://www.legal-tools.org/doc/5af172/).

[28] Bemba Decision on Sentence, para. 11, see *supra* note 9.

[29] Carsten Stahn, "Between 'Faith' and 'Facts': By What Standards Should We Assess International Criminal Justice?", in *Leiden Journal of International Law*, 2012, vol. 25, no. 2, pp. 251–82; Ambos, 2013, see *supra* note 3; Cryer *et al.*, 2014, see *supra* note 4.

[30] Cryer *et al.*, 2014, p. 36, see *supra* note 4

[31] Drumbl 2005, p. 589, see *supra* note 3.

2.2.2.10. Prevention and Individual or General Deterrence

Preambular paragraph 5 references prevention, and specifically the determination of states "to put an end to impunity for the perpetrators of these
crimes and thus to contribute to the prevention of such crimes". Prevention does not figure in the founding documents of the *ad hoc* tribunals, but
it has figured in their decisions. The ICTR's *Rutaganda* judgment finds
that the prosecution of international crimes can "dissuade forever, others
who may be tempted in the future to perpetrate such atrocities by showing
them that the international community shall not tolerate the serious violations of international humanitarian law and human rights".[32] The *Rutaga-
nira* and *Ruggiu* cases also reference deterrence along with retribution and
rehabilitation as the main purposes of punishment in equal value.[33] The
ICTY's *Delalić* case identifies deterrence as "probably the most important factor in the assessment of appropriate sentences".[34] The *Orić* and
Zelenović cases also mention deterrence.[35] Some ICTY reports and impact
studies have similarly found deterrence to be an objective and an at least
partial accomplishment of the tribunal.[36]

Scholarship specific to the ICC supports the idea of a deterrent role
in some form.[37] Among the points they have raised, they recognise that

---

[32] International Criminal Tribunal for Rwanda ('ICTR'), *Prosecutor v. Georges Rutaganda*,
Trial Chamber, Judgment, ICTR-96-3-T, 6 December 1999, para. 455 (http://www.legal-
tools.org/doc/f0dbbb/).

[33] Ambos, 2013, see *supra* note 3.

[34] ICTY, *Prosecutor v Zejnil Delalić et al.*, Trial Chamber, Judgment, IT-96-21-T, 16 November 1998, para. 1234 (http://www.legal-tools.org/doc/6b4a33/).

[35] Ambos, 2013, see *supra* note 3.

[36] Orentlicher, 2010, see *supra* note 6; Padraig McAuliffe, "Suspended Disbelief? The Curi-
ous Endurance of the Deterrence Rationale in International Criminal Law", in *New Zea-
land Journal of Public and International Law*, 2012, vol. 10, p. 257; Gary J. Bass, *Stay the
Hand of Vengeance: The Politics of War Crimes Tribunals*, Princeton University Press,
Princeton, NJ, 2000, pp. 229–31.

[37] Ambos, 2013, see *supra* note 3; Bergsmo and Triffterer, 1999, see *supra* note 2; Fife, 1999,
see *supra* note 6; Luigi Condorelli and Santiago Villalpando, "Relationship of the Court
with the United Nations", in Antonio Cassese (ed.), *The Rome Statute of the International
Criminal Court: A Commentary*, Oxford University Press, Oxford, 2002, p. 221; Roy S.
Lee, "Introduction: The Rome Conference and Its Contributions to International Law", in
Roy S. Lee (ed.), *The International Criminal Court: The Making of the Rome Statute: Is-
sues, Negotiations, Results*, Kluwer Law International, The Hague, 1999, pp. 1–7; Beth A.
Simmons and Allison Danner, "Credible Commitments and the International Criminal
Court", in *International Organization*, 2010, vol. 64, no. 2, pp. 225–56; Paola Gaeta, "Of-
ficial Capacity and Immunities", in Antonio Cassese (ed.), *The Rome Statute of the Inter-*

deterrence or prevention is generally accepted in and even a primary function of international criminal law, and debate whether the Court's mere existence can deter, or whether specific activities by the Court, states or others are required. They highlight the potential deterrent effect of the irrelevance of official capacity, as reflected in the ICC Appeals Chamber's *Bemba* decision and Trial Chamber's *Katanga* decision, as well as the potential deterrent effect of the denunciatory and educative functions of the Court, and the inculcation of a culture of respect for the law that would remove the use of violence as a "morally open" option, or what some would describe as "social deterrence". They draw parallels with the ICTY's efforts at truth-telling and its importance in deterring revenge crimes. They also acknowledge that lack of certainty of punishment, lack of speed, and selectivity are corrosive to deterrence. There is no consensus that deterrence is an absolutely achievable goal, either at the national or the international level. But in reviewing the other goals of international criminal law, there is no reason to argue that deterrence or prevention is any more complex or difficult to achieve. Any study of deterrence must keep this in mind.

As for ICC litigation, the *Katanga* sentencing decision is relatively explicit in addressing the objectives of punishment, arguing that the Court must issue penalties that will have a real dissuasive effect. The *Bemba* sentencing decision acknowledges deterrence along with retribution as the primary objective of punishment at the ICC. It elaborates on deterrence, finding that a sentence should be adequate to discourage a convicted person from recidivism (that is, specific deterrence), as well as to ensure that those who would consider committing similar crimes will be dissuaded from doing so (that is, general deterrence). The *Al Mahdi* plea agreement is relevant here, as he states to the Chamber that the crimes he committed

national Criminal Court: A Commentary, Oxford University Press, Oxford, 2002, p. 990; Orentlicher, 2005, see *supra* note 6; Daniel D. Ntanda Nsereko, "Prosecutorial Discretion before National Courts and International Tribunals", in *Journal of International Criminal Justice*, 2005, vol. 3, no. 1, pp. 124–44; Cryer *et al.*, 2014, see *supra* note 4; Drumbl, 2005, see *supra* note 3; Richard Goldstone, "Bringing War Criminals to Justice during an Ongoing War", in Jonathan Moore (ed.), *Hard Choices: Moral Dilemmas in Humanitarian Intervention*, Rowman & Littlefield, Lanham, MD, 1998, pp. 195–204; David Bosco, "The International Criminal Court and Crime Prevention: Byproduct or Conscious Goal?", in *Michigan State International Law Review*, 2013, vol. 19, no. 2, pp. 163, 170–71; Hyeran Jo and Beth A. Simmons, "Can the International Criminal Court Deter Atrocity?", in *International Organization*, 2016, vol. 70, no. 3, pp. 443–75.

would be his last wrongful acts, suggesting that his prosecution led to a specific deterrent effect.[38]

On a related note, the Chamber in the *Bemba* case found rehabilitation to be a relevant purpose, although it argued that in cases concerning the most serious crimes of concern to the international community as a whole, rehabilitation should not be given undue weight.

2.2.2.11. The Difference between Deterrence and Prevention

While international legal scholars do not always recognise or acknowledge the difference between deterrence and prevention, there are good reasons for parsing them out, and for recognising that both are at play at the ICC, even if the primary goal is prevention. Deterrence draws on the hedonistic calculus whereby individuals weigh potential gains versus costs. Law is intended to tip the balance for criminal acts towards cost, and so to deter their commission.[39] Deterrence may be divided into general deterrence, specific deterrence, targeted deterrence, and restrictive or partial deterrence.[40] Specific deterrence refers to the discouragement of subsequent criminal activity by those who have been punished. General deterrence refers to the discouragement of criminal activity through fear of punishment among the general public. Targeted deterrence attempts to deter specific individuals or groups within a society. Restrictive deterrence refers to the minimisation rather than the abandonment of criminal activity, which occurs "when, to diminish the risk or severity of a legal punishment, a potential offender engages in some action that has the effect of reducing his or her commissions of a crime".[41]

The ability of law to deter behaviour is a function of three variables relating to punishment: certainty, celerity (that is, swiftness or speed), and

---

[38] Some noted that Al Mahdi did not renounce his formerly held belief, based on Islamic teachings, that tombs should not be higher than one inch above ground; one of the prosecution lawyers challenged that if he had the opportunity, he would do the same thing again, to which he averred that he acted because he believed one is not allowed to build upon tombs, but that from a legal and political viewpoint, one should not cause damage that is more severe than the usefulness of the action.

[39] Christopher W. Mullins and Dawn L. Rothe, "The Ability of the International Criminal Court to Deter Violations of International Criminal Law: A Theoretical Assessment", in *International Criminal Law Review*, 2010, vol. 10, no. 5, pp. 771–86.

[40] Bosco, 2010, see *supra* note 37.

[41] *Ibid.*, pp. 170–71.

proportionality, parameters on which international criminal law scholars generally agree.[42] An ICTY impact study similarly finds "certainty of apprehension" to be the more decisive factor,[43] a factor that in international criminal law has at least increased from something impossible to imagine to something potentially achievable, the limited effect of which is hotly debated.[44]

Crime prevention, by contrast, includes government and community-based programmes, policies and initiatives to reduce the incidence of risk factors correlated with criminal participation and the rate of victimisation, to enforce the law and maintain criminal justice, and to change perceptions that lead to the commission of crimes. Preventative measures can be undertaken at the primary, secondary and tertiary levels. Primary prevention addresses individual and family-level factors. Secondary prevention focuses on at-risk situations in which individuals may find themselves, and promotes social programmes to reduce these risks. Tertiary prevention is pursued after a crime has occurred in order to prevent successive incidents.[45] Prevention is generally accepted as being broader than deterrence, as it includes incapacitation, rehabilitation, education, stigmatisation and moral pressure.[46]

While the boundary between the two is not always clear, and what some, for example, might call negative general prevention is likely in fact

---

[42] Mullins and Rothe, 2010, see *supra* note 39.

[43] Kimi L. King and James D. Meernik, "Assessing the Impact of the International Criminal Tribunal for the Former Yugoslavia: Balancing International and Local Interests While Doing Justice", in Bert Swart, Alexander Zahar and Göran Sluiter (eds.), *The Legacy of the International Criminal Tribunal for the Former Yugoslavia*, Oxford University Press, Oxford, 2011, pp. 7–44.

[44] Mark Findlay, "Enunciating Genocide: Crime, Rights and the Impact of Judicial Intervention", in *International Criminal Law Review*, 2013, vol. 13, no. 1, pp. 297–317; Alette Smeulers, Barbara Hola and Tom van den Berg, "Sixty-Five Years of International Criminal Justice: The Facts and Figures", in *International Criminal Law Review*, 2013, vol. 13, no. 1, pp. 7–41.

[45] New York City Alliance Against Sexual Assault, "Factsheets: Crime Prevention" (http://www.svfreenyc.org/survivors_factsheet_17.html); Australian Institute of Criminology, "Approaches to Understanding Crime Prevention", 20 May 2003.

[46] Bosco, 2010, see *supra* note 37.

to be targeted deterrence, it is important to keep these concepts as distinct as possible, so as to preserve their power.[47]

Deterrence is theoretically easier to measure because it tends to follow the impact of the application of the law on specific perpetrators. Whether a particular perpetrator reoffends is generally a matter of public record, although not all crimes are reported and therefore known. Prevention's aims are much broader. Prevention more than deterrence grapples with the truism that it is impossible to prove a negative. In fact, where deterrence attempts to change the demonstrable behaviour of a single individual, prevention attempts to change the entire social environment in which that individual may perpetrate crimes. By definition, it attempts to create an alternate reality in which certain criminal actions are no longer morally available and thus difficult or impossible to undertake. What might have been becomes the domain of a parallel universe, open to speculation but impossible to know. In assessing the legal as well as the social, political and economic impacts of any effort to prevent crimes, the ICC will need to rely on experts and organisations much better suited to these kinds of assessments than is an international court.

A further distinction can be drawn. The term 'prevention' originates from the period 1375 to 1425, from the late Middle English and Middle French, drawing from the Latin word *praeventus*, past participle of *praevenīre*, to anticipate what is to come. The modern French word, *prevenir*, to foresee and/or to forewarn, has similar roots. By comparison, the word 'deter' has a slightly later provenance, originating in the period 1570–1580, from the Latin word *dēterrēre*, to prevent or to hinder, the equivalent of to frighten (hence the link between deterrence and terror; and the link in French to *de*, meaning from, and *terror*, meaning terror, as in to flee from terror). Often when it comes to discussing crimes, the terms prevention and deterrence are considered interchangeable; this is incorrect. There are fundamental differences between them. At the risk of oversimplification, prevention is orientated around hope; that through forewarning, society may close off as a moral option the risk of crimes being committed, and build on that foundation a better version of itself. Deterrence is orientated around fear, and specifically around instilling fear of punish-

---

47 Hector Olásolo, "The Role of the International Criminal Court in Preventing Atrocity Crimes through Timely Intervention", Inaugural Lecture as Chair in International Criminal Law and International Criminal Procedure at Utrecht University, 18 October 2010.

ment in potential perpetrators. While deterrence is the most traditional goal of criminal law, prevention may be closer to what the ICC should aim to achieve, an aim to which it may be able to contribute in concert with other actors already addressing these broader social, economic and political questions of how we live together, in our national homes, and as an international community.

2.2.3.   What Is the Value of Goals?

Any examination of goals must ask what their value is and whether they represent aspirations or obligations. Article 4 recognises the ICC's international legal personality as limited to "such capacity as may be necessary for the exercise of its functions and the fulfilment of its purposes", which are described in the Preamble. This suggests that any goals springing from the Preamble constitute obligations in some form, indirectly rooted in the broad range of treaty, customary and soft law sources that support the duties of states and which underpin the ICC Statute. As such, the ICC is obliged to respect the law as much as enforce it, and this pertains in particular to *jus cogens* obligations. Like the UN Charter and all other treaties, the ICC Statute cannot derogate from *jus cogens* obligations, and therefore neither can the ICC. It is worth noting in this context that the UN Security Council is also bound to respect *jus cogens* norms, especially those enshrined in its own governing treaty, the UN Charter. The failure of the Council to do so threatens the legitimacy of the Council as much as it lessens the impact of these norms and their universality.

The ICC's duties are essentially nesting; they fit within and do not therefore exist independently of those of the states that created the Court. In turn, states have acknowledged and vested part of their duties in the ICC as an independent tool for their achievement. In Preambular paragraph 5, states acknowledge that the ICC can at best contribute to prevention; in the *Katanga* and *Ngudjolo Chui* cases, the Appeals Chamber found that states that voluntarily relinquish jurisdiction to the ICC via a state referral do not negate their obligation to prosecute international crimes.[48]

---

[48]   ICC, Situation in the Democratic Republic of the Congo, *Prosecutor v. Germain Katanga and Mathieu Ngudjolo Chui*, Judgment on the Appeal of Mr. Germain Katanga against the Oral Decision of Trial Chamber II of 12 June 2009 on the Admissibility of the Case, ICC-01/04-01/07 OA 8, 25 September 2009 (http://www.legal-tools.org/doc/ba82b5/).

2.2.4. The Legal Norm and Corresponding Duty to Prevent Crimes

The nature of any obligation to prevent crimes or deter perpetrators is of specific interest here. A general legal norm, prescribing a duty to prevent international crimes does exist in the form of the responsibility to protect doctrine. This argument depends in part on the underlying definition of a legal norm; positivist arguments erring on the safe side include only treaty obligations, where the consent to undertake an obligation is clear. This view of legal norms, however, is relatively static and does not take proper account of the dynamism and fluidity of modern international lawmaking. The alternate view is that the norm and corresponding duty are in the process of emerging because the emergence of a norm is not a one-off occurrence, but an ongoing process. The general duty to prevent international crimes exists in one form now; ongoing state practice and *opinio juris* will inexorably shape and polish that norm, as will the rough and tumble of international relations, as legal norms themselves are nuanced and influenced by every interaction between states and non-governmental organisations ('NGOs'), among states, between states and the UN Secretariat, and between UN experts and academics.

It matters whether or not a general legal norm and corresponding duty exist, but the exact form may matter less. The responsibility to protect doctrine, endorsed by the UN General Assembly and the UN Security Council, already constitutes soft law. Soft law "covers all those social rules generated by states or other subjects of international law which are not legally binding but which are nevertheless of special legal relevance". Lord McNair coined the term soft law to describe instruments with "extra-legal binding effect", whose "compliance pull can be significantly higher than hard law norms".[49] With the increasing influence of soft law, "the formerly strict division of sources into legally binding ones and those that lack binding force is getting blurred".[50]

The legal norm and corresponding duty to prevent draw from and build on obligations to prevent conflicts, prevent human rights violations and prevent crimes, and directly through the endorsement and support of the responsibility to protect doctrine itself over the past 10 and more years.

---

[49] Daniel Thürer, "Soft Law", in *Max Planck Encyclopedia of Public International Law*, 2103, vol. 9, pp. 270–71.

[50] Rüdiger Wolfrum, "Sources of International Law", in *Max Planck Encyclopedia of Public International Law*, 2013, vol. 9, pp. 299–313.

First, the legal norm and corresponding duty to prevent international crimes draws on the UN Charter itself, in particular its Preamble and opening articles, which serve as what the legal theorist Hans Kelsen has described as the basic norm against which all other norms are tested.[51] The Preamble and opening articles set out the purposes and principles of the UN system, namely: the prevention of conflict and the promotion of peace; the promotion of principles of justice and of respect for obligations arising from treaties and other sources of international law; the promotion of respect for human rights in all their forms; and the promotion of international co-operation in solving international problems, with a particular emphasis on the obligation to act in good faith in all of the above.

These purposes and principles are considered to have the character of *jus cogens* norms.[52] Other *jus cogens* norms are largely believed to include the outlawing of aggression and of genocide, the principles and rules concerning the basic rights of the human person, including protection from slavery and racial discrimination[53] and the prohibition of torture,[54] the prohibition of the use of force,[55] and the principles and rules of humanitarian law.[56] These *jus cogens* norms are further buttressed by norms of customary international law and soft law, which are in constant interplay and which reflect obligations that may not be formally binding but may, as noted above, have extra-legal compliance pull.

---

[51] Hans Kelsen, *Pure Theory of Law*, University of California Press, Berkeley, 1967.

[52] Jochen A. Frowein, "Ius Cogens", in *Max Planck Encyclopedia of Public International Law*, 2013, vol. 9, pp. 443–46.

[53] International Court of Justice ('ICJ'), *Barcelona Traction, Light and Power Company, Limited (Belgium v. Spain)*, Judgment, Second Phase, 5 February 1970, para. 34 (http://www.legal-tools.org/doc/75e8c5/). On genocide: ICJ, *Reservations to the Convention on the Prevention and Punishment of the Crime of Genocide, Advisory Opinion*, ICGJ 227, 28 May 1951; ICJ, *Case Concerning Armed Activities on the Territory of the Congo (Democratic Republic of the Congo v. Rwanda)*, Order, 18 September 2002 (http://www.legal-tools.org/doc/a204bc/); ICJ, *Case Concerning Armed Activities on the Territory of the Congo (New Application: 2002), Democratic Republic of the Congo v. Rwanda*, Judgment, 3 February 2006 (http://www.legal-tools.org/doc/1d7775/).

[54] ICTY, *Prosecutor v. Anto Furundžija*, Appeals Chamber, Judgment, IT-95-17/1, 21 July 2000 (http://www.legal-tools.org/doc/660d3f/).

[55] ICJ, *Military and Paramilitary Activities in and against Nicaragua (Nicaragua v. United States of America)*, Judgment, 27 June 1986, para. 100 (http://www.legal-tools.org/doc/046698/).

[56] ICJ, *Legality of the Threat or Use of Nuclear Weapons*, Advisory Opinion, ICJ Reports, 8 July 1996, para. 226.

2.2.5. Application of the Legal Norm and Corresponding Duty to Prevent Crimes

This chapter now examines how the ICC's efforts should fit with the obligations and efforts of other members of the international community, in particular states. It presents 10 matrices to break down the legal framework by which the obligation to prevent international crimes may be analysed and applied. How it is applied depends on the capacity of each actor concerned, and this is true for the ICC as much as it is for states and other actors; an honest assessment of that capacity is essential, as will be seen below. This chapter further provides two considerations for further context: first, that legal norms must be applied on a case-by-case basis, and second, that these legal norms represent a duty of conduct, not result.

2.2.5.1. Case-by-Case Basis

The responsibility to protect doctrine, as set out in paragraph 139 of the 2005 World Summit Outcome Document, is a good illustration of why legal norms must be applied on a case-by-case basis. Paragraph 139 sets out nine conditions for its application by states: 1) collective action; 2) in a timely manner; 3) through the UN Security Council; 4) in accordance with the UN Charter; 5) including Chapter VII; 6) on a case-by-case basis; 7) in co-operation with relevant organisations as appropriate; 8) should peaceful means be inadequate; and 9) should national authorities manifestly fail to protect their populations from genocide, war crimes, ethnic cleansing and crimes against humanity.[57] The inclusion of "on a case-by-case basis" is redundant; a list of nine separate conditions already suggests that each situation and its unique combination of factors must manifest a similarly unique solution.

While the application of a case-by-case basis approach inevitably raises fears of bias, double standards and fundamental shortfalls in protection, it seems unavoidable. The application of each legal norm arguably requires: establishment of the hypothesis, that is the conditions under which an actor should be guided by the given legal norm; the disposition, indicating the rights and duties of the participants in relations arising under the circumstances envisioned in the hypothesis; and the sanction, or

---

[57] United Nations General Assembly, 2005 World Summit Outcome, UN doc. A/RES/60/1, 24 October 2005, paras. 138–40.

the consequences for actors who violate the prescriptions of a particular norm.[58] This kind of formula highlights the idea that norms may be universal, but that for each it still must be established to whom they apply, under which circumstances they arise, and what sanction may attach for failure to meet them. Even *jus cogens* norms therefore have limits in their application, a conjecture that finds support in their actual implementation, which is likewise on a case-by-case basis. This accords with the responsibility to protect doctrines focus on case-by-case application, and reinforces the idea that the norm of prevention could be considered to be a legal norm already, even if the circumstances in which it applies or the sanctions which attach may not *a priori* be clear.

2.2.5.2. Duty of Conduct

Closely interlinked to the case-by-case approach is the question of the duty of conduct. The concept has its roots in human rights law and in the duty to protect, which provides that states have a positive obligation in certain circumstances to prevent private actors from infringing on the rights of other individuals. States may commit violations of human rights law where they fail to exercise due diligence to prevent, punish, investigate or redress the harm caused by the acts of private persons or entities.[59] The UN Human Rights Committee further enunciates the due diligence standard, similar to the concept from the national law of torts, as an obligation of conduct, not of result.

2.2.5.3. The ICJ *Bosnia v. Serbia* Decision and Its Implications

The case-by-case approach and the duty of conduct come together in the International Court of Justice's ('ICJ') *Bosnia v. Serbia* decision, finding the government of Serbia responsible for failing to prevent genocide in

---

[58] Stevan Gostojić, Branko Milosavljević and Zora Konjović, "Ontological Model of Legal Norms for Creating and Using Legislation", in *Computer Science and Information Systems*, 2013, vol. 10, no. 1; Daniel Kroslak, "To the Law Structuring Theory (An Attempt at Semantic Analysis in the Evolution Perspective", in *Juridical Review: A Theoretical Journal for the Questions of State and Law*, 2008, vol. 91, no. 1, pp. 5–15; Ulf Linderfalk, "The Effect of *Jus Cogens* Norms: Whoever Opened Pandora's Box, Did You Ever Think About the Consequences?", in *European Journal of International Law*, 2008, vol. 18, no. 5, pp. 853–71.

[59] Sheri P. Rosenberg, "Responsibility to Protect: A Framework for Prevention", in *Global Responsibility to Protect*, 2009, vol. 1, no. 4, pp. 442–77.

Bosnia. In setting out the conditions for preventing genocide, the Court held that the hypothesis (*the conditions under which a person should be guided by the legal norm*) of preventing genocide would come into play once the person (likely in this case to be working for or representing a state) has actively identified a reasonable suspicion that a relevant individual harbours specific intent to commit genocide or that there is a serious risk of genocide being committed. The Court addressed the disposition (*the rights and duties of the participants*) as requiring states to "employ all means reasonably available to them", falling somewhere between the employment of due diligence and avoiding "manifest fail[ure] to take all measures within its power, which might have contributed to preventing genocide".[60] The sanction (*consequences for persons who violate the prescriptions*) is, at minimum, the sanctions that the Court can impose on states, provisional or otherwise, to ensure enforcement of the Convention. The sanction, of course, potentially includes whatever measures the UN Security Council can take.

The application of these conditions will vary not only from one country situation to the next, but from one actor seeking to prevent genocide to the next. Each will be equipped with different knowledge underpinning "a reasonable suspicion that a relevant individual harbours genocidal intent" or that there is a "serious risk of genocide being committed". Likewise, each actor will possess vastly different "reasonably available means" to prevent genocide. In assessing a state's range of action, the ICJ endorses a state self-assessing 1) its capacity to effectively influence those who may commit genocide, which will vary greatly from one state to the next; 2) its geographical distance and the strength of its political and other links to those who may commit genocide; and 3) whether its prospective actions may fall within or outside of the limits of the law, the latter which is forbidden.

How these means may interact among different actors in an ever-changing country situation dictates the obvious, that there must be a case-by-case approach. Further, the ICJ's finding that actors must "employ all means reasonably available to them", falling somewhere between the employment of "due diligence" and avoiding "manifest fail[ure] to take all

---

[60] ICJ, *Case Concerning Application of the Convention on the Prevention and Punishment of the Crime of Genocide (Bosnia-Herzegovina v. Yugoslavia)*, Judgment, 11 July 1996, para. 430 (http://www.legal-tools.org/doc/356fe2/).

measures within its power", suggests a duty of conduct, a duty to try without knowing the likelihood of success.

2.2.5.4. The Matrices

The nine matrices set out below draw on the ICJ's *Bosnia v. Serbia* decision, as well as the Draft Articles on State Responsibility, and the foundational responsibility to protect documents to create a framework for assessing the actions of states or others to prevent crimes.

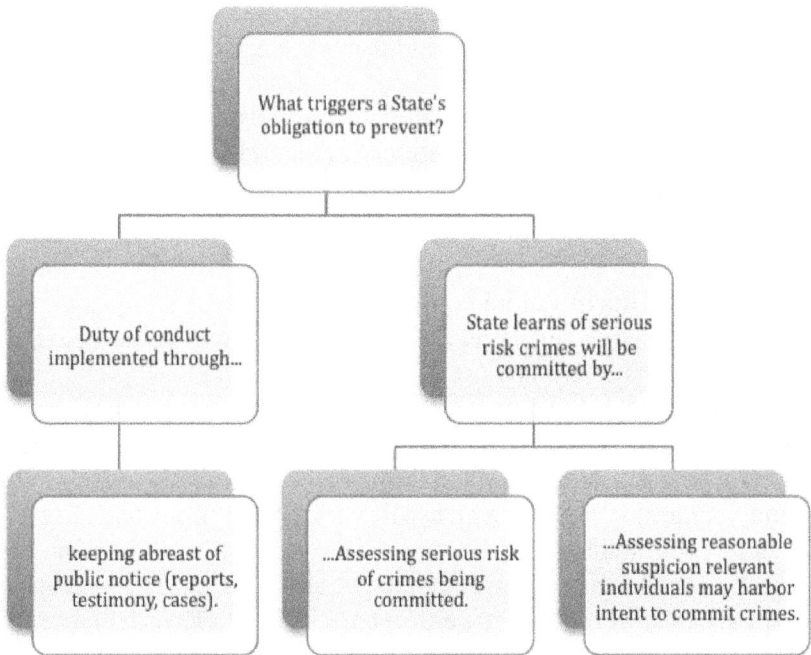

Matrix 1 is drawn entirely from the ICJ's *Bosnia v. Serbia* decision. It could be compared with a similar matrix from the Draft Articles on State Responsibility, which examines what constitutes a violation and how to assess whether an obligation is violated.

This first matrix from the Draft Articles would be accompanied by the following, which briefly lays out the assessment injured states must make in triggering potential action in response to an internationally wrongful act.

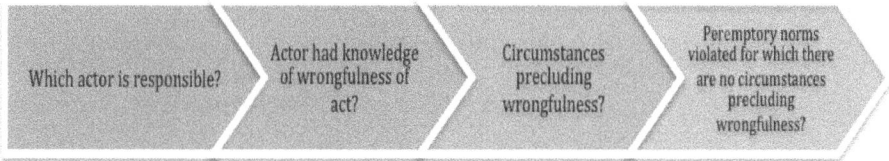

This set of three matrices, from the ICJ decision and from the Draft Articles, are complementary because they establish an assessment process that looks at the actions, intentions, capacities and responsibilities of the potentially offending state or states.

Matrix 2 continues with the logic of the ICJ decision, in setting out the range of efforts in which states are expected to engage, if they find that there is a serious risk of crimes being committed, or they have a reasonable suspicion that relevant individuals may harbour intent to commit crimes.

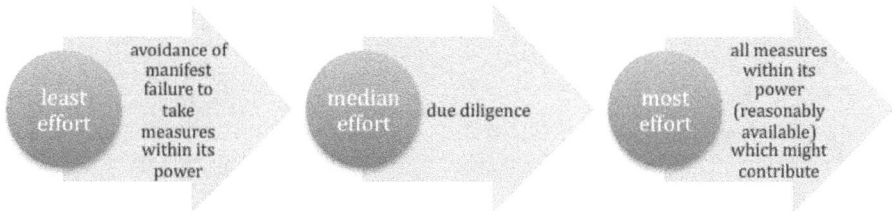

Matrix 3 rounds out the ICJ decision breakdown, arguing that in assessing their range of action, a state must self-assess: 1) its capacity to effectively influence those who may commit genocide, which will vary greatly from one state to the next; 2) its geographical distance and the strength of its political and other links to those who may commit genocide; and 3) whether its prospective actions may fall within or outside of the limits of the law, the latter which is forbidden.

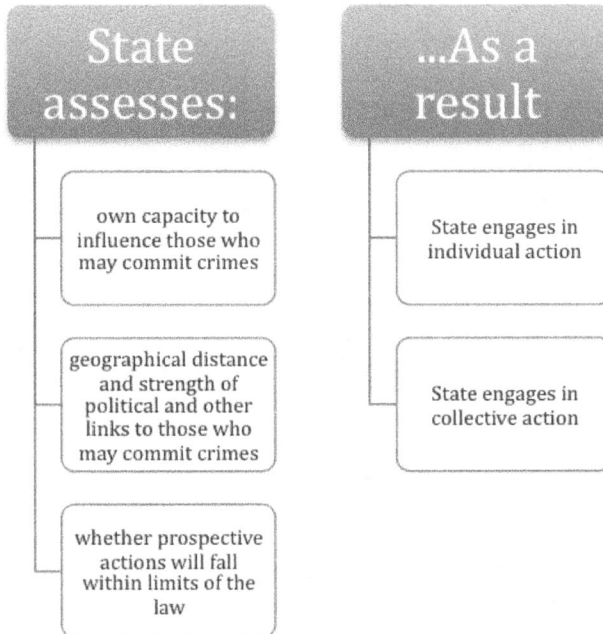

State assesses:	...As a result
own capacity to influence those who may commit crimes	State engages in individual action
geographical distance and strength of political and other links to those who may commit crimes	State engages in collective action
whether prospective actions will fall within limits of the law	

By comparison, the Draft Articles on State Responsibility lay out more detailed descriptions of the dos and don'ts of state action in response to internationally wrongful acts.

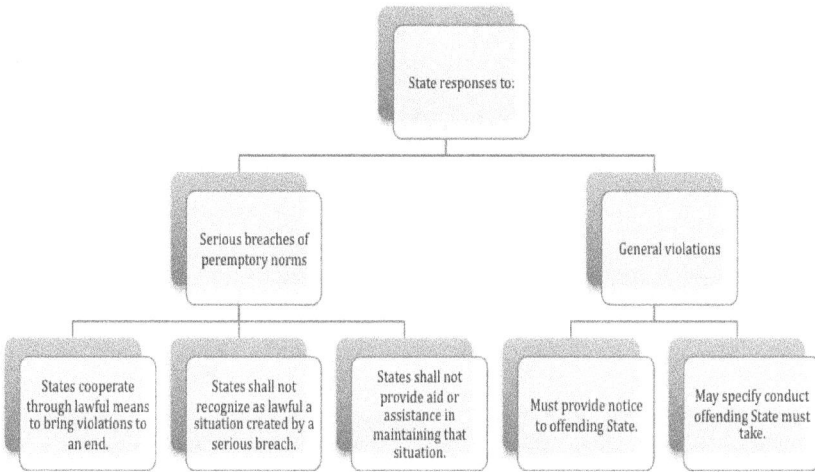

The Draft Articles envision strict limits for countermeasures.

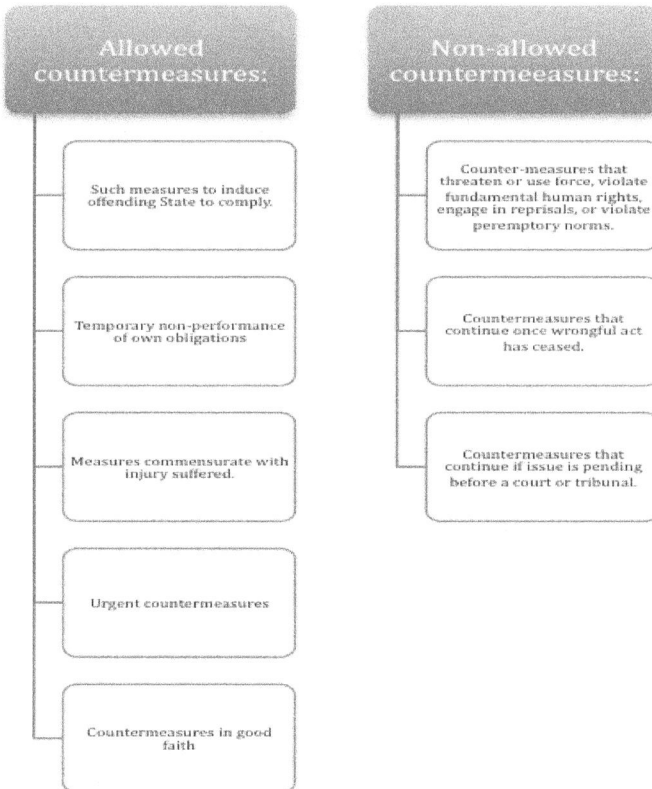

Matrices 4 and 5 move away from the ICJ decision and the Draft Articles and pick up references from foundational responsibility to protect documents.

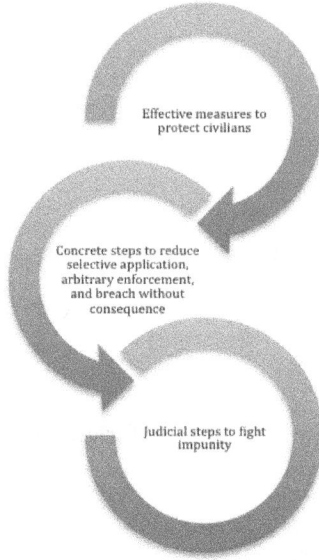

Effective measures to protect civilians

Concrete steps to reduce selective application, arbitrary enforcement, and breach without consequence

Judicial steps to fight impunity

If national authorities fail to protect civilians from the commission of international crimes, collective action comes into play. Preference is given to consensual and peaceful measures, leaning towards Chapter VI and VII action as at least a first step.

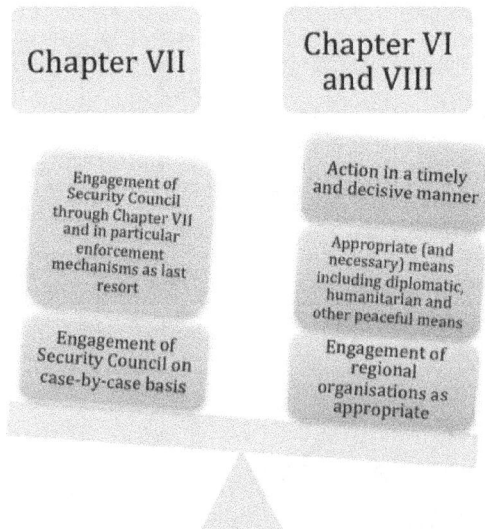

Chapter VII

Chapter VI and VIII

Engagement of Security Council through Chapter VII and in particular enforcement mechanisms as last resort

Action in a timely and decisive manner

Appropriate (and necessary) means including diplomatic, humanitarian and other peaceful means

Engagement of Security Council on case-by-case basis

Engagement of regional organisations as appropriate

Matrix 6 reflects the circularity of interaction in the international community, and that no members are exempt from it.

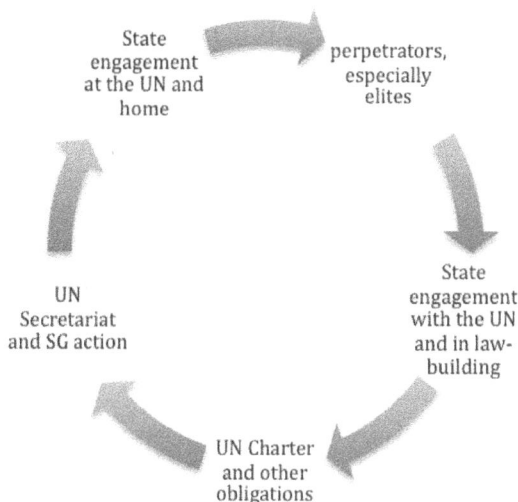

These matrices make it fairly clear that, if one must consider as the ICJ suggests, the "means reasonably available to an actor", the actors in the international system with the greatest power to prevent crimes or deter perpetrators are states. As made clear in the ICC Statute's Preamble, the Court can only contribute to prevention. For the ICC, the key is that contribution lies in its independence and interdependence. Its greatest strength in contributing to prevention or deterrence is in the independent execution of its core functions. But it must be aware of and co-ordinate where appropriate with other actors such as states, if it wishes to maximise the impact of those core activities.

2.3. A Framework of Indicators

Third, this chapter considers the role of indicators in assessing the potential deterrent or preventive effect of the actions of the ICC or others. These indicators are intended for use by any actor engaging in efforts to deter perpetrators or prevent crimes, the ICC included. They should be able to help the ICC and others assess how best to direct and assess their efforts in this regard, including in relation to the all-important question of when, and how early, to act. As Diane Orentlicher writes in relation to the ICJ *Bosnia v. Serbia* decision: "The [ICJ] put to rest states' all-too-familiar claim that it is unclear whether they must act to prevent genocide in the face of ambiguous facts that are unambiguously menacing: if they wait until it is legally certain, they have waited too long to prevent it".[61] If states with the obligation to prevent genocide cannot be legally certain about a situation, then they must look to indicators that help to interpret the 'ambiguous facts' that stand between them and a decision on when and how to act.

As for how states may derive or test their suspicions, the ICJ offers that it may come from notice from public reports, such as UN reports, or testimony before the ICTY (or arguably testimony at the national or international level generally). Both of these tests require active commitment on the part of states because of the ICJ requirement that a state's obligation arises "at the instant that the state learns of, or should normally have learned of, the existence of a serious risk that genocide will be committed". This implies an obligation to keep abreast of these potential developments as a member state of the Genocide Convention and, indeed, many states do monitor human rights or related developments worldwide, and all states have access to the kind of public notice that UN and other reports on crisis situations provide.

2.3.1. What Are Indicators?

The concept of indicators is difficult to define. The use of ambiguous end goals such as truth, forgiveness and reconciliation can make the identification of relevant indicators difficult and assessment of their achievement even more arduous. What is needed in this case is a place to start,[62] a way to "simplify raw data about a complex social phenomenon".[63] To this end, some scholars divide indicators into external parameters relating to state

---

[61] Susana SáCouto, "Reflections on the Judgment of the International Court of Justice in Bosnia's Genocide Case against Serbia and Montenegro", in *Human Rights Brief*, vol. 15 no. 1, 2007, pp. 2–6.

[62] Iain Scobbie, "Some Common Heresies about International Law", in Malcolm D. Evans (ed.), *International Law*, 2nd ed., Oxford, Oxford University Press, Oxford, 2006, pp. 59–87.

[63] Kevin E. Davis, Benedict Kingsbury and Sally Engle Merry, "Introduction: Global Governance by Indicators", in Kevin E. Davis, Angelina Fischer, Benedict Kingsbury and Sally Engle Merry (eds.), *Governance by Indicators: Global Power through Quantification and Rankings*, Oxford University Press, Oxford, 2012, pp. 6–7.

co-operation and internal parameters relating to the judicial institution's functioning.[64]

The production of indicators is often a collective process, and can be an essential part of standard-setting and decision-making, even to the point where it can "alter the forms, the exercise, and perhaps even the distributions of power in certain spheres of global governance", lending governing power to actors who promulgate them.[65]

Indicators, including in the form of early warning, reinforce the overlap of the ICC's mandate with those of others, and provide common ground upon which to act. Following on the UN Charter and on the responsibility to protect doctrine, nine groups of indicators are here drawn from conflict prevention and management, human rights violations prevention, crime prevention and even disease prevention. Each of these fields has something unique.

2.3.2. Conflict Prevention and Management

Conflict prevention and management first bring to the discussion the idea that conflict is a result of a normal and not of an abnormal system, that conflict is logical and is rooted in everyday politics and not in "ancient hatreds, the pathology of particular rulers, or the breakdown of normally peaceful domestic systems".[66] Conflict prevention must then address the structure of conflict and what supports its continuation (or re-emergence) over a longer period of time, with an eye toward creating enabling conditions for a more stable environment,[67] of which law is an essential com-

---

[64] Pierre Hazan, "Measuring the Impact of Punishment and Forgiveness: A Framework for Evaluating Transitional Justice", in *International Review of the Red Cross*, 2008, vol. 88, no. 861, pp. 27–29.

[65] Davis *et al.*, 2012, see *supra* note 63.

[66] Luc van de Goor and Suzanne Verstegen, "Shooting at Moving Targets: From Reaction to Prevention", in in Alfred van Staden, Jan Rood and Hans Labohm (eds.), *Cannons and Canons: Clingendael Views of Global and Regional Politics*, Royal Van Gorcum, Assen, 2003, pp. 272–73.

[67] David Carment and Albrecht Schnabel, "Conflict Prevention – Taking Stock", in David Carment and Albrecht Schnabel (eds.), *Conflict Prevention: Path to Peace or Grand Illusion?*, United Nations University, Tokyo, 2002, p. 11; Andrea Kathryn Talentino, "Evaluating Success and Failure: Conflict Prevention in Cambodia and Bosnia", in David Carment and Albrecht Schnabel (eds.), *Conflict Prevention: Path to Peace or Grand Illusion?*, United Nations University, Tokyo, 2002, pp. 70–72.

ponent.[68] This undermines the purported peace–justice conflict,[69] or at least emphasises that maintaining peace, or preventing conflict, is as difficult an objective to achieve as is building accountability, or preventing crimes.[70]

Conflict prevention and management also contribute to the concept of early warning, which has its basis in the UN Charter, and which finds support from the African Union, the Carnegie Commission on Preventing Deadly Conflict, the Clingendael Institute, the European Union, the Forum on Early Warning and Early Response and the International Commission on Intervention and State Sovereignty, among others.[71] Early warning theories, studies and discussions provide essential input for the development of indicators for the prevention of international crimes.

2.3.3. Human Rights Law and Violations Prevention

Human rights law and activities focusing on preventing violations bring to the table the idea that, while international crimes "are at the tail-end of the spectrum of severity of offending, [p]articularly genocide, […] other kinds of gross human rights violations, are among the most serious crimes".[72] Human rights violations may continue at a lower level for a long period of time. The willingness of the international community to tolerate or even encourage them can frequently open the door to interna-

---

68 Carnegie Commission on Preventing Deadly Conflict, *Preventing Deadly Conflict: Final Report*, Carnegie Corporation, Washington DC, 1997.

69 Goldstone, 1998, see *supra* note 37; James Meernik, "Justice, Power and Peace: Conflicting Interests and the Apprehension of ICC Suspects", in *International Criminal Law Review*, 2013, vol. 13, no. 1, pp. 169–90.

70 Gareth Evans, "Preventing Deadly Conflict: How Can We Do Better?", President of International Crisis Group to Foreign Policy Association 'Off-the-Record' Lecture Series, New York, 6 December 2006; van de Goor and Verstegen, 2003, see *supra* note 66; United Nations, UN High-level Panel on Threats, Challenges and Change, *A More Secure World: Our Shared Responsibility*, United Nations, New York, 2004, p. 203.

71 African Union, "The Continental Early Warning System (CEWS)", 23 November 2015; Carnegie Commission, 1997, see *supra* note 68; van de Goor and Verstegen, 2003, see *supra* note 66; European Union, European Commission in Cooperation with the General Affairs and External Relation Council, "Early Warning Checklist", 2006; Centre for Conflict Research and the West Africa Network for Peacebuilding, "Conflict Analysis and Response Definition: Abridged Methodology", 2001.

72 Catrien Bijleveld, "So Many Missing Pieces: Some Thoughts on the Methodology of the Empirical Study of Gross Human Rights Violations", Free University Amsterdam, Working Paper for the Expert Meeting at Maastricht University, Netherlands, 13–14 April 2007.

tional crimes. In this way and others, the field of human rights provides support for the concept of early warning mechanisms, as well as a number of specific subsidiary indicators of potential crimes. It is essential to look at the relationship between human rights violations and violent conflict, underscoring a connection between human rights law and conflict prevention and management.[73] The United Nations, including the Security Council, the Economic and Social Council, the International Committee applying the International Convention on the Elimination of all Forms of Racial Discrimination, the Office on Genocide Prevention and the Responsibility to Protect, and the High Commissioner for Human Rights also recognise the connection between human rights violations and the prevention of crimes and of conflict, in particular the maintenance of international peace and security, and have contributed useful indicators to the list.

2.3.4. Disease Prevention

Disease prevention brings to the table the idea that it is not uncommon for fields to borrow methodologies from other disciplines, in particular biology and epidemiology.[74] Experts in disease prevention track very closely the impact of their efforts on the spread of disease, which may make it more precise than other areas of prevention, such as conflict prevention. The Carnegie Commission in the area of conflict prevention invokes a public health model in emphasising primary prevention. The spread of crimes has likewise been compared to the spread of an epidemic, and negative situational forces are described as infectious, making good people behave in pathological ways alien to their nature.[75]

Disease prevention, like crime prevention, can focus on universal prevention, targeting the population in general as well at the individual level those who seem to exhibit problem behaviours that could be indicators of disease or of criminality. There may be some parallel with the ICC Office of the Prosecutor's policy focusing on those bearing the greatest

---

[73] Eileen F. Babbitt and Ellen L. Lutz (eds.), *Human Rights and Conflict Resolution in Context: Colombia, Sierra Leone, and Northern Ireland*, Syracuse University Press, New York, 2009.

[74] Bijleveld, 2007, see *supra* note 72.

[75] Philip Zimbardo, *The Lucifer Effect: Understanding How Good People Turn Evil*, Random House, New York, 2007, p. 195; Malcolm Gladwell, *The Tipping Point: How Little Things Can Make a Big Difference*, Little Brown, Boston, 2000.

responsibility for the most serious crimes, coupled with Article 27 of the ICC Statute's irrelevance of official capacity. In this context, leaders of states or organisations in particular circumstances may be viewed as individuals who are high risk for criminal behaviour.

Rarely do practitioners talk about complete elimination of disease, if only because it seems unreasonable to expect that disease can be completely eradicated. The fact that experts have mapped multiple levels of disease prevention also suggests that they do not believe they can catch all disease at the earliest level of prevention, before the disease has taken hold. The same can be said, at least from experience, about international crimes. Even at the national level, practitioners do not speak of the complete eradication of serious crimes.

2.3.5. Crime Prevention

Finally, in relation to national crime prevention, in addition to arguments explored earlier about the origins of the concepts of deterrence and prevention, there is a clear link to human rights law and violations as well as to conflict prevention and management. George Kelling and Catherine Coles's 'broken windows' theory, in particular, as well as that of Jane Jacobs on the life and death of cities, postulate that order arises out of the "small change" of urban life, the day-to-day respect with which we deal with others and the concern that we exercise for their privacy, welfare and safety.[76]

When it comes to international crimes, the context in which they take place is a culture of impunity, in which everyday human rights violations are disregarded or even encouraged. Lack of respect for human rights norms is a major indicator for possible future international crimes. This is logical in part because there is a fine line between what constitutes human rights violations and international crimes, a distinction often more legal than literal. Human rights violations are the 'broken windows' of international criminal law enforcement: according to the broken windows theory, broken windows in a neighbourhood show neglect, in particular from law enforcement authorities, who overlook small infractions such as vandalism, and likely therefore larger ones as well. Broken windows signal that criminals are likely to get away with their actions; that no one in a

---

[76] George L. Kelling and Catherine M. Coles, *Fixing Broken Windows: Restoring Order and Reducing Crime in Our Communities*, Martin Kessler Books, New York, 1996, p. 9.

position of authority cares to police the neighbourhood. If human rights violations are the broken windows in this case, perpetrators who infringe with impunity on the civil, political, economic or social rights of their victims will take the message that if these broken windows are not fixed, bigger crimes for greater gains can be committed. Broken windows also send the message to the victims of human rights violations that if these are not fixed, if law enforcement is not interested in investigating their complaints or holding the perpetrators accountable, the risk of greater victimisation is heightened. In this way, the lack of redress for victims of human rights violations or, in the broader sense, the lack of a law enforcement mechanism to take human rights victims and their complaints seriously are also other major indicators of potential international crimes.

2.3.6. The Indicators

Those indicators of possible commission of international crimes are broken down into nine key areas: 1) human rights violations; 2) impunity; 3) social harm; 4) the system, in particular looking at the question of bad apples (individuals in the system) versus bad barrels (the system itself); 5) individual versus group decision making; 6) the role of elites; 7) the role of propaganda and the infectious idea as an indicator, looking at propaganda's goals of moral disengagement, mobilisation and denial; 8) the role of evidence and arrest warrants; and 9) the role of the international community. In relation to the role of the system (indicator 4), one must examine the problem of self-perpetuation, in particular through the application of internal logic and anonymity.

This chapter does not allow sufficient space to fully explore how the fields of conflict prevention, human rights law, criminal law and even disease prevention support the derivation of these nine categories of indicators. This is explored at greater length elsewhere, in the author's Ph.D. suffice it to say, they do find extensive support across the boundaries of these different disciplines. The presence of one or more of these indicators is a strong warning sign that international crimes may be on the verge of being committed, if they are not underway already. An actor does not have to come from any of these fields to apply the relevant indicators, and most actors to whom these indicators are directed bridge these and other fields in their day-to-day activities and in their overall mandates. The ICC is one such institution, but is far from being the only one.

2.4. Policy Recommendations to Prevent Crimes and Deter Perpetrators

Finally, this chapter offers targeted policy recommendations that will render more scientific the approach to preventing crimes, and create more objective benchmarks for assessing efforts to prevent crimes in the future. In particular, it closes with seven key lessons for the ICC and others interested in the prevention of international crimes. These seven lessons build on two key elements: that knowledge or reasonable belief that serious crimes have taken place are essential, and for there to be such knowledge or reasonable belief early warning undoubtedly has an important role to play.

Regarding the first element, this knowledge is essential for both those inside and outside the situation. It is essential that perpetrators know that their actions are monitored and understood from the outside. In relation to Rwanda, "the people who did this thought that whatever happened, nobody would know. It didn't matter, because they would kill everybody, and there would be nothing to see".[77] The same proved true during the Holocaust, during which a Nazi SS militiaman admonished prisoners:

> However this war may end, we have won the war against you; none of you will be left to bear witness, but even if someone were to survive, the world will not believe him. [...] And even if some proof should remain and some of you survive, people will say that the events you describe are too monstrous to be believed.[78]

The enemy of knowledge is anonymity of perpetrators, protection from the systems within which they work, and the use of propaganda to cover up, deny or distract attention from crimes committed.

Propaganda in particular is what some have called an "infectious agent".[79] It is a near universally recognised accelerant of conflict and violations of international law, intended to keep people, both inside and outside of a situation, from understanding or believing that crimes have taken or could take place. Hence, the 'big lie', the lie so colossal that no one would believe that someone could have the impudence to distort the truth

---

[77] Philip Gourevitch, *We Wish to Inform You that Tomorrow We Will Be Killed With Our Families: Stories From Rwanda*, Picador, New York, 1998, p. 200.

[78] Primo Levi, *The Drowned and the Saved*, Summit Books, New York, 1988.

[79] Gladwell, 2000, p. 18, see *supra* note 75.

so infamously, or something that must have been dreamed up because "things whose existence is not morally permissible cannot exist".[80] The work of philosopher Harry G. Frankfurt provides valuable insight into the nature of propaganda in his works, *On Bullshit* and *On Truth*. 'Bullshit' is not about truth or falsity, but about what the speaker intends to achieve by speaking 'bullshit.' Similarly, propaganda draws on elements of truth, in particular historical facts or events. It cannot always be called outright lies. The goal in invoking these facts is to create a false or, perhaps more accurately, an alternate, reality, in which a particular group for example is deemed to represent a threat to others, and to justify crimes against them.[81]

Regarding the second element, for early warning to work, the international criminal law community must take greater cognisance of human rights regimes and monitoring, and must seek partnerships from outside its own area of competence, from criminologists, legal theorists, sociologists, philosophers, conflict experts, human rights advocates, epidemiologists and others, to synthesise a way of thinking about prevention that makes the most of the resources that currently exist to address this challenge.

On the basis of those two key elements, the following seven lessons are offered for the ICC and others interested to prevent international crimes, which in turn build on two key elements.

2.4.1. Lesson One: The Importance of Monitoring Human Rights Violations

The first lesson is the importance of the human rights regimes and monitoring of human rights as a gateway to commission of international crimes. While the Office of the Prosecutor cannot monitor human rights violations worldwide, it can monitor human rights violations in the states within its jurisdiction, or, given the scope of the task, considering there are currently 124 states parties and growing, can work with key partners outside the Court, NGOs, states and others, to set up a monitoring network that would make public the results of its work, use the results to lobby

---

[80] Levi, 1988, p. 165, see *supra* note 78.

[81] Harry G. Frankfurt, *On Bullshit*, Princeton University Press, Princeton, NJ, 2005; Harry G. Frankfurt, *On Truth*, Alfred A. Knopf, New York, 2006.

states against violating human rights, and remind them that escalating to ICC Statute crimes could lead to investigations and prosecutions.

2.4.2. Lesson Two: The Importance of Understanding the System

The second lesson is the importance of understanding the system in each situation under preliminary examination or under investigation.[82] Understanding the system may be particularly important, not just for the investigations phase but also for the issue of arrest warrants. It is the system that will protect an individual under an arrest warrant, and if the ICC has a partial understanding of the role of that individual within the system, what steps the system will take to protect that individual, and how the system (and the state that co-exists with or otherwise represents the system abroad) interacts with other states in the international community, it will be difficult to isolate the individual wanted for arrest. Studying the system more directly may also help to identify situations of priority, in particular in their earliest stages.

Monitoring systems requires some sense of how they work, and this subject itself probably deserves further elaboration, because like situations, there will not be a single recipe for all of them. However, some of the indicators provided by Philip Zimbardo, Martha K. Huggins and their colleagues may be useful. Huggins lists 10 criteria for a system.[83] Above all, she emphasises and encourages criminologists to deal with serious crimes like torture from a social organisation perspective, and that such scholarship would envision torture as systemic and resulting from the normal operation of various types of state, bureaucratic and social organisation. This latter point cannot be overemphasised. If crimes are treated as the result of a broken system, then the goal of the international community in intervening is to fix the system; for example, to offer human rights or international law training, to train the judiciary and other lawyers, and so on. If crimes are treated as the result of a healthy system being directed to commit crimes toward a desired political end, members of the international com-

---

[82] Zimbardo, 2007, see supra note 75; Gladwell, 2000, see *supra* note 75; Kelling and Coles, 1996, see *supra* note 76; Martha K. Huggins, "Torture 101", Paper for the American Association for the Advancement of Science, Science and Human Rights Program, Washington, DC, 28 June 2004; Goldstone, 1998, see *supra* note 37; Carnegie Commission, 1997, see *supra* note 68; van de Goor and Verstegen, 2003, see *supra* note 66; European Union, 2006, see *supra* note 71.

[83] Zimbardo, 2007, see *supra* note 75; Huggins, 2004, see *supra* note 82.

munity must face the situation in an honest way, in appreciating that crimes result from a conscious choice and not by accident, and in reacting accordingly.

Huggins's concern is also broader: that the system is not only normal but even self-perpetuating. In this sense, the system almost literally takes on a life of its own. In this case, the removal of a few individuals from the system may not be sufficient to change it. Changing the system should be viewed as different from changing a state's policy, in the sense that the system is much more entrenched. If the system's 'instinct', if it may so be called, is self-preservation, the challenge to an institution like the ICC which addresses individual criminal responsibility is much larger, and the opponent much more difficult to vanquish.

Justice Goldstone makes a similar point, in arguing "[i]t is naive for anyone to assume that in a transitional society such institutions and practices will die a natural death".[84] Zimbardo sets out another view of the elements of a system when he cites the Milgram studies, which illustrate a process whereby 'good people' are trapped into committing evil acts.[85] This is arguably another way that a system is self-perpetuating, by slowly integrating individuals who would be less likely to participate if it were simply a matter of intellectual consideration and decision-making.

Related to the issue of the system is the question of legitimacy.[86] Legitimacy is absolutely essential for the commission of crimes:

> States do not maintain their control of a society solely through the use of force and coercion, but also because citizens have adopted ideas and values that support the status quo. People support the state because they accept certain ideas about how things ought to be.[87]

Philip Gourevitch documents the role of legitimacy in his book:

---

[84] Goldstone, 1998, pp. 202–3, see *supra* note 37.

[85] Zimbardo, 2007, p. 273, see *supra* note 75.

[86] *Ibid.*; Alex Alvarez, "Destructive Beliefs: Genocide and the Role of Ideology", in Alette Smeulers and Roelof Haveman (eds.), *Supranational Criminology: Towards a Criminology of International Crimes*, Intersentia, Antwerp, 2008; Gourevitch, 1998, see *supra* note 77; Isabel Fonseca, *Bury Me Standing: The Gypsies and Their Journey*, Vintage Books, New York, 1995; Erna Paris, *Long Shadows: Truth, Lies and History*, Bloomsbury, London, 2000; Goldstone, 1998, see *supra* note 37; Carnegie Commission, 1997, see *supra* note 68; European Union, 2006, see *supra* note 71. ·

[87] Alvarez, 2008, p. 49, see *supra* note 86.

> During the genocide, the work of the killers was not regard-
> ed as a crime in Rwanda; it was effectively the law of the
> land, and every citizen was responsible for its administration.
> That way, if a person who should be killed was let go by one
> party he could expect to be caught and killed by someone
> else.[88]

Isabel Fonseca cites examples of authorities legitimising attacks on the
Roma, and Erna Paris discusses the whitewashing of French complicity in
Nazi crimes, noting that by

> [i]nvent[ing] the story that the Vichy regime did not exist in
> reality [that it was illegitimate] De Gaulle was trying to
> avoid having to try the majority of the French people. His
> reasoning was that you couldn't incriminate people on behalf
> of a state that simply did not exist![89]

This underscores why the international community cannot be neutral. A system that commits a crime like genocide depends for its survival
as well as for the continuation of its criminal or genocidal policies on a
lack of serious opposition both internally and externally. Such a system
will probably be monitoring external indicators more closely than the international community is monitoring internal indicators within that country.
Without any serious indication that its legitimacy will be challenged, criminal policies will continue. Or, as the Serbian writer Drinka Gojković argued:
"Why should we talk about Serbian responsibility for the Bosnian war
when the whole world takes this bloodied man [Milošević] as a partner?"[90]

The responsibility to protect regime aims to reverse this process that
legitimises the commission of serious crimes by arguing that a government's capacity to provide for its population's welfare is a paramount criterion for recognising its legitimacy; failures of such responsibility remove the government's right to non-interference and permit, and even
may compel, external involvement to protect the subject population.[91]

---

[88] Gourevitch, 1998, see *supra* note 77.

[89] Paris, 2000, p. 377, see *supra* note 86.

[90] *Ibid.*

[91] Benjamin N. Schiff, "The ICC and R2P: Problems of Individual Culpability and State Responsibility", in Henry F. Carey and Stacey M. Mitchell (eds.), *Trials and Tribulations of
International Prosecution*, Lexington Books, Lanham, MD, 2013, p. 154.

2.4.3. Lesson Three: The Importance of Raising Greater Awareness That War and Violence Are Rational

The third lesson is the importance of raising greater awareness of the fact that war and the use of violence is rational, with rational even if amoral motives that can be countered. In this sense, the famous statement of the German military theorist Carl von Clausewitz that war is the continuation of politics by other means could arguably be extended to conclude that serious crimes are the continuation of policy by other means. Most agree that, as conflict prevention expert Bruce Jentleson puts it:

> The dominant dynamic is not the playing out of historical inevitability, but rather the consequences of calculations by parties to the conflict of the purposes served by political violence. It is in seeking to influence this calculus that preventive statecraft has its potential viability.[92]

The Carnegie Commission also acknowledges that "[w]ar and mass violence usually result from deliberate political decisions, and the Commission believes that these decisions can be affected so that mass violence does not result".[93] The International Commission on Intervention and State Sovereignty and the experts from Clingendael reach similar conclusions; in the Commission's case, it focuses on serious crimes as the "product either of deliberate state action, or state neglect or inability to act, or a failed state situation",[94] where the Clingendael experts focus on finding "the purpose and reasons for conflict [...] [in the] long-term embedded social processes that define the conditions of everyday life".[95]

In other words, the use of violence, and the commission of serious crimes, is not inherently an irrational act, but rather the opposite; a proven means to an end. As Gourevitch describes it:

> Genocide [...] is an exercise in community building. A vigorous totalitarian order requires that the people be invested in the leaders' scheme, and while genocide may be the most perverse and ambitious means to this end, it is also the most

---

[92] Bruce W. Jentleson, "The Realism of Preventive Statecraft", in David Carment and Albrecht Schnabel (eds.), *Conflict Prevention: Path to Peace or Grand Illusion?*, United Nations University, Tokyo, 2002, p. 28.

[93] Carnegie Commission, 1997, p. 3, see *supra* note 68.

[94] *Ibid.*, pp. xi–xii.

[95] Van de Goor and Verstegen 2003, p. 276, see *supra* note 66.

> comprehensive…In fact, the genocide was the product of or-
> der, authoritarianism, decades of modern political theorising
> and indoctrination, and one of the most meticulously admin-
> istered states in history.[96]

Primo Levi reaches a similar conclusion, writing in *The Drowned and the Saved*: "Wars are detestable, they are a very bad way to settle controversies between nations or factions, but they cannot be called useless: they aim at a goal, although it may be wicked or perverse".[97] He quotes Nazi sources supporting this argument, and country expert Stephen Ellis makes a similar argument about the use of so-called "useless violence" in Liberia:

> The observation that there is a 'cultic' element to violence of
> this type does not imply that the militias fight primarily as a
> form of ritual behaviour. […] Clearly, the prime motive is to
> gain wealth and power through violence, with the cultic as-
> pects being a means of spreading terror and also of psycho-
> logically strengthening fighters, using a lexicon of symbols
> which is widely understood.[98]

A related point is the role of elites in planning crimes.[99] For example, Malcolm Gladwell writes about the role of "the infectious agent itself, and the environment in which the infectious agent is operating".[100] Political elites are more frequently presented with both the opportunity and the motive to commit international crimes, they have more to gain, and they may more easily access the means to commit crimes on a large scale. This is not to say that all political elites will commit crimes, but a more critical eye should be cast on their activities. They also face different circumstances in different countries, and within different systems may commit serious crimes, only in different forms. Bill Berkeley argues that "[e]thnic conflict in Africa is a product of tyranny. By 'product' I mean in both an immediate sense – it is a tactic that tyrants use to divide and rule – as well as in a deeper, historical sense: ethnic conflict is a legacy of tyranny",

---

[96] Gourevitch, 1998, p. 95, see *supra* note 77.

[97] Levi, 1998, p. 105, see *supra* note 78.

[98] Bill Berkeley, *The Graves Are Not Yet Full: Race, Tribe and Power in the Heart of Africa*, Basic Books, New York, 2001, p. 38.

[99] Carment and Schnabel, 2002, see *supra* note 67; Carnegie Commission, 1997, see *supra* note 68; Gladwell, 2000, see *supra* note 75; Berkeley, 2001, see *supra* note 98; Levi, 1998, see *supra* note 79.

[100] Gladwell, 2000, p. 18, see *supra* note 75.

which he describes as a product and legacy of colonialism. He continues: 'Hate mongering in Africa, no less than elsewhere in the world, is an acquired skill'.[101] According to this logic, tyranny in Africa produces certain types of serious crimes, in particular crimes against a regime's own population.

On planning, it may be useful to examine again the link between root and proximate causes. Root causes are not directly responsible for conflict, or for serious crimes, and may exist in many situations and not manifest conflict or crimes. However, understanding better the exploitation by political demagogues of long-standing grievances is important for tracking the progress from the root causes to the violence itself and may give the international community some advance warning of which situations are the most volatile and require attention the most urgently.[102]

Another angle on planning that deserves further consideration is the comparison between the planning of ICC Statute crimes and the planning of traditional organised crime, which have a number of parallels. The planning and implementation of serious crimes also involves the elites drawing others into commission often through coercion, force or deception.[103]

2.4.4. Lesson Four: The Importance of Raising Greater Awareness That Confrontation Can Bring Change

The fourth lesson is the importance of raising greater awareness of the knowledge that confrontation can bring change and break the cycle of violence. It may be possible to tip an epidemic of accountability, just as it is possible to tip an epidemic of impunity. The elements should be similar, in that "[e]pidemics are a function of the people who transmit infectious agents, the infectious agent itself, and the environment in which the infectious agent is operating".[104] If an epidemic tips, it is due to change in one or more of these three areas. In the case of spreading accountability, the key issues are who are the people who transmit infectious agents, what are

---

[101] Berkeley, 2001, p. 11, see *supra* note 98.

[102] Carnegie Commission, 1997, p. 4, see *supra* note 68.

[103] Levi, 1998, see *supra* note 79; Gourevitch, 1998, see *supra* note 77; Fonseca, 1995, see *supra* note 87; Zimbardo, 2007, see *supra* note 75; Huggins, 2004, see *supra* note 82.

[104] Gladwell, 2000, p. 18, see *supra* note 75.

the infectious agents, and what is the environment in which the infectious agents operate.

2.4.5.   Lesson Five: The Importance of Raising Greater Awareness That the International Community Must Take a Strong Stand

The fifth lesson is the importance of raising greater awareness of the knowledge that the international community must take a strong stand against serious crimes, that it cannot be neutral, and that a joint approach is necessary. To draw from on the oft-quoted words of Martin Niemöller, the German anti-Nazi theologian and Lutheran pastor who was sent to the Sachsenhausen and Dachau concentration camps for resisting Nazi repression of the Church, serious crimes underscore our interdependence, at the national level and internationally. He famously wrote:

> First the came for the Socialists, and I did not speak out –
> Because I was not a Communist.
>
> Then they came for the Trade Unionists, and I did not speak
> out –
> Because I was not a Trade Unionist.
>
> Then they came for the Jews, and I did not speak out –
> Because I was not a Jew.
>
> Then they came for me – and there was no one left to speak
> for me.[105]

What he describes is a rational progression that demonstrates that serious crimes are not necessarily driven by the characteristics of any single victim group, so much as by the political calculations of the perpetrators. In the case of the Nazis, they systematically eliminated different groups that they viewed as a threat to their regime. The point Niemöller emphasises is that the commission of serious crimes affect all of us, not just the direct victims, and they affect all of us not only because of the moral effect of the crimes, but because impunity for serious crimes leads to more crimes, as the calculation of the perpetrators that the crimes will pay dividends is reaffirmed. Niemöller's point was reiterated more recently by Kyaw, lead singer of Rebel Riot, a Burmese punk band, who released a new song slamming religious hypocrisy and an anti-Muslim movement known as 969. Radical monks are at the forefront of a bloody campaign against Muslims, and few in an otherwise Buddhist nation have spoken out. "If

---

[105]   This version of the text is that at the United States Holocaust Memorial Museum.

they were real monks, I'd be quiet, but they aren't", says Kyaw. Michael Salberg, director of international affairs at the US-based Anti-Defamation League has pointed out "[the radical monks] are nationalists, fascists. No one wants to hear it, but it's true. [...] It's not perpetrators that are the problem here", he says, pointing to conditions that paved the way for the Holocaust in Germany and the genocide in Rwanda. "It's the bystanders".[106]

In its follow-up to the outcome of the Millennium Summit, the UN General Assembly acknowledged that when it comes to addressing events that lead to "large-scale death or lessening of life chances", such as internal conflict, civil war, genocide and other large-scale atrocities, "collective security institutions have proved particularly poor at meeting the challenge posed by large-scale, gross human rights abuses and genocide". This is both a normative and operational challenge. The General Assembly places additional emphasis on the importance of key actors in the international community working together, arguing, "[c]ollective security institutions are rarely effective in isolation. Multilateral institutions normally operate alongside national, regional and sometimes civil society actors, and are most effective when these efforts are aligned to common goals".[107] The report points to the lack of political will, not the lack of early warning, as the biggest problem, arguing that:

> The biggest source of inefficiency in our collective security institutions has simply been an unwillingness to get serious about preventing deadly violence. The failure to invest time and resources early in order to prevent the outbreak and escalation of conflicts leads to much larger and deadlier conflagrations that are much costlier to handle later.[108]

Jentleson expresses no surprise at the lack of political will, arguing that "[i]nertia and inaction are much more natural states for democratic governments not confronted by clear and present dangers than mobilization and action".[109]

---

[106] "Punk Bands Break Myanmar's Silence on Religious Attacks", in *The Hindu*, 5 August 2013.

[107] United Nations General Assembly, Follow-up to the Outcome of the Millennium Summit, UN doc. A/59/565, 2004, para. 23.

[108] *Ibid.*

[109] Jentleson, 2002, p. 33, see *supra* note 92.

According to Gourevitch and other experts, the lack of a planned or strategic approach, combined with the lack of political will, resulted in the international community's contradictory responses to the Rwanda genocide, in which first the international community ignored the genocide, then returned to Rwanda in the form of a United Nations peacekeeping operation that seemed to residents more willing to defend corpses from dogs than to defend civilians from perpetrators. The international community then focused intensive energy on the refugees fleeing to the Democratic Republic of the Congo, even though among them were large numbers of perpetrators of the genocide, a process that intensified the Congo war.[110] Likewise, General Roméo Dallaire, who was in charge of the United Nations mission in Rwanda during the genocide, argues:

> Almost fifty years to the day that my father and father-in-law helped to liberate Europe, when the extermination camps were uncovered and when, in one voice, humanity said, 'never again', we once again sat back and permitted this unspeakable horror to occur. We could not find the political will nor the resources to stop it.[111]

Gareth Evans of the International Crisis Group and others also emphasise the importance of leadership in the context of "co-operative internationalism".[112] The role of Kofi Annan as the mediator following the 2008 Kenya election violence is a good example of this kind of leadership. Unlike other situations such as Darfur, members of the international community engaged in the Kenya situation agreed that Annan should be the sole interlocutor on behalf of the international community *vis-à-vis* the Kenyan authorities. At the same time, Annan made clear the links between his work and that of the ICC, to demonstrate the synergy of a comprehensive approach, and that there was no conflict between peace and justice. Those following the Kenya situation generally agree that the identification of a single interlocutor as well as Annan's truly comprehensive approach prevented the kind of forum shopping that would have undermined Annan's ability to conclude a strong agreement, including support for an ICC investigation of those most responsible for the most serious crimes. The ICC and other actors through their work can encourage and

---

[110] Gourevitch, 1998, see *supra* note 77.

[111] Roméo Dallaire, *Shake Hands with the Devil: The Failure of Humanity in Rwanda*, Random House Canada, Toronto, 2003, p. xviii.

[112] Evans, 2006, see *supra* note 70.

support the international community to identify single interlocutors in other situations as well and to stick with them.

Kenneth J. Campbell also pushes civil society in particular to work harder to generate that political will. He writes: "We must accept that government leaders are politicians who respond to political pressure. To be disappointed by this is to be disappointed that the sun is hot or the desert dry. This is how political will is created".[113] While it is paradoxical, he calls on civil society to be optimistic and realistic at the same time, and to "rebut the cynics and critics who would paralyze us with unwarranted pessimism".[114] He calls on civil society and others to raise the costs of committing genocide and the costs of doing nothing to stop it.

2.4.6. Lesson Six: The Importance of Raising Greater Awareness of the Credible Threat of Prosecution as a Deterrent

The sixth lesson is the importance of raising awareness of the credible threat of prosecution as a deterrent. Jentleson emphasises the importance of a commitment to a peaceful and just resolution of the conflict rather than partisanship or sponsorship of one or the other of the parties, but emphasises that

> [f]airness is not necessarily to be equated with impartiality if the latter is defined as strict neutrality even if one side engages in gross and wanton acts of violence or other violations of efforts to prevent the intensification or spread of the conflict.[115]

Human Rights Watch seconds this in writing about Rwanda that the UN Security Council made the mistake of believing that "to take a strong position against the genocide could compromise the appearance of neutrality essential to serving as go-between in negotiations between the two parties".[116] In other words, a conflict cannot be fairly resolved, or resolved at all, if in efforts to resolve it, victims are ignored or "gross and wanton acts of violence" are overlooked.

---

[113] Kenneth J. Campbell, "Lack of Political Will", in Samuel Totten (ed.), *Impediments to the Prevention and Intervention of Genocide. Genocide: A Critical Bibliographic Review*, vol. 9, Transaction Publishers, New Brunswick, NJ, 2013, p. 36.

[114] *Ibid.*, p. 34.

[115] Jentleson, 2002, p. 38, see *supra* note 92.

[116] Human Rights Watch, *Slaughter Among Neighbours: The Political Origins of Communal Violence*, Yale University Press, New Haven, 1995, p. 26.

Just as serious crimes are committed through the normal functions of the system and the state, so these functions must be turned to the protection of civilians if the cycle of violence is to be broken. The justice system should be in the first line of defence. As Raimo Vayrynen writes: "The methods of conflict resolution must incorporate the established structures of a society and seek to exert influence from within in order to change the likelihood of violence".[117]

Andrea Talentino notes: "There is a tendency to judge the absence of a speedy solution as a failure. This is particularly true in cases when preventive efforts are to be undertaken where violence is already taking place".[118] This argument is certainly true for the judicial process, which is always slower than even its advocates wish it would be. But Vayrynen emphasises its continuing importance:

> Practical experiences [...] indicate that incentives alone are not enough to stop recalcitrant actors from continuing their misdeeds. Promises and rewards must be backed up by threats and, if they fail, even by punishments [...] Successful preventive action requires that one makes threats of sufficient credibility and sufficient potency to persuade an adversary to cease or desist from an objectionable course of action.[119]

This is certainly true of judicial action, which is in a unique position to deliver such threats, if there is the political will to support it.

Goldstone concurs, citing the positive effect of the ICTY indictments on the Dayton peace process, first in removing recalcitrant participants from the process, and second in sending a message to the other participants not to cross the line into commission of serious crimes. The ICTY's deterrent effect is also documented in a 2010 impact study, which emphasises the importance of justice for survivors and for persuading perpetrators to cease or desist from an objectionable course of action.[120] In the nearly 20 years since the ICTY's creation, the study notes that Bosnian Serbs, originally the most resistant group when it came to accepting the

---

[117] Raimo Vayrynen, "Challenges to Preventive Action: The Cases of Kosovo and Macedonia", in David Carment and Albrecht Schnabel (eds.), *Conflict Prevention: Path to Peace or Grand Illusion?*, United Nations University, Tokyo, 2002, p. 65.

[118] Talentino, 2002, p. 71, see *supra* note 67.

[119] Vayrynen, 2002, p. 48, see *supra* note 117.

[120] Orentlicher, 2010, see *supra* note 6.

ICTY's existence and findings, are increasingly coming to terms with crimes committed by fellow Serbs. On the level of daily interactions, Damir Arnaut, a senior legal adviser to the Bosniak member of the Bosnia and Herzegovina Presidency says: "It helps that there are judicial findings. [...] When you talk about other issues, this elephant isn't in the room anymore".[121] Carsten Stahn agrees that

> [u]ltimately, judicial fact-finding might also limit the mystification of acts and perpetrators. Through their evidentiary filters and their publicity, international criminal proceedings may render certain facts less contestable. In this way, they may leave less room for the denial of atrocity.[122]

The ICC needs greater support from the international community in building on the potential deterrent threat of prosecutions. Conflict prevention experts recognise the importance of a preventative strategy being backed by a credible threat to act coercively.[123] Jentleson cites the Republic of the Congo and Chechnya as two examples where actors used force because they knew that no significant cost would attach to its use.[124] As a more recent example, Syria certainly comes to mind, among others.

2.4.7. Lesson Seven: Impunity and Non-Deterrence Are Too Costly, Economically and Otherwise

The seventh lesson is that impunity and non-deterrence are too costly, economically and otherwise.[125] For this reason, Cyanne E. Loyle and Christian Davenport urge scholars and practitioners, on the one hand, to increase their efforts to collect conflict data more broadly and to improve their intelligence infrastructures to do so, but at the same time to recognise that atrocity prevention strategies have lower thresholds of data needs and therefore can be implemented before the components of the conflict are conclusively determined.[126] In other words, the international commu-

---

[121] *Ibid.*, p. 96.

[122] Stahn, 2012, see *supra* note 29.

[123] Carment and Schnabel, 2002, see *supra* note 67.

[124] Jentleson, 2002, see *supra* note 92.

[125] *Ibid.*; Carment and Schnabel, 2002, see *supra* note 67.

[126] Cyanne E. Loyle and Christian Davenport, "Data Limitations as an Impediment to Genocide Intervention", in Samuel Totten (ed.), *Impediments to the Prevention and Intervention of Genocide. Genocide: A Critical Bibliographic Review*, vol. 9, Transaction Publishers, New Brunswick, NJ, 2013, pp. 113–31.

nity does not need to wait for the final verdict. Unlike military intervention, atrocity prevention strategies can be implemented even when the full picture is not clear, to try to prevent crimes in the earliest phase possible. This is an assessment with which Maureen S. Hiebert agrees, when she argues that preventative measures must be applied much earlier than trials can take place, and that the international community must take the lead and not leave it all on the shoulders of international tribunals.[127]

Dallaire addresses the cost of prevention in the context of Rwanda and the genocide, arguing the original US assessment for the UN mission, UNAMIR 1, for which the United States promised to pay and did not, would have been no more than $30 million, and the cost of UNAMIR 2 would have been only slightly more. By comparison, United States support for the Rwandan refugee camps in Goma, DRC, after the genocide, cost more than $300 million over two years. Dallaire adds:

> If we reduce to the petty grounds of cost effectiveness, the entire argument over whether the US should have supported the United Nations in Rwanda, the United states government could have saved a lot of money by backing UNAMIR. As to the value of the 800,000 lives in the balance books of Washington, during those last weeks we received a shocking call from an American staffer, whose name I have long forgotten. He was engaged in some sort of planning exercise and wanted to know how many Rwandans had died, how many were refugees, and how many were internally displaced. He told me that his estimates indicated that it would take the deaths of 85,000 Rwandans to justify the risking of the life of one American soldier. It was macabre, to say the least.[128]

Similarly, Nuremberg prosecutor Telford Taylor, who writes about the Vietnam War, cites the costs of the Vietnam War as one reason that war should not have been prosecuted:

> Colonel Donovan has estimated the cost of the air war alone, to the end of 1968, as over $7 billion for bombs dropped and aircraft lost. Over half of this sum was spent on bombing North Vietnam from early 1965 to late 1968. The bombing

---

[127] Maureen S. Hiebert, "Do Criminal Trials Prevent Genocide? A Critical Analysis", in Samuel Totten (ed.), *Impediments to the Prevention and Intervention of Genocide. Genocide: A Critical Bibliographic Review*, vol. 9, Transaction Publishers, New Brunswick, NJ, 2013, pp. 223–45.

[128] Dallaire, 2003, p. 498, see *supra* note 111.

in South Vietnam has, of course, been the principal cause of civilian casualties and the 'generation' of refugees.[129]

Of course, the most substantial cost of conflict and of serious crimes is arguably the loss of human life. The Office of the Prosecutor may have opportunities to link up with experts who can help to provide more concrete information about the cost of ICC Statute crimes. Helping to make this kind of information more widely known could help to build greater support for the work of the ICC.

---

[129] Telford Taylor, *Nuremberg and Vietnam: An American Tragedy*, Quadrangle Books, New York, 1970, p. 162.

3

Serbia and the International Criminal Tribunal for the Former Yugoslavia: Deterrence through Coercive Compliance

Sladjana Lazic*

3.1. Introduction

The International Criminal Tribunal for the former Yugoslavia ('ICTY') was established in May 1993 by a UN Security Council Resolution as an *ad hoc* tribunal tasked with ensuring that crimes and violent conflicts, at that time still ongoing in the area of the former Yugoslavia, are "halted and effectively redressed", and peace restored and maintained.[1] The hope for its prosecutorial deterrence was reiterated once again in the ICTY's first annual report to the Security Council where it was stated that one of the main aims behind founding of the Tribunal was to "establish a judicial process capable of dissuading the parties to the conflict from perpetrating further crimes".[2] The Tribunal was supposed to accomplish its mandate by prosecuting *those most responsible* for four types of offences: grave breaches of the 1949 Geneva conventions; violations of the laws or customs of war; genocide; and crimes against humanity. During a little more than 20 years of activity,[3] the Tribunal indicted 161 individuals, 80

---

* Sladjana Lazic holds a Ph.D. in political science from the Norwegian University of Science and Technology, Trondheim, Norway. Her areas of specialisation include peacebuilding, transitional justice, peace and conflict studies, Balkan area studies and ethnography.

1 United Nations Security Council, Resolution 827, 25 May 1993, UN doc. S/RES/827 (http://www.legal-tools.org/doc/dc079b/).

2 United Nations, Annual Report of the International Criminal Tribunal for the former Yugoslavia to the Security Council and the General Assembly, UN doc. A/49/342, 29 August 1994, para. 13.

3 In 2003 the Security Council adopted the ICTY's Completion Strategy which envisioned a focus on the most senior leaders alleged to be the most responsible for the committed crimes, and that all investigations and indictments should be completed by the end of 2004, all the trials at first instances by 2008, and all other kinds of work by 2010; United Nations Security Council, Resolution 1503, 28 August 2003, UN doc. S/RES/1503 (http://www.legal-tools.org/doc/05a7de/). Its last charges were raised in 2004 and confirmed in 2005, while the closing date of the Tribunal was later on postponed with United

of whom were sentenced, and is now working towards the completion of its mandate after which all the remaining functions of the ICTY will be taken over by the International Residual Mechanism for Criminal Tribunals ('MICT').[4]

Twenty-one (13 per cent) of those 161 defendants have been citizens of the Republic of Serbia, including two former presidents of the country, all of whom were accused of crimes committed during the wars in Croatia (1991–1995), Bosnia and Herzegovina (1992–1995) and Kosovo (1998–1999). The lack thus far of empirical exploration of the ICTY's deterrent impact on Serbia[5] is not a surprise bearing in mind the difficulties of proving any effects of this kind of institution in general,[6] and especially of establishing causal relations between justice administered and the absence of crimes.[7] Most of those interviewed for this study claimed that the Tribunal has not had any deterrent impact either on Serbia or the neighbouring countries. These claims are supported with widely known facts that some of the worst atrocities in the former Yugoslavia happened after establishment of the Tribunal, and even with claims that the Tribunal did not stop wars elsewhere in the world. In the context of these claims, deterrence is thus understood as an absolute value – either it exists or it does not. This chapter takes a more nuanced approach to assessing the deterrent impact of the ICTY by understanding it not in the sense of an absolute absence of crimes, but in the sense of *altering policies, behaviours and attitudes in a way which could imply*

Nations Security Council, Resolution 1966, 22 December 2010, UN doc. S/RES/1966 (http://www.legal-tools.org/doc/e79460/).

[4] The ICTY branch of the MICT started operating on 1 July 2013 in accordance to the Security Council Resolution 1966 which imply temporal overlap with the ad hoc tribunals for the first several years of the MICT's work.

[5] Diane Orentlicher, *Shrinking the Space for Denial: The Impact of the ICTY in Serbia*, Center for Transitional Processes, Belgrade, 2008, briefly mentions deterrence, but restrains herself from pursuing that line of inquiry by claiming that she could not reach significant conclusions based upon the evidence available at that time.

[6] Oskar N.T. Thoms, James Ron and Roland Paris, "State-Level Effects of Transitional Justice: What Do We know?", in *International Journal of Transitional Justice*, 2010, vol. 4, no. 3, pp. 329–54.

[7] Kate Cronin-Furman, "Managing Expectations: International Criminal Trials and the Prospects for Deterrence of Mass Atrocity", in *International Journal of Transitional Justice*, 2013, vol. 7, no. 3, pp. 434–54; SONG Sang-Hyun, "Preventive Potential of the International Criminal Court", in *Asian Journal of International Law*, 2013, vol. 3, no. 2, pp. 203–13.

growing importance of international criminal justice principles in individual and societal considerations. These changes are tracked along the procedural steps relevant for the prosecutorial work of the Tribunal: investigations; indictments; trials; convictions/acquittals; and returns/ releases of the indicted.

Following these benchmarks, this chapter will specifically examine the *sui generis* experience of the ICTY's deterrence practice in Serbia around two sets of indictments related to the 1998–1999 Kosovo conflict. Those are: 1) the indictment from 27 May 1999 against Slobodan Milošević, then sitting president of Federal Republic of Yugoslavia, and four other senior officials[8] for murder, persecution and deportation during the conflict and subsequent North Atlantic Treaty Organisation ('NATO') campaign in Kosovo; and 2) the indictment from 20 October 2003 against four military and police generals (Lukić, Đorđević, Pavković and Lazarević) indicted on five counts of crimes against humanity and breaches of the customs of war during the violent conflict in Kosovo in spring to summer 1999. With the exception of Milošević's and Đorđević's cases, the other indictees ended up being joined in one trial process in July 2005 known as the *Milutinović et al.* case – later on changed into *Šainović et al.* – or as usually referred in the media, the Kosovo six.[9] Milošević's trial and Đorđević's trial were led separately. These two sets of indictments are representative of the types of perpetrators the Tribunal intended to deter in Serbia: political (regime) leaders responsible for violence against civilians, and commanders who either ordered, or permitted and failed to punish, commission of mass crimes by their subordinates. The focus on these two sets of indictments allows for seeing how the Tribunal's legitimacy and impact changed over time, as well as for tracking how the change of international and domestic socio-political conditions in Serbia affected relations with the Tribunal and consequently the Tribunal's actual and potential deterrent effect.

---

[8]   The other four indicted officials were: Milan Milutinović, president of Serbia; Nikola Šainović, deputy prime minister of the Federal Republic of Yugoslavia; Dragoljub Ojdanić, chief of staff of the Yugoslav army; and Vlajko Stoiljković, minister of internal affairs of Serbia.

[9]   ICTY, *Prosecutor v. Nokola Šainović et al.*, Appeals Chamber, Judgment, IT-05-87/1-A, 23 January 2014 (http://www.legal-tools.org/doc/81ac8c/).

3.2. Argument and Structure of the Chapter

The chapter consists of five sections. The first section briefly introduces the context in Serbia and its relationship with the Tribunal. The second and the third sections address the deterrent impact of the ICTY along the procedural lines relevant for prosecution by examining the two sets of indictments. By looking at sequences of events which played themselves out before, during and/or after the above-mentioned procedural steps, this section tracks possible changes in behaviour, and discourses of those directly prosecuted, those similarly placed, and/or the general public, as well as any policy changes in relation to the prosecution of war crimes. Each of the sets of indictments is treated separately in order to account for temporality and changes of domestic and international socio-political constellations. The fourth section addresses the cumulative effects of the Tribunal's administration of justice with regard to both legal and social deterrence. The fifth section is reserved for implications of the empirical findings and concluding remarks. The empirical evidence consists of the analysis of the secondary literature and the public record (media reports, official documents, non-governmental organisation ['NGO'] reports), supplemented with interviews I conducted with those I call professional observers (for example, civil society/NGO representatives, political actors, representatives of international organisations in Serbia), ex-combatants (volunteers and conscripted), and a few former military officers who were active soldiers during the recent conflicts in the Balkans.

Analysis of the empirical material shows how in the pre-2000 period the ICTY's impact manifested itself solely as *an acknowledgment of a potential judicial threat*, but became more concrete after 2000. This was due not only to the change of the domestic political context and arrival of political actors who sought international legitimacy in a global socio-political environment that supported the idea of institutionalised international criminal justice more than it did during the 1990s, but also due to deeper involvement and intervention of the Tribunal that evolved from an 'empty threat' (non-executed indictments) during the 1990s to full (albeit slow and domestically contested) administration of justice in the 2000s. The deterrent curve (measured through the policy changes, institutional performance, behavioural and attitudinal developments of those similarly placed to the prosecuted and the general public) trended upward, though not without hurdles, especially between 2003 and 2009. From 2010 onwards there is a slight downscaling (see section 3.4.) in the deterrent curve, which coincides with the European Union ('EU') softening of political and economic pressure after Serbia officially obtained candidate status, with the Tribunal entering its final years, and with the arrival in power of right-wing political forces in Serbia.

3.3. Serbia and the ICTY during and after Milošević's Rule

The timeline of the Tribunal's impact on Serbia can be divided into two stages. The first one coincides with the Tribunal's entry into the situation in 1993 and ends with Slobodan Milošević's transfer to the detention unit in The Hague in 2001. During this first stage, which coincides with the violent conflicts in Bosnia, Croatia and Kosovo, the Tribunal was in its institutional infancy and trying to impose itself as a relevant institution both in Serbia and internationally. At the same time, the ethnic semi-democratic regime[10] of then Serbia (as a part of the Federal Republic of Yugoslavia) led by Milošević was already implicated in crimes and held itself in power through a combination of ethnonationalist mobilisation and perceived fear of other nations, minorities and the 'New World Order', both of which were supported and propagated by nationalist intellectuals and political elites alike.[11] In 1998–1999, police and military forces met an Albanian insurgency in what was at that time the province of Kosovo with violent reprisals against both guerrilla fighters and civilians. This led to the NATO bombing campaign against Serbia, which after more than 70 days managed to force the withdrawal of Serbian troops from Kosovo. The relationship between the regime and the Tribunal during this stage remained mostly confined and never went further than the threat of investigation and indictments. The discourse, which the regime-controlled media in Serbia reproduced, framed the ICTY as yet another instrument which Western powers used for the establishment of the 'New World Order' and for the defeat of Serbia.[12] Despite the indictments, none of the citizens of Serbia and the Federal Republic of Yugoslavia appeared in

---

[10] An ethnic semi-democracy is a type of a hybrid regime between authoritarianism and semi-democracy and between post-socialism and nationalism. See Florian Bieber, "Serbia in the 1990s: The Case of an Ethnic Semi-Democracy", in Sammy Smooha and Priit Järve (eds.), *The Fate of Ethnic Democracy in Post-Communist Europe*, Open Society Institute, Budapest, 2005, pp. 167–89.

[11] Ibid.; Christopher K. Lamont, *International Criminal Justice and the Politics of Compliance*, Ashgate, Aldershot, 2010, p. 63.

[12] Author's interviews.

front of the Tribunal during this period, and the threat of international prosecution did not galvanise domestic accountability processes. The regime disputed the authority of the United Nations Security Council to establish the Tribunal, and rejected the jurisdiction of the Tribunal by claiming that it violated state sovereignty.[13]

The second stage starts with Milošević's transfer to the detention unit in The Hague in June 2001, which happened after the ideologically diverse democratic opposition led by Zoran Đinđić of the Democratic Party and Vojislav Koštunica of the Democratic Party of Serbia had taken power in October 2000. The transfer is taken as a benchmark because it was the first sign that the new political leaders might start co-operating with the Tribunal. In addition, Milošević's transfer to The Hague marked a new stage in enforcement of international criminal legal norms through, at first, increased social and political coercion from the United States which made its financial support to Serbia conditional on co-operation with the ICTY, and then later through so-called EU conditionality politics, which enforced full co-operation with the ICTY in arresting those indicted as one of the requirements for Serbia's Stabilisation and Association Process.[14]

This period (2003–2009) marked a convergence of effects, which complemented and amplified each other: specific and general legal deterrence coming from the Tribunal; social deterrence coming from both the international community and the Serbian civil sector; and in response, the often hectically negotiated interests of the new regime in Belgrade that sought international legitimacy and financial support. These effects converged in an international environment in which what has been described as the 'justice cascade' concept gained more power than it had had at any time prior to the 2000s.[15] Nowadays, professional observers nostalgically label this period the 'best time' for the prosecution of war crimes and dealing with the past in Serbia, and claim that it ended soon after the arrest and delivery of the last indicted fugitive to the ICTY

---

[13] Lamont, 2010, p. 63, see *supra* note 11.

[14] *Ibid.*; Jelena Subotic, *Hijacked Justice: Dealing with the Past in the Balkans*, Cornell University Press, Ithaca, 2009; Marlene Spoerri, "Justice Imposed: How Policies of Conditionality Effect Transitional Justice in the former Yugoslavia", in *Europe-Asia Studies*, 2011, vol. 63, no. 10, pp. 1827–51.

[15] Kathryn Sikkink, *The Justice Cascade: How Human Rights Prosecutions Are Changing World Politics*, W.W. Norton, New York, 2011.

(2009). This speaks more to the current state of war crimes prosecutions in Serbia, the expectations and subsequent disappointment, than about the effectiveness of the ICTY's 'golden days' from 2003 to 2009, especially when bearing in mind that this period was still marked by struggles to accept fully the jurisdiction of the ICTY and arrest all of the indicted. After the last arrest, social and political pressure from the EU declined (notably after Serbia became a candidate for membership in March 2012), and the number of newly raised indictments by the Serbian war crimes prosecutors decreased. At the same time, the systematic obstruction of public access to war files by the Serbian army and police increased (see section 3.4.). These attempts at curbing the space for prosecutorial actions are part of the state war narrative which evolved from a complete denial of war crimes to attribution of crimes to individual perpetrators who present a deviation from the societal norms (for example, 'paramilitaries', 'crazy people'), and thus denial of any systematic state involvement, let alone state-organised commission of crimes. The case of Serbia's relationship with the ICTY and recent developments are explained in more detail in section 3.4. They show the need to carefully consider and calibrate the relationship between compliance with the relevant norms on the one side, and deterrence (as a short-term effect) and prevention (as a long-term impact of war crimes prosecutions) on the other.

3.4. Milošević: Deterrence Impact in the Context of Prosecutorial Procedural Steps

As previously mentioned, the worst atrocities in the former Yugoslavia – the 1995 genocidal killings in Srebrenica (Bosnia), Operation Storm (Croatia) and atrocities in Kosovo – happened despite the Tribunal's existence and even despite several indictments,[16] which were raised prior to the 1995–1999 period. All of the respondents used these arguments when claiming the limited success or even complete failure of the ICTY to deter perpetrators and put an end to violent conflicts in the Balkans. These facts show that "establishing a credible judicial process capable of dissuading" was not an easy task for a newly created and unprecedented

---

[16] The ICTY issued and confirmed its first indictment against Dragan Nikolić, a commander of Sušica detention camp in eastern Bosnia and Herzegovina, by November 1994. Prior to the events in Srebrenica, the Tribunal also confirmed the indictment against Tadić (Omarska prison camp) and he made his initial appearance before the Trial Chamber on 26 April 1994.

international court. As Richard Goldstone and Gary Bass point out, it is very "difficult for a tribunal to have a deterrent effect if that tribunal is being created in the middle of the conflict".[17] This is especially true bearing in mind that the first two prosecutors were supposed to lobby for international support at the same time as they were acquiring evidence through a 'pyramidal prosecutorial strategy' in order to build cases against high-ranking perpetrators.[18] Additionally, the peacemaking strategy for ending the conflict in Bosnia included negotiating with Milošević, which prevented the ICTY from indicting him in 1995 under command responsibility for crimes committed in Bosnia[19] and even granted *de facto* impunity for the residents of Serbia.[20] Some claimed that this undermined the Court's deterrent impact since it allowed Milošević to return to his policies of ethnic cleansing in Kosovo, while others were convinced that by signing the Dayton Peace Accord of November 2005 and pledging to "co-operate fully" with the ICTY, Milošević not only legitimised the Tribunal but also put a sword of Damocles over his own head.[21]

Despite formally accepting the Tribunal's jurisdiction through the Dayton Peace Agreement, Milošević and the Federal Republic of Yugoslavia continued to oppose the Tribunal on the grounds that the ICTY Statute violated state sovereignty.[22] Milošević's government indeed transferred two suspects to the ICTY but found a legal excuse for this *sui generis* case of co-operation with the Tribunal in the fact that neither of the two were Yugoslav citizens, therefore providing a legal basis for their transfer.[23] Accordingly, the evidence suggests that this low level of Tribunal intervention and interaction with Serbian authorities did not

---

[17] Richard J. Goldstone and Gary J. Bass, "Lessons from Recent Criminal Tribunals", in Sarah B. Sewall and Carl Kaysen (eds.), *The United States and the International Criminal Court: National Security and International Law*, Rowman and Littlefield, Lanham, MD, 2000, p. 53.

[18] Frederiek de Vlaming, "The Yugoslavia Tribunal and the Selection of Defendants", in *Amsterdam Law Forum*, 2012, vol. 4, no. 2, pp. 89–103.

[19] Kenneth A. Rodman, "Darfur and the Limits of Legal Deterrence", in *Human Rights Quarterly*, 2008, vol. 30, no. 3, pp. 529–60.

[20] Lamont, 2010, p. 78, see *supra* note 11.

[21] Rodman, 2008, pp. 539–40, see *supra* note 19.

[22] Lamont, 2010, p. 66, see *supra* note 11.

[23] At the same time, Milošević continued to effectively ignore indictments against Serbian citizens who had been indicted by the ICTY in October 1995 (the so-called Vukovar Three). See *Ibid*.

create enough pressure for the Serbian regime to start domestic processes to try those responsible for violations of international criminal law during the violent conflicts in Bosnia and Croatia. According to the reports, during the 1991–2003 period there were only eight cases (16 persons indicted)[24] of war crimes prosecutions in front of the regular courts, and some serious doubts were expressed with regard to the regularity of these processes.[25]

Most of the professional observers from Serbia agreed that prior to the Milošević arrest, the Tribunal appeared as an institution with no teeth. One explained:

> the key reason for that was the fact that *there was no good reason to take the Court seriously! Because before that there was nothing [like that] with the exception of Nuremberg and Tokyo*. And when it comes to those two cases [Nuremberg and Tokyo trials], here in the Balkans it was reasoned: "We are not the Nazis, we're not killing each other in an industrial way". [...] Simply, the Court was considered to be a political act of the international community which would be withdrawn as soon as some political changes happened here, like removal of Milošević for example or the end of the war in Bosnia. Everyone took it that way because that's how it was explained to them here in Serbia. But even if it wasn't for that, *simply there was no precedent in history to show the existence and strength of institutionalised international criminal justice*. The judgments of the Tadić and Čelebići cases were not enough, not to mention that they were even unknown here; those [the judgments] were covered up, hushed. [my emphasis]

Another professional observer from Belgrade claimed that "not even the international community believed that the Court could do anything. They all thought that in the best-case scenario the Tribunal would prosecute a

---

[24] In addition, there were 12 cases in which the prosecuted crimes were not qualified as war crimes even though they should have been. Military courts processed and convicted 17 persons (mostly prisoners of war from the Croatian forces) for war crimes but those sentences were not executed.

[25] Organization for Security and Co-operation in Europe ('OSCE'), *War Crimes Proceedings in Serbia (2003–2014): An Analysis of the OSCE Mission to Serbia's Monitoring Results*, OSCE Mission to Serbia, Belgrade, 2015, pp. 17–18; Humanitarian Law Center, *Ten Years of War Crimes Prosecutions in Serbia: Contours of Justice*, Humanitarian Law Center, Belgrade, 2014, pp. 77–81.

few direct executors and then close its doors, thus leaving 'the big shots' untouched". For a while even the states on the Security Council were not fully prepared to provide political backing to the Tribunal.[26] In addition, the performance of the Tribunal during the first six years of its existence did not give enough proof that its threats of prosecution were high cost enough to prevent or deter atrocities. The Tribunal was productive in issuing indictments,[27] but lacked international support and co-operation from the former Yugoslav republics in enforcing the indictments by apprehending those suspected of committing war crimes. As some of the respondents mentioned, not only Radovan Karadžić and Ratko Mladić remained at large despite the indictments, albeit removed from politics and in hiding,[28] but at the same time Milošević enjoyed the status of a "factor of peace and security" in the Balkans due to his role in the Dayton Peace Agreement. In addition, Milošević and his regime had a complete monopoly on informing the citizens of Serbia about the Tribunal, its purpose and work. The "steady diet of anti-ICTY propaganda" which the regime served to its citizens during the first seven years is usually considered to have had a lasting influence on the citizens' perception of the criminal accountability and their relation with the ICTY even after the political changes in 2000.[29] An frequently mentioned misstep on the part of the

---

[26] SONG, 2013, p. 206, see *supra* note 7.

[27] From 1994 to 1996 the Tribunal publicly issued 44 indictments, which resulted in only 8 arrests by the end of 1996. Between 1997 and 1999 the Tribunal issued additional 17 indictments and a similar number between 2000 and 2002. The number of arrests started to increase with time, especially after Stabilisation Force in Bosnia and Herzegovina forces became involved in apprehension of the indicted after 1996–1997. Lilian A. Barria and Steven D. Roper, "How Effective are International Criminal Tribunals? An Analysis of the ICTY and the ICTR", in *International Journal of Human Rights,* 2005, vol. 9, no. 3, pp. 349–68.

[28] The ICTY indictment and the decision of the major brokers of the Dayton Peace Accord to negotiate with Milošević politically marginalised and legally excluded Mladić and Karadžić not only from Dayton but also later on from post-Dayton Bosnia. Karadžić was forced to resign in July 1996 (but for a while continued to exercise some political influence from behind the scenes), and Mladić was dismissed from the Bosnian army in November the same year. Even though during these dismissals there was no direct reference to the ICTY, it is considered that international pressure for their removal from political life in Bosnia was grounded in the existence of the indictments. See Payam Akhavan, "Justice in The Hague, Peace in the Former Yugoslavia? A Commentary on the United Nations War Crimes Tribunal", in *Human Rights Quarterly,* 1999, vol. 20, no. 4, p. 746.

[29] Orentlicher, 2008, p. 38, see *supra* note 5; Eric Gordy, "Rating the Sloba Show: Will Justice Be Served?", in *Problems of Post-Communism,* 2003, vol. 50, no. 3, pp. 53–63; ICTY,

Tribunal's work in this regard that many local professional observers mentioned was the late creation of the Tribunal's outreach programme. However, having in mind the regime's control over the Serbian media during the 1990s, it is questionable whether and how much an earlier establishment would have helped in informing the Serbian public about the Tribunal's mandate.

3.4.1. The First-Ever Indictment against a Sitting President of a State

After the justice and foreign minsters of Milošević publicly denied the Tribunal's jurisdiction, Chief Prosecutor Louise Arbour reminded him on 15 October 1998 that the jurisdiction of the Tribunal was not conditional upon his consent or his negotiation with anyone else, and that she intended to resume investigations in Kosovo.[30] However, it was not until the massacre of Kosovars in Račak in January 1999, and the US allegation that it constituted a crime against humanity, that the peace talks in Rambouillet were set.[31] Even though Arbour was denied access to Kosovo, Milošević was still afraid of a potential secret Tribunal indictment against him and refused to attend talks in Rambouillet, while his delegation tried to build into the talks amnesties for the crimes in Kosovo.[32] This shows how although the idea of institutionalised international criminal justice was slowly gaining momentum, especially in light of the adoption of the ICC Statute in July 1998, the threat of possible prosecution was still not strong enough to dissuade the regime from further commission of crimes.

When the peace talks failed while the violence continued unabated, NATO began its air strike campaign against Serbia on 24 March 1999. Two days after, Arbour sent yet another warning letter to Milošević repeating her intention to investigate the crimes.[33] On 27 May Arbour

---

"Prosecutor Seeks Assurance from President Milosevic Regarding Kosovo Investigations", Press Release, CC/PIU/353-E, 15 October 1998.

[30] ICTY, Press Release, 15 October 1998, see *supra* note 29.

[31] Gary J. Bass, *Stay the Hand of Vengeance: The Politics of War Crimes Tribunals*, Princeton University Press, Princeton, 2000, pp. 271–72.

[32] *Ibid.*, p. 272.

[33] ICTY, "Justice Louise Arbour, the Prosecutor of the International Tribunal, Writes to President Milosevic and Other Senior Officials in Belgrade and Kosovo to Remind Them of Their Responsibilities under International Law", Press Release, JL/PIU/389-E, 26 March 1999.

publicly announced the indictment against Milošević, which reflected her wish to halt atrocities in Kosovo, but also reflected her concern that he might get away.[34] The indictment presented a significant shift from the Tribunal's previous work with regard to the speed of prosecutorial action, but even more so with regard to Arbour's strategy to go directly after high-level accused instead of pyramidally building her cases.[35] Reactions to Arbour's decision were mixed: some welcomed it while others were concerned that it would hinder peace.[36] Despite furious reactions at that time from Serbia,[37] many of my respondents nowadays claim that "[n]o one took that indictment seriously [in Serbia]. That was such a precedent! No one believed that Milošević would end up transferred to The Hague or that Serbia would co-operate with such an institution".[38]

That the Tribunal's existence and ability to raise indictments were not part of everyone's calculations around the Kosovo conflict was also proven with the words of one of the 'Kosovo six' – General Vladimir Lazarević. When asked by a journalist in 2004 whether he had ever considered that he himself might end up in front of the Tribunal (and especially after Milošević had transferred Dražen Erdemović), Lazarević said that neither he nor his soldiers had had time to think of Milošević or Erdemović in "such a situation":

> I remind you, what was at stake in Kosovo [was a] secession of territory, an armed rebellion. Regular Army, operational structure and Prishtina corps, of which I was the Chief of Staff, had the task to prevent secession. 60 per cent of the territory of Kosovo in 1998 was occupied by terrorists. Thousands of civilians, police officers, 38 soldiers were killed, the border obsessed by terrorists from Albania. Every day and every night hundreds of terrorists from Albania

---

[34]   Orentlicher, 2008, p. 18, see *supra* note 5.

[35]   Another prosecutorial innovation by Arbour, which Carla Del Ponte was viewed in some quarters as using excessively, were sealed indictments. However, most of those interviewed for this study considered the sealed indictments as controversial and prone to political manipulation.

[36]   Lamont, 2010, pp. 80–81, see *supra* note 11.

[37]   Ivica Dačić, Milošević's spokesperson, accused the prosecutor of being a tool of US politics and even a war criminal herself, and claimed how the only purpose of the indictment was to stall the peace process. See AP Archive, "Yugoslavia: Milosevic Indictment: Government Reactions", in *AP Archive*, 27 May 1999; Neil King, "Milosevic Indictment Raises Stakes and Pressure on NATO", in *Wall Street Journal*, 28 May 1999.

[38]   NGO representative from Belgrade.

entering Kosovo. Who would think about Erdemović and Milošević in such times?! I was an officer tasked to prevent the overflow of terrorism from the territory of Albania and to preserve human lives, to enable so to say functioning of life in Kosovo in 1998. When the war came [NATO bombing], then especially when the bombs were falling and people dying on all sides, none of us had thought [about the extradition of Erdemović] but had precise tasks to do.[39]

Lazarević's words show the need to take into consideration the nature of the conflict and its domestic ideological framing. As suggested elsewhere, governments facing guerrilla insurgencies and attempting to establish territorial control are more likely to commit atrocities because their calculations are significantly altered by "overriding interest".[40] Even in those situations, commanders who allow or fail to punish their subordinates for committing crimes (rather than explicitly ordering them) are possibly more susceptible to being deterred by an increasing risk of prosecution, which would alter their cost-benefit calculation.[41] But Lazarević's words suggest that the perceived risk of prosecution was not high enough, or known enough, to affect his calculus, and/or that incentive to offend or to fail to prevent and punish was a stronger motivator than the perceived threat of prosecution.

Some of the professional observers claimed that the only visible deterrent effect of the Tribunal that we could speak of during the conflicts was the change in *modus operandi* when it comes to the commission of crimes. A representative of a human rights NGO from Belgrade said:

> If we take a look at the way in which the crimes had been committed from the beginning of the war in Yugoslavia, from summer of 1991 when the operation around Vukovar started and then all the way until 1999 [...] *If nothing else the perpetrators started hiding their crimes*, and as time was passing they were doing that more and more. [...] It appears to me that they did that first of all because of the Tribunal. So, I think that is the proof of that deterrent effect. The Court could not prevent them from [further] commission of the crimes, but if nothing else it prevented them to do that openly and in front of the cameras. [my emphasis]

---

[39] "Pucanj u prazno", in *Vreme*, 8 July 2004.

[40] Cronin-Furman, 2013, p. 445, see *supra* note 7.

[41] *Ibid.*

This explanation, repeated by a few other professional observers, has been in a way confirmed by the former head of the State Security Service Radomir Marković in 2001. In his statement Marković explained how during one of the meetings with Milošević, the then head of public security, General Vlastimir Đorđević, "raised the issue of the removal of the bodies of Kosovo Albanians in order to remove all possible civilian victims who could be the subjects of an investigation by the Hague Tribunal".[42] The attempt to hide the crimes indeed speaks to the fact that the high-ranking perpetrators were put on notice that they too could be called to account. The question is, however, whether we can talk about these acts as moments of "restrictive deterrence"[43] or just as *an acknowledgment of illegality of their actions*. As explained elsewhere, restrictive deterrence exists "when, to diminish the risk or severity of a legal punishment, a potential offender engages in some action that has the effect of reducing his or her commissions of a crime".[44] This might include "reducing the frequency, severity, or duration of their offending, or displacing their crimes temporally, spatially, or tactically".[45]

Even if hiding crimes does not qualify as a form of restrictive deterrence, another form could be a decrease in the number of casualties and the incidence of violence. Figure 1 shows that the peak in the number of casualties during the Kosovo conflict was reached on 27 April 1999 when 262 Albanian civilians were killed. Arbour publicly indicted Milošević and others a month after. A gradual decrease of both the number of incidences and the number of casualties during May and June cannot be attributed only to Arbour's indictment, bearing in mind that the NATO military intervention was ongoing from 24 March and that this could have had a stronger deterrent influence on the actors.

The conflict in Kosovo ended on 12 June 1999 after 78 days of NATO bombing. Milošević agreed to withdraw his troops from Kosovo, yet declared victory in front of his domestic constituency. The standing ICTY indictment meant that Milošević was risking arrest if he left

---

[42] "Serbia's Kosovo Cover-Up: Who Hid the Bodies?", Balkan Insight, 23 April 2015.

[43] David Bosco, "The International Criminal Court and Crime Prevention: Byproduct or Conscious Goal?", in *Michigan State Journal of International Law*, 2011, vol. 19, no. 2, pp. 163–200.

[44] *Ibid.*, p. 71.

[45] Kim Moeller, Heith Copes and Andy Hoechstetler, "Advancing Restrictive Deterrence: A Qualitative Meta-synthesis", in *Journal of Criminal Justice*, 2016, vol. 46, pp. 82–93.

Yugoslavia. As early as July 1999, even the second republic of the Federal Republic of Yugoslavia – Montenegro – announced its wish to arrest and deliver Milošević and any other war crimes suspects to the Tribunal if they appeared on its territory.[46]

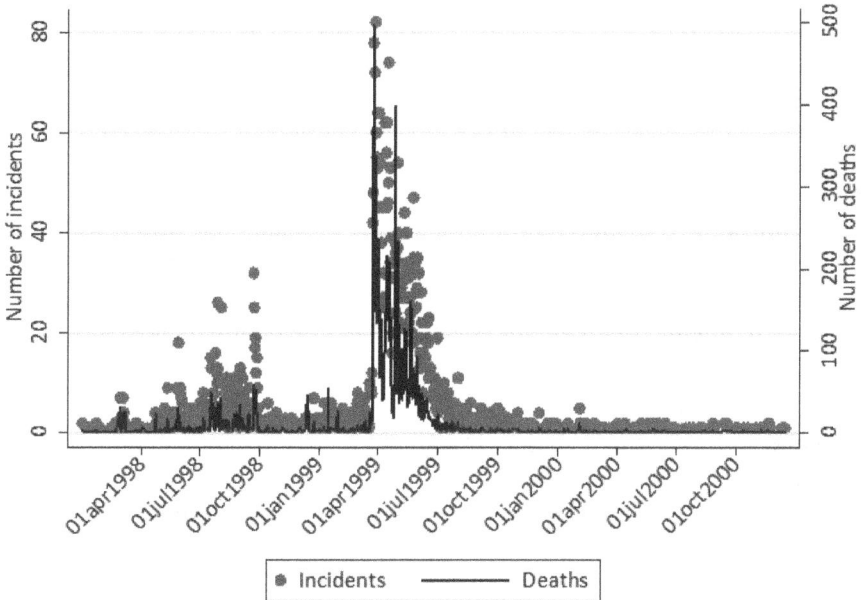

Figure 1: The Kosovo Memory Book Database.

As the evidence documents, up to 2000 the Tribunal's intervention in Serbia was contained to the level of investigations and the threat of indictments without the ability to detain those indicted. The Tribunal's weak pre-existing deterrent impact in the case of Bosnia[47] only bolstered Belgrade's doubt of the Tribunal's legitimacy and its refusal to co-operate. The international courts' dependence on state co-operation is a problem often mentioned in the literature and it is particularly exacerbated in case of non-democratic regimes such was the one that ruled Serbia during the

---

[46] "Montenegro Speeds Up Drive to Break from Serbia", Associated Press, 11 July 1999.

[47] Patrice C. McMahon and Jennifer L. Miller, "From Adjudication to Aftermath: Assessing the ICTY's Goals beyond Prosecution", in *Human Rights Review,* 2012, vol. 13, no. 4, pp. 421–42.

1990s. This superficial involvement of the Tribunal – investigations and indictments – together with the novelty of the court as an institution within the international arena did not manage to produce more than *the acknowledgment of the illegality of the actions* on the side of the Serbian regime through attempts to cover up the crimes and build amnesties into peace process.

3.4.2. Change of Regime and Milošević's Arrest and Transfer

Due to Serbian citizens' growing political support for opposition parties, a devastated economy, the loss of Kosovo and electoral fraud, Milošević was removed from power in October 2000 – though not without protest, and with help from international actors who made a decision to support regime change in Serbia.[48] Milošević was arrested on 31 March 2001,[49] but the evidence suggests that he would not have been transferred to The Hague if it were not for the pressure of Western governments on the United States to make Congressional economic aid to Serbia conditional on co-operation with the Tribunal.[50] This has been considered to be a decisive reason why Zoran Đinđić, the prime minister, transferred Milošević extrajudicially on 28 June of the same year, despite protests from certain parties in the ruling coalition, smaller public expressions of dissatisfaction among citizens,[51] and the first political crisis, which sparked from within the new ruling Democratic Opposition of Serbia coalition between Đinđić and Koštunica.[52] Koštunica called the act of Milošević's transfer to The Hague a "limited coup d'état" whose "consequences should be circumscribed".[53] Many of the professional observers consider that Koštunica's establishment of a short-lived truth commission and his insistence that those accused of war crimes should be prosecuted in front of domestic courts, along with his refusal to arrest those indicted and a persistent emphasis on voluntary surrenders, were some of ways in which he attempted to circumscribe the impact of the ICTY.

---

[48] Lamont, 2010, see *supra* note 11.

[49] Milošević was charged domestically for financial manipulation in regard to embezzlement and abuse of the office, but there were no domestic charges for war crimes.

[50] Authors' interviews; Orentlicher, 2008, see *supra* note 5; Subotic, 2009, see *supra* note 14; Lamont, 2010, see *supra* note 11.

[51] Orentlicher, 2008, see *supra* note 5; Subotic, 2009, see *supra* note 14.

[52] Orentlicher 2008, pp. 40–44, see *supra* note 5.

[53] "Državni udar bez države", in *Vreme*, 12 July 2001.

3.4.3. "The Trial of the Century" and a Reality Show in the Courtroom

Milošević made his first appearance in front of the Trial Chamber on 3 July 2001. In Serbia his trial became "not only a legal and political event – it is also a television show, and a tremendously popular one".[54] Milošević's and later Vojislav Šešelj's trials were televised as reality shows. The extensive media coverage also allowed both these former political leaders to use the courtroom much of the time as yet another platform for communication with their constituencies, and at times even for running, or at least influencing, electoral campaigns back in Serbia.

Three months after the beginning of Milošević's trial in April 2002, the Federal Law on Cooperation with the ICTY was passed,[55] accompanied by establishment of the National Council for Cooperation with the Tribunal that was in charge of co-ordinating responses to the ICTY's requests.[56] One of the problematic aspects of the law was a clause that prohibited state organs from surrendering to the Tribunal those Serbian citizens who would be indicted after its enactment.[57] This was an attempt to give an appearance of compliance while at the same time preventing the Tribunal from creating further disturbances by indicting those implicated in the crimes who still held positions in the state structures.[58] This clause was changed with later amendments to the law[59] made during the state of emergency, which was enforced after the assassination of Đinđić in March 2003. However, various strategies continued to be applied in order to prevent both the ICTY prosecutor and later the Serbian war crimes prosecutor from expanding the network of those implicated in crimes with new indictments, either by lobbying to prevent indictments for command responsibility or by blocking access to

---

[54] Gordy, 2003, p. 58, see *supra* note 29.

[55] "Zakon o saradnji Srbije I Crne Gore sa MKSJ", in *Službeni list SRJ 18*, 2002.

[56] "Formiran Nacionalni Savet za Saradnju sa hagom", in *B92 Online News*, 27 April 2002.

[57] Human Rights Watch, "Yugoslavia: Cooperation Law Inadequate", 12 April 2002. Despite the law's imperfections, it still managed to stir significant reactions in Serbia, especially among those who had been previously indicted. The former minister of police, Vlajko Stoiljković. whom Arbour indicted along with Milošević, killed himself in front of Parliament and left a letter in which he condemned the government for co-operating with the ICTY. Koštunica blamed the international community for this death.

[58] Interviews with professional observers.

[59] "Zakon o saradnji Srbije I Crne Gore sa MKSJ", in *Službeni list SCG 16*, 2003.

official documents.

Due to the international community's pressure to co-operate, on 17 April 2002 the federal government published the names of 23 persons previously indicted by the ICTY (10 of whom were citizens of the Federal Republic of Yugoslavia) and invited them to surrender voluntarily within three days. For those who would do so, the government guaranteed release pending the trial. After the designated three-day period there would be no more voluntary surrenders but arrests and transfers to the Tribunal. [60] Six of the indicted surrendered themselves, including Dragoljub Ojdanić (25 April 2002) and Nikola Šainović (2 May 2002) who were indicted together with Milošević. Milan Milutinović, indicted along with Milošević, continued to serve as president of Serbia and was the last to surrender from the initial five indicted by Arbour in May 1999. He did so on 20 January 2003 at the end of his mandate as president.

During Milošević's trial, Serbia was internally shaken with the assassination on 12 March 2013 of the prime minister by the Zemun gang, an organised crime group that was related to paramilitary and security forces implicated in crimes in Bosnia and Kosovo. This assassination showed the strength of those (still unreformed) forces within the security services that were not under democratic control and which opposed not only co-operation with the Tribunal but also a crackdown on organised crime.[61] It was exactly this convergence between organised crime and war crimes, together with the state of emergency, that finally pushed the government to amend the 2002 Law on Cooperation and remove the clause barring extradition to The Hague. As a result of the state of emergency, four accused surrendered to the Tribunal and the fifth was arrested, while the government even requested the ICTY to bring forward indictments against certain individuals who could present a potential

---

[60] "Savezna vlada saopštila spisak optuženih za ratne zlocine", in *B92 Online News*, 17 April 2002.

[61] As noted elsewhere, during the trial of the Zemun gang, the Serbian prosecutor claimed that the motives of the accused were stopping Đinđić's anti-organised crime campaign, ensuring that no more accused were sent to the Tribunal, and bringing hardline nationalists back to power. However, despite media reports stating that one of the organisers of the assassination (Milorad Ulemek Legija, a former special police commander whose unit Red Berets was implicated in war crimes in Bosnia and Kosovo) was concerned about a secret Tribunal's indictment, there is not enough proof to claim whether that or the threat to organised crime was his primary motivation for the murder of the prime minister. See Orentlicher, 2008, pp. 45–47, *supra* note 5.

danger to its stability.[62] Compellingly enough, according to some reports, this was also a moment when the majority of the Serbian public supported co-operation with the Tribunal.[63] As part of these reformist advances that followed Đinđić's assassination, in July of the same year Serbia also adopted the Law on the Organisation and Justification of State Organs in Proceedings against Perpetrators of War Crimes[64] which established an Office of the War Crimes Prosecutor, a War Crimes Chamber affiliated with a district court in Belgrade, and the Section for Discovering War Crimes affiliated with the police. Around this time, the State Union of Serbia and Montenegro also declined to sign a bilateral immunity agreement with the United States, which would guarantee non-surrender of US personnel to the International Criminal Court, despite the US threat to withdraw military aid to Serbia.[65]

Milošević's trial ended abruptly without a judgment after he died in his prison cell in March 2006. His death raised, yet again, some conspiracy theories about the Tribunal being an anti-Serb court, but it also raised the question of the duration of the trials in front the Tribunal. A common belief among the professional observers is that the Tribunal allowed both Milošević and Šešelj to turn the courtroom into a 'theatre' by allowing them to represent themselves, and that this led to prolongation of the trials and discredited the Tribunal to a certain extent. Even those in favour of the Tribunal's work and legacies mention lengthy delays of the trials and the so-called 'controversial acquittals' (the cases of Perišić, Haradinaj, Gotovina and Šešelj) due to uneven judicial application of principles of joint criminal enterprise, as factors that have had diminished both the Tribunal's legitimacy among citizens of the former Yugoslav area and the Tribunal's effectiveness in producing a deterrent effect and building towards longer-term prevention.

How problematic ending Milošević's trial without a verdict and how fickle interpretations of the past without a credible and binding judgment could be surfaced in the recent controversy about language in the Karadžić judgment. The controversy arose when the British journalist

---

[62] *Ibid.*, p. 48; Lamont, 2010, see *supra* note 11.

[63] Orentlicher, 2008, see *supra* note 5.

[64] See also later revisions of the war crimes law.

[65] Serbia adopted the Law on Cooperation with the International Criminal Court, Official Gazette of the Republic of Serbia, No. 72/09 on 31 August 2009 (http://www.legal-tools.org/doc/0fd4f6/).

Neil Clark used a paragraph from Karadžić's judgment stating that "there was no sufficient evidence presented in this case [Karadžić's trial] to find that Slobodan Milošević agreed with the common plan"[66] in order to claim that the Tribunal had "exonerated" Milošević. Even though the Trial Chamber, the former prosecutor in Milošević's case, and the current prosecutor of the Tribunal reacted by saying that it was not possible to draw conclusions about one case based on another, Milošević's former party allies, who are at the same time members of the current Serbian government, picked up Clark's claim as an excuse to declare Milošević's innocence and even suggested building him a monument.[67]

3.5. The Kosovo Six and Further Territorial Disintegration

The public announcements of the indictments against the four generals on 20 October 2003[68] (just before the general election scheduled for December of that year) attracted significantly more attention than Milošević's initial indictment, triggered considerable protest even among the pro-European Democratic Opposition of Serbia government,[69] and also created a stalemate in relations with the ICTY that lasted well over a year.

This could be explained by two factors. First, after the creation of the legal framework for co-operation with the ICTY, the likelihood of actually being transferred to The Hague grew significantly. Second, however, the contingencies of political life in post-2000 Serbia demanded a constant negotiation between 'patriotic' and pro-European national interests and did not favour the interests of the Tribunal. The change of the regime in 2000 was a negotiated transition in the sense that many remnants of the past, ideological as well as structural, were left to coexist

---

[66] Neil Clark, "Milosevic Exonerated, as the NATO War Machine Moves On", in *RT News*, 2 August 2016.

[67] Sasa Dragojlo, "Milosevic's Old Allies Celebrate His 'Innocence'", in *Balkan Insight*, 16 August 2016.

[68] According to Belgrade media reports, Carla Del Ponte had even attempted to hand these indictments earlier that month but the prime minister Zoran Živković had declined to receive them.

[69] The indictment was described as "an attack: and an "unseen nonsense" which 'destabilized democratic order in the country". See "Mićunović: Optužnice destabilizuju demokratski poredak u zemlji", in *B92 OnlineNews*, 26 October 2003, and "Čanak: Haška optužnica protiv četvorice – 'neviđena budalaština'", in *B92 Online News*, 26 October 2003.

and interact with reformist attempts. Not only was the reform of the security forces going slowly – Nebojša Pavković, one of the Kosovo Six and a close Milošević ally, remained at the head of the Yugoslav army until 2002 – but also the anti-Hague sentiment continued to exist on the political scene not only through the political parties of Milošević (Socialist Party of Serbia) and Vojislav Šešelj (Serbian Radical Party) but also through the party of Koštunica (Democratic Party of Serbia). As noted elsewhere, in the 2003 parliamentary elections three indictees (Milošević, Pavković and Šešelj) were leading their parties' lists, while two other indicted generals (Lazarević and Lukić) figured on the Liberal Party list.[70] This was despite the fact that even before the indictments were announced, the generals had been alleged as being involved in the commission of crimes in Kosovo. Although under investigation by the Tribunal, most of them kept high-ranking positions in post-2000 Serbia.[71] Even Đinđić said, when asked in 2001 about keeping Lukić in a high position, that the Democratic Opposition of Serbia was aware of Lukić's position with regard to Kosovo and that his name might show up in one of the indictments; but that was "less of a problem for us than if he was involved in a chain of drug, oil, or weapon dealers. […] So from the ones [police officers] we had available, he was the most appropriate despite all awareness that he is not an angel".[72] When the indictment was announced in 2003, Lukić was the deputy minister of the interior and enjoyed significant public support due to his role in the crackdown on organised crime after Đinđić's assassination.

The case of the generals is a good example not only of this negotiation between patriotic and pro-European interests, but also of the limits of the consequentialist logic behind conditionality,[73] which in the long run could possibly undermine the preventive impact of war crimes

---

[70] Subotic, 2009, p. 76, see *supra* note 14.

[71] As early as October 2001, the names of the four generals were mentioned in the report of Human Rights Watch, "Under Orders: War Crimes in Kosovo", 26 October 2001. The report stated that the campaign in Kosovo was clearly co-ordinated from the top, and alleged that the four generals were important part of that organisational structure, and at the same time urged both Serbian authorities and the international community to hold accountable all those who committed crimes.

[72] "Pucanj u prazno", in *Vreme,* 8 July 2004.

[73] Nikolas Milan Rajkovic, "The Limits of Consequentialism: ICTY Conditionality and (Non) Compliance in Post-Milosevic Serbia", in *Review of European and Russian Affairs,* 2008, vol. 4, no. 1, pp. 27–72.

trials.

The then prime minister, Zoran Živoković, reacted to the indictment harshly and alleged that both he and Đinđić had had a deal with the ICTY chief prosecutor Carla Del Ponte not to raise any more indictments for command responsibility. At the same time, he claimed that Serbia had no reason to protect those who committed war crimes and that serious measures were being undertaken in order to locate and arrest both Mladić and Karadžić, but that arrest of the generals was not the state's priority.[74]

As Nokolas Rajkovic explains, the 2003 elections showed the re-emergence of anti-Hague sentiments, and this allowed nobody but the Serbian Radical Party of Šešelj and Democratic Party of Serbia of Koštunica to benefit.[75] The former based both its presidential and parliamentary election platforms on an anti-Hague agenda and got the highest number of votes, but was not able to form a government. Koštunica, on the other hand, managed to form a minority government by securing a parliamentary majority with support from Milošević's former party. After he took the premiership, Koštunica announced a hardening of Serbia's approach to co-operation with the ICTY, and did not arrest or deliver any of the accused during the first 10 months in office.[76]

3.5.1. Arrests, Surrender and Transfer to The Hague

The transfer of the generals was postponed until the last possible moment – when it became obvious that Serbia's feasibility study for the Stabilisation and Association Process might be endangered due to lack of co-operation with the ICTY. As noted elsewhere, on 20 January 2005 the European Union's commissioner for enlargement explicitly linked a positive assessment of the study with Serbia's progress in co-operation with the ICTY.[77]

At the end of January the government found a (temporary) solution for co-operation with the ICTY in the form of the voluntary surrender of the indicted 'Serbian heroes'. Lazarević was the first to do so. On that occasion, Koštunica said that the government respected and appreciated

---

[74] "Premijer Srbije: Hapšenja I izručenja nisu prioritet", in *News Bulletin of the Ministry of Foreign Affairs*, 20 March 2003.

[75] Rajkovic, 2007, see *supra* note 73.

[76] *Ibid.*

[77] *Ibid.*

this "patriotic, moral, and honourable decision" of the general, which was in line with the long-standing tradition of the Serbian army and its officers who always "fight for the interests of their country".[78] The president of the National Council for Cooperation with the Tribunal expressed his hopes that the other indictees would follow Lazarević's "brave move" and by the same token promised legal as well as financial help to those who surrendered and to their families.[79] The voluntary surrenders were discursively framed as acts of patriotism[80] and sacrifice, and the consequent trials as yet another battle, which the generals were fighting for their country. This public framing, together with unofficial financial rewards for those who would surrender and material compensation for their families, "strengthen[ed] the public's perception of an 'unjust tribunal'".[81]

3.5.2. From a Reality Show to a 'Non-Event'

Unlike Milošević's trial, the actual trial of the Kosovo Six, which began in July 2006 and ended in August 2008, became a 'non-event', as Denisa Kostoviceva explains (with regard to Mladić's case),[82] even though it was a process in which the whole former political and military leadership of Serbia was put on trial for crimes in Kosovo. A programme director of one of Belgrade's human rights NGOs said: "For me that was one of the most important cases for Serbia because it was creating a broader narrative of what happened and how the state was implicated [in the crimes], but besides that initial attention for their surrender there was no interest of the public or the politicians for that trial, well not until the judgment at least".

In the period after October 2003, when the indictment against the four generals was publicly unsealed and for the duration of the trial, Serbia saw further territorial disintegration: Montenegro separated peacefully from Serbia in 2006, and Kosovo declared its independence in

---

[78] "General Vladimir Lazarević iduće nedelje ide u Hag", in *Bilten vesti*, 28 January 2005.

[79] "Ljajić: SCG korak bliže evropskim integracijama", in *Bilten vesti*, 28 January 2005.

[80] Rajkovic, 2007, see *supra* note 73.

[81] Humanitarian Law Center, *Transitional Justice Report: Serbia, Montenegro, and Kosovo 1999–2005*, Humanitarian Law Center, Belgrade, 2006.

[82] Denisa Kostovicova, "The Trial of Ratko Mladic at the Intentional Criminal Tribunal for the former Yugoslavia Shows Once Again That It Is Possible to Have Justice without Reconciliation", in *LSE European Politics and Policy (EUROPP) Blog*, 30 July 2012.

2008 without a major outburst of military or police violence. Some considered that these facts could be proof of the ICTY's deterrent effect.[83] At that time, according to the closing strategy, the ICTY prosecutor was not allowed to raise any new indictments, but the war crimes prosecutor in Belgrade was in the position to do so. In addition, bearing in mind all the previous reforms and developments already noted, it seems plausible to entertain the idea that the ICTY's demonstrated capacities resulted in some specific as well as general legal deterrence, which the European Union and Serbian civil sector reinforced with social deterrence, through financial conditionality and social pressure. These influences were at least some of the reasons behind stabilisation and the absence of (mass) violence around Montenegrin and Kosovo independence. Thus, the question is whether the cumulative effect of the Tribunal's retributive efforts with regard to both legal and social deterrence was one of the reasons behind the absence of violence despite further territorial reduction, or whether any deterrent impact is more attributable to the Special Court for War Crimes in Belgrade and its Office of the Prosecutor or rather from some of the actions of non-prosecutorial actors like the European Union.

The first question on the impact of the ICTY received a strong negative response. All the professional observers disagreed with the proposition that the peaceful outcomes of these developments could be in any way attributed to the effects of impact of the ICTY's (cumulative) prosecutorial work:

> I think that would be overstretching. Because I think [at that time] there was no further potential for the [violent] conflicts: we have, conditionally speaking, democratic governments in the states of the region, societies were already exhausted with the previous wars. [...] So I wouldn't relate the lack of new wars to the ICTY's effects. I wish I could ascribe that to one of the effects of the ICTY's work, but [...] I think that would be too much overstretching.[84]

An officer from the security service also denied that the peaceful outcome was in any way connected with the work of the ICTY. In his opinion, the lack of bloodshed could only be attributed to big world powers who at that time "did not find any interest" in new wars. At the same time, he agreed that the existence of a court tasked with prosecuting violations of

---

[83] Orentlicher, 2008, p. 20, see *supra* note 5.
[84] Interview with NGO representative from Belgrade.

the customs of war could "scare people" but only if "the justice is not on the side of the powerful". Otherwise, in his opinion, the court would just create resentment and even a wish for revenge.

Looking at the public statements of state officials around the time of the independence of Montenegro and Kosovo, there were no explicit references to the ICTY's work, its judgments or the war crimes they addressed. However, there were rather explicit and repetitive invocations of Serbia's intent and obligation to respect international law and look for solutions (especially with regard to Kosovo independence and the outbreak of violence in Kosovo in 2004) from within the parameters of the law and the United Nation Security Council resolution 1244. These invocations of international law were usually wrapped up in the discourse on European Union integration and Serbia's respect for European values. Consequently, the answer to the second question on the effect of non-prosecutorial actors, such as the European Union, receives a more positive reaction than the effect of the ICTY, or the effect of the War Crimes Chamber which is considered to be too susceptible to political influences.

3.5.3. Judgments: Sentencing and Acquittals

The Trial Chamber, presided by Judge Iain Bonomy, read the judgments on 26 February 2009. Šainović, Pavković and Lukić were found guilty of counts one to five of the indictment by commission as members of a joint criminal enterprise, and sentenced to 22 years' imprisonment each; Ojdanić and Lazarević were found guilty of counts one and two of aiding and abetting and sentenced to 15 years' imprisonment each. Milutinović was acquitted.

A former military officer, who talked about the ICTY as an instrument of Western powers used for controlling the post-Yugoslav region, said that he does not understand on what grounds Lazarević was convicted, and that the principle of command responsibility was for the first time introduced to international law in the case of the former Yugoslavia. He strongly disagreed with the comparison with Nuremberg because "the extent of crimes cannot be compared", and claimed that if the principle of command responsibility was equally applied then "most of the leaders in Europe and America would be found guilty, including the proven war criminals who still lead Kosovo".

3.5.4. "They Are Now Free Men": 'Heroes' Are Coming Home

Three of the five sentenced of the Kosovo Six have been released after serving two-thirds of their sentences. [85] Only the military general Ojdanić[86] admitted guilt and expressed regret after the decision of the Appeals Chamber. However, after his return to the country Ojdanić expressed his "disappointment in international law and international justice", adding that he did not commit any war crime, that during the Kosovo conflict crimes were committed "on all the sides and that he always advocated that criminals [should] be punished". Šainović, the former deputy prime minister of the Federal Republic of Yugoslavia, has returned to politics and is now a member of the Socialist Party's main board. While both Ojdanić and Šainović were welcomed by their supporters and party colleagues when they returned to Serbia following their release, Lazarević also got the attention of the state. Not only were two ministers sent by airplane to bring him back to Serbia after his release, but the minister of the interior also declared that Lazarević should be a role model for future generations. The prime minister, Aleksandar Vučić explained his position with regard to the convicted general:

> General Lazarević was convicted based on command responsibility. The general neither personally committed any crime, nor does he have blood on his hands. [...] Based on the Hague Tribunal's ruling, General Lazarević is responsible for the crimes [committed] in Kosovo. And what did General Lazarević do? [He was] fulfilling his military duties. Whether he really participated in war crimes? The court said it, I am not meddling into that. [...] I am not sure that anyone in Serbia thinks that General Lazarević is really a criminal. As far as I am concerned, as a president of the government I am behaving as a legalist I and respect certain decisions. Perhaps there is a difference between my personal opinion and what I have to do as the president of the government.[87]

---

[85] The police generals Đorđević and Lukić are serving 18- and 20-year sentences in Germany and Poland respectively, while the military general Pavković is serving 22 years in Finland.

[86] Police general Đorđević, prosecuted in a separate case, also admitted guilt. See ICTY, *Prosecutor v. Vlastimir Đorđević et al.*, Trial Chamber, Judgment, IT-05-87/1, 23 February 2011 (http://www.legal-tools.org/doc/653651/).

[87] "Intervju", in *B92 Online News*, 1 April 2016.

3.6. Cumulative Deterrence Effect of the ICTY

ICTY supporters mention as its most significant, though indirect, impact the strengthening of the rule of law through enhancing domestic capacities to prosecute war crimes, and providing impetus for regional co-operation in war crimes prosecutions. At the time of its establishment supporters of war crimes prosecutions hoped that the War Crimes Chamber could become more threatening than the ICTY, which was temporally constrained and had a limited focus on "the most responsible". However, this hope retreated lately. Since it was established in 2003, the Office of the War Crimes Prosecutor has indicted 184 individuals in 64 cases, of which 84 have so far been convicted. Nevertheless, the Office of the War Crimes Prosecutor and the War Crimes Chamber have also faced a lot of criticism for being susceptible to political pressure and for prosecuting only low-ranking perpetrators while the mid- and high-level perpetrators remain unpunished and shielded from prosecution.[88] By the end of 2014 none of the indicted had had a high-ranking position at the time of the commission of the crimes, and fewer than 10 per cent had held a position which allowed them to issue orders, that is middle-level or above.[89] Starting from 2010 there has been a significant decrease in the number of new cases,[90] which is usually attributed to political pressure from police and military services, and/or the political authorities. One of the frequently mentioned problems in the reports and interviews of professional observers with regard to prosecution of the higher-ranking positions, especially in relation to Kosovo, is a systematic obstruction of access to public files,[91] and uneven judicial and prosecutorial practice with regard to the application of international criminal law rules on command responsibility.[92] This perception is shared not only among the professional observers but also among a portion of ordinary citizens. A public opinion survey from 2011 showed that the citizens of Serbia think that the Office of the War Crimes Prosecutor has no courage to launch all necessary proceedings for war crimes – including against high-ranking

---

[88] OSCE, 2015, see *supra* note 25.

[89] *Ibid.*, p. 15.

[90] *Ibid.*

[91] Maija Ristic, "Will Serbia Ever Try Generals for Kosovo Crimes?", in *Balkan Insight*, 8 August 2016.

[92] OSCE, 2015, see *supra* note 25.

army and police officers (43 per cent) – and that the its work (50 per cent) and decisions (47 per cent) are influenced by the authorities.[93] As one of the NGO representatives explained, the obstruction of access to public files did not happen right after 2000, but only after some NGOs started pressing charges against members of the police, and especially after the War Crimes Chamber started acting upon those charges. She elaborated:

> For me, this is at the same time a good and a bad thing. In a way, this sends a message that there is awareness that what has been done was wrong, hence there is a need to hide it. But at the same time, there is this persistent problem of impunity among those who were educated to respect the international law – high- and mid-ranking officers of the army and the police. [That] together with the state welcoming those who were convicted in The Hague as heroes who "just did their job" does not send a positive message that something like that won't happen again.

3.7. Conclusion and Recommendations

The analysis above shows that the ICTY was limited as an agent of deterrence *during* the Yugoslav conflicts. Its deterrent prospects and capabilities were hampered both by its own institutional limitations and by its complex relationship with local political stakeholders in Serbia, as well as with international stakeholders. This set of circumstances prevented the creation of a credible judicial process that would dissuade the parties to the conflict from perpetrating further crimes. The empirical evidence indeed implies certain moments which could anecdotally speak to some level of awareness of the local actors about the illegality of their actions, but this awareness did not lead to halting further atrocities at the state level.

In the period after 2000, however, the deterrent impact has been primarily a result of what is identified as the diffuse or indirect power of the Tribunal,[94] or what could be considered general deterrence or even prevention. The effect is indirect because it is mediated and enforced through transnational networks of governmental and non-governmental

---

[93] Organization for European Security and Co-operation and Beogradski centar za ljudska prava, "Attitudes Towards War Crimes Issues, ICTY and the National Judiciary. Public Opinion Survey", October 2011.

[94] McMahon and Miller, 2012, p. 438, see *supra* note 47.

actors engaged in promoting and enforcing respect for international criminal justice, peace and democracy, [95] rather than arising as an exclusive and direct result of the Tribunal's existence *per se* and of its prosecutorial work. Most of those interviewed agreed that without the existence of the ICTY complete impunity would have prevailed, but also that the ICTY alone could not have done anything if it were not for the European Union's policy of conditionality. As shown above, the change of institutional structures and discourses which speak to deterrence has been most of the time dressed up in Serbia's devotion to European values and its determination to gain membership in the European Union instead of relating those changes with the morals and principles behind war crimes prosecutions.

This underscores how the ICTY's prosecutorial power has depended upon the support of a wider network of global (and local) actors and their enforcement of the principles and norms that the ICTY, with its existence and work, entails and claims to promote. This is no surprise bearing in mind the nature of the contemporary global governance regimes that makes it impossible for one institution or a norm to operate in a vacuum, unaffected by other institutions, actors and norms. If the goal is to be effective in deterring and preventing further and future crimes, we cannot solely rely on the existence and work of the international courts. We should ensure, as the ICC president SONG Sang-Hyun puts it, that "international criminal justice must work in concert with other mechanisms". [96] This demands a long-term co-ordinated effort of all involved in the process, from local to national and global levels.

What seems to be particularly needed for the effectiveness of general deterrence is a *sustained commitment to universal accountability* in order to combat the prevalent perception (in particular among the ordinary citizens) of the selectivity of international criminal justice. The perceived selection bias (which can be abused as significant symbolic capital for political manipulation) shows, once again, the need for international courts to acquire their legitimacy among the ordinary people (and elites alike) in those countries where they have jurisdiction, by explaining their goals and procedures as directly as possible. [97]

---

[95] *Ibid.*
[96] SONG, 2013, p. 212, see *supra* note 7.
[97] Gordy, 2003, p. 61, see *supra* note 29.

The legal, institutional and discourse changes in Serbia which could speak of deterrence are still, in most of the cases, stronger at a symbolic level (showing the willingness) than on a practical level (showing effectiveness) of respect for international criminal justice and the fight against impunity. Several authors have pointed out in various ways how coercive compliance, as the main characteristic of Serbia's relationship with the Tribunal, has potentially undermined the internalisation of the accountability norm since it shifted the focus from legal obligations to pragmatic bargaining. [98] Apart from showing the limitations of consequentialist logic, this also gives grounds for concern, particularly with regard to prevention. However, it is still too soon to draw any broad conclusion. At the bottom line, this shows that the seed of accountability for violations of international criminal law has been planted, but that it still needs constant cultivation. Deterrence is not a once-and-for-all goal, but a process that needs constant and consistent reaffirmation.

3.7.1. Policy Implications for Serbia

One of the most pressing aspects in relation to deterrence that came out both in interviews with professional observers and through analysis of empirical material of discourse and policies is the need to enforce and explain better the concept of superior criminal liability. This is particularly important bearing in mind the theoretical assumptions that leaders who fail to prevent the commission of crimes are those who are the most susceptible to a deterrence impact.[99] The need to both enforce and explain this concept can be seen not only in the public discourse around the return of the convicted generals but also in the ambivalent practice and the legal framework that Serbian judges and prosecutors apply when it comes to superior criminal liability.[100] While some of the respondents described this fact as an omission of the ICTY outreach programme and/or a failure of Serbian political elites, others claimed that intellectual elites and the media could be more important in this regard, especially given the lack of popular (citizens') trust in both politicians and the Tribunal. As one respondent explained, it is questionable how much

---

[98] Subotic, 2009, see *supra* note 14; Lamont, 2010, see *supra* note 11; Rajkovic, 2007, see *supra* note 73.

[99] Cronin-Furman, 2013, see *supra* note 7.

[100] OSCE, 2015, pp. 57–60, see *supra* note 25.

the outreach of a "disliked institution" or politicians who are perceived as corrupt can do: "at the end of the day, that is our job – civil sector and media – and intellectual elites to keep pushing this story [accountability]".

Related, but not limited, to this is the need to provide a legal and social environment that would make it unfavourable for political and other actors to interfere with judicial processes by tampering with witnesses or denying access to public documents and files. This could be done by developing checks and balances that strengthen the institutional independence of the judiciary and thereby of the rule of law, through the continual support to civil society in their role as whistle-blowers and sources of social pressure, and through sensitising media campaigns. There is some hope that this can be accomplished and that the accountability mechanisms and processes in Serbia will not die away. These include:

1. A still very active and vigorous civil society that continues to push accountability for war crimes onto political agendas.[101]

2. A campaign demanding transitional justice to be an integral part of Serbia's European Union accession negotiation.[102]

3. The European Union's adoption of its policy framework in support of transitional justice, which accentuates as its goals, among others, ending impunity and strengthening the rule of law.[103] Even though this document is more normative than an operationalised strategy, it still offers a policy base within which certain concrete action could be taken.

4. Serbia's adoption of its National Strategy for War Crimes Processing in February 2016.

3.7.2. Implications of Serbia's Experience for General Deterrence

Perhaps the most significant transferable knowledge from the interaction of the ICTY with Serbia that could guide future policy decisions about the

---

[101] Humanitarian Law Center, 2006, see *supra* note 81.

[102] Michael Davenport, "Transitional Justice in the EU Accession Context", The Delegation of the European Union to the Republic of Serbia, 22 January 2015; David Tolbert, "Transitional Justice Should Be Part of Serbia's Accession to the EU", in *Accession Through Justice*, February 2016.

[103] EU Foreign Affairs Council, "The EU's Policy Framework on Support to Transitional Justice", 16 November 2015.

international (and hybrid) criminal courts lies in the necessity of providing a broad front of actors who would, in a collaborative and concerted way, enforce the principle of accountability. At the same time, the case of Serbia shows the need for the policy choices to take into consideration limits of consequentialist logic that drives deterrence expectations. While getting acceptance of the international criminal courts' jurisdiction in affected countries, and providing custody of the accused, will probably continue to present challenges for enforcement of the accountability norm, Serbia's case strongly implies another pressing task for both scholarship and policy. And that is: how do we move beyond acceptance and arrests towards sustainable internalisation of the norm and prevention?

4

Exploring the Boundaries of the
Deterrence Effect of the
International Criminal Tribunal for Rwanda

Mackline Ingabire[*]

4.1. Introduction

This chapter explores the phenomenon of deterrence of the commission of genocide and other international crimes in the Rwandan context. Rwanda, located in East Africa, has experienced the international crimes of genocide, crimes against humanity and war crimes. As a result, the United Nations Security Council established the International Criminal Tribunal for Rwanda ('ICTR') in 1994 through UN Security Council resolution 955.[1]

As a methodology for this research, the available data on whether a deterrence effect has occurred because of the ICTR's establishment have been drawn from a wide range of materials. A significant number of ideas were drawn from individuals who were interviewed in key informant interviews and from those who participated in focus group discussions. The focus group discussions conducted included prisoners in the Nyarugenge central prison situated in the capital city, Kigali; prisoners in Ntsinda prison in the eastern part of Rwanda; members of youth groups composed of people born between 1990 and 2000 from different backgrounds; members of the survivors' group Ibuka that works in Kigali and is the

---

[*] **Mackline Ingabire** holds an LL.M. in Criminal Justice from the University of Cape Town, South Africa, and an LL.B. from the University of Rwanda. In 2011 she was a legal researcher at the International Criminal Tribunal for Rwanda ('ICTR'). She served as a co-ordinator of a Rwandan national task force on the transfer of cases from the ICTR to the Rwandan judiciary. She was a part-time lecturer at two private universities and worked as a corporate adviser to Horizon Group in Kigali, Rwanda. In 2016 she was appointed as a senior state attorney in Rwanda's Ministry of Justice in the legal advisory services. After three months at the ministry, she was appointed acting division manager for International Justice and Judicial Co-operation in the same ministry up to October 2016.

[1] United Nations Security Council, Establishment of the International Criminal Tribunal for Rwanda (ICTR) and adoption of the Statute of the Tribunal, Resolution 955, S/Res/955, 8 November 1994 (http://www.legal-tools.org/doc/f5ef47/).

umbrella organisation co-ordinating all survivors' groups; and officials in the Ministry of Defence. The key informant interviews conducted included: one with the permanent secretary in the Ministry of Justice; staff in the Ministry of Justice heading the Access to Justice Department; and with two national prosecutors, held separately. The information from both categories of interviews largely underpins this chapter. However, some literature surveys were also conducted, especially with regard to the history of Rwanda, information on the genocide and other international crimes, and prosecutions by different mechanisms. The perceptions of respondents are evaluated in relation to both court-based and non-court-based and contextual factors to measure deterrence. Most respondents in this research have tended to agree that there was indeed a deterrent effect from the ICTR, although they add that there was much more expected than was delivered.

4.1.1. Overview of the Chapter

Following the introduction, section 4.2. presents an overview of Rwanda and, in particular, the roots of the genocide. The colonial policy of divide and rule, and the subsequent post-independence tensions between republican intellectuals and monarchist loyalists are discussed. A description of the geographic location of Rwanda is included in this section to give the reader a picture of how Rwanda fits into broader global dynamics. Information about the genocide itself is included to clarify how its founders justified the establishment of the ICTR. The social and administrative situation of post-genocide Rwanda also helps to clarify how impunity would have dealt a resounding blow to the international justice project had the international community turned a blind eye to the situation. Both retributive and deterrent rationales for the ICTR in its mandate are expounded in this section.

Section 4.3. explores the extent to which the ICTR has left in Rwanda a legacy of deterrence as a standalone mechanism of the administration of justice. This section sets out the ICTR's accomplishments which form the foundation of its deterrence effect. The Rwandan community is acutely aware and clearly recalls this Court due to the indictments it issued, the personalities of the suspects who were arrested under its auspices, and the subsequent trials and sentences, both convictions and acquittals. Respondents in interviews paid much attention to the element of severity of the sentences handed down by the ICTR. Respondents strongly criticised the perceived lightness of the Tribunal's sentences given to high-profile suspects, as well as the time the processes took. Despite these criticisms, the Rwandan community regards the ICTR very highly, when it comes to the very strong precedents established.

This comes out as well in section 4.4., which looks side-by-side at the deterrence impact of the ICTR and of the judicial mechanisms of national courts, both ordinary and specialised courts, as well as the establishment and function of an alternative form of the restorative justice judicial mechanism of *gacaca*. The elements of deterrence are equally examined to present the extent to which national prosecutorial factors have effectively either contributed to deterrence by the ICTR or filled gaps in areas where the Court is regarded as not having fared so well. Respondents were positive about the heavy sentences which national and *gacaca* courts handed down, even though they generally tried cases of low-profile suspects, rather than high-level suspects. They were also positive about the high certainty of prosecution of those suspected of committing crimes and living in Rwanda as a mark of effectiveness, but were more sceptical of the ability of national mechanisms to access genocide fugitives, for which they appreciated the role of the ICTR. Regarding the speed of trials, respondents were divided on how the national mechanisms performed when viewed independently of the ICTR, but were more positive on this aspect when viewed in comparison to the slower ICTR. The section also explores non-judicial factors which contributed to the deterrence effect of the ICTR in Rwanda and the Great Lakes region, including the public policies of relevant governments.

Finally, section 4.5. synthesises the findings and proposes a few recommendations for policymakers and the International Criminal Court ('ICC'). These include recommendations that policymakers should, from the beginning, consider the need for an effective combination of national and international mechanisms when responding to international crimes because they achieve more deterrence and that, for continuing deterrence in Rwanda, access to the ICTR archives should be readily available.

4.2. Introducing Rwanda and the Rwanda Genocide

Located in East and Central Africa, Rwanda is a small landlocked country bordering Burundi to the south, Tanzania to the east, Uganda to the north and the Democratic Republic of the Congo to the west.[2] It lies 1,200 kil-

---

[2] Alphonse Mutabazi, "Rwanda Country Situational Analysis", Camco, May 2011.

ometres from the Indian Ocean and 2,000 kilometres from the Atlantic Ocean.[3]

European historians and anthropologists who have studied the Kingdom of Rwanda describe it as having a static social structure with coherent and fixed class distinctions, political hierarchy and occupational diversity, and with different social (or ethnic) groups carrying out different economic activities. For instance, the Tutsi were believed to carry out cattle-keeping whereas the Hutu were believed to be specialised in farming. These economic positions arguably determined the relationship of the particular group to political power in the kingdom:

> In this idealized imagery Tutsi pastoralists were seen as recent immigrants from the north, arriving around 1500 CE, while Hutu agriculturalists were assumed to have preceded Tutsi immigrants into the area by some five hundred years. To complete the image, the 'aboriginal' population, referred to as Twa, was portrayed as subsisting in the forest areas.[4]

The historians Jerome Lewis and Judy Knight believe that the pygmoid people, the ancestors of the present-day Twa, were the first inhabitants to settle in the area known as Rwanda today.[5] There followed the Bantu-speaking Hutu agriculturalists who arrived, probably from the east, and began clearing and settling the hills.[6] Finally, around 1500, a pastoral people with herds of cattle moved into the region, most likely from southern Ethiopia, where other pastoralists such as the Oromo lived, and these are believed to have been the ancestors of the present-day Tutsi.[7]

---

[3] National Institute of Statistics of Rwanda, Ministry of Finance and Economic Planning, "Fourth Population and Housing Census, Rwanda 2012. Thematic Report: Fertility", January 2014.

[4] Alison Des Forges and Timothy Longman, "Legal Responses to Genocide in Rwanda", in Eric Stover and Harvey M. Weinstein (eds.), *My Neighbour, My Enemy: Justice and Community in the Aftermath of Mass Atrocity*, Cambridge University Press, Cambridge, 2004, p. 26.

[5] Jerome Lewis and Judy Knight, Les Twa du Rwanda. *Rapport d'évaluation de la situation des Twa et pour la promotion des droits des Twa dans le Rwanda d'après-guerre*, World Rainforest Movement, International Working Group for Indigenous Affairs and Survival International, Copenhagen, 1996.

[6] Paul J. Magnarella, "The Background and Causes of the Genocide in Rwanda", in *Journal of International Criminal Justice*, 2005, vol. 3, no. 4, p. 801.

[7] Edith R. Sanders, "The Hamitic Hypothesis; Its Origin and Functions in Time Perspective", in *Journal of African History*, 1969, vol. 10, no. 4, pp. 521–32.

Recent history, however, indicates that before the nineteenth century all three groups "corresponded to occupational categories within a single differentiated group, the Banyarwanda".[8] Individuals moved between
the categories depending on how property increased or decreased, and in-
termarriages were common.[9] The Hutu/Tutsi/Twa identities were not
purely ethnic or racial, but rather partly political, occupational and ances-
tral. It was during colonial rule by the Germans and Belgians that the divisions along the Tutsi/Hutu lines were sown and flourished to later cul-
minate in genocide.[10]

4.2.1. Roots of the Genocide

In 1957, a group of nine Hutu intellectuals published the Hutu Manifesto,
which complained of the political, economic and educational monopoly of
the Tutsi and characterised them as invaders.[11] The manifesto called for
promoting Hutu in all fields and argued for the use of ethnic identity cards
to monitor the race monopoly.[12] Later, tensions escalated and set off an
outbreak of violence between a Tutsi-dominated political party, Union nationale rwandaise (Rwandan National Union), and a Hutu party, Parti du
mouvement de l'émancipation Hutu (Hutu Emancipation Movement Party)
following the 1959 coup in which the king, Mwami Kigeri V, was de-
posed.[13] Belgium ultimately intervened, but rather than merely restore order
the colonialists reversed their support from the Tutsi to the Hutu majority,
promoting the need for stability.[14] The ensuing violence left more than
20,000 Tutsi dead and sent even more fleeing to neighbouring countries.[15]

---

[8] African Rights, *Rwanda, Death, Death, Despair and Defiance*, African Rights, London, 1995.

[9] *Ibid.*

[10] *Ibid.*

[11] Catharine Newbury, *The Cohesion of Oppression: Clientship and Ethnicity in Rwanda, 1860–1960*, Columbia University Press, New York, 1988.

[12] Charity Wibabara, *Gacaca Courts versus the International Criminal Tribunal for Rwanda and National Courts: Lessons to learn from the Rwandan Justice Approaches to Genocide*, Nomos, Baden-Baden, 2014.

[13] *Ibid.*

[14] Paul Christoph Bornkamm, *Rwanda's Gacaca Courts: Between Retribution and Repara-tion*, Oxford University Press, Oxford, 2012, p. 11; Gérard Prunier, *The Rwanda Crisis: History of Genocide (With a New Chapter)*, Fountain Publishers, Kampala, 1995, p. 47.

[15] Different sources provide different figures. For instance, Anastase Shyaka, a Rwandan re-searcher, asserts that "approximately 30,000 Tutsis were massacred between 1959 and

More suffering, oppression and killing of Tutsi followed the 1959 insurgence. Available literature indicates that recorded periods in which the Tutsi experienced conspicuous hostility from their Hutu kin were in 1963, 1966 and 1973.[16] The government of President Grégoire Kayibanda intensified the systematic isolation of the Tutsi, and many were forced to flee the country.[17] "As the head of the state, Kayibanda fostered the notion of Tutsi and Hutu identities as being dissimilar races, with the Hutu being indigenous to Rwanda and the Tutsi non-indigenous".[18] As Charity Wibabara notes:

> The process of ethnicization had begun in the 1933–1934 census conducted by Belgians, which officially categorized the Hutu as indigenous and the Tutsi as non-indigenous. Also, during the 1934 census, the Belgians further promoted separation of the groups when they required the ethnicity of each citizen to be stated on state-issued identity cards. It is this census that determined 85% of the population as Hutu, 14% Tutsi and 1% Twa out of a population of 1.8 million Rwandans in 1933.[19]

Juvénal Habyarimana, the second post-independence president, "further reinforced the separation of the dominant groups in Rwanda by putting emphasis on the ethnic identity of each citizen to be stated on state-issued identity cards subsequent to the Belgian colonial policy".[20]

1966 and around 500,000 Tutsis found refuge in Uganda, Tanzania and Zaire now the Democratic Republic of Congo (DRC)". See Anastase Shyaka, "Understanding the Conflicts in the Great Lakes Region: An Overview", in *Journal of African Conflicts and Peace Studies*, 2008, vol. 1, no. 1, p. 6. See also the United Nations, *The United Nations and Rwanda 1993–1996*, vol. 10, United Nations Department of Public Information, New York, 1996, pp. 8–9.

[16] Diogène Bideri, *Le massacre des Bagogwe: Un prélude au génocide des Tutsi, Rwanda 1990–1993*, L'Harmattan, Paris, 2008; Antoine Mugesera, *Imibereho y'abatutsi kuri Repubulika ya mbere n'iya kabiri (1959–1990)* [On the Life of the Tutsi during the First and Second Republic (1959–1990)], Les Editions Rwandaises, 2004.

[17] Wibabara, 2014, see *supra* note 12.

[18] Bideri, 2008, pp. 40–41, see *supra* note 16.

[19] Wibabara, 2014, p. 21, see *supra* note 12.

[20] *Ibid.*, p. 29.

4.2.2. Events Leading to the War and the Subsequent Genocide

The post-independence politicians and leaders in Rwanda used ethnicity as a political tool to prevent power-sharing and democracy, and the promotion of ethnic hatred as a means of consolidating power. Incidences of human rights violations, such as arbitrarily arresting and killing carried out by Hutu leaders and politicians against Tutsi, became routine after 1959. As a result, the violent atmosphere led to constant though not massive numbers seeking refuge in neighbouring countries. In the years immediately preceding the genocide, the Tutsi who sought refuge in the 1960s became the subject of a repatriation drive, a subject that was a predominant factor in the 1990 war. It is alleged that "by the late 1980s, the number of Tutsi in exile had increased to over 400,000 refugees".[21] The peaceful return of Rwandan refugees failed when the government insisted that Rwanda was overpopulated, thereby condemning them to perpetual refugee status.[22]

On 1 October 1990 the Tutsi-led Rwandan Patriotic Front ('RPF') invaded the country. In response to the invasion, which was meant to raise the issue of repatriation of the Tutsi to a national level, some Hutu intellectuals[23] and politicians issued the famous "ten commandments", "forbidding Hutu from interacting or entering into a wide range of relations with the Tutsi enemy, whether in marital affairs, business, or state affairs".[24] The political establishment in Kigali regarded the formation of the RPF as a direct threat to Hutu power.[25] Another response to the RPF invasion was the formation of various parties comprised mainly of Hutu extremists with the purpose of consolidating themselves in power. They advocated Hutu unity to fight the Tutsi, within and outside Rwanda, who were regarded as the common enemy of both the state and the Hutu.[26]

---

[21] *Ibid.*

[22] African Rights, 1995, see *supra* note 8.

[23] For instance, Hassan Ngeze, a journalist employed by Radio RTLM, wrote and subsequently published the sixth issue of the newspaper *Kangura* (December 1990), vilifying the Tutsi in consideration of the "Hutu ten commandments".

[24] Wibabara, 2014, p. 31, see *supra* note 12.

[25] Cyrus Reed, "Exile, Reform, and the Rise of the Rwandan Patriotic Front", in *Journal of Modern African Studies*, 1996, vol. 34, no. 3, pp. 479–501.

[26] Ogenga Otunnu, "An Historical Analysis of the Invasion by the Rwanda Patriotic Army (RPA)", in Howard Adelman and Astri Suhrke (eds.), *The Path of a Genocide: The Rwandan Crisis from Uganda to Zaire*, Transaction Publishers, New Brunswick, NJ, 1999.

4.2.3. The Genocide

One of the political repercussions of the RPF invasion was the initiation of political talks organised by the international community, which were conducted in Arusha, Tanzania, which lent its name to the Arusha Peace Agreement. The talks culminated in the signing of the 1993 agreement, guaranteeing power-sharing between the two factions.[27] "Many Hutu extremists who did not believe in making any compromises between the Hutu and Tutsi, disagreed with the peace process and were thus at odds with its implementation".[28] The escalations of violence in response led to the Tutsi genocide, and in less than a hundred days, between 800,000 and 1 million people were dead.[29]

4.2.4. Immediate Causes

Political rhetoric, disseminated through the media, laid the foundation for the genocide. According to the youth respondents, "[o]ne of the causes of genocide was the teachings of the former political elite which preached hatred among people". The media is said to have been "a channel through which the teachings of divisive politics of President Habyarimana had been sown into the young and old of the Rwandan Hutu population".[30]

A major catalyst for the genocide occurred the night of 6 April 1994, when a missile shot down the private plane of Habyarimana on its return to Kigali from a peace conference in Tanzania, killing Habyarimana and President Cyprien Ntaryamira of Burundi.[31] Hutu extremists immediately began slaughtering Tutsi and moderate Hutu in Kigali. The international community and the United Nations peacekeepers failed to act to prevent the violence at this critical moment when genocide and other international

---

[27]   See Peace Agreement between the Government of the Republic of Rwanda and the Rwandese Patriotic Front (Arusha Accords), 4 August 1993.

[28]   Wibabara, 2014, p. 32, see *supra* note 12.

[29]   Nicholas Jones, *The Courts of Genocide: Politics and the Rule of Law in Rwanda and Arusha*, Routledge, London, 2011, p. 22; Bornkamm, 2012, p. 16, see *supra* note 14; Mackline Ingabire, "An Analysis of the Legal Regime Governing Transfer of Cases from the International Criminal Tribunal for Rwanda (ICTR) to the Rwandan Domestic Justice System", LL.M. Thesis, University of Cape Town, 2010, p. 3.

[30]   Interview with staff at the Ministry of Justice, August 2016.

[31]   Linda Maguire, "Power Ethnicized: The Pursuit of Protection and Participation in Rwanda and Burundi", in *Buffalo Journal of International Law*, 1995, vol. 2, pp. 49–90.

crimes were being committed in Rwanda.[32] In the view of the survivors' group, the international community's abandonment intensified the genocide. The group cited the example of the École Technique Officielle in Kigali from where the UN peacekeepers withdrew. They said:

> Many Tutsis had gathered here [at ETO] seeking protection of the UN, but they left them despite seeing that their killers were surrounding the premises. People cried and begged that they don't leave them but the UN peacekeepers shot in the air to disperse the crowds of refugees and paved their way for them to exit. There were many people including children instead, some of the international community members carried their dogs off leaving the Tutsis, shortly to be slaughtered by the Interahamwe.

There is a commonly held view that the genocide committed against the Tutsi could have been prevented had the international community reacted decisively.[33] For instance, according to the respondents in the focus groups discussions for survivors and for Nyarugenge prison detainees: "The UN had to save face for not preventing the genocide by establishing the court for Rwanda". The Rwandan Patriotic Army stopped the genocide and on 19 July 1994 established a transitional government of unity for a term of five years.[34]

4.2.5. Victims

Indisputable evidence exists to show that Tutsi were the main targets against whom a genocide was planned and executed in 1994,[35] but those Hutu who sided with the Tutsi were also targeted and killed. The genocide caused

> massive loss of human lives (more than one million deaths), many refugees, near-total destruction of infrastructure, a huge number of vulnerable people (widows, widowers, or-

---

[32] Roméo Dallaire, then a major general in the Canadian army, was the commander of the UN Assistance Mission in Rwanda at the time of the genocide. See Roméo Dallaire, *Shake Hands with the Devil: The Failure of Humanity in Rwanda*, Random House Canada, Toronto, 2003.

[33] Timothy Gallimore, "The Legacy of the International Criminal Tribunal for Rwanda (ICTR) and its Contributions to Reconciliation in Rwanda", in *New England Journal of International and Comparative Law*, 2008, vol. 14, no. 2, pp. 239–63.

[34] Republic of Rwanda, "National Service of Gacaca Courts", 18 June 2012.

[35] African Rights, 1995, see *supra* note 8.

phans, children as heads of households, homeless individuals, etc). There were many cases of trauma arising from the genocide and other crimes against humanity as well as a large number of detainees suspected of having perpetrated the Genocide.[36]

The genocide ended when the RPF took power.

4.2.6. Incidences of Violence and Accompanying Crimes and Gross Human Rights Violations

After the plane crash, killings targeting Tutsi began. Moderates, including the former prime minister and 10 Belgian peacekeepers were murdered.[37] Roadblocks were manned immediately where victims were identified based on the national identity cards, and murders, rapes, looting, torture and other forms of violence started in Kigali.[38] The killing spread throughout the country in the days that followed. Churches, hospitals and schools were the killing sites.[39] Crimes were carried out in the most brutal way – "victims were put to death [by] use of machetes, axes, knives, sticks, tools, iron bars and sometimes firearms".[40] The survivors' group reported details about women being raped, tortured and killed. Children were not spared either; boys especially were singled out and murdered. Property was looted, victims buried in mass graves and crimes against dead bodies were very common.[41]

Prior to the ICTR's establishment, the 1994 UN Security Council adopted resolution 935, requesting the secretary-general to establish a commission of experts to analyse the situation.[42] The commission confirmed that "genocide and other systematic, widespread and flagrant vio-

---

[36] Republic of Rwanda, 2012, see *supra* note 34.

[37] *Ibid.*

[38] Focus group discussion with survivors.

[39] Scott Straus, "How Many Perpetrators Were There in the Rwandan Genocide? An Estimate", in *Journal of Genocide Research*, 2004, vol. 6, no. 1, pp. 85–98.

[40] Wibabara, 2014, p. 35, see *supra* note 12.

[41] Republic of Rwanda, 2012, see *supra* note 34.

[42] United Nations Security Council, Requesting the Secretary-General to Establish a Commission of Experts to Examine Violations of International Humanitarian Law Committed in Rwanda, UN doc. S/RES/935, 1 July 1994.

lations of international humanitarian law had been committed in Rwanda".[43] The government of Rwanda has reported that

> [a]part from direct involvement of the state machinery and a large proportion of the political class, the Genocide was perpetrated in a climate of ethnic polarisation deliberately provoked by its masterminds.
>
> The rapidity of its execution, the extreme nature of criminality, the massive participation of citizens of all ages and socio-professional conditions, the presence of the international community representatives and military contingents as well as the media all emphasise the uniqueness of this Genocide.[44]

4.2.7. Prosecution of Genocide and Other International Crimes Committed in Rwanda

After the genocide, three transitional justice processes were put in place: the ICTR, the national ordinary courts, and later the *gacaca* courts.[45] The ICTR tried those bearing the highest responsibility[46] and had primacy over the national mechanisms.[47] Some trials occurred in foreign national courts under the principle of universal jurisdiction. The current minister of justice, Johnston Busingye, credited countries which have tried genocide suspects on the basis of universal jurisdiction. He said:

> While other countries that were willing to prosecute those suspects applied their national courts to prosecute genocide suspects on the basis of the principle of universal jurisdiction. Those countries include Belgium, Switzerland, Germany, Canada, USA, Finland, Norway, Sweden, the Netherlands, and France.[48]

---

43 Statute of the International Criminal Tribunal for Rwanda ('ICTR Statute'), adopted 8 November 1994, Preamble (http://www.legal-tools.org/doc/8732d6/).

44 Republic of Rwanda, 2012, see *supra* note 34.

45 *Ibid.*

46 United Nations Security Council, Completion Strategy of the International Criminal Tribunal for Rwanda, UN doc. S/2003/9466 October 2003, para. 6.

47 ICTR, Rules of Procedure and Evidence, adopted 29 June 1995, Rules 8–13 ('ICTR RPE') (http://www.legal-tools.org/doc/c6a7c6/).

48 Extracts of a Speech by the Hon. Minister of Justice, at African Union Conference of All Heads of Intelligence, Kigali, August 2016.

At the national level, at the beginning specialised chambers in ordinary courts tried all the crimes.[49] But in 2001 a law established *gacaca* courts; these were alternative (restorative) mechanisms of justice to also try genocide and crimes against humanity. Suspects were put into four categories under the Gacaca Law, which had exclusive jurisdiction over category two, three and four offences.[50] Later a 2004 Gacaca Law reduced the categories to three: category one (those bearing the highest criminal responsibility), and categories two and three covering those bearing less and the least responsibility.[51] Then, in 2008, the Gacaca Law was amended, expanding jurisdiction of the *gacaca* courts to cover some category one suspects.[52]

The sections that follow discuss each of the three mechanisms and their respective impact on deterring the commission of international crimes.

4.3. International Criminal Tribunal for Rwanda

This section examines the extent to which the ICTR has left a legacy of deterrence as a standalone mechanism of administration of justice relating to Rwandan society. It provides information on the functioning of the ICTR and its achievements, which formed the basis for its deterrent effect. It discusses factors on which respondents rely to express their views on the extent to which the Tribunal has deterred crimes, and specifically describes how respondents view the rationale for establishing the ICTR, how evidence was collected, the impact of indictments, apprehension and prosecutions of suspects, the speed of the tribunal, its sentencing practices, and the location of the Tribunal. The certainty of apprehension and prosecution of high-profile perpetrators by the ICTR, in the view of respond-

---

49   Republic of Rwanda, Organic Law 08/96 of August 30, 1996 on the Organization of Prosecution for Offences Constituting the Crime of Genocide or Crimes Against Humanity Committed Since October 1, 1990 ('Organic Law 08/96').

50   Republic of Rwanda, Organic Law 40/2000 of 26 January 2001 Setting Up Gacaca Jurisdictions and Organizing Prosecution of Genocide Crimes or Crimes against Humanity Committed between October 1, 1990 and December 31, 1994 ('Organic Law 40/2000') (http://www.legal-tools.org/doc/0bdf0f/).

51   Republic of Rwanda, Organic Law 28/2006 of 27 June 2006 Modifying and Complementing Organic Law No. 16/2004 of 19/06/2004 Establishing the Organisation, Competence and Functioning of Gacaca Courts Charged with Prosecuting and Trying the Perpetrators of the Crime of Genocide (http://www.legal-tools.org/doc/f770b5/).

52   Republic of Rwanda, Organic Law 13/2008 of 19 May 2008.

ents, is shown to have achieved deterrence. However, on the severity of punishment and speed, respondents indicate that the ICTR needed improvement.

4.3.1. The Functioning and Accomplishments of the ICTR

In November 1994 the UN established the ICTR to "prosecute persons responsible for genocide and other serious violations of international humanitarian law committed in the territory of Rwanda and neighbouring States, between 1 January 1994 and 31 December 1994".[53] The Tribunal is now closed and the residual Mechanism for International Criminal Tribunals ('MICT') will handle any subsequent issues. The UN established the Tribunal in Arusha, Tanzania, where it worked from 1995 until its closure on 31 December 2015. It had an office in Kigali, Rwanda, and an Appeals Chamber located in The Hague, the Netherlands.[54] The Tribunal was afforded the necessary resources, including adequate staff, which increased gradually from 163 in 1995 to a peak of 1,100 in 2004–2005 and 2006–2007, 600 for the period 2008–2011, and 400 for the period 2012–2014. The number had decreased by the second half of 2015 to about 95. When operating, the annual budget stood at an average of $270 million.[55] Given the resources at hand, the ICTR was arguably positioned to achieve all its goals, including deterrence of offences in its jurisdiction. The sections that follow present the views of respondents questioning whether the ICTR achieved its goals despite this enormous capacity.

The ICTR indicted 93 individuals,[56] delivering guilty verdicts on at least one count of genocide, crimes against humanity or war crimes for 64 of them.[57] The Tribunal acquitted 14 individuals and transferred the cases

---

[53] United Nations Security Council, Resolution 955, see *supra* note 1.

[54] ICTR RPE, as amended on 13 May 2015, see *supra* note 47. The RPE have undergone 23 amendments.

[55] United Nations Mechanism for International Criminal Tribunals ('MICT'), Symposium on the Legacy of the International Criminal Tribunal for Rwanda, Arusha, 6–7 November 2014.

[56] Hassan B. Jallow, "Statement", United Nations the International Criminal Tribunal for Rwanda 20th Anniversary Commemoration, Arusha, Tanzania, 8 November 2014. A total of 95 individuals were indicted, but two indictments were withdrawn by the prosecutor.

[57] ICTR, *Prosecutor v. Jean Kambanda*, Indictment, ICTR-97-23, 16 October 1997 ('Kambanda Indictment') (http://www.legal-tools.org/doc/3bca5b/); Erin Shaw and Maxime Charron-Tousignant, "Justice for Genocide? A Retrospective on the Work of the Interna-

against 10 others to national jurisdictions. Three individuals died prior to trial, and three others were referred to the MICT because they remain fugitives from justice.[58] The sentences imposed ranged from nine months (imposed on a protected witness who testified at the trial of Jean de Dieu Kamuhanda) to life imprisonment (imposed in 17 cases). Of the 34 cases where individuals were sentenced to – and served – a period of confinement, the average sentence was 25 years. Most of the convicts are serving their sentences in Mali or Benin, and two are in France.

4.3.2. The Deterrent Effect of the ICTR

In assessing the deterrent effect of the ICTR, this section considers the rationale for establishing the ICTR, indictments and prosecutions, apprehension of suspects, ability to collect evidence, speed of trials, sentencing practices, survivors' sense of security and location of the tribunal. Overall, respondents viewed the ICTR as fairly successful on the certainty of prosecution, although only with high-level perpetrators. The ICTR was not viewed as successful in the other measures of deterrence, namely celerity and severity.

4.3.2.1. Rationale for Establishing the ICTR

The UN established the ICTR with both retributive and deterrent purposes. A major goal was ending commission of international crimes; prosecuting those responsible and thereby "contribut[ing] to the process of national reconciliation and to the restoration and maintenance of peace".[59] In the *Kambanda* case, the Trial Chamber further elaborated on the Tribunal's purpose of prosecutions. On 8 April 1998 it reasoned when sentencing Jean Kambanda that the motive was retributive, on one hand, and

> deterrence, namely dissuading for good those who will attempt in future to perpetrate such atrocities by showing them that the international community was not ready to tolerate

---

tional Criminal Tribunal for Rwanda", Canada, Parliamentary Information and Research Service, Ottawa, 2016.

[58] Shaw and Charron-Tousignant, p. 7, see *supra* note 57.

[59] ICTR Statute, Preamble, see *supra* note 43.

---

the serious violations of international humanitarian law and
human rights.[60]

Respondents identified several key reasons for the establishment of
the ICTR. These included a duty by the international community to hold
those responsible for commission of international crimes, as a complementary mechanism to the national mechanisms because the national
mechanism lacked capacity (no legal framework and capacity to apprehend the fugitives), and as a supplementary mechanism to the national efforts to prosecute international crimes. There was a need identified to
avoid a victor's justice perception of the proceedings, and they also saw it
as evidence of remorse for the international community's failure to intervene or prevent the crimes. For example, one youth respondent commented:

> Rwanda had been devastated by the war and the genocide.
> The most important reason at the time is that the country did
> not have the capacity to prosecute the people accused of
> planning and perpetrating the genocide. Besides, the persons
> were so vengeful and therefore, putting Rwandans in charge
> of prosecuting the people accused of planning and perpetrat-
> ing the genocide would be tantamount to handing down un-
> fair court sentences.[61]

However, respondents did not see reconciliation motives as the reason for
establishing the ICTR as the Tribunal had itself suggested. The fact that
respondents strongly appreciated the basic *raison d'être* of the Tribunal is
indicative that the Tribunal had a deterrent impact.

4.3.2.2. Indictment and Prosecution by the ICTR

Respondents from all the groups interviewed indicated that they had
knowledge of the work of the Tribunal from the time indictments were issued to the subsequent trials. Respondents could name individuals indicted, tried, convicted and acquitted, and which specific crimes the ICTR
had tried. However, their knowledge cannot be presumed to be representative of all Rwandans given comments by critics of the ICTR's outreach
programme. The survivors' focus group discussion pointed out that:

---

[60] ICTR, *Prosecutor v. Jean Kambanda*, Trial Chamber, Judgment, ICTR-97-23, 4 September 1998, para. 28 (http://www.legal-tools.org/doc/49a299/).

[61] Focus group discussion.

> Poor outreach programmes-umusanzu were established by the ICTR. It only contained documents in English yet was meant for Rwandans, the majority of who speak Kinyarwanda [...] [they] may say that it was a court established for Rwanda but [it] was a foreign one in operation.

Nonetheless, respondents recognised the specific deterrence effect of the ICTR's indictments and trials. A respondent in the Ministry of Justice answered as follows:

> The influence [of the ICTR] was about the identification of suspects who were abroad, gathering information related to the offences that they were suspected to have committed, increase of the number of international arrest warrants sent by ICTR to other foreign countries where those suspects were hidden.

A participant in the prisons group noted:

> The trials in the ICTR have given lessons to the leaders that they, too, are not exempted even when they flee from the country. The ICTR made acts of the Rwandan genocide known globally and all those who are still hiding in foreign countries fear that they be tried some time, and this is because of the ICTR; the ICTR established that genocide occurred and defined most acts such as rape as an act of genocide and this was accepted globally.

These respondents approved of the Tribunal's effectiveness in specific deterrence of crimes under its jurisdiction by indicting and prosecuting suspects, especially high profile leaders. However, respondents later doubted the Tribunal's real impact given the relatively low number of those indicted and tried. This comes across strongly, when discussing the contribution of national mechanisms in comparison to the ICTR (see section 3.4.).

4.3.2.3. Apprehension of the Suspects: A Measure of Certainty

Respondents were in unison on the impact of the ICTR when it comes to the certainty of apprehension of the genocide fugitives. For instance, a respondent from the survivors' focus group discussion said:

> I am of the view that the ICTR also had its share of contribution. [...] I challenge you to think of the scenario where the ICTR had not been established, other than those who argue that genocide was permitted by the government, it would

have left the people accused of genocide to have free movement all over the world. Yes, the Court has not managed to
prevent their movement, but they do so in hiding. They are
conscious of some force that is looking for them so that they
could be arrested for prosecution. This puts them in a position of weakness. For that reason, it was not easy for them to
have the power to re-organise their forces to militarily attack
the country. The realisation that the Court had been given the
power to prosecute persons like Bagosora, that sent a strong
message to even the accused who were still at large and not
yet known to be aware that their days were numbered.

This comment echoes the views of respondents in the earlier section on
the rationale of establishing the ICTR in emphasising the Tribunal's impact in deterring offenders. In both cases, respondents pointed out that the
national mechanisms had neither access nor capacity to bring to justice
those who had fled the country, which the ICTR had.

4.3.2.4. Collection of Evidence

Collection of evidence affects the prosecution of the suspects of crimes
and the Tribunal's jurisdiction. Respondents thought that evidence contributes to the establishment of an accused's level of criminal participation,
and therefore determines the sentence. Proportionality of sentences to
crimes committed was viewed as achieving individual as well as general
deterrence. The individual is incapacitated by imprisonment while those
who are like-minded get the message that such acts are punishable. For
example, a respondent from the survivors' group stated:

Remember it [the ICTR] had investigators who were perpetrators who at some point interfered with evidence. This
would not have been possible if it had been located in
Rwanda. This led to wrong decisions by the ICTR such as
acquittals. Even when the survivors demonstrated here
against most acquittals or light sentences, it had less impact
because it is far; had the judges been here and seen the
demonstrations perhaps they would have understood better
and judged differently later on.

Respondents from the Ministry of Defence similarly argued that the
ICTR investigators did not adequately gather evidence and that the ICTR
judges and lawyers did not understand the cultural context in which witnesses testified. For example a ministry respondent stated:

> The ICTR during trial made certain blunders especially when examining or cross-examining witnesses, the judges or court actors did not understand or respect the Rwandan cultural context. Most witnesses at some point refrained from testifying in the court. I understand the need to have foreign judges to safeguard impartiality but a mix would have mitigated the harm.

Respondents were not convinced by the way the Tribunal collected its evidence. They perceived that the Tribunal collected insufficient evidence, resulting in issuance of light sentences and acquittals and hence was less deterrent.

4.3.2.5. Speed of Trials

Respondents from the public prosecution on the speed of trials by the ICTR said: "Despite the huge budget, overqualified personnel, the ICTR tried a drop-75 persons in the 20 years of its existence". The respondent meant that for a period of 20 years, the ICTR tried very few suspects. A respondent from the Ministry of Justice added: "The Court took too much time on single cases. The speed was so agonizingly very slow". Looking at the number of trials the Tribunal completed in the 20 years of its existence and the views of respondents, it would be hard to argue that the speed (or lack thereof) of the Tribunal's work did not reduce its deterrent effect.

4.3.2.6. Sentencing: Inadequate Severity

Generally, respondents indicated their dissatisfaction concerning the ICTR's sentencing practices. Deterrence theory is premised on the assumption that crimes are committed due to the gains expected and that they are prevented when the costs in terms of punishment are likely to be higher than the gains.[62] To this end, the sentencing practice of the ICTR was viewed to the contrary by respondents. For example, a response from the Ministry of Justice stated:

> The court could have had difficulty in understanding certain cases. For instance, acquitting persons like Z and Nzirorera

---

[62] Jeremy Bentham, "Punishment and Deterrence", in Andrew von Hirsch, Andrew Ashworth and Julian Roberts (eds.), *Principled Sentencing: Readings on Theory and Policy*, Hart Publishing, Portland, 2009, pp. 53–56.

projects a mismatch of sentencing. I wonder whether the
Court put to use all means at its disposal in order to dig deep
into the facts and arrive at the substantial evidence of what
these two persons did during the genocide. For instance, the
role of Z was not in execution. He was a mastermind in
preparation and encouraging people to commit genocide. In
fact, the role of Z looms very large and so much more than
the role of Jean Kambanda as the latter's role was at the level
of execution. Z and others, like Bagosora and Nzirorera,
were masterminds. Ignoring such a role in punishing the
crime of genocide is equivalent to ignoring the roots of the
genocide. I do not remember even if there was anyone punished for the crimes of planning and preparation of genocide.
Masterminds in the execution effort who were tried in
Rwanda were handed down sentences of life and/or 25 or 30
years of imprisonment. In the ICTR, the punishment was really very minimal compared to the crime committed.

Respondents from the survivors' group wondered whether the ICTR
considered proportionality and gravity of the crimes committed. The survivors questioned how planners like Théoneste Bagosora were sentenced
to 30 years, which they considered lenient. The youth group also considered sentences handed down by the ICTR to the 'big fish' such as Atha-
nase Seromba to be very light in view of the crimes they committed.

The Rwandan government and the general public, as shown in the
view of respondents, frequently criticised the ICTR for handing down
what they perceived to be light sentences to those it has tried. They perceived the sentences as disregarding the gravity of the crimes prosecuted
and of the criminal culpability of those convicted, and therefore they felt
the ICTR's actions as being less deterrent.

4.3.2.7. Security of Survivors

One measure of deterrence is whether survivors have a sense of security.
Almost all those interviewed about the ICTR's contribution to the safety
of survivors did not see its role as relevant in this regard, and most of
them therefore did not comment on this. On the contrary, respondents in
the survivors' group confirmed that the ICTR indeed made them feel secure, and argued that without the ICTR's prosecutions people accused of
genocide would have had "free movement all over the world". Even for
those not prosecuted, they were in hiding, and "for that reason it was not

easy for them to have the power to reorganise their forces to militarily attack the country" or to use the media to organise a comeback. Other respondents noted:

> The Court provided security to the survivors who would fear to travel anywhere in the world for fear of being killed or hurt by the suspects roaming the planet. Conversely, the suspects fear to come out of their hiding to do harm for fear of being identified and be tracked down and arrested. Besides, the establishment of the Court sent a strong signal that persons suspected of participating in the Genocide cannot have a safe haven anywhere".

Others argued that, without the ICTR, justice imposed by the new government in Kigali would only have been viewed as victor's justice against the Hutu, and that the international community would not have accepted the *gacaca* process at all. Others added that national processes would have been less known without the ICTR's high-profile work, and that this greater awareness contributed to increased security for victims. Finally, others noted that the ICTR could provide very practical protection to some victims, relocating them to Belgium or other countries.

For these reasons, the survivors' group and other victims strongly voiced their perceptions that the ICTR's actions contributed to the safety of victims, and therefore to its deterrent effect.

4.3.2.8. Location of the Tribunal

Respondents expressed strong views that the Tribunal failed to deter offenders because of its location, distant from the scene of the crimes. They perceived this choice as reflecting the fall-out from relations between Rwanda and the ICTR as it was being established. The survivors' group argued that the ICTR's distance limited their contributions. Respondents from the Ministry of Defence also stated:

> Locating the ICTR in Arusha made it unknown to Rwanda. ICTR was largely a foreign court and as Rwandans we deserved better from international community after experiencing a terrible genocide. International courts should be based in the victim country for accessibility purposes. How many Rwandans apart from maybe survivors and those who were witnesses in the Tribunal?

Respondents in the survivors' group strongly perceived that the Rwandan public could not understand the ICTR's work with it located so far away, and this lessened the benefit of its activities. Interestingly, they sensed the situation of the ICC as potentially different, arguing that "the ICC location could be anywhere since it is international". For them, the ICTR's role was in part to mitigate what was lacking in Rwanda, and this meant being present in Rwanda.

The perceived benefits of national trials in relation to those of the ICTR, including their relative locations, are discussed below.

4.3.2.9. Perceptions on the Deterrent Effect of the ICTR on the Commission of International Crimes in Rwanda and in the Region

To summarise the ICTR's deterrent effect, before moving on to national mechanisms, respondents had understandably mixed perceptions. In the prisoners' focus group discussion, one respondent calculated that three out of five respondents agreed that the ICTR prevented similar crimes, and two of five thought specifically that the ICTR could prevent genocide. Some felt it did not help that the ICTR failed to elicit remorse from those it prosecuted, unlike the *gacaca* proceedings. Victims in general had more positive impressions of the ICTR as opposed to government representatives, who argued against the ICTR's deterrent effect. As one respondent from the Ministry of Defence concluded:

> Given what is happening in our region, we cannot say that ICTR has a deterrent effect. Even for Rwanda, the progress made so far depends on efforts made by Rwanda itself. One of the reasons for the lack of deterrent effect being the penalties imposed by that court, which are not dissuasive.

A respondent from the Ministry of Justice added:

> The incidents currently happening in Burundi is an indicator that the Great Lakes region did not learn from the events in Rwanda. The event of post-election violence in Kenya in 2007 is another indicator of the absence of learning from history or events in other countries. In the Congo, there are often isolated incidents, but they need attention to avert a major crisis.

The section that follows shows other national court-based factors that contributed to deterrence of international crimes in Rwanda.

4.4. National Judicial Process and *Gacaca*

In this section, the discussion explores the contribution of the ordinary national court system and the traditional court system, also known as the *gacaca* court system, in deterring crimes which are the subject matter of this research. It briefly establishes the background of each national mechanism to give the context, discusses relevant laws, highlights achievements in statistics, and then addresses the debate of the respondents on whether the national mechanisms deterred crimes or not. This analysis includes the extent to which respondents believed that the national efforts either effectively contributed to deterrence by the ICTR or filled in gaps in areas where the Tribunal is regarded as not having fared so well. This analysis considers the possibility that the ICTR also played an indirect role in fostering deterrence through national mechanisms.

4.4.1. The Parallel National Judicial Mechanism

4.4.1.1. National Courts

In Rwanda, the first national justice process is represented in the ordinary national courts and military courts (collectively referred to as ordinary courts). The Supreme Court is the highest court of jurisdiction that has competence to deal with cases on appeal from both the High Court and the Military High Court.

When the genocide ended, the new government determined to end violence and impunity. About 120,000 suspects of genocide and crimes against humanity were imprisoned.[63] The capacity of the judiciary to deal with the huge number of detainees in the aftermath of genocide was severely limited because most judges, lawyers, investigators and other judicial officers were either dead or in exile, and the physical infrastructure of the justice system was a shambles.[64] The brutality of the massacres and the great need for justice stimulated the new government into developing

---

[63] Republic of Rwanda, 2012, see *supra* note 34.

[64] National Public Prosecution Authority, "NPPA Quarterly Progressive Report, July 2015–March 2016", May 2016; Mark A. Drumbl, "Collective Violence and Individual Punishment: The Criminality of Mass Atrocity", in *Northwestern Law Review*, 2005, vol. 99, no. 2, pp. 539–607.

laws and establishing institutions to adjudicate and punish perpetrators for the same reasons that led to the establishment of the ICTR.[65]

As a first step, rebuilding judicial capacity took significant time and resources. The ICTR, according to the respondents, also contributed to capacity building of legal personnel through its outreach programmes, such as training for prosecutors, internship programmes for law students, establishment of a library in which books and case law of the ICTR would be accessed, and various workshops.[66] Funds from donors helped with restoring physical spaces, distributing basic office supplies, compiling copies of the laws, and providing transport to prosecutors for investigating crimes and interviewing witnesses.[67]

4.4.1.1.1. Initial Legal Framework

Prior to 1996, Rwanda's Penal Code did not expressly punish genocide or crimes against humanity.[68] Although Rwanda had signed the Genocide Convention in 1975, the enacting provisions had not been incorporated into national law. Respondents in this study also alluded to this fact when explaining reasons for establishing the ICTR:

> Rwanda at the time [of the establishment the ICTR] lacked a legal framework to try genocide cases because even when it had ratified the genocide convention it had made reservations on planning. The perpetrators of the genocide against the Tutsi, based largely on the loopholes that existed in the Rwanda legal framework, believed that because of the absence of any punishment framework in Rwanda for perpetrators of genocide, they would not be punished as a result. I base this argument on the reservation by the sitting government of Rwanda on Article 9 of the Convention Against the Genocide. Besides, there was no domestic law providing for

---

[65] Kasaija Phillip Apuuli, "The ICC Arrest Warrants for the Lord's Resistance Army Leaders and Peace Prospects for Northern Uganda", in *Journal of International Criminal Justice*, 2009, vol. 4, no. 1, pp. 179–87.

[66] Interview with permanent secretary, the Ministry of Justice; Interview with two national prosecutors.

[67] National Public Prosecution Authority, 2016, see *supra* note 64.

[68] Republic of Rwanda, 2012, see *supra* note 34.

> the crime of Genocide and the mechanism of punishing such
> a crime.[69]

This was a gap at national level, which the ICTR filled, according to the respondents.

The transitional General Assembly enacted Organic Law 08/96 of 30 August 1996 on the Organisation of Prosecution for Offences Constituting the Crime of Genocide or Crimes Against Humanity Committed Since 1 October 1990 ('Organic Law 08/96'). This law is said to have had three main purposes: 1) to reduce the burden on the courts; 2) to facilitate prosecutions by encouraging people to provide information; and (3) to enhance the reconciliation process through public admissions of guilt.[70] The law served to deter offenders given the prosecutions that followed the enactment, trials held in the communities encouraging the participation of the population, the severity of punishment the law provided and subsequent apprehensions of suspects. The enactment of Organic Law 08/96 might be viewed as a product of external influences, including the ICTR's influence. Rwanda had had no experience of trying international crimes and the fact that the ICTR was already in place before this law prompted legislators to consult other jurisdictions, especially the ICTR, before enacting the law.[71]

Organic Law 08/96 established specialised chambers within the courts of first instance to try people accused of genocide, crimes against humanity and war crimes. The temporal jurisdiction in this law was from 1 October 1990 to 31 December 1994, which is broader than the ICTR's temporal jurisdiction that was limited to events in 1994, but the national court jurisdiction was still not open-ended, a move that could have increased their deterrent effect. Respondents viewed limited temporal jurisdiction as a weakness in either instance. Respondents in the focus groups discussion of Nyarugenge central prison pointed out:

> The accused before the ICTR were prosecuted for crimes
> committed only from 1 January to 31 December 1994, while
> most of us because we were tried in our communities, we
> were prosecuted for crimes dating back in 1990s. We find

---

[69] Interview with permanent secretary, Ministry of Justice, Kigali.

[70] Lawyers Committee for Human Rights, "Prosecuting Genocide in Rwanda: A Lawyers Committee Report on the ICTR and National Trials", July 1997.

[71] Interview with national prosecutor, Kigali.

this unfair, because all along those were our leaders, who
planned all these things.

Following the deterrence theory of making the cost of committing a
crime higher and lowering the benefits of crime, in this case it seems to be
the opposite: limited temporal jurisdiction means less cost in terms of
treatment and punishment, for more serious crimes, and so likely less deterrence.

Organic Law 08/96 also based prosecution of ordinary crimes in the
Penal Code carried out in the context of the genocide or the commission
of crimes against humanity.[72] Such crimes included murder, inflicting
physical injury, rape, deprivation of liberty as well as theft and other offences against property as provided for in various other articles of the
Penal Code of 1977.[73] This will be demonstrated with the few cases sam-
pled. The 'double qualification' aimed at enabling the application of both
Organic Law 08/96 and the Penal Code.[74] This was to avoid occurrence of
the violation of the non-retroactivity principle of Organic Law 08/96. This
was rather innovative. The task for the prosecutor was to qualify the
crimes according to the Rwandan Criminal Code, and then prove whether
the crime constituted a crime of genocide or crime against humanity.

Another contribution of this law was to categorise suspects into four
categories.[75] Category one encompassed the leaders of the genocide:
"planners, organisers, instigators, supervisors and leaders of the crime of
genocide or of a crime against humanity". The law was later amended to
make rape a category one crime. Category two included people who killed
or intended to kill under the orders or direction of others. Category three
included those who committed serious assaults, while category four applied to individuals who committed property crimes. The law was amended several times with the effect that the ordinary courts continued trying
those in category one only, whereas some category one, and all category
two and three offenders were tried in the *gacaca* courts.

The categorisation and especially the inclusion of rape is said to be
a direct influence of the ICTR jurisprudence. This position was supported

---

[72] Organic Law 08/96, Article 1, see *supra* note 49.
[73] Republic of Rwanda, Decret-Loi No. 21/77, Penal Code of 1977, Articles 312, 318, 360,
388 and 396 (http://www.legal-tools.org/doc/71507b/).
[74] Republic of Rwanda, 2012, see *supra* note 34.
[75] Organic Law 08/96, Article 2, see *supra* note 49.

during research by some of the respondents while holding a key informant interview with the national prosecutor and in the focus group discussion with the youth. In their view, one of the contributions of the ICTR was to qualify acts of genocide, especially including rape, as an act of genocide. Rwanda, prior to Organic Law 08/96, had no legal instrument on the international crimes as indicated by various respondents and writers; therefore, the ICTR did influence most of the provisions drafted in 1996 and other subsequent laws. Respondents from the Ministry of Defence added:

> The first law on genocide largely borrowed definitions from the ICTR Statute. Rape was also considered in our penal code as an act of genocide and this had never happened before the ICTR[.] In the first years due to the conduct of ICTR proceedings in any national courts handed severe punishment as to oppose light sentencing by the ICTR.

The law provided for a form of plea bargaining, which was quite unusual in a civil law system but a practical necessity to deal with the staggering number of those detained for their participation in the genocide and to facilitate unity and reconciliation. This, too, is an ICTR influence. Rwanda being purely a civil law system had its first experience with plea bargaining in the *Kambanda* case.[76] In an interview held with the national prosecutor, he explained that the ICTR practices such as plea bargaining were borrowed in the national system:

> The 1996 law provided for plea bargaining for all but those found guilty of category one crimes. This exception for category one is also arguably an ICTR emulation of not reducing the sentence even when there is a guilty plea. For example, in the *Kambanda* case before the ICTR, the accused entered a guilty plea with the Prosecution; however, he was sentenced to life imprisonment.[77] The ICTR Trial Chamber held that the motive in sentencing the accused was, on the one hand, retributive and deterrent, and on the other to dissuade others who may attempt in the future to perpetrate such atrocities.

It is this spirit of sentencing that continued to manifest in interviews with respondents. The five respondents in Nyarugenge central prison noted:

---

[76] Kambanda Indictment, see *supra* note 57.

[77] *Ibid.*

> We confessed to our crimes, provided information implicat-
> ing others, asked for forgiveness and even some [three] of us
> testified in the ICTR as prosecution witnesses. Well, this had
> no impact on the sentences handed to us, most of us are serv-
> ing life sentences.[78]

Under Organic Law 08/96, an accused person not in category one could receive a reduced sentence in exchange for an accurate and complete confession, an apology to the victims, implication of others and an offer to plead guilty.[79] The procedure of guilty pleas is reported to have played a significant role in genocide trials based on the objectives it was designed to complete: revealing the truth about the genocide; speeding up genocide trials; and contributing to national reconciliation.[80] This procedure was later carried to *gacaca* courts and carried retributive, deterrent and reconciliation messages. Respondents indicated that: "Confessions facilitated reconciliation. The information provided during the confessions was a lesson to the population about the dangers of committing international crimes".[81]

Currently, an improved legal framework is in place to ensure that genocide suspects are afforded legal counsel.[82] The ICTR has greatly contributed to the establishment of this law and also provision of legal aid to this category. This is based on Rwanda's journey to transfer cases from the ICTR. When it was decided that the ICTR should wind up its work, this necessitated the transfer of residual cases to national courts for trial after it has closed.[83] Rwanda attempted but failed to have cases transferred even when it supported the ICTR prosecutor's five initial requests for referral to its national courts.[84] This meant that Rwanda had to work on sev-

---

[78] Focus group discussion, Nyarugenge prison.

[79] Organic Law 08/96, Article 6, see *supra* note 49. Confessions were required to include a complete and detailed description of the offences, "including the date, time and the scene of each act, as well as the names of victims and witnesses".

[80] Republic of Rwanda, 2012, see *supra* note 34.

[81] Focus group discussion, prisons.

[82] Republic of Rwanda, Law 47/2013 of 16 June 2013, Transfer of Cases to the Republic of Rwanda, Article 17.

[83] United Nations Security Council, Resolution 1503, 28 August 2003, UN doc. S/RES/1503 (http://www.legal-tools.org/doc/05a7de/).

[84] ICTR, *Prosecutor v. Yussufu Munyakazi*, Appeals Chamber, Decision on the Prosecution's Appeal against Decision on Referral under Rule 11bis, ICTR-97-36, 8 October 2008 (http://www.legal-tools.org/doc/d3defa/); ICTR, *Prosecutor v. Gaspard Kanyarukiga*,

eral issues including fair trial guarantees, improved detention facilities, and establishing a legal framework to achieve the transfers from the ICTR.[85]

To refer any case, the ICTR required minimum standards to be met by Rwanda and any other United Nations member state interested in trying these cases before any transfer could be affected. Rule 11 *bis* provided for the criteria followed by a trial chamber designated to refer a case to authorities of a state. In deciding whether to refer a case, relevant trial chambers had to satisfy themselves that the accused would receive a fair trial, and that the death penalty would not be imposed as punishment on conviction. Before applying for a referral, the ICTR Office of the Prosecutor reviewed an alleged status and the extent of participation of the accused in the crimes, the connection that the accused may have had with other cases, as well as the availability of evidence and investigative material for transmission to the relevant domestic courts.[86]

Finally, transfers from both the ICTR and other jurisdictions have been secured, meaning that Rwanda has met the requirements; this reflects the influence of the ICTR and the international community on furthering Rwanda's national capacity to prosecute, and deter, international crimes.[87]

Trial Chamber, Decision on Prosecutor's Request for Referral to the Republic of Rwanda, ICTR-2002-78, 6 June 2008 (http://www.legal-tools.org/doc/e03d5c/); ICTR, *Prosecutor v. Ildephonse Hategekimana*, Appeals Chamber, Decision on the Prosecution's Appeal against Decision on Referral under Rule 11bis, ICTR-00-55B, 4 December 2008 (http://www.legal-tools.org/doc/e79867/); ICTR, *Prosecutor v. Fulgence Kayishema*, Trial Chamber, Decision on the Prosecutor's Request for Referral of Case to the Republic of Rwanda, ICTR-01-67, 16 December 2008 (http://www.legal-tools.org/doc/c3581e/); and ICTR, *Prosecutor v. Jean-Baptiste Gatete*, ICTR-00-61, Decision on the Prosecution's Appeal against Decision on Referral under Rule 11bis.

[85] Ingabire, 2010, see *supra* note 29.

[86] United Nations Security Council, ICTR Completion Strategy Report, UN doc. S/2007/323, 31 May 2007, para. 35.

[87] Information from the Ministry of Justice of Rwanda indicates that the following cases have been transferred to Rwanda: Dr. Leon Mugesera deported from Canada on 24 January 2012; Jean Uwinkindi transferred by ICTR on 19 April 2012; Charles Bandora extradited from Norway on March 10 2013; Bernard Munyagishari transferred by ICTR on July 24 2013; Emmanuel Mbarushimana extradited from Denmark on 7 July 2014; Ladislas Ntaganzwa transferred by ICTR on 2 March 2016; and Leopold Munyakazi deported in September 2016.

4.4.1.1.2. Sentences

Penalties in Organic Law 08/96 range from imprisonment to the death penalty. Articles 14 and 17 of that law provide details on the sentencing regime of the ordinary courts. The highest penalty was death for those falling under category one. As noted above, they were not eligible to have their sentence reduced even if they admitted guilt before trial. Category two perpetrators were sentenced to life imprisonment, unless they offered a confession and guilty plea after prosecution, in which case they received a sentence of twelve to fifteen years. If they offered a confession and guilty plea *prior* to prosecution, the sentence range was further reduced to a period of between seven and 11 years. For category three perpetrators, the sentences had no set range but a reduction in sentence was available in exchange for a confession and guilty plea. Those who pleaded guilty after prosecution received a one-third reduction of the normal sentence, and those who pleaded guilty before prosecution received a half reduction.

4.4.1.2. Implementation

Some 606 convicts were sentenced to death, but only 22 of them were executed.[88] The rest were on death row awaiting execution, which was later commuted to life imprisonment after the 2007 abolition of death penalty.[89] There had been a moratorium for quite some time when Rwanda passed legislation abolishing the death penalty, a step that was applauded given that it was such a short time after the genocide and so it was expected that the general public still approved of a severe punishment. The death penalty was replaced with life imprisonment or life imprisonment with special measures. The abolition of the death penalty by Rwanda, some argue, was due among other reasons to the ICTR's influence.[90] Rwanda had always wished to try all genocide perpetrators as indicated by its efforts to secure transfers. The fact that the ICTR did not permit transfer to a jurisdiction where the law permitted a death sentence might have influenced Rwanda's legislative action to abolish death penalty.

---

[88] Ligue Rwandaise pour la Promotion et la Défense des Droits de l'Homme ('LIPRODHOR'), "Situation des droits de la personne en 2005", Kigali, 2006.

[89] Republic of Rwanda, Organic Law 31/2007 Relating to the Abolition of the Death Penalty, 25 July 2007 (http://www.legal-tools.org/doc/bdc59f/.

[90] Lawyers Committee for Human Rights, 1997, see *supra* note 70.

On 27 December 1996, two and half years after the genocide, a first instance court in Kibungo opened the first trial for genocide and crimes against humanity committed in Rwanda.[91] By 30 April 1997 judgments had been entered for 56 defendants in 22 trials.[92] Four defendants were acquitted. Of those convicted, courts sentenced 35 people to death, 14 people were sentenced to life imprisonment, and three received prison sentences from one to five years.

The United Nations special representative, Michel Moussalli, reported in early 2000 that the genocide courts had tried a total of 2,406 people.[93] Of these, 19 per cent were acquitted. Some 14 per cent were sentenced to death, about 30 per cent received life imprisonment, and 34 per cent were sentenced to imprisonment of between one and 20 years. Confessions and guilty pleas speeded up the processing of thousands of prisoners in this same period. About 500 prisoners confessed in 1997, but the number had grown to 9,000 by the end of 1998. By the end of 1999, 15,000 people had confessed. By early 2000, more than 20,000 had.[94]

By 12 December 2002 courts had tried 8,363 cases of genocide, crimes against humanity and war crimes,[95] and by the end of 2004, a total of 10,026 individuals had been tried by the ordinary courts.[96] When *gacaca* courts started trials in the pilot phase in 2005, ordinary courts continued prosecuting only category one genocide cases, but at a significantly lower rate and no longer in the specialised chambers. Rwanda's ordinary courts tried 10,248 genocide cases from December 1996 to March 2008. After March 2008 very few genocide trials were heard in ordinary courts since most of the cases had been transferred to *gacaca* courts to reduce the caseload in ordinary courts. Currently, the genocide cases in the ordinary courts are primarily those transferred from ICTR or other foreign jurisdictions.

---

[91] National Public Prosecution Authority, 2016, see *supra* note 64.

[92] Lawyers of Committee on Human Rights, 1997, see *supra* note 70.

[93] William A. Schabas, "Genocide Trials and Gacaca Courts", in *Journal of International Criminal Justice*, 2005, vol. 3, no. 4, pp. 879–95.

[94] *Ibid.*

[95] National Public Prosecution Authority, 2016, see *supra* note 64.

[96] Wibabara, 2013, see *supra* note 12.

4.4.1.3. Deterrent Effect of Ordinary Courts Trials

4.4.1.3.1. Whether the Atrocities Stopped as a Measure of Deterrence

At the end of genocide, about 120,000 persons were apprehended and therefore prevented from continuing atrocities. Apprehending and prosecuting such large numbers can be said to have achieved specific deterrence. Proponents of this theory argue that individual deterrence can be achieved by taking from the perpetrator the physical power of offending (by imprisonment or execution) thereby incapacitating them; taking away the desire to offend; and making them afraid of offending.[97]

4.4.1.3.2. Impact of Severe Punishment and Guilty Pleas

The procedure of confessions and severe sentences of the death penalty and life imprisonment under Organic Law 08/96 sent a message to other like-minded individuals not to attempt similar crimes and likely advanced general deterrence in Rwanda. Respondents confirmed this in their view:

> The accused and the onlookers realised that the category of
> the crimes for which the accused were being prosecuted
> were crimes that one cannot hide even when they were exe-
> cuted in circumstances that the truth would be revealed.[98]

The respondents' views are supported by deterrence theories that the condemnation of the crime and application of punishment serve as an example and stop those of like mind who would be willing and are in position to commit such crimes.[99]

Given the severity of punishments handed down by the ordinary courts and *gacaca* courts, the cost of crime is indeed high. The high costs, the level of apprehension and prosecution by national courts have likely largely deterred offenders. This thinking is supported by Richard Posner in his economic analysis of law. He asserts that crimes are committed be-

---

[97] Bentham, 2009, p. 52, see *supra* note 62; Emile Durkheim, "What is a Social Fact? and Rules for the Observation of Social Facts", *The Rules of the Sociological Method: And Selected Tests on Sociology and Its Method*, ed. Steven Lukes, Free Press, New York, 1982, pp. 50–59. Cesare Bacarria, "On Crimes and Punishments", in John Muncie, Eugene McLaughlin and Mary Langan (eds.), *Criminological Perspectives: A Reader*, Sage, London, 1996, p. 12.

[98] Focus group discussion with survivors.

[99] Ingabire, 2010, see *supra* note 29.

cause the expected economic benefits outweigh anticipated costs.[100] Various human rights bodies in different fora have advanced the issue of whether severe punishment is against human rights principles. However, the issue here is whether the severity of punishment deterred offenders in Rwanda or not. From the respondents' views, the answer is in the affirmative.[101] By contrast, the perception is that the ICTR's more lenient sentencing practice may not deter perpetrators of the 'greatest mischief', in Jeremy Bentham's words.

4.4.1.3.3. Impact of Trials Taking Place at the Crime Scene

Respondents indicated that one of the weaknesses of the ICTR was that prosecutions took place in a distant land and that most Rwandans never had a chance to see justice dispensed by the Tribunal. National prosecutions therefore filled this gap. In relation to national prosecutions and the *gacaca* court system respondents stated:

> *Gacaca* courts left an indelible image on the life of the communities in Rwanda and on the individuals who were prosecuted. The reason is that the courts were organised and implemented on the foundation of the legal principle of "prosecuting crimes from the place where they were committed".[102]

Supporting this view is Timothy Gallimore's discussion on deterrence; he argues that to achieve deterrence, "[m]imetic structures of violence that are embedded in the minds of people in places where massive violence occurred should be attacked if deterrent goals are to be achieved".[103] One way of achieving this is to hold trials at the scene of crime, as was done by ordinary courts. Those mimetic structures happen when "[p]erpetrators of genocide especially leaders, become public heroes or gain notoriety among the population who may see them as desirable characters to be celebrated and emulated".[104]

---

[100] Richard A. Posner, "An Economic Theory of the Criminal Law", in *Columbia Law Review*, 1985, vol. 85, no. 6, p. 1193.

[101] Focus group discussions with prisoners; focus group discussions with survivors.

[102] Focus group discussion with survivors.

[103] Gallimore, 2008, p. 240, see *supra* note 33.

[104] *Ibid.*

The way national trials were conducted destroys such structures. This is because leaders, who were the planners and initiators of genocide, were prosecuted before those they had led and so no longer had the power and influence they once had when perpetrating the crimes; it is thus deterrent.[105]

As Antonio Cassese argues, the best judicial forum for prosecution of crimes is the court of the territory where crimes have been committed.[106] Reasons for prosecution to be carried out in a place where crimes were committed include:

> The crime has breached the values and legal rules of the community existing in that territory, and has offended against the public order of that community; it is there that the victims of crime or relatives normally live; it is there that all, or at least most, evidence can be found; the trial is conducted in the language normally shared by the defendant, his defence, the prosecutor and the court and the international criminal tribunals take excessive length proceedings.[107]

4.4.1.3.4. Legitimacy

National trials, especially by ordinary courts and *gacaca* courts, are a more acceptable mechanism in comparison with the ICTR and therefore are viewed as better achieving deterrence. The ability of the *gacaca* court system to achieve deterrence is, however, viewed to be more than that of the ordinary courts.[108] In the view of respondents, the ICTR was a remote mechanism. This relates to Nils Christie's assertion that the root problem of the system is that conflicts were stolen from their legitimate owners, the victims, and became the property of professionals rather than people.[109] It is also paradoxical for a society "reeling from violence to be disenfranchised from the redressing of that violence which, instead, becomes

---

[105] Ingabire, 2010, see *supra* note 29.

[106] Antonio Cassese, "The Rationale for International Criminal Justice", in Antonio Cassese (ed.), *The Oxford Companion to International Criminal Justice*, Oxford University Press, Oxford, 2009, p. 123.

[107] *Ibid.*, p. 129.

[108] Interview with Ministry of Defence; focus group discussion with survivors; focus group discussion with prisoners.

[109] Nils Christie, "Conflicts as Property", in *British Journal of Criminology*, 1977, vol. 17, no. 1, p. 8.

a task suited to the technocratic savvy of the epistemic community of international lawyers".[110] The national prosecutions amply filled this gap left by the ICTR.

4.4.1.3.5. Number of Perpetrators Tried

The ordinary courts tried a large number of perpetrators in comparison to those tried by the ICTR. To achieve deterrence, perpetrators need to be held accountable. By the level of the numbers that were prosecuted, it would not be far-fetched to assert that specific deterrence was achieved. When referring to the ICTR, respondents commented on the small number of prosecutions in the ICTR.[111]

4.4.2. Alternative (Restorative) Justice – *Gacaca* Courts

4.4.2.1. Introduction

The name *gacaca* has its genesis in a Kinyarwanda word *umucaca* meaning a type of soft grass. Rwandans in the past more often preferred to gather and sit on *imicacaca* (plural) to discuss various societal issues.[112] Historically, *gacaca* gatherings were meant to restore order and harmony within communities by acknowledging wrongs, restituting and having justice for those who were victims, and reforming the offenders. The king and men of integrity would preside over such functions and help warring parties to come to terms.[113]

After the enactment of Organic Law 08/96, the ordinary courts tried some cases but the pace was slow. At that pace, the government realised that it might take at least 100 years to try all the suspects.[114] When it became clear that the number of cases was beyond the capacity of the judicial system, Rwanda established *gacaca* courts to facilitate transitional justice and to relieve pressure on the national courts.[115] The government conceived the idea in 1998–1999 during consultation meetings convened

---

[110] Drumbl, 2005, p. 597, see *supra* note 64; see also Ezzat A. Fattah, "Victimology: Past, Present and Future", in *Criminologie*, 2000, vol. 33, no. 1, pp. 17–46.

[111] Interview with national prosecutor, Kigali.

[112] Republic of Rwanda, 2012, see *supra* note 34.

[113] *Ibid.*

[114] National Public Prosecution Authority, 2016, see *supra* note 64.

[115] Des Forges and Longman, 2004, see *supra* note 4.

by the president.[116] In these meetings, people from different backgrounds, including human rights organisations, participated. However, the decision to opt for *gacaca* as a judicial system caused significant controversy with strong arguments in favour and against. Proponents of traditional *gacaca* argued that the population needed to be involved in settling genocide cases and that there was a need to reconstruct the social fabric which could only be achieved through *gacaca*. The opponents of *gacaca*, especially those from human rights organisations, argued that this system would not observe all the principles of a fair trial.[117]

4.4.2.2. Legal Framework

Against the background of Organic Law No. 40/2000 of January 2001, *gacaca* courts were established to prosecute genocide crimes and crimes against humanity committed between 1 October 1990 and 31 December 1994. The law's purposes were to help expedite the prosecution of genocide suspects, to provide the truth about the genocide, to eradicate the culture of impunity, and to facilitate reconciliation and encourage communities to confront their own involvement in the genocide.

The law initially provided that *gacaca* courts had exclusive jurisdiction over category two, three and four offences. Persons under category one continued to face prosecution in national courts. This law was later modified by several amendments that, among other changes, gave the *gacaca* courts jurisdiction over some category one crimes. A similar plea or confession practice as in the national court process allowed for reduced sentences.

4.4.3. The *Gacaca* Court System

Over 12,000 courts were established throughout Rwanda and presided over by people of integrity called *inyangamugayo* as judges, of whom there were more than 169,000.[118] The *gacaca* courts' activities were carried out at three levels of jurisdiction: the *gacaca* courts at the level of the cell, *gacaca* courts of the sector and *gacaca* appeal courts. Nationwide, there were 9,013 *gacaca* cell courts, 1,545 sector courts and 1,545 courts

---

[116] Republic of Rwanda, 2012, see *supra* note 34.

[117] Human Rights Watch, "Justice Compromised: The Legacy of Rwanda's Community-Based Gacaca Courts", 31 May 2011.

[118] Republic of Rwanda, 2012, see *supra* note 34.

of appeal. The judges were elected from the cell, or a local grouping of the population with a maximum of 200 people aged 18 years or older.[119] They could not be government officials, legal officers, politicians, active soldiers or part of the police force.[120] However, they were required to be at least 21 years of age and "honest Rwandans", as defined by the statute.[121] The procedure of confession, guilty plea, repentance and apologies was a keystone of the *gacaca* trials. The procedure served the punitive and restorative goals of justice. The trials were open to the adult Rwandans in every community, whose participation was seen as key in moving the nation past the atrocity.[122]

4.4.4. Achievements of the *Gacaca* Courts

In just 10 years, *gacaca* courts tried 1,958,634 cases, about 37,000 convicts serving their sentences in various prisons.[123] Around 1.2 million cases were category three, which consisted of suspects accused of crimes of a relatively lesser degree such as looting and destruction of property. During this period of the *gacaca* courts, out of the 60,552 category one case files, 53,426 suspects were convicted of genocide charges and the remaining 7,126 were acquitted. Of the 577,528 category two cases, 361,590 suspects were convicted and 215,938 acquitted, and of the 1,320,554 category three cases, 1,266,632 defendants were ordered to pay reparations and 54,002 of the suspects were acquitted.[124]

Notable from the *gacaca* trials is that they assisted in clearing the backlog of genocide cases and delivered expeditious trials. These resulted

---

[119] Organic Law 40/2000, Articles 6, 9, 10, see *supra* note 50.

[120] *Ibid.*, Article 11.

[121] Republic of Rwanda, Organic Law 16/2004, Establishing the Organisation, Competence and Functioning of Gacaca Courts charged with Prosecuting and trying the perpetrators of the Crime of Genocide and other Crimes against Humanity, Committed between 1 October 1990 and 31 December 1994, 19 June 2004, Article 8 (http://www.legal-tools.org/doc/eb49aa/).

[122] Hollie Nyseth Brehm, Christopher Uggen and Jean-Damascène Gasanabo, "Genocide, Justice, and Rwanda's Gacaca Courts", in *Journal of Contemporary Criminal Justice*, 2014, vol. 30, no. 3, pp. 333–37.

[123] Republic of Rwanda, 2012, see *supra* note 34.

[124] *Ibid.*; Wibabara, 2013, see *supra* note 12.

in acquittals, reparations, imprisonment and community service as an alternative to imprisonment.[125]

4.4.5. Perception of the Deterrence of Gacaca Courts

4.4.5.1. Prosecution of Genocide Suspects

The respondents appreciated the role of *gacaca* in trying a large number of suspects of genocide and other international crimes. The youth focus group discussion pointed out:

> The ICTR was less deterrent compared to Gacaca courts given the number of cases tried –more than 1 million in 10 years compared to less than one hundred of the ICTR, after learning the meaning of deterrence – individual as well as general deterrence, I observe that the ICTR achieved the individual deterrence given the few accused it tried, but did not deter other offenders in Rwanda like Gacaca did yet general deterrence should have been achieved. Gacaca punished to achieve individual deterrence but also taught lessons on reconciliation.

The focus group discussion prisoners argued:

> Those tried by *gacaca* have learnt lessons of what one gets if he/she treats the community well or commits crimes against it. We learnt through *gacaca* about dangers of hating each other and mistakes of believing everything that leaders say. Even the community has learnt this, it is yes because people are aware with experience of gacaca that no escape if one commits such crimes.

The youth focus group discussion respondents argued:

> Previous governments in Rwanda turned a blind eye to crimes so much so that there was such a level of impunity that whoever committed a crime would go free in public, as long as the committed crime was favored by the political elite. Presently, there is a strong judicial system.

---

[125] Wibabara, 2013, see *supra* note 12.

4.4.5.2. Apprehension

On certainty of apprehension to achieve deterrence, the respondents indicate that *gacaca* courts made this more certain, especially for those residing in the country. The youth focus group discussion respondents mentioned that:

> Even when it may occur that a certain clique may preach hatred to the extent that a certain group of people believe it, either the clique or its followers would be harbouring fear as to what might happen to them once they are identified. If it so occurred that, an individual may think of committing a crime such as genocide, the considerations of the repercussions of prosecution would cause the person to abandon the idea altogether.

4.4.5.3. Evidence Collection

Respondents attested to the information collected during *gacaca* trials as being of high evidential value. Evidence collected from *gacaca* courts was also used in the ordinary courts. Respondents in the survivors' focus group discussion argued that:

> *Gacaca* proceedings provided evidence, the truth was revealed during Gacaca trials, revealed where victims were buried in mass graves and so got decent burial after. In the section on ICTR, criticism of ICTR lacking evidence due to its location, was reversed in the *gacaca* proceedings. There was much evidence resulting into the number of convictions and sentencing practice by these courts.

4.4.5.4. Speed of Trial

Gacaca courts are credited nationally with having tried so many cases in the shortest period, and with minimum resources, according to the Ministry of Justice officials.

4.4.5.5. Severity

In the previous section, it was noted that deterrence is premised on proportionality principles where the higher criminal responsibility calls for equivalent sentence that is harsher than sentences for lesser crimes. This is reflected in various laws on *gacaca* and sentences. Respondents appreciated the sentences by *gacaca* courts. As respondents in the prison focus group discussion noted:

> *Gacaca* sentences were heavy, imagine like me [convict speaking] I am a mother, I was given a life sentence, my children needed to grow up under my care but that is not possible, so I think people seeing such sentences would not want to be like me.

Youth focus group discussion respondents added:

> The ICTR [was] established to try planners of genocide-big fish but the sentencing was lenient, for example, Seromba who planned and killed thousands of his congregation was given a light sentence but when you see ordinary crimes tried under Rwandan courts are punished more severely or I should say the perpetrators of genocide who were tried in *gacaca* were given higher punishment than the ones tried by the ICTR.

4.4.5.6. Safety of Survivors

On this issue, the *gacaca* courts did not score as well as on other factors. Respondents in the survivors group argued:

> I would answer that they contributed up to 40 per cent of security. Let me begin with a no. Since the commencement of *gacaca*, there are a big number of survivors who were murdered. There are those who were killed because they had proved to be giving credible evidence of what happened during the genocide. There are those who were judges in the *gacaca* courts. And, there are those who were victimised for their participation in the *gacaca* courts. Even up to today, there are those who are killed and the factual reason for their deaths is not established as being associated to their status of survivors.

Another added:

> Perhaps I should respond to the question as a psychologist who lived the *gacaca* experience as a counsellor and a survivor, at the same time. I was told on a number of occasions by the survivors, who were encouraged to testify before the *gacaca* courts, that after their delivering of testimony they felt like having undressed themselves in public. They felt that they had exposed themselves to harm from those sus-

> pects who were still at large or their relatives or yet their sympathisers. Members of the detained or convicted persons regard the survivors as the cause for the imprisonment thus the absence of a family member from their family. For this reason, they behave with hostility towards the survivor or/and the family of the survivor. There is general security to all Rwandans because the country is governed under the rule of law principle. This security is enjoyed by everyone. *Gacaca* courts individually did not provide security for the survivors in particular.

Some survivors felt, however, that accountability from *gacaca* courts contributed to safety because of increased awareness of perpetrators that they could be punished.

In sum, respondents showed that the nature of conduct of *gacaca* proceedings exposed the survivors and made them vulnerable to reprisals from suspects of genocide. On the contrary, the ICTR had an effective mechanism of witness protection as provided by its rules of procedure.

4.4.5.7. Trial at the Crime Scene

The benefits of trials taking place at the crime scene are more real in the *gacaca* trials and this has been clearly illustrated by respondents in the prisons' focus group discussion: "*Gacaca* trials took place in cells, sectors and villages where perpetrators were living, and this is a humbling experience that no one wants". Therefore, specific deterrence, and likely general deterrence, was furthered.

4.4.6. Non-Judicial Factors

Deterrence is also affected by non-judicial factors that do not stem from the actions of the courts. Respondents perceived that these external or contextual factors included non-discriminatory policies, inclusive politics, general positive governmental policies, good leadership, integration of former prisoners, a strong system of apprehension, the development of the economy and effective legal mechanisms.

4.4.6.1. Non-Discriminatory Policies

The importance of non-discriminatory policies is reflected in the comments of a focus group discussion youth:

> We Rwandans have reached at a level where genocide cannot find root in our society. Before the genocide, some Rwandans were limited to enjoying certain rights, such as education, in their country. I am of the view that presently, all Rwandans equally enjoy rights in the country, such participation in the governance of the country, education. There is no such a thing like having a particular ethnic group or religious group governing the country, such factors which would cause the society to degenerate leading to genocide. We all participate in leadership, we freely take careers in activities like business, we have access to education, etc. For those reasons, I find no factor that would lead to division thus leading to genocide.

Another said:

> Another factor that facilitated to occurrence of genocide, which is worth mentioning, is the identification of people within the ethnic groups such that such identification was evident by national identity cards. Presently, there is such identification in the national identity cards. For this reason, genocide cannot be carried out again.

4.4.6.2. Inclusive Politics

Again, a focus group discussion youth pointed out:

> On the basis for this group to be notified and summoned to be present here is the fact of us being youths. The youth in the past were taught to hate each other. Presently, we are grouped into co-operatives or youth groups and taught to develop ourselves and the country. The youth being the force to reckon with in the effort to prevent genocide, we are here as a youth to discuss the subject of this research and therefore, we are the force that is in charge of preventing the genocide re-occur in Rwanda.

Respondents from this group added:

> We have a good institutional framework that fosters unity and reconciliation such as the Unity and Reconciliation Commission, Commission against Genocide, Itorero, etc. which promote unity and reconciliation and fights genocide ideology.

4.4.6.3. Good Governmental Policies

In relation to good policies in the country, the survivors' group said:

> Good policies such as education for all where there is no discrimination and policies to conserve memorial sites; this keeps our history alive and teaches young generations about what happened. There is institutional framework on prevention of genocide such as the commission on genocide, unity and reconciliation, *itorero ryigihugu*, abolition of ethnicity in the national identity cards there by promoting nationalism-*ndumunyarwanda*, development programmes where people are encouraged to work and so are no longer seeing their neighbours as a source of misery and poverty or necessary to kill them to have a livelihood like it was during the genocide, nationalism politics-*ndi umunyarwanda*, diversity, for example, I am a tall black woman and work with slim women, men, Rwandans in various things this itself prevents hate crimes like genocide.

4.4.6.4. Good Leadership

The survivors' group added that "as long as you have good leadership then you are sure that genocide or such crimes cannot occur. Today there are different players such as NGOs, a multiparty system, all these help to ensure rule of law".

4.4.6.5. Reintegration of Former Prisoners

The focus group discussion prisoners pointed out:

> The Army and that of Rwanda Defence Forces, a mixed army, I don't think today if the army can be commanded to exterminate either Tutsi or Hutu. The genocide had been possible before because only Hutu were allowed to join the army but today anyone can join.

4.4.6.6. Strong System-Strong Army

The survivors' group underscored this:

> Where we have a firm leadership, the Democratic Forces for the Liberation of Rwanda [a rebel group composed largely of genocide fugitives operating in the DRC] is aware that it cannot easily win a war should it want to come to Rwanda,

the impossibility of easy attack deters the offenders. The certainty of apprehension by Rwandan police and prosecution thereafter makes it harder for criminals and so deters them. In Namibia, the Herreros were killed while their government was looking on but that cannot happen here in Rwanda – the government can defend its people.

4.4.6.7. Development of Economy

The Ministry of Defence group mentioned:

> [A] developed economy is one that has deterred the commission of international crimes. People are very busy trying to develop themselves economically that they have no time for hating each other. Poor people in the past were easily swayed into committing crimes because they sought economic gains from their crimes.

4.4.6.8. Legal Mechanism

Rwanda removed the reservations on the Genocide Convention, has various laws on genocide and so has the capacity to try genocide and other international crimes whenever they may arise, so this is also a deterrent.

4.5. Conclusion and Recommendations

The ICTR, as an international mechanism put in place after gross violations of human rights and international humanitarian law in Rwanda, has achieved some degree of deterrence and other goals of criminal justice, in the view of the respondents. Prosecution of high-profile perpetrators has indeed achieved both individual and general deterrence. Respondents indicated that Rwanda had neither capacity nor access to these high-profile suspects after the 1994 genocide, but the ICTR did. The capacity (qualified personnel, resources) and access (co-operation of states) resulted in apprehension and prosecution of those tried by the ICTR, which achieved specific deterrence. The individuals tried received prison sentences and thus were individually deterred from continuing to commit crimes. Specific deterrence is crucial to the rule of law and to a sense of security and safety for the population. General deterrence is also said to have been achieved because perpetrators and those who were like-minded became aware through ICTR prosecutions that the international community was not tolerant of such violations, and this sent many into hiding, which prevented further crimes. The minuscule number of cases tried by the ICTR, however, is said to have lessened its overall deterrent effect. Other impediments to achieving complete deterrence by the ICTR in the view of respondents were: its slowness, imposing light sentences, distant location and alienating Rwandans in its processes, even though it was a Tribunal meant for them.

The national mechanisms' contribution to the deterrent effect of the ICTR is immense in the view of the respondents. The national mechanisms, which began after the establishment of the ICTR, seemed to have been designed to correct the weaknesses seen in the ICTR process. In fact, the concurrent jurisdiction seems to be the ideal approach for deterring international crimes, since both the national mechanisms and the ICTR have unique roles in deterring such crimes. Respondents had positive reactions to the heavy sentences that the national and *gacaca* courts handed down, even though they generally tried low-profile cases rather than high-level suspects. Respondents also viewed the high certainty of prosecution of those suspected of committing crimes and living in Rwanda as a mark of effectiveness, but pointed to the national mechanisms' inability to access genocide fugitives, for which they appreciated the role of the ICTR. Respondents pointed to many benefits of having trials at the scene of the crime, especially the community-based *gacaca* proceedings. Trials are said to have achieved reconciliation through guilty pleas and confessions, and to have achieved general deterrence where mimetic structures, as described by Gallimore, were destroyed because former leaders were tried in their communities. The power that the leaders had over the communities to influence them into committing crimes ceased, as discussed in the focus groups discussions for prisoners. This kind of deterrence could not have been achieved had the ICTR been the only mechanism because those trials were far from the crime scene. Regarding the speed of trials, respondents appreciated the fact that so many cases had been tried in a short period; *gacaca* courts alone tried almost two million cases in 10 years in comparison to the slower ICTR. However, impediments to deterrence by national mechanisms include limited capacity and challenges to fair trial rights such as the right to defence counsel.

The non-judicial factors that contributed to the deterrence effect of the ICTR and national mechanisms in Rwanda include the public policies of non-discrimination by the current government and a strong government system. Respondents are confident about their government's ability to

prevent the reoccurrence of gross violations of human rights and international humanitarian law that happened in 1994. They point to Rwanda
having a strong army and police force that can do that. The legal system
and judicial capacity are also shown to have improved in order to be able
to prosecute such crimes in the event that they happen. The improvement
of the judicial system is partly attributed to the ICTR through Rwanda's
requests for transfers of cases.

The deterrence of the commission of international crimes is seen to
have been achieved by the ICTR and national mechanisms and by non-
judicial factors. The ICTR had the human and resource capacity needed to
apprehend high-profile suspects, and was viewed as rendering justice in
an impartial way, thereby avoiding victor's justice that a national mechanism was suspected of providing. The national prosecutions contributed to
deterrence through proceedings that took place at the crime scenes with
access to evidence, and were conducted in a language and a manner accepted by the population, thereby being perceived as more legitimate to
the victims and perpetrators. The speed of the trials and the heavy sentences by national courts further affected deterrence. Without the combination of courts and factors, any deterrent effect would have been relatively minimal from the ICTR alone. Going forward, policymakers should
consider from the beginning the need for an effective combination of national and international mechanisms based on the Rwandan experience.

Another recommendation which also came through respondents is
to make the work of the ICTR more known to the Rwandan population
even when the ICTR has closed. The survivors have mentioned that this
could be through the

> archives of the ICTR – it is still debatable where they should
> go. But I am recommending they come to Rwanda. Archives
> are UN property, but as long as they are not transferred to
> Rwanda, they will not be accessible to Rwandans, but more
> specifically to the survivors just like the court was not.

5

Difficulties in Achieving Deterrence by International Criminal Tribunals: The Example of the International Criminal Tribunal for Former Yugoslavia in Kosovo

Dafina Bucaj[*]

5.1. Introduction

The ability of a legal system to discourage certain conduct through threats of punishment or other expressions of disapproval is defined as deterrence.[1] Scholars have created a division between general deterrence and specific deterrence. General deterrence is concerned with potential future offenders, namely the ability to deter criminal behaviour in society at large. Specific deterrence, by contrast, is intended to prevent recidivism among those already investigated and prosecuted, namely dissuading these specific individuals from the commission of future crimes.[2] In this sense, deterrence is also seen as a means of preventing future crimes although, as explained in this volume's chapter on deterrence theory, prevention is a broader concept that includes deterrence through prosecutorial action, but also includes government and community-based programmes, policies and initiatives intended to exclude the commission of crimes as a socially acceptable option.

---

[*] **Dafina Bucaj** holds a Masters degree in international law from the University of Cambridge, United Kingdom. She obtained a law degree from the University of Prishtina and a Bachelors degree in journalism from the same university. She is currently an Assistant Lecturer of International Law at the Faculty of Law, University of Prishtina and a Legal Adviser for the First Deputy Prime Minister of Kosovo.

[1] Payam Akhavan, "Justice in The Hague, Peace in the Former Yugoslavia? A Commentary on the United Nations War Crimes Tribunal", in *Human Rights Quarterly*, 1999, vol. 20, no. 4, pp. 713–71.

[2] International Criminal Tribunal for the former Yugoslavia ('ICTY'), *Prosecutor v. Zdravko Mucić*, Trial Chamber, Judgment , IT-96-21-T, 16 November 1998, para. 1232 ('Čelebići Camp Judgment') (http://www.legal-tools.org/doc/6b4a33/).

In relation to mass atrocities, scholars use the terminology developed by the International Criminal Tribunal for Rwanda ('ICTR'),[3] which in the *Kambanda* case held that the primary purpose of the Tribunal must be directed towards deterrence, namely "dissuading for good those who will attempt in future to perpetrate such atrocities".[4] This is based on the assumption that a threat of or actual meting out of punishment may cause potential perpetrators (or reoffenders) to adjust their behaviour. The punishment, which is directed towards leaders who contemplate engaging in criminal policies, may affect their behaviour, if the leaders engage in a so-called cost-benefit calculation.[5] Nevertheless, the connection between international prosecutions and the actual deterrence of future atrocities has been a relatively untested assumption for many years,[6] with the exception of some recent studies on the deterrence of the International Criminal Court ('ICC').[7] To date there are few general studies conducted on the deterrent effect of the international tribunals.

With regards to the International Tribunal for the former Yugoslavia ('ICTY'), past studies have focused on many aspects of the work of the Tribunal such as the long-term impact of the ICTY on: post-conflict peace building; the stigmatisation and marginalisation of ultranationalist leaders and ideologies allied with ethnic hatred and violence; the potential shoring-up of support for indicted leaders who have been supported by local political institutions in an expression of ethnic solidarity; the role of the broader public in distancing itself from indicted leaders despite a common ethnic affiliation; and the impact of indictments in reinforcing

---

[3]   ICTY, *Prosecutor v. Dragoljub Kunarac et al.*, Trial Chamber, Judgment, IT-96-23 and 23/1, 22 February, 2001, para. 842 (http://www.legal-tools.org/doc/fd881d/); United Nations Security Council, Establishment of the International Criminal Tribunal for Rwanda ('ICTR') and adoption of the Statute of the Tribunal, Resolution 955, S/Res/955, 8 November 1994 (http://www.legal-tools.org/doc/f5ef47/); United Nations Security Council, SCOR, 54th session, 4063d, UN doc. S/PV.4063, 1999.

[4]   ICTR, *Prosecutor v. Jean Kambanda*, Trial Chamber, Judgment, ICTR-97-23, 4 September 1998, para. 28 (http://www.legal-tools.org/doc/49a299/).

[5]   Payam Akhavan, "Beyond Impunity: Can International Criminal Justice Prevent Future Atrocities?", in *American Journal of International Law*, 2001, vol. 95, no. 1, pp. 7–31.

[6]   David Wippman, "Atrocities, Deterrence, and the Limits of International Justice", in *Fordham International Law Journal*, 1999, vol. 23, no. 2, p. 473.

[7]   Hyeran Jo and Beth A. Simmons, "Can the International Criminal Court Deter Atrocity?", in *International Organization*, 2016, vol. 70, no. 3, pp. 443–75.

the martyred image of nationalist saviours, and in turn the impact on the ICTY's reputation as a legitimate institution.[8]

Among these studies, few have examined the overall deterrent effect of the ICTY, and there is no country-specific study of Kosovo, which is the purpose of this chapter, evaluating the deterrent effect of the ICTY in the Kosovo-related conflict. The cornerstone of this chapter is to see whether the ICTY has satisfied this particular primary purpose for which it was initially created, and to evaluate the extent to which the Tribunal has contributed to the achievement of deterrence through factors such as ending and preventing further war crimes, altering the climate of impunity, and establishing a reliable historical record concerning the conflict.[9]

This chapter draws on a mixture of desk and empirical research conducted in Kosovo, as one of the situation countries with the most recent armed conflict in the former Yugoslavia and where the ICTY has had jurisdiction to try the highest-level perpetrators. Given the ending of the mandate of the ICTY,[10] the study is conducted *ex post facto*, aiming to contribute to a comparative approach of the potential of the international criminal tribunals to effectuate deterrence in conflict countries.

Respondents to the study include a variety of people from different categories of the society in general such as victims of war (including witnesses at the ICTY), representatives of civil society organisations ('CSOs') dealing with transitional justice, including from the Serb minority community, and legal professionals such as university professors, judges, prosecutors and defence lawyers. The research took the form of personal interviews and focus groups, where the respondents were asked to address issues such as:

- The effectiveness of the ICTY;
- Whether the ICTY has contributed towards ending mass violations;
- The effect on fighting a culture of impunity;
- The impact of the indictments on specific deterrence;

---

[8] Akhavan, 2001, see *supra* note 5.

[9] Ivan Simonovic, "The Role of the ICTY in the Development of International Criminal Adjudication", in *Fordham International Law Journal*, 1999, vol. 23, p. 457.

[10] United Nations Security Council, Resolution 1966 (2010), UN doc. S/RES/1966, 22 December 2010 (http://www.legal-tools.org/doc/e79460/).

- The effectiveness of deterrence through the sentences imposed by the ICTY;
- The contribution of the Tribunal to changing people's mentality and preventing future crimes;
- The effect of the ICTY in triggering national trials and legal reforms;
- The possible social deterrent effect of the Tribunal through the establishment of a reliable historical record; and
- The problems and deficiencies of the ICTY, namely what the Tribunal could have done better.

There are several related issues that this chapter aims to explore in measuring the ICTY's deterrence. It has four main sections, complemented by a contextual background and conclusions. In the first section, the study focuses on the capacity and the effect of the Tribunal in the short term, namely its ability to end or influence mass violations. This section showcases the failure of the ICTY to bring an end to ongoing massive violations through evidence of the occurrence of such violations even after the Tribunal was fully functional and cases were already in progress.

The second section analyses the Tribunal's ability to affect deterrence and to create a culture of impunity as a short-term result of its work. In conducting the evaluation, emphasis is put on certain elements of the work of the Tribunal on which deterrence is dependent, such as the capacity of the indictments to deter, the severity of the sentences and the work of the Tribunal in instilling a culture of resisting impunity. The section draws a comparative analysis of the impact of the components of the Tribunal's work from indictments to sentences. The conclusion drawn is that sentencing is the most important test of the potential deterrent effect of the ICTY. As the last segment of the section develops, the ICTY has been inadequate in general in the impact of both indictments and sentences to establish a culture of fighting impunity.

The third section elaborates on the additional factors and segments of the work of the Tribunal, which can have a long-term deterrent effect, such as establishing a historical record, achieving impact in triggering national trials and domesticating legal norms. This section in particular elaborates on the impact of the Tribunal in setting the groundwork for long-term deterrence. As the section shows, there are elements to the work of the Tribunal which do not have immediate effect, but that nevertheless can have more deterrent effect in the long term. However, as the fourth section shows, the ICTY has failed in some of those aspects while succeeding in others. The chapter also explores the deficiencies of the Tribunal, expressed in the form of criticism of its work that may have a negative impact on deterrence.

Finally, the conclusion synthesises the findings that can be summarised as unsatisfactory results of the work of the Tribunal, putting an emphasis on the failure of the Tribunal to end massive violations, and its difficulties in achieving deterrence in the short term through indictments. Although the conclusion criticises the Tribunal's sentencing record, it also notes its contribution to the establishment of a culture of fighting impunity. More positive results on the longer-term setting of the grounds for deterrence have been observed, though followed with plenty of criticism. Based on the experience of Kosovo, the chapter includes recommendations for how the ICC and other tribunals might contribute to future deterrence efforts through more standardised sentencing policies that meet the threshold of severity, fewer politically influenced indictments, and improved outreach programmes.

5.2. Contextual Background: The ICTY and Kosovo

Transitional justice has been characterised by the development of both retributive and restitutive processes, manifested in different forms. While it is of utmost importance that peace be restored in places of conflict with the aim of bringing an end to massive atrocities, it is likewise important that they not be repeated. The ending of impunity and bringing justice to the victims has taken a course of development parallel to the peace restoration processes. Indicting and sentencing major authors of mass atrocities are intended as a repressive measure for the perpetrator and aim at bringing justice to the victims of the violations. The internationalisation of criminal responsibility and the transcending of the borders of the responsibility to prosecute have been milestones in the development of international criminal justice. Article 6 of the Charter of the International Military Tribunal at Nuremberg, the Geneva Conventions and the Genocide Convention categorised crimes against peace (aggression), war crimes, crimes against humanity and genocide as international crimes. Following the Second World War, these changes contributed to the concept that these acts occurring within national borders are so unacceptable that they violate international law, and thus are no longer a responsibility of a sole state but are a universal responsibility. Nowadays, based on international treaties and customary international law, the international community arguably has an obligation to bring perpetrators of war crimes to justice.[11]

International efforts to bring perpetrators of war crimes to justice have been realised with the establishment of several international and hybrid courts and tribunals to deal with war crimes, such as the International Military Tribunal of Nuremberg, the ICTY, the ICTR, the Special Court for Sierra Leone ('SCSL'), the Extraordinary Chambers in the Courts of Cambodia ('ECCC')', the Special Tribunal for Lebanon ('STL'), the Ad Hoc Court for East Timor, and – perhaps most significantly – the ICC. Nevertheless, despite these efforts by the international community, "corralling high-level accused war criminals into the dock has turned out to be a persistent problem for international criminal courts".[12]

Prior to the establishment of the ICTY and ICTR, the idea of the establishment of an international war crimes tribunal seemed noble yet unrealistic.[13] Nevertheless, the moral guilt that the international community felt for the double failure to prevent or stop massacres in the former Yugoslavia was an impetus for the establishment of the ICTY.[14] The United Nations ('UN') Security Council established the ICTY as a measure for the restoration of peace and security under Chapter VII of the UN Charter[15] and emphasised that by "bringing to justice [...] persons responsible for serious violations of international humanitarian law [...] [prosecution] will contribute to ensuring that such violations are halted and effectively redressed".[16] While people affiliated with the ICTY and ICTR "have tout-

---

[11] Mohamed Othman, "Justice and Reconciliation", in Elin Skaar, Siri Gloppen and Astri Suhrke (eds.), *Roads to Reconciliation*, Lexington Books, Lanham, MD, 2005, pp. 249–70; Gary J. Bass, "Managing Amnesty", Paper Presented at the Transitional Justice and Civil War Settlements workshop, Bogotá, Colombia, 18–19 October 2005; Daphna Shraga, "The Second Generation UN-Based Tribunals: A Diversity of Mixed Jurisdiction", in Elin Skaar, Siri Gloppen and Astri Suhrke (eds.), *Roads to Reconciliation*, Lexington Books, Lanham, MD, 2005, pp. 55–82.

[12] Patricia M. Wald, "Apprehending War Criminals: Does International Cooperation Work?", in *American University International Law Review*, 2012, vol. 27, no. 2, pp. 229–63.

[13] Simonovic, 1999, see *supra* note 9.

[14] Catherine Cissé, "The International Tribunals for the Former Yugoslavia and Rwanda: Some Elements of Comparison", in *Transnational Law and Contemporary Problems*, 1997, vol. 7, pp. 103–6.

[15] United Nations Security Council, Resolution 827, 25 May 1993, UN doc. S/RES/827 ('UNSC Resolution 827') (http://www.legal-tools.org/doc/dc079b/).

[16] *Ibid.*, Preamble.

---

ed the tribunals' ability to prevent future crime, provide retribution, achieve restorative justice, establish an accurate historiographical record, and build precedent for future prosecutions",[17] the original emphasis was on deterrence of future violations. The headline of the discussions within the Security Council's debates relating to the ICTY was the need to prosecute in order to eradicate the "culture of impunity".[18] Consequently, the justification for the establishment of the Tribunal was convincing as being based on the assumption that that the establishment of the Tribunal should discourage possible perpetrators of future violations and change the climate of impunity.[19]

In order to understand the potential impact of not just the ICTY but of any international court in Kosovo, one must understand the history behind the conflict. Unlike some characterisations at the time and since, the conflict in the former Yugoslavia was not an expression of spontaneous blood lust, but rather the result of a deliberate incitement of ethnic hatred and violence through which certain people, often referred to as warlords, elevated themselves to positions of absolute power.[20]

Kosovo is a territory in the middle of the Balkan Peninsula. It has a majority Albanian population with long-standing claims and aspirations to join the rest of the Albanian-inhabited territories in the Balkans to form a Greater Albania. For most of the twentieth century the Albanians of Kosovo have lived under Serbian rule characterised by a heavy hand.[21] Kosovo was an integral part of the Federal Socialist Republic of Yugoslavia, which was composed of seven states and two autonomous provinces, Kosovo being one of them. The architects of the Yugoslav federal system had reasoned in 1943 that the status of republic should be reserved for nations (*narodi*) as opposed to nationalities (*narodnosti*), the former having their principal homeland inside Yugoslavia and the latter outside Yugo-

---

[17] Ralph D. Ellis and Carol S. Ellis, Theories of Criminal Justice, Longwood, Wolfeboro, NH, 1990; Barbara A. Hudson, Understanding Justice: An Intorduction to Ideas, Perspective and Controversis in Modern Penal Theory, McGraw-Hill Education, New York, 1996.

[18] United Nations Security Council, UN SCOR, 48th session, UN doc. S/INF/49, 1993.

[19] Richard Goldstone, "Conference Luncheon Address", in *Transnational Law and Contemporary Problems*, 1997, vol. 7, no. 1, pp. 1–4.

[20] Akhavan, 2001, see *supra* note 5.

[21] Noel Malcolm, *Kosovo: A Short History*, Macmillan, London, 1998.

slavia.[22] This was the beginning of discrimination against the Albanian population in Kosovo since they were not a nation, but rather a nationality, and thus did not have the right to be a nation since it was considered that the homeland of Albanians was Albania.[23] Kosovo was one of the autonomous provinces of Serbia that enjoyed "virtually all prerogatives of a republic" until March 1989, when Serbia forcefully abolished Kosovo's autonomy, precipitating a crisis, which hastened the collapse of Yugoslavia.[24]

The loss of autonomy was a catalyst for a change in the treatment of Albanians in Kosovo. Laws were passed making it a crime for Albanians to buy or sell property without special permission, tens of thousands of Albanians were dismissed from their jobs with state-owned firms, students were barred from pursuing education, and arbitrary arrests and police violence directed towards Albanians became routine, which gave Kosovo the distinction of having some of the worst human rights violations in all of Europe.[25] As the Kosovo situation never made it to the Dayton talks, the lack of trust in the international community led to the emergence of the Kosovo Liberation Army ('KLA'), with the goal of protecting the people of Kosovo through instigating attacks on the Serbian police. The attacks were answered with severe counter-attacks, destruction of entire villages and a large number of civilian casualties. Consequently, a long-standing civil conflict was transformed into outright ethnic cleansing, a military confrontation with the North Atlantic Treaty Organisation ('NATO'), and a losing battle for a historically vital province.[26]

While the warnings issued by the international community seemed to have no effect, the first step in putting an end to the war was a result of

---

[22] Frits W. Hondius, *The Yugoslav Community of Nations*, Mouton, The Hague, 1968; Zoran Pajic, "The Former Yugoslavia", in Hugh Miall (ed.), *Minority Rights in Europe: The Scope for a Transnational Regime*, Pinter/RIIA, London, 1994, p. 63.

[23] Richard Caplan, "International Diplomacy and the Crisis in Kosovo", in *International Affairs*, 1998, vol. 74, no. 4, pp. 745–61.

[24] *Ibid.*, p. 748.

[25] *Ibid.*; Helsinki Watch, *Human Rights Abuses in Kosovo 1990–1992*, Human Rights Watch, New York, 1992; ICTY, Fifth Annual Report of the International Tribunal for the Prosecution of Persons Responsible for Serious Violations of International Humanitarian Law Committed in the Territory of the Former Yugoslavia Since 1991, UN doc. A/53/219, S/1998/737, 10 August 1998 ('UNSC Fifth Annual Report') (http://www.legal-tools.org/doc/64ecb8/).

[26] Akhavan, 2001, see *supra* note 5.

the political NATO intervention. On 24 March 1999, in the absence of a UN Security Council resolution expressly authorising military action,[27] NATO began a 78-day air campaign over the former Federal Republic of Yugoslavia.[28]

On the eve of the conflict, Sandy Berger, then US national security adviser, wrote this explanation to the US Congressional leadership for the likely NATO intervention:

> NATO would be acting to deter unlawful violence in Kosovo that endangers the fragile stability of the Balkans and threatens a wider conflict in Europe, to uphold the will of the international community as expressed in various UN Security Council Resolutions, as well as to prevent another humanitarian crisis, which itself could undermine stability and threaten neighbouring countries.[29]

After the conflict, the main responsibility for restoring peace, maintaining and enforcing a ceasefire, and deterring immediate renewed hostilities lay with the NATO forces.[30] In principle, NATO did what the ICTY was not successful in doing, which was to end the mass violations and to ensure a safe environment for the citizens. Following the NATO action, the UN adopted resolution 1244, which foresaw the deployment of international security forces, known as the United Nations Mission in Kosovo ('UNMIK'), which, among other goals, held the responsibility for administering the region and ensuring peace and stability.[31]

Nevertheless, the ICTY remained one of the key institutions charged with the duty of deterring future atrocities. The potential of the ICTY in fostering general deterrence is noted by Franca Baroni:

> This is the most meaningful potential contribution that the Court can make in the former Yugoslavia, since the Court's

---

[27] Dr. Javier Solana, Secretary-General of NATO, Press Statement, Press Release 040, 23 March 1999.

[28] Following the dissolution of Socialist Federal Republic of Yugoslavia, Serbia and Montenegro claimed continuity of statehood, which was not supported by other countries and the UN, and thus the name Federal Republic of Yugoslavia was retained.

[29] Letter from Samuel R. Berger, Assistant to the President for National Security Affairs to The Honorable Trent Lott, 23 March 1999.

[30] William Moorman, "Humanitarian Intervention and International Law in the Case of Kosovo", in *New England Law Review*, 2002, vol. 36, no. 4, p. 775.

[31] United Nations Security Council, Resolution 1244, UN doc. S/RES/1244, 10 June 1999 (http://www.legal-tools.org/doc/12bfc3-1/).

role is to create a serious prospect of accountability, and to convey the message that ethnic cleansing, mass killings, systematic rape and other atrocities are wrong, unjustified by any political and social plan, and that they are not tolerated by the world community under any circumstances.[32]

5.3. The ICTY Effectuating an End to Ongoing Massive Violations: An Unrealistic Short-Term Expectation

The motivation behind the establishment of international tribunals has been to end massive human rights violations and ensure an environment where such violations would not recur. This goal entails not only stopping ongoing violations but also creating an environment that is non-conducive to mass abuses. These desires, though noble, were very unrealistic in Kosovo. As far as the aim of ending violations goes, the Tribunal's ability to influence perpetrators to end mass violations has not been shown to be effective in practice.

In order to evaluate the deterrence of the ICTY, one must understand the core elements that affect deterrence, starting with the severity of the punishment as one of the main components. When measuring the benefits of a crime, in order to achieve deterrence, the expected costs must be higher than the benefits, since an offender is expected to commit a crime only when the benefits are considered to be greater than the costs.[33] From that premise stems the assumption that individuals will make rational cost-benefit decisions, and that such analyses can be influenced by punishment.[34] Deterrence is achieved when the potential offender perceives the disincentive of the legal sanction threat to be so strong that it out-

---

[32] Franca Baroni, "The International Criminal Tribunal for rhe Former Yugoslavia and Its Mission to Restore Peace", in *Pace International Law Review,* 2000, vol. 12, no. 2, pp. 233–46.

[33] Anna Bonanno, "The Economic Analysis of Offender's Choice: Old and New Insights", in *Rivista Internazionale Di Scienze Economiche e Commerciali,* 2006, vol. 53, no. 2, pp. 193–224; J. Robert Lilly, Francis T. Cullen and Richard A. Ball, *Criminological Theory: Context and Consequences,* 5th ed., Sage, Thousand Oaks, CA, 2011; Raymond Paternoster, "How Much Do We Really Know about Criminal Deterrence?", in *Journal of Criminal Law and Criminology,* 2010, vol. 100, no. 3, pp. 765–824.

[34] Tom Buitelaar, "The ICC and the Prevention of Atrocities: Criminological Perspectives", in *Human Rights Review,* 2016, vol. 17, no. 3, pp. 285–302.

weighs the incentives of the crime under consideration.[35] This calculation
is further dependent on an individual's threshold to recognise that his or
her actions could be subjected to punishment at all, which in the context
of international humanitarian law may never be reached.[36] Thus, this is
the reason why "perpetrators commit atrocities, including genocide, when
they calculate they can get away with it".[37]

In cases of armed conflict, the possibility that rebels will lay down
their weapons and stop fighting due to fear of post-war prosecution is
highly unlikely.[38] "On the ground, those committing war crimes would
infer that regardless of their past or future violations, they will not be held
criminally accountable by the international community".[39] Even if potential wrongdoers realise that their actions will theoretically be subject to
prosecution, scholars consider that there is little credible threat of punishment for individual violators of international humanitarian law.[40] Consequently, in cases where there is a lack of credibility associated with the
warnings for punishment combined with the motivations behind the violations, it is more likely that crimes will continue to occur.[41]

Prior to the establishment of the ICTY there was no fear of international prosecution, and what is clear when looking at the history of the
ICTY is that the Tribunal had no immediate effect. The ICTY's experience seems to show that even under a perceived threat of punishment, tri-

---

[35] Bonanno, 2006, see *supra* note 33; Paternoster, 2010, see *supra* note 33; Johannes Andenaes, "The General Preventive Effects of Punishment", in Joseph Goldstein and Abraham
S. Goldstein (eds.), *Crime, Law and Society: Selected Readings*, Free Press, New York,
1966, pp. 321–42.

[36] Justin Levitt, "Developments in the Law: International Criminal Law", in *Harvard Law
Review*, 2001, vol. 114, no. 7, pp. 1943–2073.

[37] Kenneth Roth, "The Case for Universal Jurisdiction", in *Foreign Affairs*, 2001, vol. 80, no.
5, p. 150.

[38] Raymond Aron, *Peace and War: A Theory of International Relations*, Doubleday, New
York, 1981; Samuel P. Huntington, *The Third Wave: Democratization in the Late Twentieth Century*, University of Oklahoma Press, Norman, 1993; James D. Fearon, "Comments
on the Ex Ante/Ex Post Problem in Transitional Justice", Paper Presented at the Transitional Justice and Civil War Settlements Workshop, Bogotá, Colombia, 18–19 October
2005.

[39] Theodor Meron, *War Crimes Law Comes of Age: Essays*, Oxford University Press, Oxford,
1998, p. 196.

[40] Dan M. Kahan, "Social Influence, Social Meaning, and Deterrence", in *Virginia Law Review*, 1997, vol. 83, no. 2, pp. 349–54.

[41] Baroni, 2000, p. 245, see *supra* note 32.

bunals alone are unlikely to achieve general deterrence in the short term.[42] Despite the fact that the UN Security Council established the ICTY as an immediate measure to restore and maintain peace,[43] evidence clearly shows that the establishment of the Tribunal neither stopped, nor prevented future war crimes in the region since they continued to be committed in Bosnia and Herzegovina.[44] "[T]he gravest atrocity, the Serb massacre of thousands of Muslims living in and around Srebrenica, happened in July 1995, when the tribunal was fully operational and Karadzic and Mladic had both been indicted".[45] Even later on, in 1998–1999, "despite fifty-nine pending indictments before the ICTY and two publicised convictions",[46] violations of international law continued to take place in the former Yugoslavia".[47] 'Similarly, even after Milošević was indicted, forces under his control committed numerous atrocities in Kosovo despite frequent warnings by the ICTY, the UN Security Council and individual states that perpetrators would be held accountable'.[48]

Given the occurrence of mass crime violations after its establishment, many argue that the Tribunal's very reason for existence has been put into doubt, and its failures and shortcomings have been highly publicised.[49] Ivan Simonovic notes:

> Evidently, prevention failed with respect to the conflict and the area for which the Tribunal has been established. But what of the global aim of general prevention, that is, the influence upon behaviour in possible future conflicts around the world? There is no clear answer, but it seems that it depends upon whether people like Karadzic, Mladic, Martic, and Milosevic as well, are successfully brought to justice.[50]

---

[42] David J. Scheffer, "War Crimes and Crimes against Humanity", in *Pace International Law Review*, 1999, vol. 11, no. 2, pp. 319–26.

[43] UNSC Resolution 827, Preamble, see *supra* note 15.

[44] Simonovic, 1999, see *supra* note 9.

[45] Theodor Meron, "Answering for War Crimes: Lessons from the Balkans", in *Foreign Affairs*, 1997, vol. 76, no. 1, pp. 2–6.

[46] UNSC Fifth Annual Report, see *supra* note 25.

[47] ICTY, *Prosecutor v. Slobodan Milošević*, Indictment, IT-02-54, 22 May 1999 ('Milošević Indictment') (http://www.legal-tools.org/doc/041290/).

[48] Wippman, 1999, pp. 479–80, see *supra* note 6.

[49] Baroni, 2000, p. 244, see *supra* note 32.

[50] Simonovic, 1999, p. 457, see *supra* note 9.

Scholars like Payam Akhavan even consider that "it is unrealistic to suppose that the ICTY could have instantaneously deterred crimes in the midst of a particularly cruel inter-ethnic war in the former Yugoslavia".[51] The fact that atrocities persisted at high levels in the former Yugoslavia, even after the work of the ICTY began, shows only that the Tribunal's efforts have not succeeded in deterring enough perpetrators to make a visible impact on the course of events.[52] In addition, it has been argued that assessing a court's effectiveness by studying its deterrent impact on ongoing conflicts is both unwise and unfair since criminal justice systems in general have a limited capacity to deter crimes, the bases of this assumption being that that the gains from most of the crimes are often immediate, whereas legal costs are usually uncertain and far in the future.[53] If this is true for ordinary legal systems, which work in a timelier and more efficient manner, it must be even more so for international tribunals, which often start years after crimes have been committed.

As shown in numbers in the first seven years of its work the Tribunal only sentenced 15 individuals,[54] which clearly shows that ICTY had little or no effect on the first years of its establishment. Given such a small figure compared to the number of war criminals in the area,[55] one must evaluate the possible deterrence effect of the Court at a later time and from a long-term perspective, after the Tribunal has been fully functional and 'effective'.

5.4. The Court's Contribution to Deterrence and a Culture of Fighting Impunity: Short-Term Results

When looking at the ICTY as a whole, the work done and the feedback related to it are not very promising in terms of achieving deterrence. There is criticism of the Tribunal and the way it has handled the work and the end results. Respondents to this study have not viewed the Tribunal's

---

[51] Akhavan, 2001, p. 9, see *supra* note 5.

[52] Wippman, 1999, see *supra* note 6.

[53] Buitelaar, 2016, see *supra* note 34.

[54] ICTY, Sixth Annual Report of the International Tribunal for the Prosecution of Persons Responsible for Serious Violations of International Humanitarian Law Committed in the Territory of the Former Yugoslavia Since 1991, UN GAOR, 54th session, Agenda Item 53, UN docs. A/54/187, S/1999/846, 25 August 1999 ('ICTY, Sixth Annual Report') (http://www.legal-tools.org/doc/28850e/).

[55] Baroni, 2000, p. 245, see *supra* note 32.

effectiveness in accomplishing its deterrence mission as any greater. The general impression about the Tribunal not only among the victims but also among legal professionals and civil society representatives is a very pessimistic one. In the view of one of the judges, the fact that the majority of the crimes committed in the former Yugoslavia, particularly in Kosovo, were committed after the Tribunal was created is an example of the failure of the ICTY to prevent future crimes.[56]

In addition to the severity of the sentences as one of the main elements affecting the potential for deterrence, a court or tribunal's capacity to deter is also dependent on it being perceived as effective and legitimate. The test of the effectiveness of the ICTY is dependent on satisfying expectations that the Tribunal created among the citizens that "it will put the perpetrators behind bars, and the end results in that aspect are very disappointing".[57] While professionals in the legal field recognise the limited capacity of the Tribunal due to its lack of enforcement mechanisms and the nature of the crimes falling within its scope,[58] a stronger criticism and dissatisfaction with the work of the Tribunal comes particularly from the victims and civil society representatives who note that "the Tribunal has indeed failed to accomplish its biggest mission to put the perpetrators behind bars",[59] since the Court has not given a satisfactory result on the trial and sentencing of the perpetrators,[60] and the majority of the known perpetrators walk and live freely. As such, the Tribunal is often seen as a tool or mechanism created to establish peace and balance in the region rather than a body to deliver justice,[61] which questions the legitimacy of the ICTY. Therefore, there is doubt among the respondents with regards to the effectiveness of the Tribunal.

Statistical data show that the ICTY enjoyed different support at different times, which correlates with the timing of indictments and decisions based on members of which communities are being tried or sentenced.[62] In 2007, 58 per cent of the Kosovo Albanian respondents

---

[56] Interview with local judge, Prishtina, May 2016.

[57] Interview with CSO representative, Prishtina, May 2016.

[58] Interview with local judge, Prishtina, April 2016.

[59] Focus group discussion with victims, Drenas, April 2016.

[60] Interview with CSO representative, Prishtina, May 2016.

[61] *Ibid.*

[62] United Nations Development Programme, *Perceptions on Transitional Justice: Kosovo 2012*, UNDP, Prishtina, 2012, p. 170.

showed dissatisfaction with the work of the ICTY and 3 per cent satisfaction to some extent, whereas 50 per cent of the Kosovo Serbs were "satisfied to some extent". By 2012 there had been significant changes, and the numbers showed a decrease to 47 per cent dissatisfaction of Kosovo Albanians and an increase of satisfaction to 27 per cent. For the Kosovo Serb community, satisfaction fell to 35 per cent and dissatisfaction rose from 20 per cent in 2007 to 30 per cent in 2012. It is possible that the levels changed due to the work of the Tribunal. Prior to 2007 the Tribunal had indicted around eight Kosovo Albanians, members of the KLA, and the then prime minister, Ramush Haradinaj, and Fatmir Limaj (then deputy of the major political party) – two of the main political leaders. At the time when the second survey was conducted these two and the majority of the Kosovo Albanians indicted had been acquitted, which may explain the increased satisfaction of the Kosovo Albanians and decreased satisfaction of the Kosovo Serbs.

However, while it is difficult to evaluate the deterrence of the Tribunal as a whole, a more realistic approach may be to evaluate certain elements of the Tribunal's work and their potential deterrent effect. Evaluating the effect of indictments, or of sentences imposed on deterrence, or at least on instilling a culture of fighting impunity, may be a more practical and fruitful approach. This section seeks to explore precisely those elements.

5.4.1. The Power of Indictments to Deter

While the typical test of the deterrent effect of a court is dependent on its sentencing and later decisions, indictments may undermine the political influence of particular leaders by incapacitating them or discrediting their leadership. A tribunal may remove people from power, since it prevents them from committing crimes, otherwise known as the 'incapacitation ability' of a court. Supporters of international courts argue that indictments and warrants carry significant deterrent value precisely because the accused may be inhibited from travelling.[63] In the case of the ICTY, the Tribunal had noted that one of its goals is imposing "imprisonment to protect society from the hostile, predatory conduct of the guilty accused".[64] The ICTY has indicted 161 people, including the highest leaders of Serbia and the leaders of the KLA, thus having a direct impact on those people.

---

[63] Wald, 2012, see *supra* note 12.
[64] Čelebići Camp Judgment, para. 1232, see *supra* note 2.

In principle, "even if wartime leaders still enjoy popular support among an indoctrinated public at home, exclusion from the international sphere can significantly impede their long-term exercise of power".[65]

In the case of the ICTY, this effect was decreased due to the timing of the indictments, since the Kosovo-related indictments were filed years after the war had officially ended, the mass violations had ceased, most of the high-level politicians were already effectively deprived of power and reform was underway.[66] Thus the timing of the indictments is one of the criticisms of the Tribunal. The respondents argue that the Tribunal took too long to begin, and the "trials started too late".[67] This is also true for indictments for the crimes that took place in Bosnia, and the ICTY is trying people for violations in some cases more than 20 years after the event. In the view of local judges, "for war crime trials this is usually the case, it nevertheless impacts the effectiveness since now these trials no longer have an effect".[68] In addition, the duration of the trials was so long that the impact of the trials was lost. Notwithstanding the complexity of the cases, "the Court took too long to try some cases which could have been finalised in a timelier manner, and if the trials were conducted earlier the effect would have been greater".[69]

While the ICTY has removed people from the landscape, the respondents contend that the deterrent effect of the indictments is not as powerful as one may think since most of the perpetrators, the high-level politicians, "have gone out of power before they got accused"[70] and were only surrendered to The Hague after, and not at their peak of power, with a few exceptions such as in the case of Haradinaj, while he was holding the position of prime minister. From the victims' perspective, "the indictments and arrests of high profile people such as generals have been followed with a lot of pomposity",[71] but the fact that some of the leaders have been indicted by the ICTY has not satisfied its purpose to deter first

---

[65] Akhavan, 2001, p. 7, see *supra* note 5.

[66] "Ratko Mladic's Capture is a Victory for Western Diplomacy", in *Washington Post*, 27 May 2011.

[67] Interview with victims, Krushe, April 2016.

[68] Interview with local judge, Prishtina, April 2016.

[69] *Ibid.*

[70] Interview with Serbian CSO representative, Prishtina, May 2016.

[71] Interview with victim/ICTY witness, Krusha, April 2016.

and foremost, since in the end they have not been sentenced.[72] The Tribunal has also only tried the high-level politicians and leaders, whereas the actual perpetrators who have committed crimes walk free and have never been tried by anyone,[73] and this has played a significant role in this perception.

In contrast, there are those who consider that the mere issuance of an indictment, the very prospect of a trial, is itself the 'punishment' by which an international criminal court may deter.[74] Stigmatising delinquent leaders through indictment, as well as apprehension and prosecution, undermines their influence.[75] Consequently, these indicted leaders can become "international pariahs".[76] This is what is known as social censure, extra-legal sanction, or "the punishment of the society", which can take various forms such as social isolation, loss of personal contacts or a lowering of community respect.[77] At times the threat of extra-legal sanctions has been considered to have a more significant impact in deterring the general population from criminal behaviour than the threat of legal sanctions.[78]

The effectiveness of such extra-legal sanctions is difficult to prove, but there is "modest anecdotal evidence to suggest that some individual actors in the former Yugoslavia have adhered more closely to the requirements of international humanitarian law than they would have otherwise, for fear of prosecution".[79] Even though there was no immediate deterrent effect that ended mass violations since there was no actual fear of prosecution,[80] there was a noticeable change of the behaviour among the Serb forces as the threat of a NATO intervention was increasing. This was seen in intensified efforts to conceal mass graves and hide evidence

---

[72] Focus group discussion with victims, Drenas, Gjakove, Krusha, April 2016.

[73] Focus group discussion with victims, Drenas, April 2016.

[74] Robert Sloane, "The Expressive Capacity of International Punishment", Columbia Public Law & Legal Theory Working Papers, Paper No. 06-112, 2006, p. 42.

[75] Akhavan, 2001, see *supra* note 5.

[76] United Nations Security Council, U.N. SCOR, 48th session, 3217th meeting at 13, UN doc. S/PV.3217, 1993.

[77] Kirk R. Williams and Richard Hawkins, "Perceptional Research on General Deterrence: A Critical Review", in *Law and Society Review*, 1986, vol. 20, no. 4, p. 558.

[78] Paternoster, 2010, p. 817, see *supra* note 33.

[79] Akhavan, 1999, pp. 750–51, see *supra* note 1.

[80] Theodor Meron, "From Nuremberg to the Hague", in *Milano Law Review*, 1995, vol. 149, p. 107–10.

and criminal conduct.[81] As soon as the Tribunal started its work through the indictments, "some criminals began giving up their colleagues and fellow combatants, showing an impact of the Tribunal on their behaviour".[82]

In other words, one of the biggest impacts of the Court may have been connected to the indictments, namely the surrender of the indicted to the ICTY, whether willingly or as a result of international pressure. In Kosovo, the surrender of the indicted was followed with very close attention. The best examples are the media coverage that occurred with Milošević's surrender and trial, and the surrender of the KLA leaders such as Haradinaj and Limaj.[83] The media coverage may have directly affected the perception of society with regard to the effectiveness of the ICTY.

There are different approaches with regard to the power of indictments to deter. While the direct effect of indictments is questionable, despite the incapacitation effects, the indictments are considered to have a more lasting indirect effect. The attention following the issuance of indictments and potential surrender of the indictees triggers a stigmatisation effect in society, which sets the foundations for longer-term deterrence and for establishing a culture of fighting impunity. The issuance of indictments has a limited effect on perpetrators or potential perpetrators, but is likely to have a stronger impact on the society at large.

5.4.2. Severity of the Sentences Imposed: A Failed Test for the ICTY

One of the principles of modern law is that the reduction of crime committed in connection to the punishment is dependent on the punishment's certainty, severity and celerity.[84] The more applicable such characteristics are the greater are the chances for deterrence. Of the factors, "crimes are

---

[81] Ellen Knickmeyer, "Mass Graves Appear Endless in Kosovo. War Crimes Inspectors Move From Site to Site Gathering Evidence and Tallying Tales of Death", in *Indianapolis Star*, 23 June 1999.

[82] Interview with CSO representative, Prishtina, May 2016.

[83] Media coverage, and newspaper articles, and some of trials were live streamed.

[84] Robert Apel, "Sanctions, Perceptions, and Crime: Implications for Criminal Deterrence", in *Journal of Quantitative Criminology*, 2013, vol. 29, no. 1, pp. 782–87; Greg Pogarsky, "Deterrence and Decision Making: Research Questions and Theoretical Refinements", in Marvin D. Krohn, Alan J. Lizotte and Gina Penly Hall (eds.), *Handbook on Crime and Deviance*, Springer, New York, 2009, pp. 241–58.

more effectively prevented by the certainty than the severity of punishment".[85]

Akhavan and Baroni argue that for a court to have a deterrent effect, it is not necessary to punish a large number of people, with Baroni suggesting some correlation between deterrence and the number of prosecutions; namely, that if the number of prosecutions is small compared to the number of the perpetrators, the chances for effective deterrence are low.[86] Others have argued that the right punishment of the right individuals can become an instrument to instil the idea of deterrence into the popular consciousness.[87] Either way, according to the respondents of this study, the ICTY is considered to have failed in rendering sufficient decisions, both in quantitative terms given that it has only prosecuted relatively few individuals, and in qualitative terms in that it has rendered less severe sentences. In total the ICTY has indicted 161 people, of whom 83 have been sentenced,[88] which is roughly half the accused. The sentences vary from life sentences towards sentences of 30–40 years of imprisonment with a majority of sentences have been less than 30 years, including sentences as short as two years of imprisonment.[89]

In the specific situation of Kosovo as the main focus of this chapter, there were approximately 17 locations investigated for the crimes that took place. Of the crimes committed in Kosovo, there were indictments filed against 15 people, divided into six Kosovo Albanians and nine Serbian leaders. The indictees included high-ranking people such as the former Serbian president Slobodan Milošević, Milan Milutinović (former president of Serbia), Nikola Šainović (deputy prime minister of Serbia), and Ramush Haradinaj (former prime minister of Kosovo). Of the 15 indictments, six of the Kosovo Albanian indictees and one of the Serbian indictees were acquitted. The case of Milošević was terminated due to his death, whereas six of the Serbian political leaders were sentenced, and

---

[85] Cesare Beccaria, "On Crimes and Punishments", in Morris R. Cohen and Felix S. Cohen (eds.), *Readings in Jurisprudence and Legal Philosophy*, Little, Brown, Boston, 1951, pp. 346–49.

[86] Baroni, 2000, see *supra* note 32.

[87] Andenaes, 1966 cited in Akhavan, 2001, see *supra* note 5.

[88] ICTY, Key Figures of the Cases (http://www.ICTY.org/en/cases/key-figures-cases).

[89] ICTY, Judgment List (http://www.ICTY.org/en/cases/judgment-list).

one Albanian sentenced.[90] Fewer than half the indictments concluded in sentences.

According to the respondents, even in those cases that resulted in convictions, the sentences that the Tribunal has rendered are too short and disproportionate in severity to the crimes that have been committed.[91] The sentences imposed by the ICTY are considered symbolic,[92] but in a negative way. The maximum prison sentence rendered for crimes committed in Kosovo is 22 years.[93] It is contended by the respondents that not only has the Tribunal failed to create a practice that would contribute to the deterrence of future crimes, it has instead contributed to creating a culture of impunity.[94] By not imposing the "deserved sentences" and letting perpetrators, namely "known criminals such as Šešelj walk free, the Court has created a very bad example for other criminals".[95] Having spent so much time and effort in a trial such as that of Šešelj, the end results were disappointing for the victims.[96] Similar opinions also come from legal professionals, deeming the sentences rendered by the Court inadequate.[97] In addition, the Tribunal has contributed to creating distrust among the victims who "now resist coming forward and reporting their cases to the courts".[98]

The respondents are not the only ones who maintain that the sentences rendered by the ICTY are not severe enough, even less severe in comparison to the sentences rendered by other international tribunals, such as the ICTR and the SCSL. By and large, ICTR sentences are more severe than ICTY sentences, although this could be due to the fact that the ICTR has handed down more sentences for genocide.[99] The SCSL has also imposed lengthier sentences than the ICTY, varying from 15 to 52

---

[90] ICTY, Interactive Map (http://www.icty.org/en/cases/interactive-map).

[91] Focus group discussion with victims, Gjakova and Krusha, April 2016.

[92] Interview with CSO representative, Prishtina, May 2016.

[93] ICTY, *Prosecutor v. Nokola Šainović et al.*, Appeals Chamber, Judgment, IT-05-87/1-A, 23 January 2014 (http://www.legal-tools.org/doc/81ac8c/).

[94] Interviews with CSO representatives and focus groups.

[95] Focus group discussion with victims, Krusha and Drenas, April 2016.

[96] Interview with CSO representative, Prishtina, May 2016.

[97] Interview with local judge and prosecutor, Prishtina, May 2016.

[98] Focus group discussion with victims, Drenas, April 2016.

[99] Mark A. Drumbl and Kenneth S. Gallant, "Sentencing Policies and Practices in the International Criminal Tribunals", in *Federal Sentencing Reporter*, 2002, vol. 15, no. 2, pp. 140–44.

years.[100] Consequently, the sentences rendered by the ICTY are considered to be less effective, since few believe that "would-be war criminals will read the resolutions of the Security Council and stop their grave violations of international humanitarian law [...] be indoctrinated to refrain from further breaches of the law and to support the shared values of the international community if one of [their] co-fighters [...] receive[s] a 15-year prison sentence in The Hague".[101]

As such, ICTY sentences may not be perceived as sufficiently severe to deter. In addition, in the view of the respondents, it is seen as difficult to talk about deterrence when the people who surrounded Milošević and others are today the key political leaders in Serbia. Thus, from the Albanian victims' perspective, there is no deterrent effect when the same people are in power, indicating that the society has not been informed enough to condemn these people. In fact, the opposite is true in that these leaders are massively supported by society.[102] Members of the Serbian community in Kosovo, with regard to the Kosovo political leaders, take a similar view[103] because the societies in Serbia and Kosovo have not seen the political leaders sentenced.[104] As such, respondents believe that the ICTY has failed in its task of assuring deterrence.

5.4.3. Instilling a Culture of Fighting Impunity

Bearing in mind the scale of the impact of the indictments and the sentences imposed, it is rather difficult to say that the Tribunal has contributed to fighting impunity. In the opinion of some of the respondents, in comparing these numbers the Tribunal has instead created the commodity of impunity since the it has not managed to create a culture that involves a threat of punishment.[105] The expectations that the ICTY created for itself

---

[100] In a summary of the four main cases tried by the ICTR, out of nine sentences rendered, one was sentenced to 52 years' imprisonment (*RUF* case), three were sentenced to 50 years (AFRC case; *Charles Taylor* case), two others with 40 and 45 years respectively (*Kamara* and *Kallon* in CDF case and AFRC case), while only three people were sentenced to 15–25 years.

[101] Immi Tallgren, "The Sensibility and Sense of International Criminal Law", in *European Journal of International Law*, 2002, vol. 13, no. 3, pp. 561–64.

[102] Focus group discussion with victims in Krusha, April 2016

[103] Interview with Serbian CSO representative, Prishtina, May 2016.

[104] Interview with CSO representative, Prishtina, April 2016.

[105] Interview with CSO representative, Prishtina, May 2016.

do not seem to have been met. However, its work in indicting high-level people, though not meeting expectations, should not go unrecognised. The importance and the effect of the Tribunal is noted in the fact that "at least there is a body that is mandated with trying people for the massive violations of the human rights that have taken place in former Yugoslavia".[106] The respondents believe that "if the Tribunal did not exist, the situation would have been worse, as the perpetrators would not be sentenced by anyone",[107] since there "would not be any other court or body that would try these cases".[108] So in a way the existence and the work of the Tribunal have "undermined the idea that the high political leaders are immune to prosecution".[109]

The effect of the ICTY as an entity known to exist for trying war crimes is based on the fact that the Tribunal has indicted some of the key political leaders in both Serbia and Kosovo. The main example is the indictment of the former president of Yugoslavia, although the views with regards to Milošević's trial are mixed. As a former head of state, he was the highest-ranking state official indicted by a war crimes tribunal since Nuremberg.[110] Thus, the expectation was that the indictment would potentially affect the decisions to "end impunity and instill accountability on political leaders, for the decades to come".[111] At that time, the prosecution of Milošević was considered "as the litmus test for the ICTY",[112] and the expectations were very high. Milošević was never sentenced for any of his actions due to the lengthy trial and his sudden death, which resulted in the termination of the case.[113] Consequently, the ICTY never accomplished its goal of holding Milošević individually accountable, though it created the perception that no one is untouchable.

---

[106] View supported by the majority of the respondents.

[107] Interview with victims/witness, Krusha, April 2016.

[108] Interview with CSO representative, Prishtina, April 2016.

[109] Interview with judge, Prishtina, April 2016.

[110] William Miller, "Slobodan Milosevic's Prosecution by the International Criminal Tribunal for the Former Yugoslavia: A Harbinger of Things to Come for International Criminal Justice", in *Loyola of Los Angeles International and Comparative Law Review*, 2000, vol. 22, no. 4, pp. 553–62.

[111] "Why Milosevic Matters", in *Newsweek*, 7 March 2001.

[112] Sophia Piliouras, "International Criminal Tribunal for the Former Yugoslavia and Milosevic's Trial", in *New York Law School Journal of Human Rights*, 2002, vol. 18, pp. 515–19.

[113] According to recent information, the death of Milošević was a result of self-intoxication.

While segments of the ICTY's work in achieving deterrence may not have lived up to the expectations of the citizens, its impact cannot be denied. The role of the ICTY in the development of international criminal adjudication must be acknowledged.[114] A major impact of the ICTY jointly with the ICTR can be seen in introducing criminal accountability into the culture of international relations, helping to marginalise certain political leaders and other forces aligned with war and genocide, and discouraging vengeance by victims' groups.[115]

Despite the views of commentators on the ICTY's effect on a culture of accountability, there is division among the Kosovar respondents regarding the ability of the Tribunal to instil the idea of fighting impunity. When respondents look at the end results, namely sentencing, there is an opinion that the Tribunal has not contributed to fighting impunity. Instead, the view is that the Tribunal has created the commodity of impunity, since it has not managed to create the idea and the threat of punishment.[116] On the other hand, respondents recognise that the Tribunal has contributed to instilling at least "an idea of fighting impunity" since, if it had not existed, there would be no trials at all. Therefore, despite the flaws that the Tribunal has had, particularly in rendering decisions and sentencing people, respondents generally feel that its existence and the indictments have instilled an idea that justice needs to be put in place regardless of who the people are that have committed the actions complained of. If nothing else, the Tribunal has created the idea that no one is 'untouchable', by means of being indicted. If there had been no Tribunal, it is unlikely that any local court would have ever tried the high political and military leaders.[117] Therefore, the effect of the ICTY can also be seen in invoking the prosecutions in the national level in Kosovo and in Serbia.

5.5. Setting the Course for Future Long-Term Deterrence

There is little praise among the interviewees for the ICTY's work in terms of short-term deterrence since evidence shows that the Tribunal neither managed to end criminal actions nor contributed through its sentences to deterrence. This is attested to by the fact that the majority of the political

---

[114] Simonovic, 1999, p. 441, see *supra* note 9.

[115] Akhavan, 2001, see *supra* note 5.

[116] Interview with CSO representative, Prishtina, May 2016.

[117] Interviews with members of CSOs.

and military leaders who are viewed as responsible for atrocities still enjoy support and remain in power. However, in order to evaluate the full potential of the ICTY to promote deterrence, one must also look at additional components that create the preconditions for deterrence in the longer term, such as the impact of the Tribunal in the adoption of legal norms enabling future deterrence and in establishing a credible historical record which contribute to the change in mentality.

5.5.1. Domestication of Legal Norms Enabling Future Deterrence

One of the longer-term effects that the Tribunal is affiliated with is instilling humanitarian norms and respect for individual rights and incorporating norms of international humanitarian law into domestic legal systems so that the need for external punishment will be obsolete.[118] Internalisation of norms and creation of self-regulating communities have been seen to be among the long-term and transformative processes as a component of the deterrence by an international tribunal.[119] The expression of social disapproval through the legal process may influence moral self-conceptions so that "illegal actions will not present themselves consciously as real alternatives to conformity, even in situations where the potential criminal would run no risk whatsoever of being caught".[120]

The work of the ICTY and its impact can be seen from a different perspective; its role in promoting the "rule of law",[121] in the form of contributing to building trust among the population and confidence in state institutions.[122] The increased national prestige associated with accountability and the stigma attached to the failure to prosecute international crimes have also encouraged third-party states to use their courts to assert universal jurisdiction over accused war criminals. Several states have prosecuted Yugoslav or Rwandese perpetrators, even when no interna-

---

[118] Levitt, 2001, p. 1967, see *supra* note 36; Jean Hampton, "The Moral Education Theory of Punishment", in *Philosophy and Public Affairs*, 1984, vol. 13, no. 3, pp. 208–38.

[119] Buitelaar, 2015, see *supra* note 34.

[120] Andenaes, 1997, p. 323, see *supra* note 35.

[121] Minna Schrag, "The Yugoslav Crimes Tribunal: A Prosecutor's View", in *Duke Journal of Comparative and International Law*, 1995, vol. 6, no. 1, p. 187; ICTY, *Prosecutor v. Dražen Erdemović*, Trial Chamber, Sentencing Judgment, IT-96-22-T, 29 November 1996, para. 27 (http://www.legal-tools.org/doc/eb5c9d/).

[122] ICTY, Sixth Annual Report, see *supra* note 54.

tional indictments had been issued.[123] The ICTY is considered to have facilitated the need for and the conduct of such national trials. By trying the highest leaders, the Tribunal has allowed for the trial of the mid- and lower-level perpetrators.[124] The Tribunal, despite the mixed views about its work, is considered to have had some positive effect in triggering national courts into following the trials of the ICTY. While the ICTY has tried some of the key leaders, and failed to try others due to its inability to connect them to the crimes because of insufficient evidence, it is easier for the local courts to try these mid- or lower-level perpetrators. In practice, this can be seen in the establishment of the Special Chamber for War Crimes in Serbia, and in Kosovo in trials that were carried out under the international presence. Initially the UNMIK administration, then the EU Rule of Law mission, were charged with dealing with war crimes. Such courts can take their lead from the ICTY and try the lower-level accused. Despite the fact that some of the trials conducted in Serbia have been followed by a lot of criticism and at times have been perceived as fraudulent,[125] the fact that such trials have been initiated at all shows the effect of the ICTY.

Robert Sloane has argued that one of the most effective ways for international criminal tribunals to deter is by encouraging the growth of national institutions, laws and national norms, the so-called Benthamite model.[126] When talking about the international criminal tribunals, he emphasises:

> Their efficacy depends more on their ability to contribute to the growth and development of national laws, ethical norms, and institutions, as well as to encourage and, at times, compel national criminal justice systems genuinely to investigate and prosecute. For this reason, the expressive value of ICL sentences, the extent to which they convey, reinforce, and encourage the growth of national legal and moral norms that conform to ICL, matters more than the relative severity of the punishment in any individual case.[127]

---

[123] Akhavan, 2001, see *supra* note 5.

[124] Interview with CSO representative, Prishtina, April 2016.

[125] Interview with CSO representatives, Prishtina, April 2016.

[126] Sloane, 2006, p. 44, see *supra* note 74.

[127] *Ibid.*

In general, "the most effective form of law-enforcement is not the imposi-tion of external sanction, but the inculcation of internal obedience".[128] Criminal law also deters by its long-term role in shaping, strengthening and inculcating values, which encourages the development of habitual, in-ternal restraints.[129] Criminal law can also contribute to the prevention of atrocities by focusing on the long-term, transformative process that can lead to the internalisation of norms and the creation of self-regulating communities.[130] In Kosovo, this may have been the biggest contribution that the ICTY has made to a longer-term deterrent effect. When looking at the legal drafting process in Kosovo in the aftermath of independence, one can see that the country has adopted the majority of the international norms of criminal justice that are enshrined in international conventions. In particular Kosovo has borrowed and adopted practices and norms from the statute of the ICTY itself. Such norms have been also been adopted when drafting the Criminal Code and Criminal Procedure Code.[131] In var-ious national trials, direct reference has been made to the jurisprudence of the ICTY, mainly by defence lawyers or international judges,[132] leading to a new approach of relying on the reasoning and sentencing as established by the ICTY as a guiding tool for the national trials.[133] Thus, legal deter-rence affecting national trials and domestication of international norms may be the strongest suit of the ICTY yet.

5.5.2. Establishing an Historical Record

Part of the justification for the establishment of the ICTY was that through its work it would be able to establish a reliable historical record that would serve future generations in avoiding dangerous misinterpreta-tions and myths.[134] There are arguments that the work of the ICTY in es-

---

[128] Harold Hongju Koh, "How Is International Human Rights Law Enforced?", in *Indiana Law Journal,* 1993, vol. 74, no. 4, pp. 1397–1401.

[129] Kent Greenawalt, "Punishment", in *Journal of Criminal Law and Criminology*, 1983, vol. 74, no. 2, pp. 343–46.

[130] Buitelaar, 2015, see *supra* note 34.

[131] Interview with professor of law, member of the Criminal Code drafting team, Prishtina, October 2015.

[132] As elaborated in the context section, the Kosovo justice system has been assisted by the international community including executive powers, such as trials and prosecution.

[133] Interview with defendant lawyer, Prishtina, October 2015.

[134] Goldstone, 1997, cited in Simonovic, 1999, see *supra* note 9.

---

tablishing history and fact-finding is crucial in building a society that opposes the commission of such crimes and recognises the accountability of those responsible. In principle, ICTY jurisprudence may have contributed to writing history, and setting out uncontested facts that these crimes took place and that the people responsible needed to be brought to justice. In the *Tadić* case, the first prosecuted, the Tribunal wrote an authoritative account of the origins of the conflict in the Balkans, proving that the ICTY has left a qualitatively distinctive historical record.

There was also general agreement among the interviewees that one of the key components of the Tribunal's success can be seen in its work in writing the legal history for the Balkans. The Tribunal has left a written legacy of the history of the massive violations that have taken place in Kosovo and in the region. Throughout its judgments, through the testimony of witnesses and its verdicts, the Tribunal has certified an uncontested history of mass violations. The decisions of the Tribunal and its transcripts can serve as a basis for a future deterrent effect. Such is the case of Milošević where, despite not having a final verdict, the evidence gathered by the prosecution contributed to documenting the crimes he was charged with.[135]

The issue with these records is that there is not a bigger audience that would actually read them. They will be read by professionals, researchers and academics,[136] "but the possibility of any politicians or military leaders reading these files is rather low".[137] This also raises the question whether this information will ever be read by the general society since the Tribunal has failed to reach society,[138] which is one of the most criticised aspects regarding its work.

5.6.   The Tribunal's Failures: Negative Effects in Deterrence

The Tribunal's efforts in deterring future crimes are met with a twofold approach. While the Tribunal in its entirety is not perceived as a deterrent,

---

[135]   Milošević Indictment, see *supra* note 47; ICTY, *Prosecutor v. Slobodan Milošević*, First Amended Indictment, IT-02-54, 29 June 2001 (http://www.legal-tools.org/doc/b11cad/); CTY, *Prosecutor v. Slobodan Milošević*, 2nd Amended Indictment, IT-02-54, 16 October 2001 (http://www.legal-tools.org/doc/5a7da2/).

[136]   Interview with a judge, Prishtina, April 2016; interview with CSO representatives, Prishtina, April 2016.

[137]   Interview with CSO representatives, Prishtina, May 2016.

[138]   Interview with CSO representatives, Prishtina, April 2016.

there are elements to it, which have contributed to the deterrence of future crimes in the Balkans. Nevertheless, there are criticisms around some aspects of the work of the Tribunal that may serve as lessons learned for future courts and tribunals on how to increase their contribution to deterrence. The criticism of the ICTY revolves around the deficiencies in the outreach program and the flaws in legitimacy of the Tribunal due to it being perceived as political body, both of which are elements that have contributed to its failure to change the mentality on deterrence.

5.6.1. The Outreach Programme: A Major Flaw

The work of a court or tribunal needs to reach directly the ordinary citizens of the region who are the ultimate peacebuilders.[139] This requires a credible and authoritative communication of the work of the Tribunal to a wide audience in order to increase awareness of how the threatened sentences contributes to a deterrent effect. However, the ability of international courts to do so, for objective reasons such as distance from the place of the commission of the crimes and communication in the local language, has been limited.[140]

Not many people in Kosovo know what happened in the Tribunal, for what reason people were indicted and tried, and why they were received as heroes in their home countries when they were set free.[141] For many, the high level of resistance by society does not come as a surprise since, in their view, the ICTY has not done proper work in countering perceptions with facts. In the view of CSO representatives, "no one has made an effort to talk about the actual numbers and the fact that someone is responsible for the deaths of those people".[142] There is resistance on both sides towards the ICTY based on different facts; in Kosovo due to the Tribunal's attempts to balance the indictments and trials[143] and in Serbia based on the perceived imbalance.[144]

The main criticism and one of the biggest flaws is its failure to reach the people. As one of the civil society representatives argued,

---

[139] Baroni, 2000, see *supra* note 32.
[140] Sloane, 2006, see *supra* note 74.
[141] Focus group discussion with witness, Krushe, April 2016.
[142] Interview with Serbian CSO representatives, Prishtina, May 2016.
[143] Focus group discussion with victims, Krushe, April 2016.
[144] Interview with Serbian CSO representatives, Prishtina, May 2016.

"whatever has happened in the Court has remained in the Court".[145] The Court has failed to reach out to citizens to inform them about why these accused are being tried and what for are they being tried,[146] hence the reason why there is so much confusion as to what the Tribunal is actually trying to accomplish.

5.6.2. Legitimacy of the Tribunal for Achieving a Deterrent Effect

The ability of a court to deter crimes is dependent on it being perceived as legitimate, which includes proving that it is not subject to political influence, but rather is fair and unbiased. Only then can it earn the trust and respect of society at large.[147] Such discussion falls within the larger peace and justice debate, but also influences whether the ICTY will have a long-term deterrent effect. The respondents' view towards the ICTY is based on allegations that it is a politicised institution that followed the directions of its political supporters and only intervened when instructed, resulting in particular leaders being spared by the Tribunal. The political stamp is seen in its creation since the Tribunal was established due to the existence of a critical mass of political will, and many of the interviewees thought its performance produced political effects. What is more concerning is that commentators and respondents regard the ICTY as an institution that relies on the political support of the states concerned and the Security Council to perform its tasks. Thus its independence and impartiality are compromised when there are political choices in selecting which cases to prosecute as part of the political reality of the situation.[148] This study has found that this is precisely the point where the ICTY has failed to prove itself. Some of the respondents believe that the indictments were used as a form of political bargaining:

> The Tribunal used the indictments for political gains, by sending messages to people that they too can be indicted and by forcing them to comply with certain requests, whereas if they co-operate and share they can even be acquitted.[149]

---

[145] Interview with CSO representatives, Prishtina, April 2016.

[146] Interview with CSO representatives, Prishtina, May 2016.

[147] Louise Arbour, "Progress and Challenges in International Criminal Justice", in *Fordham International Law Journal*, 1997, vol. 21, no. 2, pp. 531–36.

[148] Simonovic, 1999, p. 446, see *supra* note 9.

[149] Interview with CSO representative, Prishtina, May 2016.

To those respondents, this shows that the Tribunal itself was built as a political institution aimed at restoring peace rather than contributing to justice and putting perpetrators behind bars.[150]

The main example is the indictment of Milošević,[151] which was completed 50 days after the conflict between NATO and the Federal Republic of Yugoslavia had erupted and a peaceful settlement was no longer an option, since if filed earlier the indictment would have been considered an impediment to negotiations and harmful for the prospect of peace talks.[152] Later, it was used to pressure him and maintain public support for the NATO bombing.[153] At that time Milošević had only been indicted for crimes committed in Kosovo from January to May 1999, including several crimes against humanity, including the killing of unarmed civilians and the deportation of 800,000 Kosovo Albanians.[154]

To further see the political implications, one cannot avoid the fact that the decision to send Milošević to the ICTY was made one day before an international donors' conference in Brussels was called to raise over $1.25 billion in aid to rebuild the Federal Republic of Yugoslavia and that, prior to attending the conference, the United States stated that it would attend the conference on the condition that Belgrade co-operated with the

---

[150] Interview with CSO representative, Prishtina, May 2016.

[151] Slobodan Milošević was formally indicted by the ICTY on May 24 1999, at the height of the Kosovo crisis, while he was still president of Yugoslavia, on allegations of murder and ethnic cleansing of ethnic Albanians in Kosovo. See Dorothea Beane, "The Yugoslav Tribunal and Deferral of National Prosecutions of War Criminals", in *American Society of International Law Insights*, vol. 1, no. 4, 1996, pp. 1–4.

[152] Andreas Laursen, "Nato, the War over Kosovo, and the ICTY Investigation", in *American University International Law Review*, 2002, vol. 17, no. 4, p. 765; Marlise Simons, "Milosevic to Face Charges Covering Three Wars in Balkans", in *New York Times*, 31 August 2001.

[153] Michael P. Scharf, "Indicted for War Crimes, The What?", in *Washington Post*, 3 October 1999.

[154] Miller, 2000; see *supra* note 110; Milošević was initially charged on 22 May 1999, on four counts: deportation, murder, murder and persecutions. The indictment was first amended on 29 June 2001, and then again on 16 October 2001, see *supra* note 135. These charges, among others, included "planning, instigating, ordering, committing or otherwise aided and abetted in a deliberate and widespread or systematic campaign of terror and violence directed at Kosovo Albanian civilians living in Kosovo in the Federal Republic of Yugoslavia, mass killings of hundred civilians, execution of campaigns of persecution against the Kosovo Albanian civilian population based on political, racial, or religious grounds".

ICTY.[155] The Tribunal has been a stick and carrot for Serbia. The CSO representatives contend that:

> Every time Serbia co-operated with the Tribunal, it appeared
> to be for a political reason and gain and, if there had not been
> these higher political gains, there is doubt about how much
> Serbia actually would have cooperated with the Court.[156]

Similarly, with the leaders of Kosovo, co-operation with the ICTY was insured through various tools of political pressure.[157]

Lack of trust in the Tribunal by the Kosovo Albanians has resulted in a diminution of its effects within society and a misperception of the Tribunal. Whether the Tribunal is seen as trustworthy or not also depends on the side that is being tried. One of the criticisms from both sides is the selective justice of the ICTY. Such selectivity is recognised and justified by the prosecutor for objective reasons. While in many civil law jurisdictions, all crimes are prosecuted where evidence permits, in the ICTY, the prosecutors were more selective before committing resources to investigate or prosecute, due to the difficult nature of the charges.[158] For these reasons, some commentators contend that the Tribunal often decided that the cases must be representative in terms of nationality of the victim and the perpetrator which, in the view of scholars as well as of the respondents, ought not to mean that the prosecutor should equally distribute the indictments among the national groups in the conflict.[159] In the Serbia-Kosovo conflict, the perceived attempt of the prosecutor to balance the victims with the perpetrators has damaged the credibility of the Tribunal.[160] In their view, the decision of the prosecutor on the selection of cases should be based on evidence and not some notion of moral equivalence among the parties;[161] bearing in mind that during the time when these crimes were committed, there was no such notion of equivalence, rather

---

[155] Bruce Zagaris, "Milosevic Turned Over to the ICC", in *International Enforcement Law Reporter*, 2001, vol. 17, no. 8.

[156] Interview with CSO representative, Prishtina, May 2016.

[157] Kosovo adopted a law on the co-operation with the ICTY in December 2013. The most recent Stabilization and Association Agreement between the EU and Kosovo contains a provision that ensures that Kosovo will co-operate with ICTY and the ICC.

[158] Arbour, 1997, see *supra* note 147.

[159] Simonovic, 1999, see *supra* note 9.

[160] Focus group discussion with victims, Krusha, April 2016.

[161] Shraga, 2005, see *supra* note 11.

one party was the perpetrator and the other the victim.[162] This is known as *juridical othering*, where the perpetrators claim that the perpetrators are from another group and use various devices to maintain plausible deniability.[163] Such reasoning is supported by the fact that the current government in Serbia continues to deny the crimes were committed and refuses to apologise for any actions.[164]

Respondents contend that one of the failures of deterrence is shown in the behaviour in the political arena. Most people who were part of the political elite at the time of the Milošević regime are today in Serbia's leadership, while the same is contended by the Serbian community in Kosovo with regard to the political leadership in Kosovo.[165] In an article published in May 2016, Robert Fisk highlights the irony of the current Serbian prime minister leading the nation towards EU integration, while the same being the person who once said "for every Serb killed, we will kill 100 Muslims".[166]

The importance of the context and the side that is being tried is seen from the responses of the Serbian community, who feel that "Kosovo is a really good example that the ICTY has not managed to end this practice of impunity".[167] They argue that, while the Serbian leaders have been tried by the ICTY, none of the Kosovo KLA leaders have been sentenced by the ICTY.

The fact that people in Serbia and Kosovo did not believe in the Tribunal and its legitimacy affects the possible impact of the ICTY. In Serbia people viewed it as a political body solely targeting its leaders, while in Kosovo the targeting of the leaders was considered unfair and unjust due to it being the defending side. Thus this conceptualisation of the

---

[162] Focus group discussion with victims, Krusha, April 2016.

[163] Ruth Jamieson and Kieran McEvoy, "State Crime by Proxy and Juridical Othering", in *British Journal of Criminology*, 2005, vol. 45, no. 4, pp. 504–27; Dawn L. Rothe and Christopher W. Mullins, "Beyond the Juristic Orientation of International Criminal Justice", in *International Criminal Law Review*, 2010, vol. 10, no. 1, pp. 97–110.

[164] Although the Serbian government has made an apology for the crimes committed in Srebrenica, the prime minister Aleksander Vučić had urged Russia to block a UN resolution that would have condemned the Srebrenica massacre as genocide. Robert Fisk, "Europe Has a Troublingly Short Memory over Serbia's Aleksander Vucic", in *The Independent*, 14 May 2016.

[165] Interview with Serb CSO representative, Prishtina, May 2016.

[166] Fisk, 2016, see *supra* note 164.

[167] Interview with Serb CSO representative, Prishtina, May 2016.

Tribunal has had a major impact in its perception and acceptance. Where the Tribunal itself was not accepted, it is difficult for its decisions to make a huge impact on the deterrence of the future crimes.[168]

5.6.3. Failure to Create a Mentality That Would Enable Deterrence

One of the main questions of the research is to see whether there is a perception that the ICTY has managed to contribute to deterrence through a change in societal mentality. Most of the respondents believe that there is no in-depth change. While there has been progress in terms of changes, which mostly relate to political interests of affiliation with the European Union and benefits of the European perspective, most believe that if this were to change, the same crimes would take place again.[169] The victims in particular fear that "they are not sure that similar crimes will not occur in the future".[170] There is a high level of ethnic tension that is still present.[171] Where "all the same people who were in power during the war times are in power nowadays, and the same military leaders are in power today",[172] this shows that change is yet to happen in the mentality of the society. According to the respondents, "the same individuals have gone through metamorphoses and are leading the main processes now both in the Serbian leadership and in Kosovo".[173]

When looking at the deterrence of future crimes, there are several elements the respondents point out. First and foremost, regardless of the work the ICTY has done, the victims contend that "the criminals are still walking free",[174] since the majority of mid- and low-level perpetrators were not indicted, and of the ones prosecuted, the majority were not sentenced. Thus, for the victims the feeling is that the Tribunal has not had a deterrent effect with regard to alleged but unindicted perpetrators since, if the circumstances were to change, the majority of them agree they fear that the "same crimes would occur again".[175] The same view is also shared by legal offi-

---

[168] Interview with CSO representative, Prishtina, May 2016.
[169] View expressed by the majority of the responders.
[170] Focus group discussion with victims, Krusha, April 2016.
[171] Interview with a judge, Prishtina, April 2016.
[172] Interviews with CSO representatives, Prishtina, April–May 2016.
[173] Interview with Serbian CSO representative, Prishtina, May 2016.
[174] Focus group discussion with victims, Drenas, April 2016.
[175] Focus group discussion with victims, Krusha, April 2016.

cials: "If there would be conflict again in the future, the same violations would manifest again due to the longstanding hostility".[176]

The lack of the change of mentality can be objectively observed in the declarations that have been made recently by high-standing leaders of Serbia such as Vojislav Šešelj who, upon his return to Serbia, stated: "The Hague Tribunal is the wounded beast of globalisation, which destroyed the lives of Serbian leaders, army and police commanders. Our honourable generals just defended Serbia".[177] Similarly, a declaration by the head of the Academy of Sciences, that the new reality with regards to Kosovo must be accepted, spurred immediate negative reactions from all the political leaders in Serbia.[178] There is also a tendency of increased nationalism, both in Serbia and also in Kosovo.[179]

Recently, the media spread propagandistic information that Milošević had been "exonerated" by ICTY in the decision rendered on the case of Radovan Karadžić. The 'news' that ICTY "had quietly cleared Milošević of responsibility for war crimes" spread quickly.[180] Such propagandistic efforts were immediately contradicted by many. As Gordana Knezević elaborates in detail, such allegations were not grounded and the ICTY confirmed that the Appeal Chamber did not make any determination of guilt with regards to Milošević.[181] What is more concerning, though, are the declarations by some Serbian officials such as the foreign minister Ivica Dačić and labour minister Aleksandar Vulin in response to the propaganda. They include: "We all knew that Milošević was not guilty. He should get a street [named after him] and a monument in Belgrade".

---

[176] Interview with a judge, Prishtina, April 2016.

[177] Milka Domanovic, "Seselj Revives the Rhetoric of the 1990s", in *Balkan Insight*, 13 Novemver 2014.

[178] *Balkan Insight* reports that the Serbian Academy of Sciences and Art ('SANU') chief Vladimir Kostić made a statement that that Kosovo "is not in Serbia's hands anymore either de facto or de jure", adding that someone should openly say that to the people. Shortly after, several senior Serbian officials, including President Tomislav Nikolić and Prime Minister Aleksandar Vučić, called on SANU to react.

[179] Interview with CSO representative, Prishtina, April 2016.

[180] Neil Clark, "Milosevic Exonerated, as the NATO War Machine Moves On", in *RT News*, 2 August 2016; Inserbia, "ICTY Exonerates Slobodan Milosevic for War Crimes", in *Global Research*, 3 August 2016.

[181] Gordana Knezević, "Milosevic 'Exonerated'? War-Crime Deniers Feed Receptive Audience", in *Radio Free Europe*, 9 August 2016.

These declarations were believed to be trying to whitewash Serbia's war-time past.[182]

From the perspective of Kosovo society, the main test of whether the ICTY has managed to contribute to the creation of a mentality that would enable deterrence is whether the Tribunal has managed to raise awareness among the society as to why the leaders are being tried. For Kosovo Albanian society, but similarly from the perspective of the Kosovo Serbian people, the biggest problem is that the society has no clear understanding of why specific individuals were tried. According to CSO representatives, "due to the weak outreach, the Court could not counter the narrative spread by the politicians – who continue to portray themselves as victims".[183] As the judges and legal practitioners pointed out, the "citizens are still unable to tell the difference between war crimes and frontal war".[184] This stance is taken a step further by the CSO representatives who contend that "there is unwillingness to even have that discussion, as to what party did what".[185]

Although seen as a normal transition, Kosovo society refuses to believe that there are people within the KLA that may have committed war crimes. There is a belief in the society that if a person is being tried for a war crime, they are tried for the "pure war to protect the land and the family", since the Tribunal, whether in the judgments or through the outreach programme, has failed to clarify to normal people that if a person is being tried for war crimes, they are not being tried for frontal war but rather for actions against civilians. Some of the respondents understand and advocate for such clarification, a debate that has yet to take place in Kosovo, while the rest, mainly the victims, are as yet far from understanding that. In a survey conducted by United Nations Development Programme in Kosovo, when asked if they think that members of their community have committed crimes, "the overwhelming majority of the respondents from all the communities in Kosovo do not consider that members of their

---

[182] Sasa Dragojo, "Milosevic's Old Allies Celebrate His 'Innocence'", in *Balkan Insight*, 16 August 2016.

[183] Interview with CSO representative, Prishtina, April 2016.

[184] Interview with a judge, Prishtina, April 2016.

[185] Interview with CSO representative, Prishtina, May 2016.

community have committed crimes".[186] This shows that there is yet a lot of work to be done in terms of a mentality shift.

5.7. Conclusion and Recommendations

From the arguments presented above, one may easily infer that there is no one single conclusion that can be drawn with regard to the deterrence effect of the ICTY in Kosovo. When looking at the work of the ICTY as a whole, there are different views from different people. Thus, one must look into components or segments of the Tribunal's work and evaluate their potential for effecting deterrence. In addition, deterrence can take many forms. It is important to evaluate the deterrent effect over stages because particular segments of the work of the Tribunal have influenced one type of deterrent effect but not another.

It is uncontested that the ICTY has not had any immediate effect in terms of bringing an end to massive violations. The ICTY was established and began its work in 1993, whereas the greatest human rights violations in Bosnia and Kosovo took place in the years following its establishment. The main reason for the failure of the Tribunal to end massive violations and effectuate immediate deterrence relates to the fact that deterrence is dependent on two elements: first, that there be an actual threat of punishment; and second, that the perpetrators understand that and perceive the threat as greater than the benefit of their crimes. In times of conflict, such a cost-benefit analysis is not even taken into consideration, let alone in conditions such as the ones related to the ICTY when the threat of punishment was not a realistic one. Many consider it is unrealistic to hope that any tribunal can effectuate an immediate prevention of violations. Bearing that in mind, one must look into whether the ICTY has managed to create the idea of the threat of punishments in the course of its work, which lasted more than two decades.

The ICTY has failed in its primary test, that of rendering decisions and imposing sentences that would fulfil the criteria of certainty, severity and celerity. From the subjective perspective of the interviewees, the Tribunal has not fulfilled its main mission of putting the perpetrators behind bars. Even evaluating the work of the Tribunal objectively, the sentences handed down seem less severe compared to other international tribunals. Thus it is difficult to consider the effect of the Tribunal by virtue of sen-

---

[186] United Nations Development Programme, 2012, p. 7, see *supra* note 62.

tences in effectuating specific deterrence. The sentencing policy and the jurisprudence of the ICTY are not considered to have imposed a direct threat to perpetrators such that there is a threat of punishment if similar actions were to be committed in the future.

While the sentences are not considered satisfactory or capable of deterrence, one cannot disregard entirely the effect of the indictments, even their short-term effect. This can be seen in the first instance in the capability of removing people from office and the stigmatisation effects. The main criticism regarding the Tribunal is that its indictments did not result in prison sentences. Nevertheless, the indictments themselves have contributed to creating a culture of fighting impunity. By indicting the highest political leaders in Serbia and Kosovo, the Tribunal has contributed to establishing the idea that no one is untouchable, thus shifting from a commodity of impunity. However, the criticism in relation to the Tribunal is that, regardless of the fact that it has indicted the highest leaders, they were not punished, thus creating an attempt to establish a fight against impunity in theory but not in practice. Moreover, there is the perception that the Tribunal is politicised and used the indictments as a political tool, thus affecting the legitimacy of the Tribunal as whole.

On the other hand, there are aspects of the Tribunal's work which, in addition to the indictments, are considered to have indirectly influenced long-term deterrence. One of the uncontested contributions is the work of the Tribunal in writing history and documenting all the violations that have taken place. In addition, the work of the Tribunal has had an effect in triggering trials at the national level and also domesticating legal norms of criminal justice, thus creating preconditions for long-term deterrence.

While there are positive effects of the ICTY as indicated above, there is also a lot of criticism of it. From the Kosovo perspective, one of the key deficiencies explaining why the Tribunal is considered to have failed in fulfilling its deterrence mission, in addition to not meting out what is perceived to be the right punishments, is the failure to explain to the wider society why the accused were tried and what they were sentenced for. As elaborated throughout the chapter, when analysing the deterrent effect of the ICTY in Kosovo, due regard must be paid to the ethnic context since both Albanians and Serbs only perceive the Tribunal as successful when members of the other community are tried, and not when members of their own community have been tried. The Tribunal has failed to send a clear message to society as to why certain individuals were tried and has not managed to create a separation of war crimes from war between combatants.

As long as there is still no clear difference between the two terms in society at large, and there is a perception that the Tribunal has failed to sentence the major perpetrators, one can only say that the ICTY has contributed to the creation of the idea of fighting impunity in theory, but has not created an actual practical impact in practice – a realistic perceived threat that international justice works. Bearing that in mind, it is questionable whether the ICTY has laid the groundwork and precedent for the ICC to be able to deter future crimes in the countries within its jurisdiction and beyond.

Based on the arguments presented in this chapter, there are several recommendations for international criminal institutions and the international community:

- The international community must establish more timely and efficient reactive mechanisms, and trials should take place immediately after the end of conflict since they lose effectiveness as time passes;

- Long trials are an impediment to deterrence and international bodies should conduct more timely and efficient trials, having due regard to proper administration of justice and the right to fair trial;

- International courts and tribunals should refrain from using indictments as political tools, thus preserving their legitimacy as independent and impartial bodies;

- International courts and tribunals should attempt to establish a sentencing policy to ensure severity and certainty of punishment; and

- All international courts and tribunals must ensure transparency and have strong outreach programmes that reach the ordinary people in different societies and contexts.

6

Can an International Criminal Tribunal with a Limited Mandate Deter Atrocities? Lessons from the Special Court for Sierra Leone

Eleanor Thompson[*]

6.1. Introduction

Drawing inspiration from the Preamble of the Rome Statute of the International Criminal Court ('ICC'), officials of the ICC and members of civil society have identified deterrence of grave crimes as among the Court's overarching goals.[1] Language on deterrence, the criminal law theory that the prosecution of crimes helps to prevent their further commission, both specifically by the individual who committed them as well as generally by others who are dissuaded from doing so by the threat of prosecution, has featured prominently in their public statements.[2] This rhetoric from ICC officials was largely lacking with their counterparts in the preceding international criminal tribunals and, in particular, the Special Court for Sierra Leone ('SCSL'), save for references to deterrence in the sentencing

---

[*] **Eleanor D. Thompson** is an attorney and policy advocate, currently focusing on national and regional mechanisms for human rights protection and accountability for grave crimes in Africa. In her previous work with the Coalition for the International Criminal Court, the Public International Law and Policy Group and the Open Society Justice Initiative she provided advice on national criminal justice reform and promoting international criminal justice in Africa, or developed civil society strategies for advocacy on these issues. She was also involved in the early outreach activities of the Special Court for Sierra Leone ('SCSL'). Later, as an independent consultant, she developed special legacy projects for the SCSL Registrar to highlight the Court's jurisprudence on gender crimes and crimes involving children. She holds a B.A. in Government and African Studies from Harvard University and a Juris Doctor from American University Washington College of Law. She is a member of the New York State Bar, the District of Columbia Bar and the Sierra Leone Bar.

[1] ICC, Rome Statute of the International Criminal Court, 17 July 1998, in force 1 July 2002, Preamble ('ICC Statute') (http://www.legal-tools.org/doc/7b9af9/).

[2] International Criminal Court ('ICC'), Fatou Bensouda, Prosecutor Elect of the International Criminal Court, Statement, Ceremony for the Solemn Undertaking of the Prosecutor of the International Criminal Court, 15 June 2012.

---

judgments of these courts.[3] There is no explicit reference to deterrence in the preambular language of United Nations ('UN') 2000 Security Council resolution 1315 authorising the establishment of the SCSL, nor in the statute establishing the Court. Nonetheless, some may identify a veiled reference to deterrence in resolution 1315's language on the need for a credible system of justice and accountability in Sierra Leone to end impunity, contribute to national reconciliation, and restore and maintain peace,[4] if it is assumed that peace can only be restored in the absence of the ongoing commission of grave crimes.

Beyond the architects of the Court, the SCSL Office of the Prosecutor also did not regard deterrence as one of its principal goals.[5] Rather, deterrence was taken for granted as being part of any criminal justice system – national or international. The Office of the Prosecutor's main goal and consequently its prosecutorial strategy focused on the narrow mandate given in the SCSL Statute: identifying and prosecuting those who bore the greatest responsibility for serious violations of international humanitarian and Sierra Leonean law committed in Sierra Leone after 30 November 1996.[6] As shown through an assessment of the legacy of the SCSL by Vincent Nmehielle and Charles Jalloh,[7] with this mandate, the Court represented the latest iteration in international criminal justice at the time of its establishment. Evolving from the costly and fully UN-run *ad hoc* tribunals for the former Yugoslavia and Rwanda, the SCSL's 'hybrid' billing held the promise of a more cost-efficient court with a narrow mandate

---

[3] Special Court for Sierra Leone ('SCSL'), *Prosecutor v. Alex Tamba Brima, Brima Bazzy Kamara and Santigie Borbor Kanu*, Trial Chamber, Sentencing Judgment, SCSL-2004-16-T, 19 July 2007, para. 7 ('Brima et al. Sentencing Judgment') (http://www.legal-tools.org/doc/e912c3/); SCSL, *Prosecutor v. Issa Hassan Sesay, Morris Kallon and Augustine Gbao (RUF case)*, Trial Chamber, Judgment, SCSL-04-15-T, 2 March 2009, para. 13 ('RUF Judgment') (http://www.legal-tools.org/doc/7f05b7/); SCSL, *Prosecutor v. Moinina Fofana and Allieu Kondewa*, Appeals Chamber, Judgment, SCSL-2004-14-A-829, 28 May 2008, para. 532 ('Fofana and Kondewa Appeals Judgment') (http://www.legal-tools.org/doc/b31512/).

[4] United Nations Security Council, Special Court for Sierra Leone, Resolution 1315, 14 August 2000, UN doc. S/RES/1315 (http://www.legal-tools.org/doc/95897f/).

[5] Interview with Brenda J. Hollis, Chief Prosecutor of the Special Court for Sierra Leone, Freetown, May 2016.

[6] See also Statute of the Special Court for Sierra Leone, 16 January 2002, Article 1 (http://www.legal-tools.org/doc/aa0e20/); Interview with Hollis, *ibid.*

[7] Vincent Nmehielle and Charles Jalloh, "The Legacy of the Special Court for Sierra Leone", in *Fletcher Forum of World Affairs*, 2006, vol. 30, no. 2, pp. 107–8.

that was intertwined with the local justice system and would deliver a greater sense of justice to victims because of its proximity to them.

Whether the SCSL met that promise is still disputed. Nevertheless, over the course of a decade from 2003 to 2013, the SCSL indicted 13 individuals, tried 10 of them (nine in joint cases),[8] and convicted all nine who survived to the end of trial. The first indictments were issued on 7 March 2003 for: Foday Saybana Sankoh, leader of the Revolutionary United Front ('RUF'), and his fellow RUF commanders, Sam Bockarie, Issa Hassan Sesay and Morris Kallon; Major Johnny Paul Koroma, leader of the Armed Forces Revolutionary Council ('AFRC') and other senior AFRC leaders, Alex Tamba Brima and Brima Bazzy Kamara; the head of the Civil Defence Forces ('CDF'), Samuel Hinga Norman; and then president of Liberia, Charles Ghankay Taylor (indicted under seal). These were followed by the indictment of the RUF's Augustine Gbao on 16 April 2003 and Moinina Fofana and Allieu Kondewa, both of the CDF, on 26 June 2003. The SCSL's final indictment was issued on 23 September 2003 for Santigie Borbor Kanu (also known as 'Five-Five') of the AFRC. Much to the disappointment of the majority of Sierra Leoneans, the RUF's two most senior leaders were never brought to trial. Bockarie was killed in Liberia on 5 May 2003, and Sankoh died in Freetown on 29 July 2003 after having made an initial appearance before the Court. Following confirmation of their deaths, the indictments against the two men were withdrawn later that year. Likewise, in May 2007 the Trial Chamber terminated proceedings against Norman following his death in Senegal on 22 February 2007 while undergoing a medical operation. Koroma is the sole SCSL indictee who remains at large.

The RUF defendants Sesay, Kallon and Gbao were ultimately convicted of war crimes, crimes against humanity and other serious violations of international humanitarian law. The charges included acts of terrorism, collective punishments, murder, rape, sexual slavery, other inhumane acts such as forced marriage, outrages upon human dignity, pillage, planning and the use of children to actively participate in hostilities, enslavement, committing and directing attacks against peacekeepers, and aiding and abetting attacks on peacekeepers.[9] They were sentenced to 52, 40 and 25

---

[8] The trials of individuals from the same 'faction' were consolidated for more efficiency and because the individuals were being prosecuted on the same crime base.

[9] RUF Judgment, paras. 677–87, see *supra* note 3.

years' imprisonment, respectively. Brima, Kamara and Kanu – all of whom were part of a mutiny in the national army that became the AFRC – were convicted of acts of terrorism, collective punishments, extermination, murder, violence to life, health and physical well-being or persons, outrages upon personal dignity, conscripting children under the age of 15 years into an armed group and/or using them to participate actively in hostilities, enslavement, pillage and rape.[10] Brima died on 9 June 2016 while serving his sentence, and Kanu and Kamara are currently serving 50- and 45-year sentences, respectively. The CDF defendants – Fofana and Kondewa – were convicted of violence to life, health and physical or mental well-being of persons, pillage, collective punishments and enlisting children under the age of 15 years into an armed group and/or using them to participate actively in hostilities.[11] They were ultimately sentenced to 15 and 20 years' imprisonment, respectively. Taylor's case was the sole non-joint war crimes trial conducted by the Court. He was given a 50-year sentence after being convicted of planning and aiding and abetting acts of terrorism, murder, violence to life, health and physical or mental well-being of persons, rape, sexual slavery, outrages upon personal dignity, other inhumane acts, conscripting or enlisting children under the age of 15 years into armed forces or groups, or using them to participate actively in hostilities, enslavement and pillage.[12]

Throughout the proceedings, but particularly in the investigation and indictment phases, the Office of the Prosecutor's public statements repeated a steady refrain: that the prosecution's focus was to ensure that those who bore the greatest responsibility for the crimes committed in Sierra Leone were held accountable, and that the Office would follow where the evidence led.[13] This reflected the Office of the Prosecutor's awareness

---

[10] SCSL, *Prosecutor v. Alex Tamba Brima, Brima Bazzy Kamara and Santigie Borbor Kanu*, Trial Chamber, Judgment, SCSL-04-16-T, 20 June 2007, paras. 568–72 (http://www.legal-tools.org/doc/87ef08/).

[11] SCSL, *Prosecutor v. Moinina Fofana and Allieu Kondewa*, Trial Chamber, Judgment, SCSL-2004-14-T, 2 August 2007, paras. 290–92 (http://www.legal-tools.org/doc/025645/).

[12] SCSL, *Prosecutor v. Charles Ghankay Taylor*, Trial Chamber, Judgment, SCSL-03-01-T, 18 May 2012, paras. 2475–78 ('Taylor Judgment') (http://www.legal-tools.org/doc/8075e7/).

[13] SCSL, "Prosecutor for the Special Court Begins Holding 'Town Hall' Meetings", OTP Press Release, 27 September 2002; SCSL, "Special Court Prosecutor Completes Initial Visits to South and East", OTP Press Release, 16 December 2002; SCSL, "Special Court Prosecutor Addresses Seminar Participants; Encourages Perpetrators to Talk to the TRC", OTP Press Release, 27 February 2003; SCSL, "'This is your Court'; Prosecutor Addresses

of a central limitation imposed by the Security Council on the SCSL's personal jurisdiction, which circumscribed the reach of the Court. Deterrence never became an explicit goal of the Office of the Prosecutor, even though the Court's first prosecutor, David Crane, and other Office staff began to make indirect references to it starting in October 2003, particularly during outreach to victims.[14] The absence of deterrence as a prominent goal of the SCSL perhaps reflects the *ex post facto* nature of the Court and the unlikelihood of the reoccurrence of the crimes as the chances of resurgence of armed conflict in Sierra Leone became increasingly remote over time.

Based on a review of literature on deterrence and international criminal tribunals, as well as field research, this chapter seeks to analyse the factors that influenced deterrence in light of the peculiarities of the SCSL (court-based factors) and the country and conflict context (external factors). Although it is premature to conclusively determine whether the SCSL has had a deterrent effect on the commission of atrocity crimes, the chapter draws a preliminary conclusion based on several indicators outlined in section 6.3. It is submitted that the net effect of court-based factors and Sierra Leone-specific factors, such as state co-operation on arrests and custody transfers, prosecutorial strategy on case selection, the severity of punishment, and a robust outreach programme increased the specific, targeted and general deterrent effects of the SCSL.

Section 6.2. of this chapter lays out the conflict in Sierra Leone during which the crimes were committed, as well as the political and legal context in which the SCSL was established. Section 6.3. briefly outlines the methodology applied to this case study, as well as the theoretical basis for the indicators and factors that are applied to the assessment of deterrence in this case. Section 6.4. analyses whether the SCSL had a specific or targeted deterrent effect on the commission of international crimes from the time of the Court's establishment through the various stages of

---

FBC Students", OTP Press Release, 5 May 2003; SCSL, "Chief Prosecutor David Crane Speaks to the Military", OTP Press Release, 7 November 2003; SCSL, "Prosecutor Meets Students at Milton Margai School for the Blind", OTP Press Release, 24 June 2004.

[14] SCSL, "Prosecutor Meets with War Wounded at Grafton Amputee Camp", OTP Press Release, 6 October 2003; SCSL, "Statement by Prosecutor David M. Crane: The Prosecution is Ready for the Trial of Charles Taylor", OTP Press Release, 2 June 2004; SCSL, Opening Statement of David M. Crane in the *RUF case*, 5 July 2004; SCSL, "Statement of the Prosecutor on International Women's Day", OTP Press Release, 8 March 2005; SCSL, OTP Statement Released for Inaugural World Day Against Child Labour, 12 June 2003.

its proceedings. Section 6.5. considers any longer-term and general deterrent effect of the Court, namely whether the SCSL has contributed to peace and stability in Sierra Leone. Section 6.6. presents the conclusions derived from this case study, and makes recommendations for other international criminal tribunals, namely the ICC, on possible means of increasing their deterrent effect.

6.2. The Long Road to Peace and Justice in Sierra Leone

The decade-long armed conflict in Sierra Leone epitomised a long history of state failure and weakened state institutions, brought about by "years of bad governance, endemic corruption and the denial of basic human rights that created the deplorable conditions that made conflict inevitable".[15] To halt this downward spiral and help put the country back on a course towards peace and development, several transitional justice mechanisms were deployed in the aftermath of the conflict. The first was a truth and reconciliation commission ('TRC'). The TRC was premised on an amnesty for all the combatants, which was officially seen as a necessary price in exchange for peace. The second was a special criminal tribunal, which was subsequently tacked on as a retributive measure after the limits of having only the TRC became politically too costly to bear.

6.2.1. The Conflict in Sierra Leone and Initial Attempts at Peace

With the financial and logistical backing of Charles Taylor, the RUF, led by former Sierra Leone Army ('SLA') corporal Foday Sankoh, entered Sierra Leone from Liberia on 23 March 1991 and attacked villages in Kailahun district, thus starting the war. The military's discontent with what it perceived to be inaction by the government against RUF incursions in Sierra Leone precipitated a series of coups d'état beginning just over a year later in April 1992. Even after democratic elections were held in March 1996 and civilian rule was restored, fighting continued in parts of the country. The Abidjan Peace Accords, concluded on 30 November 1996, marked the first time all fighting factions laid down arms and came together to discuss a peaceful settlement. In spite of the parties' agreement to cease hostilities, on 25 May 1997 a different group of SLA soldiers staged another coup to topple the democratically elected government of

---

[15] Sierra Leone Truth and Reconciliation Commission, "Witness to Truth: Report of the Sierra Leone Truth and Reconciliation Commission", Introduction, 2004, para. 11.

President Ahmad Tejan Kabbah. The putschists, led by Major Johnny Paul Koroma, who would later be indicted by the SCSL, formed the AFRC government.

Koroma aided the rebels' slow advance toward the Sierra Leonean capital, Freetown, by inviting the RUF to form a coalition government with the AFRC. This junta epitomised what locals had dubbed "sobels".[16] The Conakry Peace Plan of October 1997 between the Economic Community of West African States ('ECOWAS') and the junta required that the AFRC return the democratically elected government to power by April 1998. When it appeared that the junta was taking no steps to do so, the ECOWAS Monitoring Group ('ECOMOG') intervened militarily on 12 February 1998, rendering the Conakry Peace Plan void. The intervention pushed the rebels out of Freetown to Makeni in the northern region, where they set up their headquarters. There, they were able to regroup and launch another major attack, the notoriously bloody invasion of Freetown on 6 January 1999.[17]

6.2.2. The Lomé Peace Accord and Amnesty

Given that the SLA was by then defunct and its leaders had joined forces with the RUF, ECOMOG troops were the only functional military force opposing the junta. ECOMOG consisted mainly of Nigerian peacekeepers, whose intervention in Sierra Leone had the strong support of then-Nigerian president General Sani Abacha. Thus, when Abacha died suddenly, the Sierra Leone government became concerned about a potential withdrawal of ECOMOG troops from the country, and sought a new round of peace talks with the junta. These talks took place in Lomé, Togo, and culminated in the signing of the Lomé Peace Agreement on 7 July 1999.

The Lomé Agreement granted amnesty to all who had committed atrocities and gave certain RUF leaders like Sankoh key strategic positions in the government. These included control over the exploitation of the country's natural resources through Sankoh's chairmanship of the

---

[16] The term "sobel" is a combination of the words "soldier" and "rebel" because often one would see rebels wearing soldiers' uniforms.

[17] With over 2,000 houses burned in the city, Freetown was one of the three most destroyed areas during the war. The other two regions that saw the most damage were Kono (the diamond-producing region in eastern Sierra Leone) and Kambia in the north.

Board of the Commission for the Management of Strategic Resources, National Reconstruction and Development, as well as several cabinet positions.[18] Payam Akhavan suggests that "conditioning a peace agreement on an amnesty may itself be the result of a weak bargaining position".[19] This may have been the case in Sierra Leone where both the 1996 and the 1999 accords contemplated some kind of amnesty for the perpetrators of atrocity crimes; but who in this case occupied the weak bargaining position? By most indications, the party that was in the weaker position going into the negotiations was the government of Sierra Leone. The RUF and AFRC commanders were at that moment not as well placed to continue to commit atrocities on the scale that they had been without securing additional resources, but by comparison to the government side, Solomon E. Berewa reveals that the RUF were using the peace talks as a means to buy time to build up those necessary resources.[20] The peace talks also granted them high-level strategic positions in the government that gave them access to the country's mineral resources.

While the Lomé Peace Accord and the more broadened amnesty provision contained within it were being negotiated, the SCSL was not even a vague notion. The insistence by the RUF delegation, namely Sankoh, on the inclusion of amnesty before substantive negotiations began reflected his fear of the conviction against him, pending appeal, for the domestic capital offence of treason. Significantly, it also signalled what Bruce Jacobs referred to as the high "risk sensitivity" of Sankoh and perhaps the other rebels; that is, they were aware of or understood the possibility of prosecution for their acts.[21] However, that awareness was concentrated around ongoing and future domestic prosecutions rather than international prosecutions.

The risk calculations of the RUF (and SLA/AFRC) from 1996 to 1998, post-Abidjan, could naturally not have been the same risk calcula-

---

[18] Peace Agreement Between the Government of Sierra Leone and the Revolutionary United Front of Sierra Leone (RUF/SL), 7 July 1999, UN doc. S/1999/777, 1999, Article V(2) (http://www.legal-tools.org/doc/380791/).

[19] Payam Akhavan, "Are International Criminal Tribunals a Disincentive to Peace? Reconciling Judicial Romanticism with Political Realism", in *Human Rights Quarterly*, 2009, vol. 31, no. 3, p. 641.

[20] Solomon E. Berewa, A New Perspective on Governance, Leadership, Conflict and Nation Building in Sierra Leone, Author House, Bloomington, IN, 2011, pp. 108–9.

[21] Bruce Jacobs, "Deterrence and Deterrability", in *Criminology*, 2010, vol. 48, no. 2, pp. 422–23.

tions that they made in 1999 and 2000, during and after Lomé. The risk calculation changes with the increase in international criminal prosecutions, their visibility, and the growing jurisprudence on the nature of and responsibility for international crimes. For instance, while there was unqualified UN support for the first peace agreement to contain an amnesty clause for crimes committed in Sierra Leone in 1996, the so-called reservation made by the UN special representative of the secretary-general to the blanket amnesty provision in the 1999 Lomé Peace Accord, that the amnesty did not apply to serious violations of international law, was evidence of a growing international consensus on the limits of amnesty in international criminal law. The reservation, regardless of its actual legal application and reliability, would have made the possibility of prosecution even more clear. According to Priscilla Hayner's in-depth look into the Lomé peace negotiations:

> Rebel leader Foday Sankoh had signed the document before the UN representative. When he saw the UN notation he was taken aback, and said, to no one in particular, "What does this mean? Are you going to try us?" No one answered, and the signing ceremony continued.[22]

Irrespective of the questions raised by Sankoh, the RUF did not seem to be bothered by the possibility that they could be prosecuted internationally for war crimes or serious violations of international humanitarian law.[23] This could be for several reasons. According to delegates at Lomé, including Berewa, the former vice president of Sierra Leone who was then attorney general and minister of justice and the leader of the government negotiating team, the attention of the RUF delegation was not drawn to the potential limitations of the amnesty because the two sides may otherwise not have reached an agreement.[24] As to how the government negotiators approached the subject of the limitations of amnesty, Berewa explained:

> Those things are kept under the carpet. When you are negotiating these things, you won't be telling people that "we will

---

[22] Priscilla Hayner, "Negotiating Peace in Sierra Leone: Confronting the Justice Challenge", Report, Henry Dunant Center for Humanitarian Dialogue and International Center for Transitional Justice, 2007, p. 6.

[23] Interview with Solomon E. Berewa, former vice president of the Republic of Sierra Leone, Freetown, May 2016.

[24] *Ibid.*

> grant you this; we will not grant you that". You will never
> come to an agreement. Even on the question of blanket am-
> nesty, the term was not used as such. They were given am-
> nesty and immunity. Of course there was the implication that
> the negotiating body had no power to absolve them of their
> violations of humanitarian law. That was implicit without
> having it expressed.

Indeed, it seemed as if there was no open plenary discussion at Lomé of the possibility of a court to try perpetrators of violations of international humanitarian law.

Sankoh understood the personal pardon and blanket amnesty being granted through the agreement as absolving the RUF of all offences, regardless of whether they were violations of international humanitarian law or domestic law. This view would appear to be in accord with the government's position at the time or, at least, the statements of President Kabbah. In Berewa's view, as long as the RUF leader got what he wanted, which was appointment to a high-level post equivalent in status to that of vice president and control over the country's mineral resources, he could not have cared less about the rest of the negotiations, including what happened to his 'boys'. Clearly, there was a disconnect between what transpired at Lomé and the RUF's actions in the field. One RUF ex-combatant confirmed that they continued attacks after Lomé "because of lack of communication within the RUF and logistics were not in place for food. Their hunger made them go out and attack [civilians] and UN troops to get food to eat".[25]

The government delegation and mediators, as would typically occur in such contexts, left the responsibility of explaining the legal implications and limits of each provision to the RUF's lawyers. Therefore, it is likely that the RUF's disregard of the reservation stemmed from their misunderstanding or lack of awareness of it, or even because the potential benefits derived from committing additional crimes overrode their fear of prosecution in the event that the amnesty could be retracted.

6.2.3. Establishment of the Special Court for Sierra Leone

Much like in the aftermath of the Abidjan Peace Accord, the Lomé Peace Agreement did not stop the rebels from committing international crimes.

---

[25] Focus group discussion with ex-combatants, Freetown, May 2016.

In May 2000 they abducted over 500 UN peacekeepers and held them hostage. To protest this and other breaches of the Lomé Agreement, on 8 May 2000 Sierra Leone civil society staged demonstrations outside Sankoh's home in Freetown. In the process, Sankoh's guards killed 21 demonstrators and injured dozens more as the RUF leader fled his home.

Having detained Sankoh after the May 8 incident and unsure whether or not to try him, President Kabbah sent a letter to the UN secretary-general, dated 12 June 2000, asking for a tribunal to be set up to try senior members of the RUF for the crimes committed against civilians and UN peacekeepers during the civil war in Sierra Leone.[26] Putting Sankoh on trial in Sierra Leonean courts would have been political suicide for the government because of the large presence of RUF supporters and sympathisers in the country and abroad. Also, it could have jeopardised the fragile peace that existed in the country at the time. However, keeping Sankoh detained indefinitely without trial or releasing him were also undesirable options for the government. Thus, underlying the establishment of the SCSL was the notion that the SCSL as "a credible system of justice and accountability" for the atrocities committed was the only option to bring an end to the festering culture of impunity, while aiding the reconciliation process and bringing about sustainable peace.[27]

Following two rounds of negotiations between the UN and the Sierra Leone government that started in September 2000, an agreement establishing the SCSL was signed between the two on 16 January 2002. The Sierra Leone Parliament then ratified the agreement through the Special Court Agreement 2002 Ratification Act, which was adopted on 7 March 2002 and amended on 15 July 2002 before it was adopted into law.

6.2.4. The Truth and Reconciliation Commission

The other prominent transitional justice mechanism was a Truth and Reconciliation Commission ('TRC'), which had been provided for in both the Abidjan Accord and the Lomé Peace Agreement. Post-conflict Sierra Leone represented the first time a TRC and an international war crimes

---

[26] United Nations Security Council, Fifth Report of the Secretary-General on the United Nations Mission in Sierra Leone, UN doc. S/2000/751, 31 July 2000.

[27] United Nations Security Council, Resolution 1315, see *supra* note 4.

tribunal had operated simultaneously.[28] Loosely modelled on the much-lauded South African TRC, the Sierra Leone TRC was established to create a historical record of the conflict while providing a platform for both victims and perpetrators to tell their stories and thus promote reconciliation. The extent to which the TRC's simultaneous operation with the SCSL undermined or increased the latter's deterrent effect will be discussed in section 6.4.

6.3. Methodology

Under the general theory of deterrence, two specific forms operate to constitute a deontological justification for criminal law. Specific deterrence refers to an individual's inability or unwillingness to commit a crime for fear of the punishment attached to the act. General deterrence means the prevention of crime due to the proliferation of societal norms that emphasise the wrongfulness of the conduct. Deterrence theory is outlined in a preceding chapter in this volume, and so this chapter does not go into depth in unpacking the theoretical underpinnings of its assessment of the SCSL's deterrent effect.

However, one aspect of deterrence theory that has been treated differently in the literature by various authors requires examination here given its relevance to the SCSL deterrence case study. That element is what Gustavo Gallón terms "neutralisation" of the perpetrator's power to commit additional international crimes or gross violations of international humanitarian law.[29] While neutralisation seems to focus on an individual's power or ability to commit crimes, specific deterrence tends to focus on the mental calculation made by the perpetrator as to whether or not to commit crimes based on his or her fear of the potential punishment. However, the incapacitation of an individual being tried by an international criminal tribunal, as well as the freezing of a person's assets, also fall under and have been analysed under the deterrence rubric. This has led those like Gallón who argue that neutralisation – and not deterrence – should be the paramount goal of a tribunal, to conclude that neutralisation is essen-

---

[28] SCSL, "TRC Chairman and Special Court Prosecutor Join Hands to Fight Impunity", OTP Press Release, 10 December 2002.

[29] Gustavo Gallón, "Deterrence: A Difficult Challenge for the International Criminal Court", Working Paper No. 275, The Helen Kellogg Institute for International Studies, 2000.

tially a "condition for deterring".[30] As will be discussed later in this chapter, the fact that gross violations of international humanitarian law had ceased by January 2002 when the war was declared over may have taken a large part of the neutralisation aspect out of the deterrence equation in Sierra Leone.

In addition to reviewing the existing literature on deterrence and the SCSL, field research was carried out in Sierra Leone in April and May 2016. This research consisted of key informant interviews and focus group discussions with ex-combatants, victims, SCSL principals, former defence counsel for the accused and members of civil society. Interviews were also conducted in May and June 2016 with individuals connected to the SCSL who are based outside Sierra Leone. Interviews with those tried and convicted by the SCSL could not be conducted, and any resulting shortcomings in the analysis contained in this case study are acknowledged. Therefore, where this case study attributes a viewpoint or assertion to one of the SCSL convicts, this information was gathered from reliable secondary sources, such as defence lawyers who worked on that individual's case, public statements made by the individual or people who closely monitored the SCSL trials.

6.4. Indicators of the SCSL's Deterrent Effect

Previous studies on the deterrent effect of international criminal tribunals have taken mixed approaches to measuring the courts' deterrent effects. Most studies, like those of Akhavan[31], Kate Cronin-Furman[32] and Tom Buitelaar[33], have taken a qualitative approach, focusing on changes in the course of a conflict following the courts' interventions and perceived behavioural changes in the accused persons or victims' own feelings of safety. Others like Hyeran Jo and Beth Simmons have incorporated both a qualitative approach and the use of empirical evidence, such as the in-

---

[30] *Ibid.*, p. 4.

[31] Akhavan, 2009, see *supra* note 19.

[32] Kate Cronin-Furman, "Managing Expectations: International Criminal Trials and the Prospects for Deterrence of Mass Atrocity", in *International Journal of Transitional Justice*, 2013, vol. 7, no. 3, p. 434.

[33] Tom Buitelaar, "The ICC and the Prevention of Atrocities Criminological Perspectives", Working Paper No. 8, The Hague Institute for Global Justice, 2015, p. 6.

crease or decrease in the number of casualties following the court's intervention.[34]

Many of the more empirical indicators of deterrence, such as the increase or decrease in the number of international crimes or casualties of war, would not be applicable given that the SCSL was an *ex post facto* tribunal. It was established as the disarmament, demobilisation and reintegration of combatants had ended and the armed conflict in Sierra Leone was officially declared over in January 2002. As Akhavan points out:

> Justice in the post-conflict peace building phase assumes that massive victimization has already occurred [...] Because successful prevention is measured by what does not happen, it is particularly difficult to assess. This recognition is especially pertinent for tribunals that are often judged solely in terms of defendants on trial (or at least fugitives on the run), rather than the looming threat of indictments.[35]

While the end of armed conflict did not render impossible the commission of certain crimes that fell within the SCSL's jurisdiction, this chapter does not contain a statistical analysis of a change in the commission of grave international crimes in Sierra Leone before and after the Court's establishment. The closest statistical measurement would perhaps be the number of extrajudicial killings that have taken place in Sierra Leone since the establishment of the SCSL. However, that would provide a rather inaccurate comparison to the range of grave crimes committed during the conflict. Therefore, in measuring the SCSL's deterrent effect, this chapter naturally focuses on more qualitative indicators, namely: 1) discernible behavioural change on the part of the accused and like-minded individuals; 2) the increase or reduction of incidences of violence or gross human rights violations where there had been repeated cycles of violence preceding the Court's intervention; 3) victims' perceptions of whether they feel safer as a result of the prosecutions; and 4) the views of non-governmental organisations ('NGOs') and experts on whether they think that the Court has had a deterrent effect.

In this study, more weight has been accorded to the first two indicators because they provide more direct and objective data than the latter.

---

[34] Hyeran Jo and Beth A. Simmons, "Can the International Criminal Court Deter Atrocity?", in *International Organization*, 2016, vol. 70, no. 3, pp. 443–75.

[35] Akhavan, 2009, p. 637, see *supra* note 19.

Absent are the SCSL convicts' own statements on how their actions or risk calculations were affected by the trial proceedings; other sources relied on were public statements and the views of individuals who were able to closely observe the defendants' behaviour throughout the proceedings to ascertain any behavioural change. Like-minded individuals, or ex-combatant members of the RUF, AFRC, SLA and CDF, provide a minuscule, but not fully comparable glimpse into the decision-making of these armed groups. More importantly, because they are the focus of targeted deterrence, their statements on how the SCSL's operation affected their decision-making processes are key to assessing one aspect of the Court's deterrent effect. Regarding the increase or reduction of incidence of violence, Sierra Leone did experience persistent, recurring cycles of violence, but these mostly predated the decision to prosecute and the turn towards international justice. Even if there was a limited or perhaps even dramatic difference in the decrease in violence, it would be methodologically very difficult, if not impossible, to establish a causal link between the claim that violence was reduced and the deterrent effect of the Court with all its built-in temporal, personal and other jurisdictional limitations.

6.4.1. Factors Influencing Deterrence

Given that any assessment of the SCSL trials' deterrent effect may seem premature or inconclusive, in addition to using the above indicators, this case study seeks to identify factors that appear to have either increased or undermined deterrence of these crimes in Sierra Leone. Identification of these factors can provide lessons for other international criminal tribunals, principally the ICC. This case study focuses primarily on analysing the factors increasing and undermining two types of deterrence – specific and targeted – and gives cursory treatment to those factors' effect on general deterrence. These factors fall into two broad categories: court-based and non-court-based.

Scholars like Daniel Nagin and Raymond Paternoster[36] have traditionally cited certainty, speed and severity of punishment as court-based deterrence factors, with Nagin[37], Mark Kleiman[38] and others concluding

---

[36] Daniel Nagin and Raymond Paternoster, "Enduring Individual Differences and Rational Choice Theories of Crime", in *Law and Society Review*, 1993, vol. 27, no. 3, pp. 467–96.

[37] Daniel Nagin, "Criminal Deterrence Research at the Outset of the Twenty-First Century", in *Crime and Justice*, 1998, vol. 23, no. 1, pp. 1–42.

that certainty of punishment – assuming a conviction – is now considered the principal deterrence variable of the three. Restricting the certainty variable in the deterrence equation to punishment alone has two implications. The first is to disregard possible calculations in the mind of the perpetrator or would-be perpetrator that certainty of prosecution in and of itself (versus conviction) could deter criminal behaviour. The second stems from the first implication and is the questionable assumption that the certainty of prosecution by an international criminal tribunal necessarily means certainty of conviction or punishment by that court. A number of variables, including the strength of the evidence, prosecutorial strategy, the strength of the defence case, and the possibility of a plea agreement in return for a lenient sentence, all make a difference in whether a case is initiated, let alone properly prosecuted or a conviction handed down. Absent these variables, international criminal tribunals would be mere kangaroo courts. Objective analysis that the majority of those prosecuted by international criminal tribunals are convicted and punished is not enough to make that assumption true, nor, as noted by Kimi King and James Meernik,[39] is it a substitute for the subjective determination by a perpetrator or would-be perpetrator that the certainty of prosecution by an international criminal tribunal automatically means that he will be convicted by that tribunal.

Other court-based factors that are relevant in the SCSL context include the hybrid nature of the Court and the scope of its jurisdictional reach, its location, its lack of police powers, its outreach work and the place of imprisonment of convicts. Non-court-based, or external, factors include the command structure and societal hierarchy of the various factions whose leaders were tried by the Court, as well as economic factors. In fact, it is the latter – the lack of economic benefit – that may have had the most significant effect on the decisions of ex-combatants not to return to fighting, and to the commission of crimes under the SCSL's jurisdiction.

---

[38] Mark A.R. Kleiman, *When Brute Force Fails: How to Have Less Crime and Less Punishment*, Princeton University Press, Princeton, NJ, 2009.

[39] Kimi King and James Meernik, "Assessing the Impact of the International Criminal Tribunal for the Former Yugoslavia: Balancing International and Local Interests While Doing Justice", in Bert Swart, Alexander Zahar and Göran Sluiter (eds.), *The Legacy of the International Criminal Tribunal for the Former Yugoslavia*, Oxford University Press, Oxford, 2011, pp. 7–44.

6.4.2. The Specific and Targeted Deterrent Effects of the SCSL

In an era in which international criminal justice has increasing presence and visibility, can it be assumed that the risk analysis of would-be perpetrators may be more informed by an understanding that they could possibly be subject to international criminal justice? First, there would need to be a criminal justice mechanism in place or the strong possibility of establishing one to prosecute these individuals when they are making their risk analysis. Second, these individuals would have to believe that their conduct is wrong or illegal, and possess a state of mind in which they are able to make a rational assessment of their conduct. For instance, a child combatant, whether forcibly conscripted or not, likely will not have the same assessment of the offensiveness or illegality of his conduct as an adult. Thirty-three-year-old Alhaji, a former child combatant, remarked that he was "just a child" during the war and did not even know why the rebels who abducted and forcibly conscripted him had been fighting the war, let alone committing atrocities.[40] Similarly, it cannot be assumed that an individual who is voluntarily or involuntarily under the influence of a narcotic substance would be able to make the rational risk assessment inherently assumed by deterrence theory.

Alternative to incapacity, an individual's belief in the righteous and just nature of the conduct in which he is engaging is a subjective element of the mental calculation that cannot be fully captured in a purely rational risk assessment. For instance, Francis, a former CDF combatant, described his involvement in the war as follows:

> The first attack was in '91. [I was] a little boy then. You didn't even know what was happening. [...] As a Limba by tribe, at that time during the war, they had no choice but to initiate you into any kind of secret society, even if you did not know what kind of secret society you were getting involved in. Be it Gbethi or Kamajor or Ronko or whatever, they involved you in the fighting. The first thing that they said to you was that you were fighting to save yourself. The second was that you were protecting the land you were living on because a foreign – in those days, foreigners included Mende, Temne or any other tribe – could not be allowed to

---

[40] Focus group discussion with ex-combatants, Freetown, May 2016.

> invade your land for any reason, to come fight you and drive
> you out of your house or your community.[41]

The "community protection" provided by the secret society was described by another CDF ex-combatant, Nyakeh, as "one thing that made us fearless and strong enough to put up some defensive in our community".[42] Although not explored in this case study, the combatants' belief that they were under the influence of a supernatural force would have affected their assessment of both the nature of their conduct and the risk of punishment for such conduct.

Third, would-be perpetrators would have to be aware that they could be prosecuted for the types of acts that they would be engaged in. Fourth, these individuals would have to believe that they would be apprehended and brought before the relevant criminal justice mechanism, even if under different conditions to those that they would have received under the domestic system.

During the period in which the crimes in Sierra Leone were being committed and later at the time that the SCSL was being established, most of the above considerations do not appear to have factored strongly into the risk calculations of the persons who were ultimately indicted by the Court. As of the date of commencement of the SCSL's temporal jurisdiction – 30 November 1996 – the International Criminal Tribunal for Rwanda ('ICTR') and International Criminal Tribunal for the former Yugoslavia ('ICTY') were still in their infancy. Having been young *ad hoc* courts, and in many ways experiments of international criminal justice at the time, the jurisprudential and non-jurisprudential reach of the *ad hoc* tribunals in their early days was limited. Moreover, their narrow territorial jurisdictions and their very nature as *ad hoc* tribunals meant that beyond the mere notion that such courts could be established by the UN, they did not pose a threat to would-be international crimes perpetrators elsewhere. At the time, there was no widespread belief or guarantee that the UN would set up a tribunal in each country in which such crimes were being committed, or a permanent international court. Indeed, as late as during the period of the 1994 Rwandan genocide, it was not entirely certain that an international penal tribunal would be established to prosecute the crimes committed there.

---

[41] *Ibid.*

[42] *Ibid.*

The mere establishment of the SCSL in early 2002 does not seem to have resulted in a change in behaviour among most individuals who had been involved in the war, nor did they seem to be concerned that they would be prosecuted by the Court. Based on their findings in studying the ICC's deterrent effect, Jo and Simmons assert that "rebels do not respond to legal change alone; they are much more impressed with [prosecutorial] action".[43] To some extent, this may also be true with the SCSL. With the exception of Sankoh, who was in detention in a state prison, and Bockarie, who was in Liberia, all of the other senior commanders of the RUF were living openly in Sierra Leone without fear of apprehension or prosecution even as Parliament enacted legislation establishing the SCSL and incorporating its Statute into domestic law.

6.4.3. Prosecutorial Strategy: The Deterrent Effects of Selective Prosecutions

During the investigations and indictments stage from late 2002 to 2003, one perhaps gets the clearest view into the risk calculations made by persons who would eventually be tried by the SCSL. Most were blindsided by their indictments, signalling that they perceived the certainty of punishment for crimes committed during the war as very low. Norman, then minister of defence and head of the CDF, Fofana, CDF director of war, Kondewa, CDF high priest, and Sesay, interim leader of the RUF, in particular were surprised by their arrests and indictments. Their disregard of the threat of punishment posed by the SCSL's existence stemmed not necessarily from the overwhelming benefits of the commission of crimes, but instead from their determination that the risk of punishment was extremely low. The amnesty provided by the Lomé agreement and the role that they felt they played in contributing to the peace process in Sierra Leone led to a greater sense of security from prosecution by those who were actually most likely to fall within the Court's jurisdiction. The depth of Sesay's belief that he should not face punishment for crimes committed during the conflict was supported at trial through the defence testimony of late President Tejan Kabbah that Sesay had contributed to bringing the war to an end.[44] The CDF likewise perceived themselves as restorers of

---

[43] Jo and Simmons, 2016, p. 35, see *supra* note 34.

[44] SCSL, *Prosecutor v. Issa Hassan Sesay, Morris Kallon and Augustine Gbao (RUF case)*, Trial Chamber, Transcript, SCSL-04-15-T, 16 May 2008.

democracy in Sierra Leone, having defended the people and territory when the state was helpless against the RUF incursion. With ultimate "benefits" to committing war crimes like the restoration of peace and democracy and the perceived low risk of punishment due to the lofty nature of the cause for which they were fighting, absent the reality imposed by their indictments, these particular individuals may not have been deterred from engaging in the same criminal actions had the war been ongoing at the time the SCSL was established.

6.4.3.1. Use of Insider Witnesses

Assessing the deterrent effect of the SCSL at the investigation and indictment stages also provides useful insights for targeted deterrence of like-minded individuals and mid-level commanders. Even without a specific deterrence goal, prosecutorial strategy turned out to be a key factor that increased the Court's possible deterrent effect. Part of the Office of the Prosecutor's strategy included using key insider witnesses such as Gibril Massaquoi, the former RUF spokesperson and Sankoh's personal assistant, to establish the command structure and operational strategy of the RUF, as well as the relationship between the RUF and the AFRC. As such, the Office was able to build its case as to the direct involvement of the RUF and AFRC defendants in decision-making at the highest level for the planning and commission of certain crimes.

Early in the investigation stage, insider witnesses such as Massaquoi and former AFRC member George Johnson were originally suspects.[45] When questioned by the Office of the Prosecutor, then offered a chance to serve as insider witnesses, they ultimately determined that the certainty of prosecution and subsequent punishment was not only high, but also imminent. The Office's explanation that these witnesses did not meet the greatest responsibility threshold and so were treated as witnesses after they showed willingness to give a complete and honest account of the facts seems to omit or distort some of the logical steps in the process. Had the insider witnesses not believed that they fell within the personal jurisdiction of the Court nor that they would likely be convicted by the

---

[45] Kyra Sanin, "Summary Witness Profiles at a Glance. Insider Testimony on Alleged Relations between RUF and AFRC Points of Interest: Insider Witnesses and 'Dancing with the Devil'", Special Court Monitoring Program Update #58, University of California at Berkeley War Crimes Studies Center, 10 October 2005, p. 4.

Court, there would have been little incentive for them to agree to be prosecution witnesses.

Given his presence in the RUF inner circle and the AFRC Supreme Council, Massaquoi was regarded publicly and by the eventual RUF indictees as one whom the Court should have or would have otherwise prosecuted, had he not agreed to testify. The offer presented to him by the Office of the Prosecutor during the investigations phase essentially altered one of the variables in Massaquoi's risk calculation. While he still faced the risk of punishment, rather than weighing it against continuing to live off benefits he derived from previously committed crimes, he now weighed it against the benefits of a high level of witness protection that he would gain from helping to expose senior RUF commanders' responsibility for past crimes.

Turning a key suspect into a protected witness is also a means of removing that individual from the organisational power structure through which he could potentially commit further crimes. It keeps him under the watchful eye of a legal body. Responding to concerns raised by amputees in Grafton during an outreach meeting about their continued suffering from the war, the prosecutor David Crane stressed that "the Special Court can remove war criminals from society and help the rule of law take root in Sierra Leone".[46] While Crane was likely not referring to the use of key insider witnesses as a means of removing war criminals from society, comparisons can be drawn between the end effects of removal by incarceration and removal by court protection. The restrictions imposed on people in and out of detention cannot be equated. However, placing a person under heavy witness protection is akin to placing the person in the Court's custody and detention. The same would have been true for eventual SCSL convict Sesay had the Office of the Prosecutor's offer for him to become an insider witness materialised after he was arrested and brought into the custody of the SCSL.[47]

---

[46]   SCSL, "Prosecutor Meets with War Wounded at Grafton Amputee Camp", OTP Press Release, 6 October 2003.

[47]   Although the statement made by Issa Sesay to the Office of the Prosecutor after deciding to testify as a prosecution witness was not admitted into the trial record by the Trial Chamber, the Office's offer to Sesay for him to testify as an insider witness was widely known. See also interview with a defence lawyer who worked on the RUF case, August 2016.

6.4.3.2. Timing of Indictments

An important distinction can be drawn when attempting to analyse the risk calculation of a suspect already in the Court's custody at the time of indictment and one who is not. For individuals detained before or at the time the indictment was unsealed, the effect of their incapacitation through detention muddies the perceived effect that the indictment alone may have had on their risk calculations. The difficulty in bifurcating the effect of one factor from another may complicate analysis of the specific deterrent effect of the Court's issuing of indictments, but not when analysing targeted deterrence.

Individuals not already in the Court's or state's detention at the time indictments were approved would have made their determinations as to the likelihood that they would be prosecuted based on a different set of facts and factors than those who were already detained. Although it did not appear to alter the actions or movements of those who were eventually indicted by the SCSL, the mere establishment of the SCSL was enough to provoke drastic action on the part of some lower-level individuals. Their fear manifested in them fleeing to Liberia after the Court's establishment. As 23-year-old Ibrahim explained when recounting his ex-combatant father's reaction to the investigations:

> I heard about the Special Court in 2002/2003 when I was in primary school. My family was a bit disappointed to learn that the Special Court was established to try everyone that had been involved in the war, no matter where they were in Sierra Leone. As a result, my dad decided to relocate to Liberia because he had been involved in the war.[48]

Those who had fled to Liberia returned to Sierra Leone after realising that only senior leaders of each faction had been arrested and that no action had been taken against their fellow lower-level ex-combatants who had stayed in Sierra Leone.

Unlike the ICC and even the *ad hoc* tribunals, the lack of sequencing of prosecutions does not allow one to see the possible deterrent effect of earlier prosecutions on later ones. With the exception of Taylor, all of the accused who eventually stood trial were apprehended and indicted within a five-month period between 7 March and 23 September

---

[48] Focus group discussion with ex-combatants, Freetown, May 2016.

2003. In spite of the Office of the Prosecutor's internal deliberations on whether to issue one additional indictment, which Stephen Rapp revealed occurred in 2007 when he took up his appointment as SCSL Prosecutor,[49] any real expectation that the Court would issue more indictments had waned in the three and a half years since the other indictments had been issued. Thus, the looming threat of indictments, at least in the accused's and public's eyes, cannot be used to judge the deterrent effect of the Court after a certain stage in its life. The change that this produced in the risk calculation of ex-combatants was evident in the returning home of those who had run away to neighbouring countries out of fear of prosecution by the Court.

6.4.3.3. Ex-Combatants' Understanding of the SCSL's Personal Jurisdiction

For the vast majority of ex-combatants, their lack of fear of prosecution likely stemmed not from a sense of security about amnesty, but instead the understanding they gained of the Court's personal jurisdiction and the command responsibility mode of liability, as well as their own careful observations of the Court's lack of indictment of some of their seniors. Those ex-combatants who reacted hastily and fled to Liberia made their decision based only on the initial limited information of the Court's establishment. It is difficult to fully unpack the decision-making process of these individuals. Nevertheless, it can be presumed that those who made the decision to flee were either fearful of being charged or persons whose conduct during the war implied that they were at risk of facing prosecution. Whereas those who waited to gather more information, including by attending and asking questions in SCSL outreach meetings, made their calculations based on a more complete set of information that allowed them to reach the conclusion that they were likely not a direct target for prosecution. The Office of the Prosecutor's own explanations that they were focused on those bearing greatest responsibility was also an important element of this, and became a pressure point to clarify given reported ex-combatant fears of possible repercussions for them.

---

[49] Stephen Rapp, "The Challenge of Choice in the Investigation and Prosecution of International Crimes in Post-Conflict Sierra Leone", in Charles Chernor Jalloh (ed.), *The Sierra Leone Special Court and its Legacy: The Impact for Africa and International Criminal Law*, Cambridge University Press, New York, 2005, p. 25.

Through the Court's outreach efforts thereafter, ex-combatants gained a keen understanding of the Court's personal jurisdiction. Outreach by the Office of the Prosecutor began early in the life of the Court, even before the first indictments were issued in March 2003. Through town hall meetings in each district of the country and radio programmes, Office of the Prosecutor and later dedicated outreach staff explained the Court's personal jurisdiction and responded to questions from the public, including ex-combatants, as to who fell within the Court's target. As the outreach efforts intensified, ex-combatants realised that most of them did not fall in the parameters of those who bore the greatest responsibility for the crimes committed during the war. With the Court also not indicting any mid- or low-level commanders as the proceedings moved forward, ex-combatants became increasingly convinced that they would not be targeted by the Court.[50]

That ex-RUF fighter Usman had the misconception that anyone who had not been arrested by the SCSL would automatically not be investigated or prosecuted demonstrates the extent to which the Office of the Prosecutor's case selection influenced ex-combatant views about their own risk of punishment.[51]

6.4.4. Mitigating Lack of Police Powers with State–Court Co-operation

A key difference between the SCSL and the ICC is that 10 of the 13 SCSL indictees were already in the custody of the government of Sierra Leone or the SCSL at the time of their indictments, or arrested simultaneously with the public issuing of their indictments. Sankoh, Brima, Kamara and Kanu were in state detention when indicted. Norman, Sesay, Kallon and Gbao were apprehended by the SCSL and the Sierra Leone police in Operation Justice simultaneously with the public issuing of their indictments. In a proactive move, the SCSL provisionally detained Fofana and Kondewa one month before indictments against them were approved.

---

[50] Focus group discussion with ex-combatants, Makeni, April 2016.
[51] *Ibid.*

6.4.4.1. Maintaining A Positive In-State Arrest Record

Like the ICC, the SCSL's track record with the arrest and transfer of people who were not already in custody at the time of their indictments was relatively poor. Taylor's transfer to the custody of the SCSL was the only one that materialised out of a potential three. Judging from this track record, one of the factors that most increased the SCSL's deterrent effect was the government of Sierra Leone's co-operation with the Court on arrests and transfers, while one of the factors that most undermined the SCSL's deterrent effect was its need to rely on the political will of countries in the sub-region, namely Liberia, Ghana and Nigeria, to effect arrests of indicted persons outside Sierra Leone. The reliance on the goodwill of states underscores the state-centric nature of international law and also foreshadows a central issue that has now become a major concern for the permanent ICC. A third of the latter's indictments have not been enforced due to lack of political will from concerned states.

The co-operation between the SCSL and the government of Sierra Leone, particularly the Sierra Leone police, for the successful arrest or transfer of 10 individuals to the custody of the SCSL raised the stakes for both the certainty and speed of punishment for indictees and potential indictees who were physically present in Sierra Leone. With a 100 per cent success rate for apprehending individuals physically present in Sierra Leone, potential indictees in the country were on notice that if indictments were approved against them, they were almost guaranteed to be apprehended. The arrests also shored up increased feelings of safety in the minds of victims. For instance, following the arrests of Sankoh and Sesay, survivors living in the Murray Town amputee camp in Freetown at the time relaxed their fears that the men would be able to injure them further. They recalled their reaction at the time as being, "[b]ecause they are now detained, we feel relieved that they are not free to carry out any more atrocities".[52]

The evolution in the arrest strategy to make use of 'provisional detention' measures against Fofana and Kondewa gave an additional signal to potential indictees and would-be perpetrators that no window of escape would be available if the Court indicted them. The SCSL's lack of its own institutional police force, requiring reliance on state security forces, posed

---

[52] Focus group discussion with amputees, Makama Camp, April 2016.

no impediment to arrests and transfers within Sierra Leone. The integral role of the state, as well as its political will, with regard to effecting arrests was evident. This might not have been surprising considering that the Court was largely arresting former enemies of the state. The co-operation between the Court and the host state is an understated part of the SCSL's legacy, but crucial for determining the likelihood of apprehension of indictees inherent in analysing an individual's certainty of prosecution by the Court.

6.4.4.2. Challenges with Arrests and Transfers of Indictees outside Sierra Leone

When compared with the more contentious dynamic between the SCSL and other West African countries on the issue of arrests and transfers of individuals within their territory to the custody of the SCSL, the possible deterrence impact of the co-operation between the Court and government of Sierra Leone is even more noteworthy. For instance, in May 2003 the Office of the Prosecutor engaged in a very public battle with the government of Liberia, still headed by Taylor at the time, on the arrest and transfer of SCSL indictees Koroma and Bockarie. In a series of press releases starting 4 May 2003, the SCSL chief of investigations, Alan White, made public pronouncements that the Office knew the men's whereabouts in Liberia and called on Taylor to surrender them to the SCSL.[53] White went so far as to allege that Koroma was "commanding a new unit set up by President Taylor, known as the Special Monitoring Group, comprised of approximately 3,000 men from former RUF members, ATU, Marine Forces and militia forces. This unit is heavily armed and equipped with arms recently brought into Liberia from outside sources in spite of the UN arms embargo".[54]

Some characterise these claims by Office of the Prosecutor investigators as exaggeration.[55] This public show by the Office that it could tap into strong intelligence networks, even within other countries, may have been a self-serving attempt to pump up its own legitimacy within and outside of Sierra Leone. The slew of Office of the Prosecutor press state-

---

[53] SCSL, "Prosecutor Provides Location of Fugitives Koroma and Bockarie", OTP Press Release, 4 May 2003.

[54] *Ibid.*

[55] Phone interview with former Office of the Prosecutor consultant, May 2016.

ments released in quick succession and meant to show its strength did little to pressure Taylor to arrest and hand over the men to the SCSL. Moreover, Bockarie's execution in Liberia in the days that followed, likely on Taylor's orders, dampened the image that the Office of the Prosecutor was in control. Rather, in the series of events, Taylor came across as being in control, particularly when considering the implications of executing someone who could have been a potentially crucial witness against him if the SCSL decided to prosecute him. Unbeknown to Taylor at the time, the Office of the Prosecutor had not only decided to prosecute him, but also the Court had approved an indictment against him, which remained under seal until June 2003.

The Office of the Prosecutor's non-delicate handling of the diplomatic affair between the Court and the government of Liberia may have undermined its efforts to bring Bockarie and Koroma before the Court. The debacle may have also heightened in Taylor's mind the threat that he could face prosecution if the Office were able to enter into an agreement with Bockarie, for instance, to be an insider witness against Taylor, as was the case with Massaquoi against the RUF and AFRC indictees. That he was likely under investigation by the SCSL at the time did not deter Taylor from having Bockarie executed, then allegedly having Bockarie's family murdered to avoid possible DNA profiling or revelations from them as to the cause of Bockarie's death.[56]

6.4.4.3. The International Diplomacy Aspect of SCSL Prosecutions

This case study mainly focuses on the deterrent effect of prosecutions. However, the politics and diplomacy involved in the arrest and transfer of individuals to the Court had an impact on the Office of the Prosecutor's ability to carry out its prosecutorial strategy. By asking the Court to unseal the indictment against Taylor while he was attending the peace negotiations in Accra, Ghana, the SCSL prosecutor sought to use what Akha-

---

[56] See SCSL, "Prosecutor Requests Body for Identification; Calls for Surrender of Koroma", OTP Press Release, 7 May 2003; SCSL, "Special Court Takes Custody of Alleged Body of Indicted War Criminal", OTP Press Release, 1 June 2003. The alleged accidental killing took place two days after Office of the Prosecutor press statement providing the location of Bockarie and calling on Taylor to surrender him to the SCSL, a call that was reiterated the following day at an outreach event at FBC. See also SCSL, "Bockarie's Family Alleged Murdered; Office of the Prosecutor Demands Full Cooperation from Taylor", OTP Press Release, 15 May 2003.

van calls "stigmatization of those responsible for mass atrocities"[57] in order to isolate them on a regional or international level and thus diminish their political influence and the resources of the armed groups that they support. Considering the political and military influence that Taylor wielded in West Africa, and the widespread fears that he had the resources and network of followers that would allow him to support criminal activities in Liberia and Sierra Leone, the prosecutor gambled that what could possibly sway Taylor's own cost-benefit analysis was international stigmatisation and pressure.

Another vivid example of the centrality of international diplomacy to the Office of the Prosecutor's overall prosecutorial work is that it undertook advocacy *vis-à-vis* the US government to get Nigeria to hand over Taylor to the SCSL during the period in which he was in exile. Despite Taylor's own eventual transfer to the SCSL in 2006 being lauded as a major achievement due to his stature as a former head of state, Taylor lived openly under the protection of the Nigerian state for three years before he was eventually transferred to the Court. For some, this signalled uncertainty that he would ever be prosecuted by the SCSL. The UN Security Council's Liberia Sanctions Committee viewed Taylor's exile in Nigeria as undermining any possible deterrent effect of the SCSL indictment against him, particularly because he remained in contact with associates in Liberia. The committee specifically noted that:

> The presence of former president Charles Taylor in exile in Nigeria, even though the Special Court for Sierra Leone has issued a warrant for his arrest on charges of war crimes, is in itself a destabilising factor. The situation of de facto impunity arising out of this situation of exile can only undermine respect for international law and thereby lessen its deterrent effect.[58]

For other observers, certainty of Taylor's prosecution was not in question, only the timing and speed of it. The Office of the Prosecutor remained steadfast in its refusal to accept that Taylor's prosecution would operate on a timeline determined by Liberia and Nigeria rather than the prosecutor. In allowing Taylor to remain in exile in Nigeria during that three-year period, Nigeria maintained that its extension of this courtesy to

---

[57] Akhavan, 2009, p. 641, see *supra* note 19.

[58] United Nations Security Council, Liberia Sanctions Committee Report, UN doc. S/2005/360, 13 June 2005, paras. 91–92.

Taylor was to encourage him to step down from the Liberian presidency in August 2003 in the interest of securing regional peace and stability. Nigeria's move to grant Taylor exile was also viewed as a demonstration of its leadership of the ECOWAS peacemaking effort, which sought to balance the imperatives of peace in the sub-region with justice.

6.4.5. Detention

Physical restriction of an individual through detention before and during trial can be one means of preventing that individual from committing crimes, but it is not a guarantee. Particularly when dealing with structured or criminal organisations, their networks and means of operation often run deeper than requiring the physical presence of a particular individual for the commission of crimes. A former SLA soldier admitted:

> When [the SCSL] indicted the AFRC guys – 'Five-Five' and others that fell within the Johnny Paul [regime] – I was not really happy because...I would just remember the struggle that we went through and suffered together in the [battle] line during the war.'[59]

Deterrence theory assumes individual decision-making as its main driver, but the entrenched loyalty, command and control structures of military, armed groups and criminal organisations militate against individual decision-making, and thus against targeted deterrence.

Even in detention or when the organisations have been dismantled, the hierarchical structures of these organisations remain *de facto* intact. This was strongly evident in how the CDF defendants interacted with one another while in detention and during trial. Fofana and Kondewa's deference to Norman's authority was so ingrained that when Norman requested to represent himself and refused the assistance of the Court-appointed counsel, Kondewa's lawyers advised him to disengage himself from Norman when possible so as to not taint Kondewa's case because Norman was viewed by the Court as disruptive.[60] These warnings stemmed from the fear that the obvious hierarchical, yet close relationship among the CDF defendants, coupled with the fact that the trials were conducted jointly, could have created subconscious bias that would override the judges' objectivity in adjudicating the individual cases.

---

[59] Focus group discussion with ex-combatants, Freetown, May 2016.
[60] Interview with counsel for Allieu Kondewa, Freetown, May 2016.

Where this hierarchical or other authority does not result in a senior commander influencing his junior co-detainees, the commander's authority could influence non-detained members of the organisation. In fact, detention at the SCSL did not prevent Norman from being implicated in plots involving violence. In January 2004, pursuant to an Office of the Prosecutor application made under Rule 48 of the SCSL Rules of Detention, the SCSL registrar ordered that all of Norman's communications, except those with his legal counsel, be restricted for 14 days.[61] The application was made after the Court intercepted one of his telephone conversations in which there were indications that he was involved in co-ordinating activities intended to cause civil unrest in Sierra Leone.[62] Notwithstanding that the veracity of the claim against Norman remains unclear, the incident raised questions about the security implications of SCSL detainees' continued access to and influence over particularly vulnerable segments of the population. In its June 2004 report, the UN Security Council Liberia Sanctions Committee noted:

> In January 2004, Chief Sam Hinga Norman, the leader of the former Civil Defence Force which fought on behalf of the Government against RUF, who has been taken into custody by the Special Court on charges of crimes against humanity was implicated in co-ordinating activities "calculated to cause civil unrest in the country" from his prison cell. It is still possible for destabilizing forces to recruit frustrated, disengaged young people.[63]

Therefore, it is possible that a court-based deterrence factor like the ability to keep accused persons in secure detention, which is theoretically geared toward neutralisation or incapacitation, could in practice be negated or its effect diminished by context-based factors, such as the reach of the accused's social or criminal networks.

6.4.6. The Benefactor: Economically Dismantling the Atrocity Machinery

Criminal networks are generally able to sustain themselves because they have a strong financial source. As one ex-combatant succinctly stated, "to

---

[61] SCSL, "Norman Communications Restricted", Press Release, 21 January 2004.

[62] *Ibid.*

[63] United Nations Security Council, Liberia Sanctions Committee Report, UN doc. S/2004/396, 1 June 2004, para. 40.

fight [a war], you need money".[64] In fact, the economic factor may be one of the most underestimated factors in deterring the commission of crimes in armed conflict by lower-level perpetrators. Once the spoils of war become depleted, or when perpetrators do not see any material, political or other benefit arising out of their actions, the benefit variable in the deterrence equation shifts. This shift naturally alters the product of the equation, even if there is little or no perceived risk of punishment. A shift in just this one variable can determine whether an individual would be willing to commit the crimes in the future.

6.4.6.1. Prosecuting Financiers and Asset Freezing

From as early as the Lomé peace talks, the importance that the RUF placed on maintaining or acquiring additional financial backing was evident. Perhaps even more than the threat of punishment, the economic incentive of foreign aid could have been a significant factor in the RUF's willingness to temporarily cease committing atrocities and sit down to negotiate peace. Hayner notes the following comments made by Joseph Melrose, US ambassador to Sierra Leone in 1999 who was present in Lomé:

> A large part of the logic under which the facilitating group operated was the need to not throw the situation in Sierra Leone into even a greater state of chaos nor create an atmosphere in which it would be considerably more difficult to obtain the very necessary financial assistance from both institutional and bi-lateral donors that Sierra Leone desperately needed. It was pointed out to the RUF that the fact that the current Sierra Leonean government had been elected, even if under less than perfect circumstances, and enjoyed international recognition was important to remember in terms of the availability of future assistance.[65]

In reality, Taylor's individual resources and those that he was charged with managing as president of Liberia supported the RUF throughout the war.[66] Taylor can be isolated as the war's financier or, at the very least, a financial conduit or intermediary for the RUF to buyers of rough diamonds and arms dealers. Taylor's prosecution by the SCSL and those of his associates by other courts thus provide a strong basis for ana-

---

[64] Focus group discussion with ex-combatants, Freetown, May 2016.

[65] Hayner, 2007, p. 11, see *supra* note 22.

[66] Taylor Judgment, paras. 1286–2173, see *supra* note 12.

lysing whether prosecuting financiers is an effective, and even preferred, means of deterring serious international crimes.

At least two other major financial associates of Taylor have been indicted for war crimes, although not by the SCSL. Michel Desaedeleer, a Belgian-American businessman, was arrested and charged in August 2015 by Belgian authorities for allegedly committing war crimes and crimes against humanity when he illicitly traded diamonds with Taylor and the RUF in 1999 and 2000, and on occasion was present during the RUF's looting of diamonds in Kono. The money earned from the illegal trade of the diamonds that Desaedeleer was believed to have engaged in allowed the RUF to buy weapons and other equipment that they used to commit crimes. Desaedeleer's death on 28 September 2016 prior to the commencement of his trial, however, means that the effect of his prosecution on deterring the financing of international crimes cannot be analysed.

The second Taylor associate, Guus Kouwenhoven, a Dutch businessman, is being prosecuted in the Netherlands for arms smuggling to Liberia and war crimes during the Liberia civil war. Given the interconnectedness of the conflicts in Sierra Leone and Liberia, as well as Taylor's involvement in financing and supplying arms to the RUF, the information provided to the Dutch authorities by the SCSL Office of the Prosecutor to assist the former's investigations may have been a significant factor leading to Kouwenhoven's arrest and prosecution in the Netherlands.

In July 2003, following a request from the Office of the Prosecutor, the government of Switzerland froze $2 million in accounts belonging to Taylor.[67] The UN Security Council did likewise in March 2004 as part of its sanctions regime out of concern that Taylor and his associates would use funds misappropriated from Liberian state coffers to undermine peace in Liberia and the sub-region.[68] Experts do not believe there is a link between the freezing of Taylor's assets and the halting of arms movements in the region, as the asset freezing occurred after the end of the Sierra Leone war and the completion of the disarmament, demobilisation and reintegration process. Moreover, arms movements into and out of Liberia

---

[67] SCSL, "2 Million of Taylor's Assets Frozen", OTP Press Release, 23 July 2003.

[68] United Nations Security Council, "Security Council Freezes Assets of Former Liberian President Charles Taylor, Concerned They'll Be Used to Undermine Peace, Resolution 1532 (2004) Adopted Unanimously", Press Release, UN doc. SC/8024, 12 March 2004.

stopped altogether in August 2003 when Taylor left power, signalling that he no longer had direct access to power, and thus could not allow, nor control shipments into and out of the region.[69] Therefore, while the freezing of Taylor's assets could have been meant as a preventative measure against the financing of future atrocities, it does not appear to have altered either the ability or the decision-making of Taylor to finance crimes in Sierra Leone. In the end, it merely constituted a symbolic victory for the Office of the Prosecutor, as the funds were not even used to provide reparations to victims once a conviction was secured against Taylor. Kenneth Gallant pointed to this missed opportunity in his strong critique of the Office for failing to request the forfeiture of money, diamonds or other proceeds of crimes for which Taylor was convicted pursuant to Article 19(3) of the SCSL Statute.[70] Had the Office of the Prosecutor made the request and the Court successfully recovered those proceeds, it would have constituted an additional penalty that would-be perpetrators would now have to factor into their deterrence cost-benefit analysis.

6.4.6.2. Economic Disempowerment of the Perpetrator Base

In spite of efforts to directly deter atrocities by prosecuting their financiers, the effects of cutting off financial resources were felt most by the lower-level RUF and AFRC combatants; that is, those who fell under the targeted deterrence category.[71] RUF ex-combatants consistently remarked that they do not see the war as having been economically profitable for themselves or those around them, including their former commanders.[72] Reflecting on what would tempt him to take up arms in the future, Salieu, an ex-RUF fighter turn motorbike taxi driver, explained:

> What I experienced, no benefit came from it. So I don't feel that anything would be able to tempt *me* again [to go and fight]. Because if there was profit, there are people whose feet have been cut – amputees – who may have already gone

---

[69] United Nations Security Council, Liberia Sanctions Committee Report, UN doc. S/2005/360, 13 June 2005, paras. 91–92.

[70] Kenneth Gallant, "Charles Taylor, Arms Dealers and Reparations", UALR Bowen School Research Paper No. 18-08, June 2012.

[71] CDF combatants have been omitted from this discussion because their operations were not sponsored by Taylor, and because most cite their motivation for taking up arms as defence of their communities and families rather than economic or political gain.

[72] Focus group discussion with ex-combatants, Makeni, April 2016.

there. Some have lost their family, lost their houses, lost their property. Nothing was able to be refunded to them. Those that call themselves heads of the rebels, neither the NPRC [National Provincial Ruling Council] nor AFRC rebel commanders, were not able to achieve anything. Some of them are with us in town. Some are hustling in the [motor] park. So what would convince me again to go back where I was that did not make me rich?[73]

The extent to which the economic factor dictated the cost-benefit calculations of RUF ex-combatants is evident when considering that some left open the possibility of taking up arms again if it was profitable. According to Salieu: "It would be a different story if you saw a return on the resources that you wasted, but we have not see[n] that".[74] For low-level ex-combatants, particularly where the risk of punishment was almost negated by the SCSL's statutory and prosecutorial focus on the leaders of the factions, their deterrence equation eventually consisted of weighing the cost of fighting and committing atrocities versus any benefits derived from taking up arms. In practical terms, the costs involve investing their time and risking their lives to commit atrocities on someone else's behalf for little to no return instead of engaging in livelihood-generating activities. Thus, this context-based factor has increased deterrence among low- and mid-level perpetrators because most now diagnose war as simply being economically unviable for them.

6.4.7. Punishment

Whereas deterrence features prominently in domestic criminal legal theory, its place in international criminal legal theory has been more muted and inconsistent. Mirko Bagaric and John Morss[75] and Barbora Hola[76] explain this as partly stemming from international criminal law's failure to enunciate strong penal theories in the way that criminal law has. That failure may have resulted from the difficulty in definitively drawing con-

---

[73] *Ibid.*

[74] *Ibid.*

[75] Mirko Bagaric and John Morss, "International Sentencing Law: In Search of a Justification and Coherent Framework", in *International Criminal Law Review*, 2001, vol. 6, no. 2, p. 208.

[76] Barbora Hola, "Sentencing of International Crimes at the ICTY and ICTR: Consistency of Sentencing Case Law", in *Amsterdam Law Forum*, 2012, vol. 4, no. 4, p. 6.

clusions about national criminal jurisdictions' ability to deter crimes even when stout penal law theories have been articulated. According to the SCSL prosecutor Brenda Hollis: "International courts are no better or worse at general deterrence than national courts".[77] Even where deterrence is stated as a goal of international criminal law, it has more often than not been in the context of justifying punishment in the sentencing phase of trials. As Hola[78] and Mark Drumbl[79] have noted, as well as international criminal tribunal judges themselves have indicated when providing their sentencing rationale, the judges have "found inspiration in classic 'domestic' penal theories".[80] Unsurprisingly, in the sentencing judgments in all of the SCSL's joint trials, the judges situated deterrence among the principal sentencing purposes of international criminal justice.[81] The heavy sentences handed down to the nine individuals convicted by the SCSL – ranging from 15 to 52 years' imprisonment – serve two potential deterrence purposes. As described earlier, these purposes are targeted (but referred to by the judges as 'general') punishment of the offenders so as to deter others from committing the same crimes out of fear of punishment, and specific, incapacitating or removing the convicts from society so that they cannot engage in further criminal conduct.

6.4.7.1. Severity of Punishment

Sesay, Kallon and Gbao received sentences of 52, 40 and 25 years, respectively, after the Appeals Chamber overturned a conviction on one count against Gbao and upheld the other convictions against all three. Sesay's 52-year sentence represents the longest individual sentence imposed by the Court. The Appeals Chamber decided to uphold the convictions and 50-year sentences against Brima and Kanu and the 45-year sentence against Kamara. Fofana and Kondewa ultimately received sentences

---

[77] Interview with SCSL prosecutor Brenda J. Hollis.

[78] Hola, 2012, pp. 6–7, see *supra* note 76.

[79] Mark A. Drumbl, *Atrocity, Punishment, and International Law*, Cambridge University Press, New York, 2007, p. 65.

[80] SCSL, *Prosecutor v. Issa Hassan Sesay, Morris Kallon and Augustine Gbao (RUF Case)*, Trial Chamber, Sentencing Judgment, SCSL-2004-15-T, 8 April 2004, para. 12 ('RUF Case, Sentencing Judgment') (http://www.legal-tools.org/doc/f7fbfc/).

[81] Brima *et al.*, Sentencing Judgment, para. 14, see *supra* note 3; and note RUF Case, Sentencing Judgment, para. 13, see *supra* note 80; Fofana and Kondewa,, Appeals Judgment, para. 532, see *supra* note 3.

of 15 and 20 years, respectively, after the Appeals Chamber overturned their convictions on certain counts, partially sustained the convictions on others, and entered new convictions on additional counts. Taylor's 50-year sentence was affirmed by the Appeals Chamber. With the exception of Fofana, Kondewa and Gbao, who received sentences of 25 years or less, it is highly probable that the other convicts could die in prison before they can complete their sentences. In other words, their removal from society is likely to be permanent, and thus the sentences represent an attempt at specific deterrence through complete incapacitation.

Recognising the depravity of the acts of the convicts, the judges emphasised in their sentencing rationale the need for the punishment to reflect the gravity of the offences. Perhaps as a reaction to the criticism that commentators like Mark Harmon and Fergal Gaynor heaped on the ICTY for the leniency and inconsistency of its sentences in spite of the Court's clear acknowledgement of the gravity of the crimes,[82] the SCSL Appeals Chamber may have felt the need to impose lengthier sentences on the convicts to insulate itself from such criticism.

In some cases, however, the severity of the punishment could undermine the legitimacy of the Court in the eyes of both the convicted and the public, where the sentence is perceived as disproportionately severe for the crimes for which the person has been found guilty. This could lead to the perception that the Court went beyond the sentencing purposes, including deterrence, which it set out for itself based on other international criminal tribunals' precedents and its own principles. Margaret deGuzman wrote the following about the Appeals Chamber's decision to increase the sentences for Fofana and Kondewa, even though those same judges overturned part of the convictions against the two men:[83]

> Had the appellate judgment instead centered on the retributive desert of the defendants, or the need to deter them or others like them in Sierra Leone from committing future

---

[82] Mark Harmon and Fergal Gaynor, "Ordinary Sentences for Extraordinary Crimes", in *Journal of International Criminal Justice*, 2007, vol. 5, no. 3, pp. 684–89.

[83] The Appeals Chamber determined that the sentences given to the CDF accused by the Trial Chamber were inadequate. In particular, the Appeals Chamber found that the Trial Chamber had erred in considering and applying "just cause" and motive of civic duty as mitigating factors in sentencing.

> crimes, or even the goal of promoting national reconciliation,
> the result might well have been lower sentences.[84]

When the legitimacy of the Court is undermined in the eyes of the convict and a would-be perpetrator, the perpetrator may feel that he no longer has anything to lose because the Court is determined to punish him regardless of whether his guilt is proven and the crimes are indeed severe.

Having always perceived the Court as a foreign interventionist force, Kondewa, for instance, felt that the ignorance of foreign judges as to the context-specific situation of the Sierra Leone conflict meant that they could not effectively make decisions as to guilt or innocence or take into consideration mitigating factors for sentencing in order to render fair judgments.[85] Particularly given that Kondewa was not a combatant, he and others could not reconcile the mode of justice being meted out by the SCSL with that which had prevailed in their own local communities for centuries. While acknowledging the heinous acts committed by the SCSL convicts, some ex-combatants and members of war-affected communities expressed a desire to see the sentences of at least certain convicts like Kondewa and former RUF interim leader Sesay reduced.[86] Several women living in the environs of Makeni believed that the Court should have taken into consideration as a mitigating factor the assistance that they say they and their children received from Sesay to escape death, sexual violence, forced marriage and property destruction at the hands of other RUF commanders, as well as to obtain food during the war period.[87] Taking the perspective of victims, the former CDF combatant Francis pointed out:

> No matter what punishment you give [the convicts], people
> will not be satisfied. Look at those people whose hands have
> been cut. Even if you jail someone for three hundred years,
> the pain will remain because it is physical.[88]

---

[84] Margaret M. deGuzman, "The Sentencing Legacy of the Special Court for Sierra Leone", in Charles Jalloh (ed.), *The Sierra Leone Special Court and Its Legacy: The Impact for Africa and International Criminal Law*, Cambridge University Press, New York, 2015, pp. 382–83.

[85] Interview with counsel for Kondewa.

[86] Focus group discussion with ex-combatants, Freetown, May 2016; Focus group discussion with women, Mateneh, April 2016.

[87] Focus group discussion with women, Mateneh, April 2016.

[88] Focus group discussion with ex-combatants, Freetown, May 2016.

These public views on sentencing – and in turn the legitimacy of the Court – underscore the reality that sentencing will not only be interpreted through the lens of theoretical and deontological criminal justice goals, including deterrence, but also through local social justice standards.

In any assessment of an international criminal tribunal's deterrent effect, the cost of punishment must be measured not solely by the sentence handed down, but also that which the accused person will consider to be a loss resulting from his prosecution and/or detention. While deprivation of liberty is the most obvious cost, a social or economic loss may be equally or more devastating. For some, that deprivation is the loss of familial relations due to the social stigma of being a war crimes suspect or the physical separation of the accused from his or her family while in detention. The preoccupation of Kamara and Kondewa, for example, with ensuring that the Court respected their conjugal rights illustrates the importance of familial relations to the defendants.[89] In fact, Kondewa's greatest fear, loss of any of his 12 wives during his detention from May 2003 to May 2008, became a reality over the course of the five years that he was detained.[90] As it became increasingly apparent to him throughout trial that he would be convicted, the possibility that he might lose more of his wives while serving a sentence outside Sierra Leone added to the impending loss that he associated with his prosecution. Such loss would have been unpredictable at the time he committed the crimes. Nevertheless, his present understanding of the loss in real terms could be enough to dissuade him from engaging in the same acts that led to his conviction when he returns to Sierra Leone after completing his sentence.

In line with their targeted deterrence purpose, the length of the sentences sends a message to would-be perpetrators that conviction for crimes against humanity and serious violations of international humanitarian law carry a severe penalty. Shahram Dana aptly analysed the SCSL convicts' sentences as follows:

> The average sentence for opponents of the government is forty-six years, and the average sentence for supporters of the government (CDF defendants) is 17.5 years. The CDF defendants also received the lowest individual sentences.

---

[89] Interview with Mohamed 'Pa-Momo' Fofanah, former co-counsel for Brima Bazzy Kamara, Freetown, May 2016; Interview with Yada H. Williams, former co-counsel for Allieu Kondewa, Freetown, May 2016.

[90] Interview with Yada H. Williams, *ibid*.

> Among the opposition groups, the AFRC was punished most severely with an average sentence of 48.3 years. […] The average punishment for the RUF defendants was thirty-nine years.[91]

Some would interpret the large disparity in sentences given to government opponents versus government supporters as victor's justice from a court established partly by the government for the specific purpose of punishing government opponents. Holders of this view could be justified, given that the letter sent by President Kabbah to the UN requesting the establishment of a special court singled out the "RUF and their accomplices" as the targets of the court.[92] In spite of specific mention of the RUF, the AFRC convicts, on average, received lengthier sentences by the SCSL than the RUF convicts. This may be due to the fact that the Court ultimately tried more top-level AFRC commanders than it did their RUF counterparts, and the crimes committed by the most senior commanders were deemed graver. However, in a country notorious for its history of military coups d'état, imposing the heftiest average sentences on the AFRC convicts may have served the unintentional purpose of instilling fear of punishment for involvement in insurgencies among members of the nation's reconstituted military force, the Republic of Sierra Leone Armed Forces. A potential indicator of this deterrent effect is that no coup d'état has taken place nor has been attempted in Sierra Leone since the commencement of the SCSL's operations.

6.4.7.2. Place of Imprisonment

Coupled with the length of sentences is the place of imprisonment outside of Sierra Leone. With the exception of Taylor and of Fofana, who is currently living in Bo, Sierra Leone on conditional early release, the remaining convicts continue to be imprisoned in Rwanda's Mpanga prison. The lack of prison facilities in Sierra Leone meeting the required international standards for treatment of prisoners convicted by international tribunals

---

91 Shahram Dana, "The Sentencing Legacy of the Special Court for Sierra Leone", in *Georgia Journal of International and Comparative Law*, 2014, vol. 42, no. 3, p. 659.

92 United Nations Security Council, Letter dated 9 August 2000 from the Permanent Representative of Sierra Leone to the United Nations addressed to the President of the Security Council, UN doc. S/2000/786, 2000, Annex.

necessitated their imprisonment in another country.[93] Apart from the availability of such facilities in Rwanda, the fact that the ICTR had already entered into an agreement with the government of Rwanda for the enforcement of sentences of international convicts meant that Rwanda was one country that would be open to the prospect of hosting the SCSL convicts. Path dependence may also explain why the SCSL registrar did not consider other countries for the enforcement of sentences of the RUF, AFRC and CDF convicts before approaching Rwanda.

Taylor, on the other hand, is serving his sentence in the United Kingdom. As early as June 2006, a year before the opening of his trial, the UK government agreed to enforce the sentence against Taylor in the event that he was convicted.[94] This assurance from the UK government came hand-in-hand with an agreement by the government of the Netherlands to host his trial on the condition that he would be imprisoned in another country. Taylor's application to the SCSL to be transferred to Mpanga Prison was rejected. Imperatives for his imprisonment were to keep him out of West Africa, separate from the other SCSL convicts, and out of easy proximity to his associates. Both victims and ex-combatants alike have expressed satisfaction at Taylor's imprisonment outside West Africa and outside of the continent.[95] A few RUF ex-combatants have even commented that if the SCSL convicts were imprisoned in the sub-region, their desire and ability to escape would increase.[96] Usman, now a motor-bike taxi driver in Makeni, admitted that "[w]hen some of us are jailed, our only thoughts are to escape. [...] And there are terrorists in the region. If you give them money, they will easily run a mission to help the men escape from prison".[97] Much as it does not render impossible their ability to communicate with associates to plan an escape or order the commission

---

[93] Committee on Economic, Social and Cultural Rights, Standard Minimum Rules for the Treatment of Prisoner, Resolution 663 C (XXIV), 31 July 1957; Committee on Economic, Social and Cultural Rights, Standard Minimum Rules for the Treatment of Prisoner, Resolution 2076 (LXII), 13 May 1977. These Rules have been superseded by the United Nations Standard Minimum Rules for the Treatment of Prisoners (the Nelson Mandela Rules), UN doc. A/Res/70/175, adopted on 17 December 2015.

[94] Agreement between the Special Court for Sierra Leone and the Government of the United Kingdom of Great Britain and Northern Ireland on the Enforcement of Sentences of the Special Court for Sierra Leone, Cm 7208, 10 July 2007.

[95] Focus group discussion with amputees, Makama Camp, April 2016.

[96] Focus group discussion with ex-combatants, Makeni, April 2016.

[97] *Ibid.*

of crimes, the imprisonment of the convicts in Rwanda and the United Kingdom creates challenges for them to tap into or control networks in Sierra Leone and broader West Africa.

6.4.8. Release of Convicts and Societal Reintegration

Barring unforeseen circumstances, the relatively short 20- and 25-year sentences given to Kondewa and Gbao mean that they are likely to follow Fofana's lead to apply for conditional early release once they have served two-thirds of their sentences. Supposing removal of individuals from society to be one of the means by which deterrence has been effectuated, granting conditional early release to convicted prisoners naturally suggests that the Court looks to indicators of deterrence while assessing the likelihood of recidivism.

For instance, eight out of 13 prosecution witnesses interviewed before Fofana's hearing on conditional early release opposed his release altogether.[98] Eleven out of 13 witnesses expressed deep concern about their security and that of their families if Fofana were to be released to their locality. Their concerns ranged from fear of being contacted by Fofana or his agents to not feeling safe to live in the same community with him. To address these concerns, the president of the SCSL considered whether Fofana had any power, position or influence over ex-combatants in or around Bo, where he would be living. The president noted the following:

> Most of the views gathered from interviewees by the Witness and Victims Section, on whether Fofana will still be powerful and popular among CDF fighters, were that he will no longer enjoy his former status because, according to them, "Special Court for Sierra Leone used most of their former commanders and fighters as prosecution witnesses. This alone has weakened any prospect of popularity for him because lots of divisions have occurred in his absence and there is disunity among them".[99]

In line with the Court's assessment, victims' fears have not yet been realised. Between Fofana's return to Bo and the April 2016 hearing on his violation of terms of his release, none of the victims or witnesses had seen

---

[98] SCSL, *Prosecutor v. Moinina Fofana and Allieu Kondewa*, Decision of the President on Application for Conditional Early Release, SCSL-2004-14-ES, 11 August 2014, para. 26 (http://www.legal-tools.org/doc/1027ef/).

[99] *Ibid.*, para. 29.

him. Moreover, even former CDF fighters like Nyakeh see the threat of Fofana repeating his crimes as minimal because "economically, people like Moinina Fofana do not have the money to organise large ammunitions unless someone with financial power says that he will support them to co-ordinate the fight".[100]

The individual's conduct following reintegration also carries a great deal of importance for assessing the extent to which there has been deterrence. This was demonstrated in April 2016 when Fofana violated a condition of his early release agreement by misinforming the supervising authority of his whereabouts while he participated in a political meeting in Makeni.[101] Fofana, like the other SCSL convicts had been deprived of certain civil and political rights, such as the ability to participate in local or national politics. As a result of the violation, Justice Vivian Solomon of the Residual Special Court for Sierra Leone ordered that the conditions of Fofana's early conditional release be tightened. The court order's effect on his deterrence calculation will be to accord more weight to the risk of punishment for a release violation, now knowing the seriousness with which the Court will deal with them. Ultimately, the Court's determination on an application for conditional early release, as well as the continuous monitoring of the convict throughout the early release period, serves as a built-in deterrence check.

6.4.9. Operation alongside the Truth and Reconciliation Commission

The operation of the Sierra Leone TRC from early 2003 until late 2004 overlapped with the early days of the SCSL. Unlike its South African predecessor, the Sierra Leone TRC did not have the option to refer individuals to the national prosecuting authority. Additionally, a perpetrator's testimony before the Sierra Leone TRC did not have any sanctions attached to it. This was to encourage everyone – victims and perpetrators – to come forward and give accounts of what happened in order to create a historical record of the conflict in Sierra Leone and promote reconciliation. Thus, as conceived, the TRC should not have undermined or increased any deterrent effect that the SCSL would have had.

---

[100] Focus group discussion with ex-combatants, Freetown, May 2016.

[101] SCSL, *Prosecutor v. Moinina Fofana*, Disposition on the Matter of Moinina Fofana's Violations of the Terms of His Conditional Early Release, 25 April 2016, para. 81.

In reality, rumours that the TRC was sharing the testimony given at its public hearings with the SCSL prosecutor to build the latter's cases initially threatened to undermine the TRC's work by causing some reluctance on the part of both ex-combatants and victims to participate in the TRC's public hearings.[102] Ex-combatants in particular feared that any statement that they made to the TRC would be used to prosecute them at the SCSL, or to compel them to testify against their commanders at the SCSL.[103] Under the Special Court Ratification Act, the Court had the authority to order the disclosure of documents from the TRC.[104] In spite of public pronouncements by the SCSL prosecutor that the Office of the Prosecutor would not subpoena the statements of those who testified before the TRC,[105] and the TRC Secretariat's announcement that it would not share information with the SCSL, the two institutions never entered into a formal agreement on the matter. In order to appease the public, particularly ex-combatants, SCSL outreach staff made attempts to distinguish between the two institutions and emphasise that they were not sharing information. The effect that sensitisation had on ex-combatants' willingness to testify before either institution is unclear at best.[106] Thus, their unwillingness to testify cannot necessarily be attributed to fears of information sharing between the two institutions.

6.5. The General Deterrent Effect of the SCSL

Although the Office of the Prosecutor initially avoided the deterrence rhetoric, by the time judgments were being rendered, the prosecutor had fully embraced it. The evolution in language may have been the result of a policy shift by the Office due to changes in leadership or the increasing focus on the Court's legacy as it moved closer to winding up its operations. For instance, following the RUF convictions, Prosecutor Stephen

---

[102] Post-Conflict Reintegration Initiative for Development and Empowerment (PRIDE), *Ex-Combatant Views of the Truth and Reconciliation Commission and the Special Court for Sierra Leone*, 12 September 2002, p. 13.

[103] *Ibid.*, p. 19.

[104] SCSL, Special Court Agreement, 2002 (Ratification) Act, 25 April 2002, Articles 21(2) (http://www.legal-tools.org/doc/345800/).

[105] SCSL, "TRC Chairman and Special Court Prosecutor Join Hands to Fight Impunity", OTP Press Release, 10 December 2002.

[106] Post-Conflict Reintegration Initiative for Development and Empowerment, 2002, pp. 19–20, see *supra* note 102.

Rapp noted the historical significance of a Court convicting individuals for the specific war crime of attacking peacekeepers. He asserted that the conviction "sends a message that may deter such attacks against the men and women who are protecting individuals, restoring security, and keeping the peace across the globe".[107] Following the RUF Appeals Chamber judgment, the prosecutor Joseph Kamara likewise acknowledged the breakthrough that the convictions for acts of terrorism against the civilian population had, stating:

> During the Sierra Leone civil war, it was more dangerous to be a civilian than a soldier. [...] This judgment sends a signal that such tactics of warfare will not go unpunished. It may act as a deterrent against those who would use this strategy to further their own aims at the expense of the innocent.[108]

While the prosecutors' comments are applicable to any armed conflict situation, the deterrent effect of the convictions is important for Sierra Leone given the country's tumultuous history of breakdowns in the rule of law and violence. Therefore, this section assesses the effect of the SCSL on the general prevention of human rights violations and serious crimes in Sierra Leone.

6.5.1. Restoring the Rule of Law

Prior to, during and even after the armed conflict in Sierra Leone, there was a long, entrenched history of impunity for serious crimes. This was aided by a broken judicial system. When the state did prosecute individuals for serious crimes, it mainly targeted political opponents or allies who were seen as a threat to the head of state's power. Often these prosecutions involved charging political opponents with treason, then trying, convicting and executing them. For 29 individuals executed under the National Provincial Ruling Council government in December 1992, no trial is known to have taken place before their executions. Other treason trials that took place in Sierra Leone were far from meeting the minimum standards of due process. Most were carried out under authoritarian or military governments or court martial. These prosecutions were indicative

---

[107] SCSL, "Special Court Prosecutor Hails RUF Convictions", OTP Press Release, 25 February 2009.

[108] SCSL, "Prosecutor Welcomes Convictions in RUF Appeals Judgment", OTP Press Release, 26 October 2009.

of the fate of any individual who was to be prosecuted in Sierra Leone courts for their involvement in the war. This would have factored into the rebels' decision-making during the war, as well as their negotiation of amnesty and key strategic positions within government at Lomé. Considering the high certainty of punishment that Sankoh and others faced in 1999 following their convictions for treason, the priorities of the perpetrators were to avoid punishment by gaining access to power, even if it counter intuitively meant committing more atrocities.

Jo and Simmons highlight how much of a factor a country's culture of impunity plays into the accused person's or would-be perpetrator's cost-benefit analysis of whether they will be punished for the crimes.[109] They assert that "raising the risk of punishment where the rule of law is otherwise weak is precisely the *formal* role envisioned for the ICC". A similar and largely hortatory role was envisioned for the SCSL, recognising the weak judiciary and the erosion of the rule of law that existed in Sierra Leone prior to and during the war. Only small indications exist that the SCSL trials and operation in Sierra Leone have made incremental inroads into promoting the rule of law and intolerance of impunity for serious crimes and human rights violations within the country.

6.5.2. Promoting a Culture of Respect for Human Rights

The proliferation of human rights culture in a society can influence individuals' decisions on whether to engage in violence. Jo and Simmons use growth in the number of human rights organisations in a country as a quantitative indicator of general deterrence.[110] In any post-conflict country, however, human rights organisations spring up and multiply rapidly, particularly as the heavy influx of donor funds to human rights work makes such work more lucrative and prestigious than it would otherwise have been. Additionally, other entities apart from civil society organisations have engaged in awareness-raising on human rights. The increase in the number of human rights organisations operating in a country does not necessarily speak to their effectiveness, reach or influence, but it can be an indicator of potential avenues through which to promote respect for human rights.

---

[109] Jo and Simmons, 2016, p. 9, see *supra* note 34.
[110] *Ibid.*

In the Sierra Leone context, a more accurate indicator would be a qualitative assessment of the general public's level of understanding of human rights norms and accountability. The Outreach Section of the SCSL played an instrumental role in that regard. Through town hall meetings, radio programmes, the creation of Accountability Now Clubs at tertiary institutions throughout the country, cartoon booklets, and education programmes targeted at specific segments of the population, the Outreach Section engaged in dialogue with various target groups about developments in the cases, the Court itself, international humanitarian law, human rights and the rule of law generally. Patrick Tucker, head of a child-focused NGO that is a member of the Special Court Interactive Forum, remarked that the SCSL became such a well-recognised institution in Sierra Leone that some members of the public initially had the misconception that it would be a permanent court with the power to adjudicate all types of cases.[111] To the extent that the SCSL instilled more confidence in the public than the national judiciary, Sierra Leoneans began to issue the warning, "I'll take you to the Special Court" when they had a grievance against someone or felt the threat of violence from another person.

Prior to and during the trials, the Outreach Section involved NGOs, especially Special Court Interactive Forum members, in its public education and outreach work. As a result of these efforts, NGOs became synonymous with human rights in the minds of some Sierra Leoneans. In fact, Makeni motorbike taxi driver Salieu even considered that the time and efforts of these NGOs in preaching peace and lecturing on human rights would be wasted if he and his fellow ex-combatants decided to engage in violence.[112] That this attitude of respecting human rights is taking root in the minds of Sierra Leoneans, particularly ex-combatants, and influencing their decisions is a step in the right direction for long-term peace.

6.6. Conclusion

The SCSL's contributions to international criminal jurisprudence and the administration of international criminal justice have been well documented. The extent to which the Court's contributions extend to deterring international crimes has largely been unexplored, particularly using both court-based and context-specific factors as analytical measures. This case

---

[111] Interview with Patrick J.B. Tucker, Freetown, May 2016.
[112] Focus group discussion with ex-combatants, Makeni, April 2016.

study found that those factors served more to increase the deterrent effect of the SCSL than to undermine it. In other words, the SCSL's prosecutions mixed with the political and social environment that existed in Sierra Leone after the armed conflict on the whole incapacitated a small number of critical perpetrators while raising the risk of punishment felt by would-be perpetrators for committing the same or similar crimes.

6.6.1. Factors Undermining Deterrence

The case study identified the following factors as having undermined deterrence: the SCSL's lack of transnational police powers and the reliance on co-operation from other states in the sub-region for the arrest and transfer of accused persons to the Court; the Court's perceived lack of legitimacy on the issue of forfeiture of Taylor's assets; and the persistence of the hierarchical authority structures of the accused's criminal or social organisations.

6.6.1.1. The SCSL's Lack of Transnational Police Powers

The inability of international courts to operate without the co-operation of states cannot be illustrated more clearly than in international criminal tribunals' attempts to effect transnational arrests. Of the three indictees for whom the SCSL had to rely on the goodwill of other states to arrest, only Taylor was eventually apprehended by Nigeria after it first granted him exile. For the three years in which Taylor remained in exile, a question mark hung over the weight of the SCSL's power in the minds of the Sierra Leonean public. To some, this undermined the Court's legitimacy, a key factor in deterrence. Bockarie's assassination on Taylor's orders further underscores the complexities and dangers of relying on the co-operation of a state headed by an individual who is also on the Court's radar as a suspect. International legal principles on state sovereignty will continue to prevent both states and international courts from acquiring transnational police powers, and so the ICC, which is now facing a major stumbling block with the execution of arrest warrants by states, should continue seeking new avenues for engaging the Assembly of State Parties on the issue.

6.6.1.2. Lack of Proactivity of the Office of the Prosecutor on Asset Forfeiture

While it may not have undermined deterrence *per se*, the Office of the Prosecutor's lack of proactivity on requesting the forfeiture of the proceeds which Taylor had acquired through his crimes was a missed opportunity for the Prosecution to create another 'cost' of international criminal activity. In the cost-benefit analysis that comprises deterrence, every cost that can be registered is more likely to dissuade rational human beings from committing the crime to which that cost is associated. With victim reparations provided for in the ICC Statute, the ICC Office of the Prosecutor should make requests for asset forfeiture of non-indigent defendants a routine part of its comprehensive treatment of a case.

6.6.1.3. Strength of Criminal Networks and Persistence of Command Authority

Non-court-based factors should not be overlooked in assessing the deterrent effect of the Court. Concerns about Norman and Taylor inciting violence even while in detention demonstrate that where criminal organisations or networks continue to function, court-based actions against one or a few individuals within the organisation are not enough to dismantle organisational criminal behaviour.

6.6.2. Factors Increasing Deterrence

The case study reveals that the following court-based factors likely increased deterrence: prosecutorial strategy on case selection; the certainty of prosecution brought about by the timing of indictments and Sierra Leone government co-operation on arrests and transfers of persons to the custody of the Court; the severity of punishment; and a robust outreach programme. The most significant context-based factors that increased deterrence centered on the non-lucrative nature of the commission of crimes for the majority of combatants and the certainty of punishment under the domestic criminal justice system.

6.6.2.1. Prosecutorial Strategy on Case Selection

While strong criminal networks can undermine deterrence, understanding from the outset the criminal and social networks at play in a country can influence case selection by the prosecution. This includes whether and how to use individuals as insider witnesses rather than prosecuting them. For instance, Massaquoi's role as an insider witness for the prosecution in the cases against the RUF and AFRC defendants served to not only provide a path to convicting Sesay, a more senior RUF commander, but also to removing Massaquoi himself from a physical and moral position among his peers that would have enabled him to commit additional crimes.

6.6.2.2. State Co-operation and National Police Power

Easily overlooked, the "national police power" that the SCSL enjoyed because of its location in Sierra Leone and strong co-operation with the government was vital to quickly effecting arrests and maintaining the element of surprise that prevented those indicted persons who were resident in Sierra Leone from evading justice. A useful lesson for the ICC is that it should seek to ensure that a state's ICC Statute implementing legislation contains co-operation provisions that would facilitate arrests and transfers to the Court, and that thoughtful diplomacy is a priority for developing strong co-operation relationships with the states in which the indictees reside.

6.6.2.3. Severity of Punishment

While this case study does not challenge recent theories that certainty of punishment remains the most determinant factor in deterring international crimes, it does lend credence to the notion that severity of punishment is still an important factor and one that should not be overlooked in any deterrence study. Not only did the lengthy sentences imposed on those convicted persons who had opposed the government amount to their permanent ejection from Sierra Leonean society, it also served as a means of heightening fear among would-be insurgents of the punishment attached to subversive activities involving international crimes. The heavier sentences imposed by the SCSL compared to those of the ICTY and ICTR also provide a launch pad for a long-term comparative assessment of the deterrent effects of imposing lengthier sentences.

6.6.2.4. Public Outreach

Unlike the *ad hoc* tribunals that preceded it, the SCSL's strong commitment to public outreach provides an additional factor for assessing the Court's deterrent effect. Outreach added to the foundation on which the

Court would seek to build its legitimacy in the eyes of its targets, war victims, and the general public. Constantly confronted with discussions on respect for human rights, some ex-combatants have even been persuaded not to re-engage in violence. Outreach has proven to be integral to explaining the complexities of this type of court's operations and to achieving deontological goals, including deterrence. Thus, short of creating human rights discourse fatigue, international criminal tribunals' outreach efforts should involve constant engagement of various target groups, from the military to ex-combatants to affected communities. The constant engagement serves as a reminder of the Court's existence and, in turn, the threat of punishment. It also reinforces human rights and rule of law ideals that undergird a country's movement toward sustainable peace.

6.6.2.5. Unprofitability of War to Lower-Level Combatants

Although the freezing of Taylor's assets had little to no effect on the commission of crimes after 2003, the lack of economic viability of engaging in armed conflict may have been the most significant factor – court or context-based – for targeted deterrence. As the Sierra Leone TRC report made clear, having a large segment of the population made up of disaffected, unemployed young people was one of the catalysts of the armed conflict. However, the bitter experience of war coupled with the realisation that they derived no economic benefit from it have led lower-level ex-combatants to a tentative conclusion as to the expense of their actions. An international criminal tribunal may have no control over the internal economic viability of states, but they are empowered to seize assets derived from the crimes falling within their remit, and thus could have some influence over cutting off individuals' or armed groups' financial sources. Therefore, in situation countries where there is ongoing conflict, the ICC Office of the Prosecutor should focus not only on prosecuting individuals directly involved in committing atrocities, but also include financiers and use leverage with the UN to freeze individuals' assets in an attempt to cut off perpetrators' financial and operational support sources.

6.6.2.6. Threat of Domestic Punishment

The threat of the imposition of the death penalty following Sankoh's and others' convictions for treason in domestic criminal proceedings prior to Lomé had a significant impact on their cost-benefit analysis. Absent securing pardon and amnesty during the Lomé peace negotiations, this would have been the greatest cost associated with the crimes they committed during the war. Thus, the national criminal justice context, even one that appears broken, cannot be overlooked as a primary or parallel deterrence mechanism to the international tribunal. Indeed, the primacy of national jurisdictions and the complementary role of the ICC is emphasised in the Preamble of the ICC Statute.[113] The potential threat posed by domestic prosecutions and punishment underscores the importance of complementarity to deterrence. Where the ICC provides a secondary threat to that posed by the national criminal justice system, both the certainty of punishment and the cost of committing the crime increase. In that vein, Sierra Leone should enact legislation that incorporates international crimes into domestic law such that the national justice system would be able to prosecute individuals for these crimes should they be committed in Sierra Leone in the future. Likewise, efforts by the ICC, the Assembly of State Parties and NGOs to encourage and enable states to incorporate international crimes into their domestic laws and undertake investigations and prosecutions, whether under the rubric of positive complementarity or not, should continue.

---

[113] ICC Statute, Preamble, see *supra* note 1.

7

Dissuasive or Disappointing? Measuring the Deterrent Effect of the International Criminal Court in the Democratic Republic of the Congo

Sharanjeet Parmar[*]

7.1. Introduction

The International Criminal Court ('ICC') opened its first case in the Democratic Republic of the Congo ('DRC'), by charging Thomas Lubanga Dyilo with the war crime of enlisting and conscripting children under the age of 15 years and using them to participate actively in hostilities as child soldiers while commander of an armed group operating in the northeastern region of Ituri. The recruitment and use of children[1] by both the Congolese army and armed groups has been widespread throughout the modern history of violence in eastern Congo, starting with the armed rebellion against the former dictator Mobutu Sese Seko in 1997 led by Laurent Kabila who used child soldiers known as *kadogos* (literally the 'little ones').[2] Eastern Congolese children continue to be at serious risk of recruitment and use in hostilities either forcibly through abduction by armed groups or voluntarily as part of self-defence forces in their communities. This chapter evaluates whether the ICC has realised a deterrent effect on

---

[*] **Sharanjeet Parmar** is an international human rights attorney. She has worked in the Democratic Republic of the Congo since 2009 on justice and accountability issues, including the commission of serious crimes against children. She formerly worked as an Assistant Trial Attorney for the Special Court for Sierra Leone and taught in the Human Rights Program at Harvard Law School. She is presently the Anti-corruption Project Head, Essor Programme for PwC UK. She has worked in over a dozen countries across Africa and Asia on human rights, gender, peace and security issues for a number of international organisations.

[1] Under both Congolese and international law, children are considered to be human beings under the age of 18 years. République Démocratique du Congo, Loi 09/001 Portant Protection de l'enfant, 25 May 2009, Article 2; United Nations General Assembly, Convention on the Rights of the Child, UN doc. A/44/49, 20 November 1989, Article 1 (http://www.legal-tools.org/doc/f48f9e/).

[2] Filip Reyntjens, *The Great African War: Congo and Regional Geopolitics, 1996–2006*, Cambridge University Press, Cambridge, 2009, p. 105.

the recruitment and use of child soldiers in the DRC in two respects that correlate directly with these two types of ever-present risk for children. First, it assesses to what extent the Court realised deterrence among armed actors either directly in terms of those operating in Ituri or indirectly among armed actors operating in other areas of eastern Congo. Second, it assesses whether the Court realised deterrence among communities affected by violence in terms of dissuading local communities to desist from long-standing practices of child recruitment and use that have persisted as part of sustaining self-defence militias.

Following the *Lubanga* case, the ICC extended its work in the DRC to other kinds of serious violations. This chapter focuses exclusively on the crime of recruitment and use of children for explicit analytical reasons. First, realising a deterrent effect invariably involves changing attitudes and behaviours of local actors, which demands a long and sustained period of anti-impunity efforts. The Court's Ituri cases have enjoyed the longest period of activity of delivering justice to a designated geographic area. Furthermore, as of October 2016 they represent the only cases where the ICC's entire judicial processes – from indictment to judgment, sentencing and reparations – have been accomplished. Second, the crime of recruitment and use of child soldiers presents the research project with a unique opportunity to evaluate both targeted and general deterrence, the latter of which is also considered in terms of social deterrence. This particular violation enjoys strong levels of commission not only among armed actors who are most likely to be targeted by the Court for prosecutions, but equally local communities and children themselves, who view the use of child soldiers as integral to protecting themselves in the face of persistent insecurity. The operation of both targeted and general deterrence is thus integral to reducing levels of commission of this particular crime. Finally, a study of the ICC's prosecution of recruitment and use of child soldiers in the DRC provides concrete contextually relevant evidence on the nature of the relationship between targeted and general deterrence.

7.2. Chapter Overview

This chapter tests whether through the joint operation of specific and general deterrence, the ICC's Ituri case targeting Lubanga had the ultimate impact of reducing the rate of commission of the crime of recruitment and use of child soldiers in the DRC. It also considers the broader deterrent impact of the ICC by examining conflict dynamics and the commission of serious violations in Ituri and eastern DRC generally against a wider range of cases, including those of Chui, Katanga and Ntaganda.

In testing this, the chapter is presented in three parts. First, it presents its research findings on the potential targeted and general deterrence effects by the ICC. Specifically, it presents evidence from Ituri on attitudes and perceptions of armed groups and the civilian population in relation to the recruitment and use of child soldiers. Second, the chapter juxtaposes evidence on conflict dynamics and rates of commission of the crime against process tracing of key Court milestones. The resulting evidence suggests a modest deterrent impact of the Court. To understand this result, part two highlights key contextual considerations from the DRC case study that are necessary to an analytical inquiry of measuring deterrence of the ICC in a situation of ongoing armed conflict. These contextual considerations explain how a combination of carrots and sticks was insufficient to mitigate complex conflict dynamics that reduced the deterrent effect of the Court. Third, the chapter extrapolates findings from the first and second parts and proposes key conclusions for the ICC with the aim of maximising its impact on reducing recruitment and use of child soldiers, and ultimately supporting peacebuilding efforts.

Based on this three-part analysis, the chapter concludes that both direct and indirect deterrence effects are tenuous at best when the conditions driving the commission of serious crimes are more entrenched and longstanding than the anti-impunity efforts undertaken by the Court. First, in situations of ongoing armed conflict, the DRC case study illustrates how ICC cases that focus on a specific crime base will enjoy little targeted or general deterrence on the commission of crimes of other geographic areas and time periods without a sustained anti-impunity strategy that is coordinated with national efforts. Second, the DRC case study demonstrates how successfully resisting community impulses to defend themselves by using child soldiers must combine general deterrence efforts with broader political and economic reforms that respond to sustained violence dynamics.

The DRC case study concludes that assessing the deterrent effect of the ICC cannot rest on a simple exploration of direct causality between Court operations and the commission of crimes. Rather, deeper analysis is needed on how in the future the Court should situate itself within broader stability and peacebuilding efforts through the development and coordination of its prosecutorial and outreach strategies. Specifically, prosecutorial strategies should be designed with an eye on, and if possible in collaboration with, international and national actors working on judicial and non-judicial accountability mechanisms, such as trials, travel bans and sanctions regimes. Second, Court outreach programmes require deeper resources and must extend beyond communities situated within a specific case to other regions suffering from active hostilities. In sum, complementarity should be conceived of and applied not only in terms of prosecutions efforts but also in consideration of how court outreach efforts can support local action to realise broader levels of general deterrence.

7.3. Research Methodology

This study employed a combination of research methods. First, qualitative field research was undertaken through focus groups and key informant interviews to assess attitudes of actors that would be targeted by ICC prosecutions of recruitment. In Ituri, four key informant interviews and six focus group discussions were held across Bunia, Kasenyi, Djugu and Mungwalu. Interview targets included military judges and prosecutors, human rights and child protection actors, community leaders and members of local militias. Second, key informant interviews were also held with justice and child protection actors in Goma, Bukavu and Kinshasa to assess how the ICC's operations measured against issues of child protection and national anti-impunity efforts. Finally, desktop research included a detailed literature review and analysis of conflict dynamics and the collection of quantitative data on the commission of serious violations, in particular rates of recruitment and use of children by armed groups.

Central to this chapter's analysis of the impact of ICC operations is a detailed presentation of conflict dynamics and the commission of serious violations over ten years against key events in the Ituri cases. Specifically, Annex B outlines activities by armed groups against the evolution of the ICC cases involving Thomas Lubanga, Germaine Katanga, Ngudjolo Chui and Bosco Ntaganda.[3] Second, process tracing of the cases is also considered against data on child rights violations. This data relies on reporting by the United Nations ('UN') and non-governmental organisation ('NGO') agencies, in particular, the UN monitoring and reporting

---

[3] For a detailed overview of each case, including status of each case, the armed group affiliations of each accused, and a list of charges laid, see International Criminal Court, Situation in the Democratic Republic of the Congo folders at the Legal Tools Database (https://www.legal-tools.org/).

mechanism on grave violations against children and armed conflict, which is presented in periodic reports of the secretary-general's special representative on children and armed conflict and reporting by the UN Group of Experts and Human Rights Watch. Additional data considered include the numbers of children demobilised as a result of demobilisation, demilitarisation and reintegration (DDR) efforts in the DRC.

7.4. Overview of the Ituri Conflict and the ICC Cases

The four-year conflict in Ituri killed over 50,000 people and displaced more than 500,000 between 1999 and 2003.[4] Armed groups continue to operate and terrorise the civilian population to this day, though not on the same scale as during the height of the conflict. Like armed conflicts across sub-Saharan Africa, the drivers and dynamics underpinning the conflict in Ituri are multiple and complex. Set against the collapse of Zaire and the corresponding security vacuum and economic crisis, multiple factors led to this interethnic war that involved primarily the Lendu and Hema populations.[5] Profiting from overarching failed state dynamics, inter-community tensions were manipulated by local, national and regional actors – in particular Uganda – who provided military and political support to local armed groups in order to access and control economic interests in the resource-rich region. The conflict was exacerbated by the "growing rivalry between Kampala, Kinshasa and Kigali for control of the region, violence over land disputes and increasingly marked divisions between communities".[6]

Described as the "bloodiest corner of the DRC", no small moniker in a country suffering from waves of violence over decades, the conflict in Ituri involved a terrifying level of serious violations with fighting intensifying in late 2002 and early 2003.[7] Ethnic groups targeted each other for killings, summary executions, torture, rapes, and inhumane acts such as mutilations and cannibalism. The recruitment and use of children for military service, some as young as seven years old, was so widespread that

---

[4] International Crisis Group, "Congo: Four Priorities for Sustainable Peace in Ituri", in *Africa Report*, no. 40, 13 May 2008.

[5] Reyntjens, 2009, see *supra* note 2.

[6] International Crisis Group, 2008, p. 1, see *supra* note 4.

[7] Human Rights Watch, "Ituri: 'Covered in Blood': Ethnically Targeted Violence in Northeastern DR Congo", in *Human Rights Watch Report*, vol. 15, no. 11(A), July 2003.

groups were described as "armies of children".[8] The viciousness that characterised the conflict and the inability of the United Nations Mission in the Democratic Republic of Congo ('MONUC' later 'MONUSCO') peacekeeping force to contain it invariably caught the attention of the international community. In 2003 the UN Security Council authorised deployment of the Interim Emergency Multinational Force, which became the European Union's first peacekeeping mission. A relative calm did not set in until 2005, however, when MONUC finally forced disarmament of militias and the DRC government arrested five militia leaders, including Thomas Lubanga and Germaine Katanga, who had been previously granted positions in the Congolese army, Forces armées de la République démocratique du Congo ('FARDC').

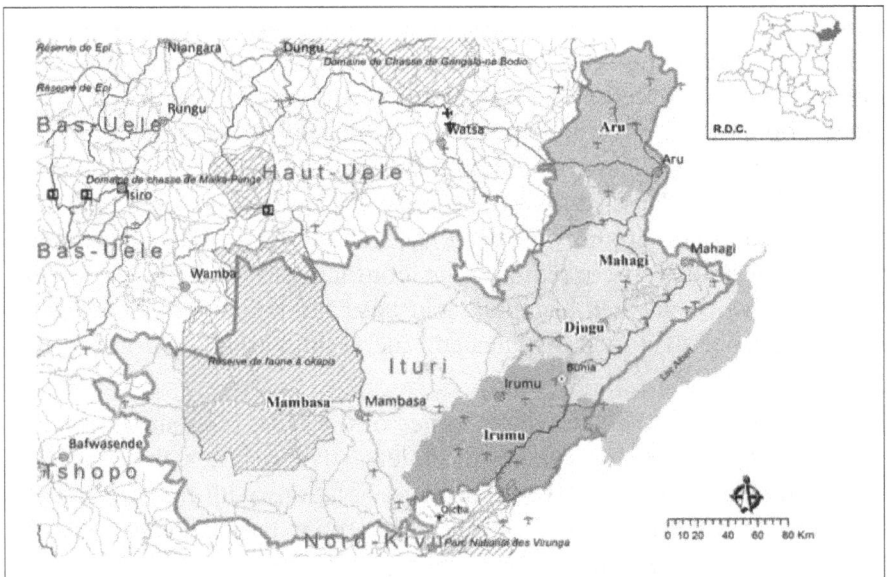

Figure 1: Ituri Region, Democratic Republic of the Congo.[9]

In response to the scale and scope of the violations committed by armed factions, the ICC opened its first situation in the Ituri region in 2004 and later brought charges against four warlords; Thomas Lubanga,

---

[8] *Ibid.*

[9] Cellule d'Analyses des Indicateurs de Développement, "Province de l'Ituri".

Germaine Katanga, Ngudjolo Chui and Bosco Ntaganda. The Lubanga case focused uniquely on the recruitment and use of child soldiers,[10] in direct response to the widespread and systematic nature in which children were used and abused by armed groups in the conflict.[11] Unfortunately, the ethnic dimension of the conflict left victims belonging to Lendu and other communities targeted for other crimes known to have been committed by Lubanga's primarily Hema Union des patriotes congolais ('UPC', Union of Congolese Patriots) feeling robbed of justice since the victims of child recruitment were children belonging to the Hema community.[12] This perceived imbalance was deepened with the broader range of charges brought against Katanga, commander of Force de résistance patriotique d'Ituri ('FRPI', Front for Patriotic Resistance in Ituri), which was allied with Chui's Lendu militia, Front des nationalistes et intégrationnistes ('FNI', Nationalist and Integrationist Front), that opposed the UPC. Ntaganda was promoted to the rank of general in the Congolese army and evaded arrest for years with the complicity of the Congolese government until turning himself in later in 2013.

This chapter examines whether the targeted approach by the ICC in the *Lubanga* case on recruitment and use of child soldiers had a deterrent effect on the practice in Ituri and other parts of eastern DRC.[13] The DRC

---

[10] The ICC Statute prohibits as a war crime conscripting or enlisting children under the age of 15 years into the national armed forces or using them to participate actively in hostilities in armed conflict of either an international or a non-international character. ICC, Rome Statute of the International Criminal Court, 17 July 1998, in force 1 July 2002, Article 8(b)(xxvi) and 8(e)(vii) ('ICC Statute') (http://www.legal-tools.org/doc/7b9af9/).

[11] For a comprehensive overview of the experiences of children associated with armed forces or groups in eastern DRC, see Amnesty International, "DRC: Children at War, Creating Hope for the Future", 11 October 2006. For a compelling and nuanced depiction of the complexity inherent to the experiences of children associated with armed forces or groups and their capacity for resilience, see Michael G. Wessells, *Child Soldiers: From Violence to Protection*, Harvard University Press, Cambridge, MA, 2009.

[12] Gender crimes were not charged in Lubanga despite the evidence thereof. Both the Women's Initiative for Gender Justice and the Legal Representative of Victims sought to broaden the charges against Lubanga to include gender crimes without success. For details, see Women's Initiatives for Gender Justice, "Gender Report Card on the International Criminal Court 2009", October 2009; Women's Initiatives for Gender Justice, "Gender Report Card on the International Criminal Court", November 2011.

[13] While the ICC Statute prohibits recruitment and use of children under the age of 15 years, the DRC has signed and ratified the Optional Protocol to the Convention on the Rights of the Child on the Involvement of Children in Armed Conflict, which prohibits recruitment and use in hostilities persons under the age of 18 years, United Nations General Assembly, Resolution 54/263, UN doc. A/54/49, 25 May 2000 (http://www.legal-tools.org/doc/669fb1/).

case study provides us with an important opportunity to assess whether and to what extent the ICC can deter a specific violation not only in a targeted crime base, but also in neighbouring geographic areas that fall equally under the Court's jurisdiction. For this reason, the chapter presents evidence on rates of child recruitment and use not only in Ituri over the course of ICC operations but also considers rates in other eastern DRC provinces where armed groups continue to operate. In addition to evaluating the reach of targeted deterrence, the Ituri cases provide an opportunity to evaluate broader general deterrence, and specifically, attitudes and behaviours by community leaders, parents and children themselves on use of child soldiers. The chapter thus weighs the normative power wielded by the Court in the face of countervailing local dynamics for children to defend their communities, exact revenge for past violations, or avail themselves of economic opportunities otherwise lacking due to chronic instability. Finally, to ensure a holistic approach, the chapter also considers broader deterrence dynamics on the overall commission of serious violations broadly in the region over the course of Court operations.

7.5. Assessing the Operation of Specific and General Deterrence in the DRC

7.5.1. Standard Claims about the ICC and Deterrence

In testing the hypothesis, this chapter evaluates standard claims made about the power of the ICC to realise a deterrent effect. These claims largely fall into three modes through which the Court is purported to achieve this effect: targeted deterrence, general deterrence, and a broader impact resulting from an inter-relationship between the two forms of deterrence. This chapter tests each claim against the qualitative and quantitative evidence collected in eastern DRC.

The claim on targeted deterrence centres on the notion of how prosecutions can deter the actions of individual armed actors who may commit crimes, or prosecutorial deterrence. The key to deterring the commission of such crimes is not necessarily the severity of punishment, but the likelihood of being caught and punished.[14] In reviewing the literature on deterrence and the Court, Hyeran Jo and Beth A. Simmons conclude: "ICC

---

[14] Hyeran Jo and Beth A. Simmons, "Can the International Criminal Court Deter Atrocity?", in *International Organization*, 2016, vol. 70, no. 3, pp. 443–75.

actions represent new information, available to all actors, demonstrating that the ICC is operational, authoritative, and that the prosecutor means to take action".[15]

Beyond deterring individuals from committing serious violations, the Court also enjoys a capacity to stimulate general deterrence on the part of the population beyond armed groups. Relying upon the "normative focal power of (an international) criminal tribunal", Jo and Simmons cite a host of commentators who point to the role of the Court in influencing behaviour.[16] Specifically, the Court wields power to stigmatise, shape social expectations, and draw bright lines around what is considered unacceptable to both the international community and local expectations in situations of political violence or armed conflict.[17] This perceived ability of the Court to influence local behaviour is particularly important when considering the crime of the use of child soldiers, which continues to be considered an undesired necessity for local communities when faced with external threats to their existence. Finally, the dissuasive power of the Court is said to be further strengthened by the inter-relationship between targeted deterrence and general deterrence. By reinforcing one another, both targeted and general deterrence "encourage member states to improve their capacity to reduce, detect and prosecute war crimes domestically".[18]

In concluding this section, it is important to note that the deterrence effect sought by international criminal law is further bolstered by international and national norms prohibiting serious violations. There exists a robust normative foundation of international laws, standards, duties and obligations on states and non-state actors that prohibit, protect, prevent, punish and remedy violations against children in armed conflict.[19]

---

[15] *Ibid.*

[16] *Ibid.*

[17] *Ibid.*

[18] *Ibid.*

[19] For a comprehensive overview of the international normative framework governing accountability for crimes against children and armed conflict, see Conflict Dynamics International, "Children in Armed Conflict Accountability Framework: A Framework for Advancing Accountability for Serious Violations against Children in Armed Conflict", June 2015. For the principles and guidelines governing the prevention, demobilisation and reintegration of children associated with armed forces or groups, see United Nations Children's Fund, "The Paris Principles: Principles and Guidelines on Children Associated with Armed Forces or Armed Groups", February 2007.

7.5.2. Process Tracing of Ituri Cases against Conflict Dynamics and Violations

By detailing key events in the Ituri cases against ongoing conflict dynamics, Annex A facilitates consideration of whether there is any correlation between Court operations and the behaviour of armed actors in the region. Spanning over 10 years, the first half of the table in Annex A covers conflict dynamics in the Ituri region itself. The second half continues by chronicling activity of armed groups in Ituri and in North Kivu, where a group of armed actors formerly associated with Congrès national pour la défense du peuple ('CNDP', National Congress for the Defence of the People) broke from the army and formed Mouvement du 23-Mars ('M23', March 23 Movement) under the joint leadership of Bosco Ntaganda, who until that time had been an ICC accused operating within the FARDC. The table thus provides important information on how and in what manner armed groups continued to operate both within Ituri and in North Kivu despite Court investigations, prosecutions, trial and convictions of the Ituri accused, and an outstanding arrest warrant for Ntaganda until his surrender to the Court.

A review of Annex A yields several notable points with respect to the behaviour and operation of armed groups in Ituri, such as the FNI and FRPI. Of note, an FNI leader reportedly sought reintegration of his faction into the army as "a sign of his fear of having to return to Kinshasa to be arrested like other militia chiefs before him".[20] However, broadly speaking, the unsealing of the ICC's Lubanga arrest warrant saw continued activity by armed groups, including by the FNI and FRPI. With the transfers of Katanga and Ngudjolo to The Hague, fighting continued between the FNI, FRPI and FARDC leaving displaced civilians to suffer in the middle. Finally, while the situation was nonetheless calmer in Ituri in 2007–2008, disarmament, demobilisation and reintegration programmes yielded far fewer children than had been expected against the estimations the numbers associated with armed groups. The United Nations International Children's Emergency Fund ('UNICEF') and other child protection agencies suspected that children were being hidden by armed actors rather than handed over for demobilisation, demilitarisation and reintegration.

---

[20] International Crisis Group, 2008, see *supra* note 4.

In North Kivu, despite the execution of the warrant against Ntaganda in 2008, ex-CNDP elements under his command continued to commit serious violations against the civilian population that year. Forces from the Lord's Resistance Army ('LRA') were reported to have done the same in the far north-eastern corner of the DRC. Human Rights Watch, an international human rights NGO, also reported widespread cases of political violence and rights violations by the DRC government in 2008. Despite investigations and arrests of key actors belonging to local armed groups, these groups continued to operate and commit violations against the civilian population. While the ICC Ituri trials were underway, violence in Ituri continued but at a much reduced level than at the height of war, with violence in the Kivus remaining constant and indeed spiking with the rise and later fall of the M23.

Beyond these broader conflict dynamics, the recruitment and use of children by armed groups also continued. After only one month following the guilty verdict in the Lubanga case in 2012, the M23 committed widespread recruitment and use of children among other violations against the civilian population. Despite the arrest and conviction of Katanga, the FRPI also continued to commit serious violations against civilians, including against children. In January 2014 the UN Group of Experts reported ongoing recruitment and use of child soldiers by several armed groups operating in eastern DRC,[21] and other violations against children in armed conflict.[22] In January 2015 MONUSCO, the United Nations stabilisation and peacekeeping mission, reported that 35 per cent of the FRPI were children. The violations thus appear to have continued unabated notwithstanding the Lubanga conviction and ongoing trial of Ntaganda, who is charged with recruitment and use of child soldiers alongside other serious violations.

---

[21] Specifically, the responsible armed actors and numbers of children identified with these groups included: Mai Mai groups (194, including 43 girls), Nyatura (112, including four girls), Mai Mai Kata Katanga (39), FDLR (30), Raia Mutomboki (25), M23 (24), Alliance des patriotes pour un Congo libre et souverain ('APCLS', Alliance of Patriots for a Free and Soveriegn People) (13), Patriotes résistants congolais ('PARECO', Resisting Congolese Patriots) (12), FARDC deserters (7 girls), Lord's Resistance Army (two girls) and ADF (one).

[22] These violations included killing of children by the armed group Nduma Defence of Congo ('NDC'); thousands of children in Ituri unable to go to school as a result of attacks by FRPI; attacks on medical facilities in North Kivu by Forces démocratiques alliées ('AFD', Allied Democratic Forces); and abductions by the Lord's Resistance Army.

Measuring the deterrent potential and impact of the ICC cannot be undertaken through a simple exploration of potential correlations between Court operations and the commission of serious violations. Rather, the exercise represented in Annex A illustrates how conflict dynamics are complex and may ebb and flow for different reasons. The crime of recruitment and use of child soldiers, in particular, is a dynamic that can be driven and mitigated by multiple factors. For this reason, the second half of this section considers qualitative evidence of attitudes and perceptions of key actors in eastern Congo on whether the Court indeed enjoyed an element of dissuasion on the commission of this crime by armed groups.

7.5.3. Local Attitudes and Perceptions of Recruitment and Use of Child Soldiers

Consultations were undertaken for this chapter with a range of international and local justice stakeholders, including military prosecutors and judges, community leaders, child protection actors, and victims of serious violations and their families, and a few members of armed groups who were in pre-trial detention. The bulk of these actors were interviewed in Ituri, though others were contacted in Goma and Kinshasa. The outcome of these consultations represents attitudes and perceptions regarding the specific and general deterrent effect of the ICC, and in particular the *Lubanga* case, on recruitment and use of child soldiers by armed groups and communities respectively. Victims and their families were also asked about their perceptions of security in their communities following the Ituri cases.

7.5.3.1. Targeted Deterrence

In terms of targeted deterrence, local actors shared the view that the *Lubanga* case raised awareness to a certain degree among some commanders of local armed groups that recruitment and use of child soldiers is a crime for which you can be punished. Interviewees explained that the ICC did play a role in this awareness through visits by the prosecutor and the diffusion of ICC proceedings in the region. Child protection actors recounted dealing with some warlords who feared being caught for using child soldiers; in apparent reference to the Ituri cases, they noted "some are horrified of experiencing the same fate as the others arrested".[23] In-

---

[23] Interview with child protection actor, Bunia, May 2016.

deed, they attributed some of the shift in use of children to the ICC *Lubanga* case, which one individual referred to as having served as "*une connotation pédagogique*" – that is, a learning moment for armed actors.[24] The impact of the Lubanga case that was most widely cited was the recent drop of children in the ranks of the Congolese army.

Despite these gains, there exists widespread consensus that a problem remains with translating awareness of the prohibition into action among the many armed actors operating in the region. According to one military justice actor, the lower-ranking elements belonging to armed groups are not still sufficiently sensitised to the ICC and the prohibition of recruitment and use of children. As another military justice actor explained, "a good number of these armed actors do not consider the practice to be a crime, proof of which is that our court is regularly seized of cases involving crimes by children who belong to local armed groups".[25] Minors are then sent to the Children's Tribunal which has jurisdiction over juvenile offenders. One local actor added that, even if some do understand the practice to be a crime, at least for self-defence militias, "members share the notion that their cause is noble – to defend the interests of their community and violations by the army or other armed groups", which trumps other considerations including precluding children from joining their ranks.[26] Child protection actors added that children continue to consist of a considerable portion of the composition of armed groups operating in eastern Congo. In sum, the perception prevails that armed groups and their leaders are not sufficiently deterred from commission of this crime, and much more awareness-raising is needed.

7.5.3.2. General Deterrence

Community leaders in Ituri belonging to different ethnic groups who were interviewed for this case study shared the view that there now exists greater knowledge that recruitment and use of children is a violation of the law. Leaders believed that this awareness has translated into lower numbers of children, particularly in self-defence militias. However, they explained that there persists a lack of detailed understanding of the laws themselves, specifically the ICC Statute and the 2009 Child Protection

---

[24] Interview with child protection actor, Ituri region, May 2016.
[25] Interview with military justice actor, May 2016.
[26] *Ibid.*

Law.[27] They also explained that important drivers behind recruitment and use of children persist today and work against deterring commission of the crime. For example, citing conflict dynamics, they explained that entire populations remain invested in defending themselves when faced by external threats, including women and children. In discussions with community leaders, focus group participants across ethnic groups shared the view of one leader who explained that while at the moment they are not recruiting children, "we retain the option of resorting to children if we must".[28]

Community leaders added that when children themselves feel exposed to insecurity, they find themselves with no choice but to defend themselves. Child recruitment and use dynamics are indeed complex. First, children remain regularly forcibly recruited by armed groups. However, child protection actors and community leaders also explained that many children across eastern DRC join voluntarily because they have been orphaned, separated from their families, seek revenge from crimes committed against their communities, and/or simply lack economic opportunities.[29] Child protection actors and community leaders presented these dynamics as contributing to the limited impact of the ICC on reducing the violation generally.

On the subject of insecurity, people living in communities affected by conflict in Ituri hold mixed views about whether they feel improved security following ICC operations. In particular, many victims and their families continue to live in areas where armed groups operate and thus do not feel secure, especially in the area of South Irumu where the FRPI still operate. In these areas, violations against the civilian population by armed groups continue. For this reason, victims do not even feel confident to talk about or engage with the ICC because of fear of reprisals. Nonetheless, despite these feelings of insecurity, many families are convinced that the place for children is in school and not in armed groups.

---

[27] In conformity with Optional Protocol to the Convention on the Rights of the Child on the Involvement of Children in Armed Conflict, see *supra* note 13, the 2009 Child Protection Law prohibits recruitment and use of children under the age of 18 years.

[28] Focus group interviews with community leaders, Ituri region, May 2016.

[29] UN Stabilisation Mission in the DRC, "Child Recruitment by Armed Groups in DRC from January 2012 to August 2013", October 2013.

7.5.3.3. Findings on the Relationship between Targeted and Broader General Deterrence

Despite these dynamics, local perceptions persist that there has been a degree of positive outcome from the ICC in that the awareness of both armed groups and local communities has been raised on the issue of child soldiers. Of note, military justice actors were of the belief that a degree of fear persists among some senior actors in armed groups of the potential for prosecutions for commission of this violation, which they attributed to a broader level of community awareness suggesting that general deterrence had in fact influenced deterrence among certain armed actors with ties to local communities. Interestingly, child protection actors nonetheless considered demobilisation, demilitarisation and reintegration to enjoy a greater impact than the ICC for awareness-raising at a general level on the importance of not having children in the ranks of armed groups. Finally, local actors uniformly referred to the strong level of antipathy among the population regarding the ICC actions, including the Ituri cases, which has undermined the legitimacy of the Court and mitigated its deterrent effect. Specifically, community members continue to feel that the accused targeted by the Court were not those most responsible for crimes in the region, and that known perpetrators of violations are yet to face justice. Based on the field research, awareness-raising, necessity and perceptions of legitimacy appear to be elements common to the manner in which both general and specific deterrence have operated among actors in Ituri.

7.6. Contextualising the Reach of the Deterrent Effect in Eastern DRC

Numerous factors can either strengthen or weaken the deterrent potential of the ICC in the DRC. This section presents these factors, which include the entrenched nature of conflict drivers, poor complementarity realisation at the national level, the efficacy of non-judicial accountability efforts, and an overarching failure to protect and realise the rights of children generally.

7.6.1. Conflict Dynamics Driving the Commission of Violations

Over five million Congolese have been killed since the country's successive conflicts first began in 1997. The underlying drivers of these conflicts are complex. On the one hand, local-level conflicts over land and competition for political power have been exacerbated by ethnic divisions between communities.[30] Overarching these divisions, illicit networks of armed groups, political actors and regional governments prevail who foment instability to enrich themselves through illicit mining and other economic activities in the resource-rich region at the expense of the civilian population. Caught between ruthless militias and an army operating for its own gain, terrified civilians face continued acts of violence, exploitation and abuse.[31] A chronically weak state with institutions that operate through layers of predation on the population further exacerbates the absence of rule of law and security.

In both Ituri and North Kivu, these factors have in the past prompted communities to organise self-defence forces to protect themselves from competing communities, armed groups and proxy militias operating for the economic gain of their local or regional backers. Years of international peacekeeping and stabilisation efforts have failed to bring calm to the region. Indeed, as noted in 2008 and still relevant today:

> There has never been a real long-term comprehensive political strategy to return peace to this peripheral region of the DRC. Rather, a series of initiatives have progressively led to a return of calm but without properly resolving the problem of insecurity in the region or the inherent causes of the conflict.[32]

Given the complexity of the local, national and regional conflict drivers, simply targeting warlords who operate in the middle of illicit networks backed by economic and political players is insufficient to adequately deter the commission of serious violations, including recruitment and use of child soldiers.

7.6.2. Persistent Impunity and Weak Local Judicial Accountability Efforts

Years of violence and conflict have weakened state institutions, including in the justice and security sectors. Interviews confirmed that a primary

---

[30] Réné Lemarchand, *The Dynamics of Violence in Central Africa*, University of Pennsylvania Press, Philadephia, 2009.

[31] Sharanjeet Parmar, "How to Tackle the DRC's Complex Anti-Impunity Agenda", in *African Arguments*, 23 April 2014.

[32] International Crisis Group, 2008, see *supra* note 4.

driver of violations against children is that perpetrators face no consequence to their actions; as one interviewee stated: "You can use children for anything".[33] The climate of impunity extends beyond daily protection issues for children to the commission of serious violations, including use and recruitment of children by armed actors. Indeed, military justice actors explained that the poor deterrent effect of the ICC is due in part to the failure of the national system to meet its complementarity obligations and build on the Lubanga case with local prosecutions for the same criminal conduct.

To date there has been not a single conviction for the recruitment or use of children in the DRC by military courts, which until recently enjoyed primary subject matter jurisdiction over international crimes and which retain personal jurisdiction over members of the military and armed groups. The UN Group of Experts has recommended the DRC government issue arrest warrants and extradition requests, where applicable, against all leaders of armed groups who have committed serious violations of international humanitarian law. The Group has also recommended implementation of the national action plan concluded in October 2012 to prevent child recruitment and other violations of international humanitarian law against children.

Recruitment and use of children is not listed as a crime in the Military Justice Code, although a 2009 Child Protection Law criminalises the practice, the extent of which is not widely known among jurists and judicial actors. Military justice actors explained that they lack the resources and the capacity to apply the ICC Statute and the 2009 law. These include lack of expertise in conducting age verification of child victims and witnesses, identifying and implementing witness protection measures, and understanding and collecting evidence around key elements of the offence. Targeting members of armed groups is particularly challenging because the FARDC does not control areas where they operate and thus cannot make arrests. Military justice actors urged action on its requests to MONUSCO to provide military support in facilitating the arrest of members of armed groups who are under investigation for the commission of serious crimes, including crimes against children. Finally, the anti-impunity agenda in the DRC has seen little progress over the years, with the Rome Statute Implementation Bill only adopted in 2015, which calls

---

[33] Interview with child protection actor, Goma, July 2016.

for the establishment of a mixed chambers yet to be acted upon.[34] More recently, charges have been laid against actors already in custody by the military justice system for recruitment and use of children, though little is known whether and how these cases will proceed.[35]

Compounding the accountability gap has been the successive use of amnesty laws in the DRC, which usually follow demobilisation, demilitarisation and reintegration programmes.[36] Coupled with the recent identification of individuals benefitting from the 2014 Amnesty Law, the third such law since 2003, which include 15 M23 members, the continued failure to hold perpetrators accountable has enabled a climate where children continue to be targeted for serious violations.

7.6.3. Impact of Military Support and Demobilisation, Demilitarisation and Reintegration on Child Recruitment

Assessments of reducing the commission of serious violations often focus on anti-impunity efforts. However, there exist additional factors that can assist in deterring international crimes, particularly in the case of the recruitment and use of child soldiers. Specifically, policies and programmes can provide *positive* incentives to dissuade the practice, which can enhance and facilitate the realisation of deterrence objectives.[37] These include demobilisation, demilitarisation and reintegration and imposing conditionality policies on bilateral or multilateral military assistance. The DRC case study illustrates, however, that when these policies are ineffective, there can be an overarching disincentive for armed groups to comply with norms.

After years of integrating armed groups that perpetuated their rebel practices of recruitment and use of children, the FARDC has seen a re-

---

[34] Sharanjeet Parmar, "Fighting Impunity for Crimes against Children in the DRC", Coalition for the International Criminal Court, 1 June 2016.

[35] "Warlords beyond Kony and Lubanga", in *CNN News*, 14 March 2012.

[36] International Center for Transitional Justice, "DRC: Lubanga Reparations Decision Should Be Celebrated, but Only When Victims Receive Compensation", 13 August 2012. "RDC: loi d'amnestie pour faits de guerre et infractions politiques", in *Radio France Internationale*, 4 February 2014.

[37] For a deeper explanation of the import of approaching a holistic approach to achieving accountability for crimes against children in armed conflict, see Conflict Dynamics International, "Practical Application of the CAC Accountability Framework: Case Example, Democratic Republic of Congo", 2015.

markable drop in recruitment and use of children in recent years.[38] The commitment to eradicate the practice by the army leadership is reflected in the DRC's signature of the action plan concerning child recruitment and other violations of international humanitarian law, which was concluded in 2012.[39] This move has been attributed in part to the UN conditionality policies requiring realisation of the action plan to accessing placements in UN peacekeeping operations, and to the US government tying conditionality to bilateral military assistance under the Prevention of Child Soldiers Act. Thus, strong operational incentives have facilitated realisation of the norm prohibiting recruitment and use of children. FARDC members explained that the occasional cases that persist are due to ignorance of lower-ranking army members. In theory, the ICC's conviction of Lubanga for the same ought to assist in dispelling such ignorance.

Eastern DRC saw successive waves of demobilisation, demilitarisation and reintegration programmes. Child protection actors and civil society working in eastern Congo criticised the operation of demobilisation, demilitarisation and reintegration since the DRC's political transition in 2003 under the Sun City Accord, particularly the practice of reinsertion of armed groups into the FARDC who are known perpetrators of crimes against children.[40] Despite the dramatic drop in numbers of child soldiers in the army, child protection actors decry continued violations of children's rights by FARDC elements, including sexual violence, forced labour, physical violence and, in some cases, killings.[41] Thus, while some progress may be seen on violations against children, their entrenched nature persists and children continue to be victimised.

Both commentators and local child protection actors have also criticised demobilisation, demilitarisation and reintegration efforts targeting

---

[38] In 2013, UNICEF's Monitoring and Reporting Mechanism unit reported cases of 113 children that were recruited by FARDC, representing 12.4 per cent of the overall number. Armed groups recruited a majority of children, representing 910 cases or 87.6 per cent.

[39] Human Rights Watch, "Submission on the Democratic Republic of Congo to the Committee on the Rights of the Child", 17 March 2016.

[40] Following the 2003 Sun City Accord, a transitional unity government was established alongside Parliament and Senate appointments based on representatives from rebel groups, while the new national army attempted to integrate members of the former warring factions. The most infamous case of known perpetrators of serious violations who were since reintegrated in the army is General Amisi, aka Tango Fort.

[41] United Nations Security Council, Report of the Secretary-General on Children and Armed Conflict in the Democratic Republic of the Congo, UN doc. S/2014/453, 30 June 2014.

children.[42] Specifically, although many children were demobilised, only a fraction of these children were successfully reintegrated into their communities resulting in many being recycled back into local armed groups.[43] Indeed, child protection actors and justice actors described how following the Lubanga case, armed groups hid child soldiers to avoid falling subject to prosecutions, which prevented the children from accessing demobilisation, demilitarisation and reintegration. By failing to be locally designed, led and executed, child reintegration did not respond to root causes underlying child recruitment nor did it strengthen the capacity of local actors to address child recruitment issues as part of longer-term peacebuilding efforts in their communities.[44] These challenges persist for current efforts to reintegrate existing armed groups, in particular the need for measures to address the specific reintegration needs of women and children associated with armed groups such as the FDLR and M23.[45]

7.6.4. Local Perceptions of the Court Undermine Its Deterrent Potential

Local justice actors reported that victims and communities in eastern Congo share a sense of disappointment with the ICC cases. These actors specifically criticised the ICC for not adequately targeting higher-level actors who were behind the commission of atrocities in eastern Congo. Local actors lamented the focus of trials on Ituri and not the entire region, the poor outcomes of the ICC cases themselves including: failure to secure convictions of all accused; failure to charge crimes in a more holistic fashion; failure to confirm the charges brought against alleged FDLR executive secretary Callixte Mbarushimana; and that after years of proceedings victims are yet to see any substantial form of reparations.[46] Such are

---

[42] Between 2002 and 2009, some 30,000 children associated with armed forces were demobilised as part of the World Bank's Multi-Country Demobilization and Reintegration Program ('MDRP'). See Yvan Conoir, "Ending War, Building Peace", World Bank, Washington DC, 2012.

[43] André Kölln, "DDR in the DRC: An Overview", Insight on Conflict, 5 December 2011..

[44] *Ibid.*; Conoir, 2012, see *supra* note 42.

[45] Enough Project, "Joint NGO Letter on DDR III process", 3 March 2014.

[46] The comments by interviewees mirror findings in reports, such as Human Rights Watch, "Unfinished Business: Closing Gaps in the Selection of ICC cases", 15 September 2011; Olivia Bueno, "In Ituri, Katanga Verdict Viewed as a Limited Success", International Refugee Rights Initiative, 21 March 2014; UN Human Rights Office of the High Commissioner, "Democratic Republic of the Congo, 1993–2003. Report of the Mapping Exercise

these perceptions, civil society actors who represent victims in ICC cases explained that victims appear reluctant to co-operate with current ICC investigations because of a prevailing lack of confidence and trust in the outcome, in particular in the ability of the ICC to relocate and provide security for witnesses and their families. CSO actors also explained that while victims expect reparations, actual ICC judicial reparations are yet to be implemented.[47] Local actors remain unfamiliar with the ICC's Trust Fund for Victims, whose work was said to not be very visible beyond Ituri. Finally, many victims have since died and their families are unhappy that ICC cases have taken so long to come to completion.

An additional note should be made on the ICC case in the Central African Republic that resulted in the conviction of Congolese businessman and politician Jean-Pierre Bemba, a former warlord and head of the main political party that lost to current President Kabila in the 2006 elections. Many Congolese continue to perceive this case as a political move wherein the current political party in power manipulated the ICC to remove one of its primary presidential rivals. Together, these factors appear to have not only eroded the normative power of the Court among the civilian population, but also the perceived politicisation and broader substantive failings of the Court have neutered the threat of prosecutions for local armed actors.

7.6.5. Poor Child Protection and Rights Realisation in the DRC Further Erode Deterrence

Due to a combination of factors, interviewees outside of Ituri expressed the view that the ICC cases have had little impact on deterring the practice of recruitment and use of child soldiers in the remainder of eastern Congo. Together, poor rights realisation for children enables armed groups to recruit with impunity while overwhelming poverty leaves children with few options but to join armed groups.[48]

Persistent insecurity in many parts of eastern Congo and the lack of state presence has also seen the predominance of practices by communi-

---

Documenting the Most Serious Violations of Human Rights and International Humanitarian Law Committed within the Territory of the Democratic Republic of the Congo between March 1993 and June 2003", April 2010, Section IV, Chapter III, Section D.

[47] International Center for Transitional Justice, 2013, see *supra* note 36.

[48] United Nations Security Council, 2014, see *supra* note 41.

ties that do not respect the rights of the child. Child marriage and forced labour are common, and adolescent girls rarely have access to education.[49] Local child protection actors explained that these practices are compounded by the socialisation of violence at the community level that has resulted from years of conflict and impunity for violations. Living in deplorable socio-economic conditions, children are not viewed as rights holders; state institutions function through corrupt practices and rarely operate to protect or promote the rights of children. Compounding the situation, the Ministries of Gender, Family and Children and of Social Affairs remain woefully under-resourced and not treated as priority sectors by the government. Together, these factors work against broader normative goals of the ICC Statute to criminalise abuse of children, including the recruitment and use of child soldiers; and in so doing, tend to undermine general deterrence sought after by court operations.

Together, the dynamics described in this section appear more entrenched and thus operate in opposition to the possible deterrent effect the Lubanga case may have wielded in eastern Congo on recruitment and use of children.

7.7. Conclusions: Final Considerations for the Operation of Deterrence and the ICC

Based on the research and analysis undertaken for this DRC case study, the following preliminary conclusions can be drawn.

7.7.1. Targeted and General Deterrence

7.7.1.1. Targeted Deterrence

The field research indicates general perceptions of an overall positive impact on awareness of both armed actors and community leaders in terms of the prohibition and criminalisation of the recruitment and use of child soldiers. General perceptions persist, however, that more is needed in terms of awareness-raising and local prosecutions of perpetrators to realise truly effective deterrence of future violations. Despite these local perceptions, the commission of these violations has persisted at alarming rates in eastern DRC, including in Ituri region itself. As a result, the deter-

---

[49]   United States Department of Labor, "Findings on the Worst Forms of Child Labor: Democratic Republic of Congo", 2012.

rent effect of the Lubanga case (and the ICC's cases targeting violations) in eastern DRC generally, appears to be rather limited.

7.7.1.2. General Deterrence

The field research indicates general perceptions of a stronger positive impact of the Lubanga case on the knowledge of community leaders on the nature of child recruitment as a violation of the law. Indeed, local actors attributed the ICC operations to a drop in child recruitment at the community level. Due to entrenched conflict dynamics, community attitudes on the import of self-preservation when faced with external threats continues to include the need to resort to child soldiers, thus reducing the general deterrence effect of the Court.

7.7.1.3. Inter-Relationship between Both

Awareness-raising of the ICC cases and general attitudes towards ICC legitimacy remain two elements that affect the manner in which general and targeted deterrence influence and operate to reinforce or undermine each other, the former in relation to awareness-raising and the latter when it comes to lack of legitimacy. Nonetheless, the DRC case study shows that for the violation of child recruitment, targeting both armed actors and local communities is important to maximising the deterrent potential of the Court.

Returning to the standard claims made about the ICC's deterrent potential, the evidence suggests that the mere presence of ICC actions may not necessarily translate into targeted deterrence. Specifically, in reviewing child recruitment rates in both Ituri and North Kivu over the course of Court operations, the DRC case study reveals that despite a high-profile prosecution for child recruitment, the targeted deterrent effect for armed actors in the same geographic area and a neighbouring region has been limited. Specifically, while rates of child recruitment dropped considerably from those at the height of the conflict in Ituri, an active armed group in the region continues to use child soldiers. Likewise, in North Kivu, armed groups continued to recruit, use and abuse children with impunity alongside key milestones in the Lubanga case. However, when it comes to a broader scope of general deterrence, it is possible to conclude via the DRC case study that the normative value of prosecuting child recruitment facilitated local efforts around demobilisation, demilitarisation and reintegration, eliminating child soldiers from the FARDC, and, orienting self-defence forces away from using children even if community leaders may not completely adhere to the norm in cases they view to be of necessity.

7.7.2. Outreach

Following on from the findings of targeted and general deterrence, the DRC case study illustrates the critical role that awareness-raising can play in realising the deterrent potential of the Court. Stakeholders repeatedly stressed the important impact the ICC has had on raising awareness among armed actors and community leaders. A strong perception persists that this improvement in awareness was a contributing factor to lower levels of child recruitment in Ituri. The ICC's outreach efforts in Ituri are thus to be commended, particularly given the challenges of working in communities where insecurity persists and local views are not always receptive to the Court. For this reason, the DRC case study strongly supports the call for sustained funding and resources of ICC outreach.

7.7.3. Prosecutorial Strategy in the Face of a Deep History of Violence

On a general level, the DRC case study demonstrates how ICC deterrence can be mitigated by a number of factors, including complex conflict dynamics that drive the commission of serious violations. When a region has seen violence for decades, anti-impunity efforts must not be short-lived, but rather sustained on a broader level over a period of time that can respond to peacebuilding and stabilisation imperatives. Consider, for example, the recommendation made by the International Crisis Group at the outset of the DRC situation that the Office of the Prosecutor should

> continue to investigate atrocity crimes committed in Ituri; ensure that this includes the principal militia chiefs who have not been arrested (Jérôme Kakwavu, Peter Karim, Cobra Matata, Floribert Kisembo Bahemuka), those responsible for the massacre at Nyakunde and senior Congolese, Rwandan and Ugandan officials who armed and supported the militias

active in Ituri; and bring charges where criminal responsibility can be established.[50]

Suffice it to say, this recommendation was made in response to underlying conflict dynamics and peacebuilding. Later in 2008, following the reintegration of armed groups, the International Crisis Group reiterated that "[i]mpunity remains the rule and many militia members who had been involved in massacres are today part of the official security forces".[51]

The economic and political drivers behind the commission of violations in eastern DRC demand a nuanced and contextually relevant prosecutions strategy. First, prosecutions need to consider their impact in conflicts where national and regional actors pursue predatory practices that fuel the commission of serious violations by armed groups. The implication of the DRC case study is that targeting warlords for prosecutions remains necessary but insufficient. Investigations must extend to economic crimes, including targeting actors who support proxy militias while sitting in business, political and regional circles of power. If not, any deterrent potential of the ICC will remain limited when the root causes behind violations persist.

Second, the DRC case study points to the importance of complementarity. Targeting potential perpetrators amid the waves of violence in eastern DRC over many years is no easy task and cannot be achieved by the ICC alone. Successfully realising complementarity requires not only initiative from national justice actors but understanding how ICC operations can strengthen and support initiatives on the ground. Recently, military justice prosecutors announced additional charges for child recruitment and use against a set of armed actors who are already in custody for other serious violations.[52] Having prosecuted this crime in the Lubanga trial, the ICC is in a strong position to assist military justice actors in this work, who admitted to lacking the technical expertise to work with child victims and try this offence.

In conclusion, the DRC case study illustrates the deterrent potential of the ICC in preventing the commission of serious violations, in particular the recruitment and use of children. However, this potential sits in a

---

[50] International Crisis Group, "Back to the Brink in the Congo", in *Africa Briefing*, 17 December 2004.

[51] International Crisis Group, 2008, see *supra* note 4.

[52] Parmar, 2012, see *supra* note 35.

very precarious place when the conditions driving the commission of serious crimes are due to long-standing conflict dynamics that can easily supersede anti-impunity efforts undertaken by the Court of a shorter duration. To ensure that the deterrent potential of the Court reaches both individual armed actors and the general population, the Court must situate itself within a sustained anti-impunity strategy that is co-ordinated with other national and international peacebuilding efforts. The victims of these crimes deserve no less.

Annex A: Timeline of ICC Events and Conflict Dynamics in Eastern Democratic Republic of the Congo

ICC Action	Conflict Dynamics and Commission of Violations
19 April 2004 State Party referral made public (Preliminary)	2004: First demobilisation, demilitarisation and reintegration programmes begins 10–14 May 2004: Peace and security negotiations for Ituri produce 'Act of Engagement' signed by seven armed group leaders (including Lubanga) and transitional government in Kinshasa. Elements within armed groups, especially UPC-L and FNI, unlikely to be satisfied with agreement – risk of return to violence and "may even escalate to a more general conflict in an effort to force concessions from the Transitional Government".[53]
23 June 2004 Formal investigation	July 2004: First major fighting since Act of Engagement near Mahagi between FNI and FAPC.[54] August 2004: Transitional government distracted by Kivus and no influence in Ituri. "At best, the situation is static, at the mercy of armed groups, who are largely self-financing".[55] December 2004: MONUC switches to more robust tactics, enforces a weapons-free zone, cordon-and-search operations with the army, demobilised 16,000 combatants.[56]
March 2006 Lubanga: warrant of arrest: unsealed	July 2006: FNI retake town of Tcheyi in north-eastern Ituri, thousands of civilians flee.[57]
August 2006 Bosco Ntaganda: indictment (sealed)	September 2006: Reports of militias (including FNI) rearming and recruiting east of Bunia, despite disarmament and demobilisation progress. Former combatants pressured to rejoin militias.[58] October 2006: Report that FRPI attacked FARDC army position

---

[53] International Crisis Group, 2004, see *supra* note 50.

[54] *Ibid.*

[55] International Crisis Group, "Maintaining Momentum in the Congo: The Ituri Problem", 26 August 2004.

[56] International Crisis Group, "Congo: Consolidating the Peace", in *Afirca Report*, no. 128, 5 July 2007.

[57] "Thousands Flee Army-Militia Showdown in Ituri", in *IRIN News*, 3 July 2006.

[58] "Recently Demobilized Militiamen Re-arming in Volatile Ituri District", in *IRIN News*, 17 September 2006.

	and fighting ensues.
November 2006 Lubanga: confirmation of charges	November 2006: Three rebel groups in Ituri agree to disarm. Expected to release 700 child soldiers.[59]
January 2007 Lubanga: decision on confirmation of charges	Ituri largely calm for most of 2007 and early 2008. February 2007: FNI rebel group surrenders weapons under demobilisation, demilitarisation and reintegration process. Estimated 500 children with FNI.[60] April 2007: FNI leader Peter Karim enters Bunia after signing disarmament agreement in December 2006. Karim hoping to secure personal interests and negotiate FNI integration into FARDC. This is seen as "a sign of his fear of having to return to Kinshasa to be arrested like other militia chiefs before him".[61] May 2007: Nkunda intensifies recruitment in his zone of control and in Rwanda.[62]
October 2007 Germain Katanga (FRPI): executed indictment; transferred to The Hague	July–October 2007: Third round of demobilisation, demilitarisation and reintegration programmes ends with fewer children than expected; UNICEF suspects that militias send children away.[63] MRC disarms en masse. FNI's fragmentation: dissident wings in Lalo and Dhera regions and Loga region of Djugu territory. FRPI also resistant to demobilisation, demilitarisation and reintegration. Resistance of FNI and FRPI explained by local community agenda, economic agenda and regional conflict dynamics.[64] November 2007: 16 senior commanders, including Karim, Ngudjolo and Cobra Matata, integrate into Congolese army and enter training at Senior Military Centre in Kinshasa.[65]
February 2008 Mathieu Ngudjolo (FNI): Trans-	Beginning of 2008, confrontations between FNI, FRPI and FARDC. Likely no more than 1,500 combatants still active in Ituri; however, remaining unwilling to surrender. Demobilisa-

[59] "Eastern DR Congo Rebels to Disarm", in *BBC News*, 30 November 2006.

[60] "Another Rebel Group Gives Up Arms", in *IRIN News*, 28 February 2007.

[61] International Crisis Group, 2008, see *supra* note 4.

[62] Human Rights Watch, "Renewed Crisis in North Kivu", 23 October 2007.

[63] "Pacifying Ituri: Achievements and Challenges Ahead", in *IRIN News*, 8 July 2008.

[64] International Crisis Group, 2008, see *supra* note 4.

[65] "Sixteen Ituri Warlords Give Up the Fight", in *IRIN News*, 6 November 2007.

ferred to the Hague; indictment made public	tion, demilitarisation and reintegration impact weak absent efforts to re-establish state authority.[66]
	February 2008: Fighting between FRPI and FARDC south of Bunia displaces more than 1,000 people.[67]
April 2008 Ntaganda (UPC, CNDP/M23): executed indictment	April 2008: FRPI reportedly recruiting new combatants and being resupplied with weapons, according to UN Security Council.[68]
May 2008 Arrest of Jean-Pierre Bemba (MLC)	September 2008: LRA attack civilians, killing 160, and abducting over 300 children in villages near Garamba National Park (Haut-Uele province, north-eastern DRC). November 2008: Nkunda CNDP rebels, under command of Ntaganda, massacre 150 people in the town of Kiwanja, North Kivu. Human Rights Watch publishes report on torture, summary executions and arrests of political opponents by the DRC government.
January 2009 Lubanga: opening of the trial	January 2009: Several thousand combatants from CNDP, PARECO and other Mai groups integrated into FARDC (following takeover of CNDP by Ntaganda).[69] Ntaganda promoted to general in FARDC. FARDC and RDF launch Operation Umoja Wetu against FDLR in North Kivu. FDLR conducts reprisal campaign against villages, including killing, raping, looting and burning.[70] March 2009: Peace agreement between government and CNDP (political and military integration.) Both sides act in bad faith over following two years.[71]
March 2012 Lubanga: verdict	Late March 2012: Ntaganda leads mutiny of 300–600 soldiers from FARDC. Suggestion the mutinies may have been sparked by rumours that President Kabila is considering the arrest of Ntaganda.[72]

[66] "Army Kills 10 Rebels in Ituri", in *IRIN News*, 29 January 2008; International Crisis Group, 2008, see *supra* note 4.

[67] "New Displacement as Army Fights Militia in Ituri", in *IRIN News*, 27 February 2008.

[68] *IRIN News*, 2008, see *supra* note 63.

[69] United Nations Security Council, Final Report of the Group of Experts on the Democratic Republic of the Congo, UN doc. S/2009/603, 23 November 2009.

[70] *Ibid*.

[71] International Crisis Group, "Eastern Congo: Why Stabilization Failed", 4 October 2012.

[72] "Understanding Armed Group M23", in *IRIN News*, 22 June 2012.

	April 2012: M23 fighters responsible for attacks on civilians, summary executions and rapes, forced recruitment of children.[73]
	3 May 2012: Colonel Sultani Makenga leads separate revolt from FARDC.
July 2012 Lubanga: sentence Ntaganda: second indictment	May 2012: Alliance between Cobra Matata's FRPI and smaller armed groups in Ituri known as Coalition of Armed Groups in Ituri ('COGAI'). COGAI later controlled much of Irumu territory and responsible for civilian violations and displacement over 2012. July–August 2012: Ethnic tensions flare, number of largely Hema civilians killed by the FRPI south of Bunia, Ituri. MONUSCO sets up additional bases in that area stretching between Bunia and Goma.[74]
August 2012 Lubanga decision on principles and process for reparations; December 2012 Ngudjolo: verdict	August 2012: Children and young men flee forced recruitment in by M23; World Vision reports 200 children forced to join M23 in North Kivu.[75] November 2012: M23 occupies Goma. Killings and other war crimes by both M23 and government forces, including forced recruitment of children by M23 reported in North Kivu.[76] Later withdraws in December after DRC government agrees to negotiate a peace deal.
March 2013 Ntaganda surrenders himself to US embassy, Rwanda for transfer to the ICC	August 2013: FARDC offensive and ongoing clashes with Cobra Matata-led FRPI displace civilians in Ituri, including over 100,000 in Irumu.[77] October 2013: Washington issues sanctions on Rwanda for recruitment of children by M23, which is deemed to be benefiting from Rwandan support.[78] October 2013: MONUSCO reports at least 1,000 children recruited since Jan 2012 in eastern Congo, with Mai-Mai Nyatura, the FDLR and M23 deemed most responsible.[79]

---

[73] Human Rights Watch, "DR Congo: M23 Rebels Kill, Rape Civilians", 22 July 2013.

[74] "Violence Hampers Aid Work in Ituri", in *IRIN News*, 21 August 2012.

[75] "Children Young Men Flee Forced Recruitment", in *IRIN News*, 16 August 2012.

[76] Human Rights Watch, 2013, see *supra* note 73.

[77] "Clashes in DRC's Ituri District Displace Thousands", in *IRIN News*, 26 August 2013.

[78] "Enfants soldats dans le M23: Washington announce des sanctions contre Kigalie", in *Radio Okapi*, 3 October 2013.

[79] "Le Monusco identifie 1000 enfants soldats dans les groups armés de l'Est", in *Radio Okapi*, 24 October 2013.

	2013: Mai-Mai Simba (also referred to as Morgan since led by Paul Sadala who goes by the alias) responsible for violations in Mambasa territory from end 2012 throughout 2013; on at least two separate occasions in 2013 found recruiting children and responsible for the rape of several young girls.[80]
	December 2013: National demobilisation, demilitarisation and reintegration plan is approved, 3,663 children expected from armed groups.
March 2014 Katanga: verdict	Repatriation of a group of ex-M23 elements with some granted amnesty in the DRC over 2014.
	April 2014: Morgan is killed, "reportedly fatally injured while surrendering to FARDC".[81]
	UN reports two cases of recruitment of children by the FARDC.[82]
September 2015 Ntaganda: trial begins	2 January 2015: Arrest of Cobra Matata, leader of FRPI; following reports that 35 per cent of FRPI were children, MONUSCO actors fail to secure release of children with commanders claiming that there were no children in their ranks.[83]
	Much of 2015: FARDC operations against FRPI, violence against civilians, displacement, and so on.

---

[80] United Nations Security Council, 2014, see *supra* note 41.

[81] United Nations Security Council, Report of the Secretary-General on the United Nations Organization Stabilization Mission in the Democratic Republic of the Congo, UN doc. S/2015/1031, 24 December 2015, paras. 11–16.

[82] Jo Becker, "Dispatches: Obama Still Arms Governments Using Child Soldiers", Human Rights Watch, 1 October 2015.

[83] United Nations Security Council, 2015, see *supra* note 81.

8

Evaluating the Deterrent Effect of the International Criminal Court in Uganda

Kasande Sarah Kihika[*]

8.1. Introduction

One of the stated objectives of international criminal law is to prevent the commission of international crimes by punishing perpetrators of atrocities, so as to send a message that criminal conduct has consequences. The fear of prosecution and punishment is expected to deter individuals from committing future violations. Acknowledging the role of prosecutions in deterring future crimes, the Preamble of the Rome Statute of the International Criminal Court ('ICC') provides that "[s]tate parties are determined to put an end to impunity for the perpetrators of international crimes and thus contribute to the prevention of such crimes".[1]

The establishment of the ICC in 2002, following the adoption of the Statute in 1998, has been hailed as a watershed moment in the quest to end the culture of impunity for international crimes. The ICC exercises its jurisdiction based on the principle of complementarity which is enshrined in Article 17 of the ICC Statute. According to the principle of complementarity, states have the primary responsibility to investigate and prose-

[*]   **Kasande Sarah Kihika** is a human rights lawyer and an Advocate of the High Court of Uganda. She currently serves as the Head of Office of the Uganda programme of the International Center for Transitional Justice ('ICTJ'). She has extensive experience and training in gender and the law, international human rights law, international humanitarian law, transitional justice and international criminal law. She has provided technical support to state and non-state actors in the areas of international criminal justice, transitional justice and gender justice. She has worked closely with the Justice Law and Order Sector in Uganda to support the establishment mechanisms that deliver redress to victims of international crimes. Before joining ICTJ, she was a Senior Programme Officer with the Uganda Association of Women Lawyers. She is a co-founder and board member of Chapter Four Uganda, a human rights organisation dedicated to the promotion and protection of human rights in Uganda. She holds a Master of Laws in International Human Rights Law from the Central European University in Budapest, a Bachelor of Laws (Hons) from Makerere University and a Postgraduate Diploma in Legal Practice from the Law Development Centre.

[1]   ICC, Rome Statute of the International Criminal Court, 17 July 1998, in force 1 July 2002, Preamble, para. 5 ('ICC Statute') (http://www.legal-tools.org/doc/7b9af9/).

cute international crimes; the ICC's jurisdiction will be invoked if national jurisdictions are unable or unwilling to genuinely investigate or prosecute perpetrators of international crimes. In January 2004 Uganda became the first country to refer a situation to the prosecutor of the ICC. The referral of the Situation Concerning the Lord's Resistance Army ('LRA') arose from the need to restore peace and stability in war-ravaged northern Uganda by putting an end to LRA mass atrocities, which included murder, torture, various forms of sexual violence, abductions, mutilations, conscription of child soldiers and destruction of property.

This chapter examines the ICC's involvement in Uganda with the aim of assessing its long- and short-term deterrent effect. Considerable literature analyses the impact of the ICC arrest warrants for the LRA leadership in shaping the legal, social and political landscape in northern Uganda. This study will not dwell on these debates. Instead, it seeks to determine the extent to which the intervention of the ICC contributed to the prevention of future atrocities by incapacitating alleged perpetrators and deterring potential perpetrators from committing future crimes, and identifying which factors undermined or enhanced the deterrent effect of the ICC. The chapter relies on a number of indicators to measure the cumulative deterrence value of the ICC's intervention in Uganda, from the point of referral of the situation of the LRA to the confirmation of charges against its leader. These indicators include the number of casualties and the incidence of violence following the intervention of the Court, perceptions of key stakeholders and victims on security in northern Uganda following the ICC's intervention, behavioural changes of combatants and perpetrators in reaction to the key procedural developments in the case, and legal, institutional and political developments in response to the ICC's intervention. It examines how the conduct of the government of Uganda elided ICC investigations into the crimes committed by state troops.

The methodology for this chapter relies on qualitative and quantitative methods. It is partly based on a review of available literature on the topic. Anonymous key informant interviews were also conducted using semi-structured questionnaires which were specifically designed for each category of respondent. Focus group discussions were also conducted for both victims and former combatants. The categories of respondents interviewed include former combatants, victims, civil society actors, justice sector actors and international justice experts. The fieldwork was conducted between March and May 2016.

The chapter is divided into six sections. Following this introduction, section 8.2. unpacks some of the assumptions that underpin the theory of deterrence and briefly examines the various types of deterrence. Section 8.3. provides a brief overview of the historical context in northern Uganda and the circumstances that led to the ICC's intervention. Section 8.4. considers the impact of the referral to the ICC and the unsealing of the arrest warrants. Section 8.5. explores the court-based and extra-legal factors that enhance or undermine the deterrent effect of the ICC along the different procedural steps taken by the Court, from the start of investigations, through the issuance of arrest warrants against the top LRA commander, to his surrender. Section 8.6. examines these same factors in relation to the one active case before the ICC. The final section concludes by summarising the key factors in order to make specific recommendations.

8.2. Unpacking Deterrence

Deterrence is regarded as one of the principle objectives of criminal justice. M. Cherif Bassiouni argues that "[t]he pursuit of justice and accountability fulfils fundamental human needs and expresses key values necessary for the prevention and deterrence of future conflicts".[2] Prosecuting perpetrators of crimes fosters a political and social culture where the commission of international crime is deemed unacceptable social behaviour.[3] The idea of deterrence presupposes that potential perpetrators are "rational calculators who carefully weigh the costs and benefits of their actions".[4] Potential perpetrators are presumed to be afraid of prosecution, and this fear is enhanced when they see perpetrators of crime prosecuted

---

[2]   M. Cherif Bassiouni, "Justice and Peace: The Importance of Choosing Accountability over Realpolitik", in *Case Western Reserve Journal of International Law*, 2003, vol. 35, no. 2, pp. 191–92.

[3]   Julian Ku and Jude Nzelibe, "Do International Criminal Tribunals Deter or Exacerbate Humanitarian Atrocities?", in *Washington University Law Review*, 2006, vol. 84, no. 4, p. 777.

[4]   Robert Cryer, Håkan Friman, Darryl Robinson and Elizabeth Wilmshurst, *An Introduction to International Criminal Law and Procedure*, Cambridge University Press, Cambridge, 2010, p. 26.

and punished.[5] This therefore dissuades them from engaging in conduct proscribed by law.

The deterrence function of the ICC's intervention depends on the political context of the situation country. In Uganda, for example, the ICC took jurisdiction after a referral by one of the parties to the conflict; this ultimately shaped the scope of its investigations and its overall deterrent effect. Hyeran Jo and Beth A. Simmons identify two channels of deterrence: prosecutorial and social deterrence.[6] They define prosecutorial deterrence as "the omission of a criminal act out of fear of sanctions resulting from legal prosecution".[7] Prosecutorial deterrence is enhanced by a high probability of prosecutions and the severity of punishment.[8] Social deterrence, on the other hand, is a consequence of broad range of factors, where potential perpetrators contemplate the extra-legal consequences of their actions and decide not to commit a crime. The social consequences of committing a crime include stigma, shame, rejection and social exclusion.[9] Convicted criminals are likely to be shunned by the community, denied opportunities for participating in community decision-making processes, and in some cases have limited prospects for employment. The deterrence effect of international criminal trials is bolstered when social and prosecutorial deterrence reinforce each other.[10]

The debate on the deterrent value of international criminal trials is not yet settled; there is insufficient data that leads to the conclusion that the prosecution of perpetrators dissuades other individuals from engaging in similar conduct.[11] Most of the available evidence of the deterrent effect of international criminal trials is anecdotal, and there are other factors that influence the decisions of individuals to commit crimes. For example, rebel commanders such as Joseph Kony, who believe that they are fulfilling a greater spiritual goal, are less likely to stop committing crimes out of fear of possible criminal sanctions. Mark A. Drumbl argues that:

---

[5]   Mark A. Drumbl, *Reimagining Child Soldiers in International Law and Policy*, Oxford University Press, Oxford, 2012.

[6]   Hyeran Jo and Beth A. Simmons, "Can the International Criminal Court Deter Atrocity?", in *International Organization*, 2016, vol. 70, no. 3, pp. 443–75.

[7]   *Ibid.*

[8]   Ku and Nzelibe, 2006, see *supra* note 3.

[9]   Jo and Simmons, 2016, see *supra* note 6.

[10]   *Ibid.*

[11]   Drumbl, 2012, see *supra* note 5.

> Commanders intoxicated by their genocidal furor [...] may believe they are doing good by eliminating the evil other [...] their attachment to the normative value of the atrocities warps whatever cost benefit analysis they may undertake.[12]

It is therefore improbable that the threat of criminal sanctions will deter such individuals. These and other factors that impact the deterrent function of international criminal trials are examined in detail in subsequent sections of this chapter.

8.3. Overview of the Conflict in Northern Uganda and Referral to the ICC

In 1987 the LRA, a spiritualist rebel group led by Joseph Kony, launched a brutal rebellion in northern Uganda against President Yoweri Museveni's National Resistance Movement ('NRM') government. The rebellion stemmed from enduring colonial legacies of political and ethnic divisions between the northern and southern parts of Uganda.[13] It was also in direct response to Museveni's National Resistance Army's[14] effort to consolidate control over northern Uganda.[15] Kony claimed that the LRA's objective was to topple the NRM government and govern Uganda in accordance with the Ten Commandments.[16] The rebellion was characterised by widespread and systematic human rights abuses, including mass abductions, forced recruitment and enlistment of child soldiers, mutilations, torture, killings, rape, sexual slavery, forced marriage, torture and destruction of property. Young boys and girls were forcibly recruited into the LRA ranks, and most of the girls were forced into conjugal relations with the commanders of the LRA. Close to two million people were forcibly interned in government-controlled internally displaced people's camps,

---

[12] *Ibid.*, p. 163.

[13] Ruddy Doom and Koen Vlassenroot, "Kony's Message: A New Koine? The Lord's Resistance Army in Northern Uganda", in *African Affairs,* 1999, vol. 98, no. 390, pp. 5–36.

[14] The National Resistance Army ('NRA') was the military arm of the National Resistance Movement. It later evolved into the Uganda People's Defence Force.

[15] Phuong Pham, Patrick Vinck, Eric Stover, Andre Moss, Richard Bailes and Marieke Wierda, *When the War Ends. A Population-Based Survey on Attitudes about Peace, Justice and Social Reconstruction in Northern Uganda*, Human Rights Center, University of California, Berkeley, Payson Center for International Development, Tulane University and International Center for Transitional Justice, New York, 2007.

[16] Chris Dolan, Social Torture, *The Case of Northern Uganda, 1986–2006*, Berghahn Books, Oxford, 2011.

ostensibly to protect them from further attacks by the LRA. This conduct was not part of the ICC investigations for political reasons examined later in this chapter. The living conditions of the camps were catastrophic; the internally displaced people did not have adequate access to clean water, sanitation, food, health care or decent housing. Family structures broke down due to the difficult living conditions. The chief of the United Nations Office for the Coordination of Humanitarian Affairs ('OCHA'), during his visit to the internally displaced people's camps, described the conflict in northern Uganda as "the biggest forgotten, neglected humanitarian emergency in the world today".[17] The government of Uganda's counter-insurgency strategy against the LRA was brutal and was characterised by serious human rights abuses including torture, rape, killings and illegal detentions.

In 2000, in response to the growing public demand for a political solution to the conflict, the government of Uganda enacted the Amnesty Act of 2000. The Act sought to end the brutal conflict by encouraging LRA combatants to lay down their arms in exchange for immunity from prosecution for the crimes committed during the rebellion against the government.[18] The top LRA commanders did not take up the offer of amnesty and instead the LRA continued its brutal armed rebellion.

In 2003 the escalating mass atrocities in northern Uganda and growing international concern over the humanitarian crisis in the internally displaced people's camps compelled the government of Uganda to refer the Situation of the Lord's Resistance Army to the ICC. However, others argue that the referral was a method used by the government to delegitimise and stigmatise the LRA, while drawing attention away from human rights abuses by its own troops. Two years later, the ICC unsealed warrants of arrest for five top LRA commanders. The warrants rendered the offer of amnesty under the Amnesty Act insignificant for the indicted commanders, and further shaped the dominant narrative about the conflict, in which the LRA were portrayed as barbaric criminals with no valid political agenda, while state troops were protected from criminal responsibility.

In 2006, hardly a year after the warrants were unsealed, Joseph Kony reached out to the government requesting peace talks and a cessa-

---

[17] Jan Egeland, Security Council Meeting Record, UN doc. S/PV.5331, 19 December 2005.

[18] Uganda, Amnesty Act, 21 January 2000, Cap 294 Laws of Uganda (http://www.legal-tools.org/doc/36fb8a/).

tion of hostilities. The talks, mediated by Riek Machar on behalf of the government of South Sudan, presented a realistic opportunity of finding a negotiated settlement to the conflict, and of restoring peace in the war-ravaged region. Previous efforts by Betty Bigombe to reach a negotiated settlement to the conflict had failed.[19] The two-year peace talks took place against the backdrop of the ICC intervention, which became a key aspect of the negotiations. Despite the collapse of the peace talks, a number of notable agreements were signed. These included the Agreement on Cessation of Hostilities,[20] the Agreement on Comprehensive Solutions for Northern Uganda,[21] and the Agreement on Accountability and Reconciliation,[22] which *inter alia* provides for the establishment of a Special Division of the High Court with jurisdiction to try the most serious crimes.

8.4. Referral to the ICC and Unsealing of Arrest Warrants against LRA Leadership

This section examines the deterrent effect of the ICC's intervention in Uganda, following the referral by the government, the launch of investigations by the Office of the Prosecutor, and the unsealing of warrants of arrest against the LRA commanders by the Pre-Trial Chamber. Evidence gathered indicates that the intervention of the ICC in Uganda precipitated two important effects, which contributed to a reduction of violence perpetrated by the LRA: the impact on the Juba peace process, and the impact on the national judicial system. The arrest warrants had a positive effect on the negotiations, which led to accountability for mass crimes becoming a central feature of the negotiations and the signing of the agreement on accountability and reconciliation. They also influenced the national judicial system by providing for the establishment of a war crimes division of the High Court as an alternative to the ICC. However, the deterrent effect of the Court was reduced by court-based and extra-legal factors, which are discussed in the next section.

---

[19] In 1994 Betty Bigombe initiated negotiations between the LRA and the government, however her efforts were not successful.

[20] Agreement between Government of Uganda and the Lord's Resistance Army, Juba Agenda Item No. 1, Juba, Sudan, 26 August 2006.

[21] Agreement between Government of Uganda and the Lord's Resistance Army, Juba Agenda Item No. 2, Juba, Sudan, 2 May 2007.

[22] Agreement between Government of Uganda and the Lord's Resistance Army, Juba Agenda Item No. 3, Juba, Sudan, 29 June 2007.

Uganda ratified the ICC Statute in June 2002 and a year later, in December 2003, the government of Uganda referred the situation of the Lord's Resistance Army to the prosecutor of the ICC.[23] One of the stated objectives of the referral was to bring peace and stability to war-ravaged northern Uganda and to put an end to the LRA atrocities. According to the government of Uganda, it referred the situation of the LRA to the ICC because it was unable to arrest and bring to justice the LRA soldiers who were based in Sudan and the Democratic Republic of the Congo ('DRC').[24] The government of Uganda observed:

> Having exhausted every other means of bringing an end to the terrible suffering, the government of Uganda now turns to the newly established ICC and its promise for global justice. Uganda pledges its full cooperation to the prosecutor in the investigation and prosecution of LRA crimes which is vital not only for future progress of the nation but also for the suppression of the most serious crimes of concern to the international community as a whole.[25]

The ICC prosecutor launched investigations in northern Uganda in 2004.[26] The investigations established that the LRA had committed crimes against humanity and war crimes, which were within the jurisdiction of the ICC. Consequently, the prosecutor lodged an application for warrants of arrest against the five top commanders of the LRA. In July 2005 the Pre-Trial Chamber granted the prosecutor's application for warrants of arrest, and in October 2005 the Pre-Trial Chamber unsealed warrants of arrest against Joseph Kony, Vincent Otti, Raska Lukwiya, Dominic Ongwen and Okot Odhiambo.[27] For 10 years the arrest warrants remained unexecuted, until January 2015 when Ongwen surrendered to US Special Forces and was transferred to the ICC to face trial. Odhiambo and Lukwi-

---

[23] ICC, President of Uganda Refers Situation Concerning the Lord's Resistance Army (LRA) to the ICC, 29 January 2004 ('Uganda Situation Referral') (http://www.legal-tools.org/doc/ff41c3/).

[24] Government of Uganda, Referral of the Situation Concerning the Lord's Resistance Army, Submitted by the Government of Uganda, 16 December 2003, p. 4; Uganda Situation Referral, see *supra* note 23.

[25] *Ibid.*

[26] ICC, "Prosecutor of the ICC Opens an Investigation into Northern Uganda", Press Release, 29 July 2004.

[27] ICC, Pre-Trial Chamber, *Prosecutor v. Joseph Kony, Vincent Otti, Okot Odhiambo and Dominic Ongwen*, Decision on the Prosecutor's Application for Unsealing of the Warrants of Arrest, ICC-02/04-01/05-52, 14 October 2005 (http://www.legal-tools.org/doc/e665e4/).

ya have been confirmed dead, and Kony and Otti remain at large.[28] It has been alleged that Otti was killed on the orders of Kony following disagreements during the Juba peace talks; however, the Court has not been able to officially confirm his death. A number of actors, including a section of civil society, have criticised the issuance of the warrants as a hindrance to peace.[29]

There are mixed reviews of the deterrence effect of the ICC intervention in northern Uganda. A majority of the respondents agreed that the ICC intervention in Uganda deterred future crimes because it created awareness and instilled fear of the consequences of committing mass atrocities in LRA and Uganda People's Defence Force ('UPDF') combatants. Although the indictments were only issued against LRA commanders, some of the respondents are of the view that they also influenced the conduct of the government army, the UPDF. Respondents observed that there was a drastic change in UPDF conduct after the warrants of arrest against the LRA were unsealed; government troops stopped committing human rights abuses overtly.

According to some of the members of the conflict-affected communities, the unsealing of the warrants of arrest brought relative peace to northern Uganda because they contributed to the relocation of the LRA from Uganda and South Sudan to the DRC. However, others are of the view that the ICC had minimal contribution to their safety because of its inability to arrest the five LRA commanders. One of the respondents observed: "I did not feel safe because I did not see it bring soldiers on the ground to fight and protect us but Kony continued and abducted many people and walked away with them freely".[30]

In a population survey conducted by the University of California-Berkeley, 38 per cent of the respondents they interviewed indicated that the ICC helped restore peace and security by "[c]hasing the LRA away".

---

[28] Raska Lukwiya was killed by the Uganda army in Kitgum district. See "Lukwiya's Death Angers LRA", in *The New Vision*, 13 August 2006.

[29] Kasaija Phillip Apuuli, "The ICC Arrest Warrants for the Lord's Resistance Army Leaders and Peace Prospects for Northern Uganda", in *Journal of International Criminal Justice*, 2009, vol. 4, no. 1, pp. 179–87.

[30] Interview with member of affected community, Gulu, March 2016.

They also believe it contributed to peace. However, 6 per cent believe the ICC undermined the peace negotiations.[31]

Some respondents noted that it is difficult to establish a direct causal link between the warrants of arrest and the reduction of LRA attacks. They argue that the reduction in the incidence of violence is a result of a combination of political factors.[32] One of the notable political factors is enactment of the Amnesty Act, which encouraged combatants to defect in exchange for immunity from prosecution. In 2000, at the height of the conflict in northern Uganda and following several failed military campaigns, the government enacted the Amnesty Act which extended amnesty to all Ugandans who renounced the rebellion.[33] Individuals granted amnesty would not be "prosecuted or subjected to any form of punishment for the participation in the war or rebellion or for any crime committed in the cause of the war or armed rebellion".[34] According to the Amnesty Commission, it has awarded 24,066 amnesty certificates to ex-combatants who abandoned rebellion, of whom 13,021 are LRA ex-combatants.[35] The mass defections of the LRA combatants ultimately weakened it.

While the LRA is no longer committing crimes in Uganda, it continues to abduct and commit serious crimes in the Central African Republic and the DRC. Instead of deterring the LRA combatants from perpetrating further atrocities, the ICC arrest warrants contributed to an escalation of LRA attacks on civilian populations in DRC and the Central African Republic. Fighting and mass abductions became part of the LRA's strategy of evading ICC arrest warrants. One of the ex-combatants interviewed

---

[31] Phuong Pham and Patrick Vinck, *Transitioning to Peace: A Population-Based Survey on Attitudes about Social Reconstruction and Justice in Northern Uganda*, Human Rights Center, University of California, Berkeley, 2010.

[32] Civil society activist interview, March 2016.

[33] Section 2(1) of the Amnesty Act provides: "Amnesty is declared in respect of any Ugandan who has at any time since the 26th day of January, 1986, engaged in or is engaging in war or armed rebellion against the government of the Republic of Uganda by: (a) actual participation in combat; (b) collaborating with the perpetrators of the war or armed rebellion; (c) committing any other crime in the furtherance of the war or armed rebellion; or (d) assisting or aiding the conduct or prosecution of the war or armed rebellion"; see *supra* note 18.

[34] *Ibid.*, Article 2(1)(d).

[35] This was revealed in the case of Supreme Court of Uganda, *Thomas Kwoyelo alias Latoni v. Uganda*, Constitutional Petition No.036/11, Arising out of HCT-00-ICD-Case No. 02/2010, 22 September 2011 (http://www.legal-tools.org/doc/9bcae5/).

reported that following the collapse of the peace talks, Kony decided to continue his rebellion "to make it hard for the ICC to arrest him".[36]

The persistence of violent acts and commission of crimes in the other countries where the LRA relocated is an indication that ICC arrest warrants had marginal deterrent effect on the LRA combatants because the benefits of engaging in mass crime far outweigh the risks of being prosecuted and punished by the ICC.[37] Other respondents reason that the ICC has had a limited deterrent effect; criminals have simply engineered new tactics of committing crimes more covertly, having become conscious of the ICC's jurisdiction.[38] One could argue that the concealment of crime demonstrates that the combatants are afraid of being arrested, prosecuted and punished by the ICC for committing international crimes, but not sufficiently afraid to stop committing crimes altogether.

According to the former combatants interviewed, the issue of the arrest warrants compelled the LRA to change its strategy and influenced the behaviour of the LRA combatants, albeit in a negative way. Kony used the warrants as a propaganda tool to retain the loyalty of the combatants. He convinced them that whereas the warrants were issued for LRA leaders, all other combatants risk being prosecuted by the ICC should they surrender or be captured.[39] Kony convinced the LRA combatants that the ICC was going to issue additional arrest warrants for other LRA commanders. As a result, combatants heeded his call to continue fighting to evade arrest.

8.4.1. Impact of ICC Warrants of Arrest on Juba Peace Negotiations

The unsealing of the arrest warrants against the top LRA commanders influenced the substance and outcome of the Juba peace negotiations. Contrary to the commonly held perception that the warrants served as a stumbling block to peace talks, the research conducted for this chapter suggests that the unsealing of the warrants incentivised the LRA leadership to commit to peace negotiations. The conditions attached to the peace talks by the LRA demonstrate that they were afraid of being arrested and prosecuted at the ICC. Further, there is evidence that following the launch of

---

[36] Ex-combatant interview, Gulu, March 2016.
[37] Expert interview, Kampala, March 2016.
[38] Interview with civil society actor, March 2016.
[39] Focus group meeting, March 2016.

investigations in northern Uganda, there was a significant reduction of violence.

In 2006 the vice president of the LRA, Vincent Otti, called for a new round of peace negotiations. The previous efforts of peace talks had failed, and most people were doubtful of the LRA's commitment to peace talks. Notwithstanding the scepticism about the new round of peace talks, South Sudan mediated the Juba peace negotiations between the LRA and the government of Uganda; this commenced in June 2006. Kony did not attend the negotiations; however, he assigned a delegation of mediators who negotiated on behalf of the LRA.

With support from Khartoum waning, and rattled by the looming ICC arrest warrants, the LRA had greater incentive to participate in peace talks, hoping that they would grant them immunity from ICC prosecution. Kony in effect used the peace negotiations as leverage against the ICC arrest warrants. Indeed, in 2006 Kony threatened to call off the peace talks if the ICC did not withdraw the arrest warrants against the LRA leaders. One of the ex-combatants interviewed noted that on one occasion Kony lamented to his soldiers that the government did not want peace talks because if it did, it would not have referred the situation of the LRA to the ICC. Kony's repeated demands for the suspension of the ICC arrest warrants as a condition for signing the final peace agreement demonstrates that he was aware and fearful of the consequences of facing trial at the ICC. A former combatant interviewed noted: "Kony was afraid of being tried by the ICC because he had the mistaken belief that he would be strangled like Saddam Hussein and that's why he kept pushing for the withdrawal of the arrest warrants".

The ICC arrest warrants influenced the substantive aspects of the negotiations. Both parties to the negotiations acknowledged that some form of accountability had to take place; what was in contention was the nature of the accountability mechanism. Eventually the LRA conceded to a national judicial process and other informal justice mechanisms as an alternative to prosecution at the ICC. This led to the adoption of the Agreement on Accountability and Reconciliation, which provides for the establishment of a special division of the High Court with jurisdiction over international crimes. The Agreement stipulates:

> Formal criminal and civil justice measures shall be applied
> to any individual who is alleged to have committed serious
> crimes or human rights violations in the course of the con-

> flict. Provided that, state actors shall be subjected to existing
> criminal justice processes and not to special justice processes
> under this Agreement.[40]

The Annex to the Agreement on Accountability and Reconciliation provides for the establishment of "a War Crimes Division of the High Court of Uganda, which has the jurisdiction to investigate and prosecute individuals who are alleged to have committed serious crimes during the conflict".[41] The subsequent legal and judicial reforms are examined in detail in the next sub-section.

In 2008 Kony failed to show up to sign the final peace agreement, marking the collapse of the peace talks that had lasted two and a half years. One of the reasons suggested was the refusal of the ICC to suspend the indictments against the LRA leaders. A cross-section of actors criticised the ICC for causing the peace talks to fail. Carlos Rodriguez noted: "No one can convince a rebel leader to come to the negotiating table if he faces the threat of trial".[42] This narrative does not account for the deep mistrust between the LRA and the government of Uganda which contributed to the failure of previous efforts to reach a negotiated settlement to the conflict.

8.4.2. Impact of ICC Intervention on the National Judicial System

The ICC intervention catalysed a series of criminal justice reforms. Notable among these was the establishment of the International Crimes Division of the High Court (formerly War Crimes Division), which was vested with the jurisdiction to prosecute war crimes, crimes against humanity, genocide, terrorism, piracy and trafficking in persons.[43] The International Crimes Division was established in fulfilment of the government's commitment under the Juba Agreement on Accountability and Reconciliation

---

[40] Agreement on Accountability and Reconciliation between Government of Uganda and the Lord's Resistance Army, 29 June 2007, Clause 4.

[41] Annexure to the Agreement on Accountability and Reconciliation signed between the Government of the Republic of Uganda and the Lord's Resistance Army, 2008, Clauses 7 and 8.

[42] Frederick Nzwili, "The Forgotten War", cited in David Lanz, "The ICC's Intervention in Northern Uganda: Beyond the Simplicity of Peace vs. Justice", The Fletcher School of Law and Diplomacy, 2007, p. 1.

[43] Uganda High Court, International Crimes Division, Practice Direction, Legal Notice no. 10 of 2011, Clause 6.

of 2007, and pursuant to the principle of complementarity. The ICC has also influenced norm-setting through the government of Uganda's enactment of the International Criminal Court Act, which domesticated the ICC Statute and provided a legal framework for the prosecution of international crimes in Ugandan courts. War crimes and Anti-Terrorism Departments have also been established in the Uganda police force and the Directorate of Public Prosecutions.[44] Currently, the First Parliamentary Council is in the process of drafting an International Crimes Division Act, which seeks to make the International Crimes Division a special court with special jurisdiction outside the High Court. The Witness Protection Bill and the National Transitional Justice Policy have been drafted and are part of the national transitional justice normative framework for Uganda. In June 2016 the Rules of Procedure and Evidence of the International Crimes Division came into force.[45] The Rules of Procedure and Evidence provide for the investigation and prosecution of international crimes in conformity with international best practices and standards. Alongside these normative developments, capacity-building and skills training for judicial officers, prosecutors and investigators have been undertaken as a result of the ICC intervention in Uganda.[46] There is co-operation between the International Crimes Division and the ICC, based on the principle of positive complementarity. The two jurisdictions have shared information. The ICC has also supported the Directorate of Public Prosecutions in developing its case against former LRA commander Thomas Kwoyelo by transmitting relevant information that it collected during its investigations in northern Uganda.[47] While there is a general view that the ICC had a downstream positive effect on the legal system in Uganda, some actors warn that the impact of the Court on national processes should not be exaggerated. Sceptics argue that government of Uganda instrumentalised the ICC to delegitimise the LRA and has it categorised as a criminal gang to suit the government's political ends. Now that these political goals have

[44]   Interview with justice sector actor, 7 April 2016; Uganda, International Criminal Law Act, 25 June 2010, Acts Supplement No. 6, Uganda Gazette, no. 39, vol. CIII, 25 June 2010 (http://www.legal-tools.org/doc/9c5540/).

[45]   Uganda High Court, International Crimes Division, Rules, Statutory Instrument no. 40 of 2016, Laws of Uganda.

[46]   Patrick S. Wegner, *The International Criminal Court in Ongoing Intrastate Conflicts: Navigating the Peace–Justice Divide*, Cambridge University Press, Cambridge, 2015.

[47]   Joan Kagezi, "The ICC and ICD", Presentation by Head of the Prosecution Division of the International Crimes Division to Members of the 9th Parliament, 2014.

been achieved, the government has adopted a hostile attitude towards the ICC, hence the call for withdrawals from the ICC by Museveni.[48] Legal experts warn that Uganda risks going back to the pre-ICC times when conflicts, gross human rights with impunity and amnesties flourished.

8.5. Factors Enhancing or Undermining the Deterrent Effect of the ICC

A series of factors affected the deterrent effect of the ICC following the launch of investigations and the unsealing of arrest warrants against the top LRA commanders. These fall into two categories: court-based, and extra-legal, social and political factors. The court-based factors include the Court's temporal and geographical jurisdiction, its enforcement capabilities and procedural requirements. The extra-legal, social and political factors include the political context, the co-operation of the Ugandan government, the changing political dynamics in Sudan, combatants' knowledge of the Court's jurisdiction, the brutal and coercive tactics used by the LRA and the spiritual indoctrination of combatants.

8.5.1. Court-Based Factors

8.5.1.1. Jurisdictional Limitations

The deterrence effect of the ICC depends on its institutional effectiveness, which further depends on the Court's temporal and geographical jurisdiction and its enforcement capabilities. The ICC has jurisdiction over crimes that were committed after it came into being in 2002, within the territory of a member state.[49] Uganda ratified the ICC Statute in 2002, the same year that the Statute came into force. By 2002 the LRA conflict had lasted more than 15 years, and both the LRA and government troops had committed mass crimes including child abductions, sexual violence and mutilations. Crimes committed prior to 2002 are beyond the jurisdictional reach of the ICC. This creates an impunity gap, which can only be addressed by national prosecutions.

However, based on the principle of complementarity, it is anticipated that the International Crimes Division of the High Court will have the

---

48 Emma Mutaizibwa, "Museveni Turns from ICC Admirer to Critic", in *The Observer*, 9 June 2013.

49 ICC Statute, Articles 11 and 12, see *supra* note 1.

primary duty to investigate and prosecute the other midlevel alleged perpetrators.

Although the LRA continues to commit atrocities in Central African Republic and the DRC, the ICC has not initiated investigations into those crimes, despite having the jurisdiction to do so. This has consequently limited the ICC's deterrent effect on the LRA.

8.5.1.2. Prosecutorial Strategy of the ICC

The ICC prosecutes individuals who bear the greatest responsibility for the perpetration of international crimes that are within its jurisdiction. This means only a small fraction of the hundreds of perpetrators will be prosecuted by the ICC. The limitations of the ICC negate the deterrent value of ICC trials, since the bulk of perpetrators are not likely to face trial, especially if national courts are unable or unwilling to genuinely investigate and prosecute the perpetrators of international crimes.

In Uganda, only five of the LRA combatants were indicted by the ICC, and so far only one of the five is in the custody of the Court. The trial of Ongwen began at the ICC on 6 December 2016. Critics of the ICC's gravity threshold and case selection criteria argue that the indictment and prosecution of a few rebel commanders could hinder future justice processes by creating the false impression that justice has already been done.[50]

8.5.1.3. Absence of Effective Enforcement Mechanisms

Given the lack of its own police force and enforcement mechanism, the ICC has to rely on the co-operation of states and Interpol to enforce its warrants. If states fail to co-operate, the warrants will remain unenforced. One of the legal experts interviewed noted that "for as long as states are non-cooperative, the ICC remains lame, and thus cannot have the deterrent effect it is supposed to have".[51] This is evident in the Bashir case in which states have been uncooperative in the enforcement of the ICC arrest warrants against him. The recent collapse of the cases against the Kenyan president Kenyatta and Ruto also demonstrate the importance of state co-operation. This co-operation includes unfettered access to its territory

---

[50] Drumbl, 2012, see *supra* note 5.
[51] Expert interview, Kampala, April 2016.

during investigations, protection of witnesses and willingness to enforce arrest warrants. So far, states largely co-operate when rebels or former leaders are before the ICC. The deterrent effect would require state co-operation in all circumstances.

In the case of Uganda, it is over 10 years since the warrants against senior commanders of the LRA were issued, yet to date only one of the indicted people is in the custody of the ICC at trial, while Kony and other LRA combatants continue to perpetrate heinous crimes in the DRC, Central African Republic and South Sudan. The lack of an effective enforcement mechanism for the arrest warrants reduces the probability of the top commanders of the LRA being prosecuted for their alleged crimes. This weakens the deterrent effect of the ICC. A former combatant noted that once it became apparent to Kony that the ICC did not have effective mechanisms to enforce the warrants, his fear of being arrested and prosecuted by the ICC diminished and he continued his brutal attacks against civilian populations.[52] This has attracted criticism from members of the affected communities. Some of them have likened the ICC to a "toothless barking dog" because of its inability to enforce its warrants of arrest. A former combatant noted that Kony was not concerned about the ICC because "it doesn't have guns to fight and arrest him".[53] The ICC's inability to enforce its warrants of arrest has created the perception that the Court is weak and ineffective, thus undermining its deterrence effect in Uganda. Respondents observe that if all arrest warrants against the LRA commanders had been executed quickly, the ICC's intervention in Uganda would have had a great deterrent effect.

8.5.1.4. Narrow Focus on Legal Rather Than Political Triggers of Violence

The framework of the international criminal justice system, which only addresses legal problems accruing from the conflict, is limited in its ability to provide a holistic solution to deter future crimes. A legal scholar interviewed observed that deterrence assumes a legal approach which excludes political issues that caused the conflict. At the end of the criminal justice process, judicial remedies may be awarded to victims and punish-

---

[52]   Ex-combatant interview, Gulu, March 2016.
[53]   *Ibid.*

ment to the perpetrator, but the political problems will remain unresolved and there will be no guarantee of non-reoccurrence of conflict.[54]

8.5.2. Extra-Legal Factors

The deterrent effect of the ICC depends on the social and political context in which the crimes were committed. Each context in which the Court intervenes is unique, with social, cultural and political factors that enhance or diminish the deterrent effect of the ICC. This section examines how these extra-legal factors impacted the deterrent effect of the ICC following the referral of the situation of the LRA to the ICC and the unsealing of the arrest warrants against the top LRA commanders.

8.5.2.1. Political Context

The Ugandan case is an example of how the political context determined the nature and scope of ICC investigations, and thereby affected the ICC's deterrent effect. After years of brutal armed conflict and overt acts of violence by both state and LRA troops, the government restricted its referral to the ICC to crimes perpetrated by the LRA. The referral and subsequent unsealing of arrest warrants against the LRA commanders framed the dominant narrative about the conflict, in which atrocities by state troops were downplayed and international attention focused on crimes committed by the LRA. The one-sided referral by the government of Uganda was a clear indication that the co-operation of the government of Uganda was limited to the investigation and prosecution of crimes allegedly committed by the LRA.[55] Although the referral was later amended to reflect the Situation in Northern Uganda, the ICC has still exclusively focused its attention on LRA atrocities. In response to critics of its one-sided investigations, the prosecutor denied excluding alleged UPDF crimes from the scope of his investigations. However, he noted that the investigations conducted had not come across acts of violence by the UPDF that were of sufficient gravity to trigger the jurisdiction of the ICC compared to those committed by the LRA.[56]

---

[54] Expert interview, April 2016.

[55] Adam Branch, *Displacing Human Rights: War and Intervention in Northern Uganda*, Oxford University Press, Oxford, 2011.

[56] Luis Moreno Ocampo, "Statement of the Chief Prosecutor on the Uganda Arrest Warrants", 14 October 2005.

The ICC's selective judicial process has brought into question the legitimacy of the ICC and created the perception that it is susceptible to manipulation by the political elite. According to some of the experts and victims interviewed for this study, the exclusive focus on LRA atrocities to the exclusion of UPDF crimes portrayed the ICC as "partial, arbitrary and lacking in legitimacy because it only targets the weakest".[57]

The legitimacy of the ICC's intervention in northern Uganda first came into question when Museveni and the former ICC prosecutor Luis Moreno Ocampo held a joint press conference to announce Uganda's referral of the situation concerning the LRA. This created the perception that Museveni was using the Court to serve his government's political interests, rather than to impartially investigate and punish the crimes and violations committed by state troops and the LRA during the two-decade conflict.[58] These perceptions have endured in the absence of investigations of crimes perpetrated by UPDF. This perceived accommodation of political power in order to secure the co-operation of the Ugandan state has undercut the Court's prosecutorial deterrence by insulating state troops from criminal accountability, thus perpetuating a culture of impunity rather than accountability. One of the experts interviewed observed that "for as long as the 'victor's justice' mentality permeates the international and domestic justice system, it will be difficult for any prosecution to have a deterrent effect either on the UPDF or on the LRA".[59]

The ICC's intervention in Uganda was also met with criticism from a broad range of civil society actors who perceived it as an obstacle to lasting peace.

8.5.2.2. Changing Political Dynamics in Sudan

The unsealing of the warrants coincided with the signing of the Comprehensive Peace Agreement between the Sudanese People's Liberation Army ('SPLA') and the government of Sudan, bringing to an end a bloody conflict which had seen Khartoum militarily support the LRA as a proxy to the fight with the SPLA. From the early 1990s, the Sudanese army offered the LRA a safe haven in Juba, with access to military training,

---

[57] Expert interview, Kampala, April 2016.
[58] Adam Branch, "Uganda's Civil War and the Politics of ICC Intervention", in *Ethics & International Affairs*, 2007, vol. 21, no. 2, p. 2.
[59] Expert interview, Kampala, April 2016.

weapons, medical equipment and other forms of logistical supplies, in exchange for the LRA's commitment to fight against the SPLA.[60] The signing of the Comprehensive Peace Agreement meant Khartoum no longer needed the LRA to fight its proxy war, which consequently led to a drastic reduction in Sudanese government military support to the LRA.[61] This development combined with the unsealing of the ICC arrest warrants compelled the LRA to shift its base of operation from South Sudan to Garamba Park across the border in eastern DRC as Kony sought to escape mounting international pressure. Whereas the shifting of LRA bases from South Sudan to the DRC led to a significant reduction in incidents of LRA attacks in northern Uganda, there was an escalation of LRA attacks and mass abduction in the DRC and Central African Republic.[62] The changing political context further motivated the LRA to pursue peace talks with the government of Uganda.

8.5.2.3. Knowledge of ICC Jurisdiction

Research conducted for this study indicates that awareness of the ICC's jurisdiction had an impact on the conduct of combatants and contributed to a reduction of violence in northern Uganda. In Uganda, knowledge of the ICC's jurisdiction has evolved over time. Prior to the unsealing of warrants of arrest against the top commanders of the LRA in 2005, only 21 per cent of the population was aware of the Court's existence. However, in 2007 two years after the unsealing of the warrants of arrest, the figure had risen to 70 per cent.[63] Research conducted in 2010 shows that knowledge of the ICC had fallen to 59 per cent. This is partly due to the inactive ICC cases which led to waning interest in the ICC, as well as the changing interests and priorities of the population affected by the conflict, most of whom focused their attention to meeting their basic needs and resettlement.[64] In the years following the unsealing of the ICC arrest warrants, the ICC's Field Outreach Office rolled out robust outreach pro-

---

[60] International Crisis Group, "Northern Uganda: Understanding and Solving the Conflict, Africa", Africa Report No. 77, 14 April 2004.

[61] International Crisis Group, "Sudan's Comprehensive Peace Agreement: The Long Road Ahead", Africa Report No. 106, 31 March 2006.

[62] Paul Ronan, "Tracking Joseph Kony: A Rebel Leader's Nine-year Odyssey", LRA Tracker, 2014.

[63] Pham and Vinck, 2010, see *supra* note 31.

[64] *Ibid.*

grammes in Uganda targeting the affected communities, to raise awareness about the Court's role and jurisdiction, to keep affected communities informed about the developments in the cases and to address misinformation about the Court. However, the lack of progress in the enforcement of the warrants led to a scaling down of the ICC outreach operations, as the Court focused its attention on other emerging situations. This created an information and knowledge gap of the ICC's involvement in northern Uganda.[65] The operations of the ICC Field Outreach Office were scaled up after the surrender of Ongwen in January 2015.

Research findings suggest that knowledge of the ICC's jurisdiction compelled some LRA combatants to change tactics to avoid being "included on the list of persons indicted by the ICC".[66] They became less overt in the perpetration of crimes. On the other hand, misinformation about the ICC's maximum sentence and prosecutorial strategy had an adverse effect. Kony and other combatants were under the mistaken belief that if they were arrested, they would be prosecuted and "hanged like Saddam Hussein".[67] Consequently, they decided to continue fighting to avoid being arrested.

8.5.2.4. Spiritual Indoctrination of Combatants

Psychological and spiritual factors have impacted the ICC's deterrent effect. According to the ex-combatants interviewed, the LRA rebellion was motivated by the desire to overthrow what they perceived as the illegitimate government of Museveni, which came to power through a violent coup. Kony claimed that his intention was to spiritually cleanse the people of Acholi and rule the country in accordance with the Ten Commandments.[68] The spiritual and ideological indoctrination of LRA combatants affected the ICC's deterrent impact, as it undermined their ability to rationally weigh the risks and benefits of committing atrocities. This is especially the case for rebel movements such as the LRA, which have a hierarchical command structure and whose soldiers are required to execute

---

[65] Lucy Hovil and Zachary Lomo, "Behind the Violence: Causes, Consequences and the Search for Solutions to the War in Northern Uganda", Refugee Law Project Working Paper, No. 11, Refugee Law Project, 2004.

[66] Ex-combatant interview, Gulu, March 2016.

[67] *Ibid.*

[68] Hovil and Lomo, 2004, see *supra* note 65.

spiritual orders from Kony without question and in fulfilment of a greater good.

Kony was also able to exercise control over the LRA fighters by invoking supernatural and spiritual powers, which he claimed guided his actions and offered protection to the LRA fighters. For example, Kony used to sprinkle oil and draw crosses on the chests of his fighters, claiming that these would shield them from bullets.[69] Through different spiritual rituals and prophecies, Kony assumed a metaphysical existence, which earned him the unquestioning loyalty of the soldiers who regarded him as messenger of the spirits[70] and was "beyond reproach and question".[71] Combatants believed that any attempt to escape was futile because Kony's spiritual powers enabled him to know about it; others believed that Kony could read their minds.[72] In view of such systematic indoctrination, the risks posed by the ICC investigations were outweighed by the fear of the likely consequences of not following Kony's spiritual rules. The LRA combatants did not perceive themselves as soldiers, but rather as teachers of God's message. This ultimately negated the deterrent effect of the ICC.

8.5.2.5. Coercive and Brutal Tactics of the LRA

The LRA is said to have used brutal tactics to retain the loyalty of abducted civilians. Children were forcibly recruited into the LRA ranks and indoctrinated to become killing machines. Most abductees were coerced under threat of imminent death to remain loyal to Kony. After the collapse of the Juba peace talks, Kony became more vicious and paranoid. He conducted systematic purging of the LRA to eliminate those he suspected of being disloyal, while promoting his sons and other combatants that he trusted. At the time, some of the combatants were reluctant to execute the orders due to fear of having their names forwarded to the ICC; however, the fear of being killed by Kony forced them to obey him. The reaction of combatants to the ICC warrants also depended on their level of awareness and literacy. Those who were informed and more literate were capable of

---

[69] Richard W. Skow, "LRA Religious Beliefs", in *New York Times*, 31 December 2010.

[70] Hovil and Lomo, 2004, p. 14, see *supra* note 65.

[71] ICC, *Prosecutor v. Dominic Ongwen*, Defence Brief for the Confirmation of Charges Hearing, ICC-02/04-01/15, 18 January 2016, p. 3 ('Ongwen Defence Brief') (http://www.legal-tools.org/doc/a0d94a/).

[72] Ex-combatant interview, Gulu, March 2016.

rationalising the implications of the ICC arrest warrants and responded in a manner that would protect them from being prosecuted. For example, some of the senior commanders who were afraid of being indicted by the ICC resorted to sending young combatants and new recruits to carry out attacks.

8.6. Surrender and Confirmation of Charges against Dominic Ongwen

On 16 January 2015 one of the LRA commanders, Dominic Ongwen, surrendered to Seleka rebels who handed him over to US Special Forces. He was subsequently transferred to the ICC to stand trial, almost 10 years since the Pre-Trial Chamber had unsealed the arrest warrants. On 26 January he made his initial appearance before the Court, and the proceedings against him were separated from the original case that also included Kony, Otti and Odhiambo. From 21 to 27 January 2016 the Pre-Trial Chamber conducted the confirmation of charges hearing in respect of the 70 charges of war crimes and crimes against humanity against him in respect of attacks committed in four internally displaced people's camps in northern Uganda between July 2002 and December 2005.[73] On 23 March 2016 the Pre-Trial Chamber confirmed all the charges against him,[74] and his trial began on 6 December 2016.

The case against Ongwen is significant for a number of reasons. First, he is the only accused at the ICC who is facing trial for crimes of which he is also a victim. It is alleged that Ongwen was abducted in 1988 on his way to school when he was around 10 years old, was forcibly recruited into the ranks of the LRA as a child soldier, and was indoctrinated to kill, mutilate and abduct civilians.[75] His fearless loyalty and ruthless execution of Kony's directives earned him rapid promotion, which saw him elevated to the rank of commander of the Sinia brigade of the LRA.[76] During the confirmation of charges hearing, the defence argued that, as a

---

[73] ICC, *Prosecutor v. Dominic Ongwen*, Prosecution's Submission of the Document Containing the Charges, the Pre-confirmation Brief, and the List of Evidence, ICC-02/04-01/15-375, 21 December 2015 (http://www.legal-tools.org/doc/621924/).

[74] ICC, *Prosecutor v. Dominic Ongwen*, Decision on the Confirmation of Charges against Dominic Ongwen, ICC-02/04-01/, 23 March 2016 (http://www.legal-tools.org/doc/74fc6e/).

[75] Ongwen Defence Brief, p. 3, see *supra* note 71.

[76] Justice and Reconciliation Project, "Complicating Victims and Perpetrators in Uganda: On Dominic Ongwen", JRP Field Note 7, July 2008.

former child soldier, Ongwen was coerced under the threat of immediate death to commit unspeakable crimes. The defence further contended that Ongwen grew up in a brutal environment, "disconnected from the social construct of a normal society in northern Uganda",[77] which left him with no room for moral development.[78] The Pre-Trial Chamber rejected these arguments and confirmed the charges.

Notwithstanding the Pre-Trial Chamber's rejection of the defence arguments, a number of nagging questions persist: whether it is possible to separate Ongwen's infractions as an adult from the brutal and traumatic child soldiering experience he endured;[79] how his traumatic experiences as a child soldier affected his ability to form the *mens rea* to commit the crimes with which he is charged; and whether former child soldiers who find themselves in terrifying environments and are left with no choice but to obey the ruthless orders of their superiors or suffer imminent death can be deterred. In the Lubanga sentencing hearing, the expert witness Elizabeth Schaur submitted that child soldiers

> often suffer from devastating long-term consequences of experienced or witnessed acts of violence. Child war survivors have to cope with repeated traumatic life events, exposure to combat, shelling and other life threatening events, acts of abuse such as torture or rape, violent death of a parent or friend, witnessing loved ones being tortured or injured, separation from family, being abducted or held in detention, insufficient adult care. [...] These experiences can hamper children's healthy development and their ability to function fully even once the violence has ceased'.[80]

According to Schaur, exposure to traumatic events as a child soldier affects individuals for the rest of their lives, and leads to multiple psychological disorders.[81] This consequently affects a former child soldier's ability to rationally weigh the risks and benefits of committing crime. Therefore, the deterrent value of criminal prosecutions on former child

---

[77] Ongwen Defence Brief, p. 3, see *supra* note 71.

[78] Justice and Reconciliation Project, 2008, see *supra* note 76.

[79] Mark A. Drumbl, "The Ongwen Trial at the ICC: Tough Questions on Child Soldiers", in *Open Democracy*, 14 April 2015.

[80] ICC, *Prosecutor v Thomas Lubanga Dyilo*, Decision on Sentence Pursuant to Article 76 of the Statute, ICC-01/04-01/06, 10 July 2012, para. 39 (http://www.legal-tools.org/doc/c79996/).

[81] *Ibid*.

soldiers is very limited. The deterrence of former child soldiers is rooted in other extra-legal processes, which facilitate their rehabilitation and re-integration into communities, and addressing the post-traumatic disorders associated with the child soldiering experience is fundamental to preventing former child soldiers from committing crimes.

The other significance of the Ongwen trial is that it is the first case at the ICC where forced marriage is charged as an inhumane act under Article 7(1)(k) of the ICC Statute. Other significant charges of sexual and gender-based crimes brought against Ongwen include forced pregnancy and sexual slavery. Sexual and gender-based crimes are among the most prevalent crimes committed by the LRA. Young women and girls were forced to serve as conjugal partners to the combatants. In addition to being raped regularly, they were required to provide domestic labour. It is of great significance that forced marriage is one of the charges brought against Ongwen. As the ICC prosecutor observes, the effective investigation and prosecution of perpetrators of sexual crimes not only renders justice to victims, but also "deters the commission of such crimes in future".[82]

Ongwen's confirmation of charges hearing elicited a range of reactions. Some respondents observed elements of negative deterrence based on victims' and returnees' comments on Ongwen's appearance and conditions of detention at the ICC. They observe that the international standards of treatment of suspects at the ICC could create the impression that crime pays, thus negating the possible deterrent effect of prosecutions. One person commented:

> Ongwen looked smart, clean and healthy when he appeared in Court. He does not look like the rebel we saw in bush and many people admired his apparent good look and it might entice some people to commit crimes instead of deterring.[83]

One of the senior ex-combatants interviewed observed that Ongwen's comfortable conditions of detention at the ICC could encourage his subordinates to lay down their arms and surrender in the hope that they will be taken care of, compared to the harsh conditions in the bush.[84] However,

---

[82] ICC, "Fatou Bensouda Publishes Comprehensive Policy Paper on Sexual and Gender-Based Crimes", Press Release, 5 June 2014; ICC, Office of the Prosecutor, "Policy Paper on Sexual and Gender-Based Crimes", June 2014.

[83] Interview with civil society expert, Kampala, March 2016.

[84] Ex-combatant interview, Gulu, March 2016.

other stakeholders are of the view that Ongwen's trial will encourage the juniors to continue fighting because they expect to face trial upon return.

There were mixed reactions from victims on whether Ongwen's initial appearance and confirmation of charges made them feel safer. Some of the ex-combatants and victims who were also abducted as children felt that Ongwen was similarly placed like them given his dual victim-perpetrator identity. However, others were of the view that Ongwen and other commanders that perpetrated grave crimes should be held accountable because of the untold suffering to which they subjected the community.[85] At a live screening of the confirmation charges hearing in Lukodi organised by the Refugee Law Project of Makerere University School of Law and the Outreach Office of the ICC, it was found that most of the members of the affected community expected the Pre-Trial Chamber to confirm the charges against Ongwen because they believe there was overwhelming evidence against him.[86] Some of the victims attending the screening expressed fear that if the charges against Ongwen were not confirmed, he would return to Central African Republic and rejoin the LRA to plot revenge attacks on the affected communities that co-operated with the ICC investigations.[87] The detention of Ongwen in The Hague prevents him from committing further crimes, which makes the victims feel safer.

Some of the ex-combatants were of the view that Kony will use the trial of Ongwen as a propaganda tool to discourage combatants from abandoning rebellion by misleading them into believing that the only way to escape Ongwen's fate is by fighting.[88]

In addition to the prosecution of Ongwen, victims continue to call for reparations, medical assistance and psychosocial support to address the physical and psychological trauma experienced during the conflict, and for the investigation and prosecution of UPDF crimes to enhance deterrence and the perception of the ICC as an impartial and credible court.

---

[85] Refugee Law Project, "Ongwen's Justice Dilemma: Part II", Refugee Law Project, Kampala, 2016.

[86] Ibid.

[87] Ibid.

[88] Ex-combatant interview, Gulu, March 2016.

8.7. Conclusion

The deterrent function of the ICC in Uganda was influenced by a series of court-based and extra-legal factors. Whereas some actors viewed the ICC's intervention as an obstacle to finding a lasting peaceful solution to the conflict in northern Uganda, evidence indicates that it presented the only threat that could motivate the LRA to seek to engage in peace talks. It is also evident that the ICC arrest warrants catalysed a series of events, including the establishment of a Special Division of the High Court with jurisdiction to investigate and prosecute serious crimes. It also contributed to norm-setting through the domestication of the ICC Statute by the enactment of the ICC Act of 2010, which provides a legal framework for the domestic prosecution of ICC Statute crimes. The major limitation has been the absence of an effective enforcement mechanism; the Court has to rely on the goodwill of states to execute its warrants. This negates certainty of prosecution which is an important aspect for deterrence. Other court-based factors that limit deterrent effect are the jurisdictional constraints of the ICC, the selective prosecutorial strategy, and the emphasis on legal issues to the exclusion of political factors. Deterrence is also affected by contextual, extra-legal factors. For Uganda, these include the political context, not only in Uganda but also in neighbouring Sudan; the level of knowledge of ICC activities; the spiritual and psychological basis of the perpetrators' actions; and the coercive tactics of the LRA.

To maximise the ICC's deterrent effect, the Court should address its structural limitations, especially its reliance on co-operation of states to enforce arrest warrants. There needs to be clear sanctions for state parties that do not co-operate with the Court. As long as arrest warrants are not executed and cases collapse due to witness interference with no consequences for the state involved, the ICC's deterrent effect will remain limited. There must be consequences for states that do not co-operate with the ICC. It is also important for the Court and other international actors to take into account contextual, extra-legal factors in assessing how best to deter perpetrators and future possible perpetrators.

9

Deterrence in Sudan:
The Limits of a Lonely Court

Olivia Bueno[*]

9.1. Introduction

When advocates and the United Nations ('UN') Security Council called for the referral of the Darfur case to the International Criminal Court ('ICC') in 2005, deterrence was very much on their minds. Leaders asserted that ensuring accountability for the serious crimes committed in Darfur would help to stop them from recurring, although this was not, and is not, the exclusive reason for seeking accountability. Twelve years on, it is an opportune moment to step back and reflect on these early assertions about deterrence and whether the intervention of the ICC has deterred criminality in Sudan generally and Darfur specifically.

At first blush, the view is grim. In the stark words of a Sudanese activist, "[t]he ICC has failed to end the hostilities".[1] Indeed, international crimes continue to be committed in Sudan. Not only does violence continue in Darfur but violence has also escalated significantly there in the past few years and, most recently, credible allegations about the use of chemical weapons have come to light.[2] In addition, a new front has

---

[*] **Olivia Bueno** is the International Refugee Rights Initiative's ('IRRI') Associate Director. She was previously Program Associate at the International Refugee Program at Human Rights First (formerly the Lawyers Committee for Human Rights). She is responsible for managing IRRI's New York office, monitoring United Nations policies and diplomatic discussions relevant to IRRI's programmes and co-ordinating outreach to and collaboration with international non-governmental organisations. She also contributes to the oversight and development of IRRI programmes and to institutional development. She has also worked on issues of refugee rights and asylum in the United States, as a part-time staff member of Human Rights First's Asylum Program and as Co-Producer of *American Purgatory*, a radio documentary on the asylum process in the United States. She holds an M.A. in International Affairs from the School for International and Public Affairs and B.A. in Russian Language and Literature from Barnard College, both at Columbia University.

[1] Interview with Najlaa Ahmed, May 2016.

[2] Amnesty International, "Scorched Earth, Poisoned Air: Sudanese Government Forces Ravage Jebel Marra, Darfur", AFR 54/4877/2016, 29 September 2016.

---

opened up in Southern Kordofan and Blue Nile. Most of those charged by the Court have yet to appear, and most visibly the Sudanese president Omar Al Bashir remains at large. In Bashir's significant travels, a number of states have shown themselves to be unwilling to execute the arrest warrant. Facing a lack of support from the international community, the ICC prosecutor, Fatou Bensouda, stated in 2014 that she was "hibernating" the Darfur case.[3]

As Najlaa Ahmed's statement makes clear, the deterrent effect of the ICC in Sudan has fallen short of the aspirations set out for it. Activists, both Sudanese and non-Sudanese, and victims interviewed for this chapter expressed frustration that the Court had not delivered as they had hoped. As an activist who campaigned extensively for the referral, hand in hand with Sudanese and international advocates, this author can attest to the high hopes held out for what the Court would be able to accomplish, and the subsequent frustrations. The crimes have not stopped. Violent attacks on civilians continue, not only in Darfur but in other Sudanese states, Southern Kordofan and Blue Nile, as well. In retrospect, however, perhaps advocates set the bar too high.

The fact that deterrence has not been as effective as was hoped does not mean that there has been no deterrent effect at all. This chapter seeks to explore the question of whether or not any deterrent effect can be perceived, and why or why not. In trying to answer the first question, the chapter looks both at the impressions and opinions of scholars and activists and at data that can point to levels of criminality – as imperfect as they are. The chapter finds that there are competing views on this question, but that the data do show a correlation between the referral of the case and a decrease in violence in the country.

In trying to answer the second question, why there has or has not been deterrence, the chapter applies theories of deterrence generally in both the domestic and international sphere to examine the elements that make deterrence more or less effective and to analyse the extent to which these are present in the Sudan situation; whether deterrence was possible in the Sudan situation; the factors that constrained the deterrent impact of the Court in practice; how might these be addressed in order to improve the Court's performance in this respect.; and whether the lack of impact

---

[3]   Worldwide Movement for Human Rights, "The ICC and Sudan: Questions & Answers", Press Release, 31 March 2015.

was the result of the Court's actions or the difficult circumstances within which it is operating. It is hoped that this analysis will help to foster a better understanding by the international community of the circumstances in which deterrence will work best, and the actions that need to be taken to ensure the greatest deterrent impact.

This chapter is intended to evaluate the deterrent impact of the Court and it is important to distinguish this from an overall assessment of the Court. Although it is important to better understand deterrence, there are many reasons other than deterrence to support international justice. In the words of Aurelia Frick, the foreign minister of Liechtenstein, "deterrence is not the only reason for us to support the ICC. In a domestic context, nobody would argue that criminal courts should be abandoned if the crime rate goes up".[4] The ICC serves other goals, including recognising the plight of victims and ending impunity, which have value in and of themselves. Thus, even if the deterrent effect is found wanting, this should not be taken to mean that the Court as a whole is not worthy of support.

9.2. Methodology

This chapter attempts to answer the question of whether or not there has been any deterrent effect as a result of the ICC's intervention in Sudan and why. It uses three approaches to explore this question. First, it looks at the issue of deterrence from the perspective of the literature that exists on the issue in the domestic context to provide a framework for exploring to what extent deterrence might be an expected outcome in the circumstances. Second, the chapter asks what Sudanese (and to a certain extent internationals following Sudan closely) perceive as the impact. In order to assess these views, the chapter relies on over two dozen interviews with Sudanese activists, refugees and experts. The majority of these were gathered in 2016, but the author has also drawn on interviews conducted earlier for an unpublished study on the broader impact of the Court. The vast majority of respondents expressed a preference to remain anonymous and are referred to only by their affiliation. A few asked to be identified and these are referred to by name. Finally, the chapter attempts to cross-check perceptions of the increase or decrease in violations against available data on the rise and fall in the frequency of violations of international humani-

---

[4]   International Peace Institute, "Proceedings of Event: Can the International Criminal Court Deter Atrocities?", 12 March 2015.

tarian law. One of the sources of objective data is a database maintained by the Armed Conflict Location and Event Data Project ('ACLED').[5] The ACLED database is compiled from a variety of sources, including reports from news agencies, civil society organisations and international organisations' security updates. Although the project prides itself on using reliable and verifiable data and has been subject to peer review, it is also subject to the limitations of the sources from which it draws.[6] In order to try to limit the potential biases of these data sources, information is crosschecked against human rights reports and the periodic reports of the UN Panel of Experts established under UN Security Council resolution 1591 to monitor implementation of the arms embargo imposed by the same resolution.

9.3. Background

9.3.1. Conflict in Darfur and Sudan

The long-running crisis in Darfur exploded in 2003, when rebels launched a series of attacks on government targets. The rebel movements involved the Sudan Liberation Army ('SLA') and the Justice and Equality Movement ('JEM'), which had been organised in 2001 and 2002 respectively, claiming to seek to rectify the marginalisation of Darfur in national structures.[7] The government responded to these attacks with a brutal counter-insurgency campaign, characterised by serious violations of international humanitarian and criminal law, including, some would argue, genocide.

The ongoing conflict builds on a number of deep-seated issues related to land distribution, governance, underdevelopment, international engagement and ideology, which cannot be addressed fully here. Briefly, however, the Darfur region suffered from neglect and underdevelopment from the British colonial period onwards. In 2000 the "Black Book" was published in Khartoum, detailing this history of marginalisation and call-

---

[5] Clionadh Raleigh, Andrew Linke, Håvard Hegre and Joakim Karlsen, "Introducing ACLED-Armed Conflict Location and Event Data", in *Journal of Peace Research*, 2010, vol. 47, no. 5, p. 110.

[6] Armed Conflict Location and Event Data Project, "Guide to Dataset Use for Humanitarian and Development Practitioners", January 2014.

[7] International Refugee Rights Initiative ('IRRI') and the Darfur Refugee Association in Uganda, "Darfurians in South Sudan: Negotiating Belonging in Two Sudans", Citizenship and Displacement in the Great Lakes Region, Working Paper 7, May 2012.

ing for action to remedy it.[8] The divisions between these groups were exacerbated by the engagement of Chadian and Libyan militants in the region in the 1980s, who promoted the spread of an Arab supremacist ideology. A critical ingredient in the violence has been tension over land. The traditional Darfurian land tenure system granted homelands to some ethnic groups leaving others landless, primarily but not exclusively Arabs and pastoralists. These tensions intensified with increasing desertification in recent years leading to increasing disputes access to pasture and water.[9]

As they have done elsewhere in Sudan, the government exploited fissures in Darfurian communities to mobilise segments of the population against the rebels. In the Darfur context, it is primarily groups that were identified as Arab who were mobilised by the government into militias known collectively as Janjaweed. As with so many similar labels, the terms 'African' and 'Arab' are simultaneously powerful markers on the ground, highly mutable and historically problematic. Most Darfuris can point to an ethnic or tribal affiliation, but these are generally associated with African or Arab identities as well. Groups such as the Baggara and the Rizeigat are generally identified as Arab, while the Fur, Zaghawa and Masaleit are identified as African.[10] There is little to support a clear genealogical division between the groups, leading Alex De Waal, an expert on Sudan, to describe the classifications as "historically bogus, but disturbingly powerful".[11]

Whatever the reasons for the rebellion, the reprisals targeted civilians perceived to be supporting the rebels rather than the rebel movements themselves. A familiar pattern of attack involved a co-ordinated action against a particular village through aerial bombardment co-ordinated with a ground attack by the Janjaweed. By the end of 2004, the International Commission of Inquiry on Darfur ('ICID') estimated that 700 villages in Darfur had been destroyed as a result of such attacks.[12] In addition, other

---

[8] Gérard Prunier, *Darfur: The Ambiguous Genocide*, Cornell University Press, Ithaca, 2005.

[9] For a more detailed discussion of the background to the conflict in Darfur, see IRRI and Darfur Refugee Association in Uganda, 2012, *supra* note 7.

[10] *Ibid.*

[11] Alex De Waal, "Counter-Insurgency on the Cheap", in *London Review of Books*, 2004, vol. 26, no. 15, pp. 25–27.

[12] International Commission of Inquiry on Darfur, Report of the International Commission of Inquiry on Darfur to the UN Secretary-General Pursuant to UN Security Council Resolution 1564 of 18 September 2004, Geneva, 25 January 2005.

serious violations including killings, torture, forced disappearances and rape were reported. This destruction caused widespread population displacement as civilians fled to urban areas and internally displaced people's camps perceived to be safer. By December 2004 an estimated 1.6 million people were displaced internally within Darfur.[13] Figures of the number of causalities at this height of the violence are highly contested, but the UN has relied on a figure of 300,000, including both direct deaths from violence and the much more numerous deaths from disease, hunger and lack of appropriate assistance.

Over time, however, the patterns of the conflict shifted. While fewer direct attacks on villages occurred, the violence became more complex as rebel movements splintered and groups not directly involved in the conflict perpetrated increasing violence. In early 2006 tensions in the SLA/M came to a head over contestations between Abdelwahid al-Nur and Minni Minawi as to who should lead the movement. Eventually this led to a split into two movements SLA-AW and SLA-MM, with each man rallying support largely along ethnic lines. In May 2006 the government of Sudan and one of the rebel factions, the SLM-MM, signed the Darfur Peace Agreement in Abuja, Nigeria. Following this, fighting and competition among the rebel factions increased. This led to an increasing sense of insecurity on the ground, as attacks on humanitarian assets and hijackings increased.[14] In late 2006–2007 the pattern of violence shifted, with fewer armed clashes between armed movements occurring. This violence was replaced, however, by fighting along ethnic lines, banditry and attacks on humanitarian organisations and the African Union Mission in Sudan ('AMIS'), which had been deployed shortly after the signing of the 2004 N'Djamena ceasefire agreement,[15] and harassment and rape of internally displaced populations.[16] In August 2006 the International Committee of

---

[13] United Nations Security Council, UN Panel of Experts, Report of the Panel of Experts Established Pursuant to Resolution 1591 (2005) concerning the Sudan, UN doc. S/2008/647, 11 November 2008.

[14] United Nations Security Council, UN Panel of Experts, Report of the Panel of Experts Establish Pursuant to Resolution 1591 (2005) Prepared in Accordance with Paragraph 2 of Resolution 1665, UN doc. S/2006/795, 3 October 2006.

[15] IRRI, "'No one on earth cares if we survive except God and sometimes UNAMID': The Challenges of Peacekeeping in Darfur", June 2016.

[16] United Nations Security Council, UN Panel of Experts, Report of the Panel of Experts Established Pursuant to Resolution 1591 concerning the Sudan Prepared in Accordance with Paragraph 2 of resolution 1713, UN doc. S/2007/584, 3 October 2007.

the Red Cross reported that 200 women had been assaulted in and around Kalma camp in the previous five weeks alone.[17]

In September 2007, in a serious escalation of the pattern of attacks against AMIS, the mission's base at Haskanita was attacked, killing 10 soldiers and wounding 12.[18] This attack was investigated by the ICC and charges were brought against three rebel leaders in connection with the incident. When the joint United Nations-African Union Mission in Darfur ('UNAMID') replaced AMIS in 2008,[19] these violations did not cease. Between January and July 2010 there were at least 10 armed attacks on UNAMID, killing five peacekeepers and wounding 19 more. In the same period 20 UNAMID vehicles were hijacked.[20] Between April and December 2013, 16 peacekeepers were killed and 32 injured in 12 incidents.[21] Since their deployment, 235 UNAMID personnel have died in Darfur, 72 of them victims of "malicious acts".[22]

In July 2011 the Doha Document for Peace in Darfur was signed by the government of Sudan and the Liberation and Justice Movement ('LJM'), a JEM splinter group, following about two years of negotiations. Like the Darfur Peace Agreement before it, the Doha Document for Peace in Darfur was undermined by the lack of consensus; it was not endorsed by the majority of rebel movements, including those with the greatest fighting capacity, and failed to bring an end to the conflict.[23]

From 2012 there has been increasing violence, with an increase in military confrontations and violence. In 2012 there were reportedly 106 aerial attacks committed in Darfur,[24] attacks for which the government can be presumed to bear responsibility as the rebels lack air capacity. In

---

[17] UN Panel of Experts, 2006, see *supra* note 14.

[18] UN Panel of Experts, 2008, see *supra* note 13.

[19] IRRI, 2016, see *supra* note 15.

[20] United Nations Security Council, UN Panel of Experts, Report of the Panel of Experts Established Pursuant to Resolution 1591 (2005), UN doc. S/2011/111, 8 March 2011.

[21] United Nations Security Council, UN Panel of Experts, Report of the Panel of Experts on the Sudan established pursuant to resolution 1591 (2005), UN doc. S/2013/79, 12 February 2013.

[22] UN Peacekeeping, "Fatalities by Mission, Year and Incident Type", up to 31 October 2016.

[23] IRRI, 2016, see *supra* note 15.

[24] UN Panel of Experts, 2013, see *supra* note 21.

2013 fighting between the government and the rebels and among tribal groups increased, newly displacing 450,000 people.[25]

In 2014 the patterns of conflict shifted again as the government of Sudan began recruiting and training militia forces under the name of the Rapid Support Forces ('RSF'). Although the RSF have their roots in the Janjaweed (indeed they have been called Janjaweed Reincarnate), the formation of the group marked a revitalisation, with the RSF being offered new weapons and formal guarantees of immunity.[26] The RSF was initially deployed to Kordofan, but then reassigned to Darfur where it participated in a major offensive against the JEM and SLA-MM rebels known as Operation Decisive Summer.[27] This offensive resulted in a marked increase in attacks on civilians. During the first six months of the year, 3,324 villages were reportedly destroyed. In the first 10 months of the year, 431,291 people were displaced, more than in any year since 2006. Abductions of humanitarian workers also reached an all-time high.[28] Intensified fighting has continued since then, with new offensives launched into Jebel Marra in early 2016.

The conflict in Sudan has not been limited to Darfur. In 2011 a new conflict erupted in Southern Kordofan and Blue Nile, along Sudan's newly formed border with South Sudan. The fighting began in Southern Kordofan, sparked by the government of Sudan's demand that the members of the Sudan People's Liberation Army ('SPLA'), who had been integrated into joint integrated units in the state, withdraw to what would soon become South Sudan, even though many were originally from areas north of the border. It built, however, on a history of abuses and marginalisation.[29] As in Darfur, civilians have borne the brunt of the conflict. In 2015 Nuba Reports estimated that more than 3,000 bombs had fallen on civilian areas in the state over the previous three years, an average of nearly three

---

[25] UN Panel of Experts, 2013, see *supra* note 21.

[26] Enough Project, "Janjaweed Reincarnate: Sudan's New Army of War Criminals", available at http://www.enoughproject.org/files/JanjaweedReincarnate_June2014.pdf, last accessed 7 September 2016.

[27] United Nations Security Council, UN Panel of Experts, Report of the Panel Experts on the Sudan Established Pursuant to Resolution 1591 (2005), UN doc. S/2015/31, 19 January 2015.

[28] *Ibid.*

[29] IRRI and the National Human Rights Monitors' Organisation, "'We just want a rest from war': Civilian Perspectives on the Conflict in Sudan's South Kordofan State", April 2015.

bombs a day.[30] This bombing has disrupted agriculture and led the Famine Early Warning Network to warn that food security was likely to reach emergency levels in 2016.[31]

Conflict is causing staggering humanitarian consequences in both Darfur and in the states of Southern Kordofan and Blue Nile. The UN Office for the Coordination of Humanitarian Affairs estimates that 5.8 million people in Sudan are in need of humanitarian assistance.[32] Approximately half the population, 1.7 million people, have been displaced from Southern Kordofan.[33] The Internal Displacement Monitoring Centre has estimated that 144,000 people were newly displaced in Sudan in 2015.[34] Between January and March 2016 approximately 100,000 people were newly displaced,[35] at least 40,000 of whom were newly displaced by fighting in the central Jebel Marra region.[36]

9.3.2. The History of the ICC's Engagement

The issue of seeking accountability for the crimes committed in Darfur was part of the discussion of these violations more or less from the outset. Mukesh Kapila, who was really the first to draw broad attention to the crisis with his statements in March 2004, suggested that the international community should set up "some sort of international court or mechanism to bring to trial the individuals who are masterminding or committing war crimes in Darfur".[37]

In September 2004, in the wake of growing international outcry about the situation in Darfur, the UN Security Council mandated the ICID to investigate reports of violations of international humanitarian and hu-

---

[30] Sudan Consortium, "Humanitarian Crisis in Sudan's Two Areas and Darfur", March 2015.

[31] Famine Early Warning Systems Network, "Conflict, Poor Harvests to Result in a Deterioration of Food Security in South Kordofan by March", December 2015.

[32] USAID, "Sudan – Complex Emergency: Fact Sheet #4, Fiscal Year. FY 2016", 23 May 2016.

[33] IRRI and the National Human Rights Monitors' Organisation, 2015, see *supra* note 29.

[34] Internal Displacement Monitoring Centre, "Sudan: Country Information 2015".

[35] United Nations Security Council, UN Secretary-General, Report of the Secretary-General on the African Union-United Nations Hybrid Operation in Darfur, UN doc. S/2016/268, 22 March 2016.

[36] UN Office for the Coordination of Humanitarian Affairs, "Humanitarian Bulletin, Sudan", Issue 19 | 2, 8 May 2016.

[37] Prunier, 2005, see *supra* note 8.

man rights law, and to make recommendations for holding the perpetrators accountable.[38]

In 25 January 2005 the Commission reported to the Security Council, finding war crimes and crimes against humanity had been committed in Darfur, but that it lacked sufficient evidence to make a finding of genocide. It recommended that the case be referred to the ICC for investigation and possible prosecutions. The Commission also compiled a list of 51 people whom the evidence implicated in the commission of international crimes in Darfur. It recommended that this evidence be handed over to the ICC. In making its recommendation, the ICID argued that securing accountability would promote peace and security by removing obstacles to peace.[39]

After some discussion of the possibility of creating an *ad hoc* tribunal to address the crimes, on 31 March 2005 in resolution 1593, the Security Council made a decision to refer the situation in Darfur to the ICC. Although resolution 1593, through which the referral was made, makes little reference to the reasons for the referral, it is clear that deterrence was a factor in the international community's decision-making. Some Security Council members referred explicitly to the role of deterrence, or prevention more broadly, in justifying their positions on the referral. For example, speaking on behalf of the United Kingdom, its ambassador Emyr Jones Parry said that the UK "hoped to send a salutary warning to other parties who may be tempted to commit similar human rights violations".[40] The French ambassador, Jean-Marc de la Sablière stated that the referral to the ICC was "the only solution […] and […] would prevent those violations from continuing".[41] Luis Moreno Ocampo, then prosecutor of the ICC, referred to prevention in his decision to open the case in Darfur following the referral, saying that the investigation "will form part of a collective effort, complementing African Union and other initiatives to end the violence in Darfur and to promote justice".[42]

---

[38] United Nations Security Council, Resolution 1564 (2004), UN doc. S/Res/1564, 18 September 2004 (http://www.legal-tools.org/doc/1ba770/).

[39] International Commission of Inquiry on Darfur, 2005, see *supra* note 12.

[40] United Nations Security Council, Security Council Refers Situation in Darfur, Sudan, to Prosecutor of International Criminal Court, UN doc. SC/8351, 31 March 2005.

[41] *Ibid.*

[42] ICC, "The Prosecutor of the ICC Opens Investigation in Darfur", Press Release, 6 June 2005.

Rhetoric related to deterrence and, more broadly to prevention, also featured in the voices of civil society who advocated for the referral. Even Alex De Waal, later a staunch critic of the ICC, called for legal action for deterrent purposes in 2004" "Legal action – trying Musa Hilal and his sponsors as war criminals – is essential to deter such crimes in the future".[43] Madgi El-Na'im of the Cairo Institute for Human Rights Studies echoed this sentiment: "Restoration of peace in Darfur is not possible unless those responsible for the grave crimes committed there are brought to justice".[44]

After a preliminary analysis of the evidence, the ICC prosecutor announced on 6 June 2005 that he would commence an investigation.[45] In the initial phase of the investigation, the government of Sudan extended some co-operation to the ICC, allowing members of the staff of the Office of the Prosecutor to travel to Sudan and interview key individuals. However, according to one prominent Sudanese commentator, "[t]his cooperation stopped short of meaningful facilitation of the ICC investigation in Darfur itself and instead appeared calculated to pre-empt the ICC proceeding and defeat them on technical grounds".[46] Citing limited access to Darfur, the Office of the Prosecutor chose to seek information sources abroad. This approach allowed the Office to carry out investigations under difficult circumstances, but also led to speculation (particularly by the government of Sudan) that actors on the ground in Sudan, whether Sudanese activists or international humanitarian NGOs, might have been passing information to the Office.

The first phase of the prosecutor's investigation focused on the responsibility of two individuals: Ahmad Harun, formerly minister of state for the interior and now governor of Southern Kordofan, and Ali Kushyab, a senior leader in the Wadi Saleh locality and member of the Popular Defence Forces. These two were accused of 51 counts of war crimes and crimes against humanity in relation to the attacks on four Darfuri villages,

---

[43] De Waal, 2004, see *supra* note 11.

[44] Cairo Institute for Human Rights Studies, the Darfur Consortium and Human Rights First, "Peace Requires Justice: U.N. Should Immediately Refer Darfur to the ICC", 2 February 2005.

[45] ICC, 2005, see *supra* note 42.

[46] Suliman Baldo, "The Impact of the ICC in Sudan and DR Congo", Expert Paper, Workshop 7 – The Impact of the International Criminal Court (ICC), at International Conference on Building a Future on Peace and Justice, Nuremberg, 25–27 June 2007.

Mukjar, Bindisi, Arawala and Kodoom in western Darfur in 2003 and 2004. The Office of the Prosecutor sought either summonses to appear or arrest warrants, leaving the judges to decide which were more appropriate. In April 2007 the Pre-Trial Chamber issued arrest warrants on the basis that there was no reason to believe the individuals sought would appear if summoned.[47] Following this, the government of Sudan broke all communication with the Court, with the Sudanese embassy in The Hague literally refusing to open the door to accept notification.[48] Although the Office of the Prosecutor made significant efforts for more than a year following these warrants convincing the government of Sudan to hand over Harun and Kushayb, or to conduct trials domestically, in particular through demarches to the governments of Jordan, Saudi Arabia, Egypt, Qatar and Indonesia and to the Arab League, these efforts were unsuccessful. One activist argued that starting with Harun and Kushayb mobilised their ethnic groups to pressure the government not to hand them over, limiting the government's scope for action.[49] Others suggested that Bashir did not want them arrested as they could have offered incriminating evidence against him; according to one source, Bashir even tentatively explored the idea of surrender, but Harun informed him, effectively: "I go to The Hague, you go with me". Sudanese activists interviewed for this research, however, showed little awareness of these efforts, focusing instead on the end point at failures to arrest.

In July 2008 the then-prosecutor Moreno Ocampo requested the Pre-Trial Chamber to issue a warrant of arrest for Sudanese president Omar Al Bashir for 10 counts of genocide, crimes against humanity and war crimes in Darfur. In March 2009 the Pre-Trial Chamber issued an arrest warrant accepting the prosecutor's charges on seven of the counts. The initial arrest warrant did not include the genocide charges, on the grounds that there was insufficient evidence to support them.[50] The prosecutor appealed and on 12 July 2010 a second arrest warrant was issued reflecting the genocide charg-

---

[47]   IRRI, "In the Interests of Justice? Prospects and Challenges for International Justice in Africa", 1 November 2008.

[48]   Sarah M.H. Nouwen, *Complementarity in the Line of Fire: The Catalysing Effect of the International Criminal Court in Uganda and Sudan*, Cambridge University Press, Cambridge, 2013.

[49]   Interview with Sudanese activist, September 2012.

[50]   ICC, *Prosecutor v. Omar Hassan Ahmed Al Bashir*, Pre-Trial Chamber, Warrant of Arrest for Omar Hassan Ahmed Al Bashir, ICC-02/05-01/09-1, 4 March 2009 (http://www.legal-tools.org/doc/814cca/).

es. Since then, the case has stalled because Bashir has refused to appear at the Court, and even when he has travelled abroad, hosting states have failed to execute the arrest warrants. This has led to litigation at the Court that has resulted in several findings of non-cooperation and referrals of member states to the Assembly of States Parties.

On 2 December 2011 Moreno Ocampo requested a warrant of arrest against Abdel Raheem Muhammad Hussein, the current defence minister and Darfur special representative of the Sudanese president at the time of the alleged crimes. On 1 March 2012 the Pre-Trial Chamber found that there was sufficient cause in relation to 41 counts of crimes against humanity and war crimes to issue an arrest warrant for Hussein.

The ICC has also issued summonses to appear against three rebel leaders, Bahr Idriss Abu Garda, Abdallah Banda Abakaer Nourain and Saleh Mohammed Jerbo Jamus. These leaders were charged with war crimes in relation to the September 2007 attack on the AMIS base at Haskanita, noted above. Abu Garda appeared before the Court in 2009, but the judges declined to confirm the charges against him, and the case never proceeded to trial, and the charges against Jerbo are no longer being pursued following the submission of evidence of his death. In March 2011 charges were confirmed against Abdallah Banda. A warrant for his arrest was issued on 11 September 2014 in order to ensure that he would appear.[51] Although the trial was to begin on 18 November 2014, Banda has yet to appear. The Office of the Prosecutor's selection of this case was widely seen as an effort to demonstrate the Court's neutrality, but it did little to convince the government. The fact that charges were not confirmed against Abu Garda has only strengthened that impression.[52]

9.4. Assessing Deterrence

9.4.1. Perceptions of Deterrence

In light of the high level of continuing violence in Sudan, it is not surprising that many Sudanese and international observers take a dim view of the effectiveness of the ICC in creating deterrence in the current Sudanese context. In response to the question of whether or not the ICC had deterred crimes, one Sudanese activist said: "In the Darfur case, it is a big no

---

[51] Worldwide Movement for Human Rights, 2015, see *supra* note 3.

[52] Nouwen, 2013, see *supra* note 48.

actually".[53] He went on to point to the reported rape of over 200 women in Tabit in October 2014 as evidence of ongoing crimes.[54] Another Sudanese activist said that there is "no deterrence. There is war in Darfur, Southern Kordofan and Blue Nile. Bashir is not worried about the ICC".[55] Others pointed to the killings of protesters during the 2013 student demonstrations in Khartoum as evidence of the lack of deterrent impact of the court. Worse yet, in the words of one activist, "[t]here is no expectation of deterrence on the ground".[56]

International commentators are hardly more enthused. Although Hyeran Jo and Beth A. Simmons have made a compelling case for a deterrent impact of the ICC globally, they caveat that finding with specific reference to Sudan, noting that "the ICC has had little effect in some countries where it has intervened with indictments (Sudan and Libya, for example)".[57] Simon Adams of the Global Centre for the Responsibility to Protect, in reviewing the deterrent impact of the Court, referred to Sudan as "the worst case example, where atrocities are ongoing, including in Darfur, six years following the indictment of President Al-Bashir".[58]

Some, however, argue that there has been some deterrence. These people do not fail to see the ongoing crimes being committed in Sudan, but they argue that the scale would be greater had the ICC not intervened. One advocate who works with victims recognised before the ICC said: "I honestly believe that the situation would be even worse if there hadn't been a referral".[59] Another advocate said: "[t]he ICC intervention has had a little impact. Bashir et al have continued to commit crimes, but they are afraid to commit them at the same scale. In an indirect way, it has helped".[60] Proponents of this view argued that the ICC investigation had kept at least minimal international attention on Darfur as the world had, in general, lost interest.

---

[53]   Interview with Sudanese activist, March 2016.

[54]   Human Rights Watch, "Mass Rape in North Darfur: Sudanese Army Attacks against Civilians in Tabit", 11 February 2015.

[55]   Interview with Sudanese activist, February 2012.

[56]   Interview with Darfuri activist, April 2016.

[57]   Hyeran Jo and Beth A. Simmons, "Can the International Criminal Court Deter Atrocity?", in *International Organization*, 2016, vol. 70, no. 3, pp. 443–75.

[58]   International Peace Institute, 2015, see *supra* note 4.

[59]   Interview with Monica Feltz, April 2016.

[60]   Interview with Sudanese activist, March 2016.

Others highlighted the erosion of the deterrent effect over time. "In the beginning, the regime and Bashir and everyone was afraid. When Bashir and the others found out that the ICC does not have police or international forces, then they returned to business as usual".[61] Another activist concurred: "They were panicking in 2008, but since then they have gotten comfortable because they have support from Africa and there is no arrest".[62] Another argued that there had been a more localised impact: "After the Harun arrest warrant, the crimes reduced. After the Bashir arrest warrant, violence went up".[63]

These differences of opinion show some of the difficulties of assessing deterrent impact. One issue is how we assess levels of violence and compare different types of violations; as has been noted above, patterns of violence in Darfur have shifted over time. How does one, for example, weigh the impact of the crackdown on civil society that followed the issuance of the arrest warrant against Bashir with the initial violations that occurred in the context of attacks on villages? The former affected fewer people directly, but resulted in a diminished capacity to monitor and respond to human rights violations which in turn impacted a greater number of people. How does one weigh attacks on villages in 2003–2004 against the crackdowns on protest in 2013 or the ongoing violence in Southern Kordofan? More philosophically, does an examination of deterrence require a counterfactual consideration: would the situation have been worse without an ICC intervention?

9.4.2. Assessing Data on Levels of Violence: Methodological Issues

In domestic contexts, criminologists often study deterrence through examination of crime rates. In the ICC context, this requires examination of the rate of commission of international crimes. Although any crime rate is subject to limitations in relation to reporting rates and other factors, this is exacerbated in the international context where there is no standard reporting or response mechanisms. How can one assess the extent of deterrence in the context of a complex (and ongoing) crisis? There is no simple answer.

First, it is difficult to get an accurate assessment of the situation on the ground, especially in a context where the government of Sudan is

---

[61] Interview with Sudanese activist, April 2016.
[62] Interview with Sudanese activist, March 2016.
[63] *Ibid.*

blocking access to information. More reporting on human rights viola-tions could mean not that violations were more visible or better docu-mented, rather than more prevalent. The lack of reporting, on the other hand, could be the result of inaccessibility of certain areas, due to insecu-rity or government restrictions. In some cases, government restrictions successfully discouraged reporting by journalists.[64] The closure of three Sudanese civil society organisations and the expulsion of 13 international NGOs following the March 2009 issuance of the first arrest warrant against Bashir caused a substantial loss to monitoring capacity. In the words of a Sudanese activist, "[t]hey expelled those organisations that were doing the monitoring".[65] After that, it "became more difficult to re-port the crimes. The government was acting in the darkness – no one was watching".[66]

This repression has also affected UNAMID, which has been criti-cised for failing to accurately report on the situation on the ground. One Sudanese activist pointed to the government's recent initiative to get rid of UNAMID as related to their desire to avoid prosecution, saying the government "doesn't need the witnesses".[67] Some have criticised UNA-MID for failing to make its human rights reporting public. Others allege that the mission systematically attempts to whitewash the dire human rights situation in Darfur.[68] Thus, where there appears to be a reduction in the level of crimes, one must remember that this may be the result of more effective obstruction, rather than a decreased level of crimes.

A second problem in assessing the rate of international crimes is their complex definition. Assessing whether an individual act constitutes an international crime often requires analysis of the context: whether the act was part of a sustained and systematic attack, and whether it was committed with the intent of destroying a group in whole or in part. In general, these assessments can be made only when a large amount of data is analysed, and cannot be assessed in the immediate stages of monitoring. Making these assessments on an immediate and ongoing basis is likely to be impractical. In addition, a wide variety of organisations conduct moni-

---

[64] Joachim J. Savelsberg, *Representing Mass Violence in Darfur: Conflicting Responses to Mass Violence in Darfur*, University of California Press, Oakland, 2015.

[65] Interview with Sudanese activist, March 2016.

[66] Interview with Sudanese activist, September 2012.

[67] Interview with Sudanese activist, March 2016.

[68] Aicha Elbasri, "We Can't Say All That We See in Darfur", in *Foreign Policy*, 9 April 2014.

toring. They do not usually monitor international crimes *per se*, but rather some of the constitutive elements of these crimes. They carry out monitoring for different purposes and to different standards. As a result, the available data addresses the question of international crimes only indirectly and is difficult to triangulate against other sources.

For example, this chapter refers to ACLED data on the number of attacks on civilians and the number of deaths caused by those attacks. While many attacks on civilians constitute war crimes, these reports make no attempt to parse out related legal issues such as the proximity of rebel forces, the intent or the gravity of the breach. Nor is this metric comprehensive; it does not include reference to other actions that might constitute war crimes such as recruitment of child soldiers.

However, an analysis of both the number of incidents and the number of fatalities resulting from those incidents (based on monthly totals) shows increases and decreases in the rates of violations over time that can be taken as an indicator of the patterns of violence.

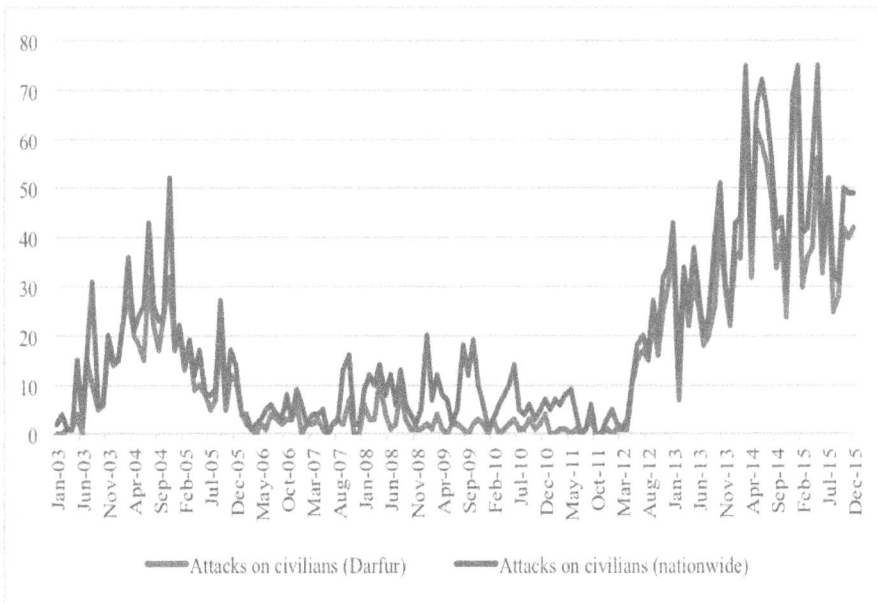

Figure 1: Number of Incidents of Attacks on Civilians.

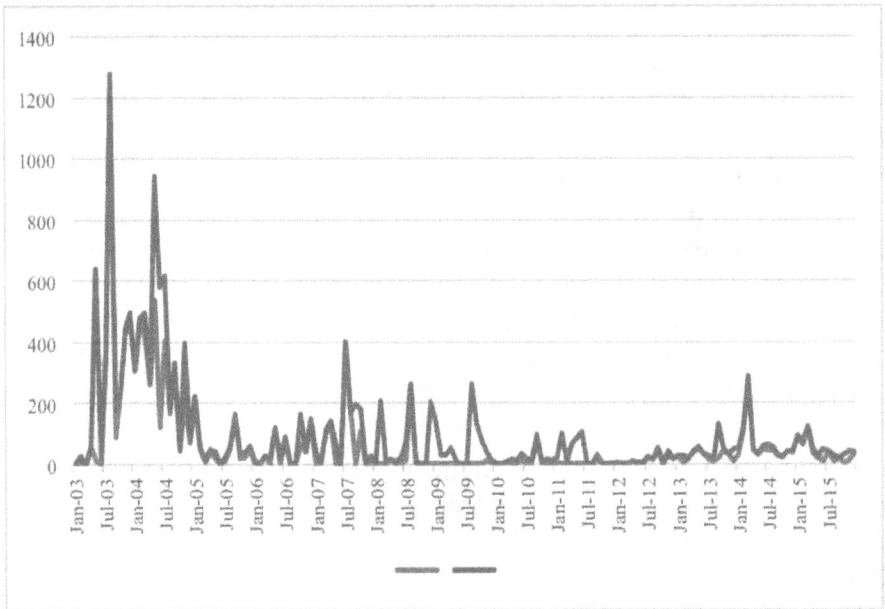

Figure 2: Fatalities as a Result of Attacks on Civilians.

These data indicate that the level of both incidents and fatalities was highest in the period 2003–2004, and that there was a significant drop in early 2005. While there are a number of ups and downs in the following years, the number of incidents does not approach 2003–2004 levels until late 2012, rising through 2014–2015.

Because of the inherent limitations in the data, the rises and falls in violence were tested against other metrics. One of these was the number of people displaced year by year, as compiled by the Panel of Experts.[69] Although displacement is not an equivalent of international crimes, in the Darfur context a large number of those displaced were driven from their homes by international crimes, thus it does give an indication of the level of such crime. These data fit the general pattern of the ACLED data, with the highest levels of violence indicated in 2003–2004, and increasing violence from 2012 leading up to the highest levels of violence since 2004 in 2014.

---

[69] UN Panel of Experts, 2015, see *supra* note 27.

Year	Number of people displaced
2003	989,920
2004	853,000
2005	no data
2006	270,000
2007	300,000
2008	317,000
2009	175,000
2010	268,000
2011	80,000
2012	114,000
2013	380,000
2014	431,000

Table 1: Number of People Displaced per Year, 2003–2014.

Data were further cross-checked against the reporting of the Panel of Experts set up under Security Council resolution 1591 to monitor the arms embargo and individual travel bans imposed by the same resolution, and historical overviews of the conflict. Although there were some challenges of categorisation and agreement between the sources, cross analysis does make some patterns clear.

First there was a major peak in violence in 2003–2004, at the time the world's attention was not focused on Darfur. The rebel attacks early in the year mobilised the brutal government counter-insurgency campaign, which had "assumed a completely new scale and exploded" by July 2003.[70] The number of people displaced in 2003–2004 and the number of casualties reported in this period are not matched by anything else in the data, and the number of incidents in this period is only matched by the period from 2014 onwards. For analysis of the deterrent impact of the ICC,

---

[70] Prunier, 2005, p. 99, see *supra* note 8.

it is important to remember that the baseline level of violations was very high, and so there was considerable room for violations to reduce without stopping altogether.

Indeed, the violence appears to drop off in early 2005, around the same time as the referral of the Darfur situation to the ICC. Of course, this correlation does not mean that the decrease was caused by the referral, and establishing causation is complicated by the coincidence of many important developments. The Comprehensive Peace Agreement ending the North-South civil war was signed in January 2005. In March 2005, the month of the referral, the Security Council also voted to impose individual sanctions on individuals obstructing the Darfur peace process and to reinforce the peacekeeping in the South. Any of these factors could have had as much or more impact than prosecutions.

It seems, however, that even if we cannot tie these changes in action to potential prosecution, we can tie them to international attention. The prominent historian of the region, Gérard Prunier, argues strongly for such a link. He argues that in May 2003 the government of Sudan "had clearly decided on a military solution to the crisis, counting on being able to crush the insurrection fast enough for it to be over before the delicate process of bringing the SPLA into Khartoum could take place".[71] In other words, the government of Sudan launched the initial assault while the eyes of the international community were fixed on the South, in the hopes that they would be able to finish the job before the international community turned its attention to Darfur.

In early 2005, however, the international community's attention shifted, likely prompted at least in part by the investigations by the ICID and the eventual ICC referral. This is likely linked to the drop in violence. Prunier argues that this represents not a change of heart on the part of the Sudanese regime, but a change in tactics. By this time, he argues, the government of Sudan "began to rely more on the parlous food and medical situation to finish off the job that the militias had started".[72] Nonetheless, given the government of Sudan's concern about prosecution, which will be discussed later, it is not unreasonable to speculate that the ICC played a role. In this context, the reduction in violence could be seen as a type of "restrictive deterrence", which causes perpetrators to limit, rather than

---

[71] *Ibid.*, p. 97.
[72] *Ibid.*, p.116.

abandon, their criminal activities.[73] Though falling short of the hopes of victims, any reduction in violence is positive.

The new violence in Southern Kordofan and Blue Nile in 2011 can also be seen as a limitation of the deterrent power of the Court. A number of those interviewed referred to the launching of this new campaign as evidence of the inability of the ICC to deter international crimes. Without doubt, the impact of the new conflict has been devastating. The National Human Rights Monitors Organisation reported that it had verified 309 attacks on civilians in 2015, leading to 46 deaths and 140 injuries as a direct result of attacks against civilians alone,[74] and the impact of the crisis there is not limited to casualties directly from bombing. An estimated 775,000 have been displaced in Southern Kordofan and Blue Nile, approximately 34,000 since the start of 2016 alone.[75] The Famine Early Warning Network has said that 4.4 million Sudanese are facing crisis levels of food insecurity or worse, with 100,000 facing emergency conditions, primarily in Darfur's Jebel Marra and Southern Kordofan.[76] Related to this, despite significant evidence that international crimes have been committed in Southern Kordofan and Blue Nile, the ICC cannot prosecute these crimes because Sudan is not a party to the ICC Statute and the Security Council referral is restricted to Darfur. This restriction is likely to negatively affect the potential for deterrence. Some Sudanese interviewed for this research argued that a new referral would be useful for addressing crimes committed in Southern Kordofan and Blue Nile.

The ACLED data cited above, however, are gathered nationwide, including from Southern Kordofan. Since these nationwide data show a lower number of incidents before 2012 and a lower number of fatalities throughout the period analysed, one can still argue that there has been some restrictive deterrence. In addition, the patterns of violence in Southern Kordofan and Blue Nile can be seen to support this. The bombing attacks tend to cause a very small number of civilian casualties, and are significantly smaller than in large-scale attacks in Darfur. This may, in part,

---

[73] Jennifer Schense, "Whether International Crimes Can Be Prevented", Ph.D. Thesis, Leiden University, forthcoming.

[74] National Human Rights Monitors Organisation and the Sudan Consortium, "Human Rights Violations in Southern Kordofan and Blue Nile: 2015 in Review", 2015.

[75] USAID, 2016, see *supra* note 32.

[76] Famine Early Warning Systems Network, "High Acute Malnutrition Remains a Concern with Early Onset of the Lean Season", May 2016.

be due to the greater military capabilities of the SPLM-N, as compared to the Darfur rebels, which has made large attacks more costly to the government. But it is also clear that the government is deploying a strategy of indirect attack. Rather than target large numbers directly, the government appears to be seeking to disrupt agricultural activities. The combined disruption of agriculture and the blockage of humanitarian aid has had devastating impact and forced many to flee, yet compared to the attacks in Darfur (which both killed many directly *and* disrupted agricultural activities), it can be seen as measured. This could be seen, again, as restrictive deterrence.

However, whatever deterrent effect there may have been appears to be wearing off as violence levels nationwide in 2014–2015 approached those of 2003–2004. The recent reporting by Amnesty International details serious violations of international humanitarian law – including credible allegations of the use of chemical weapons – in 2016.[77] This is further evidence that if there was a deterrent effect at some point, it is certainly not continuing. This view accords with those of some Sudanese activists expressed above, that the ICC initially had a deterrent effect, but that this has been undermined by a failure to secure arrests and successful prosecutions.

9.5. Is Deterrence Possible in the Current Sudanese Context?

In order to better understand why deterrence has, or has not worked, it is useful to examine the general framework for understanding deterrence that has been developed at the national level. To borrow from John Dietrich:

> Deterrence only works if potential criminals 1) make rational calculations before their actions, 2) know the laws and, ideally, accept them as legitimate limits on their behavior, 3) feel that the benefits of a given crime are relatively low, and 4) believe the costs of the crime are high as influenced by the certainty, swiftness and severity of punishment.[78]

In other words, in order for deterrence to work, the criminal has to know that a given action is illegal, should ideally accept the law making that ac-

---

[77] Amnesty International, 2016, see *supra* note 2.

[78] John Dietrich, "The Limited Prospects of Deterrence by the International Criminal Court: Lessons from Domestic Experience", in *International Social Science Review*, 2014, vol. 88, no. 3, p. 3.

tion illegal as itself legitimate, and be in a position to decide rationally against committing the crime. If the commission of the crimes is viewed as a matter of survival, it is unlikely that any sanction will be sufficient to deter the perpetrator.

9.5.1. Who Is Responsible?

One issue that has been raised as a possible limitation to deterrence in the Darfur context is the question of who is actually most responsible for the crimes committed and who has the greatest potential to stop them. In essence, do those being targeted by the ICC have the power to end the crimes being committed?

One element of this question relates to the method of commission of the crimes. Unlike a common criminal who might deploy a gun or a knife, the government of Sudan has, in the case of Darfur, acted through militias – essentially sentient weapons. In this context, questions have been raised as to whether the government has the capacity to stop the militias. They may have created and armed them, but defanging them might not be so simple. De Waal notes that "the monster that Khartoum helped create may not always do its bidding; distrust of the capital runs deep among Darfurians, and the Janjaweed leadership knows that it cannot be disarmed by force".[79] Others reported that the Janjaweed had threatened to attack Khartoum if any attempt was made to disarm them. If this is the case, as Pablo Castillo asks, "is policy reversal even an option for Khartoum?"[80] This difficulty is real. If the government were to cease support for militias in Darfur, violence would most likely not stop as the region is awash with weapons and the legacies of incitement of ethnic violence. This is not to say, however, that the government does not have influence, but to date it has not made significant effort to use that influence positively but rather uses it to incite and further inflame the situation.

Related to this point, the ICC has explicitly stated that it will only go after those who bear the greatest responsibility for the commission of the crimes, which some have suggested will have the greatest deterrent effect. This has been criticised by the ICC judges for perhaps limiting the deterrent effect of the Court as it leaves a large number of perpetrators

---

[79] De Waal, 2004, see *supra* note 11.

[80] Pablo Castillo, "Rethinking Deterrence: The International Criminal Court in Sudan", UNISCI Discussion Paper, No. 13, January 2007.

with significant influence with a relative certainty that they will not be prosecuted.[81] In the Darfur case, to an informed observer of the Court, it seems clear that the rank-and-file militia membership will not be subject to prosecution by the ICC. While it is difficult to be sure of how widely this is known, it is reasonable to assume that this would limit the impact of deterrence for this specific group.

While most Sudanese interviewed for this research agreed with the ICC's selection of cases, there was some dissension. One activist argued that Bashir was not the right person to prosecute, as it was actually the former vice president Ali Osman Taha and former security chief Salah Abdallah Gosh who bore the greatest responsibility, and thus whose prosecution would have had the greatest deterrent effect.[82]

9.5.2. Rationality

Another foundational understanding of deterrence is that the potential perpetrator is rational. Increasing the cost of perpetrating a crime is of little utility if the potential perpetrator is not making a rational assessment of costs and benefits. So, are those committing serious violations in Sudan rational? The answer would seem to be yes.

First, although some argue that irrational hatred guides the decision-making of the perpetrators of international crimes, most scholars agree that such perpetrators are rational. As Payam Akhavan points out, mass crimes take "considerable planning and preparation in addition to efficient organisation and utilisation of resources under strong and unified leadership", suggesting "that somewhere in the anatomy of genocide lies a cost-benefit analysis, however diabolical its parameters may be".[83] Others cite the efforts to hide criminal activity as evidence of rationality. Perpetrators "often attempt to conceal their crimes by burying bodies, wearing masks

---

[81] Aurelia Marina Pohrib, "Frustrating Noble Intentions: The Clash between ICC's Deterrent Effects and the Prosecutor's Policy of Focused Investigations on Perpetrators Situated at the Highest Echelons of Responsibility", in *International Community Law Review*, 2013, vol. 15, no. 2, pp. 225–36.

[82] Interview with Darfuri activist, March 2016.

[83] Payam Akhavan, "Are International Criminal Tribunals a Disincentive to Peace? Reconciling Judicial Romanticism with Political Realism", in *Human Rights Quarterly*, 2009, vol. 31, no. 3, pp. 624–30.

or setting up complex command structures to provide a degree of deniability if actions are investigated".[84]

The government of Sudan has certainly taken steps to deny and cover up its crimes. A hallmark of the conflict has been the use of ethnically based militias rather than regular government forces. In the words of De Waal, this tactic is deployed because it "immunises them against being charged in the future with committing war crimes".[85] In December 2003 the Sudanese information minister claimed "[t]here is no rebellion in Darfur, just a local conflict among specific tribes".[86] The government has also taken more direct action. In preparation for the visit of the ICID, it is reported that "the government had begun emptying mass graves existing in various parts of the province and moving the bodies to Kordofan for incineration".[87] Later the government also used access restrictions and intimidation to curtail reporting on their crimes.

There is some evidence that this concern became more intense as the potential for prosecution increased. The moving of bodies occurred in response to the creation of an international commission of inquiry tasked with making recommendations about holding the perpetrators accountable. In addition, Akhavan notes that when the government of Sudan announced a ceasefire with rebels in November 2008, local sources quoted by the BBC argued that "the government hopes that this plan will be enough to convince the international community to defer the case against Mr. Bashir".[88] One interviewee said: "After the indictment, they said go kill, rape, but don't leave evidence".[89]

The lengths to which the government of Sudan is willing to go to cover up its crimes is evidence of its concern about both public opinion and the prospect of prosecution. This concern is evidence that the government is sensitive to external pressure and would be to deterrence as well.

---

[84]   Dietrich, 2014, p. 7, see *supra* note 78.
[85]   De Waal, 2004, see *supra* note 11.
[86]   Prunier, 2005, p. 86, see *supra* note 8.
[87]   *Ibid.*
[88]   Akhavan, 2009, p. 650, see *supra* note 83.
[89]   Interview with Sudanese activist, March 2016.

9.5.3. Risk Tolerance

Another factor, in addition to the issue of rationality, is the extent to which a person is risk-tolerant or risk-averse. In making a rational decision, a potential perpetrator is usually weighing an immediate benefit against the risk of pain later. Those who are more risk-tolerant are more likely to view this risk (whatever its objective likelihood) more acceptable than those who are risk-averse. It has been pointed out that in the context of politics in conflict-prone countries, most leaders would not be in the positions that they are unless they were relatively risk-tolerant.[90] Sudan is no exception as a high-risk political environment, as numerous recent removals of high-level politicians show.

9.5.4. Knowing and Accepting the Law

It seems clear that the government of Sudan is aware of the law relating to the ICC as evidenced by the agility of their responses and their capacity to hire legal advice as needed. What is more in question is the extent to which the government sees the law as legitimate. The government has seen, and responded to, the ICC's engagement largely in political terms. In response to the Darfur referral, the Sudanese government ambassador to the UN, Elfatih Mohammed Ahmed Erwa, said that while the

> Council believed that the scales of justice were based on exceptions and exploitation of crises in developing countries and bargaining among major powers, it did not settle the question of accountability in Darfur, but exposed the fact that the ICC was intended for developing and weak countries and was a tool to exercise cultural superiority.[91]

The government continued such rhetoric, accusing the ICC of double standards and of going after only Arab and African leaders. They found a sympathetic ear from many African states and have successfully mobilised support, and the African Union issued a communiqué calling on member states not to arrest Bashir.[92]

---

[90] Dietrich, 2014, see *supra* note 78.

[91] United Nations Security Council, Resolution 1593 (2005), UN doc. S/Res/1693, 31 March 2005 (http://www.legal-tools.org/doc/4b208f/).

[92] African Union Assembly, Decision on the Report on the Meeting of African States Parties to the Rome Statute of the International Criminal Court, Doc. No. Assembly/AU/Dec.245(XIII), Rev. 1, 3 July 2009 (http://www.legal-tools.org/doc/5f9085/).

At the same time, the government of Sudan has made a number of changes to national law and set up national processes in an effort to convince the international community that it is capable of addressing these issues domestically. While these efforts are primarily a political effort to dissuade the international community from strongly supporting the ICC, they are also evidence that the government is sensitive to pressure on these issues and also that there is at least some rhetorical commitment to the law that forms the basis of the ICC Statute system. A full analysis of these measures is not possible here, but has included formation of the National Commission of Inquiry on Darfur and its questioning in 2004 of eventual ICC suspect Ahmed Harun, formation of first one, then three Special Criminal Courts on the Events in Darfur, and formation of special investigative committees (including the Judicial Investigations Committee, the Special Prosecutions Commissions, the Committees Against Rape, the Unit for Combating Violence Against Women and Children, and the Committee on Compensations).[93] In addition to setting up these special mechanisms, it has made some important changes to the legal code in Sudan. For example, in 2009 amendments to the 1991 Criminal Act were introduced incorporating war crimes, crimes against humanity and genocide for the first time. In addition, the Doha Document for Peace in Darfur, signed in 2011, includes an amnesty which, unlike that in other agreements in Sudanese history, excludes international crimes.[94] Although this is a welcome step forward in terms of facilitating eventual prosecutions, it is far from perfect. Indeed, parallel amendments to the 1991 Criminal Act amendments prohibit the trial of any Sudanese person outside the country as well as any effort on the part of a Sudanese to assist in the extradition of anyone facing such charges.[95]

Although Sudanese interviewees did not take these measures seriously as steps towards achieving justice, they argued that they could ultimately be useful if the political climate shifts. In the words of one interviewee, "[w]hat they are doing is not real justice, but at least these things are in the law".[96]

---

[93] Suliman Baldo, "Sudan: Impact of the Rome Statute and the International Criminal Court", ICTJ Briefing, The Rome Statite Review Conference, Kampala, May 2010.

[94] Nouwen, 2013, see *supra* note 48.

[95] Baldo, 2010, see *supra* note 93.

[96] Interview with Sudanese activist, December 2011.

Of course, even larger obstacles to prosecutions remain. Among them are immunities granted under Sudan's Armed Forces Act, Police Act and National Security Act, which provide that officials cannot be sanctioned in criminal or civil proceedings without prior authorisation from the heads of those forces.[97] These immunities effectively block investigation and prosecution of a large number of international crimes, as police and prosecutors who seek such authorisation most often simply never receive an answer to their requests to proceed. In addition, the Sudanese government has attacked the independence of the judiciary at home, including through purges, and has instrumentalised the law to suit its own purposes. It would seem that the government has little respect for the law as a constraint, in general, and its disdain for the ICC Statute system is merely part of this pattern.

A related question here is the extent to which the general public views the Court as legitimate. For example, in her evaluation of the impact of the Special Court for Sierra Leone, Frederike Mieth points out that the impact of that tribunal has been limited by the fact that its conception of justice is not that of ordinary Sierra Leoneans, who favoured compensation and restorative justice.[98] Similar issues have also been raised in relation to the ICC's intervention in Uganda, where a number of commentators pointed to tensions between cultural conceptions of justice focusing on compensation and restoration of social bonds and the retributive, criminal approach.

In Sudan, however, it seems that there is generally a high level of support for, and focus on, criminal accountability, although of course Sudanese victims, like their Ugandan and Sierra Leonean counterparts, also point to the need for compensation as well. In the IRRI's visit to the refugee camps in Chad in 2005, Darfuri refugees articulated accountability as a prerequisite for return. Research carried out by 24 Hours for Darfur among Darfuri refugees in Chad found an extremely high level of support

---

[97] African Centre for Justice and Peace Studies, the International Federation for Human Rights and the International Refugee Rights Initiative, "Submission to the Universal Periodic Review of Sudan 2016", 21 September 2015; Redress and Sudan Human Rights Monitor, "Human Rights Concerns and Barriers to Justice in Sudan: National, Regional and International Perspectives", February 2014.

[98] Frederike Mieth, "Bringing Justice and Enforcing Peace? An Ethnographic Perspective on the Impact of the Special Court for Sierra Leone", in *International Journal of Conflict and Violence*, 2013, vol. 7, no. 1, pp. 10–22.

for formal criminal justice procedures and for the ICC specifically. Over 90 per cent of refugees wanted Sudanese government officials, commanders and soldiers, and the Janjaweed to face formal criminal trials. Similarly, more than 90 per cent thought that the international community generally or the ICC specifically should conduct these trials. Those that argued that the arrest warrant against Bashir would have a positive effect on the situation on the ground believed that it would prevent further crimes.[99]

One of the positive impacts of the ICC's engagement in Sudan has been the increased awareness among ordinary Sudanese of the crimes that have been committed in Darfur. A lack of press coverage and public interest combined with government efforts to limit access to information left much of the Sudanese public outside Darfur largely unaware of the situation there. However, the ICC's arrest warrant for Bashir was front-page news, and it pointed, if not necessarily for the majority of Sudanese to Bashir's culpability, at least to the seriousness of the Darfur situation. Ironically, the government's own propaganda campaign against the Court raised awareness of the crimes in Darfur. In the words of an opposition politician, the National Congress Party ('NCP'), Sudan's ruling party, "have familiarised the idea that the President is a criminal".[100]

Some see this awareness, however, as unhelpful as the ultimate effect has been to rally support behind the government. One Sudanese activist argued that Bashir uses the ICC "with the Sudanese people, telling them that it is neo-colonialism and that it is targeting Muslims".[101]

9.5.5. Costs

Another element of deterrence is ensuring that the cost of criminal behaviour is sufficient to tip a rational cost-benefit analysis towards inaction. In general, deterrence theorists point to three aspects of punishment as determining how a potential perpetrator will assess it, "its *certainty* (the probability that it arrives), its *severity* (the amount of pain it delivers), and its *celerity* (how quickly it arrives after criminal conduct)".[102] Criminolo-

---

[99]   24 Hours for Darfur, "Darfurian Voices: Documenting Darfurian Refugees' Views on Issues of Peace, Justice, and Reconciliation", July 2010.

[100] Nouwen, 2013, see *supra* note 48.

[101] Interview with Sudanese activist, February 2016.

[102] Francis T. Cullen and Pamela Wilcox, *The Oxford Handbook of Criminological Theory*, Oxford University Press, Oxford, 2012.

gists suggest that of these, certainty has the greatest impact. To the extent that these general principles have been studied in Africa, they appear to apply there as they do elsewhere.[103]

The ICC has been relatively weak on all three points. Part of this is structural. Given its resource constraints, the ICC can only take on a small number of cases, which limits its ability to project certainty of investigation, much less prosecution. In the Sudan case, the failure to secure arrest of any of the suspects against whom arrest warrants were issued, and most visibly Bashir, was seen as the greatest obstacle to successful deterrence. This undermines any certainty of apprehension or actual prosecution and undermines the confidence of victims. "At first, [the victims] were very happy, but Abdel Raheem, Harun and Bashir have not been taken to the Court as there is no co-operation".[104] In the words of another activist, "[s]ome of them [witnesses] say they feel like they are abandoned. Some feel unsafe […] it is an issue".[105]

While it is not possible to determine to what extent there would be deterrence if there were arrests, it seems clear that failure to arrest is undermining both the certainty and celerity of punishment and so the potential for deterrence. In the words of one activist, "[i]f there was an arrest, there would be deterrence".[106] In the words of another, "I don't think that the ICC can deter unless there are arrests".[107]

Activists expressed frustration with the lack of consequences that have attached to the arrest warrant. In the words of one activist, "Bashir hasn't seen any real hardship".[108] As another put it, "[h]e can go to South Africa, no one disturbs him".[109] Activists were particularly disappointed that Bashir has been able to continue to travel abroad, avoiding even minimal sanction. In the words of one, "[e]very time that he comes back he claims victory".[110]

---

[103] Jo and Simmons, 2016, see *supra* note 57.
[104] Interview with Sudanese activist, 29 March 2010.
[105] Interview with Darfurian man, May 2012.
[106] Interview with activist, April 2016.
[107] Interview with Sudanese activist, April 2016.
[108] Interview with Darfuri activist, April 2016.
[109] Interview with Darfuri activist, March 2016.
[110] Interview with Sudanese activist, April 2016.

Of course, Bashir's travel has not been completely unproblematic and some point to these challenges as signs of progress. Human Rights Watch's Ken Roth points to the need for Bashir to beat a hasty retreat from Nigeria in July 2013 after civil society organisations made court filings calling on the government of Nigeria to arrest him saying, "[t]his was a disaster for legitimacy purposes. It completely undermined his effort to show that he was a respected international leader".[111]

In addition, the extent to which Sudanese actors fear prosecutorial consequences may be diminished by the ICC's weak record of securing convictions. In the one case in the Darfur situation that has proceeded to conclusion, the ICC failed to confirm charges against Abu Garda. In addition, the failure to secure convictions against the Kenyan suspects, in particular President Uhuru Kenyatta, Vice President William Ruto, Francis Muthaura and Joshua Arap Sang, perhaps because those cases focused on government officials, has particular resonance and has undermined confidence that justice will be done in Sudan. In the words of one activist, "[t]he collapse of the case against Ruto and Sang breaks my heart. There is so much evidence, but they [the ICC] aren't serious".[112]

In fact, some argue that the overall effect of threatening prosecution and not following through has been negative. Hitherto, the vague notion of international justice might have been feared, but by materialising it but not following through to the arrest, the fear was effectively neutralised. One Sudanese activist said, "[t]he failure to arrest [Bashir] made the situation worse, because Bashir's reaction was devastating, particularly the NGO expulsions and the scale of the violence also increased [...]. As a result, the environment of impunity has been established".[113]

9.5.6. Social Deterrence

It is also worth differentiating between prosecutorial deterrence (that is, the direct impact of prosecutions) and social deterrence, which reflects informal consequences of law-breaking. As Jo and Simmons note: "A judicial institution is at its most powerful when prosecutorial and social deter-

---

[111] International Peace Institute, 2015, see *supra* note 4.
[112] Interview with Darfuri activist, April 2016.
[113] Interview with Sudanese activist, September 2012.

rence reinforce one another, which happens when actors threaten to impose extra-legal costs for non-compliance with legal authority".[114]

This effect is generally stronger in the case of actors who depend more on their legitimacy in the eyes of their domestic constituency or the international community.[115] The government of Sudan was already viewed as a pariah at the outset of the Darfur crisis, sanctioned for years for support to terrorist groups and abuses related to the North-South war. Thus, the threat of the social sanctions that might come with being charged at the ICC might be expected to have had less effect on the government of Sudan than on a state previously viewed as a 'good citizen'; the government of Sudan was not losing the perks associated with good behaviour as those had already been lost.

One of the mechanisms through which it was hoped that prosecutions could deter crimes was the marginalisation of particularly problematic leaders. Some argue that this has occurred to a certain extent, undermining support for Bashir in Khartoum. "Even in the inner circles of the NCP they are seeing him as a burden".[116] This may be true among the inner circle behind closed doors, but publicly the regime has continued to back Bashir. However, others have speculated that the pressure from the ICC brings perpetrators together: "In my opinion the NCP will not be divided over the arrest warrant because moderates and hardliners in the NCP both expect to find themselves in the coming list of the Prosecutor".[117] Some argue that an arrest would change this: "[t]he arrest would make them defect [from the ruling party]".[118]

The election of Bashir in 2010 has worked against the delegitimising impact of the ICC charges. Some activists argue that not enough international attention went into monitoring and challenging those elections, allowing them to pass as acceptable despite widespread problems. The opposition now feels that one of their main arguments against the government, that it was illegitimate as a result of coming to power in a coup, has been undermined because it has now been 'democratically' elected.

---

[114] Jo and Simmons, 2016, p. 4, see *supra* note 57.
[115] *Ibid.*
[116] Interview with Sudanese activist, September 2012.
[117] Interview with Sudanese activist, July 2011.
[118] Interview with Sudanese activist, April 2016.

9.5.7. Deterrence and Rebel Forces

Both in discussions with Sudanese activists and in the review of the academic literature, the overwhelming focus has been on the cases against the government and its allies. It is important to remember that rebels have also been subjected to charges at the ICC and to assess whether there has been any deterrent impact there.

Jo and Simmons argue that the Court's deterrent impact is weaker for rebels than for governments, although rebels in need of international support tend to be more deterrable than others.[119] In the Darfur situation, rebel groups have long courted international support and based their legitimacy on their claim that they are defending their people. Compared to the government, rebels have shown a relatively high level of co-operation with the Court; in the words of one of the interviewees, "[u]nlike the government, they respect the Court".[120] The leader of JEM has stated: "We are admiring the ICC; we are fully supporting the ICC. We are ready to go to the ICC including myself and we are ready to work as a tool [for the] ICC to capture anybody".[121]

There were varying views, however, on the extent to which the rebels had been deterred. Those rebels who were charged were from a relatively small splinter group,[122] so the ICC has not yet challenged core rebel interests. Some activists claimed that the rebels did not commit abuses or felt that these should not be the focus in the light of the substantially greater scale of the government's abuses. Others argued that they continue to commit abuses and those needed to be addressed: "People say that they have committed crimes such as taxing people and looting. These should be investigated".[123]

9.6. How Could the Deterrent Impact Be Improved?

When asked what was needed in order to make the deterrent effect of the ICC work, one Sudanese activist replied: "The international community

---

[119] Jo and Simmons, 2016, see *supra* note 57.

[120] Interview with Darfuri activist, April 2016.

[121] Sarah M.H. Nouwen and Wouter G. Werner, "Doing Justice to the Political: The International Criminal Court in Uganda and Sudan", in *European Journal of International Law*, 2011, vol. 21, no. 4, p. 856.

[122] *Ibid.*

[123] Interview with Sudanese activist, February 2016.

needs to be united in supporting the ICC".[124] Indeed, the limits of the deterrent impact of the Court in the Sudan situation is in large part the story of the limits of what international justice can do without broader support from the international community.

The issue of securing arrests appears to be the most serious obstacle to deterrence in the Sudan situation. Without arrests, there is little certainty of punishment which, as we have seen, is the aspect most likely to have an effect on the calculations of a potential perpetrator. The failure to arrest is also undermining the confidence of those Sudanese who support accountability. It is unclear what the deterrent effect of the Court would be if trials proceeded, but arrests would be a critical first step.

The ICC, however, has no police force of its own and relies on state co-operation to carry out arrests. This co-operation has so far not been forthcoming in Darfur. Sudan has refused to arrest any of the suspects, and although Bashir has travelled extensively since his arrest warrant was issued, none of the states to which he has travelled has been willing to execute it. In at least 10 of the ICC prosecutor's updates to the UN Security Council on the progress of the Darfur cases, non-cooperation by both the government of Sudan and states parties to the ICC Statute has been reported to the Council. The prosecutor has called on the Security Council to take appropriate action in response,[125] but none has been forthcoming. The Council is split on the issue of Sudan, and has been for some time, and Sudanese activists are aware that "[t]he government of Sudan has been able to mobilise support from Russia and China".[126]

In interviews carried out for this research, Sudanese activists called on the Security Council to take action to follow up on the arrest warrant. Specifically, the Security Council should respond formally to the situations of non-cooperation that have been reported to it, ask for formal explanations from the states involved, and consider censuring those states if the explanations are not satisfactory. The Security Council could also consider extending the arms embargo currently in place for Darfur to the whole of the country. This action could be linked to the international law

---

[124] Interview with Sudanese activist, February 2016.

[125] Jerusha Asin, "Pursuing Al Bashir in South Africa: Between 'Apology and Utopia'", in Hendrik van der Merwe and Gerhard Kemp (eds.), *International Criminal Justice in Africa: Issues, Challenges and Prospects*, Strathmore University Press, Nairobi, 2016.

[126] Interview with Najlaa Ahmed, May 2016.

obligation to prevent genocide, taking the ICC arrest warrant as notice that genocide may be occurring and framing it as fulfilling the obligation to take immediate action to prevent further harm. This would both limit the government of Sudan's capacity to attack civilians and send a strong message to other states that they too are under an obligation to take action. The Security Council could also consider expanding its programme of individual sanctions, such asset freezes, to those who the ICC has charged with international crimes. In addition, it has been suggested that the Security Council could expand its current referral to address crimes committed in Southern Kordofan and Blue Nile. A Darfuri woman said that a referral would be useful: "It would mobilise the international community. They [the government] will be alone, now Russia is supporting them and Egypt and Yemen".[127] Another activist also suggested that this was an interesting idea.[128] This was seen as useful for both focusing international attention on the situation in Southern Kordofan and Blue Nile, and also in creating a historical record of the conflict.

But what is preventing the diplomatic community from aligning in support of the Court, and what can be done to improve the situation? One issue is a lack of legal clarity with regard to their obligations. Although many supporters of the Court argue that there is a clear legal obligation on the part of states to arrest, others argue that executing an arrest warrant would violate state obligations to respect head of state immunity. Cogent arguments have been made that Article 98 of the ICC Statute, which essentially exempts states from complying with requests from the ICC that violate other international obligations, is evidence that the drafters did not intend to impose a duty of arrest in these circumstances. Ultimately, however, the arguments of lawyers on both sides do little to clarify obligations. That clarity comes through litigation. Some advocates have already begun to do this, for example, in South Africa where the Southern African Litigation Centre brought suit asking the government to arrest Bashir. The judgment is useful, but based its findings primarily on South African national law rather than international law, and so is of limited applicability for other cases.[129] The ICC has also addressed the issue of head of state

---

[127] Interview with Darfuri activist, August 2012.

[128] Interview with Sudanese activist, February 2016.

[129] Supreme Court of Appeal of South Africa, *The Minister of Justice and Constitutional Development v. The Southern African Litigation Centre*, (867/15) [2016] ZACSA 17, 15 March 2016 (http://www.legal-tools.org/doc/d4b22b/).

immunity in its findings in relation to non-cooperation in the Bashir case. An advisory opinion of the International Court of Justice to further clarify the international law obligations might be a step forward. Such a judgment would clarify for the ICC what support it ought to expect from states, and would make it harder for states to shirk those responsibilities by arguing about a lack of clarity in the law.

A second challenge is that, whatever the legal obligation, the diplomatic community has difficulty in aligning behind the ICC. In part, this is because the stark label of criminality is at odds with the standard diplomatic approach. Joachim Savelsberg, in his study of the representation of the Darfur crisis, notes that the diplomatic field tends to generate a distinct view of the crisis. Diplomats "generally applied great caution about using dramatising labels, especially *genocide*, when they described the violence and about attributing direct responsibility, especially criminal responsibility, to central actors in the Sudanese state".[130] Savelsberg attributes this to the need for diplomatic actors to maintain not only cordial relations with, but the active participation of, their counterparts in Sudan.

However, these diplomatic actors should remember that Sudanese activists are looking to them to take a consistent stand on Sudan in general and on the arrest warrants in particular. They call on the international community to prevent Bashir from travelling, and to sanction those countries that allow him to travel.

At the same time as they blamed states for not supporting the ICC, activists also criticised the Court itself: "The ICC should have done more to build consensus and prepare for the arrest".[131] Objectively, it is difficult to know what the ICC may or may not have done privately to prepare the ground for arrest, but it is clear that whatever the strategy was, it was not very successful in mustering support. Another activist speculated that perhaps a sealed arrest warrant might have been more successful than the public arrest warrant that was issued. Although there is nothing that the ICC can do retrospectively about that, it would be useful for the Court to conduct its own assessment and to identify lessons learned that might be applicable to other cases. A key part of a prosecutor's role is to assess, among other things, the prospects of success of a particular case or set of charges. Consideration must be given to the possibility that initiating in-

---

[130] Savelsberg, 2015, p. 272, see *supra* note 64.
[131] Interview with Darfuri activist, March 2016.

vestigations that do not conclude in arrests and trials can be counterproductive.

Some Sudanese also recommended that the ICC improve its outreach. Although this would not have addressed the key frustrations around arrests, it could have mitigated disappointment by providing a more realistic picture of the capacities of the Court: "If the outreach had been better, people would have been more understanding of the limitations".[132] Some encouraged the ICC to re-engage in outreach in Sudan: "The ICC should use WhatsApp and SMS to communicate their message to Sudanese. It is possible".[133] Of course any such attempt at outreach would have to deal with considerable security concerns in the context of the government's hostility to the Court and its history of targeting those who have collaborated with it.

Another issue which was raised was the need for the Assembly of States Parties, the governing body of the ICC, to engage in support for arrest. The Assembly of States Parties could consider offering clarifications of their understanding of state obligations, for example in relation to the debate around immunities, suggesting sanctions against states parties that fail to comply and using its sessions as a forum to discuss and build consensus around arrest.

The advocacy community likewise has a role to play. In the words of one activist, "NGOs should do more to remind Bashir and the international community of the crimes being committed and the existence of the arrest warrant".[134]

The international community should also consider the need for support of transitional justice more broadly than the ICC. While international justice can play a critical role, it is not the end of the story. Research carried out in Chad indicated that 99 per cent of Darfuri refugees advocated payment of compensation.[135] In the words of one Darfuri activist: "The international community is putting the emphasis in the wrong place. What about transitional justice? What about the Mbeki Panel recommendations? Even if Bashir goes to jail, who will compensate the victims?"[136] Another

---

[132] Interview with Sudanese activist, March 2016.
[133] Interview with Sudanese activist, February 2016.
[134] *Ibid.*
[135] 24 Hours for Darfur, 2010, see *supra* note 99.
[136] Interview with Darfuri activist, March 2016.

advocated that NGOs should work on developing a framework for this: "If Sudanese NGOs work on transitional justice it would help because the ICC can't do it all. The ICC is not going to compensate two million IDPs. This is the homework".[137]

A related factor is the need to balance different priorities. Few would argue that even a very effective international criminal justice intervention could fully address any conflict; indeed, they are not really intended to do so. The international criminal interventions in Darfur take aim at the excesses committed in the course of the conflict, but they do not address the reasons that the rebel movements took up arms against the government, nor what would be needed to end the fighting. Thus, while limiting the use of the most pernicious tactics and violations of the rights of individuals in the context of war is a laudable goal, it is not the only goal. In order to address the needs of the people of Darfur, there is also a need for negotiated peace, for humanitarian aid in the short term, for reconstruction and development in the longer term, and for structural governance reforms. Diplomats generally do not have the luxury of focusing on only one of these issues and must represent their countries on a range of issues. While in the longer term international criminal justice can co-exist or support these other goals, in the short term diplomats may need to make choices about where to focus their energies and what to prioritise, and this may inhibit them from supporting ICC actions as fully as international justice advocates would like.

The international community must do a better job of integrating international justice into broader conflict responses. Immediately following the call for prosecutions cited at the start of this chapter, De Waal went on to say: "Condemnation is not a solution. The Janjaweed's murderous campaigns must not obscure the fact that Darfur's indigenous Bedouins are themselves historic victims".[138] In another early civil society statement: "Side by side with a referral of the situation of Darfur to the ICC, the international community must commit to providing substantial and sustained support to the people of Darfur".[139]

---

[137] Interview with Darfuri activist, May 2012.

[138] De Waal, 2004, see *supra* note 11.

[139] Cairo Institute for Human Rights Studies, the Darfur Consortium and Human Rights First, 2005, see *supra* note 44.

10

The Deterrence Effect of the International Criminal Court: A Kenyan Perspective

Evelyne Asaala[*]

10.1. Introduction and Background

Over time impunity for atrocities committed by and against mankind has necessitated the creation of several international criminal tribunals: the International Military Tribunals of Nuremberg and Tokyo, the International Criminal Tribunal for the former Yugoslavia ('ICTY'), the International Criminal Tribunal for Rwanda ('ICTR'), the Special Court for Sierra Leone ('SCSL'), the International Criminal Court ('ICC') and the Special Tribunal for Lebanon. One of the primary objectives underlying the creation of all these international tribunals has been to deter future atrocities. When establishing the ICTY, for example, the United Nations ('UN') underscored the need "to put an end to such crimes and to take effective measures to bring to justice the people who are responsible for them".[1] The subsequent creation of the ICTR and the SCSL was premised on similar grounds.[2] The ICC too is also determined to "put an end to impunity [...] and thus to contribute to the prevention of such crimes".[3] Legal aca-

---

[*] **Evelyne Owiye Asaala** is a Lecturer of Law at the University of Nairobi, Kenya, and is currently finalising her Ph.D. (out of seat) at the University of the Witwatersrand, South Africa. She holds a Master of Laws degree from the University of Pretoria (South Africa) and a Bachelor of Laws degree from the University of Nairobi (Kenya). She has previously worked with the Truth Justice and Reconciliation Commission of Kenya as a consultant; the Kenya National Commission for Human Rights and the Kenyan Task Force on Bail and Bond Policy and Guidelines in similar capacities; and also as a Lecturer of Law at Africa Nazarene University (Kenya). She is a member of the African Expert Group on International Criminal Law. Her areas of specialization are International Human Rights Law, International Criminal Law and Transitional Justice.

[1] United Nations Security Council, Resolution 827 (1993), UN doc. S/RES/827, 25 May 1993, para. 5 (http://www.legal-tools.org/doc/dc079b/).

[2] United Nations Security Council, Resolution 955, Establishment of the International Criminal Tribunal for Rwanda (ICTR) and adoption of the Statute of the Tribunal, UN doc. S/RES/955, 8 November 1994, para. 6 (http://www.legal-tools.org/doc/f5ef47/).

[3] ICC, Rome Statute of the International Criminal Court, 17 July 1998, in force 1 July 2002, Preamble ('ICC Statute') (http://www.legal-tools.org/doc/7b9af9/).

demics also agree on the importance of deterrence to the work of international criminal tribunals.[4] Thus, the ICC's intervention in Kenya was generally applauded since "[n]ot only would it lessen the deep-rooted culture of impunity, but it could potentially eliminate the reigning sense of betrayal and illegitimacy of the [...] government and its institutions".[5]

It is therefore entirely valid to ask whether the ICC has achieved its objective of deterrence in the Kenyan context and whether, because of the ICC process, alleged perpetrators of crimes against humanity, potential future perpetrators and the general public have been sufficiently deterred, and whether the victims feel secure to go about their daily activities. This study explores these issues from a Kenyan perspective.

Massive internal displacement and commission of serious crimes including crimes against humanity characterised Kenya's 2007 post-election violence.[6] Through the Kenya National Dialogue and Reconciliation Committee ('KNDRC'),[7] chaired by the former UN secretary-general Kofi Annan, several initiatives were launched to help Kenya address impunity for the atrocities and restore peace and development. With respect to legal redress, the KNDRC agreed on the establishment of a commission of inquiry to investigate the violence and make recommendations.[8] In its subsequent findings, the Commission of Inquiry into Post-Election Violence ('CIPEV') underscored the need for investigation and prosecution of alleged perpetrators of crimes against humanity through a special tribu-

---

[4]   Diane F. Orentlicher, "Settling Accounts: The Duty to Prosecute Human Rights Violations of a Prior Regime", in *Yale Law Journal*, 1991, vol. 100, no. 8, p. 100; M. Cherif Bassiouni, "Justice and Peace: The Importance of Choosing Accountability over Realpolitik", in *Case Western Reserve Journal of International Law*, 2003, vol. 35, no. 2, pp. 191–92.

[5]   Evelyne Asaala, "Exploring Transitional Justice as a Vehicle for Social and Political Transformation in Kenya", in *Africa Human Rights Law Journal*, 2010, vol. 10, p. 391.

[6]   Commission of Inquiry into Post-Election Violence, Final Report, 1 January 2008. According to its findings, more than 1,000 people succumbed to the violence and not less than 500,000 were displaced; European Union Election Observation Mission, Final Report: Kenya: General Elections 27 December 2007, 3 April 2008, p. 36; Internal Displacement Monitoring Centre, "Speedy Reforms Needed to Deal with Past Injustices and Prevent Future Displacement", 10 June 2010.

[7]   This was an *ad hoc* committee established during the post-election period. It comprised members drawn from the then ruling Party of National Unity, the then opposition Orange Democratic Party and a panel of eminent African personalities: Benjamin Mkapa, Graca Machel and Jakaya Kikwete. The former UN secretary-general, Kofi Anan, chaired the committee.

[8]   Commission of Inquiry into Post-Election Violence, 2008, see *supra* note 6.

nal.[9] Following failed local attempts to adopt a law establishing the special tribunal, Annan referred a list of ostensible perpetrators to the prosecutor of the ICC in July 2009.[10]

With the Court's authorisation,[11] the Office of the Prosecutor began investigations in Kenya. This led to the indictment of six individuals (the so-called 'Ocampo six') in two cases, reflecting the two sides of the political conflict: the first against William Samoei Ruto, Joshua Arap Sang and Henry Kiprono Kosgey, and the second against Francis Kirimi Muthaura, Uhuru Muigai Kenyatta and Mohammed Hussein Ali.[12] The prosecutor's choice to investigate only three Orange Democratic Movement (the then-opposition) and three Party of National Unity (the then-ruling party) individuals has been heavily criticised.[13] Although the prosecutor denied playing local party politics,[14] many observers drew the conclusion that his strategy reflected its influence. Arguably, the prosecutor chose a similar number of indictees from the two major political parties in order to show balance and thereby appease both factions. In a one-on-one interview, a member of parliament ('MP') argued that it would have been more sensible for the prosecutor to go for the heads of the two political factions as they had the overall influence on the violence.[15] Essentially, in the view of most respondents, the prosecutor went for low-ranking people in an endeavour to protect those at the top.[16]

---

[9] *Ibid.*, p. 427.

[10] International Criminal Court ('ICC'), Office of the Prosecutor, "ICC Prosecutor Receives Sealed Envelope from Kofi Annan on Post-Election Violence in Kenya", Press Release, 9 July 2009; Anthony Kariuki, "Panic as Kenya Poll Chaos Case Handed to ICC", in *Daily Nation*, 9 July 2009.

[11] ICC, Pre-Trial Chamber, Decision Pursuant to Article 15 of the Rome Statute on the Authorization of an Investigation into the Situation in the Republic of Kenya, ICC-01/09, 31 March 2010 ('Decision on ICC Statute') (http://www.legal-tools.org/doc/338a6f/).

[12] ICC, *Prosecutor v. Uhuru Muigai Kenyatta*, Case Information Sheet, Situation in the Republic of Kenya, ICC-01/09-02/11; ICC, *Prosecutor v. William Samoei Ruto and Joshua Arap Sang*, Case Information Sheet, Situation in the Republic of Kenya, April 2016.

[13] Evelyne Asaala, "The International Criminal Court Factor on Transitional Justice in Kenya", in Kai Ambos and Ottilia Maunganidze (eds.), *Power and Prosecution: Challenges and Opportunities for International Criminal Justice in Sub-Saharan Africa*, Universitätsverlag Göttingen, Göttingen, 2012, p. 136.

[14] Mutwiri Mutuota, "Ocampo: I Am Not Playing Politics", in *Capital News*, 11 April 2011.

[15] Interview with MP N, Nairobi, March 2016.

[16] Generally a cross-cutting observation in most interviews with experts, victims and journalists.

After separate confirmation of charges hearings in the *Ruto et al.* case on 1–8 September 2011 and in the *Kenyatta et al.* case on 21 September–5 October 2011, the ICC Pre-Trial Chamber confirmed charges against four of the six individuals on 23 January 2012: William Samoei Ruto and Joshua Arap Sang in the first case, and Francis Kirimi Muthaura and Uhuru Muigai Kenyatta in the second.[17] The charges against Muthaura were subsequently withdrawn on 18 March 2013. The trial against Ruto and Sang began on 10 September 2013, and the trial against Kenyatta was scheduled to begin on 5 February 2014. However, after vacating the trial date twice, on 3 December 2014 the Trial Chamber rejected the prosecution's request for further adjournment and directed the prosecution to indicate either its withdrawal of charges or readiness to proceed to trial. On 5 December 2014 the prosecution filed a notice to withdraw charges, stating it had no alternative, given the state of the evidence. The prosecution indicated it was doing so without prejudice to the possibility of bringing a new case should additional evidence become available. On 13 March 2015, noting the prosecution's withdrawal, the Trial Chamber vacated charges against Kenyatta due to insufficient evidence.[18] Subsequently, on 5 April 2016 the Trial Chamber vacated the charges against Ruto and Sang.[19] In both cases, the Trial Chamber emphasised that the prosecution could reopen the case if new evidence was found; in both cases, therefore, there were no acquittals.[20] In both cases, the Trial Chamber cited witness interference and political meddling as a reason for vacating charges rather than acquitting the individuals charged.[21] Notably, before confirmation of charges, neither Kenyatta nor

---

[17] ICC, *Prosecutor v. William Samoei Ruto, Henry Kiprono Kosgey & Joshua Arap Sang*, Pre-Trial Chamber II, Decision on the Confirmation of Charges Pursuant to Article 61(7)(a) and (b) of the Rome Statute, ICC-01/09-01/11, 23 January 2012 ('Ruto Confirmation Decision') (http://www.legal-tools.org/doc/96c3c2/); ICC, *Prosecutor v. Francis Kirimi Muthaura, Uhuru Muigai Kenyatta & Mohammed Hussein Ali*, Pre-Trial Chamber II, Decision on the Confirmation of Charges Pursuant to Article 61(7)(a) and (b) of the Rome Statute, ICC-01/09-02/11, 23 January 2012 ('Kenyatta Confirmation Decision') (http://www.legal-tools.org/doc/4972c0/).

[18] ICC, *Prosecutor v Uhuru Muigai Kenyatta*, Trial Chamber V(B), Decision on Withdrawal of Charges against Mr Kenyatta, ICC-01/09-02/11, 13 March 2015 (http://www.legal-tools.org/doc/2c921e/).

[19] ICC, *Prosecutor v. William Samoei Ruto and Joshua Arap Sang*, Appeals Chamber, Decision on Defence Applications for Judgments of Acquittal, ICC-01/09-01/11, 15 April 2016.

[20] *Ibid.*

[21] *Ibid.*

Ruto were heads of state, but in the subsequent elections of March 2013, which were relatively peaceful, the two emerged winners as head of state and deputy respectively. The cases involving them were plagued with controversy as the government of Kenya became so intransigent leading to their eventual collapse as some witnesses were reported to have died in questionable circumstances. It is within this context that this chapter seeks to establish the ICC's impact on deterrence in Kenya.

This study shows that factors that can in general enhance the ICC's deterrent effect in fact hindered deterrence because of the government of Kenya's lack of political will to render them genuine. For example, when the Pre-Trial Chamber authorised the prosecutor to open investigations into the Kenya situation, the government publicly committed itself to undertaking extensive constitutional and institutional reforms, including attempts to create a special division within the High Court with jurisdiction over international crimes. Such acts may theoretically demonstrate a commitment to justice under the rubric of positive complementarity that can enhance deterrence. However, these efforts did not come to fruition. Moreover, the government's efforts to secure an Article 16 deferral of the Kenya situation from the UN Security Council, to encourage other states parties to withdraw from the ICC coupled with the Parliament's overwhelming support for Kenya's potential withdrawal, and to intervene in the ongoing Ruto *et al.* case through its conduct at the 2015 Assembly of State Parties to the Rome Statute ('ASP'), reveal a deliberate disinterest on the part of the government to support any genuine justice initiatives and, by extension, deterrence.

This chapter therefore explores the effect of the ICC's intervention in Kenya, specifically its instigation of proceedings against high-level individuals allegedly involved in the 2007 post-election violence. Each stage of the process from preliminary examination to the trial phase and dismissal of cases is examined to consider possible deterrent effects. The perceptions of key individuals, including victims, experts and members of the Kenyan judiciary and the political establishment, are documented through in-person interviews, review of media source, and research conducted by other commentators. From an analysis of the data collected, it is possible to identify the ICC's contribution to some deterrence markers, but any deterrent effect is complicated and limited by local politics at the time and underlying systemic challenges. Despite the complex mix of factors at work in Kenya, lessons can be learned from the situation that inform recommendations made in the final section for the ICC, States, and civil society on how to maximise the ICC's contribution to deterrence in the future.

10.2. The Theory of Deterrence as Applied in the Kenyan Situation

In the introduction and this volume's chapter on deterrence theory, the notion of deterrence is conceptualised as being generated through legal, institutional and cultural influences, meaning a significant number of actors, including legal and judicial actors, can have a deterrent effect on their environment. Deterrence can be specific, general, targeted or restrictive, meaning that it can be directed at specific individuals, at more general classes of individuals or at society as a whole. Efforts on the broadest level to make criminality a less morally available option may alternately be considered general deterrence or prevention.[22] Like other international tribunals, ICC prosecutions aim to contribute to all these forms of deterrence.

Deterrence manifests itself through every stage of the judicial process: with regard to the ICC, those stages comprise preliminary investigations, institution and confirmation of charges, prosecution and, in cases where conviction follows, sentencing. Debates abound on which particular aspect delivers the greatest deterrent effect. Some commentators favour severity of punishment,[23] while others favour the swiftness of the criminal process and the certainty of punishment.[24] The severity argument does not apply in the ICC's Kenya proceedings given that some of the crimes constituting crimes against humanity would attract the death penalty, in contrast with the ICC's less severe punishment of imprisonment.[25]

---

[22] Hyeran Jo and Beth A. Simmons, "Can the International Criminal Court Deter Atrocity?", in *International Organization*, 2016, vol. 70, no. 3, pp. 443–75.

[23] Harold G. Grasmick and George J. Bryjak, "The Deterrent Effect of Perceived Severity of Punishment", in *Social Force*, 1980, vol. 59, no. 2, p. 472.

[24] Mark A.R. Kleinman, *When Brute Force Fails: How to Have Less Crime and Less Punishment*, Princeton University Press, Princeton, NJ, 2009; Valerie Wright, "Deterrence in Criminal Justice: Evaluating Certainty vs. Severity of Punishment", The Sentencing Project, November 2010.

[25] Linda E. Carter, Ellen S. Kreitzberg and Scott Howe, *Understanding Capital Punishment Law*, Matthew Bender & Company, Newark, 2012. According to Carter, the death penalty would be more effective in general deterrence in the sense that not only does it deter the would-be perpetrators but it also ingrains "the wrongfulness of the punished conduct into the societal mores".

The certainty of punishment or the swiftness of the process may be more applicable. This study argues that all the prosecutorial processes are significant to the theory of deterrence. It therefore analyses each stage with the aim of establishing how this has impacted on deterrence in relation to the Kenyan cases before the ICC.

As Claudio Corradetti, Hyeran Jo and Beth A. Simmons argue, there ordinarily ought to be a correlation "between ICC state's ratification and the reduction" of civil conflict.[26] Thus, as they argue, the ICC is a likely deterrent factor to those with a stake in either current or future governance. Nonetheless, the mere ratification of the ICC Statute was not sufficient to deter Kenyan actors. It took the actual involvement of the ICC for elements of deterrence to be witnessed.

10.2.1. Preliminary Examination

The preliminary examination phase of the Kenyan situation at the ICC took place from July 2008, when the Office of the Prosecutor made first contact with Kenyan officials, to March 2010 when the Office announced the commencement of an investigation. Within the Office, the Jurisdiction, Complementarity and Cooperation Division ('JCCD') is responsible for managing the preliminary examination process, the goal of which is to confirm the ICC's jurisdiction in all its aspects (*rationae temporis*, *rationae materiae* and *rationae personae*). Having been satisfied of the jurisdiction element, the JCCD must then analyse the issues of gravity, complementarity and the interests of justice, to assess whether the Office of the Prosecutor should open an investigation.

With regard to this phase, this section draws three conclusions: deterrence was affected first by lack of understanding as to how the ICC works; second, by a specific convergence of local politics that lessened the chances of support for domestic judicial mechanisms that could have promoted deterrence; and third, by systemic problems with domestic mechanisms that have proved difficult under any circumstances to address.

First, as for lack of understanding of how the ICC works, the Office of the Prosecutor did make its preliminary examination of the Kenyan situation public and explained it to the government. In July 2008 the Office

---

[26] Claudio Corradetti, "The Priority of Conflict Deterrence and the Role of the International Criminal Court in Kenya's Post-Election Violence of 2007–2008 and 2013", in *Human Rights Review*, 2015, vol. 16, pp. 257–59; Jo and Simmons 2016, p. 443, see *supra* note 22.

received a Kenyan delegation comprising seven government officials, and explained to them Kenya's primary obligation in relation to investigation and prosecution of alleged perpetrators of international crimes.[27] The delegation and the Office of the Prosecutor agreed that the Office would only intervene where the government failed to carry out "genuine judicial proceedings against those most responsible".[28] The Office made its preliminary examination public on 5 February 2009,[29] when it reported that it had written and requested further information from various parties, that it had received reports in response to its requests, that it had received communications from individuals and from Kenyan-based NGOs, and that it was reviewing information from open sources.[30] On 11 February 2009 the Office of the Prosecutor further confirmed in several press statements that it was monitoring domestic proceedings in relation to the post-election violence.[31] The preliminary examination stage came to an end with the official opening of the investigation in March 2010.[32]

Knowledge of the Court and the law is a prerequisite for deterrence.[33] Without this knowledge, the deterrent effect of a court is very limited. However, in the Kenyan situation, save for the experts and most politicians, almost all those here interviewed were not aware of the ICC's involvement at the preliminary examination stage. The interview with expert W confirms the limited knowledge about the ICC among the public as a major challenge to deterrence during this early stage.[34]

Many MPs and other politicians had serious misconceptions about the ICC, which affected not only their engagement on the subject, but also their consideration of national alternatives that could have strengthened deterrence in general. For example, in line with a CIPEV recommendation,

---

[27] ICC, Agreed Minutes of the Meeting between Prosecutor Moreno-Ocampo and the Delegation of the Kenyan Government, The Hague, 3 July 2009.

[28] *Ibid.*, para 4.

[29] ICC, OTP Statement in Relation to Events in Kenya, The Hague, 5 February 2008.

[30] ICC, Office of the Prosecutor, "ICC Prosecutor Reaffirms That the Situation in Kenya Is Monitored by His Office", 11 February 2009.

[31] *Ibid.*

[32] ICC, Situation in the Republic of Kenya, IC-01/09.

[33] John Dietrich, "The Limited Prospects of Deterrence by the International Criminal Court: Lessons from Domestic Experience", in *International Social Science Review*, 2014, vol. 88, no. 3, p. 9.

[34] Interview with expert W, Nairobi, April 2016.

in February 2009 the government introduced a bill to establish a special tribunal, which failed to pass. The government reintroduced it in March 2009, but despite the president and prime minister attending the session in support of the bill, it again failed, in part because the ICC was not viewed as the kind of threat that could have mustered support for a domestic alternative to supplant it, as noted in an interview with a local journalist.[35] More so, some MPs are on record as having dismissed the ICC idea as hypothetical mainly based on the perception that the Kenyan scenario was insufficiently severe to trigger the ICC's jurisdiction:

> Let not the threat of The Hague be used now and again. There are those people who have it at the back of their minds that people will necessarily go to The Hague. The Hague is not a Kangaroo court. I dare say, that probably, those envelopes that you are seeking to be opened may never be opened because, to my knowledge, that is not how the International Criminal Court operates. There have been conflicts in Sudan, Uganda, and the Democratic Republic of Congo (DRC). If you look at the history of those conflicts and the matters which have been taken before The Hague, it is not more than some people who have gone to the International Criminal Court because the threshold is so high for it to act.[36]

> In Rwanda, it took the international community to witness the mass massacre of over 1 million people to agree to set up the tribunal. That was after all the calamity had happened! We also know about the calamity that has taken place in Darfur, Sudan. It is only now that they are talking about setting up one. In Liberia, where they tried some people, the amount of calamity was also very substantial. It is also the same in the former Yugoslavia. What happened in Kenya in 2007 was tragic and really tragic. But it is not sufficient to call for the intervention of the ICC.[37]

> I want to caution this House, that it is not a given; it is not guaranteed that if we do not act domestically, one Moreno-

---

[35] Interview with a local journalist, Nairobi, May 2016.

[36] Minister of Lands, Mr Orengo, Report of Parliamentary Proceedings of 3 February 2009, Kenya National Assembly Official Record (Hansard), 3 February 2009.

[37] Mr Baiya, Report of Parliamentary Proceedings of 4 February 2009, Kenya National Assembly Official Record (Hansard), 4 February 2009.

> Ocampo, the Chief Prosecutor of the ICC will be on the next flight to Nairobi.[38]

In principle, the MPs' arguments resonate with the spirit of the ICC Statute, that the Kenya situation fails to meet the gravity test under Articles 53 and 17(1)(d). Although the threshold argument is persuasive, the then underlying political motive among Kenyan politicians was questionable. For example, when an MP observes "that it is not a given; it is not guaranteed that if we do not act domestically [...] the Chief Prosecutor of the ICC will be on the next flight to Nairobi",[39] and "[t]here are those who will come to this Floor to debate this law with the determination to ensure that this law does not pass; with the determination that, that tribunal will not be set up, because their political rivals will be headed to The Hague".[40] It is very doubtful that such political statements were informed by the intricate interpretation of the law governing threshold requirements for international crimes. Rather, it is more likely that the threshold argument among the political class was bolstered by a culture of impunity, which in turn negatively impacts on deterrence both of local mechanisms and the ICC.

Another notable aspect in this context is the dissenting decision of Judge Hans-Peter Kaul who similarly found that the ICC lacked jurisdiction, because the requirement of an organisational policy was missing, and therefore this may not have been a crime against humanity. In his dissent, Kaul dismisses the prosecutor's interpretation of the notion 'organisation' as insufficient to fulfil the threshold of Article 7(2)(a) of the ICC Statute. The relevant parts of his judgments read as follows:

> 51. I read the provision such that the juxtaposition of the notions 'State' and 'organisation' in article 7(2)(a) of the Statute are an indication that even though the constitutive elements of statehood need not be established those 'organisations' should partake of some characteristics of a State. Those characteristics eventually turn the private 'organisation' into an entity which may act like a State or has quasi-State abilities. These characteristics could involve the following: (a) a collectivity of people; (b) which was estab-

---

[38] Mr Namwamba, Report of Parliamentary Proceedings of 5 February 2009, Kenya National Assembly Official Record (Hansard), 5 February 2009.

[39] *Ibid.*

[40] *Ibid.*

---

lished and acts for a common purpose; (c) over a prolonged period of time; (d) which is under responsible command or adopted a certain degree of hierarchical structure, including, as a minimum, some kind of policy level; (e) with the capacity to impose the policy on its members and to sanction them; and (f) which has the capacity and means available to attack any civilian population on a large scale.

52. In contrast, I believe that non-state actors which do not reach the level described above are not able to carry out a policy of this nature, such as groups of organised crime, a mob, groups of (armed) civilians or criminal gangs. They would generally fall outside the scope of article 7(2)(a) of the Statute. They would generally fall outside the scope of article 7(2)(a) of the Statute. To give a concrete example, violence-prone groups of people formed on an ad hoc basis, randomly, spontaneously, for a passing occasion, with fluctuating membership and without a structure and level to set up a policy are not within the ambit of the Statute, even if they engage in numerous serious and organised crimes. Further elements are needed for a private entity to reach the level of an 'organisation' within the meaning of article 7 of the Statute. For it is not the cruelty or mass victimisation that turns a crime into a *delictum iuris gentium* but the constitutive contextual elements in which the act is embedded.[41]

Kaul further underscored the fact that the 'network' as described by the prosecution in the *Ruto, Kosgey and Sang* case was not only *ad hoc* but was also ethnically based with an amorphous alliance "of coordinating members of a tribe with a predisposition towards violence with fluctuating membership". Thus, such a network would not qualify as an organisation under Article 7(2)(a) since "members of a tribe [...] do not form a state-like 'organisation', unless they meet additional prerequisites". More so, the mere "planning and coordination of violence in a series of meetings during the time period relevant to this case does not transform an ethnically-based gathering of perpetrators into a State-like organisation".[42]

---

[41] Decision on ICC Statute, Dissenting Opinion of Judge Hans-Peter Kaul, paras. 51–53, see *supra* note 11; Ruto Confirmation Decision, para. 8, see *supra* note 17; Kenyatta Confirmation Decision, para. 7, see *supra* note 17.

[42] Ruto Confirmation Decision, para. 12, see *supra* note 12.

During this time, majority of the general public, including most of my respondents, were not fully aware of this dissent.[43] While agreeing with the dissent, expert O underscored that the philosophy underlying international criminal law was not to prosecute ordinary criminals, but rather high-level crimes whose perpetrators were likely to be heads of states and other senior state officers.[44] Where private institutions are concerned, then these should have state-like capabilities.[45] Nonetheless, expert J totally disagreed with Kaul's dissent. According to this expert, restricting the meaning of an organisation to a state or state-like entity is very limiting and likely to undermine the deterrence effect of the ICC, especially with respect to these private organisations that have the ability to commit grave international crimes, yet do not by themselves have state-like characteristics.[46]

The general feeling among MPs, as Elias Okwaro documents, that "any suspected power brokers would remain untouched"[47] further compounded this perception. For this reason, they ostensibly could not support passage of the bill.[48] Similarly, victims and others understood that any politician who thought they could be implicated opposed an ICC intervention.[49] This perception may have informed slogans such as "Do not be vague, go for The Hague", which became commonplace for MPs who supported the ICC process over a domestic one.[50] This excitement about the ICC seems also to have been "informed by previous quests to rid the state of the deep-rooted culture of impunity and the fear of possible manipulation of the special tribunal, given the apparent ethnic and political tensions".[51] With the likelihood of a local tribunal being susceptible to manipulation, there is no doubt that the majority of the MPs perceived

---

[43] Interview with expert O, Nairobi, September 2016.

[44] *Ibid.*

[45] *Ibid.*

[46] Interview with expert J, Nairobi, September 2016.

[47] Elias B. Okwaro, "The International Criminal Court and Kenya's Post-election Violence: National Justice through Global Mechanisms", in *GGI Analaysia*, No. 2/2011, July 2011.

[48] *Ibid.*

[49] Interview with victim B, Eldoret, April 2016.

[50] See Reports of Parliamentary Proceedings, 3 February–5 February 2009, *supra* notes 36–38.

[51] Asaala, 2010, p. 397, see *supra* note 13. The majority of MPs who supported the ICC over and above domestic mechanism cited the culture of impunity for past atrocities as a key reason.

such a local mechanism to be unlikely to deter certain individuals, thus necessitating the intervention of an international mechanism.

Finally, one of those charged by the ICC is also on record as having suggested that "[t]he ICC will begin hearing the Kenyan case in 2090. Who amongst us will be alive then?"[52] Underlying his reasoning was the perception that an ICC process was uncertain and almost impossible. In the light of that perception, the sense of urgency in setting up a national alternative was significantly lessened, and the subsequent cost-benefit analysis favoured a culture of impunity. For example, when a politician observed in Parliament that despite the atrocities in Sudan, "it is only now that they are talking about setting up [a tribunal]", this implies that when politicians rationally calculate the delayed cost of punishment versus the immediate benefit of gaining political power, they easily settle for the latter. Indeed, John Dietrich notes that "people tend to discount future costs when compared to current costs".[53] He further observes that although benefits for committing atrocities are also discounted over time, the benefits often occur more immediately than the potential costs.[54] Thus, in the eyes of the Kenyan political class, the ICC represented a delayed or even non-existent threat of punishment as opposed to immediate gains to be had. This in turn negatively affected the deterrent effect of the ICC on the political class that had some awareness of the Court.

Ironically, some politicians defeated the motion to establish a special tribunal on the basis of just the opposite perception: that their opponents would be the ICC's targets, in which case they preferred the ICC to a national tribunal. As one MP noted, "There are those who will come to this Floor to debate this law with the determination to ensure that this law does not pass; with the determination that, that tribunal will not be set up, because their political rivals will be headed to The Hague".[55] Expert W further perceives the failure of the then minister of justice and constitutional affairs, Martha Karua, to command confidence of both political factions as a factor contributing to the failure of the bills.[56] According to expert W, as the initiator of the motion, Karua failed to win the trust of

---

[52] Makozewe, "Uhuruto Took Themselves to the Hague", in *Kenya Stockholm Blog*, 12 September 2013.

[53] Dietrich, 2014, p. 19, see *supra* note 33.

[54] *Ibid.*

[55] Namwamba, Report of Parliamentary Proceedings, see *supra* note 38.

[56] Interview with expert W, Nairobi, April 2016.

either side of the political factions each of whom suspected her to be conspiring with their opponent.[57]

Second, the preliminary examination phase represents a missed opportunity for deterrence in the Kenya situation due to a specific convergence of local politics that lessened the chances of support for domestic judicial mechanisms that could have promoted deterrence. According to a judicial source, the fallout between the two Orange Democratic Movement leaders, Raila Amollo Odinga and William Ruto, further exacerbated political rivalry leading to eventual defeat of the bill supporting a special tribunal.[58] This judicial source further argued that while Raila supported the ICC process largely because of the perception that it would have gotten rid of his political opponents, Ruto was opposed to the idea.[59] However, the position discussed by this respondent occurred much later when the political class had changed its perspectives on learning who the ICC indictees were. It is true, though, that Raila and Ruto were political rivals, and as Raila initially supported the special tribunal, Ruto, the then minister of agriculture, enthusiastically supported the ICC process.[60]

This judicial source further noted with some irony that this was the very same Parliament that had earlier passed the International Crimes Act of 2008 ('ICA'), making national proceedings on international crimes more feasible. The defeat of the bill establishing the special tribunal can thus perhaps best be explained within the context of local politics at the time. Of course, as correctly noted by another judicial source, it may also be a possibility that Parliament passed the ICA without any due consideration or without an understanding of its implications.

Another late initiative by civil society to reintroduce the bill in Parliament emerged in August 2009, but was never discussed in Parliament. Although the lawmakers had the opportunity to take advantage of the doctrine of complementarity and establish domestic mechanisms to prosecute international crimes, local politics was instead used to undermine such ef-

---

[57] *Ibid.*

[58] Interview with a judicial source, Nairobi, March 2016.

[59] *Ibid.*

[60] "Ruto: Why I Prefer the Hague Route", in *Daily Nation News*, 21 February 2009; Vitalis Kimutai, "Ruto Wants Annan to Hand Over Envelope to Hague", in *Standard Media Group*, 21 February 2009; "Chronology of Events that Frustrated Raila's Efforts to Form Local Tribunal to Try PEV Suspects", in *Kenya Today*, 14 October 2015.

forts. An interview with a local MP further confirms that the political class perceives this as a lost opportunity.[61]

Third, the preliminary examination phase represents a missed opportunity for deterrence in the Kenya situation due to arguably systemic problems with domestic mechanisms that have proved difficult under any circumstances to address. Even when seized of the opportunity, domestic prosecution of international crimes has underperformed. National prosecution of international crimes related to post-election violence has been limited, thus compromising the deterrence effect of the local processes. A Human Rights Watch report labels domestic prosecution efforts in Kenya as a "half-hearted" effort at accountability. As such, "hundreds of [...] perpetrators of serious crimes continue to evade accountability".[62] This deficiency can be attributed to a host of challenges, including inadequate investigations by the police in terms of competencies and human and technical resources and a distinct lack of political will in some cases. Indeed, echoing the complaints of judges who presided over post-election violence-related cases, two judicial sources in an interview observed that the levels of investigations conducted in these cases were deliberately shoddy so that no conviction would be secured.[63] Citing the case of *Edward Kirui v. R*, where a police officer was caught on camera shooting to death two unarmed people taking part in a peaceful demonstration, a judicial source lamented how the police tampered with the evidence in order to salvage one of their own from a conviction.[64] A Human Rights Watch report has also made similar observations.[65] In *Edward Kirui*'s case, the sergeant in charge of the armoury testified that on that material day he issued the accused with an AK47, serial number 23008378. The firearms examiner and the then acting senior superintendent, however, testified that the weapon that killed the victim bore the serial number 3008378. This cast some doubt on the linkage of the accused to the offence, leading to an acquittal.

---

[61] Interview with an MP, Nairobi, March 2016.

[62] Human Rights Watch, "'Turning Pebbles': Evading Accountability for Post-election Violence in Kenya", December 2011.

[63] High Court of Kenya, *R v Stephen Kiprotich Leting and 3 Others,* Nairobi High Court, Criminal Case no 34 of 2008 at Nakuru; High Court of Kenya, *Republic v Edward Kirui,* Nairobi High Court, Criminal Case No 9 of 2008.

[64] Interview with a judicial source, Nairobi, March 2016.

[65] Human Rights Watch, 2011, p. 33, see *supra* note 62.

An interview with another judicial source revealed the main impediment in local prosecutions centred on the use of police officers as both investigators and prosecutors.[66] It therefore becomes almost impossible to secure a conviction against their own since cases involving the police as perpetrators are often compromised. Noting that one of the ICC indictees was the police commissioner, it would have been impossible to effectively conduct local prosecutions of international crimes through a local mechanism. In this regard, a judicial source observed, "the probability of local prosecution of 2007 post-election violence cases would have been suicidal for any person who tried to prosecute an ICC indictee".[67] This explains why there was no single conviction of any politician or police officer despite an estimated 962 cases of police shootings, which resulted in 450 deaths.[68] This further demonstrates the near absence of deterrence of local mechanisms, in particular in relation to the political class and the police, as opposed to an international mechanism, which is at least functionally independent from these local actors.

Two judicial sources further lamented the public selection of judicial officers based on their tribe as another factor compromising the deterrent effect of local prosecutions.[69] For example, in an interview with one judicial source who sat on the committee on allocation of election petitions, tribe was a factor to be considered when allocating judicial officers to the various regions.[70] Due to such practices, it was a risk to post an officer to a region that was not of their ethnic group. Tensions surrounding ethnicity were therefore significant challenges to domestic prosecution of post-election violence.

The government's decision to close all national cases, coupled with its reluctance to collaborate effectively by conducting thorough investigations, further confirms the lack of political will to effectively prosecute post-election violence at a local level. In fact, according to expert W, this withdrawal signifies an unspoken agreement that there were no crimes committed in the 2007 post-election violence and, if there were, that no evidence exists to sustain any prosecution.[71] It is for these reasons that

---

[66]   Interview with a judicial source, Nairobi, March 2016.
[67]   *Ibid.*
[68]   Commission of Inquiry into Post-Election Violence, 2008, see *supra* note 6.
[69]   Interview with a judicial source, Nairobi, March 2016.
[70]   *Ibid.*
[71]   Interview with expert W, Nairobi, April 2016.

factions of the political class and the public at the time perceived the ICC to be a greater deterrent, particularly with respect to senior government officials.

All the respondents here interviewed, however, do not attribute the ICC's intervention as a factor that deterred further atrocities in the short-term period of the post-election violence. They all agree that the end of violence was the result of the power-sharing agreement the KNDRC brokered between the Orange Democratic Movement and the Party of National Unity. Expert W further observed, in an interview, that one-party rule could not be accepted at the time.[72] It is this sharing of power that quelled the animosity which had earlier fuelled the violence. This view resonates with the reality on the ground. Indeed, the day a power-sharing deal was brokered, on 28 February 2008, coincides with the day when the violence ceased.

10.2.2. The Reporting Stage

The reporting phase of the Kenyan case before the ICC took place from 26 November 2009 to 31 March 2010. 26 November 2009 was the date when the prosecutor submitted a request to the Court for authorisation of an investigation, while 31 March 2010 was the date when Pre-Trial Chamber II issued its decision authorising the prosecutor to begin investigations. This section concludes that the reporting stage represents yet another lost opportunity for deterrence in the Kenya situation due to lack of knowledge of the Court's processes.

Where the Office of the Prosecutor initiates investigations *proprio motu*, the prosecutor must first analyse the seriousness of the information at their disposal.[73] If it is concluded that such information provides a reasonable basis to initiate investigations, the prosecutor must then submit a request to the Pre-Trial Chamber seeking authorisation to conduct investigations of that particular situation.[74] It is therefore the Pre-Trial Chamber that decides whether or not to grant such authority.[75]

---

[72] *Ibid.*
[73] ICC Statute, Article 15(2), see *supra* note 3.
[74] *Ibid.*, Article 15(3).
[75] *Ibid.*, Article 15(5).

After a preliminary examination of the Kenyan situation, the prosecutor, having concluded that the available information provided a reasonable basis to lodge investigations, submitted a request to the Court for authorisation of an investigation under Article 15 of the ICC Statute on 26 November 2009.[76] From the interviews conducted, it can be observed that the majority of Kenyans, including the political class, civil society and victims, were not keen on these preliminary stages of the ICC. As a local journalist noted in an interview, the majority of the population, including the politicians, had no clue about the ICC.[77] This underscores expert W's earlier criticism of the ICC for its limited outreach, contributing to a widespread lack of understanding of the Court's procedures. Further, some Kenyans who had information did not feel they had enough. Some victims confessed that they never knew that other than prosecution, the ICC had a reparative mandate.[78] This may have influenced their decisions on whether to interact with the ICC in one way or another.[79]

Lack of proper knowledge of the Court and its processes therefore undermined its deterrent effect in this preliminary phase.

10.2.3. Opening of Investigations

The phase of opening investigations into Kenyan cases took place from 31 March 2010, the date when Pre-Trial Chamber II issued its decision authorising the prosecutor to commence investigations, to 15 December 2010, the date when the prosecutor made an application seeking the indictment of the Ocampo six.[80] The opening of investigations signalled the swiftness and certainty of an ICC process. This informed the government's commitment to extensive constitutional and institutional reforms, but the government nonetheless denied these mechanisms the political support that would have rendered them relevant to deterrence in the short term. Its efforts to secure an Article 16 deferral at the ICC also demonstrated a deliberate disinterest on the part of the government in supporting genuine justice initiatives and deterrence at either the national or the in-

---

[76] Decision on ICC Statute, see *supra* note 11.

[77] Interview with a local journalist, Nairobi, May 2016.

[78] Interview conducted with victims, Eldoret, March 2016.

[79] *Ibid.*

[80] Decision on ICC Statute, see *supra* note 11.

ternational level. However, the institutional reforms instituted may yet have a deterrent impact in the long term if they are properly implemented.

On 31 March 2010 Pre-Trial Chamber II issued its decision authorising the prosecutor to commence investigations in Kenya.[81] Subsequent to this authorisation, there was a slow change of views – among the political class – of what had seemed to be the impossible ICC process. A local journalist explained the critical role played by the media in creating consciousness on the nature and processes of the ICC among the public and the political class.[82] In this regard, one expert correctly observed that real deterrence began with the Pre-Trial Chamber's issuance of authorisation to investigate.[83] The government undertook some key domestic reforms directly linked to the Kenyan cases before the ICC. This would in turn have a direct impact on the deterrent effect of the ICC.

For example, although the history of constitutional reforms is protracted and its genesis can be traced to 1992, it is the ICC prosecution of the 2007 post-election violence that reminded the government of the need for both institutional and constitutional reforms. Numerous efforts culminated in the promulgation of a new Constitution on 27 August 2010. Kenya's new Constitution is noteworthy for its incorporation of a robust bill of rights[84] and provisions for the creation of an independent electoral management body,[85] an independent judiciary,[86] executive[87] and Parliament,[88] a decentralised political system and a framework regulating a system of devolved government.[89] The constitutional reform process laid the ground for important institutional reforms of the justice and security apparatus and other governance institutions, geared to prevent the recurrence of human rights atrocities.

The commencement of the Kenyan cases by the ICC cracked the whip at the right time.[90] This was confirmed in an interview with two ju-

---

[81]   *Ibid.*

[82]   Interview with a local journalist, Nairobi, May 2016.

[83]   Interview with an expert, Nairobi, April 2016.

[84]   Constitution of Kenya, 2010, Articles 19–51 (http://www.legal-tools.org/doc/964817/).

[85]   *Ibid.*, Article 88.

[86]   *Ibid.*, Article 160.

[87]   *Ibid.*, Articles 129–55.

[88]   *Ibid.*, Articles 93–105.

[89]   *Ibid.*, Articles 174–200.

[90]   Asaala, 2012, p. 140, see *supra* note 13.

dicial sources.[91] According to them, the political class always thinks it is above the law. Even in their prosecution of ordinary crimes, this political class always expects the law to be interpreted in its favour. They further observed that the reality of an ICC process necessitated numerous interventions. In this context, a local mechanism would have no deterrent effect at all to the political class since this group of people has embraced a culture of impunity and could deploy all manner of tools, including alteration of the law, threats and even death to ensure their own protection. The government must therefore have thought that adopting a new Constitution would tame the ICC process. On various occasions, the government referred to the new Constitution as its new strength to prosecute the Ocampo six.[92] In fact, as will be demonstrated below, constitutional reform was one of the government's key arguments when challenging the admissibility of Kenyan cases before the ICC. It can thus be inferred that legal reforms, and in particular constitutional reform, have been used in the short term to deflect ICC action and undermine its deterrent effect. The longer-term effect of these initiatives, though, may be to anchor the ICC's deterrent effect to social institutions that can be trusted to deter future occurrences of similar atrocities. The ICC contributed to Kenya's "long-term peace, stability, and equitable development" and hopefully this stabilisation "guarantees for a future free of violence".[93] But for the present, the political class too selectively implements these progressive provisions of the Constitution and other institutional reforms to render them fully effective and meet the hope they embody.

In addition to pursuing but then limiting the impact of constitutional reforms, the then vice president, Kalonzo Musyoka, engaged in shuttle diplomacy within the region and the UN, seeking support for a deferral motion before the Security Council.[94] This reaction underscores the fear that

---

[91]   Interview with judicial sources, Nairobi, March 2016.

[92]   Lucas Barasa, "Mutula to Ocampo, Quit Kenyan Probe", in *Sunday Nation*, 19 September 2010; "Why Go to The Hague", in *Sunday Nation*, 19 September 2010. The then minister for justice and constitutional affairs called upon the ICC to quit the Kenyan probe and to allow Kenya a chance under the new constitutional court structures to deal with the cases. Cited in Asaala, 2012, p. 141, see *supra* note 13.

[93]   Sang-Hyun Song, "Preventive Potential of the International Criminal Court", in *Asian Journal of International Law*, 2013, vol. 3, no. 2, p. 203.

[94]   "ICC: Kalonzo Shuttle Diplomacy Hits New York", in *Daily Nation*, 8 March 2011; "Former VP Kalonzo Musyoka Led Cabinet Ministers in Worldwide Push to Bring ICC Cases to Kenya", in *The Standard*, 13 October 2013.

the political class had of an ICC process as opposed to a local mechanism, and their fears of possible manipulation of a local mechanism.

The victims, on the other side, expressed their hope for justice, especially when Moreno-Ocampo visited the country.[95] According to victim B, although a local mechanism would have been most effective, it was unlikely that it would have been free and fair.[96] Not only did the victims lack trust in a local mechanism but also, since the majority of alleged perpetrators were senior politicians, most were unwilling to give evidence to a local body. The victims expressed a lot of fear about witness protection. While the Witness Protection Act[97] guarantees protection to all witnesses through various mechanisms, the fact that the attorney general has the overall discretion in all the appointments to the agency in charge, and coupled with the fact that the agency is fully funded by the government, leaves the impartiality of such a programme questionable, especially regarding the protection of witnesses against the government. According to Harun Ndubi, this arrangement lacks credibility and independence as "those who are supposed to protect the witnesses are the ones the witnesses are likely to testify against".[98] This perception and the fears ingrained in probable witnesses lead to one inference: that the accuracy of any evidence that would have been given in these circumstances would have had questionable probative value.

10.2.4. Indictment

The indictment phase covers the period from 15 December 2010, when the prosecutor made two applications to Pre-Trial Chamber II seeking an indictment against the Ocampo six, to 31 March 2011, when the government challenged the admissibility of the two Kenyan cases before the ICC. The handing down of the indictments, coupled with the cross-cutting effect of a second warrant of arrest against President Omar Al Bashir of Sudan, underscored the certainty of an ICC process. This phase saw the government's initiative to create a special division within the High Court with jurisdiction over international crimes. Although the creation of this divi-

---

[95] Interview with victims, Eldoret, April 2016.
[96] *Ibid.*
[97] Republic of Kenya, Witness Protection Act, Cap 79 Laws of Kenya, 1 September 2008 (http://www.legal-tools.org/doc/b37769/).
[98] Alex Kiprotich, "Will Witness Protection Law Work?", in *The Standard*, 26 July 2009.

sion could theoretically have enhanced deterrence, the implementation of these initiatives was completely devoid of much-needed political will and the continued government efforts to secure an Article 16 deferral of the Kenya situation at the ICC, to encourage other states parties to withdraw, and the Parliament's overwhelming support for the country's potential withdrawal from the ICC, all demonstrate a deliberate disinterest on the part of the government to support genuine justice initiatives and, by extension, deterrence. The ICC's indictment strategy may have denied the process its legitimacy, thus negatively impacting on deterrence.

Having completed his investigations, on 15 December 2010 the prosecutor made two applications to Pre-Trial Chamber II in accordance with Article 58 of the ICC Statute.[99] In these applications the prosecutor asked the Court to issue summonses to appear for Ruto, Kosgey and Sang in the first case, and Muthaura, Kenyatta and Ali in the second.[100]

According to MP N, it was at this point that the ICC began losing its legitimacy.[101] While investigations form the crux of a criminal case, the perception among many Kenyans was that the ICC seemed to base all its investigations that led to indictments on reports already done by civil society and the CIPEV.[102] This appeared to compromise the much-needed independence of the Office of the Prosecutor investigations, which is essential in leading to transparent and genuine indictments. In fact, MP N further demonstrated his grievances that the ICC eventually indicted the wrong people – those second in command – instead of going for the then-leaders of the ruling party and of the opposition, Raila Amollo Odinga and Mwai Kibaki.[103] These two, according to this MP and two judicial sources, were highest in rank and with command responsibility for the violence. The poorly perceived indictment strategy deployed by the prose-

---

[99] ICC, Pre-Trial Chamber, Prosecutor's Application Pursuant to Article 58 as to William Samoei Ruto, Henry Kiprono Kosgey and Joshua Arap Sang, ICC-01/09, Office of the Prosecutor, 15 December 2010 (http://www.legal-tools.org/doc/c6cf4c/); ICC, Pre-Trial Chamber, Prosecutor's Application Pursuant to Article 58 as to Francis Kirimi Muthaura, Uhuru Muigai Kenyatta and Mohammed Hussein Ali, ICC-01/09, 15 December 2010 (http://www.legal-tools.org/doc/fd1a68/).

[100] *Ibid.*

[101] Interview with MP N, Nairobi, March 2016.

[102] *Ibid.*

[103] *Ibid.*

cutor denied the process its legitimacy thus negatively affecting deterrence.

The issuance and publication of indictments confirmed the celerity and certainty of the ICC process. This, coupled with the Court's issuance of a second arrest warrant against Al Bashir, had a catalytic effect on the government's efforts to vitiate the ICC process, especially given the fact that a majority of those indicted were senior government officers. In December 2010 the Kenyan Parliament overwhelmingly voted in favour of a motion urging the government to withdraw from the ICC Statute.[104] Realising the limited impact this would have in the international arena, the government agreed to reach out to the region and other supporters, seeking their consent for a withdrawal en masse from the ICC. Indeed, the African Union guaranteed its support for Kenya in the event of a withdrawal.

This withdrawal attempt was, however, misguided. For the most part, the government was under the illusion that such a withdrawal would have compelled the ICC to back off the Kenyan cases. On the contrary, such a step had been overtaken by events since the ICC process had begun way before the withdrawal. In an interview, an MP agrees with the prosecutor of the ICC's criticism of this move as being "short-sighted and unfortunate".[105] Expert W termed this move "a desperate attempt informed by ignorance".[106] Perhaps it was the realisation that such a move was not going to salvage the six that the government opted for another alternative. There is no doubt that the ICC's indictment of the Ocampo six and the issuance of a second warrant of arrest for Al Bashir on 12 July 2010 instilled more fear in the government, given the certainty and swiftness of the ICC process.

In January 2011 the government announced its intention to establish a special division within the High Court to deal with all post-election violence cases.[107] This was a laudable step, since such local initiatives not only enhance complementarity but are also likely to assuage fears about

---

[104] Parliament of the Republic of Kenya, National Assembly Official Report, Plenary Hansard, 22 December 2010, p. 83. The Kenyan parliament passes motion to withdraw from the ICC.

[105] Interview with an MP, Nairobi, March 2016.

[106] Interview with expert W, Nairobi, April 2016.

[107] International Centre for Transitional Justice, "Prosecuting International and Other Serious Crimes in Kenya", April 2013.

an ICC imposing itself through prosecuting future international crimes.[108] The timing of this announcement by the government, however, raised questions about its real motive.[109] Though a commendable idea, underlying this move was the misperception that this special division would lead to a deferral of the Kenyan cases to a local mechanism. While advocating for the establishment of an International Crimes Division ('ICD') modelled on the ICC within the Kenyan High Court, a Multi-Agency Task Force on the 2007/2008 post-election violence highlighted that any ICD should be conferred jurisdiction over post-election violence cases in order to try international crimes under the International Crimes Act.[110] Given that the director of public prosecutions had already withdrawn all post-election violence-related cases for lack of evidence, it was no surprise that this new local mechanism was destined to fail. As expert W correctly observed, there was no political will to establish an ICD that would effectively prosecute post-election violence.[111] With an ICC indictment on the president and his deputy, the two automatically had vested interests to ensure that the ICD would not work.[112] A local journalist described this as "a political gimmick to appease the international community. If it is ever established, its effectiveness remains doubtful".[113] Thus, underlying the establishment of an ICD was the intention to get rid of the ICC process and have the cases transferred to a domestic mechanism. While this is the underlying philosophy of the doctrine of complementarity, which states should be encouraged to adopt, the motive is sometimes misguided. Thus, while such a move by the government may seem to be in tandem with complementarity, underneath are negative efforts that can be inferred to be undermining the deterrent effect of the ICC.

An interview with an MP additionally revealed the silent perception among the political class that the heightened terrorist attacks experienced in Nairobi during this time were part of the strategies designed to engineer

---

[108] Juidicial Service Commission, "Report of the Committee of the Judicial Service Commission on the Establishment of an International Crimes Division in the High Court of Kenya", 30 October 2012.

[109] Interview with a judicial source, Nairobi, March 2016.

[110] Multi-Agency Task Force on the 2007/2008 PEV, Report on the 2007/2008 PEV-Related Cases, 2012.

[111] Interview with expert W, Nairobi, April 2016.

[112] *Ibid.*

[113] Interview with a local journalist, Nairobi, April 2016.

the deferral of the ICC's Kenyan cases to a local mechanism.[114] With respect to the Westgate attack, for example, expert O argued that the delayed government response and extensive media coverage of the situation confirmed that the government took advantage of the attack to create the perception that Kenya was in dire need of its leaders locally for national security, and therefore their periodic travels to the ICC were inappropriate.[115] This notwithstanding, it is MP N's view that the KNDRC's recommendations were in favour of a local mechanism that was reconciliatory and not retributive in nature.[116] This kind of approach, the MP further observed, was essential for national cohesion, as the violence had ripped apart the ethos of cohesiveness among the various tribes.

Interestingly, most of the victims interviewed expressed their ignorance of these debates. According to victim B, tribal animosity had heightened at this time.[117] Thus not only were the victims confused, but ethnicity informed their entry point to such debates. Depending on which ethnic leader initiated the debate, the victims would blindly follow if this leader were from their ethnic group.

Accordingly, the victims expressed mixed reactions towards these indictments. One victim from the Kikuyu community stated that his tribe felt that the indictment of Kenyatta was wrong since he may have acted in their defence.[118] The Kalenjin, Kisii and Luo victims, on the other side, faulted the indictment of Ruto and other Orange Democratic Movement politicians.[119] If these victims' observations are true, then it is arguable that ethnic ideology as a factor in the initial attacks against different communities and the resulting desire for revenge and seemingly spontaneous outburst of post-election violence may undercut the argument that the crimes were rationally calculated, at least for those at a lower level who carried them out. It is possible that the actual perpetrators never had the opportunity to rationally consider the costs and benefit of the violence. In addition, the group 'arousal effect' could easily explain the extensive nature of the violence. In such a context, explains Dietrich, acts that

---

[114] Interview with an MP, Nairobi, March 2016.
[115] Interview with expert O, Nairobi, September 2016.
[116] *Ibid.*
[117] Interview with victim B, Eldoret, April 2016.
[118] *Ibid.*
[119] *Ibid.*

would amount to atrocities become heroic, and could deny the opportunity for rational calculations.[120]

10.2.5. Admissibility

The admissibility phase covers the period from 31 March 2011, when the government challenged the admissibility of Kenyan cases, to 30 May 2011, when the Court issued its final judgment confirming their admissibility. The government's challenge on admissibility demonstrates its total lack of interest in deterrence since the government sought to rely on positive complementarity through local mechanisms while denying these same local mechanisms the much-needed political support to succeed. These actions had a cumulative negative impact on deterrence.

Kenya and Côte d'Ivoire are so far the only countries in which the prosecutor has successfully exercised *proprio motu* powers. Unlike in the Ivorian situation where the Court's intervention initially received full acceptance and support of the Ivorian government,[121] the contrary was true for Kenya.

On 31 March 2011 Kenya lodged an application before the ICC challenging the admissibility of the Kenyan cases. The government urged the ICC to take into account the comprehensive constitutional and judicial reforms that had been adopted.[122] Although admissibility was challenged against the prosecutor's exercise of his *proprio motu* powers, the Court was seized of the Kenyan cases on the basis that even though the government claimed that there were ongoing investigations, these were hypothetical promises and not investigations within the context of Article 17(1)(a)

---

[120] Dietrich, 2014, p. 9, see *supra* note 33.

[121] ICC, Situation in the Republic of Côte D'Ivoire, Pre-Trial Chamber III, Decision Pursuant to Article 15 of the Rome Statute on the Authorisation of an Investigation into the Situation in the Republic of Côte d'Ivoire, Gbagbo, ICC-02/11-14, 3 October 2011, paras. 5–8 (http://www.legal-tools.org/doc/7a6c19/).

[122] ICC, *Prosecutor v. Francis Kirimi Muthaura, Uhuru Muigai Kenyatta and Mohammed Hussein Ali*, Pre-Trial Chamber, Decision on the Application by the Government of Kenya Challenging the Admissibility of the Case Pursuant to Article 19(2)(b) of the Statute, ICC-01/09-02/11-96, 30 May 2011 para. 12 (http://www.legal-tools.org/doc/bb4591/); ICC, *Prosecutor v. William Samoei Ruto, Henry Kiprono Kosgey and Joshua Arap Sang*, Pre-Trial Chamber II, Decision on the Application by the Government of Kenya Challenging the Admissibility of the Case Pursuant to Article 19(2)(b) of the Statute, ICC-01/09-01/11-101, 30 May 2011, para. 64 (http://www.legal-tools.org/doc/dbb0ed/).

of the ICC Statute.[123] According to the Court, the government only wrote to its police commissioner asking him to institute investigations into the post-election violence suspects two weeks after lodging the application challenging admissibility.[124] In its challenge, the government also claimed that there were ongoing investigations, which was not the case. In the opinion of the Court, there were no such investigations *at the time of the proceedings*. This, coupled with the failure to specifically mention the suspects before the ICC as some of the people under the government's investigation,[125] rendered the information given by the government inadequate to sustain the challenge. The Court emphasised that an investigation or national proceedings within the meaning of Article 17(1) must encompass substantially the same conduct in respect of the same people as at the time of the proceedings concerning the admissibility challenge.[126] This was contrary to Kenya's understanding of the notion of admissibility. In its submission, the government argued that the "national investigations must [...] cover the same conduct in respect of people at the same level in the hierarchy being investigated by the ICC".[127] Given that the investigations were with respect to all crimes committed during the 2007 post-election violence, the Court was uncertain as to whether the investigations involved the same people and crimes being investigated by the ICC.[128]

There is no doubt that the Kenyan government had panicked. The ICC process that seemed impossible was now certain and swift, prompting numerous government interventions to scuttle it. A challenge on the very admissibility of the cases seemed to be a necessary tool. According to one victim, however, at this level the victims were not very keen on the ICC process; they in fact wanted it to end as more local efforts were then being exerted towards reconciliation.[129]

---

[123] Kenyatta Confirmation Decision, paras. 56, 58, 61–62, 64-66, see *supra* note 17; Ruto Confirmation Decision, paras. 65–66, 68–69, see *supra* note 17.

[124] *Ibid.*

[125] Kenyatta Confirmation Decision, paras. 56, 61, 65–66, see *supra* note 17; Ruto Confirmation Decision, paras. 66, 69, see *supra* note 17.

[126] Kenyatta Confirmation Decision, paras. 49–52, 58, 64, 66, see *supra* note 17; Ruto Confirmation Decision, paras. 53, 55 and 70, see *supra* note 17.

[127] Kenyatta Confirmation Decision, paras. 48–49, 55–65, see *supra* note 17; Ruto Confirmation Decision, paras. 59–60, see *supra* note 17.

[128] *Ibid.*

[129] Interview with victim B, Eldoret, April 2016.

10.2.6. Confirmation of Charges

The confirmation of charges in the Kenyan cases covers the period between 1 September 2011 and 10 September 2013. On 1 September 2011 the Court began the first confirmation of charges hearing against Ruto and Sang. This was concluded on 8 September 2011. Confirmation of charges hearings in the Kenyatta and Muthaura case began on 21 September and were concluded on 5 October 2011.[130] On 23 January 2012 the ICC Pre-Trial Chamber confirmed charges against Ruto and Sang, and against Muthaura and Kenyatta. The charges against Muthaura were subsequently withdrawn on 18 March 2013. The trial against Ruto and Sang began on 10 September 2013.

Confirmation of charges is a pre-trial hearing held in order "to confirm the charges upon which the Prosecutor intends to seek trial".[131] With regard to this phase, there is one major conclusion which can be drawn: that the deterrence effect of the ICC was manifest through the certainty and swiftness of the ICC process. As a result of this deterrence, Kenya's political landscape and numerous government decisions relating to the ICC were redefined through the lens of the ICC decision on confirmation of charges. It is also clear that the ICC deterrent effect alone was not sufficient to cure the problems ailing Kenya, in particular the deep-rooted problems that informed violence and which subsequent governments have failed to prevent.

The 2013 general election illustrates how its political landscape was redefined, for good and bad. The difficulty with individual deterrence in a study of this nature is the challenge of empirically establishing that prosecution has deterred an individual. The challenge lies in the almost impossible act of measuring a perpetrator's state of mind. This notwithstanding, Julian Ku and Jide Nzelibe suggest an alternative and practical approach to establishing individual deterrence. This entails measuring the "correlation between the prosecution of certain crimes and the change in the levels of such crimes",[132] which can reflect behavioural change in the perpetra-

---

[130] Ruto Confirmation Decision, see *supra* note 17; Kenyatta Confirmation Decision, see *supra* note 17.

[131] ICC Statute, Article 61, see *supra* note 3.

[132] Julian Ku and Jide Nzelibe, "Do International Criminal Tribunals Deter or Exacerbate Humanitarian Atrocities?", in *Washington University Law Review*, 2006, vol. 84, no. 4, p. 791.

tors. The subsequent trend or track of civil hostilities, particularly related to elections, is therefore one of the indicators that this study adopts in establishing individual deterrence.

Although post-election violence occurred after the 2007 general election, there was a seeming total change in the events subsequent to the 2013 general election, which were relatively peaceful. The certainty and swiftness of an ICC intervention is likely to have put potential perpetrators on notice of a probable ICC arrest and prosecution, and affected their cost-benefit analysis in favour of not committing further crimes. This would confirm Payam Akhavan's thesis that in addition to the fear and conscious moral influence of punishment, prosecution is likely to create "unconscious inhibitions against crime, and perhaps to establish a condition of habitual lawfulness".[133] This would essentially instil the rule of law into the popular consciousness,[134] and both the legal and social norms that make the ICC Statute crimes had become both punishable and unacceptable in Kenyan society.[135] In this regard, the argument of some critics that ICC prosecutions make perpetrators more resistant to deterrence and more likely to perpetrate further atrocities[136] may not hold true in the Kenyan context, at least in so far as the general election of 2013 is concerned.

Of course, it may be too soon to cite this single election as a new norm, and even if it attains such status, the possibility of having such norms suspended amid desperate struggles to defend one's community, as suggested by James Alexander, may not be impossible.[137] The lack of violence may also have been informed by other factors unrelated to the deterrent effect of the ICC. For example, while acknowledging the minimal role played by the ICC in toning down political rhetoric, which normally sparks emotions leading to violence, a judicial source also observed that

---

[133] Payam Akhavan, "Justice in The Hague, Peace in the Former Yugoslavia", in *Human Rights Quarterly*, 1998, vol. 20, no. 4, p. 746.

[134] *Ibid.*, p. 746.

[135] Song, 2013, p. 209, see *supra* note 93.

[136] Nick Grono, "The Deterrence Effect of the ICC on the Commission of International Crimes by Government Leaders", Presentation for the Conference 'The Law and Practice of the International Criminal Court: Achievements, Impact and Challenges', at the Peace Palace, The Hague, 26 September 2012.

[137] John F. Alexander, "The International Criminal Court and the Prevention of Atrocities: Predicting the Court's Impact", in *Villanova Law Review*, 2009, vol. 54, p. 1.

the public has given up to whatever fate.[138] This implies that the public is disinterested in whatever goes on during the general election. Thus, sections of the public are most likely to be indifferent to any electoral malpractices that would otherwise trigger violence.

Finally, some have argued that the actual violence was only postponed.[139] This situation is likely to change in 2017 if similar repression continues, and thus Kenya is likely to experience real violence again. An MP's observations in an interview that the grievances leading to post-election violence in 2007 are still in place further supports this theory; these grievances are complex and far-reaching. At the centre is the land question that has consistently informed all the post-election violence from 1992 to 2007. While the ICC played a role in the calmness of the 2013 election, nothing has been done to address the deep-seated problems ailing the Kenyan community. The subsequent leadership has failed to "identify and address the causes of crime so as to create an environment that will render the commission of crimes less appealing and less likely".[140] While the ICC, in some instances, was essential in creating the necessary fear in perpetrators, targeted individuals and the general public, it is important that society broadly embraces crime prevention measures by addressing the underlying issues. Given the complex nature of the conflict, coupled with the deeply rooted ideology of ethnicity and related social and economic factors, the ICC should thus not be viewed as the sole necessary deterrent factor for atrocities.

Further undercutting the argument that the ICC had a positive impact is the possibility that election violence took place in 2013 after all, contrary to the perception of calmness. An expert lamented the government's restraint of the media in order to keep the public ignorant of any negative occurrences.[141] According to this expert, the party preliminaries, which had been characterised by violence, had laid the ground for numerous violations which did occur during the 2013 election, but which went unremarked because of the government's gagging of the media.[142] This was confirmed in an interview with a local journalist who acknowledged

---

[138] Interview with a judicial source, Nairobi, March 2016.

[139] Interview with a local journalist, Nairobi, May 2016.

[140] Schense, forthcoming, see *supra* note 73.

[141] Interview with an expert, Nairobi, April 2016.

[142] Ibid.

that the media had no independence in announcing the results of the elections, but rather that the Independent Electoral and Boundaries Commission fed all the media houses with results. Since electronic voting failed, the honesty of the results announced remained doubtful. According to this journalist, Kenya experienced covert violence in 2013, and many people were unhappy with the situation, including with the Supreme Court's decision upholding the election of the president and his deputy.

Expert W, however, acknowledges that the violations of 2013 were not equal to those of 2007 primarily because of two political factors: first, the former president Mwai Kibaki was not vying for election; and second, both Ruto and Kenyatta, previously political opponents, were now united on one election ticket. As Corradetti further correctly notes, it is the indirect and unforeseen deterrent effects of the ICC that triggered this inter-ethnic electoral alliance.[143]

Finally, the indictment and confirmation of charges occurred before Kenyatta and Ruto took office. Critics argue that Kenyatta used this indictment as a basis to leverage himself to power – either on the basis of sympathy[144] or through manipulation in order to better his bargaining power against the ICC at the international level. In separate interviews, one victim and an MP both agreed that any other person winning the 2013 elections as head of state would have meant that the ICC process would be accelerated to the detriment of Kenyatta and Ruto.[145] Thus, the ICC process provided the hub around which the 2013 election and its outcome revolved. Indeed, expert W underscored the fact that it is the feeling that one needed political power in order to keep the ICC away.[146]

According to a local journalist it is at this point – the coming to power of the president and his deputy – that the ICC cases were lost.[147] The ICC should not have expected a president and his deputy to fully co-operate with the Court and give evidence that would eventually incriminate them. This observation brings into perspective the nature of the challenge the ICC faces in achieving a deterrent effect where the individuals

---

[143] Corradetti, 2013, p. 259, see *supra* note 26.

[144] "Did the ICC Help Uhuru Kenyatta Win Kenyan Election?", in *BBC News Africa*, 11 March 2013.

[145] Interview with victim B, Eldoret, April 2016; Interview with an MP, Nairobi, March 2016.

[146] Interview with expert W, Nairobi, April 2016.

[147] Interview with a local journalist, Nairobi, May 2016.

sought are government leaders who are expected to co-operate with the Court.

Since ICC prosecutions in Kenya are against government leaders, the other indicator this study adopts in establishing individual deterrence is to track the government's decision-making both at the domestic and international levels. The act of confirming charges should influence how leaders behave, particularly in relation to decisions that have a correlation to their prosecution. For example, the government engaged in shuttle diplomacy both within the African Union and the UN seeking a deferral of the Kenyan cases. These efforts bore fruit when, after confirmation of charges, the African Union wrote to the Security Council seeking a deferral of both the indictment against Al Bashir and the ongoing Kenyan cases.[148] The subsequent inaction by the Security Council in these matters prompted the African Union to express its displeasure.[149] Not only did it call upon its members not to co-operate with the ICC in effecting the arrest and surrender of Al Bashir, but it also subsequently applauded its members that adhered to this call.[150]

10.2.7. The Trial Process

The trial process covers the period from 10 September 2013 when the trial against Ruto and Sang began, and 15 April 2016 when the Trial Chamber vacated charges. Deterrence in regard to this phase was affected by three factors: first, the government of Kenya's conduct in the 2015 Assembly of States Parties to the ICC Statute; second, the availability of evidence; and third, the African Union resolution on a collective withdrawal from the ICC Statute. These factors had a cumulative effect that led to a disintegra-

---

[148] Assembly of the African Union, Decision on Africa's Relationship with the International Criminal Court, Extraordinary Session of the Assembly of the African Union, Ext/Assembly/AU/Dec.1 (2003) 3, 12 October 2013 (http://www.legal-tools.org/doc/edad86/); ICC, *Prosecutor v. Uhuru Muigai Kenyatta*, Trial Chamber V(A), ICC-01/09-02/11, 5 December 2014.

[149] Assembly of the African Union, Decision on the Meeting of African States Parties to the Rome Statute of the International Criminal Court, 13th Ordinary Session, Assembly/AU/Dec. 243-267 (XIII), Rev.1 Assembly/AU/Decl.1- 5(XIII), Assembly/AU/Dec.245 (XIII), (ICC) Doc. Assembly/AU/13(XIII), 1–3 July 2009, p. 1 (http://www.legal-tools.org/doc/5f9085/).

[150] Assembly of the African Union, Decision on the Implementation of Decisions on the International Criminal Court, 26th Ordinary Session, Assembly/AU/Draft/Dec.3(XXVI) Rev.2, 30–31 January 2016, para. 3 (http://www.legal-tools.org/doc/057db3/).

tion of the ICC investigations and prosecutions leading to a withdrawal and vacation of charges in both the main Kenyan cases. This cumulative effect was also evident in the government's eventual success in thwarting the ICC process, which has an overall negative impact on deterrence.

On 10 September 2013 the trial against Ruto and Sang began. In relation to the first factor, Kenyan government action at the Assembly of States Parties, the commencement of this trial elicited two major events that undermined the deterrent effect of the ICC trial process. The first, following on from the killings of witnesses and recanting of evidence by others was the Trial Chamber V(A) ruling allowing the use of recanted evidence.[151] This decision prompted the second event, the decision of the Kenyan government to initiate discussion at the fourteenth session of the Assembly of States Parties, which reaffirmed the non-retroactive application of Rule 68 of the Rules of Procedure and Evidence, which allows the introduction of previously recorded evidence of a witness.[152] It should be noted that the ICC Appeals Chambers then overruled the Trial Chamber. It was the Appeals Chamber's view that the Trial Chamber erred in limiting the notion of detriment under Article 51(4) of the ICC Statute, which precludes a retroactive application of an amended rule of procedure or evidence if detrimental to an accused.[153] According to the Appeals Chamber, the term 'detriment' should be interpreted broadly, so as to avoid "that the overall position of the accused in the proceedings be negatively affected by the disadvantage".[154] In which case, this disadvantage or loss, damage or harm to the accused may include the rights of that person.[155] After giving due consideration to the procedural regime applicable in the Ruto and Sang case, the Appeals Chamber found the introduction of recanted evidence detrimental to the accused person. It is also notable that the African

---

[151] ICC, *Prosecutor v. William Samoei Ruto and Joshua Arap Sang*, ICC-01/09-01/11, Trial Chamber V(A), 5 April 2016.

[152] Assembly of States Parties to the Rome Statute of the ICC, 14th Session, Official Records, Vol. I, Advance version, ICC-ASP- 14/20, 18–26 November 2015, pp. 12–13, para. 61 (http://www.legal-tools.org/doc/8b9a53/). The ASP recalled its resolution ICC-ASP/12/Res.7 of 27 November 2013 amending Rule 68 of the Rules of Procedure and Evidence to allow the use of previously recorded witness evidence. This rule entered into force on the same date.

[153] ICC, *Prosecutor v. William Samoei Ruto and Joshua Arap Sang*, ICC-01/09-01/11, Trial Chamber V(A), 5 April 2016.

[154] *Ibid.*

[155] *Ibid.*

Union submitted *amicus curiae* observations on the subject to the Appeals Chamber in support of Ruto and Sang.

Second, with regard to the availability of evidence, on 5 December 2014 the Court terminated the case against Kenyatta for lack of evidence.[156] The prosecutor has since lamented that her lack of evidence was due to the following challenges:

> several people who may have provided important evidence regarding Mr. Kenyatta's actions, have died, while others were too terrified to testify for the Prosecution; key witnesses who provided evidence in this case later withdrew or changed their accounts, in particular, witnesses who subsequently alleged that they had lied to my Office about having been personally present at crucial meetings; and the Kenyan government's non-compliance compromised the Prosecution's ability to thoroughly investigate the charges, as recently confirmed by the Trial Chamber.[157]

The availability of evidence thus played out as a key factor on deterrence. For example, as the prosecutor noted, reported instances of killing of witnesses in order to tamper with ICC evidence became a common complaint. In this regard, the ICC charged three individuals, Walter Osapiri Barasa, Paul Gicheru and Philip Kipkoech Bett for offences against the administration of justice and comprising corruptly influencing ICC witnesses.[158] Despite the Court issuing an arrest warrant against Barasa on 2 August 2013, and against Gicheru and Bett on 10 March 2015,[159] the government has been adamant that it will not co-operate with the ICC in their arrest and surrender. The president has publicly declared that "Kenya has closed the ICC chapter [...] we will not allow anyone else to be taken anywhere [...] we have our courts here [...] no other Kenyan will walk the ICC path

---

[156] ICC, *Prosecutor v. Uhuru Muigai Kenyatta*, Notice of Withdrawal of the Charges against Uhuru Muigai Kenyatta, ICC-01/09-02/11-983, 5 December 2014.

[157] ICC, Statement of the Prosecutor of the International Criminal Court, Fatou Bensouda, on the withdrawal of charges against Mr. Uhuru Muigai Kenyatta, Office of the Prosecutor, 5 December 2014; ICC, *Prosecutor v. Walter Osapiri Barasa*, Pre-Trial Chamber II, ICC-01/09-01/13, 2 August 2013.

[158] ICC, *Prosecutor v. Paul Gicheru and Philip Kipkoech Bett*, Pre-Trial Chamber II, ICC-01/09-01/15, 24 September 2015.

[159] ICC, *Prosecutor v. Walter Osapiri Barasa*, Pre-Trial Chamber II, ICC-01/09-01/13, 29 October 2015; ICC, *Prosecutor v. Paul Gicheru and Philip Kipkoech Bett*, Pre-Trial Chamber II, ICC-01/09-01/15, 24 September 2015.

as we have done".[160] This confirms the argument that "certainty of apprehension […] may be the more decisive factor if we were able to penetrate the decision-making calculus of would-be war criminals".[161] If would-be criminals are certain of government support against ICC apprehension, this vitiates the ICC's deterrent effect while encouraging the further commission of crimes. On several occasions, the prosecutor decried the government's refusal to give documentary evidence that was crucial for the cases. It can therefore be deduced that availability of evidence for the prosecution was a key deterrent factor, which the government has consistently sought to undermine.

MP N, however, blames the killing of ICC witnesses on a poor ICC witness protection programme.[162] Not only did the Office of the Prosecutor rely on witnesses procured by other institutions, they also failed to offer them effective protection.[163] MP N notes that it is during this period that Kenya experienced a drastic reduction of terrorist acts, particularly in Nairobi.[164]

Third, the government through the African Union repeatedly sought to have the case against Ruto terminated.[165] These efforts informed the January 2016 African Union resolution calling upon a ministerial committee to develop "a comprehensive strategy including collective withdrawal from the Court".[166] Not everyone took these actions seriously. An MP, in an interview, described the African Union as a big joke.[167] According to

---

[160] KTN NEWS, "Jubilee Leaders Descended on Afraha Stadium for Much Hyped Prayer Rally", 16 April 2016.

[161] Schense, forthcoming, see *supra* note 73.

[162] Interview with MP N, Nairobi, March 2016.

[163] Ibid.

[164] *Ibid.*

[165] Assembly of the African Union, Decision on the Progress Report of the Commission on the Implementation of Previous Decisions on the ICC, Assembly/AU/Dec.547(XXIV), Doc. Assembly/AU/18(XXIV), 2015, para. 17 (d); Assembly of the African Union, Decision on the Progress Report of the Commission on the Implementation of decisions on the ICC, EX.CL/Dec.914 (XXVIII), Executive Council 28th Ordinary Session, 2016, para. 2.

[166] Assembly of the African Union, Decision on the Implementation of Decisions on the International Criminal Court, Assembly/AU/Draft/Dec.3(XXVI)Rev.2, 26th Ordinary Session, 30–31 January 2016, para. 8(4) (http://www.legal-tools.org/doc/057db3/); Assembly of the African Union, Decision on the Progress Report of the Commission on the Implementation of Decisions on the International Criminal Court (ICC), EX.CL/Dec.914(XXVIII), Executive Council 28th Ordinary Session, 2016, para. 2 (vii) d.

[167] Interview with an MP, Nairobi, March 2016.

this MP, the attempt by the African Union to use a regional mechanism to sabotage the ICC was ill-informed. While agreeing with the MP, a local journalist retorted that this withdrawal action did not come by surprise.[168] It was the journalist's view that the African Union comprises "godfathers of impunity", the majority of whose members engage in similar atrocities with impunity. Indeed, an expert criticised the African Union for continuously creating weak institutions.[169] Another judicial source, however, quickly qualified this by condemning Africa as its own enemy. He cited South Sudan as an example of how Africa brings doom upon itself. According to this expert, the Constitutive Act mandates the African Union to maintain peace and security.[170] Therefore, there should not be any conflict between the ICC and the African Union as the latter should be encouraged to embrace complimentary mechanisms that assist it in achieving its objective.

While some found the African Union's arguments and efforts laughable, others found them believable. A victim shared the sentiment with some judicial sources that underlying the African Union's reaction is the perception that the ICC is biased towards Africa, and that, while atrocities greater in magnitude than those witnessed in Africa are occurring in other parts of the world, the ICC seems only concerned with African cases. This echoes the work of some academics that for both "legal and political reasons" international prosecutions are likely to "almost exclusively" target offenders in weak or failed states.[171] These beliefs can undermine the perceived legitimacy of the Court, as Dietrich asserts, because "deterrence works best when criminals accept both the law and the courts as legitimate".[172] This legitimacy is informed by the idea of "fair and equal treatment".[173]

All these negative efforts finally culminated in the Trial Chamber vacating charges against Sang and Ruto on 15 April 2016. Emerging from the interview with an MP, the political class has begun to view the ICC as

---

[168] Interview with a local journalist, Nairobi, May 2016.

[169] Interview with an expert, Nairobi, April 2016.

[170] African Union, Constitutive Act of the African Union, 11 July 2000, Articles 3(e), (f) (http://www.legal-tools.org/doc/496299/).

[171] Ku and Nzelibe, 2006, p. 785, see *supra* note 132.

[172] Dietrich, 2014, p. 9, see *supra* note 33.

[173] *Ibid.*

mere "hot air".[174] Continuing public utterances by the political class that is likely to spur violence indicates the dimming deterrence effect of the ICC. For example, the MP Moses Kuria has publicly incited his constituents thus: "that is why I asked you to come with your *pangas* [machetes]. Those *pangas* are not just for clearing bushes. Use them to slash those opposed to the NYS [National Youth Service] project".[175] Seemingly, the cost-benefit calculations of a probable ICC prosecution among the Kenyan political class continue to favour the culture of committing atrocities for political ends. These acquittals, according to an MP, not only confirm this changed perspective on the ICC among the political class but also render the deterrent effect of the ICC to zero.[176] Indeed for ICC deterrence to operate the potential perpetrators must believe in the certainty of an ICC prosecution and punishment and that the incentive to offend must not be so strong as to outweigh the risk of punishment.[177] The contrary is however true in the Kenyan context. Thus, if anything triggers violence in the aftermath of 2017 election, Kenya is likely to experience one of the worst forms of violence since ICC deterrence no longer exists. The political class, which contains the potential perpetrators, already disregards probable ICC prosecution and punishment.

According to one victim, with all those initially under ICC indictment now free, the deterrent effect of the ICC has come to naught.[178] Citing the ICC's perceived lack of genuineness, victim B further lamented the ICC's withdrawal of all key Kenyan cases. According to victim B, this indicated that the ICC had finally succumbed to the pressure exerted by the African Union at the expense of the entire population of the victims.[179] In the opinion of victim B, the ICC was caught in the dilemma of choosing between effectively prosecuting the Kenyan cases or losing the entire African region, and they chose the latter.[180] Terming it a dangerous move,

---

[174] Interview with an MP, Nairobi, March 2016.

[175] Kenya Broadcasting Corporation, "Tobiko Orders Muthama, Ngunyi Be Charged over Hate Speech", 6 October 2015.

[176] Interview with an MP, Nairobi, March 2016.

[177] Kate Cronin-Furman, "Managing Expectations: International Criminal Trials and the Prospects for Deterrence of Mass Atrocity", in *International Journal of Transitional Justice*, 2013, vol. 7, no. 3, p. 442.

[178] Interview with a victim, Nairobi, April 2016.

[179] Interview with victim B, Eldoret, April 2016.

[180] *Ibid.*

a victim further observed that Africa could now engage in grave violations with impunity.[181] According to yet another victim, if the ICC was acting for the good of the Kenyan nation, it would not have terminated these cases but delayed them at least until Kenyatta and Ruto were out of power.[182] Interestingly, several other victims affiliated with Kenyatta and Ruto's political party expressed their joy over the termination of the ICC cases in support of their party leaders.[183]

In this regard, several MPs, experts and some victims forecast the 2017 elections will be extremely violent. An MP and an expert further point out some telltale signs that Kenya is in an incubation period to a probable escalation of violence, including ongoing interethnic violence in Molo and Njoro, deployment of tanks in opposition areas, suppression of democracy by intimidating the opposition, alleged grand corruption in key institutions – the Supreme Court and the Independent Electoral and Boundaries Commission – allegedly in favour of one community, the Kikuyu, and the unequal standards in the war on graft.[184] The fact that sections of the public lack confidence in the Independent Electoral and Boundaries Commission and the Supreme Court, coupled with the likelihood of not having these two institutions properly constituted before 2017 general election amid a likely hotly contested election, further dims the picture. These are recipes for violence where more lives are expected to be lost.[185] Presumably, having failed to achieve its retributive objective in the Kenyan context, the ICC is unlikely to deter future similar crimes that may arise out of the desire for ethnic revenge.

A judicial source, however, disagrees with the probability of there being violence in 2017.[186] According to this source, the major historical protagonists in successive post-election violence in 1992, 1997 and 2007 are the Kikuyu and Kalenjin communities.[187] Not only are these two

---

[181] Interview with a victim, Nairobi, April 2016.

[182] Interview with victim B, Eldoret, April 2016.

[183] "Integrated Victims Cry Foul", in *Kenya Broadcasting Corporation*, 5 February 2016. All the victims interviewed by the KBC expressed their joy over this termination.

[184] Expert W observed that the government seems to be vigilant in fighting corruption where individuals from the opposition are involved as opposed to alleged corruption scandals involving individuals in the ruling party, Jubilee.

[185] Interview with MP N, Nairobi, March 2016; Interview with expert W, Nairobi, April 2016.

[186] Interview with a judicial source, Nairobi, April 2016.

[187] *Ibid.*

communities in government leadership, but the Kalenjin have also achieved their original objective, the driving away of the Kikuyu community from the Rift Valley region.[188] This source further observes that as a result of the election-related violence, one can hardly find a region within the Rift Valley settled only by the Kikuyu.[189] The majority of the Kikuyu community have sold their land and moved away.[190] As such, there may be no Kikuyu to be fought, come 2017. This judicial source opines that the initiators of the 2007 violence rationally calculated the cost-benefits of the violence and decided to pursue their goal of expanding their territory. Violence was therefore inevitable regardless of the costs when compared to the larger benefit of acquiring land while driving out the Kikuyu community.

Victim B, a Kikuyu, however disagrees with this judicial source.[191] In victim B's opinion, not all Kikuyus have left the Rift Valley.[192] In fact, the majority of those who left – including the interviewee – have since gone back.[193] The only reason why there may be no violence is that no single Kikuyu is likely to register as a voter in the Rift Valley. As such, there will be no Kikuyu to fight during elections.[194]

10.2.8. Convictions

Although there have been no convictions in the Kenyan cases, conviction is a key process in measuring the deterrent effect of the ICC. First, there is the transnational effect of Lubanga's conviction on 14 March 2012, which intensified the government's efforts towards a deferral of the ICC cases. Lobbying within the region and the UN intensified during this time, perhaps because of the realisation of the increased prospects of an ICC conviction. Again, complaints by the prosecutor about mysterious deaths and recanting of evidence broadened during this time. On the same note, it is also feared that a conviction of either Kenyatta or Ruto would have creat-

---

[188] *Ibid.*
[189] *Ibid.*
[190] *Ibid.*
[191] Interview with victim B, Eldoret, April 2016.
[192] *Ibid.*
[193] *Ibid.*
[194] *Ibid.*

ed political martyrs.[195] Their local sympathisers are likely to have engaged in more violence in protest.[196] If this were the case, then MP N's suggestion that jailing does not necessarily solve the deep-rooted problems would make sense, thus necessitating a cohesive and more conciliatory approach as opposed to retribution. Of course, this is again speculative, as there were no full trials or convictions in the Kenya situation at the ICC.

10.3. Kenya's Challenges at Experiencing the Deterrent Effect of the ICC

One key factor hinders Kenya from experiencing the deterrent effect of the ICC: the lack of political will informed by a culture of impunity among the political class. The political class perceives itself to be above the law and not only lacks respect for local institutions, only showing some respect when convenient, but has also initiated numerous efforts to undermine the deterrent effect of the ICC. A judicial source may be therefore correct when observing that if Kenya is to experience the deterrent effect of prosecuting post-election violence-related cases, one must first tame the mind of the political class through sanctions or some other form of external pressure.[197]

Lack of political will emanates from poor leadership. As correctly observed by an MP, successive post-independence governments have been at the centre of the problems ailing the nation.[198] The inequality in resource allocation and the inability to find any redress from weak institutions makes the situation sad. The high proportion of unemployed youths, who form the majority of the youth, worsens the situation. This group that seemingly has lost hope and can easily be procured to supply the required manpower necessary for violence.

This confirms Ku and Nzelibe's observation that more atrocities are committed in weak or dysfunctional states because "they have more *opportunities* to do so, and not because they have a greater *inclination* to commit such atrocities".[199] Strong institutions act as a constraining factor

---

[195] Interview with MP N, Nairobi, March 2016.

[196] *Ibid.*

[197] Interview with a judicial source, Nairobi, March 2016.

[198] Interview with an MP, Nairobi, March 2016.

[199] Ku and Nzelibe, 2006, p. 780, see *supra* note 132.

on the ability of potential offenders to mobilise violent groups and engage in large-scale humanitarian atrocities. Weak states, by contrast, lack the necessary "structures needed to facilitate the rule of law and government control".[200] While powerful states have strong state institutions and are therefore likely to adhere to the ICC's standards and requirements of investigations at the domestic level, thus reducing the chances of such countries getting to the ICC, Kenya's institutions and the legal system are fragile and susceptible to political interference. For example, although Kenya is headed for another hotly contested election in 2017, the most critical institutions – the Independent Electoral and Boundaries Commission and the Supreme Court – suffer a lack of public trust due to allegations of corruption. This total lack of trust in key domestic institutions is likely to contribute to more violence that may lead to violation of rights. Civil society, which would have offered an alternative to channel constructive political demands, is also weak and lacks political trust.

10.4. Conclusion

This chapter demonstrates that the ICC has had some deterrent effect in Kenya, albeit of limited impact and duration. During its initial stages, this impact was not significant due to three factors: first, lack of knowledge of the Court's procedures and prosecutorial strategies among the public and the perpetrators; second, a specific convergence of local politics that lessened the chances of support for domestic judicial mechanisms that could have promoted deterrence; and third, systemic problems with domestic mechanisms that have proved difficult under any circumstances to address.

Over time, the certainty and swiftness of the Court procedures dawned on the population, and while levels of violence, particularly during the 2013 elections, seemed to decline, the ICC's actions at the same time catalysed anti-ICC sentiments not just among the local political class but also regionally. Central to these views was the fear of a probable ICC trial and conviction. While perpetrators running as electoral candidates were arguably discouraged from using outright violence to attain power, the two indicted candidates still sought power to shield themselves from justice, and some argue still engage in clandestine atrocities to achieve their aims.

---

[200] *Ibid.*, p. 812.

The government also committed itself to undertake extensive constitutional and institutional reform processes. This could theoretically have demonstrated a commitment to justice under the rubric of positive complementarity. Nonetheless, these efforts did not come to fruition because they were not genuine. Coupled with the government's efforts to secure an Article 16 deferral of the Kenya situation at the ICC, to encourage other states parties to withdraw, and Parliament's overwhelming support for Kenya's potential withdrawal from the ICC, these reveal a deliberate disinterest on the part of the government to support genuine justice initiatives at any level and, by definition, undermined deterrence. Thus this chapter demonstrates that factors that can in general enhance the ICC's deterrent effect in fact hindered deterrence because of the government's lack of political will to render them genuine.

Additionally, the certainty of the ICC's intervention is what subsequently informed the government's initiative through the African Union resulting in a resolution for a regional withdrawal from the ICC, and its initiatives through the Assembly of States Parties to cripple the ICC's ability to move forward with its Kenyan cases in the face of witness tampering and interference. Indeed, some of the victims interviewed perceived the withdrawal of all cases as succumbing to African Union pressure. Following the termination of all the key Kenyan cases, the deterrent effect of the ICC has waned. It is therefore feared that this may trigger more violence when the opportunity presents itself.

This chapter has further demonstrated that the ideology of ethnicity is still rife in Kenya, despite ICC efforts ostensibly to address the situation even-handedly, and despite the government's response mechanisms. This ideology is likely to play out in the 2017 general election, as the seeds of hatred and discord for certain tribes has manifestly been planted in the population. The incentive of achieving the objective of this ideology – to get rid of certain tribes or teach them a lesson - might, yet again, lead to the perpetuation of more atrocities.[201] This problem is further compounded by the limited nature of the ICC's deterrent effect. Following the termination of all Kenyan cases, part of the population has expressed its fear over the uncertain nature of the ICC process and for the impunity gap now created.

---

[201] Tom Buitelaar, "The ICC and the Prevention of Atrocities Criminological Perspectives", Working Paper 8, The Hague Institute for Global Justice, 2015, p. 14.

10.5. Recommendations

This study makes the following recommendations, both specific – based on the Kenyan context – and general in nature.

10.5.1. Recommendations on the Office of the Prosecutor's Prosecutorial Strategy

The Office of the Prosecutor should avoid even the appearance of whole-sale reliance on investigations done by domestic and other institutions. It should ensure that it is understood that it undertakes its own independent investigations from the grassroots, and identifies its own witnesses. For example, it is damning that the prosecution of the police failed totally both at the ICC and locally. No single police officer has been convicted at the ICC and at the local level despite an estimated 962 cases of police shootings, which resulted in 405 deaths.[202]

10.5.2. Recommendations to the Court

In situations like Kenya, according to an MP, the ICC should encourage and facilitate a holistic approach that remedies the deep-rooted causes of violence. Focusing only on retribution is superficial. It should increase its outreach role to enable people to understand it better. For example, one of the reasons why the ICC initially had no deterrence to the public and political class is that they did not understand the Court's operations and the Office of the Prosecutor's strategy. This contributed to numerous failed local attempts at prosecution, which may have assisted in capacity building of local institutions but could have further informed how to address the root causes to violence.

At the regional level the ICC should closely and actively engage with regional political institutions. For example, the Court should have continuously engaged the African Union member states with respect to its procedures and decisions, and sought their opinion on some controversial matters. This could, for instance, include their physical audience or reports on all the African-based situations and cases. This would enhance co-operation between the Court and African states parties and would also keep African states aware of the Court and its activities.

---

[202] Commission of Inquiry into Post-Election Violence, 2008, pp. 472–75, see *supra* note 6.

The ICC should, through an amendment of its Rules of Procedure and Engagement, seek to bar people indicted by the Court from assuming political power in their respective countries. Otherwise, it is impossible to expect an indictee to effectively co-operate with the court in his or her own case. Finally, through collaboration with the UN Security Council, the ICC should seek to adopt some police powers.

10.5.3. Recommendations to State Parties

States parties to the ICC Statute should be encouraged to embrace positive complementarity and shun negative complementarity. The ICC should be actively involved in reviewing acts of states in various situations and cases in order to ensure positive complementarity. They should seek to hold each other accountable for more genuine efforts to promote justice.

10.5.4. Recommendations to Civil Society

Kenyan civil society should be encouraged to bolster its presence as it offers a viable alternative to aggrieved members of the political class or the public to channel their grievances.

11

The Deterrence Effect of the International Criminal Court in Côte d'Ivoire

Kounkinè Augustin Somé[*]

11.1. Introduction

The International Criminal Court ('ICC') entered a situation in Côte d'Ivoire following the post-electoral crisis of 2010–2011 during which serious crimes were committed. Violence ensued after the Constitutional Council declared the incumbent president Laurent Gbagbo the winner in a closely contested election, while the opposition and international community claimed that the opposition leader Alassane Ouattara had actually won. Both the opposition and the international community viewed the subsequent confirmation of Gbagbo's re-election by the Constitutional Council on 3 December 2010 and swearing in on 4 December 2010 as illegitimate acts.[1] Indeed, global and regional intergovernmental bodies, including the Economic Community of West African States ('ECOWAS'), the African Union's Peace and Security Council and the United Nations ('UN') Security Council formally recognised Ouattara's election.[2] Violence accompanied by egregious violations of human rights by both sides began even as Gilbert-Marie Aké N'gbo, the prime minister appointed by Gbagbo, named his cabinet which began running the polarised country.

---

[*]   **Kounkinè Augustin Somé** LL.B. (Ouagadougou), D.E.A. (Nantes, Paris XII) LL.M. (Pretoria-American University, Cairo), is a graduate in international human rights law with specialisation in human rights and democratisation in Africa and humanitarian assistance. He has experience in the areas of human rights, democratic governance and peace building. He has worked with the Parliament of Burkina Faso as a Parliamentary Legal Affairs Officer and has over 12 years' experience of human rights fieldwork with the United Nations. He was the Winner of the Vera Chirwa Award (2013) on human rights, instituted by the University of Pretoria (Centre for Human Rights) to recognise an alumnus/alumna who epitomises the true human rights lawyer by making a difference to the protection of human rights or the strengthening of democratisation in Africa. The author would like to thank Dr. Godfrey Musila who kindly reviewed an earlier draft of this chapter.

[1]   Constitutional Council of Côte d'Ivoire, CI-2010-EP-34/03-12/CC/SG, Decision, 28 November 2010.

[2]   United Nations Security Council, Resolution 1975, UN doc. S/RES/1975 (2011), 30 March 2011, para. 1 (http://www.legal-tools.org/doc/05ed67/).

Five months later, on 11 April 2010, forces loyal to Ouattara arrested Gbagbo.[3] After a short period of detention in the northern part of the country, he was transferred to the ICC on 30 November 2011 where, jointly with the former leader of the pro-Gbagbo Congrès panafricain des jeunes et des patriotes ('Young Patriots') and youth minister in his government, Charles Blé Goudé,[4] he stood trial on charges of crimes against humanity of murder, attempted murder, other inhumane acts, rape and persecution.[5]

Côte d'Ivoire has been a state party to the ICC since 15 February 2013, when it ratified the ICC Statute. However, to vest jurisdiction in the Court to investigate and try crimes committed during the conflict that started on 19 September 2002, the Gbagbo government deposited an *ad hoc* declaration on 18 April 2003 in accordance with Article 12(3) of the ICC Statute granting jurisdiction to the Court.[6] Following his assumption of power in May 2011,[7] Ouattara recommitted his country to the declaration on 14 December 2010 and requested that the Court investigate crimes committed since March 2004,[8] the date on which government forces massacred over 105 opposition protesters in Abidjan.

On 23 June 2011 the Office of the Prosecutor invoked Article 15 of the ICC Statute and requested Pre-Trial Chamber III to authorise an investigation into crimes committed in Côte d'Ivoire in the post-election period starting on 28 November 2010, the date of the contested election. Four months later, on 3 October 2011, the Pre-Trial Chamber granted the prosecutor's request on the terms specified, and with regard to crimes that may have been committed in the future if such crimes were linked contextually to those committed before that date.[9]

---

[3] "Ivory Coast's Gbagbo Arrested – Live Updates", in *The Guardian*, 11 April 2011.

[4] Charles Blé Goudé was transferred to the ICC on 22 March 2014.

[5] International Criminal Court ('ICC'), *Prosecutor v. Laurent Gbagbo*, Pre-Trial Chamber, Decision on the Confirmation of Charges against Laurent Gbagbo, ICC-02/11-01/, 12 June 2014 ('Gbagbo Confirmation Decision') (http://www.legal-tools.org/doc/5b41bc/).

[6] République du Côte d'Ivoire, Déclaration de reconnaissance de la Compétence de la Court Pénale Internationale, 18 April 2003 (http://www.legal-tools.org/doc/036bd2/).

[7] Ouattara was sworn in on 6 May 2011 and an inauguration ceremony held of 21 May 2011.

[8] For Ouattara's letter, see République du Côte d'Ivoire, NR 0039-PR, 14 December 2010.

[9] ICC, Pre-Trial Chamber, Decision Pursuant to Article 15 of the Rome Statute on the Authorisation of an Investigation into the Situation in the Republic of Côte d'Ivoire, ICC-02/11-14, 3 October 2011 (http://www.legal-tools.org/doc/7a6c19/).

This was the second time that the prosecutor had invoked his *proprio motu* powers under Article 15 of the ICC Statute to trigger the jurisdiction of the ICC and initiate an investigation, having done so a year earlier in relation to the situation in Kenya in November 2009.

On the Pre-Trial Chamber's orders, the prosecutor filed additional information on 4 November 2011 pursuant to Rule 50(4) of the Rules of Procedure and Evidence to support authorisation to investigate crimes committed before 28 November 2010. Based on these new elements, the Pre-Trial Chamber expanded the investigation on 22 February 2012 to include crimes within the jurisdiction of the Court allegedly committed between 19 September 2002 (in respect of which the declaration was made in 2003) and 28 November 2010 (the date of the contested election).[10] This period covers crimes allegedly committed after the attempted coup in 2002 by Forces Nouvelles rebels led by Guillaume Soro, who would later on join Gbagbo's government as a minister and subsequently become prime minister under Gbagbo following agreements brokered in January 2003 and March 2007. Based on these two successive decisions, the ICC has jurisdiction over crimes against humanity and war crimes committed in Côte d'Ivoire from 19 September 2002.

11.1.1. Content and Structure

This chapter discusses the deterrent effect of the ICC in Côte d'Ivoire. It is not possible to provide a comprehensive view that tracks the procedural steps of the Court's process from entry into the situation to the post-conviction stage when issues of sentences and reparations are settled, and so its focus is limited to deterrence at the trial stage, which is as far as the ICC process has reached at the time of writing. The backdrop is the fluid and evolving situation in Côte d'Ivoire, where the national judiciary has convicted tens of pro-Gbagbo partisans for crimes unrelated to the ICC in 2014,[11] and where trials for crimes against humanity, especially that of

---

[10] ICC, Pre-Trial Chamber, Decision on the Prosecution's Provision of Further Information Regarding Potentially Relevant Crimes Committed between 2002 and 2010, ICC-02/11-36, 22 February 2012 (http://www.legal-tools.org/doc/de6177/).

[11] Simone Gbagbo was sentenced to 20 years in prison for "crime against the authority of the state, participation in an insurrectionary movement and disturbing public order" during the post-election crisis of 2010. General Brunot Dogbo Blé, former commander of the Republican Guard, and Admiral Vagba Faussignaux, former navy commander, were also sentenced to 20-year terms.

Simone Gbagbo, the wife of Laurent Gbagbo, are ongoing. This chapter therefore endeavours to assess whether the mere existence of the ICC is a deterrent in the current context of Côte d'Ivoire, and whether prosecutions of key leaders have a deterrent effect to the extent of discouraging the commission of crimes now and in the future. To reach a conclusion, the author interviewed different categories of respondents, including alleged perpetrators and like-minded individuals, victims, subject matter experts from civil society, members of the Ivorian judiciary and members of international organisations operating in the country.

The chapter is composed of five sections. The current introductory section briefly recalled the background of the ICC's entry into the situation in Côte d'Ivoire. Section 11.2. gives details of the Ivorian crisis and an overview of the ICC intervention focusing on the case against Laurent Gbagbo and Blé Goudé and that of Simone Gbagbo. Section 11.3. summarises the views and perceptions of the respondents about the deterrent effect of the ICC and its intervention in Côte d'Ivoire. Reflecting these views and perceptions, section 11.4. discusses factors that impact on the deterrent effect of the ICC in Côte d'Ivoire. The final section concludes this chapter with some recommendations for the ICC and the international community in the future.

11.2. The Ivorian Crisis and an Overview of ICC Intervention

What came to be known as the Ivorian crisis has its roots in a failed coup attempt against Laurent Gbagbo in 2002, two years after his election following a short transitional government led by retired General Robert Guéi, who had taken over in 1999 after the ousting of Henry Konan Bédié in a coup d'état. The 2002 coup was led by a coalition of rebel forces mainly from the north of the country led by Gillaume Soro. The Forces Nouvelles had mobilised against the government in response to nationalistic fervour stoked by Bédié under the slogan "*ivoirité*", through which he sought to mobilise southerners against the northern population, seen as largely immigrant. The *ivoirité* criterion of parentage had been used to block the former prime minister Alassane Ouattara from running for the presidency in 1995 on the grounds that he was of Burkina Faso ancestry. For someone to seek the presidency, the law required that both parents must be Ivorian. Between 2002 and 2010 Gbagbo presided over an unstable government, but managed to stay in power by sharing power negotiated in a series of peace agreements that would yield a commitment to and a timeline for holding elections, which were postponed several times before they were eventually conducted in 2010.

11.2.1. Gbagbo and Blé Goudé

Gbagbo and Blé Goudé are currently on trial on four counts of crimes against humanity. Arriving at the Court three years apart, the charges against each were confirmed in separate hearings. Following his arrest in a bunker in Abidjan, the Ivorian authorities handed over Gbagbo to the ICC on 30 November 2011 and he made his first appearance before the Pre-Trial Chamber five days later on 5 December 2011. On 12 June 2014 the Pre-Trial Chamber confirmed four charges of crimes against humanity, namely murder, rape, inhumane acts or, alternatively, attempted murder, and persecution.[12] The Ivorian authorities handed over Blé Goudé to the ICC on 22 March 2014 pursuant to an ICC arrest warrant issued on 21 December 2011. At the end of the confirmation hearing held between 29 September and 2 October 2014, the Pre-Trial Chamber confirmed the same four charges against him. As in Gbagbo's case, the prosecution alleged that the crimes were committed in Côte d'Ivoire between 16 December 2010 and 12 April 2011 or thereabouts.[13]

On 11 March 2015 the Trial Chamber granted the prosecutor's request to join the two cases on the grounds of ensuring efficiency and expeditious proceedings, which is a right of the accused. According to a press release,[14] the Trial Chamber also noted that, although their alleged participation in or contribution to the conception and implementation of the common plan or purpose was not the same, the conduct of Gbagbo and Blé Goudé was closely linked. A further justification was that largely the same evidence had been and would be disclosed and presented in both cases. It would therefore serve the interests of justice and it would not prejudice the accused to avoid duplicating presentation of a significant body of evidence, to avoid hardship and reduce witness exposure. The

---

[12] Gbagbo Confirmation Decision, see *supra* note 5.

[13] ICC, *Prosecutor v. Charles Blé Goudé*, Pre-Trial Chamber, Decision on the Confirmation of Charges against Charles Blé Goudé, ICC-02/11-02/11-186, 11 December 2014 (http://www.legal-tools.org/doc/0536d5/).

[14] ICC, "ICC Trial Chamber I Joins the Cases Concerning Laurent Gbagbo and Charles Blé Goudé", Press Release, ICC-CPI-20150311-PR1097, 1 March 2015.

joint trial began on 28 January 2016 and, as of October 2016, several prosecution witnesses had testified.[15]

11.2.2. Cases against Simone Gbagbo

The third person to be indicted for crimes committed during Côte d'Ivoire's post-election violence in 2010 was Simone Gbagbo, the former First Lady. At the Prosecutor's request, the Pre-Trial Chamber issued a sealed arrest warrant on 29 February 2012, which was unsealed on 22 November 2012. Simone Gbagbo, like Laurent Gbagbo and Blé Goudé, was charged under Article 25(3)(a) as an indirect co-perpetrator of crimes against humanity that targeted Ouattara supporters. According to the arrest warrant, she allegedly was part of a group of which Laurent Gbagbo and Blé Goudé formed part, that conceived a plan to keep Laurent Gbagbo in power by all means, including through the use of violence which she knew would result in the commission of crimes against humanity. Côte d'Ivoire refused to surrender her and filed an admissibility challenge on 1 October 2013, which the Pre-Trial Chamber rejected on 11 December 2014.[16] Côte d'Ivoire argued in its application that proceedings relating to the same charges (crimes against humanity) against the same person (Simone Gbagbo) were ongoing in Côte d'Ivoire, a proposition that did not convince the Pre-Trial Chamber, which concluded that the "domestic authorities were not taking tangible, concrete and progressive steps aimed at ascertaining whether Simone Gbagbo is criminally responsible for the same conduct that is alleged in the case before the Court". It consequently ordered Côte d'Ivoire to surrender the suspect to the ICC without delay. Three days after the pre-Trial Chamber's decision, on 14 December 2014, Côte d'Ivoire appealed; the Appeals Chamber subsequently confirmed the lower chamber's decision on 27 May 2015, declaring the case against Simone Gbagbo admissible before the ICC.

A couple of months before the Appeals Chamber rendered its decision, the authorities in Abidjan put Simone Gbagbo and 82 other individuals on trial, charged with disturbing public order and attacks on national

---

[15] ICC, *Prosecutor v. Laurent Gbagbo and Blé Goudé*, Trial Chamber, Decision Adopting Amended and Supplemented Directions on the Conduct of the Proceedings, CC-02/11-01/15, 4 May 2016 (http://www.legal-tools.org/doc/7c836b/).

[16] ICC, Case Information Sheet: Situation in Côte d'Ivoire, *Prosecutor v. Simone Gbagbo*, ICC-02/11-01/12, 24 February 2016.

security. She was convicted on 10 March 2015 and sentenced to a prison term of 20 years.[17] Other accused drawn from the ranks of pro-Gbagbo supporters and members of the militia were sentenced to varying prison terms. While one may speculate about the reasons for the refusal to surrender Simone Gbagbo to the ICC, it is possible that, as is frequently the case for post-conflict governments, trials are staged in the aftermath with the aim of generating legitimacy for a post-conflict government while galvanising its core constituency. The trial of Simone Gbagbo, a highly visible and divisive figure in Ivorian politics, and one who was seen by some as a key pillar of the fallen regime, could have such an effect. Indeed, her case in which 15 individuals were reportedly acquitted, together with that of her husband and Blé Goudé in The Hague, was cited by some respondents and commentators to support a thesis of partial justice that had thus far targeted only one side of the conflict. This deep-seated perception of unfairness undermines the moral standing of the ICC and has a far-reaching impact on how it is viewed in Côte d'Ivoire, and could as a result undermine its deterrent mission. One observer we talked to during this study commented:

> The prosecutorial strategy adopted by the ICC in Côte d'Ivoire [...] (one side first, the other after) affects its deterrent effect because this strategy is not convincing. It would be beneficial for the ICC to also prosecute the winners' camp. The Court has opened room diverse in interpretation [...] This strategy gives the impression that the ICC has already chosen its camp. This creates doubts.

Ouattara's suggestion that Côte d'Ivoire will not surrender any other national to the ICC also supports the view that the government sees the ICC's job as done.[18] Some could see a more sinister motivation in the refusal to surrender Simone Gbagbo. One expert has argued that she has been kept to forestall any indictments or demands for surrender of individuals in the Ouattara camp should the prosecutor of the ICC indict them. In essence, she is some sort of 'buffer' to public opinion and pressure for Ouattara to co-operate with the Court on any future demands to surrender individuals from his own camp.

---

[17] Jeune Afrique, "Verdict 'scandaleux' Condamnés à verser 965 milliards de dommages et intérêts à l'Etat: vers la saisie des biens des pro-Gbagbo?", 11 March 2015.

[18] "Alassane Ouattara: No More Ivorians Will Go to ICC", in *BBC News*, 5 February 2016.

On 9 May 2016, three years after Côte d'Ivoire had claimed to have the capacity to prosecute Simone Gbagbo for crimes against humanity and three months after Ouattara reportedly affirmed that no other national would be surrendered to the ICC, Simone Gbagbo's trial for international crimes committed during the post-election violence in 2011 opened in Abidjan. She is on trial for "crimes against civilian populations, crimes against prisoners of war, and crimes against humanity".[19] She was initially accused of genocide, crimes against civilians, crimes against prisoners of war, murder, rape, assault and battery, collusion, coercion and attempt offences, assaults and crimes against humanity. In a joint statement, several non-governmental organisations ('NGOs') – the International Federation for Human Rights ('FIDH'), Ligue ivoirienne des droits de l'homme ('LIDHO', Ivorian Human Rights League) and Mouvement ivoirien de droits de l'Homme ('MIDH', Ivorian Movement for Human Rights) who claim to represent almost 250 victims – announced their decision to boycott the trial on the grounds that their "lawyers have not had access to all stages of the proceedings". In this regard, Patrick Baudouin, honorary president of the FIDH, declared on the plaintiffs claiming damages on behalf of the victims:

> The denial of our basic rights as organisations representing the victims has deprived them (the victims) of expressing their views on the conduct of the procedure. They were deprived of the exercise of all rights related to their status as victims participating fully in the legal proceedings.[20]

11.3. Perceptions about Deterrent Effect of the ICC

Although there are common trends in perceptions about the ICC's role in Côte d'Ivoire, this section details group perceptions, particularly those that may have a bearing on the deterrent effect of the ICC by reason of being viewed as a 'serious' court that affects the behaviour of civilians, political leaders, armed actors and the military or security forces. Perceptions matter at multiple levels. With respect to deterrence, a court that is viewed as efficient, fair and responsive in the sense of acting appropriately and speedily to investigate and mount trials where there is credible

---

[19] Chambre d'accusation de la Cour d'appel d'Abidjan, Arrêt no. 29, Affaire Ministère Public contre Simone Ehivet épouse Gbagbo, 27 January 2016.

[20] Patrick Baudouin, "Avocats des parties civiles, nous ne participerons pas au procès de Simone Gbagbo", in *Jeune Afrique*, 30 May 2016.

evidence of commission of crimes within its jurisdiction would in all likelihood act as a stronger deterrent than one that is not. Indeed, perceptions among sections of the population, and particularly perpetrators or those likely to commit crimes, that the court is a willing, able and speedy actor are likely to influence behaviour and cause them to alter their calculations. In this regard, as Mark A. Drumbl warns, the probability of being apprehended plays a significant role in the calculations:

> One reality that deterrence theory must contend with is the very low chance that offenders ever are accused or, if accused, that they ever are taken into the custody of criminal justice institutions. Selectivity is especially corrosive to the deterrent value of prosecution and punishment. [...] Moreover, being brought into custody to face trial is one thing: actually being convicted is another.[21]

Some commentators argue that the mere existence of the ICC has a deterrent effect because it sends the message to perpetrators and potential perpetrators that they will face justice should they commit crimes.[22] In a global context, however, M. Cherif Bassiouni observes that deterrence may not work with certain tyrants of the past, but it certainly does for those younger individuals that are usually used by others, and that the ICC provides the conditions and incentives for them to disobey unlawful orders.[23] It is argued that while the mere existence of the ICC, and particularly the fact that it is a permanent court, is dissuasive, this effect can only be enhanced when the Court acts competently and firmly when crimes are committed, and conducts its proceedings in a manner that communicates seriousness to the world and to perpetrators.[24] On fairness and deterrence, one commentator writes that there are perceptions that portend risks for the impact of the ICC and whether it can act as a deterrent: "They relate to public perceptions of just how fair the drive for international justice is, and how effective local procedures can be. Perceptions matter. Not con-

---

[21] Mark A. Drumbl, *Atrocity, Punishment, and International Law*, Cambridge University Press, New York, 2007, pp. 169–73.

[22] Action Mondiale des Parlementaires, "Une Cour Pénale Internationale de dissuasion – Objectif Fondamental".

[23] *Ibid.*

[24] *Ibid.*

fronting them can nourish longer-term grievances that could re-emerge as violence'.[25]

In the case of Côte d'Ivoire, representatives of civil society and the international community have expressed the view that a prosecutorial strategy that has so far involved charging only one side of the conflict portrays the Court as biased, warranting its dismissal as a political actor. However, the fact that the ICC is seen as biased does not necessarily erode its power to persuade if it acts decisively and conducts proceedings competently and in a timely manner.

The respondents interviewed for this study appreciate the deterrent effect of the ICC differently. Collectively, respondents are informed of the existence of the Court even if it exists in a world removed from that which most of them inhabit, and has not, until recently, been part of their daily realities. For a proportion of them, the ICC is considered to be a court that upholds justice for the weakest in society. For others, it is a court of law for countries that have ratified the ICC Statute, with a mandate to try the most serious crimes, crimes against humanity, mass atrocities and crimes of genocide. Another segment is aware of the Court's restorative function, whereby victims of human rights violations can receive reparations. For this group, the Court has made the fight against impunity a reality. For a small section of interviewees, the political dimension of the Court's work is highlighted with the Court being seen as a neo-colonial body essentially created for use against Africans or less powerful states. They argue that the ICC lacks credibility because of the selective nature of its work both in terms of targets and the crimes it can prosecute. The following sections highlight the views of six categories of respondents" the perpetrators and similarly placed individuals and groups, victims' organisations, civil society, state institutions and international organisations.

11.3.1. Perpetrators

Due to lack of direct access to those currently on trial before the ICC or domestic courts, their legal counsel was contacted. Also interviewed were people who had fought on both sides of the conflict, including Young Pa-

---

[25] Alex Vines, "Does the ICC Help End Conflict or Exacerbate It?", Expert Comment: Chatham House, Royal Institute of International Affairs, 23 February 2016.

triots and members of Commando invisible.[26] Generally, interviewees in this category felt as a whole that the Court has a deterrent effect. However, this effect is limited by the continuing policy of the prosecution that is selective and does not include everyone who has committed offences. One of the interviewees indicated: "It is a deterrent; however, this deterrent effect is limited by the prosecution system that is selective and does not target all kinds of criminals". Also, the complementarity with national courts and the limited number of offences within the Court's jurisdiction are an obstacle to its deterrent effect. It is the view of some interviewees that the Court could be described as ineffective in view of the repeated commission of serious crimes falling within its jurisdiction. Moreover, the low number of states parties to the ICC Statute is explained by the politicisation of the Court and its lack of credibility. All these highlighted weaknesses contribute to diluting the deterrent effect of the Court in the view of these interviewees.

Some in this group hold the view that for more effective international criminal justice, the Court should have primacy over national courts. In addition, the prosecutorial strategy should be inclusive and not target only a portion of the protagonists of the conflict. It would also be more deterrent if its jurisdiction was to be expanded to include other crimes, presumably suggesting that the failure to prosecute crimes that do not rise to the level of international crimes undermines the ICC's potential for deterrence. They further express the view that the Court should be more independent to be able to fight more effectively against impunity. On the other hand, for them, lending the Court executive powers through the creation of an armed force is unrealistic.

These respondents proposed solutions to enhance the deterrent effect of the Court. For instance, they suggested that the deterrent effect of the ICC would be enhanced through depoliticisation of its work and through the implementation of coercive measures against states that refuse to co-operate with the Court in its investigations and prosecutions. One respondent stated: "The ICC must show that it is a truly independent [court] from political powers; in addition, there should be action against states that refuse to co-operate". A legal commentator has echoed this

---

[26] Commando invisible is a militia which is believed to have fought alongside pro-Ouattara forces and contributed to the fall of Gbagbo. Its leader, known as IB, was killed on 27 April 2011 during a Forces Nouvelles commanders' intervention.

concern that the enforcement measures provided for in the ICC Statute – reliance on the Security Council and Assembly of States Parties –have turned out to be weak in appropriate cases.[27] In the case of Côte d'Ivoire, at least one instance in which enforcement measures could have been invoked but were not relates to the refusal of the government to surrender Simone Gbagbo on orders of the Chambers, which had taken the view that Côte d'Ivoire's admissibility challenge failed ICC Statute criteria.

11.3.2. Similarly Placed Individuals to Those on Trial

This category of respondents includes people close to Laurent Gbagbo's camp, either as members of his political party, including the youth branch, or militiamen who fought for him during the crisis. People believed to be close to Ouattara's side were also interviewed and include his party members and elements that were part of Commando invisible that fought on his side during the conflict. People in this classification have knowledge of crimes punishable by the ICC. For them, massive violations of human rights, crimes against humanity, the destruction of cultural heritage registered by United Nations Educational, Scientific and Cultural Organisation, war crimes, violent crimes, rape, economic crimes, ecological crimes, and exploitation of minors in armed conflict constitute grave acts punishable by the Court.

For a segment of this category, the ICC is a very important institution that must exist. However, to achieve its objectives, the Court needs to be strengthened in its ability to be fair, transparent and equitable. By its very existence, it deters the commission of crimes. This effect would be enhanced if the Court rigorously exercised its powers. For another subgroup, the existence of the ICC is not a deterrent for potential perpetrators because this justice is not equally made and it is selective.

Some respondents believe that the presence of the Court during the Ivorian electoral crisis in 2011 helped to prevent potential violations of human rights because all major actors were aware of the Court's existence. But it is also their view that crimes committed with this knowledge are likely to have been 'crimes of passion'. It was thought that the existence of the ICC had no impact on the quantum of violations of human rights

---

[27] Gwen P. Barnes, "The International Criminal Court's Ineffective Enforcement Mechanisms: The Indictment of President Omar Al Bashir", in *Fordham International Law Journal Volume*, 2011, vol. 34, no. 6, pp. 1584–1619.

because the perpetrators acted out of anger and were motivated by revenge. Others consider that the ICC's power to dissuade perpetrators was wholly absent during the crisis. This is explained by its silence during this time and its intervention only at the end of hostilities. One interviewee commented: "It intervened after all was spoiled; a post-crisis intervention". Some interviewees felt that the Court could be encouraging impunity in the procedures used by the Office of the Prosecutor, in part because it is considered as "victors' justice", which targets only the vanquished. Evidently, the deterrent effect of the ICC is mixed for this segment of interviewees, especially those close to Laurent Gbagbo's camp. One such interviewee compared this with the situation in domestic justice processes where crimes continue to be committed despite severe sentences being passed.

On the effectiveness of the Court, the responses of interviewees fell into two categories. While some believe that the Court was effective, others thought that it was not credible and that it was partial, slow and unfair. Opinions were equally divided on the government's decision not to surrender any more citizens to the ICC, in reference to Ouattara's statement in early 2016. Some respondents considered it to be the expression of the sovereign functions of the state, while others saw the move as flight by the government, and an unfair decision that could even be described as irresponsible.

Turning to the question concerning the ability of the Ivorian justice system to prosecute crimes within the Court's jurisdiction, some interviewees believed that Côte d'Ivoire now had the capacity to prosecute international crimes, but concerns lingered on whether the prosecution services would operate independently of political influence. For other respondents, the justice system is not independent and is corrupt; consequently, Côte d'Ivoire cannot try these crimes impartially.

Notwithstanding these differences, respondents in this category were unanimous on the factors that diminish the deterrent effect of the ICC: the lack of extension of the instruments, mechanisms and actions of the Court, the length and slowness of procedures, political manipulation, and failure to apply the principles of justice, partiality and political influence. As a solution, all the respondents in this category advocated the development of a healthy collaboration between the ICC and states in order to avoid conflicts; the development of effective communication channels; demarcation from the ruling regimes; strengthening of self-referrals to the prosecutor; effective and efficient management of the affairs of the Office of the Prosecutor; and strengthening investigation and prosecution beyond declarations of intent. This was summarised by one political figure interviewed:

> This is because there is not enough communication about the activities of the ICC. In Côte d'Ivoire, there is the Ivorian Coalition for the ICC, for instance, which has worked in this direction; otherwise Ivorians are not sufficiently informed. There must therefore be enough resources to help organisations carry out a lot of awareness of the ICC on the ground. This would allow Ivorians to know that the ICC is not there for a particular category of people.

11.3.3. Victims' Organisations

Interviewees for this category included victims and various organisations responsible for some of the victims of the crises in Côte d'Ivoire. The existence of the ICC was for some of them a guarantee of security for victims because the Court works neutrally and influences states. For others, the ICC created or exacerbated insecurity for victims because it acted in a partisan manner, and this could create security risks for victims and witnesses, as was the case at a hearing in March 2016 when the name of a witness was revealed over the public address system. They were of the view that targeting a section of perpetrators encourages the commission of crimes by actors who no longer fear that they run the risk of being caught and prosecuted, not to mention being punished.

On the deterrent effect of the Court, some interviewees believed that it was not truly a deterrent because the Office of the Prosecutor's approach had generated disenchantment among pro-Gbagbo supporters and the temptation for revenge was high. For another segment of interviewees, the Court has a deterrent effect by its mere existence and the quality of the work it does.

Regarding the location of the Court and how its distance from the theatre of violence factors into deterrence and the safety of victims, responses were mixed. The conduct of trials in situation countries where crimes had been committed carries enormous security risks for victims and attacks or intimidation from supporters of suspects are heightened. However, access to justice is critical for victims, and attempts should be made by the ICC to hold trials in Africa, with South Africa cited as a potential host of the ICC.

11.3.4. Civil Society

Civil society groups interviewed included both local and international NGOs working on broad human rights issues but also on specific themes such as transitional justice, the fight against impunity and accountability. For them, the ICC has not helped mitigate the massive violation of human rights during the Ivorian crisis. The Court's existence, and the fact that the government had deposited a declaration triggering its jurisdiction in 2003, does not appear to have had a bearing on the conduct of the parties to the conflict. This is due in part to lack of knowledge about the Court among belligerents and the general public.

Overwhelmingly, respondents were of the view that the existence of the ICC alone has had no impact on the number of victims that the conflict eventually generated. For them, the deterrent effect of the ICC was more noticeable after the issue of the arrest warrants and the conduct of trials. Some took the view that the status of those targeted by the ICC (in this case a former president and an influential minister) and the severity of punishment that may be handed down by the Court could have a deterrent effect on potential perpetrators.

The interviewees believed that through its action in Côte d'Ivoire, the ICC can help end impunity provided lessons are drawn from the trial and successfully internalised, but this depends on whether all actors are prosecuted and on the Court acting impartially and fairly. On the issue of lessons, commentators were hopeful, as civil society representatives were, that Côte d'Ivoire and the ICC could both learn from the experience. Noting that the descent into violence in 2010 showed that Côte d'Ivoire leaders failed to avoid the mistakes made in Liberia, a neighbouring country whose former President Charles Taylor is serving 50 years in jail for war crimes, one commentator argues that the ICC prosecutions can secure peace but hopes that the ICC itself can learn from this experience.[28] However, civil society representatives are cognizant of the fact that the prosecution is unlikely to succeed if Côte d'Ivoire does not co-operate fully with the Court, something that could result in non-prosecution by the ICC, thus perpetuating impunity. Ouattara's statement that the Côte d'Ivoire

---

[28] Vines, 2016, see *supra* note 25.

government will not surrender more nationals to the ICC should be seen in this light. While acknowledging that targeting only one side to the conflict creates perceptions of bias, one commentator was of the view that Côte d'Ivoire's "à la carte approach to the ICC might enhance stability",[29] but the judicial authorities must take deliberate steps to investigate and prosecute individuals from Ouattara's group.

In terms of the government's position that it would not surrender Ivorians to the ICC, respondents believed that the legal system does not sufficiently take into account the serious crimes as defined by the ICC Statute. This decision could also be described as political and simply serves to appease sections of the population that are hostile to the Court. For them, the state cannot fail to comply with its international commitments.

Regarding the impact of the ICC on general election held in 2015, some respondents believed that the presence of Gbagbo and Blé Goudé at the ICC contributed to a peaceful election. They were unanimous on the important role that civil society has to play in enhancing the deterrent effect of the Court, which includes contributing to outreach to educate the public since access to information about the work of the Court is critical for deterrence.

11.3.5. Views of State Actors within the Criminal Justice System

The accountability process aimed at addressing crimes and human rights violations committed in Côte d'Ivoire has been patchy, selective, underfunded, uncoordinated and has proceeded without an overarching policy and requisite political will.[30] Until April 2016, when Simone Gbagbo was put on trial for crimes against humanity, Côte d'Ivoire had taken minimal steps to prosecute serious crimes committed during the post-election violence in 2010 as crimes under the jurisdiction of the ICC. Other than the surrender of Laurent Gbagbo and Blé Goudé to the ICC, investigations at the national level into international crimes committed by both sides to the conflict had been slow, and targeted only the pro-Gbagbo groups. It is reported that other than the mass trial of 83 pro-Gbagbo individuals including Simone Gbagbo for crimes against state security, not a single trial for

---

[29] *Ibid.*

[30] On the domestic accountability project in Côte d'Ivoire with particular reference to prosecutions, see International Center for Transitional Justice, "Disappointed Hope: Judicial Handling of Post-Election Violence in Côte d'Ivoire", April 2016.

crimes against humanity has been concluded in ordinary civilian courts. Moreover, the special inquiry and investigation unit established in 2013 to investigate and prosecute serious crimes linked to the 2010 election, Cellule spéciale d'enquête et d'instruction, is beset with serious challenges, including a lack of prosecutorial strategy and political will, that have undermined its work. By 2014 the military court had tried only four cases, with five others under investigation. This is the context in which interviews for this chapter with officials from relevant state institutions were conducted.

Interviewees include those that drove the state institutions, serving judicial professionals and high-level state advisers on justice issues. It was their view that it was too early to study or judge the impact of the ICC in Côte d'Ivoire, particularly from the perspective of deterrence. However, they recognised that the ICC helped to secure a peaceful election in October 2015. They thought that, on balance, the Court was important because it helped to fight against impunity and serious crimes, prosecuted individuals who would otherwise not be prosecuted in national courts, and thus contributed to ending the culture of impunity.

For them, the creation of an armed force of the ICC to help the Court enforce its orders was not necessary to reinforce the deterrent effect of the Court. Joining the ICC is voluntary, and it is essential to strengthen co-operation between the Court and states and to provide sufficient resources to enable it to conduct its investigations and prosecutions of serious crimes.

On the complementarity of the ICC with national courts, the respondents did not regard the actions of national courts as impacting negatively or undermining the deterrent effect of the ICC. It was rather the expression of the sovereignty of states. Also, in response to the views of others that the ICC should also prosecute lesser crimes which would net smaller fish, respondents did not think that the expansion of the Court's jurisdiction was a solution because the ICC would lose its special character and be overburdened. It was their view that what was needed was to enhance the resources available to the ICC.

On continuing the strategy adopted by the ICC in Côte d'Ivoire, interviewees described it as selective. This gives the impression that the Court is biased. For them it was important that all those responsible were able to answer for their actions before the Court, and that prosecutions took place concurrently.

For these respondents, lack of access to information about the Court had a direct bearing on deterrence and, despite the existence of the Court, many crimes were still occurring because of ignorance of the Court and the contempt of some for it. They unanimously recognised that the ICC had weaknesses that reduced its deterrent effect, which included the principle of legality and non-retroactivity which limits its temporal jurisdiction, administrative delays, lack of funding and the politicisation of the Court's work, particularly at the level of prosecutions.

To address these shortcomings, some respondents proposed the creation of a court in Africa. However, they stated that it should be created to complement the ICC and national jurisdictions, and not to sidestep international justice and perpetuate impunity. Others believed that this step is unnecessary and that what is required is to strengthen national courts and the implementation of the principle of complementarity that regulates the relationship between the ICC and national courts.

To enhance the deterrent effect of the ICC, they proposed that it would require a more robust outreach programme, the pursuit of those who bore the greatest responsibility, impartiality in the conduct of trials, the strengthening of co-operation between the ICC and states, and strengthening capacity of national courts to conduct free and fair trials. It would also be vital to provide the ICC with substantial resources, expand the recruitment field of competent judges and strengthen regional accountability mechanisms such as the African Court of Justice and Human Rights.

11.3.6. International Community

In African situations in particular, the international community has become an essential partner in processes created to establish accountability for human rights violations and international crimes. In Côte d'Ivoire, the international community, through the UN and individual donor states, has played an important role during the Ivorian crisis that touches on accountability. Various UN agencies, including the Office of the High Commissioner for Human Rights and the United Nations Operation in Côte d'Ivoire ('UNOCI') in particular, have been involved not only in documenting crimes but also in building the capacity of national institutions to investigate and prosecute crimes and in providing resources to finance specific activities. However, as UNOCI winds down its work, its potential role and that of the international community decreased significantly in 2014 when the Security Council dropped the rule of law from its mandate.[31] The lack of finances that bedevils the accountability process in Côte d'Ivoire is due in part to the diminishing role of the UN at a time when its input is still most needed, and a reported exclusion of transitional justice from the €23 million pledged by France to the rule of law programme to be disbursed over three years (2014–2017).[32] In preparation for its closure by June 2017 as directed by the latest Security Council resolution on Côte d'Ivoire,[33] UNOCI is finalising a plan to transfer residual functions to other partners. It is important that sufficient resources continue to be devoted to support and consolidate the gains in the area of the fight against impunity.

The interviewees in this category, who included officials of the African Union Office in the country and professionals from UNOCI, had different views on the deterrent effect of the Court. For some, the ICC was theoretically dissuasive. It was a weapon against impunity. For others, however, the Court was not a deterrent because of the lack of binding force, policy and political influence in the judicial chain, and the Office of the Prosecutor's prosecutorial strategy. To strengthen the deterrent effect of the Court, the ICC should be invested with executive powers (an armed force) to be able to enforce its decisions. This opinion was not shared by all respondents as some believe that the only weapon that the ICC had that could enhance its deterrent effect was the co-operation of states. This should be strengthened to achieve the objectives of the Court.

In terms of complementarity of the Court with national courts, some respondents proposed that the ICC should have primacy over national courts. For others, the Court was not created to replace national courts; it should therefore keep the complementarity and work to strengthen the capacity of national courts. Regarding the Court's jurisdiction, respondents were unanimous that the enlargement of the offences within the sphere of

---

[31] On the current mandate of UNOCI, see United Nations Security Council, Resolution 2162, Renewing Mandate of United Nations Operation in Côte d'Ivoire, UN doc. SC/11450 (2014), 25 June 2014 (http://www.legal-tools.org/doc/8ab882/).

[32] International Center for Transitional Justice, 2016, see *supra* note 30.

[33] United Nations Security Council, Resolution 2284, UN doc. S/Res/2284 (2016), 28 April 2016 (http://www.legal-tools.org/doc/639da2/).

jurisdiction of the Court could make it more of a deterrent, but that a broader mandate could overwhelm the Court. The Court should rather work on enhancing its credibility and confidence to have a greater deterrent effect. Also, the Office of the Prosecutor strategy should be reviewed for fairness.

Some also believed that it is not feasible to indict serving heads of state, who have all the state resources at their disposal which they deploy to undermine the investigations with potentially disastrous results. In case of failure, indictment of serving heads of state alters the deterrent effect of the Court. Also, the principle of independence of the ICC was not fully respected and its independence was compromised by the factors given above. All these weaknesses affected its deterrent effect. Despite these shortcomings, the respondents pointed out that the Court was effective and called on people not to lose hope given the massive and complex nature of crimes punishable by the ICC, which were in any case imprescriptible.

On forms of dissuasive international criminal courts, the interviewees proposed the integration of measures relating to universal jurisdiction as a palliative, and refuted the idea of creating another Court. They proposed strengthening the ICC in financial, material and human resources, and working with civil society organisations to enhance accountability and to eliminate duplication of effort in the areas of training and outreach.

11.4. Factors That Impact on the Deterrent Effect of the ICC in Côte d'Ivoire

Factors that influence the deterrent effect of the ICC can be classified into court-based and external or contextual factors. Respondents mainly highlighted external factors which negatively affected the deterrent effect of the Court. These included politics, national trials, outreach and mechanisms to enforce decisions. The only court-based factor that was alluded to by respondents was the prosecutorial strategy.

11.4.1. Court-Based Factors

11.4.1.1. Prosecutorial Strategy

If certainty and speed of action on the part of the ICC are central to its deterrence, then a prosecutorial strategy that emphasises co-operation and thus forbearance from proceeding against pro-Ouattara partisans is detrimental to the Court, in part because it is viewed as indecisive and weak, but also because it elicits perceptions of unfairness from the public as illustrated above. The ICC's inability to secure the custody of Simone Gbagbo is detrimental for the Court for the same reasons, as it has fallen victim to what one commentator referred to as Abidjan's *à la carte* approach to the ICC. It is evident to many that the perceived partiality of the justice process, which is linked to the exercise of prosecutorial strategy in selection of cases, weighs heavily against the ICC's esteem and its capacity to dissuade in Côte d'Ivoire. On the fact that the ICC has indicted only individuals in the Gbagbo camp, Human Rights Watch sees this one-sided focus of charges as having a negative bearing on impact. They argue: "The absence of cases to date for crimes committed by pro-Ouattara forces means that so far the OTP has missed the mark in selecting cases in a manner likely to maximise impact in the country".[34]

In terms of which crimes charged so far arise from events in Abidjan, respondents further suggested that reflecting the patterns of violence and charging individuals from all parties involved in conflict are good for deterrence, with one noting that prosecuting only one side "does not convince anyone" about the fairness and seriousness of the ICC. Ouattara's assertion in February 2016 that he will not transfer any other Ivorian to stand trial at the ICC guarantees that this will remain unchanged. This step, while guaranteeing that pro-Ouattara perpetrators are unlikely to be tried at the ICC, at least while he holds office, essentially removes the ICC from the list of options for justice after the Gbagbo and Blé Goudé trial. If it stands, it renders moot any discussion of deterrent effect of the ICC or, at best, it fatally undermines the deterrent edge of the Court *vis-à-vis* Côte d'Ivoire where the only serious initiative to prosecute perpetrators for crimes against humanity has only begun, and as in the case of the ICC also targets only pro-Gbagbo supporters, including Simone Gbagbo.

---

[34] Human Rights Watch, "Making Justice Count: Lessons from the ICC's Work in Côte d'Ivoire", August 2015.

11.4.2. External Factors

11.4.2.1. Politics

The saga that is playing out at the ICC around the Gbagbo and Blé Goudé trial is tinged with domestic politics, and the defence has sought to capitalise on this. This 'politicisation' of the ICC process has had an impact on how it is viewed, and by extension could reduce its deterrent effect. The fact that trials both at the ICC and in Côte d'Ivoire have targeted only one side has created the impression of continuity of the two distinct legal spheres, and that both processes have been politicised to the detriment of the opposition. Indeed, the current trial of Simone Gbagbo for crimes against humanity is overshadowed by the earlier trial for crimes against security of the state, with its overwhelming political overtones. Some commentators have noted Abidjan's calculated approach to the question of justice, driven in part by the desire to consolidate power while being less than assiduous in investigations that target government supporters and collaborators in the 2010 conflict.[35] Beyond a handful of trials, investigations have been slow and the government appears to increasingly take actions that favour reconciliation, including the release of some of those convicted with Simone Gbagbo in the first trial, and encouraging the return of influential pro-Gbagbo partisans exiled after the conflict in 2010. On 1 July 2016 the minister for solidarity, social cohesion and reparation of victims, Mariatou Koné, reportedly stated while receiving returning exiles that an amnesty law is being drafted.[36]

11.4.2.2. Complementary National Trials

If the ICC's deterrent effect is enhanced or the Court's power to dissuade individuals from committing crimes is greater when opportunities to enjoy impunity nationally are eliminated through robust national prosecutions, then the absence of such an initiative in Côte d'Ivoire not only lowers the esteem of national courts and the ICC but also undermines its ability to dissuade individuals from committing crimes. Many respondents believed that the capacity of national courts to prosecute crimes should be enhanced, although some took the view that the ICC should have primacy

---

[35] International Center for Transitional Justice, 2016, see *supra* note 30.
[36] "Côte d'Ivoire: retour de quatre pro-Gbagbo, dont l'ancien ministre de la défense Kadet Bertin", in *Jeune Afrique,* 1 July 2016.

over national courts. With the question of fairness being central to perceptions of national and ICC prosecutions, preference for the ICC over national courts was perhaps informed by its perceived capacity for fairness. Indeed, the view of some respondents that the subject matter jurisdiction of the ICC should be expanded was partly informed by the desire to "widen the net" and to try other perpetrators from both sides of the political divide.

11.4.2.3. Outreach

During its early years, the ICC adopted an approach of keeping a low profile which was highly detrimental to its image. The Court's silence or limited and ineffective communication has resulted in false rumours and misconceptions about its work. The Office of the Prosecutor was motivated to keep a low profile by security concerns for both witnesses and Office staff. Although one may think that this is a sensible approach, it proved damaging. The work of the Court was not well known, and decisions of the Office of the Prosecutor with major ramifications were not explained to the public. The lack of information on why the Office pursues one case and not another, or why it only brings certain charges, can give the impression of a lack of transparency. This impression may induce the perception that the Court is not impartial and independent.

In Côte d'Ivoire, it is claimed that the Court's outreach programme has been less than adequate and that its law, processes and work are not well known. Its interaction with civil society mirrors that in other situations: civil society representatives complained that the Court no longer collaborates with the Coalition ivoirienne pour la Cour pénale internationale (Côte d'Ivoire Coalition for the ICC), and that it has ignored advice from local organisations that have intimate knowledge of the situation, including its politics, actors and challenges. This is baffling given the limited resources at the disposal of the outreach office, which is inadequately staffed. Its field outreach officer arrived only in October 2014, three years after the ICC began its work and during which period it had conducted several sessions attended by a total of 500 people drawn from the community, media, legal community and civil society.[37] The scope of outreach is framed by the cases and is thus narrow, yet it confronts a prosecutorial charging policy that has elicited concerns of bias on the part of the

---

[37] Human Rights Watch, 2015, p. 46, see *supra* note 34.

ICC. Overall, it is reported that "the Court's outreach strategies have been ill-equipped to engage polarised opinion about the court in Côte d'Ivoire".[38]

11.4.2.4. Mechanisms for Enforcing Decisions

In an interview with the *New York Times* on 2 April 2006, the former ICC prosecutor Luis Moreno-Ocampo, explained his helplessness in the face of state intransigence: "I'm a stateless prosecutor – I have a 100 states under my jurisdiction and zero policemen".[39] Unlike the *ad hoc* tribunals which had primacy over national jurisdictions and are reinforced by the obligations imposed on states to co-operate with the tribunal by the UN Security Council, the ICC lacks executive powers and has a weak enforcement mechanism, consisting of the Assembly of States Parties for situations triggered by the Office of the Prosecutor and states, and the Security Council itself for those it refers.[40] The failure by the ICC to take custody of Simone Gbagbo, coupled with the announcement that no other Ivorian will face justice at the ICC, portrays the Court as weak and undermines its power to persuade perpetrators. Indeed, in the face of a weak criminal justice system in Côte d'Ivoire, Abidjan's declaration could plant the seed of impunity and undermine the ICC's broader preventative goal, when the ICC is marginalised through non-cooperation and yet national authorities are either unable or unwilling to prosecute.

11.5. Conclusions and Recommendations

11.5.1. Conclusion

This study has considered the deterrent effect of the ICC in Côte d'Ivoire, a state that accepted the jurisdiction of the Court in 2003 by *ad hoc* declaration, and renewed it in 2010 before eventually ratifying the ICC Statute in 2015. The situation in Côte d'Ivoire is still evolving, the case facing Laurent Gbagbo and Charles Blé Goudé having started at the end of January 2016. The review of the Court's processes thus related to an assessment of whether the mere existence of the ICC is deterrent in the Côte

---

[38] Human Rights Watch, 2015, p. 46, see *supra* note 34.

[39] Elizabeth Rubin, "If Not Peace, Then Justice", in *New York Times*, 2 April 2006.

[40] ICC, Rome Statute of the International Criminal Court, 17 July 1998, in force 1 July 2002, Article 87(7) (http://www.legal-tools.org/doc/7b9af9/).

d'Ivoire context, and whether the indictment of key leaders, confirmation of charges and the eventual commencement of the trial have produced a deterrent effect at each stage such that perpetrators, like-minded individuals, and the general public are dissuaded from committing crimes.

While it is often asserted that the mere existence of the ICC can be a deterrent, particularly in a broader African context where the ICC has been active since 2006, this chapter has established that the ICC may not have featured in the calculations of the protagonists as the country descended into violence for five months that eventually left 3,000 people dead after the Court's initial intervention. It is instructive to note that the Court's jurisdiction had been triggered seven years earlier. It seems that contests for political power in deeply divided societies like Côte d'Ivoire – where ethnicity features prominently in electoral politics and where factors exist such as deep-seated hatred and sentiments of revenge distort rational calculation by individuals – overcome the ICC's power to dissuade.

The study also finds that the ICC is considered by many as having a deterrent effect, as evidenced by the peaceful election in October 2015. Among factors cited by respondents as reinforcing the deterrent effect of the ICC are the status of individuals targeted, and that Gbagbo's presence in the dock has sent a strong message that even the most powerful are not beyond the reach of the ICC. However, there is a widespread feeling that the ICC, more specifically the Office of the Prosecutor, has adopted a sequencing strategy that leads to the conclusion that the Court has effectively targeted only one side of the conflict. As reinforced by Abidjan's declaration that it will not surrender any more citizens to the Court, it means that this situation will not change. This chapter also established that the ICC process is seen as politicised, and this perception of partiality undermines the Court's esteem in the eyes of many in Côte d'Ivoire, particularly when the government has refused to hand over Simone Gbagbo and has adopted a stance that could be detrimental to the Court's work when the current case is concluded. The study also analysed court-based and contextual factors that enhance or undermine the ICC's deterrent effect, including prosecutorial strategy, outreach and structural flaws in the ICC Statute, including limits in jurisdiction and politics.

11.5.2. Recommendations

11.5.2.1. Assembly of States Parties

To strengthen the ICC's co-operation framework, and to enhance respect for decisions of the Court that have a bearing on deterrence, the Assembly of States Parties should establish coercive measures against states that refuse to co-operate. Even compared with the UN Security Council, which fails to enforce decisions arising out of situations it refers to the Court, the Assembly of States Parties' enforcement modality is considerably weaker, yet it is the mainstay of the ICC's enforcement mechanisms. In addition to bilateral pressures, consideration should be given to wider measures, including recourse to the Security Council.

The paucity of resources constrain the operations of the Court and limit the scope of its work in terms of situations it can take up and cases at the level of prosecutorial strategy. It is recommended that the Assembly of States Parties provides financial, human and material means to increase the Court's capacity to intervene and, for the prosecutor, the means to invest in the prosecution of a larger number of perpetrators from any particular situation to reflect the pattern of crimes, and to avoid the appearance of partiality caused by sequencing over a long period of time.

11.5.2.2. The ICC

In view of the importance of outreach in the construction of perceptions, consideration should be given to early entry by the ICC's outreach team into situations when jurisdiction is triggered. Resources can be maximised through a more structured relationship with civil society organisations, particularly local organisations such as the Coalition ivoirienne pour la Cour pénale internationale that have a closer and often better understanding of the context in which the ICC operates. The ICC should strengthen its collaboration with civil society and increase training and sharing of information.

Prosecutorial strategy should reflect the patterns of crimes and varied responsibility for such crimes. The Office of the Prosecutor's sequencing strategy, while providing the prosecution with an opportunity to advance its work in a particular situation by securing co-operation, undermines the Court by nourishing perceptions of bias among sections of the population in target countries, as is the case in Côte d'Ivoire. The Office should act impartially and fairly, conducting its operations competently and in a manner that inspires confidence. The belief and trust within the general public that the ICC acts speedily, efficiently and conducts competent prosecutions are core to its deterrent effect.

Finally, the ICC, its Assembly of States Parties and the international community should support national courts in situation countries to investigate and prosecute perpetrators of all international crimes. The conduct of national prosecutions is ultimately positive for the ICC's deterrent effect at many levels: perpetrators who do not face justice at the ICC will not have a safe haven; where national courts prosecute, part of the 'harmful politics' operates at the national level rather than international level where it undermines the ICC; and in a co-operative situation, the ICC is unlikely to be seen as avoiding where national courts act speedily and competently in respect of individuals wanted by the ICC.

12

The Deterrence Effect of the International Criminal Court in Mali After the 2012 Crisis

Seydou Doumbia[*]

12.1. Introduction

Analysing the deterrent effect of the International Criminal Court ('ICC') in post-crisis Mali requires the consideration of several factors: historical, social, political, economic, geopolitical, geostrategic, ethnic, cultural and religious aspects. There is no need to give a detailed account of each of these factors, but listing them shows the complexity of the issues and the means to better assess the relevance of the proposed solutions to these crises, with the emergence of the ICC as a new strategy for justice, deterrence, peace and security. The discussion in this chapter focuses on whether the ICC has a deterrent effect on the perpetrators of crimes under its competence. The deterrent effect of the ICC refers to the fear of punishment for international crimes. It also extends to the fight against impunity and consequently to the prevention of violations of international law, as stated in the Preamble of the ICC Statute.

This chapter first traces the history of the crisis in Mali and the various solutions provided by successive political regimes, and then reflects on perceptions from different stakeholders on the effectiveness of the ICC. It analyses the factors affecting its effectiveness before making recommendations.

The chapter's methodology comprises a review of documentary sources on the rebellions in northern Mali, both written and audio-visual, and of opinions expressed during nearly a dozen workshops on security issues, transitional justice and governance. Meetings were also held with direct actors in the conflicts, both soldiers of the Malian army and fighters

---

[*] **Seydou Doumbia** is a lawyer registered with the Mali Bar, a human rights specialist, a lawyer before international criminal tribunals (the International Criminal Tribunal for Rwanda and the International Criminal Court), an expert trainer, an international consultant, an investigator and Executive Director of the non-governmental organisation Victory which deals with the promotion of schools in rural Mali.

from armed non-state groups. It also reviews the perceptions of politicians, government and national parliamentarians, prominent judicial personalities including lawyers and judges, victims, civil society members, journalists, diplomats, international organisation representatives and ordinary citizens.

The goal of collecting the perceptions of all actors involved in the conflict is to understand how they view the relevance of the ICC as a solution that could positively affect the conflict and the establishment of lasting social peace, and to further understand the various factors influencing the ICC's effectiveness. This chapter draws the conclusion that if the conflict continues, it is certainly because the solutions adopted have not been efficient until now. That is why Malians hope that the ICC will remedy the recurrent crisis in northern Mali. The ICC's success relies on all parties understanding its role, and conceiving complementary roles that will give the ICC true effectiveness.

12.2. Chronicle of a Persistent Rebellion in Northern Mali and Institutional Responses

The origins of the successive crises in Mali are very deep. The most significant facts take their origins from French colonisation. Since then, the northern part of Mali has experienced five major crises, which its leaders have managed differently. The most recent drew the attention of the international community because it involved serious threats to regional and even world stability.

After decades of failed Tuareg secessionist rebellions, the separatist Mouvement national de libération de l'Azawad ('MNLA', National Liberation Movement of Azawad) declared the end of military operations in northern Mali after reaching its objectives: to take control of the regions of Gao, Kidal and Timbuktu, and to form a new state. A separatist Islamist group, Ansar Dine, which does not share the MNLA's objectives and which has attempted to introduce *sharia* law in Mali, also took part in the fighting and claimed to have taken Timbuktu from the MNLA.

12.2.1. The Successive Crises from Independence

This section does not endeavour to provide a full chronology of main events, many of which can be easily accessed elsewhere, but rather to provide a snapshot of historical events to understand better how the ICC's intervention fits into the current dynamics in Mali.

Figure 1: Mali.

12.2.1.1. French Colonial Occupation of Northern Mali

The colony of French Sudan was established in July 1891, and comprised most of Malian territory. French troops occupied Timbuktu, but faced strong resistance in the city in December 1893. In 1911 French troops crushed a first revolt, but numerous others followed which the French suppressed with the support of rival Tuareg confederations and Arabs. It would not be an exaggeration to say that this conflict dynamic has remained largely unchanged, sowing the seeds of other rebellions to come, including the Fellagha rebellion of 1962, and rebellions in 1990, 2006, 2010 and, most recently, 2012. These rebellions saw the birth of multiple rebel movements, and repeated failed attempts to alternately suppress or address Tuareg grievances.

12.2.1.2. Rebellion Extension (2012)

In August 2011 a major event changed everything: the arrival of heavily armed Tuareg on Malian territory from Libya via Algeria and Niger. The MNLA was established on 16 October 2011 when Mouvement national de l'Azawad merged with Alliance Touareg Niger-Mali, a more intransigent movement. The main objective was to end Mali's perceived illegal occupation of Azawad territory. In January 2012 the MNLA accused the government of military provocation and of not meeting a series of promises, and launched rebel attacks on Menaka. The movement stated that its objective was "to achieve peace and justice for the community of Azawad" and "stability for their region".[1]

The army mutiny in Gao and Bamako on 21 March 2012 to protest against the misconduct of the war and the lack of resources led to the announcement on the following day of a group of soldiers, members of the Comité national pour le redressement de l'État et la restauration de la démocratie ('CNRDRE', National Committee for the Recovery of the State and the Restoration of Democracy), of a coup and the overthrow of President Amadou Toumani Touré. The CNRDRE announced the suspension of the constitution, the establishment of a curfew and closed borders. Condemnation came from all directions – from human rights organisations to the United Nations ('UN') Security Council through to the Economic Community of West African States ('ECOWAS'), the African Union and the United States, among others. The MNLA reaffirmed its aim to obtain independence for Azawad, which it proclaimed on 6 April 2012 and called for a unilateral ceasefire. ECOWAS excluded Mali from the Community on 2 April 2012 and placed the country under embargo. After 3 April the African Union further penalised the post-coup Malian military regime by suspending Mali as member of the organisation.

On 6 April 2012 Tuareg rebels, supported by the Islamist group Ansar Dine, proclaimed independence of the Azawad territory in the north of the country. The major cities of Kidal, Gao and Timbuktu fell under rebel control. The transitional president, Dioncounda Traoré, was sworn in on 12 April 2012, under the agreement signed by the junta with ECOWAS,

---

[1]   "Chronologie du conflit au nord du pays", in *IRIN News*, 5 February 2012.

providing for the transfer of power back to civilians. The MNLA and An-sar Dine merged on 27 May 2012 and proclaimed an independent Islamic state governed by *sharia* law in northern Mali. This agreement was termi-nated a few days later by the MNLA, because it believed that *sharia* was contrary to its values. On 8 June 2012 the Tuareg rebels of MNLA left the city of Timbuktu. The Islamists of the Movement for Oneness and Jihad in West Africa took full control of Gao after chasing out the Tuareg sepa-ratists.

The Islamist destruction of shrines and holy places of Islam in Tim-buktu began on 30 June 2012, two days after the registration of Timbuktu on the United Nations Educational, Scientific and Cultural Organisation's ('UNESCO') List of World Heritage in Danger. From 11 July 2012 the Islamists took control of the entire north of the country, and enforced *sha-ria* law, including amputation of the hands of thieves and death by stoning for adulterers.

On 18 July 2012 the Malian authorities referred the situation in Mali to the ICC with regard to the crimes allegedly committed "since Jan-uary 2012".[2] This referral comes on the back of Mali's accession to the ICC Statute on 16 August 2000, which grants the ICC jurisdiction over the Mali situation since the ICC Statute's entry into force on 1 July 2002.

Islamists consolidated their positions in the north and took control of Douentza in Mopti region on 1 September 2012. On 4 September 2012 the president requested the intervention of a West African military force to reconquer the north. The UN Security Council in the framework of res-olution 2085 (20 December 2012) authorised the deployment of the Afri-can-led International Support Mission in Mali ('AFISMA') as Mali re-quested and ECOWAS endorsed.[3]

12.2.2. Institutional Responses to Various Crises

From independence to date, Mali has experienced three different Repub-lics: under Modibo Keïta (1960–1968), under Lieutenant Moussa Traoré (1968–1992) and under democratic management methods of the Tuareg

---

[2] République du Mali, Ministère de la Justice, Letter to Prosecutor, International Criminal Court, Concerning the Situation in Mali, 13 July 2012.

[3] United Nations Security Council, Resolution 2085, UN doc. S/RES/2085 (2012), 20 De-cember 2012 (http://www.legal-tools.org/doc/386f9f/).

issue.[4] The three Republics shared the Tuareg issue in common, but each attempted to handle it differently.

Under the First Republic, the young state could not tolerate any secessionist inclination that would undermine national cohesion and unity; the Nigerian experience of Biafra was still fresh in everyone's mind. In this respect, the first rebellion was quelled militarily and the north placed under military administration, with military personnel in place from the governor to teachers, doctors and administrative staff. It is likely that during this period military personnel committed many crimes against civilian Tuareg in the north. This left a negative image in the popular consciousness and fed Tuareg hatred and phobia of the army, leading them to request in successive agreements the demilitarisation or withdrawal of the army from the northern region, or otherwise some form of relief from the military system, something essential to the honour of the Tuareg but unacceptable to the sovereign state.

Under the Second Republic, the state opted to manage the conflict through notable minority families in the north, essentially in an attempt to contain the Tuareg. Unfortunately, unlike the south where development was more evenly distributed, notable families in the north excluded the Tuareg tribes on the borders, bypassing them in all development projects and practising a paternalistic form of management at the expense of potential beneficiaries.

Under the Third Republic, the government challenged the supremacy of the notable families for the benefit of all cantons and nomadic groups. The government took the decision to integrate former rebels into the army and security forces, which were previously the exclusive domain of the notable families. The integration of rebels into the army was a double-edged sword. On the positive side, it empowered new military chiefs as spokespeople for their communities, who came mostly from tribes considered before as a subordinate class. This ended the need for these communities to rely on the notable families for solving problems. On the negative side, it marked a serious threat to the state in that Tuareg knowledge of the army and its operations empowered them to try to take by force the resources they felt were owed to them and which, in the end, the relatively

---

[4] Youssouf Sissoko, "Mali: Jeudi 22 Septembre 1960–Jeudi 22 Septembre 2016, 56 long chemins vers la paix au nord: La rébellion arabo-touareg, toujours l'un des gros handicaps pour le développement harmonieux du Mali", in *MaliActu.net*, 23 September 2016.

poor state of Mali could not provide in sufficient measure. Their participation also brought to the fore existing Tuareg prejudices towards other ethnic groups that they considered as 'blacks', inferior and unable to govern. The state of Mali was too weak to enforce democratic rule as the only way to inspire change.

This chronicle allows a better understanding of the context and specificity of the Malian crisis. The repetitive nature of the crisis in northern Mali certainly demonstrates the inadequacy or, at least, the insufficiency of the management methods chosen to contain it. In addition to traditional actors of various rebel groups living in northern Mali and opposed to government forces, the rebellion has become more complex with the involvement of other external forces supported by those inside with new jihadist ideologies. The 2012 crisis and its evolution through new strategies to resolve it clearly highlights the need for reflection on the relevance of international solutions, in this case to instil fear of legal sanctions by the ICC or national jurisdictions for perpetrators of crimes.

12.3. Factors Affecting Malian Perceptions on the Effectiveness of National Justice and the ICC

The occupation of northern Mali from the beginning of 2012 by armed groups led to the state administration, including justice mechanisms, deserting this part of the country. The Supreme Court of Mali, following a government report on the situation in the north, rendered two decisions of "withdrawal and designation of jurisdiction" to pull out the jurisdictions in the north and appoint the High Court of District III of Bamako to deal with the cases under their jurisdiction.[5] In another decision, the Supreme Court, in the context of a gradual return of government officials in the north, returned their competence to these jurisdictions.[6] In between lay a critical gap of two years. Aside from their dysfunctional character, justice mechanisms suffer from a great lack of legitimacy due to corruption and deficit of independence.

Mali had ratified the ICC Statute on 16 August 2000, and the government referred its situation to the ICC on 13 July 2012. After a preliminary examination of the situation, the Office of the Prosecutor decided on 16 January 2013 to investigate alleged crimes committed on the territory

---

[5] Supreme Court of Mali, Judgments No. 46 of 16 July 2012 and No. 04 of 21 January 2013.
[6] Supreme Court of Mali, Judgment No. 11 of 16 February 2015.

of Mali since January 2012. The three northern regions of Gao, Timbuktu and Kidal were the primary subject of concern of these investigations, as well as to a lesser extent Bamako and Mopti/Sevare in the south.

On 18 September 2015 the ICC issued an arrest warrant against Ahmad Al Faqi Al Mahdi. On 26 September 2015 the authorities of Niger, which already had Al Mahdi in custody, transferred him to the ICC, and he thereafter appeared before the Pre-Trial Chamber on 30 September 2015. The Office of the Prosecutor argued that Al Mahdi was allegedly responsible for war crimes committed in Timbuktu, consisting of intentional attacks on 10 buildings dedicated to religion and historical memorials (nine mausoleums and a mosque). All the buildings and monuments attacked were under the protection of UNESCO, and most of them were on the World Heritage list. These attacks constituted crimes under Article 8(2)(e)(iv) of the ICC Statute, and were charged for the first time in this case. Al Mahdi pleaded guilty and apologised for cultural properties war crimes committed in Timbuktu. The Court sentenced him to 12 years' imprisonment.

12.3.1. Perception of Malians of the Effectiveness of the ICC

12.3.1.1. Perceptions Gathered During Workshops

The comments reported here reflect widely held perceptions in Mali on national justice and the expected role of the ICC as a solution to the crisis. During a workshop on transitional justice held in April 2016 and at other conferences, several interventions from participants had the same content: "If the Malian justice system is inefficient and corrupted, it is still possible to call for the ICC to address impunity". Another civil society actor said: "Prejudices need to be repaired here in Mali and the ICC could be above small arrangements that we experience within the national justice system and that would prevent justice from functioning correctly".[7]

During another workshop on transitional justice organised by Justice, Prévention et Réconciliation ('JUPREC'),[8] a member of the panel

---

[7]   Marie-Laure Tapp, "Justice nationale, justice internationale… Justice, où te caches-tu?", Lawyers Without Borders, 6 June 2016.

[8]   JUPREC is a project of a Canadian consortium of Avocats sans frontières Canada, Centre d'étude et de coopération internationale, and École nationale d'administration publique du Québec.

was asked whether, as a former ICC judge, she believed in the ICC's deterrent effect. She first replied negatively before she recognised that the ICC had a deterrent effect. At first stating that the ICC did not have the desired deterrent effect, she cited the Burundi situation, where President Pierre Nkurunziza, defying the international community and the ICC, is categorically opposed to the deployment of international forces in his country. She also recalled the unexecuted international arrest warrant against the Sudanese president, Omar Al Bashir, as well as the dismissal of charges against the president of Kenya, and the lack of prosecutions against members of the Rwandan Patriotic Front of President Paul Kagame for the atrocities committed in 1994 during the capture of Kigali and the start of the genocide in Rwanda. An open discussion followed in which several judges, academics, leaders of political parties, lawyers and members of the Truth, Justice and Reconciliation Commission ('TJRC') maintained that the ICC still has a deterrent effect, with some claiming that it is only fear of prosecution by the ICC that prevents Nkurunziza from openly using all means at his disposal against the political opposition. Some participants argued that the ICC only targets weak countries, that it only pursues the defeated in armed conflicts and never the winners, and that the principle of complementarity is a source of inefficiency. Despite these criticisms, there was unanimity that the ICC is necessary for the stability of African countries plagued by recurring violence.

Elsewhere in Timbuktu and Gao, during a workshop on 'Capacity-building of the Actors of the Criminal Chain' in April and May 2016, participants voted on the effectiveness of the ICC in the punishment of crimes in Mali's post-crisis period. Again, the answers were unanimous that the action of the ICC is very beneficial to prevent the recurrence of conflict in northern Mali, although concerns were also raised that selective intervention criteria inhibited deterrence of all actors, as the ICC is concerned only with the most serious crimes committed by the highest authorities. Again, participants mentioned that the ICC would benefit from being better known to have a dissuasive effect on the perpetrators of crimes, especially if we consider the imprescriptibly of the crimes under its jurisdiction.

12.3.1.2. Victims and Victim Advocacy Organisations

In answering a question on what she thinks of the ICC's potential role in the Mali situation, a very committed victim defending the cause of victims in Gao replied:

> Now that the ICC is here, we are not afraid anymore to denounce our looters and rapists. We will tell everything. The tragedy is that the ICC will not prosecute everyone as their leaders and instigators are left. How are they to be found and punished?

Another official of one of the largest and oldest national organisations of human rights exclaimed:

> For me, the ICC is the white elephant; this big thing that frightens for nothing. See the case of Al Mahdi for example; he is simply prosecuted for destruction of memorials, while he is notoriously known for being one of the most important of the jihadists' police officials. And then he played a leading role in the implementation of decisions of their courts. The ICC has proof of all of this. What does it expect? To prosecute all these crimes? [...] The worst in all this is that the leaders of the Malian army are worried neither by the ICC nor by national jurisdictions. Yet, we know that soldiers of our own national army have committed serious crimes against the civilian population, they have also raped women and violently killed civilians not involved in hostilities. Are these not war crimes?

12.3.1.3. Armed Groups

Addressing the same question of the deterrent effect of the ICC, prisoners under house arrest in Bamako gave an unequivocal answer. Twenty out of the approximately 300 prisoners are being prosecuted for breaches of internal and external security of the state, conspiracy, rape and terrorism, among other charges. They have clearly stated that they fear the ICC more than the national jurisdiction. They cited several reasons: the ICC's distance, especially from their families, and the fact that, as one put it: "If we are in Mali, arrangements are always possible, either with the government or with the judges directly". As an example, one of the prisoners recalled that some of their leaders had been released in exchange for some prisoners without any judgment.

During interviews in Mopti with three individuals responsible for the 'Platform' group of fighting forces participating in the demobilisation, disarmament and reintegration process argued:

> The worst enemy of Mali is Mali itself [...] You can't claim to have it both ways. We can't fight against impunity and release the well-known perpetrators of serious crimes at the same time. The case of Wadoussène is very explicit. Mali will never get out of the spiral of violence in the north if the international community does not take responsibility, given the obvious inability of Malian justice. The other thing is that Mali must win respect as a state with a national army worthy of the name, with patriotic soldiers, well-trained and well-armed. The release of Wadoussène has spilled much ink.[9]

At the end of these interviews and interactions, the main point was that the ICC can deter armed groups from committing the most serious crimes only by punishing severely all the authors of crimes, both from the rebel groups and the regular army as well. Also, for the ICC to have a deterrent effect would require it to be devolved to the country where crimes are perpetrated and for the judges to adjudicate within the accused's community and before their people, or to create a hybrid jurisdiction like that of Sierra Leone.

12.3.1.4. Defence and Security Forces

At the level of the Kati garrison, one of the largest military bases in the country, a colonel of the national army was not embarrassed to say:

> If our men killed civilians, it was for a good cause. How would you distinguish between a civilian and a military? These white-skinned people are all soldiers and civilians at the same time; it's part of their war tactic. The rules of humanitarian law, okay! But we were not in a conventional war.

---

[9] The terrorist Mohamed Aly Ag Wadoussène was imprisoned for having participated in the kidnapping of two French nationals in northern Mali (Philippe Verdon and Serge Lazarévic in Hombori on 4 November 2011) and in the massacres of Aguelhok. For further details, see Georges Diarra, "Mali: Libération du terroriste Wadoussène sans jugement: IBK piétine encore la justice malienne", in *MaliActu.net*, 12 December 2014. To allow the release of the last hostage in the Sahel, France twisted the arm of the president to exchange Wadoussène with Lazarévic, a situation that was not well received by people who see this as a promotion of impunity in Mali.

> Mali should not, under any circumstances, deliver Malian soldiers responsible for abuses during the war to the ICC because this betrayal could be the cause of other problems within the country. In addition to the humiliation inflicted by the jihadists, if the Malian military should appear before the national jurisdictions or before the ICC, the fact would worsen the situation. Besides, no country has ever delivered elements of its regular forces to the ICC for trial. It did not happen in Rwanda and Côte d'Ivoire. In this regard, the ICC is just "*un Tribunal des vaincus*" [...] like in Rwanda.

A senior officer of the national gendarmerie in Timbuktu argued:

> The fight against impunity through the ICC is easier said than done, because on one hand, the states themselves do not play the game; co-operation to track the perpetrators to justice is quite biased. Our state requests the ICC when they are defeated, when the national justice system is unable to cope with the situation; on the other hand, they practise a policy of double standards in the prosecution. Equality before the law is not respected. They want to prosecute some authors and not others. This leads to revenge. The same applies to national justice. This is what largely explains the history of the red berets [forces close to President Touré who allegedly also committed crimes].

12.3.1.5. Legal Actors

The perceptions of prosecutors and judges in the north and in Bamako are of particular interest. The president of the Court of Appeal of Mopti, the highest court, close to the location of the rebellion, stated:

> The authors of violations of fundamental human rights, rape, war crimes and crimes against humanity never pay the full price of their crimes. Mali is encouraging rebellion by giving bonuses to criminals, integrating them into the national army, giving them all kinds of favours. It is the state itself which encourages impunity. An amnesty law is possible in the light of what we perceive from the government when releasing criminals. Unless the state takes full charge of all the victims, Mali is not immune to a civil unrest demanding justice. That is why the intervention of the ICC is not only useful but necessary to stop the cycle of rebellions in Mali.

The Malian press echoed such concerns.[10] Beyond the issues expressed here, the major worry was how far national solutions would take the country, and whether most Malians could see in the TJRC or other national mechanisms a viable solution to the recurrent crises.

The president of the Court of Mopti also argued that while criminal justice will always play its role and occupy a place in the restoration of social balance, with its effectiveness depending on how it is employed, one must recognise that in the Mali situation more is expected from international justice. The ICC should play a key role in avoiding a repetition of the crisis. It has more means to effectively investigate and prosecute those who are guilty of serious crimes. He added that, in his opinion, national justice serves criminals because of corruption and its capture by political power, as opposed to the ICC. This fuels impunity and furthers the frustration of the victims. Convicted prisoners are released because of political decisions without consulting judicial authorities. That is why the ICC should not be complementary to national justice, but must prevail over it. He advocated raising further awareness on the merits of the ICC as a solution to the crisis and insisted on the imprescriptibly of the prosecuted crimes in order to discourage young people from enrolling in fighting forces.

For a prosecutor of the same jurisdiction, the primary role of justice is to resolve conflicts and to demonstrate the public power of the state to establish social peace. The failure of the Malian government therefore demands the intervention of the ICC as a reminder that not everything is allowed. In particular, politics has inhibited the full exercise of national justice, breaking the morale of local judges. National jurisdictions are therefore not able to effectively take care of these disputes. Unfortunately, the ICC is not competent to prosecute crimes of all kinds in the northern part of the country, and is therefore also limited.

In conclusion, despite the anomalies of the ICC, no other mechanism can claim its role. It is for states parties to the ICC Statute to show the necessary confidence that will pre-empt some countries from considering withdrawing from the institution. The ICC, for its part, should create equal justice for all without exception. The deterrent effect of the ICC is very clearly shown through the attitude of the most powerful countries in

---

[10] Alpha Mahamane Cissé, "Nina Wallet en N°2 du CJVR: Une nomination qui fait polémique", in *Maliweb*, 19 October 2015.

the world like the United States. If these countries do not want to be part of the ICC, it is not because they can judge their nationals, but because they fear prosecution of their nationals in other countries. Nonetheless, the ICC remains a bogeyman with some power to dissuade the dictators of this world from perpetrating international crimes.

12.3.1.6. The Government

A technical adviser in charge of human rights at the Ministry of Justice and Human Rights of Mali was interviewed. He argued that "[t]he government has faith in the effectiveness of the ICC to deter criminals in northern Mali. That is why the president, the minister of justice and the entire government did not hesitate to call the ICC to investigate crimes committed in the north during the occupation of this part of our country". He added that jihadists should know that even if the Malian government had no adequate means of repression to stop their interventions, the international community could play this role.

12.3.1.7. The National Assembly

At the National Assembly, a member of parliament noted: "We nearly voted in two amnesty laws. It would be a serious mistake for the future of our country. Fortunately we changed our minds in time". This short revelation says enough about the risks of promoting impunity.

12.3.1.8. Local Religious Authorities

Local religious authorities in Timbuktu and Gao consider that the deterrent effect of the ICC to dissuade criminals is real. As an example, they cite the case of Al Mahdi. They are happy with the remorse he expressed for the destruction of the mausoleums of Timbuktu, and they admit that only an international jurisdiction could have obtained such a result. They also underline that since his arrest none of the people recognised as having participated in the destruction of World Heritage Sites in Timbuktu have been seen in the area. This is evidence that they are afraid to join him in prison. These authorities also hope that Al Mahdi will be prosecuted for other serious crimes that the Islamists have committed during the occupation of Timbuktu.

In a rather sharp intervention, the president of the High Islamic Council, Mahamoud Dicko, a religious leader of the first rank and a great preacher, recognising the importance of the ICC's presence to punish the miscreants who claim to speak on behalf of the religion, underlined the government's failure to protect Islam. In an article published in the newspaper *Le Prétoire* on 21 July 2016, he criticised the government's position on the introduction of the interim authorities in the north, in accordance with the terms of the Algiers Peace Agreement. He argued: "You cannot lose a war and want to command".[11] Dicko said that Mali should rely on international solutions since it has failed to ensure its own security. In fact, it is well known that international partners who were involved in the Algiers Peace Agreement suggested the introduction of an interim administration in the northern areas as an alternative to the escalation of violence. The interim administration will be composed of credible representatives of all belligerents and members of victim groups or civil society known for their integrity.

12.3.2. Common Factors Determining the Effectiveness of National Justice and the ICC

The effectiveness of any justice system, whether national or international, is determined by the degree to which states accept their responsibility to protect citizens as a preventative measure, the strength of diplomatic action, the mobilisation of military forces as necessary, and the availability of financial resources from the international community. These factors are interrelated.

12.3.2.1. The Universal Principle of the State's Responsibility to Protect Citizens

The principle of the state's responsibility to protect its citizens is referred to for genocide prevention as well as crimes against humanity, war crimes and ethnic cleansing, together with incitement to commit such crimes. According to the principle, which is a underpinned by the United Nations, prevention implies a shared responsibility and the related obligation to co-operate between the involved states and the international community.

The state has an obligation to avoid and end genocide and atrocities. The international community also has a role to play, without prejudice to

---

[11] Harber Maiga, "Mali: Mahamoud Dicko au sujet des autorités intérimaires: 'Nous n'avons pas à remettre en cause leur mise en place'. 'Vous ne pouvez pas perdre une guerre et vouloir vous imposer…'", in *MaliActu.net*, 21 July 2016.

the principle of the sovereignty of states. The principle of state sovereignty cannot be invoked by a state to refuse external intervention if the state has failed in its responsibility to ensure the well-being of its population.[12]

The final document of the 2005 UN World Summit defines three bases of the responsibility to protect.[13] These three pillars were announced by the UN secretary-general in his 2009 report on the responsibility to protect.[14] They are:

1. The obligation mainly belonging to the state to protect citizens;
2. The obligation of the international community to encourage and help states to fulfil this responsibility; and
3. The obligation of the international community to use all diplomatic, humanitarian and other means to protect populations against those crimes.

If a state is clearly not protecting its citizen, the international community must be ready to implement collective action to protect those populations in accordance with the United Nations Charter.

In Mali, in conformity with the United Nations Charter, and in accordance with Article 1 of the United Nations Convention on the Prevention and Punishment of Genocide, it was the responsibility of the state to ensure the protection of its citizens. Having failed in this responsibility, the duty to protect fell on the international community. The implementation of this principle can have a deterrent effect in bringing the Malian state before both national and international jurisdictions, due to its failure to protect its citizens as a result of its negligence of and non-compliance with national and international laws.

12.3.2.2. Mobilisation of International Military Forces and Financial Resources

There is no peace without justice, and no justice without security; likewise, no development is possible without security. If justice, whether na-

---

[12] United Nations General Assembly, Convention on the Prevention and Punishment the Crime of Genocide, 9 December 1948, Article 1 (http://www.legal-tools.org/doc/498c38/).

[13] United Nations General Assembly, World Summit Outcome, UN doc. A/RES/60/1, 16 September 2005, paras. 138–40.

[14] United Nations General Assembly, Integrated and Coordinated Implementation of and Follow-up to the Outcomes of the Major United Nations Conferences and Summits in the Economic, Social and Related Fields, UN doc. A/63/677, 12 January 2009.

tional or international, can only be exercised in a secure environment, security being understood in the sense of preserving the physical integrity of people and their property, then security becomes the primary determinant of the effectiveness of justice.

In this regard, the stabilisation of Mali after the crisis was only possible thanks to the mobilisation of several forces deployed in northern Mali, and in particular the intervention of the French military in Operation Serval. Requested by the acting president of Mali and with the approval of the international community, including regional organisations like ECOWAS, the intervention began on 11 January 2013 with air strikes and the deployment of troops. France has laid the groundwork for further military deployments to help Mali; several military operations will take over to contribute to the stabilisation of the country.

The initial French intervention was followed by AFISMA and a military mission led by ECOWAS to provide assistance to one of its members. Authorised by UN Security Council resolution 2085, it sanctioned the deployment of AFISMA for an initial period of one year to help restore the capacity of the Malian armed forces, to preserve the civilian population. It was also tasked to dislodge Islamist groups including Al-Qaeda in the Islamic Maghreb, Movement for Oneness and Jihad in West Africa and Ansar Dine, which had taken control of northern Mali after driving out the separatist Tuareg rebels of the MNLA. AFISMA was replaced by the UN Multidimensional Integrated Stabilisation Mission in Mali ('MINUSMA'), officially deployed on 1 July 2013, which the Security Council established through resolution 2100 and renewed through resolutions 2164 and 2295 to support the political process in the country and carry out a number of security-related tasks.[15] The French military Operation Barkhane complemented MINUSMA, as an operation intended to root out jihadists and Salafist armed groups in the Sahel region. It was launched on 1 August 2014 and took over from the previous Operations Serval and Epervier.

Strong economic and geostrategic interests underpin the French intervention, which may undermine its perceived legitimacy. For example,

---

[15] United Nations Security Council, Resolution 2100 (2013), UN doc. S/RES/2100, 25 April 2013 (http://www.legal-tools.org/doc/c8983e/); United Nations Security Council, Resolution 2164 (2014), UN doc. S/RES/2164, 25 June 2014 (http://www.legal-tools.org/doc/f14aa0/); United Nations Security Council, Resolution 2295 (2016), UN doc. S/RES/2295, 29 June 2016 (http://www.legal-tools.org/doc/825dbd/).

many believe that France's interests in the region are strongly linked to their need to mine uranium and drill for oil. This may be balanced out by the growingly international nature of the intervention. It is interesting to note that, between these various operations, 20 states have forces present in Mali and the immediate region,[16] and training support comes from the European Union. The presence of so many countries as well as non-state actors and forces underscores how the military aspect has been so prominent in the international intervention in Mali.

The value of the intervention may also be undermined by eventual limits to the ability of an international force to attain and sustain real control over a huge desert area solely by military action, especially in the face of significant drugs and weapons trafficking on the border with Algeria, and ongoing cross-border activities of Islamist groups, as reflected in hostage-taking in Amenas in Algeria. Sustainable peace requires a dialogue with all Malian stakeholders willing to work to rebuild the country.

12.3.2.3. Diplomatic and Financial Mobilisation of the International Community

Great diplomatic efforts have been needed to handle the normalisation process of the situation in the Sahel in general and in Mali in particular, including a focus on justice issues as a key pillar of any long-lasting solution. The European Union has pursued diplomatic efforts in co-operation with national, regional and international actors, and is conducting a permanent dialogue at the highest level with the authorities in charge of the political transition in Mali.[17] Justice in this context has largely taken a back seat. The European Union has promoted the reinforcement of international co-ordination to address the crisis and is a key member of the international group supporting and monitoring the situation in Mali, co-led by the African Union and the UN. It also closely works with ECOWAS, Algeria and Mauritania.

---

[16] These are Bangladesh, Benin, Burkina Faso, Burundi, Cambodia, Cape Verde, Chad, China, France, the Gambia, Ghana, Guinea, Guinea-Bissau, Liberia, the Netherlands, Niger, Nigeria, Senegal, Sierra Leone, and Togo, with further logistical support from Côte d'Ivoire, Belgium, Canada, Denmark, Germany, Morocco, Russia, Spain, the United Kingdom and the United States.

[17] European Union, External Action, Fact Sheet: "The European Union and the Sahel", 6 February 2014.

Fund-raising to support Mali has been as important as military action against rebel groups. As part of the aid harmonisation process in Mali, the Collective Group of Technical and Financial Partners was created to bring together all the technical and financial partners involved in the country. They have played a leading role in solving the crisis.

In an information sheet entitled "The European Union and the Sahel", the European Union sought to define a global approach to the crisis in the Sahel region, with reference to the strategy presented to the Council of Europe in March 2011. The European Union's strategy is based on the assumption that development and security are interrelated and can be mutually reinforced, and that the ongoing complex crisis in the Sahel requires a regional response. This strategy has been useful in reinforcing a coherent approach to the crisis, particularly in relation to Mauritania, Niger and Mali. The European Union allocated over €660 million to the region under the tenth European Development Fund (2007–2013). As part of its strategy for the Sahel, the European Union has also mobilised additional financial resources for development-related projects and security. With a budget of €167 million, these projects are organised around four pillars: 1) development, good governance and resolution of internal conflicts; 2) political and diplomatic action; 3) security and rule of law; and 4) the fight against violent extremism and radicalisation.[18] Undeniably, the idea of a global solution to the crisis in the Sahel region and the four pillars of the EU strategy are key to resolving the crisis in Mali.

The commitment of civil society organisations has undoubtedly been an important aspect in mastering the security situation and therefore in achieving effective and efficient legal solutions to end the crisis. On 1 September 2014 the Consortium of Civil Society Organisations to End the Crisis met to discuss the terms of their commitments for Mali.[19] Thirteen organisations took part. The Consortium reported its concerns about the political and security situation on the national territory for more than three years and found that, despite various UN resolutions, the efforts of the Malian government, and the involvement of African countries and the international community, the Malian people remain perplexed as to the possibility of favourable outcome. According to the Consortium, the security

---

[18] European Union, 2014, see *supra* note 17.
[19] Consortium of Civil Society Organisations to End the Crisis, "Voix commune de la société civile", 1 September 2014.

situation in the northern region continues to be characterised by insecurity in all areas, bomb attacks, and occupation of most areas by rebel groups, jihadists and drug dealers. The population does not have access to basic social services and the economy is struggling to restart. The return of the administration and the army is limited to a few centres. Violations of the rights of the people continue to be perpetrated in many communities left behind in the violence. Development programmes are frozen. This keeps people in a position of idleness and uncertainty, not allowing for reconciliation, as had been expected.

Today, several international organisations, with the support of the MINUSMA, constitute the spearhead of judicial activity in northern Mali. These include the International Development Law Organization, the American Bar Association and the Canadian consortium JUPREC through its national partners. In this context, the Division of Human Rights of MINUSMA launched its first forum on the participation of victims and the role of civil society in the process of transitional justice at the Ahmed Baba Centre in Timbuktu on 21 March 2015. This activity's main objective was to build the capacities of human rights organisations and victims' associations for their role and participation in transitional justice mechanisms. Several UN organisations and NGOs, including UN Women, the World Food Programme and the International Committee of the Red Cross, support these activities.

12.3.2.4. Specific Factors Determining the Efficiency of National Justice

Regardless of the relative lack of focus on justice mechanisms, justice is expected to play a decisive role. During a working visit to Mali on 9–13 November 2015, the former German minister of justice, Herta Däubler-Gmelin, said: "Justice – a fundamental pillar of democracy – is at once at the heart of the Malian crisis and its solution".[20] Justice is hindered by government instability and multiple changes of ministers of justice; since December 2013, in a period of less than three years, Mali had four ministers of justice. This lack of stability in the management of justice affairs does not favour the implementation of the objectives assigned to a justice system in crisis – of contributing to national stability.

---

[20] Friedrich-Ebert-Stiftung, "Justice après la Crise – l'ancienne ministre de la justice, Herta Däubler-Gmelin au Mali", 12 November 2015.

On 17 December 2015 the Ministry of Justice and Human Rights launched an emergency programme (2015–2018) for strengthening the judiciary and implementing the Algiers Peace Agreement and national reconciliation, at a total cost of more than 59.9 billion CFA francs ($97 million). This programme seeks to overcome the persistent shortcomings in the Malian legal system by providing the means and opportunity to the justice sector to move towards a fundamental change in meeting the expectations of the people. The general objective is "to improve the quality and credibility of the judicial system to a strong justice in a strong state".[21] The emergency programme has three components: the consolidation of justice and the rule of law; protection of human rights and promotion of the fight against impunity, corruption and financial crime; and, communication on justice. Since its launch, technical and financial partners of Mali, notably the Canadian Cooperation Office, USAID, the European Union and the Dutch Cooperation Office, have deployed significant efforts to achieve the programme's objectives.

It is clear though that much remains to be done. To date, none of the courts of northern Mali operates normally because of the lack of staff for those that do not work at all and insufficient competent staff. For example, intermediate courts like those in Timbuktu and Gao have only one clerk each. The reform of the justice sector mainly suffers from a lack of political will to make justice an instrument of peace and security contrary to the objectives of the emergency programme for strengthening the judiciary.[22]

This must be underpinned by a strong state with strong institutions, led by competent and honest people, guaranteeing security and well-being to all citizens for self-fulfilment. In such a state, fundamental human rights are preserved for all. Corruption, impunity, favouritism, nepotism, injustice and a failure to value merit are the opposite of strong state-building. Many reports agree that Mali is one of the most corrupt countries in the world. None of the government institutions escapes this desig-

---

[21] Maliki Diallo, "Renforcement du système judiciaire: Plus 59 milliards pour le programme d'urgence", 18 December 2015.

[22] The emergency programme for strengthening the judiciary advances structural reform, which aims at systematic institutional strengthening of Mali's justice sector. Its objective is to contribute to building and strengthening a system of independent justice, impartial and fair to all Malian citizens. It has three components: improving the performance of judicial structures; rebuilding the values of justice and the fight against impunity; and improving access to justice and security protection.

nation, a real brake on democracy. Never in history has a governance slogan sounded so loud: we must put the right person in the right place.

Däubler-Gmelin summed up the prospect of resolving the crisis in Mali in brief, addressing the responsibility of the justice sector, judges and magistrates to overcome the crisis during the roundtable with the National Institute of Judiciary Training. At the Constitutional Court, she discussed its role as a "watchdog of democracy",[23] using the example of the experience of the Constitutional Court of Germany. At a roundtable that brought together the National Commission for Human Rights and the minister of justice, Däubler-Gmelin pointed out the importance and urgency of the reform of justice whose challenge is to make justice more accessible, fairer and more credible to all Malians.

This must also be supported by stronger separation of powers within the state, the independence of judicial power, respect for the laws of the Republic, and the effectiveness of the principle of equality before the law, which are essential in any democracy. Article 81 of the Malian Constitution states:

> The judicial power is independent from the executive and legislative powers. It shall be exercised by the Supreme Court and other Courts and Tribunals. The power of the judiciary is the guardian of the liberties defined by this Constitution. It guards the rights and liberties defined by this Constitution. It is charged to apply, in its proper domain, the laws of the Republic.[24]

Article 82 further provides: "Magistrates shall not be suppressed in the exercise of their duties, but the authority of the law".[25] It is painful to note that there is no real judicial power in Mali, as the independence of the judiciary is compromised by the intrusion of the executive. The consequence is a concentration of all powers in the hands of the president. The modernisation of the Malian government must begin with the revision of the Constitution in reducing presidential power, increasing the effectiveness of the separation of powers, and ensuring the real independence of the judiciary.

---

[23] Friederich-Ebert-Stiftung, see *supra* note 20.

[24] Republic of Mali, Constitution, 12 January 1992, Article 81 (http://www.legal-tools.org/doc/e8a50c/).

[25] *Ibid.* Article 82.

12.3.2.5. Specific Factors Determining Efficiency of the ICC

United Nations Security Council resolutions are a key basis of respect for international law. On 5 July 2012 the Security Council held a meeting on peace and security in Africa and unanimously adopted resolution 2056 submitted by France, supporting the efforts of ECOWAS and the African Union to resolve the crisis in Mali.[26] This resolution had a significant impact on the way forward for the Malian crisis, even if serious violations of international law are ongoing and the country is far from peace. The major challenge to the implementation of international law lies in the difficulty of giving a restrictive character to its mechanisms. Resolutions, charters, conventions, declarations and so forth can produce the desired effect only if they apply real punishment to the offender. This requires political will, and in the case of the ICC for states parties to co-operate and thereby to give free rein to all the necessary acts of procedure of the Court, from investigations to prosecutions and the execution of sentences.

Arising from perceptions of the effectiveness of the solutions to overcome the crisis in northern Mali, the most frequent criticisms and expectations are based on the need for:

- Revising the principle of complementarity;
- Extending the *rationae materiae*, *rationae personae* and *rationae temporis* competences as a deterrent measure; and
- Applying the principle of equality before the Court.

These measures may seem bold to some extent and one could ask why progressive changes should be introduced while states are struggling to comply with existing provisions.

The crisis in Mali was particularly violent and continues to seriously mobilise the international community, given the extreme weakness of the Malian government. The weakness of African states should reinforce the international community's will to examine situations on a case-by-case basis, to assume solutions that take into account the specific situation of each country in crisis, and to redouble diplomatic efforts to achieve universal ratification of the ICC Statute and full implementation of its provisions.

---

[26] United Nations Security Council, Resolution 2056 (2012), UN doc. S/RES/2056, 5 July 2012 (http://www.legal-tools.org/doc/2dda16-1/).

12.4. Conclusion

The political and security crisis that Mali has experienced since January 2012, which paralysed institutions and the administration, threatening the existence of the state itself, has deep roots. Informed observers note among the major causes is the non-compliance with the law. Malian democracy, once considered a model, concealed serious breaches of the law, and controversial democratic governance.

The stabilisation of Mali is now only possible thanks to security, humanitarian, institutional, technical and financial support from the international community. There is a high price being paid for this dangerous intervention, with many peacekeepers injured or killed. However, this intervention has limited the jihadist offensive and blocked the rebellion, even if the resistance continues to spread terror, using the techniques of asymmetric war.

The national legal system, deeply disorganised, is slowly recovering, but great efforts are still needed to put men and women to work. With the support of many partners in the implementation of credible justice, responding to the deep aspirations of peace, justice and security, the Malian government, though strongly challenged, must take the right measures by effectively implementing the proposed reforms.

In this context, the intervention of international justice through the ICC was applauded. The Malian people remain hopeful that the ICC will be the remedy to overcome impunity and deter people from taking up weapons again in the future. The victims are most comfortable with the principle of imprescriptibly of crimes committed, because they want those who bear the responsibility of past rebellions to be prosecuted, even after a hundred years. The TJRC of Mali also supports this popular will.

The hope of the people is compromised by the perceived deficiencies in the ICC Statute: the principle of complementarity, and the limits of its competence *rationae materiae*, *rationae personae* and *rationae temporis*. It is easy to recognise that the ICC should revise its rules if it wants to really be effective, to be a tool of deterrence, prevention, peace and security, and therefore a development catalyst in the most serious and complex situations such as the one in Mali. The ICC should be able to investigate and prosecute crimes committed before its creation; it should be able to prosecute all violations and not just the most serious; and it should be able to prosecute anyone whose participation was significant in the commission of crimes regardless of their rank in the hierarchy of their organisations. That is why the ICC also needs to be located on the ground where crimes are committed. The ICC is far from being able to address all Malian concerns, but states parties to the ICC Statute should start to think about the possibility of giving the institution a real deterrent force.

The international community through the UN Security Council should commit to making international criminal law an effective tool for peace and security around the world, through the adoption of stronger and more coercive resolutions as well.

12.5. Recommendations

The recommendations here are primarily directed to the UN Security Council, the states parties to the ICC Statute, the government of Mali, Malian and international civil society organisations, and technical and financial partners.

12.5.1. United Nations Security Council

The UN Security Council is the main organ providing international standards for peace and security in the world. As such, it must make greater efforts in the production of standards and other effective binding, preventative and deterrent measures. A dynamic international diplomacy should be put at the disposal of such an international legislative policy. Regional and sub-regional institutions such as the African Union and ECOWAS should adopt the same policy.

12.5.2. States Parties to the ICC Statute

The states parties to the ICC Statute intend to confer to the ICC the power to act as a real tool of peace and security worldwide. This will be more evident when all countries trust the institution and accept it as a remedy for violence. For this, they must conduct more active diplomacy with the aim of convincing all states to ratify the ICC Statute in order to respond to the widespread need for security in the sub-region, by giving to the ICC the opportunity to investigate and freely prosecute all violations in all countries and regions in crisis.

It is equally important that states parties to the ICC Statute provide the means for the credibility of the institution by showing more impartiality in the prosecutions. All failures, all violations of international humanitarian law must receive deserved punishment, including for the winners of armed conflicts. A debate must be launched to expand the scope of the competence of the Court.

And finally, states parties must make clear their political will to fully co-operate in achieving the goals of the ICC, including from the financial point of view.

12.5.3. Malian Government

Referring a case to the ICC is not enough. The government of Mali must address the operationalisation of its legal system, which is broken. It must build on the support of the international community and civil society organisations to confer credibility to justice. The reforms in the field of security and justice must be implemented and closely monitored. The government must fully co-operate to allow investigations of members of the army, who have committed serious crimes during the crises, thus complying with the fight against impunity. The government should revise its prevention and crisis alert methods.

12.5.4. Malian and International Civil Society Organisations and Technical and Financial Partners

The technical and financial partners and the organisations of national and international civil society have not only a technical and financial support role to play in enabling the implementation of reforms leading to peace and security, including the legal treatment of populations, but also a monitoring role in the fight against corruption, ensuring compliance with the laws and principles of political and economic good governance.

13

———

Findings and Recommendations

Jennifer Schense[*] and Linda Carter[**]

The Chinese philosopher Lao Tzu is credited with the saying, "A journey of a thousand miles begins with a single step". The editors and authors of this volume have taken this philosophy in stride, in aiming to showcase new information and ideas that will advance the dialogue about how international crimes can be deterred. No one expects such an endeavour to succeed overnight, or even in the early days in the life of international justice, but neither can it succeed without sober and clear-eyed reflection about what has been achieved thus far, what obstacles have arisen and how successes – even limited or temporary ones – can serve as the foundation for more lasting change over the long term. All the participants in this project have approached this endeavour from the perspective of committed advocates of justice for all. In that spirit, all will continue in their own ways to contribute to the ongoing dialogue.

Looking over the 10 case studies comprising this study, two crucial elements and seven themes deserve further reflection and discussion. The-

---

[*]   **Jennifer Schense** is the founding director of the House of Nuremberg and of Cat Kung Fu Productions, both dedicated to creating films and other popular, cultural works reflecting on justice. She has also worked with the International Criminal Court ('ICC') Office of the Prosecutor in the Jurisdiction, Complementarity and Cooperation Division since 2004, and is currently contributing to the ICC Registry's external relations and networking strategy. Prior to her work at the ICC, she served as the Legal Adviser for the NGO Coalition for the International Criminal Court from September 1998 until September 2004, and served for one year as a fellow at Human Rights Watch. She is currently completing her Ph.D. in international criminal law at Leiden University. She received her Juris Doctorate from Columbia Law School in 1997, and her B.Sc. in Russian language and Russian area studies from Georgetown University in 1993.

[**]   **Linda Carter** is a Distinguished Professor of Law Emerita at the University of the Pacific, McGeorge School of Law, California, USA, where she teaches and researches on issues of domestic and international criminal law. Her most recent publications include, as co-editor, *International Criminal Procedure: The Interface of Civil Law and Common Law Legal Systems* (Edward Elgar, 2013) and, as co-author, *The International Criminal Court in an Effective Global System* (Edward Elgar, 2016). She has also participated in programmes in various international venues in teaching, research and programme development roles. She taught in the Nuremberg Summer Academy in 2016. She is a member of numerous professional organisations, including election to the American Law Institute.

---

se common elements and themes ground the recommendations that this volume offers in particular to policy-makers, whether in the employ of states or elsewhere, as well as to the International Criminal Court ('ICC') as it moves forward. The concrete suggestions proposed are intended to move us a few steps further down the path to global accountability, respect for the law and value of each other as human beings.

To begin with an observation succinctly set out in the Kosovo chapter and to paraphrase it as simply as possible:

Deterrence = actual threat + perception of threat of accountability

To further clarify, actual threat is generated according to deterrence theory by the certainty, severity and speed of investigations and prosecutions. The perception of the threat must outweigh the perception of potential benefits. The Sierra Leone chapter echoes this analysis, arguing that there must be a criminal justice mechanism in place or the strong possibility of establishing one to prosecute individuals concerned when they are making their risk analysis, and these individuals must be aware they could be prosecuted. Without the reality and the perception, there can be no deterrence. Both of these elements are explored in more detail in the next two sections, using examples from chapters on specific country situations. Following this discussion, the seven themes that emerged from the case studies are developed. As a final section, this chapter makes recommendations for international and national policy-makers and the ICC.

Preliminarily, it is important to recognise that deterrence is a multifaceted concept. *Specific deterrence* refers to the cessation of criminal activity by a perpetrator who is prosecuted. In the case of international criminal tribunals, this is a limited group of individuals – those who have been or are being prosecuted in an international or national forum. *General deterrence* is a utilitarian concept that the punishment of a perpetrator will deter others who might contemplate criminal conduct. This form of deterrence sweeps broadly and contemplates an impact on all persons within a society and even within the broader international community. More nuanced aspects of deterrence are *targeted deterrence* and *restrictive deterrence*. Targeted deterrence is the effort to impact on the criminal activity of specified individuals or categories of individuals. In this study, targeted deterrence is often the issue as military and political officials, similarly situated to those who are prosecuted, are identified as the groups that it is hoped the tribunals will most deter. Restrictive deterrence also arises in the case studies; it is a partial form of deterrence that causes individuals to limit, even though they do not entirely cease, their criminal activities.

Another categorisation of deterrence is either as *prosecutorial* or as *social* deterrence. Prosecutorial deterrence was the primary focus of this study and includes specific, general, targeted and restrictive deterrence – all forms of deterrence generated by court or prosecutorial actions. Social deterrence refers to the impact of actors or entities, other than prosecutions, on furthering deterrence. This can include national institutions, such as a legislature, and social pressures such as from community values. The case studies identified social deterrence where it was relevant to their specific country.

The case studies that explored the various forms of deterrence were designed to gather three types of information: 1) statistical data on incidence of violence; 2) actual deterrence of perpetrators or would-be perpetrators; and 3) perceptions of perpetrators, similarly situated political and military leaders, victims, and the broader community represented by academics, non-governmental organisations ('NGOs') and other military and civilian experts. The search for evidence of deterrence is elusive. Perceptions of individuals and groups are key to deriving insights about deterrence from the work of the tribunals. Correlation between statistical data and the work of international tribunals is difficult, if not impossible, to establish and evidence from convicted perpetrators of specific deterrence is necessarily limited in quantity and hard to obtain or verify. However, the qualitative research into the perceptions of a wide range of constituencies about the effect of the tribunals provides an extraordinary window into how deterrence works and how it can be better achieved. The painstaking work of the authors of this book through all forms of research, but especially through interviews and focus group sessions, yielded a significant body of information and a greater understanding of both actual and perceived deterrence.

The 10 countries chosen for the case studies were selected to examine multiple international criminal tribunals and also proceedings in multiple stages with varied results. Serbia and Kosovo are two of the situations under the aegis of the International Criminal Tribunal for the former Yugoslavia ('ICTY'). These cases are largely concluded, so the interviewees could reflect on reactions at each phase of the prosecutions. Prosecutions have similarly concluded in the Rwanda and Sierra Leone situations before the International Criminal Tribunal for Rwanda ('ICTR') and the Special Court for Sierra Leone ('SCSL'). By considering three of the earlier tribunals, it is possible to compare and contrast factors affecting deterrence. Moreover, the experience with the earlier tribunals provides a foundation for analysing ICC situation countries. The Democratic Republic of the Congo ('DRC') and Uganda were the earliest cases before the ICC, but with different experiences in the progress of prosecutions. Kenya and Darfur (Sudan) are situations where the ICC issued arrest warrants or summonses, but the proceedings encountered problems in moving forward. Two of the newer situations, Côte d'Ivoire and Mali, allow study of the early phases of interaction with an international criminal tribunal.

Taking into account the differences among the situations and the types of deterrence, the next two sections develop the findings on the elements of actual and perceived deterrence. It is problematic to measure or reach conclusions on actual deterrence, but the perceptions of crucial groups of individuals in each case study on a deterrent effect from the work of international criminal tribunals as well as what impeded deterrence provides a significant amount of information for future efforts.

13.1. Actual Deterrence: Performance of the International Criminal Tribunals

One of the most difficult challenges in measuring actual performance is the problem of correlation. To what degree can specific actions be linked to specific consequences? The authors have generally acknowledged that there is no perfect correlation to be obtained. In some cases, the facts seem to point away from a correlation, as in Serbia and in Kosovo, where it is argued that the worst atrocities in the former Yugoslavia happened despite the ICTY's existence. Likewise, in the DRC, following the guilty verdict in the Lubanga case in 2012 for war crimes of recruiting and using child soldiers, although rates of child recruitment in Ituri dropped considerably from those at the height of the conflict, the rebel group Mouvement du 23-Mars ('M23') continued with widespread recruitment and use of children, as did other armed groups elsewhere in the DRC. Despite Germaine Katanga's arrest and conviction, Force de résistance patriotique d'Ituri ('FRPI', Front for Patriotic Resistance in Ituri) continued to commit serious violations; in January 2015 the United Nations Organisation Stabilisation Mission in the DRC (MONUSCO) reported that 35 per cent of FRPI recruits were children. Most situations will present a similarly mixed picture when it comes to correlation. All in all, the authors found that any direct correlation – while appealing as a concept – was not finally a useful measure of deterrence in their situations.

In some cases, the facts seem to point towards a correlated deterrent effect, but one that cannot be wholly or even necessarily attributed to the tribunal's intervention. The decrease in incidences of violence and casualties in Kosovo after the May 1999 ICTY indictment of Slobodan Milošević could be correlated or coincidental, as the author notes, following as it did as well the NATO military intervention. Likewise, Darfur statistics show a drop-off in incidents and fatalities in early 2005, around the time of the Darfur referral to the ICC, but this seeming correlation does not necessarily mean that the ICC deterred crimes. It is interesting to note, though, that Kosovo respondents believed generally that "if the tribunal did not exist, the situation would have been worse, as the perpetrators would not be sentenced by anyone" since there "would not be any other court or body that would try these cases". Respondents in the Darfur situation also argued that the scale of violations would have been greater had the ICC not intervened.

Rwanda presents a similar example. In the view of respondents, in particular victims, the certainty of apprehension and prosecution of high-profile perpetrators by the ICTR is shown to have achieved deterrence. However, on severity of punishment and speed factors, respondents indicate that the ICTR needed improvement compared with national processes. For an interesting counterpoint to this general argument, it is worth noting the views of the five respondents in Nyarugenge central prison regarding those national processes, who informed the author: "We confessed of our crimes, provided information implicating others, asked for forgiveness and even some [three] of us testified in the ICTR as prosecution witnesses. Well, this had no impact on the sentences handed to us, most of us are serving life sentences".

A Ministry of Justice respondent described the unique contribution of the ICTR as "the identification of suspects who were abroad, gathering information related to the offences that they were suspected to have committed, and an increase of the number of international arrest warrants sent by ICTR to other foreign countries where those suspects were hidden", a category of suspects less readily available for national proceedings. The chapter goes on to demonstrate that the ICTR's impact cannot be examined in isolation from the extensive efforts undertaken by Rwandan authorities to investigate and prosecute the authors of the genocide through national proceedings, both in formal courts and in *gacaca* trials. As respondents in the prison focus group discussion noted on the impact of national proceedings: "*Gacaca* trials took place in cells, sectors and villages of perpetrators where perpetrators were living and this is a humbling experience that no one wants". Correlation between the ICTR's impact and deterrence cannot be undertaken without reference to these other factors.

Kenya reflects some positive developments as well. As the author argues, the ICC may have cracked the whip at the right time. It arguably prevented widespread violence during the 2013 election, although there is some debate about whether this violence went underground or was sublimated, only to threaten to arise again in the upcoming 2017 election. A similar argument has been made in relation to Côte d'Ivoire, in which some respondents argued that the ICC helped to ensure peaceful elections in October 2015.

Cracking the whip is an interesting analogy as well because, to extend the analogy, whipping a horse to goad movement may lead to unintended and unpleasant consequences; in the fight against impunity, those who enjoy impunity will almost certainly kick back. In the Kenya situation, the author argues that the Kenyan political class, accustomed to feeling itself above the law, was spurred into action in two directions: first, constitutional reform in Kenya that was used in the short term to undermine ICC action, but that in the longer term could have a more powerful deterrent effect; and second, intensive regional diplomacy to generate African support for an Article 16 deferral of the Kenya situation at the UN Security Council and to lobby for restrictive legal actions at the ICC Assembly of States Parties. The correlation between ICC action and Kenyan response is fairly clear, but a correlation with deterrence of crimes is much less so. A similar situation may be shaping up in Burundi, currently under ICC preliminary examination. The Rwanda chapter touches on the current Burundi situation, citing a respondent from the Ministry of Justice, who added from his or her perspective: "The incidents currently happening in Burundi are an indicator that the Great Lakes region did not learn from the events in Rwanda. The event of post-election violence in Kenya in 2007 is another indicator of the absence of learning from history or events in other countries. In the Congo, there are often isolated incidents, but they need attention to avert a major crisis".

The Mali chapter notes that the former ICC judge from Mali had cited the impact of ICC activities in other situations as scaring the Burundi president, Pierre Nkurunziza, into not engaging in criminal activity, but more recently Nkurunziza has stated that he will withdraw Burundi from the ICC Statute so they can be totally free to take whatever steps they deem necessary. The unintended consequence of ICC activities on Burundi and elsewhere may be the creation of a broader culture of impunity in that country situation. Time will tell.

The Kosovo, Serbia and Darfur situations pose the question whether the responsive cover-up of crimes can be considered a form of restrictive deterrence or only an acknowledgement (if a back-handed one) that the actions being covered up are illegal. As a reminder, restrictive deterrence exists "when, to diminish the risk or severity of a legal punishment, a potential offender engages in some action that has the effect of reducing his or her commission of a crime".[1] This might include "reducing the frequency, severity, or duration of their offending, or displace their crimes temporally, spatially, or tactically".[2]

In Kosovo, Serb forces noticeably changed their behaviour as the threat of a NATO intervention loomed, as seen in intensified efforts to conceal mass graves and hide evidence and criminal conduct. Some individuals also began to give up their colleagues and former combatants, a move more likely to have a restrictive deterrent effect than strict cover-up of crimes. In Darfur, the government of Sudan engaged in repeated efforts to cover up crimes.

In Serbia, one civil society representative opined:

> If we take a look at the way in which the crimes had been committed from the beginning of the war in Yugoslavia, from summer of 1991 when the operation around Vukovar started and then all the way until 1999. [...] There is, at least that's my impression, that the role of the Tribunal was that [...] if nothing else, the perpetrators started hiding their crimes, and as time was passing they were doing that more and more. [...] It appears to me that they did that first of all because of the Tribunal. So, I think that is the proof of that deterrent effect. The Court could not prevent them from [further] commission of the crimes, but if nothing else it

---

[1]   Jack P. Gibbs, "Deterrence Theory and Research", in Gary B. Melton (ed.), *The Law as a Behavioral Instrument*, University of Nebraska Press, Lincoln, 1986, p. 89.

[2]   Kim Moeller, Heith Copes and Andy Hochstetler, "Advancing Restrictive Deterrence: A Qualitative Meta-Synthesis", *Journal of Criminal Justice*, 2016, vol. 46, p. 82.

prevented them to do that openly and in front of the cameras.

While this testimony and others suggest strongly that high-ranking perpetrators were put on notice that they, too, could be called to account, it likely is more of a cover-up than actual restrictive deterrence.

It is thus problematic to attempt to measure or correlate deterrence with the work of international criminal courts. At best, it is possible to document parallel events, either a decrease or an increase in violence, but there are too many actors and too many variables to find a direct or even an indirect effect conclusively. This is not surprising as proving actual deterrence in domestic criminal justice systems is similarly vexing. However, the perceptions of deterrence or lack of deterrence, discussed in the next section, are more identifiable and useful in evaluating the impact of international tribunals.

13.2. Perceived Deterrence: Perceptions of Performance of the International Criminal Tribunals

Perhaps the most important common thread among the case studies has been the importance of perception. As the introduction noted, it is common sense that perpetrators, victims, bystanders and others act on their perceptions, for good or bad. Rational actor theory supports the argument that if perpetrators perceive that potential prosecutions threaten them, this perception will affect their choices. It matters less in the short term if these perceptions are correct, but more in the long term, as mainstream criminology supports the idea that primarily certainty of punishment, not swiftness or severity, has a deterrent effect.

As the introduction further noted, on the qualitative side, authors collected and evaluated information on three key factors: 1) discernible change in behaviour and perceptions on the part of suspects, accused and 'like-minded' individuals, including political and business elites and rebels; 2) changes in views and perceptions of victims about how or whether the relevant tribunal's effect has contributed to their safety; and 3) views of NGO members and experts on whether the tribunal has had a deterrent effect. Not all respondents canvassed for these studies shared the same perceptions, which of course is not surprising, but can make it more difficult to assess what had the greatest effect on actions subsequently taken.

The authors identified a number of court-based factors that affected perceptions of deterrence, including: whether the tribunal concerned was situated in-country or elsewhere; the limits of the tribunal's jurisdiction (temporal, subject matter and personal); whether the tribunal concerned undertook appropriate and effective outreach; the speed and number of indictments; whether the tribunals concerned successfully concluded cases and convicted and sentenced individuals; the length of sentences handed down; effectiveness of enforcement; prosecutorial strategy; legitimacy; resources; and whether the person convicted expressed genuine remorse. They also identified a number of non-legal or contextual factors that were similarly influential, including: the impact of the use of propaganda; the truth-telling capacity of trials; the contribution of trials to strengthening the national judiciary; group dynamics; the role of elites in the society; cross-situation influences; political and social norms; a culture of impunity; the level of awareness; legitimacy and perceptions of legitimacy; the existence and strength of national institutions; and the role of the international community. The number of both court-based and contextual factors complicates each situation and renders each situation somewhat unique as different factors are dominant in each case.

As an example of the complexity of court-based factors, some observers in Kosovo found indictments had a punitive effect, in showing that their subjects were not untouchable, but found the subsequent sentences to be insufficiently severe. At the same time, they found that the ICTY contributed to writing history and documenting violations, and triggering trials at the national level. However, in both the Serbia and Kosovo situations, observers found that outreach efforts failed to translate the ICTY's contribution to the historical record to a broader audience beyond scholarly readers. In Rwanda, respondents likewise found the sentences to be insufficiently severe, and the trials to have taken too long and addressed too few alleged perpetrators. They also criticised the ICTR's location outside of Rwanda as making it inaccessible, although perceived this choice as reflecting the fall-out in relations between Rwanda and the ICTR as it was being established, a factor that ostensibly places blame on both sides. At the same time, they acknowledged that the ICTR accessed some high-profile perpetrators who might otherwise have gone free, as they were outside the reach of Rwandan authorities, and acknowledged shortcomings in national proceedings, in particular in relation to witness protection in the *gacaca* trials. In response to a question about increased security as a result of *gacaca*, respondents in the survivors group argued:

> I would answer that [*gacaca*] contributed up to 40 per cent of security. Let me begin with a no. Since the commencement of *gacaca*, there is a big number of survivors who were murdered. There are those who were killed because they had proved to be giving credible evidence of what happened during the genocide. There are those who were judges in the *gacaca* courts. And, there are those who were victimised for their participation in the *gacaca* courts.

Victims in general had more positive impressions of the ICTR, as opposed to government representatives, who viewed the ICTR's deterrent effect as more limited.

In Mali, local religious authorities in Timbuktu and Gao consider the deterrent effect of the Al Mahdi case to be real, and especially heightened by his expression of remorse; at the same time, others interviewed believe that the ICC has been too selective in its investigations thus far to deter, for example, members of government forces who have as yet gone unexamined. These comparisons serve as testament to the fact that many moving parts affect perceptions of the work of the courts and tribunals, and why tracking and assessing them is a serious challenge.

It is important to note in this regard that even the process of identifying these factors is likewise a matter of perception. Authors synthesise the views of their respondents through their own perceptions and understandings. In this regard, perception plays an outsized role in evaluating the work of the tribunals, from a number of angles – how the participants, perpetrators and victims perceive a situation and the international community's response to it, and how responders and observers perceive these situations and respond in turn. In this context, a common factor in many chapters, that of selectivity or even politicisation, is truly in the eye of the beholder. For example, the Kosovo chapter documents respondents' views of several ICTY cases in which the view is correlated with the ethnicity of the respondent and the accused. In general, Kosovar Serbs viewed prosecutions of ethnic Serbs as unfair while Kosovar Albanians viewed prosecutions of ethnic Albanians as unfair. In each case, the respondents believed the ICTY was targeting their side of the conflict selectively. This is not necessarily good news for the international tribunals concerned, as this perception of selectivity or politicisation affects the legitimacy of the courts and tribunals, whether or not it is objectively true.

With this background on actual and perceived deterrence in mind, the more detailed themes that can be distilled from the case studies are explored in the next section.

13.3. Themes from the Case Studies

13.3.1. The Importance of Outreach

All of the situations canvassed amply demonstrate the importance of thorough, engaged, imaginative and interactive outreach on the part of the international courts and tribunals. This outreach is essential to spreading knowledge that serious international crimes have taken place and to contributing to early warning as a mechanism of deterrence. The role that an international court can play, in providing objective information in the form of evidence and warrants, is unique. It can also serve as a platform for raising awareness in general about the law.

In the DRC, community leaders in Ituri interviewed acknowledged that there now exists greater knowledge that recruitment and use of children is a violation of the law, something that has translated into lower numbers of children recruited, as well as having translated into a degree of fear among some senior actors in armed groups of the potential of prosecutions. This knowledge has complemented the greater impact of disarmament programmes on lowering the levels of child recruitment. The community leaders added, though, that there persists a lack of detailed understanding of the law itself and a fair amount of antipathy towards the ICC over its choice of targets, highlighting that more work remains to be done on outreach.

In Kenya, the author notes that lack of understanding of how the ICC works substantially diminished its deterrent effect, in combination with a specific convergence of local politics, and systemic problems with domestic mechanisms. Many members of parliament ('MPs') and other politicians had serious misperceptions about the ICC, which affected decisions about national as well as international justice. One MP argued:

> If you look at the history of those conflicts and the matters
> which have been taken before The Hague, [the actions of the
> accused from Kenya are less serious than those] who have

> gone to the International Criminal Court because the thresh-
> old is so high for it to act.

Another MP said:

> In Rwanda, it took the international community to witness
> the mass massacre of over 1 million people to agree to set up
> the tribunal. That was after all the calamity had happened!
> We also know about the calamity that has taken place in
> Darfur, Sudan. It is only now that they are talking about set-
> ting up one. In Liberia, where they tried some people, the
> amount of calamity was also very substantial. It is also the
> same in the former Yugoslavia. What happened in Kenya in
> 2007 was tragic and really tragic. But it is not sufficient to
> call for the intervention of the ICC.

The perception that ICC intervention was impossible affected greatly the
steps taken by national politicians on justice issues. Others undermined
national justice initiatives on the opposite misunderstanding, that the ICC
would try all their adversaries, so that a competing national tribunal
should not be supported. Another misunderstanding about the ICC arose
from the perception that the ICC did not conduct independent investigations, but only recycled civil society and other reports, a perception that
undermined the legitimacy of the Court; this led to assumptions that the
ICC targeted the wrong people.

In Kosovo, the author found that not many people know what happened in the ICTY, and for what reason people were indicted and tried,
and therefore, why they were received as heroes upon their return home.
Civil society representatives argued, "No one has made an effort to talk
about the actual numbers and the fact that someone is responsible for the
deaths of those people". Or as another put it, "Whatever has happened in
the Court has remained in the Court". As a result, people both in Serbia
and Kosovo viewed the ICTY as a political body targeting solely its leaders.

In Uganda, a majority of respondents agreed that the ICC intervention in Uganda deterred future crimes because it created awareness and
instilled fear of the consequences of committing mass atrocities in Lord's
Resistance Army ('LRA') and Uganda People's Defence Force ('UPDF')
combatants. Respondents observed that there was a drastic change in UP-
DF conduct after the warrants of arrest against the LRA were unsealed;
government troops stopped committing human rights abuses overtly.

In Côte d'Ivoire, respondents, including those similarly placed to the defendants, argued there was not enough communication about the ICC's activities. Aside from the activities of Coalition ivoirienne pour la Cour pénale internationale (Côte d'Ivoire Coalition for the ICC), they felt they were not sufficiently informed. Civil society members felt the ICC had not helped mitigate the massive violation of human rights that took place during the Ivorian crisis, that belligerents did not have sufficient information to affect their conduct or to be deterred.

In Rwanda, some respondents argued that the ICTR did not conduct sufficient outreach, and in particular in languages other than English. At the same time, respondents acknowledged that without the ICTR, justice imposed by the new government in Kigali would likely have been perceived as victor's justice against the Hutu, and that the international community would not have accepted the *gacaca* process. Others added that national processes would have been less known without the ICTR's high-profile work, and that this greater awareness contributed to greater security for victims. Finally, others noted that the ICTR could provide very practical protection to some victims, relocating them to Belgium or other countries.

What is clear from these situations is that outreach, as with any form of true communication, must be a two-way street, a conversation, and must be agile enough to consider responses (positive and negative), understand their cultural grounding, and respond with clarifications and further information that will help ensure that the court or tribunal concerned is truly understood.

13.3.2. Outreach Versus Propaganda

A related theme to general outreach and knowledge is the impact of outreach by the tribunals and courts versus the impact of propaganda employed to counter that outreach. Of course, these terms are both relatively loaded; one could argue in the broadest sense that both constitute a form of outreach, with the purpose of informing but also convincing a broad audience of the rightness of action taken by whoever is propagating that outreach. Nevertheless, what could be called propaganda because of the intent to sway national audiences away from the cause of international justice is important to understand because it seriously affects perceptions.

Sierra Leone offers a particularly interesting example of the impact of controlling the flow of information. The chapter notes that when rebel leader Foday Sankoh signed the peace agreement, he saw the UN notation overriding a blanket amnesty, and asked with some alacrity whether it meant he could be prosecuted. His question was ignored. Others confirm that the attention of the Revolutionary United Front ('RUF') delegation was simply not drawn to the potential limitations of the amnesty provisions. In this case, deliberate withholding of information had an impact on the perception of perpetrators about the threat of accountability. Many of those later indicted were blindsided, signalling their low awareness of the risk. In contrast, some of those at no risk of prosecution responded to the establishment of the SCSL by fleeing to Liberia. Interestingly, others who remained in Liberia learned from court outreach sessions that the prosecutorial strategy of targeting those bearing the greatest responsibility would leave them safe. Eventually, those who fled to Liberia returned when they felt sufficiently safe from prosecution. Ironically, the Lomé Agreement amnesty provision provided a false sense of security to those who were actually most likely to be targeted for prosecution.

Kenya is one situation where traditional propaganda came seriously into play. As the chapter's author notes, while some found the African Union's arguments and efforts laughable, others found them believable, and shared the sentiment that the ICC is biased against Africa. This translated into assumptions on the part of some victims and others that the ICC withdrew its Kenya cases due to political pressure. Serbia is another situation where controversy arose with the issuance of the Radovan Karadžić judgment, from which some drew the conclusion that Milošević had been effectively exonerated for lack of sufficient evidence that he agreed with the common plan. In Uganda, Joseph Kony used the ICC warrants as a propaganda tool to frighten his combatants into continuing loyalty.

The Darfur situation demonstrates that a cover-up of crimes, also addressed later in these conclusions, served as a form of propaganda. A cover-up affects the perceptions of observers because lack of adequate information skews understanding of what is truly going on. The author on Darfur notes how the government of Sudan effectively blocked access to information for journalists, NGOs, the UN and others, rendering it more difficult to advocate for action on ongoing crimes. As one Sudanese activist noted: "It became more difficult to report the crimes. The government was acting in the darkness – no one was watching". This led to some oth-

erwise reliable observers reaching the conclusion that criminality had diminished, with the result that the international community's attention
shifted elsewhere. It is perhaps ironic in the Darfur situation that the government's extensive propaganda campaign had the unintended effect of
raising awareness of the Sudanese public about the Darfur situation, and
familiarised them to the idea that President Omar Al Bashir was an alleged criminal.

Recognising the existence and role of propaganda or counter-
messages to the actual work of the international tribunals is necessary in
the quest for deterrence as international courts and the international community need to take it into account in determining how, when and to
whom the information about the Court's work should be disseminated.

13.3.3. The Noble Cause

Propaganda finds fertile ground in the noble cause. It is arguable that no
perpetrators believe that their actions are immoral or wrong. The chapters
almost invariably demonstrate that perpetrators feel motivated by the
rightness of their cause. As Mark A. Drumbl has written, perpetrators may
believe they are doing good by eliminating the "evil other"; their
attachment to the normative value of their actions warps their perceptions
of the costs and benefits of their actions.[3]

In the DRC, local actors noted that many people did not consider
recruiting child soldiers to be a crime; at least for self-defence militias,
"members share the notion that their cause is noble – to defend the
interests of their community and violations by the army or other armed
groups", which trumps other considerations, including precluding children
from joining their ranks. Respondents in Kenya reacted similarly, noting
that in self-defence, acts that would amount to atrocities become heroic,
and despite the emergence of a new norm making them illegal,
suspending such norms amid desperate struggles to defend one's
community would be a possibility.

In Kosovo, people refused to believe that the Kosovo Liberation
Army ('KLA') may have committed war crimes, believing instead that the
KLA was engaged in a "pure war to protect the land and the family". In

---

[3] Mark A. Drumbl, *Atrocity, Punishment, and International Law*, Cambridge University
Press, New York, 2007, pp. 169–73.

Serbia, when asked by a journalist in 2004 whether he had ever considered that he might end up in front of the ICTY, General Vladimir Lazarević said he did not have time to think of such things, as he was occupied with fighting terrorism, preserving human lives and the functioning of life in Kosovo. The Serbian government-organised voluntary surrenders of the indicted "Serbian heroes" followed a similar playbook, with the "patriotic, moral and honourable decision" of indicted persons to appear before the ICTY being presented as a brave continuation of their fight for their country, for which they and their families were financially compensated. Once they completed their sentences, the Serbian government welcomed them back as heroes and many found places again in politics and public life. Prime Minister Aleksandar Vučić explained his position in regard to Lazarević thus: "Based on the Hague Tribunal's ruling, General Lazarević is responsible for the crimes [committed] in Kosovo. And what did General Lazarević do? [He was] fulfilling his military duties. [...] I am not sure that anyone in Serbia thinks that General Lazarević is really a criminal".

In Mali, at the Kati garrison, one of Mali's largest military bases, a national army colonel offered: "If our men killed civilians, it was for a good cause. How would you distinguish between a civilian and a military? These white-skinned people are all soldiers and civilians at the same time; it's part of their war tactic. The rules of humanitarian law, okay! But we were not in a conventional war". In Sierra Leone, Sam Hinga Norman, then minister of defence and head of the Civil Defence Forces ('CDF'), Moinina Fofana, CDF director of war, Allieu Kondewa, CDF high priest, and Issa Sesay, interim leader of the RUF, were particularly surprised by their arrests and indictments. They saw their risk of punishment as extremely low because they believed they had contributed to the peace process. Even the late President Ahmad Tejan Kabbah testified that Sesay had contributed to bringing the war to an end. The CDF likewise perceived themselves as restorers of democracy in Sierra Leone, having defended the people and territory when the state was helpless against the RUF incursion. In Uganda, LRA members came to believe that they were engaged in a struggle to overthrow an illegitimate government, which came to power through a violent coup, and to spiritually cleanse the people of Acholi and the country.

From these examples, it is clear that the "noble cause" phenomenon is not uncommon in conflict and post-conflict situations. Understanding this hurdle to full acknowledgement of international crimes may help with outreach and, ultimately, with achieving a deterrent effect.

13.3.4. Legitimacy and Selectivity

Legitimacy also emerges as a major issue relating to perception; if people in situation countries perceive the international court or tribunal concerned as illegitimate, it affects their willingness to engage with the institution in any way, and it diminishes deterrence. As the Darfur chapter noted, borrowing from John Dietrich:

> Deterrence only works if potential criminals 1) make rational calculations before their actions, 2) know the laws and, ideally, accept them as legitimate limits on their behavior, 3) feel that the benefits of a given crime are relatively low, and 4) believe the costs of the crime are high as influenced by the certainty, swiftness and severity of punishment.[4]

For the respondents interviewed for the chapters in this study, a key issue relating to perceived legitimacy of the international courts and tribunals was selectivity. As Drumbl has noted, selectivity and indeterminacy are especially corrosive.[5]

The ability of a court to deter crimes is highly dependent on it being perceived as a legitimate court, which includes proving that it is not subject to political influence, but rather is fair and unbiased, in order to earn the trust and respect of the societies at large.[6] In Kosovo, some respondents viewed the ICTY as illegitimate because they felt it only intervened when instructed, resulting in particular leaders being spared from the Tribunal at specific times. This impression was deepened by the ICTY's obvious reliance on the political support of states and the Security Council. Further, ICTY efforts to undertake cases in both Serbia and Kosovo led to the perception that the prosecutor chose cases on the basis of some kind of moral equivalence between the parties, not on the basis of

---

[4] John Dietrich, "The Limited Prospects of Deterrence by the International Criminal Court: Lessons from Domestic Experience", in *International Social Science Review*, 2014, vol. 88, no. 3, p. 3.

[5] Mark A. Drumbl, "Collective Violence and Individual Punishment: The Criminality of Mass Atrocity", in *Northwestern University Law Review*, 2015, vol. 99, no. 2, pp. 539–610.

[6] Ivan Simonovic, "The Role of the ICTY in the Development of International Criminal Adjudication", in *Fordham International Law Journal*, 1999, vol. 23, p. 440.

evidence,[7] with parties on either side of the divide ultimately unhappy.

The Côte d'Ivoire situation, though, illustrates the flip side of the coin, why sequencing cases between two sides of a conflict can be dangerous. In this case, as the author notes, national trials are often staged with the aim of generating legitimacy for a post-conflict government while galvanising its core constituency. Simone Gbagbo's trial, as a key pillar of the fallen regime, may fall into that category; ICC cases focusing also on key figures in the fallen regime support the perception by some respondents that justice has only targeted one side of the conflict. As one respondent argued:

> The prosecutorial strategy adopted by the ICC in Côte d'Ivoire [...] (one side first, the other after) affects its deterrent effect because this strategy is not convincing. It would be beneficial for the ICC to also prosecute the winners' camp. The Court has opened room diverse in interpretation [...] This strategy gives the impression that the ICC has already chosen its camp. This creates doubts.

President Ouattara's repeated assertion that he will surrender no further Ivorian nationals to the ICC, as he sees the ICC's job as done, does not help. While some Ivorians, including "presumed perpetrators" from the Congrès panafricain des jeunes et des patriotes ('Young Patriots') and Commando invisible, did contend that the ICC had a deterrent effect, they felt it was limited by an overly selective prosecution policy that did not include all persons who committed offences. Other civil society representatives hedged that the ICC's sequenced approach could work, but only if Ivorian authorities take deliberate steps to investigate and prosecute individuals from Ouattara's group.

In Serbia, respondents found that the government exercised a similar strategy to Ouattara's, to try to limit further indictments from the ICTY. Serbian respondents also contended that the ICTY diminished its own legitimacy by allowing lengthy delays of the trials and through the so-called "controversial acquittals" (cases of Perišić, Haradinaj, Gotovina and Šešelj) due to uneven judicial application of principles of joint criminal enterprise. The death of Milošević in custody without judgment fuelled conspiracy theories about the Tribunal being an anti-Serb court, as

---

[7]   Minna Schrag, "The Yugoslav Crimes Tribunal: A Prosecutor's View", in *Duke Journal of Comparative and International Law*, 1995, vol. 6, no. 1, p. 187.

well as underscoring the perception that the ICTY was not judicially effective, that trials were too long, and that both Milošević and Šešelj were allowed to turn the courtroom into "a theatre" by allowing them to represent themselves.

In the DRC, respondents felt that the ICC did not adequately target higher-level actors behind the commission of atrocities, focused only on Ituri and not the entire region, failed to secure convictions of all accused, did not charge crimes in a more holistic fashion, failed to confirm charges brought against Callixte Mbarushimana, and failed to award reparations to victims. Some respondents also viewed the Bemba case, involving a Congolese militia leader and politician who intervened militarily in the Central African Republic at the behest of its then president, as demonstrative of politicisation of the Court.

In Kenya, the ICC prosecution's choice to investigate only three Orange Democratic Movement (the then-opposition) and three Party of National Unity (the then-ruling party) individuals, has been heavily criticised. Although the prosecutor denied playing local party politics, many observers drew the conclusion that his strategy reflected its influence. Arguably, the prosecutor chose a similar number of indictees from the two major political parties in order to show balance and thereby appease both factions. In a one-on-one interview, a Kenyan MP argued that it would have been more sensible for the prosecutor to go for the heads of the two political factions as they had the overall influence on the violence. Essentially, in the view of most respondents, the prosecutor went for lower-ranking people in an endeavour to protect those at the top.

In Kosovo, respondents argued variously that the ICTY took too long to start cases in the first place, started trials too late, and focused on high-level trials to the detriment of pursuing direct perpetrators who still walked free. In Sierra Leone, respondents interpreted the sentences issued, significantly lengthier than the ICTY's, as too severe on government opponents versus government supporters, and therefore as victor's justice. In Darfur, respondents mainly felt frustrated about the lack of arrests and the continued high visibility and activity of those under arrest warrants. In Uganda, respondents questioned the ICC's selection of cases and argued that it undermined the Court's legitimacy, as it focused on LRA atrocities to the exclusion of UPDF crimes.

In Rwanda, the chapter argues that between the ICTR and numerous national proceedings, the ICTR and national authorities achieved at the very least restrictive deterrence, in that large numbers of perpetrators were almost immediately in detention, and large numbers of convictions were thereafter achieved, promoting specific deterrence. Both the ICTR and national authorities focused exclusively on the genocide's perpetrators. Some have argued that the very narrow focus of this approach makes it unclear how it would apply to other crimes of a similar scale or gravity in the future, which speaks to the potential question of selectivity. Respondents viewed limited temporal jurisdiction as a 'weakness' in both the instances of the ICTR's work and that of specialised national chambers, the latter which were limited by law to the 1 October 1990 to 31 December 1994 period.

The selectivity argument will likely continue to plague international courts and tribunals, so long as they do not have the resources and structure to cast their net widely and quickly. It is unfortunate, as the various situations studied demonstrate, that international courts and tribunals often end up in 'damned if you do, damned if you don't' situations, where there is no easy solution to avoiding perceptions of selectivity from at least some categories of potential respondents. But awareness of and sensitivity to the charge of selectivity is at least a good place to start.

13.3.5. Short-Term Versus Long-Term Effects

It is a common conclusion in the chapters of this volume that a deterrent effect has been achieved, but often it is short-term and ephemeral. Darfur is a good example; some argue that "[i]n the beginning, the regime and Bashir and everyone was afraid. When Bashir and the others found out that the ICC doesn't have police or international forces, then they returned to business as usual". The deterrent effect diminished when no arrests followed the issuance of warrants. Others argued that the shift of international attention to Darfur in 2005 drove down the crime rate, and the subsequent loss of interest in the situation allowed it to rise again, with violence levels in 2014–2015 approaching those of 2003–2004. The failure of states to co-ordinate sustained pressure on a criminal situation, and to co-operate with international courts and tribunals, in particular in implementing arrest warrants, was one of the most commonly cited causes of the loss of any deterrent effect.

On the other hand, more promising deterrent effects are found on a long-term basis. For example, the Kosovo chapter speaks of the ICTY as creating the "preconditions for deterrence", which include establishing an historical record in the ICTY proceedings and incorporating international norms into the domestic legal system that, in turn, facilitate national trials. In almost every case study, building national capacity to try international crimes is cited as a benefit from the involvement of the international tribunal and the broader international community. The impact of national accountability for international crimes could prove to be a strong long-term deterrent.

13.3.6. Building a Culture of Accountability

Building a culture of accountability is an overarching theme in the chapters of this book. It provides an answer at least in part to the question of how to ensure that deterrence is more than a temporary and somewhat unplanned effect. Building a culture of accountability in an effort to deter crimes is not the responsibility of international courts and tribunals alone. As has been noted in the ICC Statute and elsewhere, a court like the ICC can, through its core work of investigations and prosecutions, contribute to deterrence. Trials do not take place in a vacuum, but in a social environment that results from the interaction of numerous political, social, economic, cultural and legal factors. The best and most lasting effect will arise from joint and sustained efforts not just to deter perpetrators, but to prevent crimes. As the former ICC president Sang-Hyun Song has written, prevention may be the goal that the ICC and other courts should aim to contribute to advancing in the future.[8] As discussed in the chapter on the theoretical basis for deterrence, prevention is a much broader concept that includes "government and community-based programmes, policies and initiatives to reduce the incidence of risk factors correlated with criminal participation and the rate of victimisation, to enforce the law and maintain criminal justice, and to change perceptions that lead to the commission of crimes". Prevention is a long-term goal to which the ICC may be able to contribute in concert with other actors already addressing these broader social, economic and political questions of how we live together, in our national homes, and as an international community.

---

[8] Sang-Hyun SONG, "Preventive Potential of the International Criminal Court", in *Asian Journal of International Law*, 2013, vol. 3, no. 2, pp. 203–13.

One of the most effective ways to achieve deterrence and prevention is by encouraging the growth of national institutions, laws and national norms. This is consistent with the idea that "the most effective form of law-enforcement is not the imposition of external sanction, but the inculcation of internal obedience".[9] Criminal law can contribute to the prevention of atrocities by focusing on the long-term, transformative process that can lead to the internalisation of norms and the creation of self-regulating communities.[10]

In some situations, progress is already visible. In Kosovo, this may have been the biggest contribution that the ICTY has made to a longer-term deterrent effect. Kosovo has adopted the majority of the international norms of criminal justice; in particular, Kosovo has "borrowed" and adopted practices and norms from the statute of the ICTY itself.[11] Moreover, in various national trials, direct reference is made to the ICTY's jurisprudence, leading to a new approach of relying on the reasoning and sentencing as established by the ICTY as a guiding tool for the national trials. In Sierra Leone, small indications exist that the SCSL trials and operation in Sierra Leone have made incremental inroads into promoting the rule of law and intolerance of impunity for serious crimes and human rights violations within the country. As one ex-combatant put it, he considered the time and efforts of NGOs preaching peace and lecturing on human rights would be wasted if he and his fellow ex-combatants returned to violence, suggesting that an attitude of respecting human rights is beginning to take root. And in the DRC recently, military justice prosecutors announced additional charges for child recruitment and use against a set of armed actors who are already in custody for other serious violations.[12] Having prosecuted this crime in the Lubanga trial, the ICC is in a strong position to assist military justice actors in this work, who admitted

---

[9] Harold Hongju Koh, "How is International Human Rights Law Enforced?", in *Indiana Law Journal*, 1993, vol. 74, no. 4, pp. 1397–401.

[10] Tom Buitelaar, "The ICC and the Prevention of Atrocities Criminological Perspectives", Working Paper No. 8, The Hague Institute for Global Justice, 2015, p. 14.

[11] Dafina Buçaj, "Acceptance of International Criminal Justice through Fragmented Domestication: The Case of Kosovo", in Susanne Buckley-Zistel, Friederike Mieth and Marjana Papa (eds.), *After Nuremberg: Exploring Multiple Dimensions of the Acceptance of International Criminal Justice*, International Nuremberg Principles Academy, Nuremberg, 2016.

[12] Sharanjeet Parmar, "Fighting Impunity for Crimes against Children in the DRC", Coalition for the International Criminal Court, 1 June 2016.

to lacking the technical expertise to work with child victims and try this offence.

In Rwanda, the chapter cites the large number of detainees in the genocide's aftermath and the severely limited capacity of the judiciary (with most judges, lawyers, investigators and other judicial officers dead or in exile and the physical infrastructure of the justice system in shambles) as having stimulated the new government into developing laws and establishing institutions to adjudicate and punish perpetrators. The ICTR contributed significantly to this capacity building through its outreach programmes, including training programmes for prosecutions, internship programmes for Rwandan law students, and establishment of a library in which books and case law of the ICTR could be accessed. The national prosecutor also noted that the adoption of the genocide and crimes against humanity law reflected consultations with the ICTR, as well as with other jurisdictions. Respondents from the Ministry of Defence added: "The first law on genocide largely borrowed definitions from the ICTR Statute. Rape was also considered in our penal code as an act of genocide and this had never happened before the ICTR". The law further reflected the ICTR's influence in establishing a form of plea bargaining, which had not existed in Rwanda before, but facilitated handling the large number of cases of those detained for their participation in the genocide. With ICTR assistance, provision of defence counsel was also improved.

However, in other situations, there is still a long way to go. In Côte d'Ivoire, the accountability process aimed at addressing crimes and human rights violations committed in Côte d'Ivoire has been patchy, selective, underfunded, uncoordinated and has proceeded without an overarching policy and requisite political will. Investigations at the national level into international crimes committed by both sides to the conflict has been slow, and targeted only the pro-Gbagbo partisans. Other than the mass trial of 83 pro-Gbagbo partisans including Simone Gbagbo for "crimes against state security" described in the chapter, no single trial for crimes against humanity has been concluded in ordinary civilian courts in Côte d'Ivoire. Moreover, the special inquiry and investigation unit established in 2013 to investigate and prosecute serious crimes linked to the 2010 election, Cellule spéciale d'enquête et d'instruction, is beset with serious challenges including a lack of prosecutorial strategy and political will that has undermined its work. By 2014 the Military Court of Côte d'Ivoire had tried only four cases, while five others were under investigation. The international community has an essential role to play in establishing accountability, but again, maintaining focus is critical. In Côte d'Ivoire, as the United Nations Operation in Côte d'Ivoire ('UNOCI') winds down its work, its potential role and that of the international community has decreased significantly in 2014 as the UN Security Council has dropped rule of law from its mandate. The lack of finances that bedevils the accountability process in Côte d'Ivoire is due in part to the diminishing role of the UN at a time when its input was and still is most needed.

In the DRC, years of violence and conflict have weakened state institutions, including in the justice and security sectors. Interviews confirmed that a primary driver of violations against children is that perpetrators face no consequence to their actions; as one interviewee stated: "You can use children for anything". Indeed, military justice actors explained that the poor deterrent effect of the ICC is due in part to the failure of the national system to meet its complementarity obligations and build off of the Lubanga case with local prosecutions of the same. Recruitment and use of children are not listed as a crime in the Military Justice Code though a 2009 child protection law criminalises the practice, but whose contours are not widely known among jurists and judicial actors. Military justice actors explained that they lack the resources as well as the capacity to apply the ICC Statute and/or the 2009 law. These include lack of expertise in conducting age verification, protection measures, understanding and collecting evidence around key elements of the offence, and so forth. Targeting members of armed groups is particularly challenging because Forces armées de la République démocratique du Congo does not control areas where they operate and thus cannot effectuate arrests. Military justice actors urged action on its requests to MONUSCO to provide military support in facilitating the arrest of members of armed groups who are under investigation for the commission of serious crimes, including crimes against children. Finally, the anti-impunity agenda in the DRC has seen little progress over the years, with the Rome Statute Implementation Bill only adopted in 2015 and calls for the establishment of mixed chambers yet to be acted upon.[13] More recently, charges have been laid against actors already in custody by the military justice system for recruitment and

---

[13] Sharanjeet Parmar, "How to Tackle the DRC's Complex Anti-Impunity Agenda", in *African Arguments*, 23 April 2014.

use of children, though little is known whether and how these cases will proceed.[14]

Similarly, in Kenya, even when seized of the opportunity, domestic prosecution of international crimes has underperformed. National prosecution of international crimes has been limited, thus compromising the deterrence effect of the local processes. This deficiency can be attributed to a host of challenges, including inadequate investigations by police in terms of competencies and human and technical resources as well as a distinct lack of political will in some cases. Indeed, echoing the complaints of judges who presided over post-election violence cases, two judicial sources in an interview observed that the levels of investigations conducted in these cases were deliberately shoddy so that no conviction would be secured. This explains why there was no single conviction of any politician or police officer despite an estimated 962 cases of police shootings, which resulted in 450 deaths. The government's decision to close all national cases coupled with its reluctance to collaborate effectively by conducting thorough investigations further confirms the lack of political will to effectively prosecute post-election violence at a local level. Despite this, the Kenyan government's panicked reaction to the ICC intervention led to the promulgation of a new constitution that is noteworthy for its incorporation of a robust bill of rights and provisions for the creation of an independent electoral management body, an independent judiciary, executive and parliament, a decentralised political system and a framework regulating a system of devolved government. The constitutional reform process laid the ground for important institutional reforms of Kenya's justice and security apparatus and other governance institutions, geared to prevent the recurrence of human rights atrocities. Whether these reforms will be genuinely implemented in the face of strong indicators of potential election violence in 2017 remains to be seen.

Similar to Kenya, the Darfur situation has seen the government of Sudan make a number of changes to national law and set up national processes in an effort to convince the international community that it was capable of addressing these issues domestically. While these efforts were primarily a political effort to dissuade the international community from strongly supporting the ICC, they are also evidence that the government is sensitive to pressure on these issues and also that there is at least some

---

[14] Parmar, 2016, see *supra* note 12.

rhetorical commitment to the law that forms the basis of the ICC Statute system. Of course, even larger obstacles to prosecutions remain. Among them are immunities granted under Sudan's Armed Forces Act, Police Act and National Security Act, which provide that officials cannot be sanctioned in criminal or civil proceedings without prior authorisation from the head of those forces. These immunities effectively block investigation and prosecution of a large number of international crimes, as police and prosecutors who seek such authorisation most often just never receive an answer to their requests to proceed. Although Sudanese interviewees did not take these measures seriously as steps forward to achieving justice, they could ultimately be useful if the political climate shifts. In the words of one interviewee: "What they are doing is not real justice, but at least these things are in the law".

In Uganda, the ICC arrest warrants influenced the substantive aspects of the peace negotiations. Both parties to the negotiations acknowledged that some form of accountability had to take place; what was in contention was the nature of the accountability mechanism. Eventually the LRA conceded to a national judicial process and other informal justice mechanisms as an alternative to prosecution at the ICC. This led to the adoption of the Juba Agreement on Accountability and Reconciliation of 2007, which provides for the establishment of a special division of the High Court with jurisdiction over international crimes. The ICC also influenced norm-setting through the government of Uganda's enactment of the International Criminal Court Act, which domesticated the ICC Statute and provided a legal framework for the prosecution of international crimes in Ugandan courts. While there is a general view that the ICC had a downstream positive effect on the legal system in Uganda, some actors warn that the impact of the Court on national processes should not be exaggerated. Whether these instruments will be used to achieve accountability at the national level remains to be seen.

Mali, too, once considered a model, is facing a difficult situation with paralysed institutions and administration. Three respondents responsible for the 'Platform' group of fighting forces participating in the demobilisation, disarmament and reintegration process argued: "The worst enemy of Mali is Mali itself". For the president of the Court of Appeal of Mopti, the highest court, close to the theatre of the rebellion in northern Mali:

> The authors of violations of fundamental human rights, rape, war crimes and crimes against humanity never pay the full price of their crimes. Mali is encouraging rebellion by giving bonuses to criminals, integrating them into the national army, giving them all kinds of favours. It is the state itself which encourages impunity.

It is clear though that much remains to be done. To date, none of the courts of northern Mali operates normally because some courts have stopped functioning entirely, on the one hand, and those that have continued working suffer from insufficient staff and lack of competent staff, on the other. For example, the intermediate courts like Timbuktu and Gao have only one clerk each. The reform of the justice sector in Mali mainly suffers from a lack of political will.

The Serbia situation provides some middle ground. Professional observers nostalgically label the period from 2003 to 2009 as "the best time" for the prosecution of war crimes and dealing with the past in Serbia, and claim that it ended soon after the arrest and delivery of the last indicted fugitive to the ICTY in 2009. This speaks more to the current state of the war crimes prosecution in Serbia, expectations, and the resulting disappointment with its failures. After the last arrest, the social and political pressure from the European Union declined (notably after Serbia became a candidate for membership in March 2012), as well as the number of newly raised indictments by the Serbian war crimes prosecutor, while the systematic obstruction of public access to war files by the Serbian army and police increased. These attempts at curbing the space for prosecutorial actions are part of the state war narrative which evolved from a complete denial of war crimes, to attributions of crimes to individual perpetrators who present a deviation from the societal norms ('paramilitaries', 'crazy people' and so on) and thus negation that there was any systematic state involvement not to mention state-organised commission of crimes. The Serbia situation is a perfect illustration of how the factors needed to spark deterrence can come together, but then misalign and fall apart. The challenge is to maintain the focus and commitment necessary to sustain the deterrence effect.

13.3.7. Gaming the System

Closely related to the theme on building a culture of accountability, these studies demonstrate the importance of understanding and reacting strategically to the systems that support the commission of international crimes. As Justice Richard Goldstone noted: "It is naive for anyone to assume that in a transitional society such institutions and practices will die a natural death".[15] Or perhaps as expressed in the Kenya chapter, to deter crimes, one must first tame the mind of the political class through sanctions or some other form of external pressure. In the DRC chapter, the author concludes that deterrence effects will always be tenuous when the conditions driving the commission of serious crimes are more entrenched and long-standing than the anti-impunity efforts undertaken by the Court. She advocates investigation and prosecution of actors who make money off commission of crimes, to undercut the systems that support them.

In Sierra Leone, the Court's failed efforts to bring RUF rebel leaders Sam Bockarie and Johnny Paul Koroma before the Court, leading to Charles Taylor's execution of Bockarie, highlighted the lengths to which a perpetrator might go to ensure the survival of the system he put in place to draw benefit from the commission of crimes. The CDF head Hinga Norman demonstrated the reach of some suspects when he was subject to an order from the registrar, restricting his communications, because the Court had intercepted phone calls which indicated he was co-ordinating activities intended to cause civil unrest in Sierra Leone.

In Serbia, one of the largest challenges the ICTY faced was under-cutting Milošević's status as a "factor of peace and security" in the Balkans due to his role in the Dayton Agreement, one which he used to shore up his system, which organised his commission of crimes for political and economic gain. The ICTY's failure to ever effectively counter his propaganda machine through its own outreach is one of the respondents' main criticisms of the Tribunal.

In Kenya, the system's intervention manifested directly in witness interference and political meddling that eventually led to the vacating of charges for President Uhuru Kenyatta and Vice President William Ruto. The fact that they were able to manipulate the political system to get elected to these posts after they were charged with international crimes demonstrates the strength of the established system in Kenya.

---

[15] Richard Goldstone, "Bringing War Criminals to Justice during an Ongoing War", in Jonathan Moore (ed.), *Hard Choices: Moral Dilemmas in Humanitarian Intervention*, Rowman & Littlefield, Lanham, MD, 1998, pp. 202–3.

In the Darfur situation, the system has protected Al Bashir and others, facilitating their travel abroad and continued recognition from other governments and regional organisations. While some speculated that the Sudanese regime was tiring of Al Bashir, in the opinion of many respondents, the ICC's pressure brought the perpetrators together because they all expected that otherwise, they would also be subject to prosecutions. The same ICC pressure facilitated the coming together of erstwhile political opponents in Kenya as well.

In Côte d'Ivoire, perhaps ironically, the challenge has been moving from co-operation to confrontation with a new regime that entered power with support from the international community, but that now takes a more defiant stance on cooperation with the ICC.

13.4. Recommendations and Conclusion

Based on the case studies and the themes from this research, the following specific recommendations are proposed:

1. *Selectivity.* The impact of selectivity in prosecutorial choices, or the perception that such exists, whether or not it actually does, is significant in many of the situations studied here. The perception of selectivity undermines the credibility of the tribunal and lessens any deterrent message. At the ICC, the Office of the Prosecutor should be cognizant of this likely perception and devise strategies to effectively explain the reasoning behind who is prosecuted and for what crimes. This may necessitate greater outreach at the initial stages of proceedings.

2. *Outreach.* Throughout the case studies, there is a plea for greater outreach to the affected communities. Outreach is necessary for accurate knowledge. Knowledge, in turn, is key to handling issues related to selectivity, politics and even the nature of the proceedings in the courts. A better understanding of a court's processes leads to a greater perception of legitimacy for the court, which is essential for any deterrent effect. For the ICC and the international community, it would reap benefits in the credibility of the Court, and a contribution to deterrence, to invest more resources in outreach efforts.

3. *Co-operation and co-ordination.* The multitude of actors and institutions, national and international, involved in a conflict or post-conflict situation creates some confusion, but also important oppor-

tunities. This is true for establishing rule of law, democratic institutions, peace and security, and a deterrent effect. Recognising that deterrence can only be achieved through the combined efforts of international and national entities means that there is a need to co-operate and to co-ordinate efforts.

4. *National capacity*. Related to combined efforts, it is clear from the case studies that fostering national capacity to prosecute international crimes cannot be overlooked or relegated to a lesser status. Instead, deterrence is dependent upon the actual and perceived ability to hold individuals accountable. International tribunals are designed only to try a limited number of the highest-level perpetrators. A greater sense of certainty, severity and celerity in punishment necessitates a greater number of prosecutions, which must occur at the national level.

5. *Long-term, not short-term goals*. Several of the case studies emphasised a perception of a greater deterrent effect when viewed through a long-term, rather than a short-term, lens. Deterrence is dependent upon creating a culture that identifies international crimes and rejects impunity for them. This is not a short-term project. Moreover, with the recognition that an international criminal tribunal at most can only *contribute* to deterrence, it becomes clear that many institutions must be established or strengthened, governments must have the political will to protect their citizens, and the social norms of the society must incorporate an intolerance for international crimes. These changes do not happen overnight and should be assessed at intervals with an eye towards a long-term effect.

Through the findings and recommendations in this chapter, and the extensive information in the case studies, this project was designed to contribute to an important dialogue on deterrence, how to measure it, and how best to position international criminal courts to assist in a global effort to prevent international crimes. As elusive as demonstrating deterrence can be, it remains an aspiration of international justice. From this project, it appears that international criminal courts can make a limited contribution to a deterrent effect through prosecutions, and that impact can be strengthened by focusing especially on communication with all constituencies.

It is important to remember, though, that the courts also achieve other goals. A retributive response to international crime is immediate for the perpetrators and contributes to a sense of justice throughout the world. The international courts further serve an expressivist role. As Carsten Stahn has noted: "The virtue of international criminal jurisdiction lies increasingly in expressivist features, such as the condemnation of certain types of violations or pattern of crime or performative aspects, such as the demonstration of fairness in proceedings".[16] Drumbl has also emphasised the importance of recognising goals in addition to retribution and deterrence where international criminal courts can make a lasting contribution:

> The expressivist punishes to strengthen faith in rule of law among the general public, as opposed to punishing simply because the perpetrator deserves it or because potential perpetrators will be deterred by it. Expressivism has greater viability than either deterrence of retribution as a basis for a penology of extraordinary international crime.[17]

As further studies and dialogue occur on the ICC or any other international criminal tribunals, the multiple goals of the courts, the varied constituencies, and the numerous interlocking actors and institutions should all factor into the calculus for any goal, including deterrence. Perhaps the most important lesson of this study is that perceptions of individuals affected by a court's work provide us with invaluable insight into what might increase the impact of an international criminal court, including contributing to a deterrent effect.

Although progress towards deterrence may take two steps forward and one step back as it edges forward, it is worth the journey. It has been noted that the Nuremberg trials arguably had their greatest impact several generations after their conclusion. On this final note, the impact of international courts and tribunals has yet to be fully felt, and cannot at this stage be fully predicted. Perhaps as M. Cherif Bassiouni has suggested, as well as Hunjoon Kim and Kathryn Sikkink, those interested in deterrence should be keeping their eyes especially on the younger generations of political, military and other leaders, coming of age together with the age of accountability.[18] It is their response to these developments, more than that

---

[16] Carsten Stahn, "Daedalus or Icarus? Footprints of International Criminal Justice Over a Quarter of a Century", Grotius Centre for International Legal Studies, Leiden University, 2016, p. 5.

[17] Drumbl, 2007, p. 173, see *supra* note 3.

[18] Parliamentarians for Global Action, "A Deterrent International Criminal Court – The Ultimate Objective", 6–7 December 2004; Hunjoon Kim and Kathryn Sikkink, "Do Human

of the leaders who are the subject of current investigations and prosecutions, which will determine the strength of the deterrence effect of the international courts and tribunals in the future.

Rights Trials Make a Difference?", in Paper Presented at American Political Science Association Annual Meeting, Chicago, September 2007, pp. 35–36.

INDEX

A

accountability, 42, 53, 68, 72, 92–94, 134, 150, 162–64, 167, 179–80, 189, 224, 231, 234, 239, 245, 248, 265, 269, 274, 281, 291, 299–300, 316, 318, 324, 343, 387–88, 390, 392, 428, 440, 447, 449, 452–53, 457

administration of justice, 66, 96, 106, 178, 362

admissibility, 18, 348–49, 354–55, 378, 384

African Union Mission in Sudan, 296

Akhavan, Payam, 72, 141–42, 153, 186, 314, 357

Alekšovski, Zlatko, 16

Al Mahdi, Ahmad Al Faqi, 16–17, 408

amnesty, 184–88, 197, 201, 223, 229, 248, 261, 268, 272, 317, 394, 412, 414, 440

Arab League, 302

Arbour, Louise, 73, 169

armed groups, 193, 206–7, 228, 231, 233–35, 237–51, 254–55, 257, 260–61, 407, 411, 417, 430, 437, 441, 450

arms embargo, 204, 294, 309, 324

arrest warrants, 5, 45, 48, 110, 225, 247, 264–65, 269–70, 272–74, 277–80, 282, 285, 289, 302–3, 320, 326, 387, 430–31, 445–46, 452

Arusha Peace Agreement, 102

Asaala, Evelyne, **329–72**

awareness, 9, 51, 53–54, 57, 83, 90–91, 114, 134, 168, 175, 182, 186, 188, 223, 242–43, 245, 252–54, 271, 282, 284, 302, 319, 341, 386, 413, 435, 437–41, 446

awareness-raising, 223, 243, 245, 253–54

B

Bashir, Omar Al, 292, 302, 349, 384, 409, 441

Bassiouni, M. Cherif, 265, 330, 381, 457

behavioural changes, 191, 264

Bemba, Jean-Pierre, 16–17, 251

Bentham, Jeremy, 112, 126

Benthamite, 165

Bensouda, Fatou, 179, 287, 292, 362

Bosnia, 64, 67, 69–71, 77, 80, 152, 156, 176

Bosnia v. Serbia, xiv, 32, 34, 39

Bucaj, Dafina, **141–78**

Bueno, Olivia, **291–328**

C

Carnegie Commission, 42–43, 48–49, 51–53

Carter, Linda, **1–11**, **427–58**

case selection criteria, 278

Cassese, Antonio, 20, 23, 127

celerity, 25, 108, 158, 176, 319–20, 351, 456

certainty of prosecution, 97, 108, 138, 194, 198, 204, 226, 289

Ćerkez, Mario, 22

certainty of punishment, 6, 24, 178, 194, 197, 223, 226–27, 229, 324, 334, 434

child soldiers, 231–33, 237, 239, 241–42, 245–46, 248–54, 258, 264, 267, 286–87, 307, 430, 441

Chui, Ngudjolo, 28, 234, 237

civil law, 18, 120, 171

civil society, 3, 55–56, 66, 93, 143, 154, 168, 179, 189, 191, 223, 249, 251, 264, 271, 273, 281, 287, 294, 301, 305–6, 321, 328, 334, 343, 346, 350, 372, 376, 382, 387–88, 392, 395, 398, 402, 408, 415, 419–20, 425–26, 433, 438, 444

civilian population, 170, 222, 233, 235, 241, 244–46, 251, 339, 410, 417

Clausewitz, Carl von, 51

Code of Hammurabi, 16

command responsibility, 70, 80, 84, 88, 90, 201, 351

community leaders, 234, 238, 242, 244, 252–54, 437

conditionality, 68, 84, 86, 91, 248, 249

H

Harmon, Mark, 214
historical record, 15, 20, 143–44, 164, 166, 190, 220, 325, 435, 447
holistic solution, 279
Huggins, Martha K., 48
Human Rights Watch, 1, 13, 57, 79, 83, 129, 148, 235, 241, 249–50, 258–61, 304, 321, 343, 393, 395–96, 427
humanitarian crisis, 149, 268

I

ideology, 9, 135, 294, 353, 358, 370
imminent death, 284, 286
independence, 39, 86–87, 93, 96, 100–1, 166, 169, 318, 349–50, 359, 368, 392, 404–5, 407, 422
indeterminacy, 22, 443
indictments, 58, 63, 65–67, 69–70, 72, 74, 77, 80–84, 86, 96, 107–10, 142–45, 152, 154–56, 158–59, 161, 163, 165, 168–69, 171, 177–78, 181, 192, 197, 200–3, 226, 271, 275, 304, 349–51, 353, 379, 435, 442, 444, 453
indirect deterrence, 233
individual sanctions, 310, 325
Ingabire, Mackline, **95–139**
institutional limitations, 90
interests of justice, 335, 377
interests of victims, 18, 19
International Criminal Court (ICC): intervention, 269, 271, 275, 304–5, 340, 357, 376, 438, 451
International Commission on Intervention and State Sovereignty, 42, 51
International Committee of the Red Cross, 297, 420, 466
International Court of Justice (ICJ), 30, 32, 40, 326
international criminal justice, vii, 65–66, 71, 73, 91–92, 145, 179–80, 195–96, 213, 224, 263, 279, 328, 383
International Crisis Group, 42, 56, 235, 240, 246, 254–55, 257–59, 282
international humanitarian law, 22–23, 105, 107, 109, 137, 139, 146, 151, 157, 161, 164, 181, 187–88, 190, 216, 224, 247, 249, 263, 294, 312, 426

International Nuremberg Principles Academy, viii, ix, 448
international peace and security, 15, 20, 21, 43
international support, 70, 72, 323
investigations, 5, 7, 10, 16, 18, 47–48, 63, 65, 73, 77, 197, 199–200, 204, 210, 229, 240–41, 251, 264–66, 268–70, 274, 276–81, 284, 288, 301, 310, 327, 331, 333–34, 343, 345–47, 350, 354, 361, 369, 371, 383, 388–89, 392, 394, 408, 423, 426, 428, 436, 438, 447, 451, 458
irrelevance of official capacity, 24, 44

J

jihadists, 410, 412, 414, 417, 420
Jo, Hyeran, 6, 24, 142, 191–92, 239, 266, 304, 334–35
judicial reforms, 275, 354
jus cogens, 28, 30, 32

K

Karadžić, Radovan, 20, 72, 82, 84, 174, 440
Katanga, Germaine, 16, 234, 236–37, 430
Kaul, Hans-Peter, 338–39
Kelsen, Hans, 30
Kenya, 3, 11, 56, 115, 278, 321, 329–72, 375, 409, 430, 432, 437–38, 440–41, 445, 451, 454–55
Kihika, Kasande Sarah, **263–89**
Klaus Rackwitz, viii, ix, 465
Kleiman, Mark, 193
Kordić, Dario, 22
Koskenniemi, Martti, 3, 15
Kosovo, 3, 11, 64–65, 67, 69–70, 73–78, 80, 82–83, 85–89, 141, 153, 145, 147–50, 152, 154–56, 158–63, 165–68, 170–77, 428–31, 433, 435–36, 438, 441–43, 445, 447–48
Kosovo Liberation Army, 148, 441
Kosovo Six, xv, 82–83, 85, 88
Krštić, Radislav, 20

L

Lao Tzu, 427
Lazic, Sladjana, **63–94**

TOAEP Team

Associate Professor YANG Lijun, Chinese Academy of Social Science
Professor Marcos Zilli, University of Sao Paulo